Law as Performance

Tirades against legal theatrics are nearly as old as law itself, and yet so is the age-old claim that law must not merely be done: it must be "seen to be done." *Law as Performance* traces the history of legal performance and spectatorship through the early modern period. Viewing law as the product not merely of edicts or doctrines but of expressive action, it investigates the performances that literally created law: in civic arenas, courtrooms, judges' chambers, marketplaces, scaffolds, and streets. It examines the legal codes, learned treatises, trial reports, lawyers' manuals, execution narratives, rhetoric books, images, (and more) that confronted these performances, praising their virtues or denouncing their evils. In so doing, it recovers a long, rich, and largely overlooked tradition of jurisprudential thought about law as a performance practice. This tradition not only generated an elaborate poetics and politics of legal performance. It provided western jurisprudence with a set of constitutive norms that, in working to distinguish law from theatrics, defined the very nature of law. In the crucial opposition between law and theatre, law stood for cool deliberation, by-the-book rules, and sovereign discipline. Theatre stood for deceptive artifice, entertainment, histrionics, melodrama. And yet legal performance, even at its most theatrical, also appeared fundamental to law's realization: a central mechanism for shaping legal subjects, key to persuasion, essential to deterrence, indispensable to law's power—as it still does today.

JULIE STONE PETERS (B.A. Yale, Ph.D. Princeton, J.D. Columbia) is the H. Gordon Garbedian Professor of English and Comparative Literature at Columbia University, an Affiliated faculty member at Columbia Law School, and a Global Professorial Fellow at Queen Mary University School of Law. A scholar of law and humanities and media history, she studies performance, film, digital, and legal cultures across the *longue durée*. Her books include *Staging Witchcraft Before the Law: Skepticism, Performance as Proof, and Law as Magic in Early Modern Witch Trials* (Cambridge UP, 2024), *Law as Performance: Theatricality, Spectatorship, and the Making of Law in Ancient, Medieval, and Early Modern Europe* (OUP, 2022, finalist for the Joe A. Callaway Prize, David Bevington Award, and Media Ecologies Association Book Award), and *Theatre of the Book: Print, Text, and Performance in Europe 1480–1880* (Oxford University Press, 2000, winner of the MLA's Harry Levin Prize and English Association's Beatrice White Prize, and finalist for the Barnard Hewitt Award).

LAW AND LITERATURE

The Law and Literature series publishes work that connects legal ideas to literary and cultural history, texts, and artifacts. The series encompasses a wide range of historical periods, literary genres, legal fields and theories, and transnational subjects, focusing on interdisciplinary books that engage with legal and literary forms, methods, concepts, dispositions, and media. It seeks innovative studies of every kind, including but not limited to work that examines race, ethnicity, gender, national identity, criminal and civil law, legal institutions and actors, digital media, intellectual property, economic markets, and corporate power, while also foregrounding current interpretive methods in the humanities, using these methods as dynamic tools that are themselves subject to scrutiny.

"Peters pursues the puzzle of law's *vividae rationes* with her characteristic erudition, analytic acuity and verbal verve. Exhaustive and meticulous, *Law as Performance* brilliantly transforms the cold gray Janus face of the jurist into the terpsichorean and tempestive figure of justice being done."

—Peter Goodrich, Director, Program in Law and Humanities, Cardozo Law School

"Peters brilliantly excavates the 'performance of law'. This volume is a treasure trove of ideas and images."

—Judith Resnik, Arthur Liman Professor of Law, Yale University

"Wonderful history, not only because of the deftness of its arguments but also because of the rich anecdotal detail that enlivens nearly every page. A marvelous book."

—William Chester Jordan, Dayton-Stockton Professor of History, Princeton University

"1001 nights of legal and intellectual adventures: a brilliant work of relentless scholarship."

—Jesús R. Velasco, Augustus R. Street Professor of Spanish and Portuguese, Yale University

"Extraordinarily detailed and entirely persuasive. A fine achievement."

—Stanley Fish, Davidson-Kahn Distinguished University Professor of Humanities and Law, FIU

Compelling scholarship that matches evidence and argument across 2,000 years of legal practice.

—Joseph Roach, Sterling Professor of English and Theater, Yale University

"Peters traces the role of courtroom theatre with impressive erudition and a verve that makes her book read as compellingly as a novel."

—Ingrid Drake Rowland, *Continuity and Change*

"Justice can't be done to the depth and breadth of Peters' arguments and ideas."

—Marett Leiboff, *Journal of Social History*

"*Law as Performance* is an adventure and a provocation that will energize the field and re-map its contours."

—Subha Mukherji, *Comparative Drama*

Law as Performance

Theatricality, Spectatorship, and the Making of Law in Ancient, Medieval, and Early Modern Europe

JULIE STONE PETERS

OXFORD
UNIVERSITY PRESS

OXFORD
UNIVERSITY PRESS

Great Clarendon Street, Oxford, OX2 6DP,
United Kingdom

Oxford University Press is a department of the University of Oxford.
It furthers the University's objective of excellence in research, scholarship,
and education by publishing worldwide. Oxford is a registered trade mark of
Oxford University Press in the UK and in certain other countries.

First Edition published in 2022
First published in paperback in 2026

Published in the United States of America by Oxford University Press
198 Madison Avenue, New York, NY 10016, United States of America

British Library Cataloguing in Publication Data
Data available

Library of Congress Control Number: 2021949555

ISBN 978–0–19–289849–4 (Hbk.)
ISBN 978–0–19–790395–7 (Pbk.)

DOI: 10.1093/oso/9780198714163.001.0001

Printed and bound by
CPI Group (UK) Ltd., Croydon, CR0 4YY

MIX
Paper | Supporting
responsible forestry
FSC® C013604
FSC
www.fsc.org

The manufacturer's authorized representative in the EU for product safety is
Oxford University Press España S.A. of Parque Empresarial San Fernando de Henares,
Avenida de Castilla, 2 – 28830 Madrid (www.oup.es/en or product.safety@oup.com).
OUP España S.A. also acts as importer into Spain of products made by the manufacturer.

For Kaia and Nathaniel

Acknowledgments

A number of institutions have supported this project as it evolved, most notably the Columbia and Harvard English Departments and the Guggenheim Foundation. I am indebted to them, as well as to the many librarians who have offered vital assistance: Ian Beilin and Jeffrey Wayno, to whom I have repeatedly turned for their erudition and their ability to answer the most obscure of questions; Insaf Ali, Mayra Alvarez, Nancy Friedland, Hollyann Kozlowski, Meredith Levin, the indefatigable Nikhil Raghuram, John Toffanelli, and Sherry Wei.

This book would not have been possible without the extraordinary group of research assistants with whom I've had the good fortune to work during the project's various phases. Two of these served more as colleague-consultants than as assistants: the medievalist Eugene Petracca, whose vast learning saved me from many errors; and the classicist Francesco Cassini, who made several key scholarly discoveries. Their translations appear throughout this book. Nathan May, on whose brilliant research skills I came to depend, became the project's mainstay. Clara Beccaro spent hundreds of hours, often working around the clock. Others who made significant contributions include Berra Akcan, Toby Berggruen, Josue Chavez, Lauren Green, Nicholas Lopez, Sofia Riva, Chloe Schneewind, and Melanie Shi. I am profoundly grateful for what each brought to the project.

While no portion of this book has previously appeared in print, I have published a number of essays that developed its theoretical armature, and have received invaluable feedback on these from collection editors: Elizabeth Anker, Maksymilian Del Mar, Lawrence Douglas, Mitchell Greenberg, Bernadette Meyler, Subha Mukherji, Austin Sarat, Simon Stern, Martha Merrill Umphrey, and Richard Weisberg. Many of these essays began as talks or seminar presentations: at the American Comparative Literature Association, Amherst College, Harvard Law School, John Jay College of Criminal Justice, the NEH Summer Institute for College and University Faculty, New York University, Queen Mary College (University of London), the Stanford Law School Law and Humanities Workshop, Trinity College Cambridge, UC Berkeley, the UCLA Center for Medieval and Renaissance Studies, the University of Lisbon Faculdade de Letras, and the University of Toronto Law School. I am indebted to my interlocutors there, as well as to the many students with whom I have discussed this work both in and out of the classroom.

I am also thankful to those who responded generously to my queries, made helpful suggestions, small and large, or otherwise offered their time and wisdom: April Alliston, Laurie Barron, Daniel Blank, Sarah Cole, Jean-Michel David,

Francesco De Angelis, Frédéric Elsig, Alison Feit, David Freedberg, Thomas Fudge, Rhonda Garelick, Darren Gobert, Max Harris, Jean Howard, Rebecca Kastleman, Laura Kendrick, Pamela King, John Kuhn, Maureen Miller, Molly Murray, Alan Nelson, Andy North, Adam Peters, Lisa Peters, Sarah Rose, Kirsi Salonen, Wolfgang Schild, Karl Shoemaker, Andrew Solomon, Alan Stewart, Eloisa Thompson, Jerome Wakefield, Hannah Weaver, Lauren Whitney, W. B. Worthen, and Claire Zion.

I am especially grateful to those who took time to read and respond to my unduly long chapter drafts or (in some cases) the entire manuscript: Leanne Bablitz, Christopher Baswell, Maksymilian Del Mar, Helene Foley, Thomas Fudge, Peter Goodrich, Eleanor Johnson, Bernadette Meyler, C. D. C. Reeve, and the anonymous OUP readers. I owe a particular debt to the OUP Law and Literature series editors, Robert Spoo and Simon Stern, who not only enthusiastically welcomed my contribution and read multiple drafts, but went to extraordinary lengths to track down image permissions, troubleshoot, and generally offer support and friendship. I feel very lucky to be included in their series, as well as to be working with the OUP editorial team, most notably Jacqueline Norton, Aimee Wright, and Philip Dines, and with Jayaprakash P. (JP), whose expert and gracious guidance has helped speed the book through production.

My interlocutors also, of course, include the many colleagues, friends, and relatives whose conversation sent me down new pathways, inspired revelations, opened worlds, or illuminated the shadows, or whose friendship offered consolations intellectual and otherwise during the journey: too many to name, but they are here between the lines. I am grateful to Sandra Peters for the magical sanctuary in Mexico where this book finally took shape, and to the memory of Melvin Peters who created that sanctuary and whose spirit still resides there. It is to the memory of Sandra Stone that I owe whatever poetry may be in these pages. Above all, I am indebted to Nathaniel Berman, my greatest interlocutor, supporter, partner in all senses, and to Kaia Berman Peters, ever-astonishing daughter and comrade: my ultimate inspiration and moral compass.

Contents

List of Illustrations

Note on Citations, Texts, and Translations

To keep notes short, I have attempted to give the minimum information necessary for readers to pursue my references without having to consult the Works Cited at the end of this volume. I give volume and page, folio, or signature numbers after short titles. Where information in brackets follows these, it gives additional information, such as book, chapter, or line numbers, or traditional section identification numbers. References to early texts are to the earliest extant printed editions unless otherwise noted. References to Loeb Classical Library editions are to the most recent revisions, available online at www.loebclassics.com.

Throughout, I have generally preserved original orthography, modernizing only the letters u, v, i, j, and s, and eliminating ligatures. In translations—as in quotes originally in English—I use brackets to indicate substantial changes to individual words, such as modification of number or tense: for instance, the Latin *curiae* (courts) might appear as "cour[t]" in my translation to indicate the change to singular; *perago* (I accomplish or perform) might appear as "I perform[ed]" to indicate the change to past tense. Where translations are my own or where the phrasing of a text is important to my claims, I include the original in the notes. I am grateful to all those who have made my work easier by providing the many extraordinary translations on which I have drawn.

Introduction

Tothill Fields (1571): Law versus Theatre in "the Last Trial by Battel"

On June 18, 1571, over four thousand spectators gathered in Tothill Fields, Westminster for an extraordinary event: a trial by battle.[1] All around the field (or "lists") were scaffolds "for people to stande and beholde" (1152). Trial by battle was long obsolete: the last in England had been in 1456 (a nasty fight involving penis and nose biting). Perhaps this one would be equally riveting. Following tradition, the litigants would not themselves take the field. Instead, "champions" would represent them. After a public ceremony of casting down the "Gauntlet[s]" (1151), the champions were "sworn . . . to perform the battle" (fol. 301b), and the fight was on. The contrast between the two champions added further spice to the spectacle. The defendant's champion, George Thorne, was "a bigge, broade, strong set fellowe." The plaintiffs' champion, fencing master Henry Nayler, was, on the contrary, very "slender" and certainly "not . . . tall." But he was handsome: altogether "a proper . . . man" (1151). It would be lithe skill plus sex appeal against brute force, David against Goliath. Moreover, Nayler had something even more important than skill and sex appeal: exceptional theatrical flair. This he had gained in part from performing regularly as a "prize player" in public fencing matches in the London theatres.[2] As "servant to the . . . Earle of *Leicester*" (1151) he was also

[1] For "the last trial by battel," see Blackstone, *Commentaries* (2016 ed.), 3:223. All in-text citations to this event refer to John Stow's *Chronicles of England* (1580 ed.), 1151–2; or the first English translation of Sir James Dyer's reports: *Reports of Cases* (1794), fol. 301a–302a. These are the two principal accounts. Stow's first appeared in his *Summarye of the Chronicles* (1573). Dyer's first appeared in *Cy ensuont ascuns novel cases* (1585). Holinshead repeats Stow's account with a few minor embellishments (*Firste [Laste] Volume of the Chronicles* [1577 ed.], 1858–60). Before arriving on appeal in the Court of Common Pleas, the case had already been adjudicated in at least three courts. The two plaintiffs were technically "demandant[s]" (petitioners) here, but to simplify, I refer to them as the "plaintiffs" and to the respondent as the "defendant." For later accounts, see Filmer, *Chronicle of Kent*, 69–70; Furley, *History of the Weald of Kent*, 173; and Berry, *Noble Science*, 6.

The Church had opposed "trial by battle" (also called "trial by combat" or "wager of battle") since the ninth century, and it had been largely discarded as a mode of proof by the fourteenth. The 1571 event, however, was not in fact the last attempt to try a case by battle: litigants continued to occasionally invoke their right to battle—for instance in 1631, 1638, and (astonishingly) 1817—but courts managed to forestall actual combat.

[2] The manuscript recording the activities of the Masters of Defence identifies thirty prizes that were played in public playhouses and fifteen more in places that were to become public playhouses (Berry, *Noble Science*, 2, noting that "these prize playings were a form of drama, competing with plays for audiences in some of the same ways and places").

Law as Performance: Theatricality, Spectatorship, and the Making of Law in Ancient, Medieval, and Early Modern Europe. Julie Stone Peters, Oxford University Press. © Julie Stone Peters 2022. DOI: 10.1093/oso/9780192898494.003.0001

probably an actor in Leicester's troupe, performing alongside the master of the bawdy jig Richard Tarlton, who studied fencing with Nayler and was to become the most famous comic actor of his era.[3]

Nayler's dramatic march to Tothill Fields on June 18th and his costume change in the field suggest how much he had learned from his experience as a showman. At 7 a.m., dressed in flamboyant crimson satin, with a fashionably slashed doublet and a black velvet hat sporting a colossal red feather, he had begun his parade through the streets of London. As he marched—preceded by a fife-and-drum orchestra and followed by a Yeoman of the Queen's Guard bearing a horn-tipped staff and leather shield (1152)—he held aloft a sword with Thorne's glove dangling from its tip. Proceeding through the Palace of Westminster, pausing before the great doors of Westminster Hall (the hall of law), he then paraded along King Street, through "the Sanctuary," onto Tothill Street. Taking his time (to increase anticipation and keep Thorne waiting), he arrived at Tothill Fields and then disappeared into his tent. When a herald at last called upon the plaintiffs to produce their champion, Nayler emerged in full glory. Having stripped off his fancy doublet and plumed *chapeau*, he now appeared in a sort of medieval-Roman-gladiator costume, "in red sandals over armour of leather, bare-legged from the knee downward, and bare-headed, and bare arms to the elbow." A knight carrying "a red b[a]ton of an ell long, tipped with horn" and the Yeoman "carrying a target made of double leather" led him into the field, where he proceeded to march around its perimeter and finally into the center "of the lists," to the admiration of the thousands of spectators (fol. 301b–302a).

This was clearly theatre: a cross between Roman circus, medieval joust, and carnival; entertainments of the kind Tothill Fields regularly hosted.[4] But it was also law. For there was a real case to be decided: one so dull that no one could possibly mistake it for entertainment (a dispute over title to a property somewhere in Kent, involving "a writ of entry *sur disseisin*, in the nature of assise . . . " [yawn]) (fol. 301a). Not only was it a real case: it was a real court. For the entire Court of Common Pleas had decamped to Tothill Fields, furniture and all. There the court was to "sitte" just as it sat in Westminster Hall. A "stage . . . representing the court" contained an exact replica (1152): a "place or seat for the Judges of the Bench was made without and above the lists, and covered with the furniture of the same Bench [as] in *Westminster Hall*." There was even "a bar made there" for the lawyers (the "Serjeants at law"). To begin proceedings, three "Justices of the Bench," including Sir James Dyer, Chief Justice of the Common Pleas, wearing

[3] Tarlton started his theatrical career in the Earl of Leicester's troupe. Probably around the same time, he became Nayler's fencing student and eventually became a fencing master under Nayler's sponsorship. See Berry, *Noble Science*, 5–6 and 12–13.

[4] Tothill Fields was a traditional site of jousts and duels. It had hosted a weekly market and annual fair since at least the thirteenth century (extended to a month-long fair in the fourteenth century), and had a pleasure ground with a maze and bearbaiting spectacles.

"their robes of scarlet, with the appurtenances and coifs," took their places on the bench. The two serjeants-at-law took their places at the bar. And three "*Oyes*" ("Hear-ye"s) proclaimed that the trial had begun (fol. 301b). Thorne "approach[ed] the bar before the Justices with three solemn congies [bows]" and was instructed to stand to the right of the court. Nayler "approach[ed] the bar before the Justices with three solemn congies" and was instructed to stand to the left of the court (fol. 301b–302a).

All was proceeding just as it did in Westminster Hall. Except that they were sitting in the middle of Tothill Fields surrounded by four thousand spectators about to watch two champions in a prize fight, with coifed, scarlet-robed judges presiding as umpires. What happened next was a surprise: a woefully anticlimactic one. After the champions had paid their respects to the court and stood awaiting instructions, Dyer "solemnly called" the plaintiffs to appear by the side of their showy champion (Nayler) (fol. 302a). Everyone waited expectantly . . . , but no one appeared. Twice. Default judgment for the defendant. There was, after all, to be no combat. The Judge ordered Nayler to give Thorne back his glove. However, Nayler was not ready to concede defeat. Standing before the crowd in his Roman gladiator's costume, with undiminished bravado, he looked up at the judge and said "no!" Even for those who could not hear, the scene must have appeared as a showdown between the scarlet-robed, becoifed judge (standing for law) and the costumed showman (standing for theatre). His Lordship might command anything else, said Nayler, but he would *not* give the glove back. Thorne would have to win it! *En garde*! Thorne must at least "playe wyth hym halfe a score blowes." Did he not realize that they had to "shew some pastime to the Lorde chiefe Justice and the [spectators] there assembled"? Thorne sullenly declared that he "came to fighte, and woulde not playe" (1154). Dyer "commend[ed] *Nayler* for his valiaunt courage,"—perhaps noting the difference in size between the combatants. But he was sorry, there was indeed to be neither fighting nor playing: the show was over. The champions were "bothe quietly t[o] departe the fielde" (1154). And the spectators were to go home (fol. 302a).

Dyer's (or his clerk's) account of the event left out one small detail: the parties had settled the day before. In exchange for a payoff of five hundred pounds, the plaintiffs would give up their claim to the property.[5] However, the Queen—who had somehow gotten in on the action—had declared that everyone must nevertheless appear in Tothill Fields and *make believe* that the combat would go forward: the spectators would gather; the champions would appear; the plaintiffs would then forfeit by not showing up. The spectacle would dramatize the

[5] Stow explains: "the matter was stayed, and the parties agreed, that [the defendant] being in possession, shoulde have the lande, and was bound in five hundred pounde, to consider the Plaintifs, [which] upon hearing the matter, the Judges should award" (1151–2). This was *de facto* a settlement, even if technically the case was merely stayed and there was to be another hearing that would make the settlement official.

defendant's rightful ownership without actually requiring the judges to preside over a bloody spectacle.[6] This charade raised a question: what was the nature of the event that had taken place? Was it a trial? Or was it merely a piece of theatre? Had the court really "removed" to Tothill Fields? Or was it merely acting on a "stage ... *representing* the court of the common pleas"?

Dyer's account, included in his official collection of law reports, treated the case as if it were just like any other case. The account devotes pages to the legal facts and issues, the case's progress through various courts, and the decisions of each of those courts. But then the report suddenly switches genre to describe in rich detail the throwing down of the gauntlet and the spectacle at Tothill Fields: the stage carpentry, the *mise-en-scène*, Nayler's costume. Attempting to provide a legal justification for the spectacle, the report explains: it was "for [the defendant's] assurance [that] the order should be kept touching ye combate" (1152). The plaintiffs' failure to appear was to clinch the settlement. In this sense, the drama in Tothill Fields was to have real and binding legal force. In fact, the public spectacle would do what apparently the Chief Justice of the Court of Common Pleas and the Queen herself could not do: ensure the validity of the legal decision. At the same time, the spectacle decided nothing. In fact, it represented a lie: there had been no actual verdict. The plaintiffs had *not* lost but had in fact pocketed a rather tidy sum. Moreover, the event's theatricality far exceeded its potential legal utility. Surely there were simpler and less costly ways of securing the settlement than constructing scaffolding for four thousand spectators, erecting a large stage, and mounting on it a replica of the Court of Common Pleas, furniture and all.

Whatever the Queen's or Dyer's intentions, that costly, elaborate theatricality—a theatrical supplement exceeding any legal necessity—helped to articulate the contradictory meanings of the event. It implicitly drew a set of parallels: between the prize fight that was to take place in the field and the verbal fights that took place in court; between the costumed champions and the costumed judges, in their ceremonial robes and coifs; and between the real Common Pleas in Westminster Hall and the one on the "stage ... *representing* the court of the common pleas." In replicating the seating arrangements of the Common Pleas and many of its forms, the event made it hard for spectators to miss the analogy. The event seemed, initially at least, to collapse the difference between these. Perhaps there was really no difference between a court and a "stage ... *representing* [a] court"? Perhaps there was no difference between a trial and a prize fight, a spectacular diversion, a bit of theatre? However, at the same time, the arc of the event also seemed to act out precisely the opposite message. It taught a lesson to the four thousand

[6] Given that the parties had pursued the suit fervently for at least a decade, through multiple courts and before multiple juries, it seems surprising that they would simply settle unless the Queen forced them to do so. She appears to have been heavily involved in the case, both weighing in on the decision and lending her Yeoman of the Guard to Nayler. But she was almost certainly not present at the combat, since no one mentions her presence there.

spectators who went to Tothill Fields expecting the show-of-a-lifetime. It seduced the crowd with the promise of law-as-sport, inflaming its desire for spectacle only to chasten it. The lesson was: do not expect trials to be like prize fights. Law is not entertainment. The verdict was thus a victory not only for the defendant against the plaintiffs and their all-too-showy champion but for law against theatre. Law, not spectacle, had decided the case.

Law as Performance: Legal Theatricality and Antitheatricality as Idea and Practice

The thwarted Tothill Fields trial by battle stands for several principles that are at the heart of this book. In their shortest (most schematic form) they are as follows. *First* and most obviously, while legislators, judges, texts, institutions, ideas, and social practices produce and enact law, so does performance—a word whose multiple meanings I discuss below. *Second*, law's aesthetic power is essential to its force. Scholars of law and literature have often stressed that "there are fundamental differences between law and literature" or law and aesthetic forms generally; "most obviously, law coerces people"; it produces "command[s] backed by state power."[7] And yet, the show in Tothill Fields (like modern-day judicial reality TV) produced a coercive "command backed by state power." Law and its aesthetic representation are not always radically distinct kinds of things, their differences often more a matter of degree than of kind. *Third*, stagers often deploy performance to enact law, articulate doctrine, or enforce a decision. But performance has a tendency to take on a life of its own—its contradictory political trajectories and layered performance poetics defying attempts to harness it to legal orthodoxy. *Fourth*, whatever else legal performance may figure or express, it also (perhaps always) confronts its own status as performance, understood as power or problem, figured as inherently antithetical to law or inherently inseparable from it, embraced or reviled. Theatricality is itself one of the subjects of legal performance.

Behind such legal theatricality lies a long and rich tradition of jurisprudential thought about law as a performance practice. This is the "legal idea" to which I refer above and whose history this book seeks to recover: an idea explicitly articulated in countless texts and, at the same time, communicated through actions, staging, events. My study traces the history of this idea through the early modern period while at the same time exploring some of its manifestations in practice. As an idea, it was once overwhelmingly influential,

[7] Gewirtz, "Narrative and Rhetoric in the Law," 4 ("fundamental differences"); West, "Adjudication Is Not Interpretation" (unlike "other things we do with words" such as literature, adjudication "is imperative, [a] command backed by state power" [207]); and see Petch, "Borderline Judgments" ("law has direct and material social consequences that literature does not" [7]).

engendering an elaborate poetics of legal performance—a set of performance rules and norms—and a highly developed critical vocabulary for thinking about the ethics and politics of legal performance. Performance is at the center of a tradition of thought that ancient, medieval, and early modern theorists and practitioners transmitted across centuries, continually elaborating it and altering it to suit changing conditions. It appears in explicit discussions of how to perform in the courtroom (in rhetorical manuals and judges' and lawyers' guides to practice). But it also appears in more fragmented form in codes and collections of customary law, statutes, law reports, legal opinions, procedural treatises, proposals for judicial reform, chronicles, trial reports, execution narratives, memoirs, letters, visual images.

Such texts helped to articulate what became truisms about the value of legal spectacle and spectatorship. Punishment was to be visible to terrify evildoers. Judicial proceedings were to be transparent and accessible to the people (at least some were). Proverbially, law was not merely to be done but "seen to be done." At the same time, they pointed to the dangers of legal spectacle and spectatorship. The lure of beauty or riches could seduce the judge. Spectacle could blind one with its splendor. The best performers used theatre to deceive. The attribute of Justice's blindfold—which began to appear in visual representations in the late fifteenth century—could exalt Justice or act as an accusation: sometimes idealizing her impartiality (neither courtroom histrionics, false pity, nor the splendor of riches could sway her); sometimes satirizing her blindness. In a portrayal of "Worldly Justice" in the Dutch jurist Joost de Damhouder's popular civil practice manual (1562) (fig. 0.1), she is "Janus-faced": one side wears a blindfold; the other's eyes are open.[8] The image registers the blindfold's ambiguities. On the one hand, as Damhouder explains, the blindfold may represent blindness to justice: Worldly Justice is often blind to just causes; her eyes bound by a blindfold, she cannot see her way to clemency. On the other hand, as the image and its captions suggest, the blindfold may represent true Justice's immunity to the seductions of the eye. Sighted (on the left), she is swayed by "Favor, Kin, Silver, Lawyer[s], [Greedy] Guardians" who try to bribe her as the flames of "Hell" lick at their feet.

[8] *Praxis rerum civilium* (1567), sig. ****1v (and for Damhouder's extended explanation of the image, sig. ****2r-****8v). The image originally appeared in the 1562 edition of his *Praxis rerum criminalium*, and appears in different versions in the many editions in various languages that follow this one. I am indebted here to the discussions in Resnik and Curtis, *Representing Justice*, 72–4 (and 62–75, 91–105 generally on Justice's blindfold); Huygebaert et al., ed., *Art of Law*, 116–19 specifically on the Damhouder image and 147–50 on Justice's blindfold generally; and see Prosperi, *Justice Blindfolded*; and Hayaert, "Paradoxes of Lady Justice's Blindfold." For similar negative representations of Justice's blindfold, see, for instance, the 1494 image of the Fool blindfolding Justice (sometimes attributed to Albrecht Dürer) in Sebastian Brant's *Ship of Fools*, or the image of the Tribunal of Fools in Schwarzenberg, *Bambergische Peinliche Halsgerichtsordnung* (1508); and see the discussion (and reproduction of both images) in Resnik and Curtis, 67–9. The negative blindfold also draws on the traditional iconographic contrast between Jewish Synagoga (blindfolded) and Christian Ecclesia (clear-sighted).

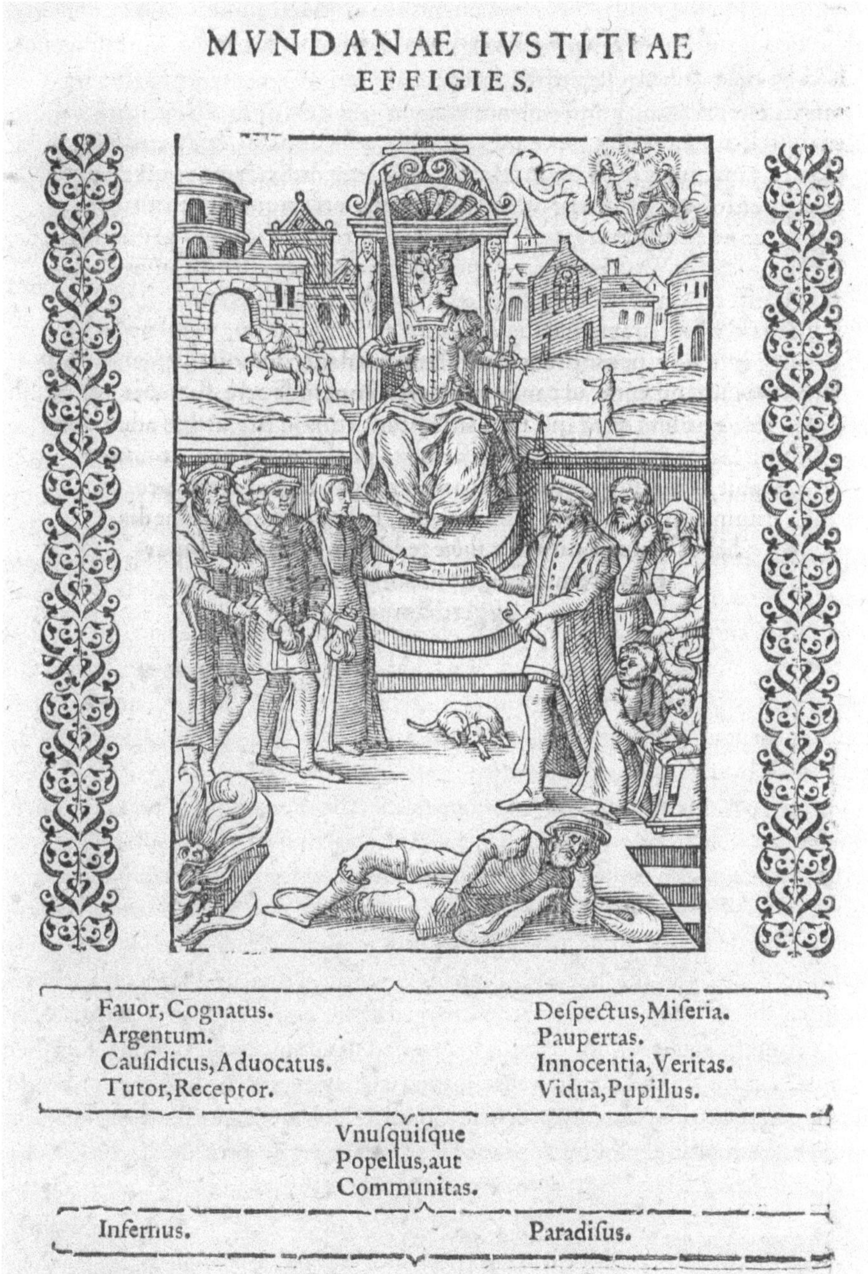

Fig. 0.1 Janus-faced, half-blindfolded "Worldly Justice" in Dutch jurist Joost de Damhouder's *Practice in Civil Cases* (1567): "Favor, Kin, Silver, Lawyer[s] . . . " against "Misery, Poverty, Innocence, Truth, [the] Widow, [the] Orphan."

Damhouder, *Praxis rerum civilium* (1567), sig. ****1v. Rare Book Collection, Lillian Goldman Law Library, Yale Law School.

Blindfolded (on the right), she metes out justice to "the Despised, Misery, Poverty, Innocence, Truth, the Widow, the Orphan" without regard for worldly goods, blessed by the heavenly Trinity that hovers above.

One can find a similar ambivalence about legal visibility in a trope with a much longer history than blindfolded Justice, a trope that appears insistently in legal thought, from ancient to modern times, in everything from learned commentaries to rude quips: the trope of law as theatre. Ancient Athenians identified trials as tragedies, and likened legal speakers to actors: both actors and legal orators needed the art of *hypokrisis* (delivery), which outlined the proper use of voice, body, and movement. Ancient Romans elaborated on the likeness in their transformation of *hypokrisis* into the arts of *actio* (bodily action) and *pronuntiatio* (vocal expression). For them and their heirs, the theatre of law was where justice and truth might be revealed and enacted. In this sense, law itself was a "Theatre of Justice and Truth," as the title of Giovanni Battista de Luca's magisterial treatise declared.[9] But law as theatre could, alternatively, be a place of lies, perverting the course of justice. For in teaching legal speakers the art of *hypokrisis*, actors taught them the art of falsehood. In a famous anecdote, Solon-the-lawgiver attacked Thespis-the-actor for telling lies. If theatre was allowed, he said, it would soon spread its lies to the most solemn of legal acts.[10] For Plato, the theatre of law was not merely a place of lies but the site of mob rule. There the "theatrocracy" (*theatrokratia*)—run by a rabble that ruled the lawcourts through applause—augured the end of law, the beginning of nihilism, and the inevitable return to a brutish state of nature.[11]

In this view, theatre and law were opposites. Theatre was the realm of artifice, ostentation, vulgar entertainment, melodrama, narcissistic self-display, hysteria, perfidy. Law was the realm of dispassionate reason, objectivity, discipline, and the sovereignty of truth. Legal speakers were not to attempt to hoodwink Justice, blinding her with histrionic arts. One was not to do anything "fitter for the stage than the court" (as the lawyer Abraham Fraunce wrote in 1588) or let one's theatrical tricks show.[12] Those who charged their opponents with theatricality were saying: "I stand for law." But law, one had to admit, could not do altogether without theatre. It had to showcase justice, visibly represent its own force and dignity, induce deterrent awe in the populace, produce docile legal subjects through example, deploy the passions of the crowd, provide a theatre for

[9] De Luca, *Theatrum veritatis, et iustitiae* (1669–81).

[10] Plutarch, *Lives* [Loeb], 1:489 [Solon, 29]. The story is the inspiration for Kezar, ed., *Solon and Thespis*, a collection of essays on early modern law and drama.

[11] Plato, *Collected Dialogues* (ed. Hamilton and Cairns), 1294 [*Laws*, 700c–701c]. The term theatrocracy appears surprisingly rarely in later discussions, but see Nietzsche's *Case of Wagner*, where it denotes the dominion of theatre over the other arts ("a faith in the *precedence* of the theater, in the right of the theater to *lord it* over the arts, over art") (*Birth of Tragedy and the Case of Wagner*, 182); Rancière, *Philosopher and His Poor*, especially 45–7; and Weber, *Theatricality as Medium*, 31–53.

[12] Fraunce, *Arcadian Rhetorike*, sig. K3v.

vengeance, promise catharsis as closure. The legal actor had to employ just enough theatre, but not too much. The trope thus registered two opposing attitudes: legal theatricality (law needs theatre); and legal antitheatricality (law must avoid theatre at all costs). It marked these out as antinomies, but also revealed them as, often, perilously proximate. Recognizing law as a performance practice, it identified theatre as both a source of law's power and an embarrassment.

As I suggest throughout this book, such debates about legal theatricality are not just jurisprudential footnotes but lie at the heart of legal theory, defining what counts as law and what does not. "What is law?" (legal philosophers have asked since the beginning of time). "Not theatre!" Except when it is. My study is thus not only a history of law as a performance practice; it is also a history of legal performance as a constitutive idea in western jurisprudence. Modern legal historians and philosophers have largely ignored performance, whether as legal practice or legal problem. This is understandable. Most legal transactions were (and are) spectacularly unspectacular, involving paper-pushing (or the equivalent), forms and formulae, deals in back rooms with no spectators to applaud or hiss. Trials were not single spectacular events but made up of a series of actions—formal accusation, investigation, interrogation, compilation of evidence, decisions on proper procedures and methods of proof—most of which took place in private chambers. Even public proceedings could be decidedly dull, lasting for weeks or (sometimes) years. In the penal sphere, fines, imprisonment, and exile were far more common than the kinds of spectacular public punishments we associate with ancient Rome or medieval and early modern Europe.[13] Legal events that took theatrical form, as the Tothill Fields trial by battle did, were rare happenings. And yet such events played an outsized role in people's perceptions of what law stood for (as sensational trials do today). Such events, along with accounts of what they meant and how to do them, served—and serve—as the narrative and conceptual backdrop to the day-to-day life of law.

If legal historians and philosophers of law have largely ignored this tradition, scholars in a number of other fields have nevertheless recognized its potential importance and explored some of its many facets. Law and literature has long looked to early play texts and theatrical representation for what they may tell us of historical legal performance practices and ideas. Cultural history has vividly conveyed both the drama and the meaning of the medieval and early modern spectacle of punishment. Historians of rhetoric have shown us the importance of judicial oratory in rhetorical theory and practice. In recent decades, classicists have devoted their attention to performance in a number of domains, among them the ancient lawcourts. And scholars in law and humanities generally have

[13] See Caviness, "Giving 'The Middle Ages' a Bad Name," 194 (and generally); Dean, *Crime in Medieval Europe*, 180 and "Criminal Justice in Mid-Fifteenth-Century Bologna," 26–7; Jordan, *From England to France*, 24–7; and Tedeschi, *Prosecution of Heresy*, 151.

turned increasingly to the exploration of law as a visual, embodied, spatial, sensory, and affective practice.[14] I am heavily indebted to such studies, on which I draw liberally throughout this book. I hope that our work will, collectively, contribute to reimagining legal history as the history not only of doctrines and institutions but of felt and lived experience. This book attempts to give an account of a set of discourses and practices that were (I argue) central to that history for millennia, and continue to be so today.

That said, I did not actually set out to write a book that would cover more or less two thousand years. It was to be a collection of historical forays: studies of specific legal events that I hoped would, together, demonstrate a set of diverse methodologies for interpreting legal performance. Having completed most of the studies that would make up that book, I thought I should perhaps add a chapter of prehistory that could serve as historical scaffolding, explaining the long tradition of thought about legal performance that undergirded the specific events I was examining. A paragraph on Plato became a chapter; my chapter of prehistory became two, then three (and so on). The material seemed to demand that I follow it. As my chapters alarmingly split and multiplied, I found myself plunging recklessly into unfamiliar periods and places, moving far farther into the past than I had ever dreamed of going. That "chapter" of prehistory is this book: the prequel (in a sense) to the book I had originally envisioned.

Although I did not set out to write such a book, in the course of doing so I did come to feel that studying the *longue durée* offered valuable perspectives that my initial shorter time span would not have provided. Among other things, only by looking at widely different periods can one see past period exceptionalism and recognize that what may appear unique to one period is in fact part of a longer tradition. Only a longer trajectory can show how formative ideas and practices travel and mutate, continually generating new ones. Only such a trajectory can show tradition to be a thing that is not static or unidirectional: a thing that does not change in a from–to fashion or form a seamless totality, but waxes and wanes, crosses borders, disappears and re-emerges in utterly new guises; a thing that is messy, multifarious, and often very untraditional.[15] More specifically, it was only

[14] I cite much of this scholarship throughout. See especially Chapter 1, note 8 and Chapter 2, note 7 (on studies of ancient legal performance); Chapter 3, notes 4 and 44 (on judicial oratory in the history of rhetoric); Chapter 4, note 164 (on studies of the spectacle of punishment); and Chapter 5, note 6 (on studies of early modern theatre and law). Several important studies of law, theatre, and performance in later periods are nevertheless in dialogue with this project. See e.g. the discussions of law in Joseph R. Roach's extraordinary *Cities of the Dead* (especially 55–62, 239–82); Leiboff, *Towards a Theatrical Jurisprudence*; Read, *Theatre & Law*; and the essays in Umphrey, Douglas, and Sarat, eds., *Law and Performance*; Bove, ed., *Théâtre & justice*; Leiboff and Nield, eds., *Law's Theatrical Presence*; and Biet and Schifano, eds., *Représentations du procès*. For further discussion of law and performance as a proto-field, see my "Mapping Law and Performance."

[15] For a classic account of "tradition" in this sense, see Hobsbawm and Ranger, ed., *Invention of Tradition*; and for an inspiring parallel discussion, see Greenblatt, ed., *Cultural Mobility: A Manifesto* (especially 1–23 and 250–3).

after traversing large swathes of legal history that I began to see fully what before I had seen only in fragments: just how enduringly important performance—and spectatorship—have always been for law.

Law as Spectatorship: Public Trials, Open Courts, and the "Audience"

Even at trials "behind closed doors" there was always at least one spectator: a judge "holding audience." But trials were also often held in "open Court," at the "open barre" before "publique Audience[s]."[16] I use historical phrases here in part as a reminder that terms such as "open" or "public" can mean very different things in different contexts. As Subha Mukherji has stressed, phrases describing courts as closed or open register perceptions as much as realities.[17] Nevertheless, such terms—however imprecise—can offer clues about trial audiences, whose nature is often elusive. We do know a good deal about the audiences that gathered in the Athenian Agora or Roman Forum. But, while historians of medieval and early modern law have given us detailed accounts of the practices, procedures, personnel, doctrines, and jurisdictional powers of a dizzying multitude of early courts, they rarely mention trial audiences. In the course of writing this book, I often found myself searching in vain in the vast literature on medieval and early modern law for answers to specific questions: who, precisely, was allowed into a particular courtroom? Who was actually there? Where did they sit? How did they behave? What was the space like?[18] I have striven to answer such questions where I can, particularly where they illuminate scenes I analyze closely. In doing so, I have repeatedly stumbled upon basic facts and suggestive details that are at odds with

[16] See Lambarde, *Just Lawyer*, 10 ("open Court"); Prest, "William Lambarde," 472 (quoting Lambarde on the "open barre"); and Tuvill, *Essaies Politicke, and Morall*, fol. 1r ("publique Audience"); and for "huys clos" (behind closed doors), see La Roche-Flavin, *Treze livres des parlemens de France* (1617 ed.), 296 [Bk 4, 67].

[17] See Mukherji's excellent discussion of the idea of the open court in *Law and Representation*, 174–205 ("[o]penness is at once a spatial perception and a function of the 'public'" [194]). In law, the word "public" often means "state-sponsored" (rather than individual or "private"). A history of the "open" or "public" trial (as concept and reality) is still to be written. For brief, general accounts, see Herman, *Right to a Speedy and Public Trial*, 1–30; and Radin, "Right to a Public Trial."

[18] Attention to physical space, action, and atmosphere is rare in traditional legal history. There have been, however, a number of studies of early courthouses, courtrooms, their spatial arrangements, and their iconography. Those to which I am most indebted include: Resnik and Curtis, *Representing Justice*, (see especially 1–87, 134–6, on medieval and early modern civic space, the rise of town halls, and their images and architecture); Graham, *Ordering Law* (especially 1–71 on medieval and early modern English courtrooms); Deimling, "Courtroom: From Church Portal to Town Hall" (a brief but very helpful account of ecclesiastical court locations); and the brief description of typical late medieval courtroom arrangements in Brundage, "'My Learned Friend,'" 186. For an anthropological approach to medieval and early modern legal ritual that pays considerable attention to space, see Garapon, *L'âne portant des reliques*. The chapter on trials in Dillon, *Language of Space*, 155–77 (closely analyzing space in, primarily, the trial of Mary Queen of Scots) offers a useful model for both legal and performance historians; and see my "Staging the Last Judgment in the Trial of Charles I."

certain textbook narratives. Most notable among these is the classic account of the disappearance of public trials on the Continent some time in the twelfth century.[19] These facts and details appear throughout my book, but a very short summary may be helpful to those who might say (as one learned colleague did), "but there were no trial audiences outside of England!"

Few would dispute the fact that judgment in early medieval Europe often took place "in an atmosphere of public witness" before "a communal audience" (as Wendy Davis and Paul Fouracre put it).[20] And few would dispute the fact that many courts in late medieval *England* remained relatively open public venues. But most would insist that things were quite different on the Continent after the twelfth-century "legal revolution."[21] According to the now standard account, around the time that the Church founded the Inquisition, Roman and canon law began spreading their tentacles across the Continent, transforming the old customary accusatorial legal systems into inquisitorial systems. Trials moved behind closed doors almost everywhere but England. Gone were the old traditions: proof through witnesses and community testimony; public, collective judgment; protections against false accusation. The judge-as-Inquisitor became the sole accuser, interrogating witnesses in secret and extorting confessions through torture. The only forms of public justice that remained came too late, after torture and confession had confirmed guilt: in vast public sentencing proceedings; and in the spectacular displays of brutality that exhibited so-called justice to the people, treating staggering savagery as sacred ritual.

This account has a good deal of truth to it (even in this grossly schematic form): many trials were closed to all but a few officials; judges usually interrogated witnesses (at least initially) in chambers. However, in the chapters that follow I question various elements of it: showing the ongoing importance of oral argument before various kinds of audiences; qualifying standard representations of inquisitorial trials and late medieval punishment rituals as controlled expressions of absolute power; and examining public or semi-public trials and trial spectators. What is indisputable is that there were "trial audiences outside of England," in later periods as in earlier ones.

A few notes and images must stand here as placeholders for my more extended discussion of public trials in Chapters 3, 4, and 5.[22] In the later Middle Ages and well into the early modern period, many courts continued to hold trials in church porticos, public squares, marketplaces, on city walls, or in other open public spaces. In a lengthy discourse on why trials must

[19] See e.g. Peters, *Torture*, 41–4; Evans, *Rituals of Retribution*, 37; Deane, *History of Medieval Heresy and Inquisition*, 100–1; Dülmen, *Theatre of Horror* (throughout, but especially 34–9); Cohen, *Crossroads of Justice*, 54, 75; Merback, *Thief, the Cross, and the Wheel*, 132–3 (132 for "behind closed doors"); and my more extended discussion in Chapter 4, 146.

[20] Davis and Fouracre, ed., *Settlement of Disputes*, 216.

[21] For discussion of the twelfth-century "legal revolution," see Chapter 3 and 4, 93–4, 146–8.

[22] See especially Chapter 3, 92–3, 110–11, 119, Chapter 4, 150–76, and Chapter 5, 200–4, 228–32, 238–50.

be open to the public in his 1617 treatise on the French parlements, judge Bernard de La Roche-Flavin notes that there are "tribunals of justice [in] many places in public squares in the towns of France," some "uncovered, exposed to the Sun, winds, & rain," holding trials in "open session" [*à huys ouvert*]."[23] Even courts that met indoors were often open to the street. One *c.*1497 image (fig. 0.2) shows a lively scene in a Hamburg municipal courtroom: judges, parties, bailiffs, prisoners, and onlookers crowd around the judges' bench or mill around inside the courtroom; many more gathered outside peer through the giant window at the scene within.[24] An image in Damhouder's criminal law manual shows a more dramatic scene: a supplicant begs the judge for mercy on bended knee, while spectators watch through the windows at the back (fig. 0.3).[25] Even heresy and witch trials—which were supposed to be among the most secret—were not always so secret. At the heresy trial of Jan Hus in 1415, there were hundreds of people in the audience.[26] At Françoise Fontaine's witch trial in Louviers, France in 1591, "a great number of people" watched the spectacle through windows.[27]

In many of the royal palaces converted to "palaces of justice" between the fourteenth and sixteenth centuries, large crowds gathered to watch trials: for instance, in the Quarantia courts in the Ducal Palace in Venice; or in the judicial parlements (appeals courts) in Paris, Rouen, Toulouse, Aix-en-Provence, Dijon, and elsewhere in France.[28] As La Roche-Flavin writes, justice is "rendered publicly in the great halls of the Palaces, which one calls 'halls for Audiences'" because, "if [justice] . . . is not seen by all, that is not justice."[29] We can see such audiences in an image of the Toulouse Parlement, in which dozens of attendees crowd around the gated bar, jockeying for elbow room (fig. 0.4).[30] Writing in the mid-fifteenth

[23] "Les places publiques des villes" are "sans aucune couverture, & à descouvert, exposée[s] au Soleil, vents, & pluyes," though occasionally, "au tour de ces places, ou tribunaux de la justice, il y avoit des couverts, co[m]me nous voyons es environs de plusieurs places des villes de France." "[E]n ces Basiliques, ou places publiques, [on] donnoit Audiance [aux Advocats] à huys ouverts." La Roche-Flavin, *Treze livres des parlemens de France* (1617 ed.), 296 [Bk 4, Ch 66–7]). La Roche-Flavin was presiding judge in the Chambre des Requêtes in the Toulouse Parlement.

[24] Hamburg Staatsarchiv, Cl. VII. Lit. LaNr. 2 Vol. 1 c, reproduced in Reincke and Bolland, ed., *Die Bilderhandschrift des Hamburgischen Stadtrechts von 1497* (unpaginated, image B; and see, similarly, image C). With thanks to Wolfgang Schild for helping me locate this image.

[25] Damhouder, *Praxis rerum criminalium* (1562), sig. ***4v.

[26] See my extended discussion in Chapter 4, 165–76.

[27] A "grand nombre de peuple . . . estoit aux fenestres de lad. cohue" (noisy courtroom). Bénet, ed. *Procès verbal fait pour délivrer une fille possédée*, 68.

[28] Both the Quarantia courts in Venice and the French parlements had political functions as well, but from the late Middle Ages, their main order of business was judicial. On these courts generally and for the fact that their doors were open to the public, see Viggiano, "Giustizia, disciplina e ordine pubblico," especially 833–4; and Shennan, *Parlement of Paris* [1998 ed.], especially 18, 68, 100–1, 105–6; and below.

[29] "[L]a justice se rend publiquement es grandes sales des Palais, qu'on appelle les sales des Audiances de la grand Chambre" (*Treze livres des parlemens de France*, 299 [Bk 4, sec. 75]). "[L]a justice si elle . . . n'est veüe de tous, ce n'est pas justice" (298 [Bk 4, Ch 74]).

[30] Bertrand, *Opus De Tholosanorum Gestis* (1515) (title page). The image shows François I confirming offices in the Toulouse Parlement, but represents the Parlement more generally. The Toulouse Parlement was the first of the provincial parlements, established *c.*1420–37.

Fig. 0.2 A busy Hamburg municipal courtroom (*c.*1497), with a group of petitioners and onlookers clustered beside the judges' table (far right), and a large crowd at the window.

Staatsarchiv Hamburg, 111-1 Senat, Nr. 92693: Stadtrecht, 1497 [Altsignatur: Cl. VII Lit. L a Nr. 2 Vol. 1 c].

Fig. 0.3 A supplicant begs the judge for mercy on bended knee, as spectators watch the scene through the windows in Joost de Damhouder's *Practice in Criminal Cases* (1562).

Damhouder, *Praxis rerum criminalium* (1562). The Bodleian Libraries, University of Oxford, Douce D 230, sig. ***4v.

Fig. 0.4 A crowd of attendees in the Toulouse Parlement's courtroom in jurist Nicolas Bertrand's *Acts of the Toulousians* (1515).

Bertrand, *Opus de Tholosanorum Gestis* (1515). The Bodleian Libraries, University of Oxford, Vet. E1 d. 46, frontispiece.

century, jurist Thomas Basin claimed that trials in the parlements of Normandy and Paris often had as many as fifteen hundred spectators.[31] A little over a century later, Etienne Pasquier claimed there were nine or ten *thousand* spectators at one of the trials he argued in the Paris Parlement.[32] Throughout these pages, I offer testimony to the presence of audiences—sometimes large ones—at trials on the Continent, as in England: in (for instance) repeated references to "the Court, *and* the whole Audience"; in images of trial spectators; and in descriptions of trials as vast "spectacles" in which (as in Tothill Fields) participants were expected to "perform" for the "crowd."[33]

Performance, Theatricality, Gender, Law, and the Question of Anachronism

Although early cultures did not have a single word for what we call "performance," they did have many words that served a similar function. Throughout, I look closely at these words, viewing them as crucial clues to the ideas and attitudes that lay behind discussions of legal performance. Most notable among them were terms specifically focused on bodily expression: "*hypokrisis*," "*actio*," "*pronuntiatio*," "delivery" (and variants). For the Spanish humanist Juan Luis Vives, "*actio*" denoted not only bodily action but—like the modern word "performance"—the full range of display skills and "active" aesthetic practices whose end (he said) was "action," including oratory, theatre, dance, and music.[34] Words that described audiences—"*spectatores*," "*publica*," "*auditorium*," and cognates—similarly served to link different kinds of events, all of which had spectators.[35] The word *actus* could denote an action generally, but in certain contexts pointed specifically to actions displayed for an audience: the reason that public disputations in England were called "acts." While the English word "performance" denoted the accomplishment of any kind of action (as it often does today), it could also specifically identify actions for spectators, including legal ones: Nayler and Thorne were (as we have seen) "sworn... to *perform* the battle at *Tothill*"; Inns of Court students regularly

[31] "Libellus de optimo ordine forenses lites audiendi et deferendi," 35 (in Basin, *Histoire des règnes de Charles VII et de Louis XI* [1859 ed.], vol. 4); with thanks to Jody Enders' *Rhetoric and the Origins of Medieval Drama*, 40–3, 96, for introducing me to Basin, whom I discuss briefly in Chapter 3 and at greater length in Chapter 4, 153–7.

[32] Pasquier, *Oeuvres d'Estienne Pasquier* (1723 ed.), 2:314, and see my extended discussion of this case in Chapter 5, 244–50.

[33] Charrier, *Memorable action judiciaire* (1559), 5 ("la Cour, & tout l'Auditoire"; emphasis added); and see similar examples and references to "performing," "spectacle," and the "crowd" throughout.

[34] Vives, *Vives On Education*, 23; *De [tradendis] disciplinis* (1612 ed.), 223 (arts whose essence is "actio,... quae activae dicantur").

[35] The word "*auditorium*" at once denoted the people gathered to listen and the place where something was heard, and (more narrowly) a judicial hearing.

"performed" in moots.[36] Theatrical analogies similarly stressed the relationships among different kinds of performance events, most notably (for my purposes) legal and theatrical ones: the Roman Forum was a "theatre [*theatrum*] [of] eloquence" (as Cicero put it); for later commentators, a trial or punishment might be a "spectacle" or "pagean[t]," "a[n] enterlude upon a stage," "a theatre for [staging] comedies or satires."[37] Words such as *scaenicus*, like our "theatrical," both identified representations that took place in theatres and described events or behavior that resembled those representations (usually to decry their histrionics or mendacity).

All of these words served to point to performance as a distinctive form of expression, palpably different from both textual expression and ordinary being and doing. At the same time, the trope of the *theatrum mundi*—expressed in such assertions as "all the world's a stage" or "the make-believe [is] true"—identified performance as a universal ontological condition: all doing and being was, in fact, performance in the "great theatre of the world."[38] In bearing this double meaning, the constellation of early terms designating performance and theatricality aligns surprisingly well with the double meaning of the words "performance" and "performativity" in contemporary critical usage. On the one hand, "performance" may *describe* a *particular* form of expression: what Richard Schechner famously called "showing doing"; those special actions that expressly or overtly display, signify, present, demonstrate, or enact something for a real or imagined audience.[39] On the other hand, "performance" (or its adjunct "performativity") may *diagnose* a *universal* ontological condition: the fact that what appears as natural is in fact produced and reproduced through performance on the stage of life.

These two ideas about performance are different, yet they converge, particularly when overt performance seems to reveal the performativity of everyday life or display the world as theatre. Early legal performance often seems to do just this.

[36] Middle English borrowed the verb "to perform" from the French, using it to designate both "to carry out (an action)" and "to furnish" (often in legal contexts). For the later history of the word and its variants, see my discussion in "Law as Performance," 200–1. And see Chapter 6 for many examples in which "perform" and "performance" specifically denote the display of action or skills (there, in legal contexts).

[37] Cicero, *Brutus, Orator* [Loeb], 23 [*Brutus*, 6] (describing the orator Hortensius). For "spectacle," see e.g. Basin, *Histoire de Louis XI* (1963–72 ed. [orig. 1471–3]), 2:269; Pernoud, ed., *Retrial of Joan of Arc* (orig. 1450s), 240; and *Most Wonderfull and True Storie* (1597), 24. For "pageantes," Phillips, *Examination and Confession of Certaine Wytches* (1566), sig. A3r. For "enterlude...," Buchanan, *Detectioun of the duinges of Marie Quene of Scottes* (1571), sig. F1r. "Ne doit la court estre ung theatre pour y faire comedies ne satires" (chief royal prosecutor of France in 1495; quoted in Houllemare, *Politiques de la parole*, 457).

[38] Readers will of course recognize Shakespeare's *As You Like It* [2.7]. "The make-believe [is] true" is a rough translation of the title of Lope de Vega's play, *Lo fingido verdadero* (*c.*1608), in which, the actor Genesius (later Saint Genesius) becomes a Christian by performing the role of a Christian. And see Calderón's *El gran teatro del mundo* (*c.*1634).

[39] "'Showing doing' is performing: pointing to, underlining, and displaying doing." "The underlying notion is that any action that is framed, enacted, presented, highlighted, or displayed is a performance" (*Performance Studies* [2013 ed.], 28, 2). Schechner famously describes such actions as "twice-behaved"; "restored"; in the "subjunctive" mode, expressing an "as if...". Schechner, *Between Theater and Anthropology* (e.g. 3, 6, 35, 37, 41, 52, 55, 104, 112, and throughout).

For instance, in his defense of Titus Annius Milo, on trial for murder, Cicero pointed to Milo as a vision of stoic masculinity and declared that Milo's manliness forbade that he weep publicly: Cicero himself would have to weep Milo's secret tears, which he proceeded to do, weeping copiously throughout the speech.[40] Cicero seems quite aware of the norms he is deploying (as a device for gaining sympathy for the not-altogether-sympathetic Milo). If a time-traveling twenty-first-century critic were to arrive in Rome in 52 BCE to reveal to Cicero that his speech had "exposed the norms of quotidian gender performance" (overcoming the not insignificant translation challenges), Cicero might say: "so I did!" But his display of gender performativity did not serve in any sense as critique. For acts of unmasking the *theatrum mundi* or the performative constitution of things are political wild cards. Like performance generally, they rarely have a single political meaning but are instead many-vectored, ambiguous, ambivalent, politically polymorphous (and sometimes altogether perverse) things.[41]

Sadly but unsurprisingly, while early commentators might recognize gender as (in part) a thing that was made through performance, very few thought this meant that gender roles were malleable, least of all in law. Virtually all commentators (ancient to early modern) understood judges, lawyers, and other kinds of legal actors to be, necessarily, men. There were exceptions. Female rulers could preside as judges or intervene in cases.[42] Valerius Maximus lists a few "women who pleaded before magistrates for themselves or others" in ancient Rome. Among these was the "infamous" Carfania, whose appearance in medieval law books I discuss in Chapter 4, Maesia of Sentium, who pleaded before "a great concourse of people, going through all the forms and stages of a defence not only thoroughly but boldly," and Hortensia, who "pleaded the cause of women before the Triumvirs resolutely and successfully, ... [r]eviving her father's eloquence" and winning her case.[43] In the year 1500, Giustina Rocca served as judge (*arbiter*) in the Tribunal of Trani (Italy) in a highly public family inheritance dispute ("all the people rushed to see such a female wonder sit on the bench of the tribunal and proffer the sentence").[44] In one mid-fourteenth-century text, the Virgin Mary

[40] See *Pro Milone*; and my discussion in Chapter 2, 78–80.

[41] For an extended discussion, see my "Legal Performance Good and Bad."

[42] Pope Gregory's *Decretals* (one of the major sources of canon law) actually specifies that illustrious women with power and authority are an exception to the general rule, and may act as judges in cases between their subjects. See Mastroberti, "Sul caso della tranese Giustina Rocca" (quoting the *Decretals*, Bk 1, Title 43, Ch 4).

[43] Valerius, *Memorable Doings and Sayings* [Loeb], 2:211 [8.3].

[44] "[T]ota penitus civitas confluit, ut videret tale monstrum mulierem in bancho sedentem pro tribunali, et sententiam ... proferentem." Lambertini, *Tractatus de iure patronatus* (1533); passage quoted in full in Mastroberti, "Sul caso della tranese Giustina Rocca," 108 (and see 107–10 on Giustina generally). I have translated "monstrum" as "wonder" because Lambertini's attitude is otherwise positive, but the word could, of course, have far more negative associations. Lambertini's short account is the only source for the story. Giustina's grandchildren were the parties and asked her to arbitrate, presumably because she had substantial legal knowledge and (as Lambertini puts it) had

declares that, while "women generally are not admitted to the office of advocate," they may defend orphans, widows, and the miserable: perhaps pointing to additional instances in which women served as advocates.[45] It seems not merely possible but probable—given the still largely untold history of transgender life—that among the male judges and lawyers were some who had once been identified as female, and others who continued to live in the borderlands of gender.

However, Justinian's sixth-century *Digest*—which served as the most important source of Roman law through the early modern period—declared:

> [o]n the ground of sex, [the praetor] forbids women to [represent] others. There is a reason for this prohibition, to prevent them from involving themselves in the cases of other people contrary to the modesty in keeping with their sex and to prevent women from performing the functions of men.[46]

Few men would have disagreed with the view that Leonardo Bruni expressed in a letter to the humanist Baptista di Montefeltro (*c.*1405), explaining that she might study piety and morality but must by no means study rhetoric, for studying rhetoric meant studying law:

> [W]hy should... a thousand... rhetorical conundrums consume the powers of a woman, who will never see the forum? That art of delivery, which the Greeks call *hypocrisis* and we *pronunciatio*,... so far is that from being the concern of a woman that if she should gesture energetically with her arms as she spoke and shout with violent emphasis, she would probably be thought mad and put under restraint. The contests of the forum, like those of warfare and battle, are the sphere of men.... She will, in a word, leave the rough-and-tumble of the forum entirely to men.[47]

As Bruni's letter suggests, the masculine pronoun in such texts is not generic or falsely universal: it is often assertively, aggressively masculine, precisely because

accomplished many "admirable things." Lambertini notes that she required the losing party to pay her for her services. Scholars have sometimes painted Giustina as a lawyer regularly working in the Trani Tribunal ("Avvocatessa del Foro di Trani"), and she may in fact have served as a diplomat between Trani and Venice, but this seems to have been the only case in which she appeared in court. For "Avvocatessa," see "Giustina Rocca," *Enciclopedia delle donne*, http://www.enciclopediadelledonne.it/biografie/giustina-rocca/ (accessed March 28, 2021).

[45] See Shoemaker, "Devil at Law," 582, quoting the *c.*1360 manuscript of the *Processus Sathanae* (Trial of Satan) in the Bibliothèque Nationale.

[46] Justinian, *Digest of Justinian* (trans. Watson, 1998 ed.), 1:79 [3.1.1.5]. For a twelfth-century update, see Bulgarus' letter to papal chancellor Haimeric: "Women can neither be judges nor bring claims for others, but can only claim for themselves. They cannot intervene on another's behalf save when they are conducting their own business" (quoted in Brasington, *Order in the Court*, 109). In some places (such as ancient Athens and some parts of medieval Europe), women could not in fact represent themselves but had to sue through a representative.

[47] Bruni, "Study of Literature" (in Kallendorf, ed., *Humanist Educational Treatises*), 105.

women refused (as we will see) to "leave the rough-and-tumble of the forum entirely to men." In replicating the masculine pronoun (as I do with some frequency), I am attempting to mark this history, which is far from past.

If "performance," "theatricality," and gendered pronouns do a fairly good job of representing historical experience, other terms have proven less tractable, including some that commonly serve as broad historical rubrics. Among these are traditional terms of periodization ("ancient," "medieval," "early modern"), place names ("Europe," "England"), as well as some of the most common keywords of legal history: "trial," "judge," "juror," "forensic," "litigant," "lawyer," "witness," "public," "courtroom," and, not least, "law." I use all of these (alongside their approximate historical equivalents) in the uncomfortable recognition that modes of categorizing legal phenomena change from one period to another—indeed, one jurisdiction to another—and that modern terms only partly express the conventions of the shifting legal histories I trace. I use "courtroom" as a general term, but, as I have noted, trials took place in many kinds of spaces, some of them "rooms" in only the loosest sense: piazzas, church porticos, marketplaces, city walls. I use the word "law" despite the fact that what counts as law may be murky at times. The double meaning of the word "court" (*curia*)—both royal court and lawcourt—reminds us how hard it may be to disentangle law from political power. The event in Tothill Fields reminds us how hard it may be to disentangle law from entertainment. That entanglement is, of course, one of the themes of this book.

Representations of Legal Performance versus Legal Performance as Representation

Although defining the parameters of both law and performance may sometimes be difficult, I have tried to keep my eye squarely on performance in legal arenas, often in the face of frustratingly limited evidence. We know a great deal about ancient, medieval, and early modern law, and quite a bit about certain legal rituals: compurgation or oath-taking ceremonies; gestures and actions that created legal status or contractual relationships.[48] We have countless tomes of doctrine and commentary, court records, and reports of words spoken in courtrooms: formal speeches; judges' pronouncements; attacks and counterattacks by disputants or their lawyers, sometimes rendered in vivid direct speech. We have a vast body of depositions, often in the form of highly dramatic narratives. But although such sources may describe events in the world at large, they are frustratingly silent on precisely the things I have sought to identify: how events in specifically legal

[48] See e.g. Stacey, *Dark Speech*; Mostert and Barnwell, ed., *Medieval Legal Process*; Davies and Fouracre, *Settlement of Disputes*; and many scattered references in Hibbitts, "Coming to Our Senses" and "Making Motions."

arenas looked, sounded, felt; the movement of legal actors in space and time; their use of body language and performance style; the mood and behavior of the audience; the visceral experience of being present there; in short, performance by and before the law. What Paul Brand writes of the medieval English courtroom might be said of early legal events generally: the "courtroom was [a] place of actions, gestures, and movement, [but] [t]hese are only very occasionally recorded."[49]

The absence of such evidence is the reason that scholars of early law so often turn to literary texts to understand what legal events felt and looked like, while recognizing that the interpreter must do a good deal of work to separate fact from fiction. What can we learn of real courtrooms from a text like Hermann von Sachsenheim's *The Moorish Woman* (1453), where the judge is "Queen Venus," the lead prosecutor is the "Moorish woman," and the defendant a knight who has violated the laws of love?[50] Probably a great deal, as the study of "law in literature" has long held. But in the temptation to interpret the politics and poetics of such a complex, verbally intricate, and narratively wild text, it is very easy to lose sight of the things real people did in real legal arenas and the things they believed to be true. Legal performances have their own politics, their own performance poetics, their own forms of complexity, intricacy, and wildness.

For that reason, I have resisted using palpably fictional texts as sources and tried to focus where I can on legal events as, themselves, modes of representation. Nevertheless, I do spend a good deal of time on representations *of* law: images and texts that represent reality as their makers saw it. These reveal conceptions of and attitudes toward legal performance that are central to my account. Like others trained in literary, visual, and performance studies, I often attend to seemingly insignificant details that are, it turns out, not insignificant at all. Thus, while my range is broad, I sometimes dwell on smaller scale moments as emblems or microcosms of larger forces, particularly in the "close readings" of performance that appear at various points in this book.[51] This practice of dwelling on small but significant moments is not just a critical habit but represents one important claim of this book: that it is not only sovereigns, legislatures, and judges who create law through grand edicts; so do law's subjects, not only through words but through

[49] Brand, *Earliest English Law Reports*, 4:xxxviii (referring only to English law reports, but his comment applies to trial records generally). See, similarly, Musson, *Public Order and Law Enforcement* (medieval law clerks "were content to provide only the bare minimum of information necessary to keep a record of the trials" [188]); and Musson, "Visualising Legal History," 203–5 (on the utility of images for filling in what trial records rarely record).

[50] *Die Mörin*: see the discussion of this text in Westphal, "Bad Girls in the Middle Ages," 108–16.

[51] For a more extended discussion of the (sometimes subtle) distinction between representations of legal events and legal events as, themselves, representations, see my "Law as Performance." For examples of close reading in this book, see the analysis of two of Cicero's speeches in Chapter 2, 75–80; of Jan Hus's defrocking and the Innsbruck reappointment ceremony in Chapter 4, 169–76 and 182–3; and of Pasquier's defense of Jean d'Arconville in Chapter 5, 244–50.

actions large and small. Law is by nature a living thing and the people who live under it change it: sometimes imperceptibly; sometimes dramatically. In this sense (to borrow Peter Goodrich's phrase), performance is a form of "minor jurisprudence."[52] And sometimes not minor at all.

Chapter Summaries

In retrospect, the fact that my paragraph on Plato swelled beyond all expectation should not have been a surprise. Medieval and early modern commentators return again and again to certain passages in ancient texts: Plato's discussions of lawcourt rhetoric, sophistry, and theatrocracy; Aristotle's of the "depravity" of audiences and "corruption" of the courts and the sad necessity of "warp[ing]" the jury. They repeatedly reference certain anecdotes, treating them as foundational stories: Demosthenes' response when asked to name the three most important elements of oratory ("Delivery, . . . delivery, . . . delivery"); Aeschines' performance of the speech that had sent him into exile, and his commentary on Demosthenes' delivery of it, "[if only] you had heard the beast himself[!]"; the contest between Cicero and the actor Roscius to determine whether Cicero could express more in words or Roscius in gestures; the scene of Cicero in the theatre, mesmerized by "the actor-man's eyes . . . blazing behind his mask" and the "sobs of mourning in his voice."[53] Those who offered the tradition its founding ideas came from or studied in far-flung places in Europe, Africa, and Asia: Egypt, Stagira, Calahorra in Rioja Baja (Spain), Numidia (Algeria), Persia, Baghdad, Damascus, Córdoba (via "Greater Libya").[54] I begin in ancient Athens and Rome not because these are self-evidently the birthplaces of European culture (as historians used to say). I begin there because their distinctive legal practices—in which prominent trials took the form of mass spectacles, and an orator's star performance before a cheering audience could make the difference between life and death—gave rise to an extensive body of thought and a set of recurrent questions about the poetics, politics, and practice of legal performance.

Those questions are at the heart of Chapter 1, "Theatre, Theatrocracy, and the Politics of Pathos in the Athenian Law Court." Here, examining a variety of legal orators alongside such major figures as Plato and Aristotle, I look at ancient Greek debates about the value and meaning of legal performance. On the one hand, legal

[52] Goodrich, *Law in the Courts of Love: Literature and Other Minor Jurisprudences* (and see Goodrich and Zartaloudis, ed., *Cabinet of Imaginary Laws*, a collection of "jurisliterary inventions" that are themselves forms of minor jurisprudence).

[53] For the sources of these discussions and anecdotes and later elaborations, see Chapter 1, 32–3, Chapter 2, 65, 80, 86; Chapter 3, 104–6; Chapter 4, 156–7, note 39; Chapter 5, 207 and note 28, 210–11, 214–16, 220, 237, 243; and Chapter 6, 264.

[54] These are places where, respectively, Plato, Aristotle, Quintilian, Augustine, Al-Farabi, and Averroës (Ibn Rushd), were either born or spent significant time studying.

theatricality appears in these debates as potentially toxic: exciting evil passions, encouraging mob rule, riding roughshod on reason. On the other hand, it appears as a powerful instrument that, rightly used, may rouse virtuous anger, pity, and fear, channeling these not toward catharsis but toward righteous judgment.

Chapter 2, "The Roman Advocate as Actor: *Actio*, *Pronuntiatio*, *Prosopopoeia*, and Persuasive Empathy in Cicero and Quintilian," takes up a different set of questions about the ethics of emotion in legal performance. For Cicero and Quintilian, the crucial question is not whether you should manipulate the theatre of the forum but how: how to display your clients as victims; how to play your audience; how to weep in court convincingly. They offer detailed accounts of the techniques advocates can employ to fully identify with their clients' anguish and communicate its reality in court: "let us not plead the case as though it were someone else's," insists Quintilian, but "take the pain of it on ourselves."[55] At the same time, they raise critical questions about the integrity of practiced empathy, the doubtful value of highlighting one's own representational frame, and the ethics of instrumentalizing suffering in the name of justice.

If my first two chapters focus on a set of foundational texts in two specific urban legal cultures, the chapters that follow turn to "minor" texts and events in widely divergent legal cultures across western Europe. Chapter 3, "Courtroom Oratory, Forensic Delivery, and the Wayward Body in Medieval Rhetorical Theory" shows the ongoing importance of theories of forensic oratory and (specifically) delivery to medieval theorists. After looking at portrayals of judicial performance in rhetorical treatises, procedural manuals, guides to legal deportment, satiric portraits of the lawyer-as-robed-vulture (and more), I turn to the work of four rhetorical theorists who rewrite (and upend) ancient rhetorical theory. In their work, law appears not as a set of rules or the sovereign's fiat but as visceral, intimate bodily experience: sometimes divine; sometimes indecorous, subject to accident, hopelessly leaky, sublimely obscene.

Chapter 4, "Irreverent Performances, Heterodox Subjects, and the Unscripted Crowd from the Medieval Courtroom to the Stocks and Scaffold," explores the gap between normative visions of legal events and their often disorderly realities: heterogeneous crowds; participants who went off-script; those who mooned the judge, spit at the Inquisitor, killed the executioner, or jeered like the mockers of Jesus. I explore here the open spaces and public venues that made trials into arenas for challenging the discipline and order that law was supposed to represent. I then turn to a detailed analysis of two trials—Jan Hus's heresy trial of 1415, and the Innsbruck witch trial of 1485—showing, in these, how defendants could use performance to recast the meaning of such events and sometimes their outcomes. In the chapter's last section, I revisit classic accounts of the medieval spectacle of

[55] Quintilian, *Orator's Education* [Loeb], 3:63 [6.2.34–5].

punishment: often characterized as "solemn religious ritual" and "theater of devotion," but in fact toppling expectations, defying intentions, turning to irreverent sport, and sometimes verging on sacrilege.

The last two chapters turn to the early modern period, in which theatres had become fixtures of the urban landscape, and lawyers seemed to have bred like "caterpillers" (the "streets [were] paved with them"!)[56] Chapter 5, "Performing Law in the Age of Theatre (*c.*1500–1650)," explores both the renewed identification of law with theatre and the legal cultures that helped give rise to that identification. As humanists borrowed from antitheatrical discourses to denounce the use of "Histrionical-Rhetorical Gesticulation" for law, those who celebrated the courtroom as a "great & magnificent theatre" invested the trope with a variety of contradictory political meanings.[57] Manuals dedicated to delivery appeared alongside a newly encyclopedic-anatomical science of non-verbal communication, teaching their users how to scrutinize nuances of body parts, gesture, and intonation: techniques they applied to courtroom performance critique. In courts like the Paris Parlement, celebrity lawyers like Etienne Pasquier blurred the boundaries between law and entertainment, flipping hostile crowds with dazzling theatrical legerdemain.

Chapter 6, "Legal Performance Education in Early Modern England," takes up the question of how one learned such performance skills. Looking at both the Inns of Court and the universities, it examines the tutoring, books, and above all the exercises that trained young men not just in how to be a lawyer but how to look like one. Often excruciatingly difficult but also sometimes uproariously funny, the exercises bore a distinct resemblance to the revels that satirized them, which themselves bore an uncanny resemblance to the real practice of law. If moots and disputations trained future lawyers in crucial skills, they also trained them in impersonation, dissimulation, and make-believe, training that shaped not only their identity as lawyers but their sense of the fundamental meaning of the profession of law.

Throughout this book, I often highlight the strangeness of history in a belief in the value of encounters with the unfamiliar, which train us to resist viewing everything in our own image, force us not to take anything for granted, and remind us: things were not always as they are; nor need they always be. At the same time, I trace a set of enduring tropes, concerns, and questions about law as performance. Changing kaleidoscopically as perspectives have changed, these have nevertheless persisted across centuries, outlasted the rise and fall of legal empires, and (as I suggest in a brief Epilogue) are still with us today. They appear

[56] *Att.-Gen v. Kinge* (21 May 1596) in Hawarde, *Les reportes del cases in Camera Stellata*, 45; *Recueil general des caquets de l'acouchee*, 140 ("les ruës de Paris en sont pavées").

[57] Agrippa, *Vanity of Arts and Sciences* (1676 trans.), 65 ("Histrionical-Rhetorical Gesticulation"). Faye d'Espeisses, *Recueil des remonstrances* (1591 ed.), 25 ("ce grand & magnifique theatre").

in the interstices of formal legal thought and practice: in discussions of the role of emotion, sensations, or the lure of charisma in legal persuasion; the means of producing law-abiding subjects and the justifications for legal violence; the virtues and evils of legal democracy; the meaning of "the rule of law"; and much more. Questions about the use and abuse of theatricality for law lurk behind some of our most important legal doctrines: show trials are bad (too much theatre), but secret trials are even worse (not enough theatre); trials must be public (they need spectators) but not too public (lest they become public spectacles); evidence may dramatize, but not too dramatically; performance must be probative but not prejudicial. Knowing the history of the ideas about performance that underlie these and many other doctrines may give us keys to understanding our own cultures of legal performance, and the more overt and less docile kinds of performance we call theatricality: seeing into their mechanisms; observing how they exert power over us; pondering their consequences. This book seeks to provide such a history.

1

Theatre, Theatrocracy, and the Politics of Pathos in the Athenian Lawcourt

Introduction: Aeschines vs. Demosthenes

In 330 BCE, the Athenian orator and statesman Aeschines addressed the stadium full of jurors and spectators gathered to hear him destroy his arch-nemesis Demosthenes in court: "I ask you to imagine for a little time" (he exhorts his listeners) "that you are not in the lawcourt, but in the theatre."[1] In that theatre, they were to imagine a scene sure to take place unless the jurors prevented it: before the more than ten thousand spectators gathered from around the Hellenic world in the Theatre of Dionysus for the annual performance of the tragedies, the Athenian people would offer Demosthenes a golden crown for his service to Athens.[2] Demosthenes (declared Aeschines) was a coward who had fled the

[1] Aeschines, *In Ctes.* 427 [3.152–3] (translation of passage modified throughout paragraph). Throughout this chapter I cite first to a page number (with volume number if necessary), followed by the standard passage identification in brackets. I use the following abbreviations for frequently cited texts not otherwise identified, conforming to the abbreviation style in Hornblower, Spawforth, and Eidinow, ed., *Oxford Classical Dictionary* (2012 ed.), xxvi–liii. For Loeb editions, I use the most recently updated versions at www-loebclassics-com.

De cor. = Demosthenes, *De Corona* [*On the Crown*] in Demosthenes, *De Corona, De Falsa legatione, XVIII, XIX* [Loeb].

De falsa = Demosthenes, *De falsa legatione* [*On the False Embassy*], in Demosthenes, *De Corona, De Falsa Legatione, XVIII, XIX* [Loeb].

Hyp. = Hyperides, in Burtt, trans., *Minor Attic Orators* [Loeb].

In Alc. = Pseudo-Andocides, *Against Alcibiades*, in Maidment, trans., *Minor Attic Orators* [Loeb].

De legat. = Aeschines, *On the Embassy*, in Aeschines, [*Speeches of Aeschines*] [Loeb].

In Ctes. = Aeschines, *Against Ctesiphon*, in Aeschines, [*Speeches of Aeschines*] [Loeb].

In Tim. = Aeschines, *Against Timarchus*, in Aeschines, [*Speeches of Aeschines*] [Loeb].

Isoc. = Isocrates, *Isocrates* [Loeb].

Lys. = Lysias, *Lysias* [Loeb].

Meid. = Demosthenes, *Against Medias*, in Demosthenes, *Orations XXI–XXVI* [Loeb].

Poet. = Aristotle, *Poetics* [Loeb].

Pol. = Aristotle, *Politics*, trans. Reeve (2017 ed.).

Rh. = Aristotle, *Rhetoric*, trans. Reeve.

Pl. = Plato, *Collected Dialogues* (ed. Hamilton and Cairns).

[2] To briefly summarize the facts of the case: in 336 BCE, a man named Ctesiphon proposed that Athens offer Demosthenes a crown (his second). Aeschines planned to sue, but for various reasons—including Philip of Macedon's assassination that year—he delayed his suit until 330. He prosecuted not Demosthenes but Ctesiphon (an easier target), charging him with lying and knowingly violating certain legal provisions in offering Demosthenes the crown. But everyone knew that Aeschines' intended target was Demosthenes. For particularly detailed accounts of the Aeschines–Demosthenes conflicts, see Harris, *Aeschines and Athenian Politics*, and Buckler, "Demosthenes and Aeschines."

Law as Performance: Theatricality, Spectatorship, and the Making of Law in Ancient, Medieval, and Early Modern Europe. Julie Stone Peters, Oxford University Press. © Julie Stone Peters 2022. DOI: 10.1093/oso/9780192898494.003.0002

battlefield in Chaeronea, as hundreds of Athenians were slaughtered. To crown him would not only patently violate several laws: it would be a foul outrage against justice itself. "[I]magine" (Aeschines urges his auditory) "that you see the herald coming forward," leading Demosthenes in glory: "the man who is responsible for making [our] children orphans." There in the theatre, "truth, ashamed, will refuse to be silent, and we shall seem to hear it crying out: . . . 'This man, if man he can be called, the Athenian people crown, . . . for his "virtue," . . . for his "nobility,"'" this so-called man is "'the basest . . . coward and deserter.'" If Demosthenes receives the crown, surely "the relatives of the dead will shed more tears over . . . the blindness of the city" than even "over the tragedies and the sufferings of the heroes soon afterward to be presented on the stage." If Demosthenes receives the crown, "what Greek" (asks Aeschines) will "not mourn as he [sits] in the theatre [?]" "No!" he implores, "by Zeus and the gods, do not, my fellow citizens, do not, I beseech you, set up in the orchestra of Dionysus a memorial of your own defeat [!]" (*In Ctes.* 427–9 [3.152–6]).

It would not have required a great leap of the imagination for the spectators to imagine the court as the Theatre of Dionysus: the city in fact often held major political trials there.[3] Moreover, for well over a decade Aeschines and Demosthenes had been denouncing each other for turning the lawcourt into a theatre. Aeschines had in fact once been an actor, and he remained (said Demosthenes) a bit-part "player," "third-rate acto[r]," "monkey of melodrama," "bumpkin tragedy-king," a "charlatan" with "the feigning voice of an actor" who might "hop[e] to overawe you by an exhibition of histrionic talent" but whose only skills were *hypokrisis* and hypocrisy.[4] Demosthenes (said Aeschines) was a "mountebank, an impostor," a "juggler," and "charlata[n]" who attempted to entrap juries with his "wicked arts of rhetoric," his buffoonery and histrionics ("his tears and the straining of his voice," his "groans for Hellas"!)[5] In these attacks, each claimed to represent truth against theatrical lies, law against histrionics. From our historical distance, it is hard to understand how the central issue at stake in the case—whether Demosthenes should be able to parade across the stage of the Theatre of Dionysus in his shiny golden crown—became an issue at all, let alone gave rise to such intense passions. It generated a defense

[3] The Theatre of Dionysus was next to the entrance to the Odeion of Pericles, one of the main operating courts and quite possibly where Aeschines delivered his speech. He seems likely to have gestured toward the theatre as he asked the spectators to imagine they were there. On the permeability of legal and theatrical spaces, see Blanshard, "Permeable Spaces of the Athenian Law-Court." On the physical space of the courts generally, see Boegehold, *Lawcourts at Athens*.

[4] *De cor.* 193 [18.266] ("player"); *De cor.* 179 [18.243] ("monkey of melodrama," "bumpkin tragedy-king"); *De falsa*, 403, 407 [19.247, 19.250] ("third-rate acto[r]," "charlatan"); *De cor.* 207 [18.287] ("feigning voice of an actor"); *De falsa*, 469 [19.337] ("exhibition of histrionic talent"). A "third-rate acto[r]" was quite literally the minor third actor in the typical fourth-century troupe of three.

[5] *In Ctes.* 415 [3.137] and 471 [3.207] ("juggler"); *De legat.* 279 [2.156] ("wicked arts of rhetoric"); *In Ctes.* 473 [3.210] ("tears . . . "); *In Tim.* 279 [2.156] ("groans for Hellas"). And see Demosthenes, *De cor.* 199 [18.276] (quoting Aeschines' attack: "mountebank," "impostor"); *De falsa*, 403 [19.246] ("charlata[n]").

speech—Demosthenes' "On the Crown"—that is often viewed as the greatest oration of the greatest orator the world has ever known.[6] It led to disgrace for Aeschines and glory for Demosthenes. But the crown at issue in the case was not only Athens' highest mark of honor. It also served as a metonymy for broader concerns about the role of theatricality in politics and law. The crowning (in Aeschines' analysis) was not merely a piece of theatre, but stood for theatricality itself: for the victory of lies over truth, of demagogic crowd-appeal over law.

Scholars have long noted the mutual influence of ancient tragedy and judicial oratory.[7] In the past few decades, a burgeoning literature on cultures of performance in the ancient world has emerged, much of it looking at ancient Greek legal oratory.[8] My debt to this work is immense. However, my central concerns are somewhat different from those of most classicists. Writing as a scholar of law-and-humanities and performance, I have attempted to situate the texts and practices this chapter examines not only in their cultural context but also in relationship to standard genealogies of theatrical theory and to the longer history of legal theory and practice this book explores. Textbook theatre theory tends to treat Aristotle's *Poetics* and the sections on theatre in Plato's *Republic* as the origin and progenitor of the entire history of European theatrical theory, as well as much practice. There are good reasons for this: virtually every theatre theorist from Donatus to Brecht (and beyond) either draws on or contests Plato's or Aristotle's claims about the nature and purpose of theatre. Moreover, these claims long ago migrated from their original aesthetic context, their terms appearing in simplified form in

[6] See e.g. Smith, "Oration on the Crown," 496.

[7] See, for instance, such early discussions as Thomson, *Euripides and the Attic Orators*, or Genet, *Recherches sur le développement de la pensée juridique*, or more recent discussions of the relationship between poetic and legal rhetoric in, for instance, Buxton, *Persuasion in Greek Tragedy* or Eden, *Poetic and Legal Fiction*. See also the discussion in Bers, *Genos Dikanikon* and "Performing the Speech" (debunking the view that trial speeches derive from tragedies or tragedies from trials but affirming claims about the mutual influence of tragedy and judicial oratory). Among the studies that have particularly informed my understanding of ancient Greek legal oratory are: Todd, "Law and Oratory at Athens"; Yunis, "Rhetoric of Law in Fourth-Century Athens"; Harris, "Law and Oratory"; and Lang, *Life, Death, and Litigation in the Athenian Agora*. Among those that have particularly informed my understanding of ancient Greek rhetoric and oratory generally are: Kennedy, *Art of Persuasion in Ancient Greece* (and his updated abridgement: *New History of Classical Rhetoric*, 3–80); and Pernot, *Rhetoric in Antiquity*, 1–56.

[8] On performance in an array of ancient Greek social institutions and texts generally, see e.g. Farenga, *Citizen and Self*; the essays in Goldhill and Osborne, ed., *Performance Culture and Athenian Democracy*; the essays in Peponi, ed. *Performance and Culture in Plato's Laws*; Duncan, *Performance and Identity in the Classical World*; and Hall, *Theatrical Cast of Athens*. On legal performance, see Hall, *Theatrical Cast*, 353–92 (chapter on "Lawcourt Dramas," to which I am particularly indebted), Serafim, *Attic Oratory and Performance*; and the essays in Papaioannou, Serafim, and Da Vela, ed. *Theatre of Justice* (particularly Worthington, "Audience Reaction," Griffith-Williams, "Would I Lie to You?" Apostolakis, "Pitiable Dramas," Carey, "Style, Persona, and Performance"; and, for a useful corrective to the usual alignment of theatrical with lawcourt oratory, Harris, "How to 'Act.'"). Studies specifically of Aeschines' and Demosthenes' oratorical performances include Duncan, *Performance and Identity*, 58-89 ("Demosthenes versus Aeschines"); Hanink, *Lycurgan Athens*, 129–58 ("Courtroom Drama: Aeschines and Demosthenes"); and Easterling, "Actors and Voices."

remarks on public performance more generally: festive, religious, political, and (not least) legal. Plato's critique of theatre and of imitation generally has influenced centuries of tirades against both theatre and theatricality, in law as in other domains. Both theorists and popular discourse regularly draw on the concept of "catharsis" to explain events (in particular, legal events) in which emotional release leads to deliverance from conflict and trauma, bringing reconciliation and harmony. Infamous murder trials, war crimes tribunals, truth commissions, the punishment of perpetrators of atrocity (it is said) provide catharsis for both victims and society at large.

This chapter attempts, among other things, to revisit the theoretical foundation on which such claims rest. It seeks to do so by looking not primarily at ancient theatre theory but at ancient theories of the trial, exploring both practices and ideas about the nature and function of legal-oratorical performance. By way of contextualizing this exploration, I briefly discuss the more general Athenian association of the lawcourt with the theatre (both positive and negative), the assumptions that lay behind this association, and the conditions that helped produce it. I then turn to an examination of Plato's, Aristotle's, and others' discussions of lawcourt performance: their comparison of the lawcourt to the theatre and of trials to tragedies; their analysis of the use and abuse of pathos and *hypokrisis*; their ideas about the role of jurors and bystanders as spectators; their claims about the relationship between legal theatricality and justice. Their discussions of legal theatricality laid the groundwork for the long tradition of thought about legal performance that this book explores. At the same time, I argue, these discussions might serve to reshape our habitual understanding of Plato and Aristotle as performance theorists, offering us an alternative set of foundational texts for theatre and performance theory that provide a very different—and far more radical—account of how performance works and what it does.

Theatricality and Antitheatricality in the Athenian Lawcourt

Trial as Theatre

As scholars have noted, Athenians routinely figured the lawcourt as a kind of theatre: a place in which litigants performed their "tragic" (or sometimes comic) "dramas."[9] On trial for bribery, the general Iphicrates famously pleaded: "my opponent's actor is better" but "my play [is] superior."[10] An orator who failed to use body, face, and eyes expressively, said Aristotle's student Theophrastus, was

[9] See, for instance *Meid.* 105 [21.149] ("melodrama"); and *Hyp.* 389 [1.12] ("tragic phrases"), 483 [4.26] ("theatrical complaints and accusations"); Lycurgus in Burtt, trans., *Minor Attic Orators* [Loeb], 141 [fragment 3: "play tragic parts"].

[10] Plutarch, *Moralia, Volume X* [Loeb], 177 ("Precepts of Statecraft," 801f) (translation modified).

like "an actor with his back turned."[11] A witness who appeared out of nowhere was like "[a god] from the machine," declared Demosthenes.[12]

The spatial arrangements and proceedings of Athenian trials contributed to the association.[13] Not least among these was the typically massive Athenian audience of jurors (normally five hundred and one male citizens, but ranging in size from two hundred to six thousand), with a large number of additional spectators standing outside the railing surrounding the court.[14] While those outside the railing were not jurors, they generally contributed vocally to the trial, and were viewed as "judges" of sorts: "while you are passing judgement on the defendant," declares the prosecutor in a case against the demagogic orator Aristogiton, "the bystanders [outside the railing] and everyone besides are passing judgement on you."[15] The fact that trials requiring juries of over a thousand might be held in the Theatre of Dionysus cemented the association.

Several practices and norms tended to intensify the theatricality of Athenian trials. While speakers often cited the laws, arguing that their opponents had violated them, there were generally no expert judges to declare them right or wrong, only jurors to decide.[16] There were, moreover, essentially no procedural or evidentiary rules except time limits (measured by a water clock). Virtually everything was admissible: irrelevant, inflammatory, unreliable, mendacious, and (above all) *ad hominem* testimony, which was an essential part of any legal argument. Since litigants could not be prosecuted for perjury (only witnesses could), they routinely lied in court. And since parties normally argued their own cases, with high-profile litigants regularly going head-to-head, trials often had the air of a cross between a political debate and a reality show.[17] The fact that the

[11] Theophrastus, *Theophrastus of Eresus*, 2:559 (fragment 713: quoted in Cicero's *On the Orator*).

[12] Demosthenes, *Orations XXVII–XL* [Loeb], 521 ["Against Boeotus," 40.59].

[13] I have relied, in particular, on Boegehold, *Lawcourts at Athens*, and Lanni, *Law and Justice*, for the details below on Athenian courts and procedures. On theatrical judging, see Marshall and Van Willigenburg, "Judging Athenian Dramatic Competitions," 92, 95. Helpful discussions of delivery and gesture in ancient Greece can be found in Boegehold, *When a Gesture Was Expected*, Bers, *Genos Dikanikon* and "Performing the Speech," Fortenbaugh, "Theophrastus on Delivery," Edwards, "*Hypokritēs* in Action," and Kennedy, *Art of Persuasion*.

[14] Private cases were heard by juries of a few hundred citizens; public cases required at least five hundred and one jurors. See Allen, *World of Prometheus*, 46, and the discussions in Lanni, *Law and Justice*, 83, 86 and Boegehold, *Lawcourts at Athens*, 15–16, 24–6 and throughout (six thousand jurors viewed as the right number on one occasion [24]). See the discussion of different kinds of cases in Allen, *World of Prometheus*, 45–7. See Boegehold, *Lawcourts at Athens*, 195–6, on the railing. I use the term "jurors" for *dikastes/dikastai* (though many scholars refer to them as judges, and they effectively combined the functions of judge and juror). I reserve this word for those who voted on the case and use the word "spectators" to refer to the trial audience as a whole.

[15] Dinarchus in Burtt, trans., *Minor Attic Orators* [Loeb], 277–9 [1.19]; and (similarly) 195 [1.30]; 221 [1.66]; 275 [2.15]; *De cor.* 207 [19.309]; and *In Ctes.* 353 [3.56–7].

[16] Specialized lawcourts such as the homicide courts did often have smaller juries of experienced magistrates. See Lanni, *Law and Justice*, 31, 36–7, 83–5.

[17] Although representatives (*sunêgoroi*) sometimes argued for litigants, it was illegal to do so for pay, so there were no lawyers in the modern sense. On the *sunêgoroi*, see Rubinstein, *Litigation and Cooperation*.

stakes were high added to the drama: a lawsuit was the central mechanism of resolving disputes over property, career, reputation, and citizenship, and losers often faced a choice between exile and death.

All of these elements meant that swaying the mass jury was the most important element in winning a case. Since there were no rules for order in the court, the audience signaled approval and disapproval, as in the theatre, with handclapping, catcalls, whistling, hissing, shouts, hooting, heel-drumming, and a rude sound made with one's mouth.[18] With anywhere from two hundred to six thousand jurors, the noise could be deafening. Speakers repeatedly begged the spectators not to interrupt.[19] As Demosthenes put it, the "audience controls . . . the speaker" with its "discriminating favour" (*De Corona*, 199–201 [18.277]). But a skilled litigant also knew how to control the crowd, as the speeches suggest: "which [is] Timarchus—. . . love[r], or . . . prostitut[e]?" cried Aeschines in his speech against Timarchus. "Prostitute!" roared the crowd (*In Tim.* 127 [1.159]). "Come, men of Athens, what do you think? Is Aeschines Alexander's hireling, or Alexander's friend?" Demosthenes demanded in "On the Crown." "Hireling!" shouted the crowd (*De Cor.* 51 [18.52]).[20]

The key tool for controlling the crowd was the art of rhetoric. Teachers of rhetoric often served effectively as legal advisors: most of the great "Attic orators" were also professional legal speechwriters ("logographers"); some also helped clients with memorization and coaching in *hypokrisis* (Demosthenes among them).[21] *Hypokrisis*—sometimes translated as "delivery," sometimes as "acting a part on stage"—included intonation, vocal modulation, pronunciation, facial expression, movement and gesture: that is, all those elements that could not be expressed in the words of a speech alone but could produce their effects only through live performance. *Hypokrisis* was crucial to both the art of the actor (the *hypokritēs*) and the art of the orator.[22] In perhaps the most frequently repeated

[18] On the noisy legal audience and its ability to determine outcomes, see Bers, "Dikastic Thorubos." On audience vocal expressions in the theatre (similar to those in the lawcourt), see *De cor.* 193 [18.265] ("cat-called," "hissed"); *Meid.* 151 [21.226] (spectators "hissed and hooted" Meidias), and the discussion in Hall, *Theatrical Cast*, 364–5.

[19] See e.g. *Hyp.* 377 [Speech A, fragment 2]. For detailed advice on how to handle such interruptions, see [Aristotle], *Rhetoric to Alexander* [Loeb], 543–9 [1432b–1433a].

[20] Here, I have inferred the crowd's answer from the speakers' reactions: Aeschines' "You see, Timarchus[!]" (*In Tim.* 127 [1.159]); Demosthenes' "You hear what they say [!]" (*De cor.* 51 [18.52]). On Demosthenes' addresses to the audience, see Serafim, "'Conventions' in / as Performance."

[21] Teachers of rhetoric often became logographers and vice versa. For instance, Isocrates started his career as a logographer and later set up rhetorical academies in Cius (around 404 BCE) and Athens (around 392 BCE). On the logographers, see Bers, *Genos Dikanikon*; and Yunis, "Rhetoric of Law," 193.

[22] Duncan notes that the fourth century saw the rise of both the professional actor and the professional logographer (*Performance and Identity*, 82): perhaps not a coincidence. Certainly, Aeschines was not the only actor-turned-orator. Because of their mobility and oratorical skills, actors often served as diplomats, for instance the comic actor Satyrus, who joined Aeschines and Demosthenes on one of their embassies to Philip (*De legat.* 279 [2.156–7]). Their ability to memorize and recite from the tragedies was particularly useful in the lawcourt. See the discussion in Hall, *Theatrical Cast*, 347–9, 366–7.

story about Demosthenes (possibly apocryphal), when he was asked to name the three most important elements of rhetoric, he answered: "first, delivery; second, delivery; third, delivery."[23] Theophrastus insisted that delivery was essential to persuasion: "the movement of the body and the pitch of the voice [must be] in harmony with the entire science."[24] Especially in the absence of help from nature (or the nature of the subject), *hypokrisis*—the art of performance—was a crucial tool for altering appearances, creating an illusion of dignity, mastery, and truth.[25] But successful *hypokrisis* was not merely acting: it was *good* acting. It demanded restraint. Its adepts did not "lea[p] to the platform" (*In Tim.* 61 [1.71]). They did not indulge in "vulgar dancing around and joking... in court."[26] Mastering the art of *hypokrisis* entailed creating an impression of oratorical artlessness and spontaneity. One early fourth-century fragment suggests that orators should feign memory loss in order to seem more spontaneous.[27] Legal inexperience was a common trope.[28]

If the gestures, movements, vocal registers, intonations, and attitudes that *hypokrisis* taught were crucial to successful legal oratory, so were other aspects of appearance such as costumes, props, and staging: not technically features of *hypokrisis* but potentially just as influential. The litigant was, for instance, to appear well groomed and modest, but not too trendy: the young and wealthy Mantitheus asks the jury to overlook the fact that he wore his hair fashionably long.[29] Litigants had to avoid clothing that might risk provoking the common charge of effeminacy: at one point, Aeschines urged the jurors to pass around Demosthenes' feminine mantles and soft shirts; it was, he charged, impossible to tell whether they belonged to a man or woman (*In Tim.* 107 [1.131]). While demonstrating weakness was generally unwise, in a prosecution for assault one might display one's wounds, as one of Demosthenes' clients did, showing the senate "the marks of the blows."[30] According to Herodotus, at the general Miltiades treason trial, he "could not speak in his own defence, his thigh being mortified," so "he was laid before the court on a bed [as] his friends spoke for him."[31] In another case, one of Lysias' clients showed the jury the "two sticks" he

[23] Different sources tell this anecdote differently. For the classic versions, see Cicero, *On the Orator* [Loeb], 2:169 [3.213] and *Brutus* [Loeb], 125 [142]; and Plutarch, *Moralia, Volume X* [Loeb], 10:419 ["Lives of the Ten Orators," 845b].

[24] Athanasius quoting Theophrastus: *Theophrastus of Eresus*, 2:559 [fragment 712].

[25] As Hall notes, since beauty, physical prowess, and fitness were "construed ethically," there was a presumption in their favor: anyone wishing to refute that presumption in the lawcourt had the burden of proof (*Theatrical Cast*, 378–9, 381).

[26] *Hyp.* 417 [2.7] (translation modified).

[27] See Hall, *Theatrical Cast*, 356.

[28] For extended discussions, see Hesk, "Rhetoric of Anti-Rhetoric," and *Deception and Democracy*, 202–41; Bers, *Genos Dikanikon*; Ober, *Mass and Elite*, 170–7; and Duncan, *Performance and Identity*, 58–89.

[29] *Lys.* 385 [16.18].

[30] Demosthenes, *Private Orations XLI–XLIX* [Loeb], 301 [47.41].

[31] Herodotus, *Books V-VII* [Loeb], 291–3 [*Persian Wars*, 6.136]).

used to support himself, urging the jury "rather to believe your own eyes than [my opponent's] words."[32]

Athenian legal practice also exploited visual display. In a bid for pity, defendants often paraded their children or aged parents across the stage of the court (the *bema*), claiming that if they were executed or sent into exile, the family before the jurors' eyes would starve. Litigants sometimes brought others on stage as well, not merely as witnesses but as (effectively) material evidence. To defend against the charge that he had sent his slave to repossess a mine by force, one of Demosthenes' clients brought the slave on stage to show that this was impossible: "behold him! This is the man who dispossessed Pantaenetus; this is the man who was stronger than the friends of Pantaenetus, and stronger than the laws," he declared, displaying the apparently frail slave to the jury.[33] Alleging that Aristogeiton, when imprisoned, stole the pocketbook of another prisoner, the victim had resisted, and Aristogeiton had attacked him and bitten off and swallowed his nose, the prosecutor produced the victim himself, palpably noseless, to prove the truth of his allegations.[34] In an even more sensational trial, fourteen people had testified under oath to the fact that a man named Cratinus had murdered a female slave by crushing her head. But Cratinus found the slave (whom the accuser had hidden away) and, in a dramatic *coup de theatre*, revealed her on the *bema* during the trial (*Isoc.* 3:285–7 [18.52–4]).

Consciously or unconsciously, litigants channeled the tragedies they saw onstage. In a speech in which a son accused his stepmother of poisoning his father, the son identified the stepmother as a "Clytemnestra," recalling Aeschylus' representation of Orestes' case before the court of the Areopagus (where, in fact, as a murder case, the real case might have been tried).[35] Litigants could dramatize their cases by taking on others' *personae*. One man, for instance, spoke in first person in the voice of his widowed mother, charging her father with squandering her children's inheritance after her husband's death: "And you thought fit to turn these, [my] children" (pointing to his siblings and raising his voice to an effeminate pitch) "out of their own house, in worn-out clothes, without shoes or attendant or bedding or cloaks, ... turning [them] into beggars."[36]

[32] *Lys.* 525–7 [24.12, 24.14].

[33] Demosthenes, *Orations XXVII–XL* [Loeb], 405 [37.44]. For discussion of this example and several of those that follow, see Hall, *Theatrical Cast*, 378.

[34] Demosthenes, *Orations XXI–XXVI* [Loeb], 553 [25.60–2] (the speech is probably not Demosthenes'; see 515).

[35] Antiphon in Maidment, trans., *Minor Attic Orators* [Loeb], 23–5 [1.17] ("Prosecution of the Stepmother for Poisoning": probably not delivered but a model for using tragedy to buttress legal oratory).

[36] *Lys.* 669 [32.16–17]. The context implies the use of the mother's voice and the gesture toward his siblings. See the discussion in Hall (*Theatrical Cast*, 383), who remarks: "If recast in iambic trimeter it could be imported more or less directly into a suppliant scene in a tragedy."

Against Histrionics

Jurors expected such theatrics, which could be essential to winning a case. But they also frowned upon them. If *hypokrisis* was the art of both the orator and the actor, it was also the art of the hypocrite.[37] Just as sophism perverted truth with the seductive arts of rhetoric, *hypokrisis* perverted justice with the seductive arts of theatre.[38] Litigants routinely warned juries to be wary of theatrical illusions: actors merely playing characters or faking injuries. One of Demosthenes' clients, a young upper-class Athenian suing for assault and battery, claimed that the witnesses for the defense only "pretend to play the Spartan" in their single-soled shoes and short cloaks, to mask their "wickedness [and] indecency."[39] Litigants might urge jury members to "believe your own eyes," as Lysias' client did, showing the jury his two sticks. But they also sometimes urged them *not* to believe their eyes: do not believe show (*opsis*), but deeds.[40]

If *opsis* could deceive, so could pathos: just as legal actors could trick the unwary spectators' eyes, so could they hoodwink hearts. Litigants aware of the power of transferring tragedy to the lawcourt were ready to accuse others of creating legal pseudo-tragedy, as Aeschines and Demosthenes did routinely: my opponent (says Lycophron) "writ[es] tragic phrases" (*Hyp.* 389 [1.12]); Olympias' allegations (says Euxenippus) are "theatrical complaints and accusations" (*Hyp.* 483 [4.26]); Demades "play[s] tragic parts made for others," says his antagonist.[41] In the *Apology*, Socrates famously expressed his disdain for the customary pity-begging display of the defendant's aged parents and children. Describing his prosecutor Meletus, Socrates declares: "in standing his trial upon a less serious charge than this," Meletus

> made pitiful appeals to the jury with floods of tears, and had his infant children produced in court to excite the maximum of sympathy, and many of his relatives and friends as well[.] I on the contrary intend to do nothing of the sort. [For] anyone who stages these pathetic scenes... brings ridicule upon our city.
>
> (*Pl.* 20 [34c, 35b])

Plato's "Athenian stranger" (his alterego in the *Laws*) echoes Socrates, arguing that the magistrates in the utopian Magnesia must ban such legal dramatics: no

[37] The word *hypokrisis* conjoins the idea of playing a part with the suffix "-crisis": to decide, determine, judge. In a sense, *hypokrisis* involves playing a part for the purposes of judgment. See "hypocrisy, n." in *OED Online*. For further discussion, see Easterling, "Actors and Voices," 160.

[38] The paradigmatic attack on the sophists' rhetoric is Plato's *Gorgias* (discussed below). See also *Isoc.* 2:159–77 ("Against the Sophists" [13]).

[39] Demosthenes, *Private Orations L–LVIII* [Loeb], 153 [54.34].

[40] See, for instance, *Lys.* 125 [6.18].

[41] Lycurgus in Burtt, trans., *Minor Attic Orators* [Loeb], 141 [fragment 3].

more "indulg[ing] in degrading appeals for mercy or unmanly pathos" (*Pl.* 1494–5 [949b]).

Plato's Theatrocracies

Theatrocracy and Theatrical Sophism versus the Laws

In a famous passage in Book 3 of the *Laws*, Plato (speaking through the Athenian stranger) launches into an excoriation of what he terms "theatrocracy" (*theatrokratia*): the rule of theatre, which he opposes to the philosopher's rule of law.[42] The passage begins with an extended narrative describing the degeneration of musical standards. In former times, he explains,

> [t]he competence to take cognizance of [musical laws], to pass verdicts in accord with them, and, in case of need, to penalize their infraction was not left, as it is today, to the catcalls and discordant outcries of the crowd, nor yet to the clapping of applauders; the educated made it their rule to hear the performances through in silence, and for the boys, their attendants, and the rabble at large, there was the discipline of the official's rod to enforce order. Thus the bulk of the populace was content to submit to this strict control in such matters without venturing to pronounce judgment by its clamors.

However, in the course of time, several men "ignorant of what is right and legitimate" took over, and "license set in." "Possessed by a frantic and unhallowed lust for pleasure, they contaminated" one form with another, as if

> there is no such thing as a right and a wrong, [their] standard of judgment being the pleasure given to the hearer, be he high or low. [They] inspired the multitude with contempt of... law, and a conceit of their own competence as judges. Thus our once silent audiences have found a voice, in the persuasion that they understand what is good and bad...; the old 'sovereignty of the best'...has given way to an evil 'sovereignty of the audience' [*theatrocracy*].
>
> (*Pl.* 1294 [700c–701a])

This critique of the rule of the audience echoes a similar passage earlier in the *Laws* in which Plato discusses poetic contests:

[42] See Cartledge, "'Deep Plays,'" on Plato's coinage of the term—"meaning literally the sovereign rule of the theatre-audience"—to "refer to the dictatorship of the mass (or mob) of poor Athenian citizens who formed the majority of the spectatorship, as they formed the ruling majority of the Athenian democratic state (9); and see Meineck, *Theatrocracy* (on Greek theatre as a social and political force). For a detailed discussion of Plato's theatrocracy complementary to my own, see Folch, *City and the Stage*, especially 117–31.

> A judge who is truly a judge must not learn his verdict from the audience, letting himself be intimidated into it by the clamor of the multitude and his own incompetence, nor yet, out of cowardice and poltroonery, weakly pronounce a judgment which belies his own convictions.... [T]he judge takes his seat not to learn from the audience, but to teach them, and to set himself against performers who give an audience pleasure in wrong and improper ways.
> (*Pl.* 1256 [659a–b])

The decay of aesthetic judgment to which he refers in these passages is not merely evil in itself but poses further evils, heralding among other things the decay of legal judgment. For the musical theatrocracy (he explains in the passage that follows) is the first stage of a more catastrophic legal theatrocracy: "If the consequence had been even a democracy, no great harm would have been done, so long as the democracy was confined to art." But musical theatrocracy (he writes) has led to a wholesale "escape [from] obedience to the law":

> [A]s things are with us, music has given occasion to a general conceit of universal knowledge and contempt for law, and liberty has followed in their train,... a reckless excess of liberty.... So the next stage of the journey toward liberty will be refusal to submit to magistrates, and on this will follow [the] effort to escape obedience to the law.... The spectacle of the Titanic nature of which our old legends speak is re-enacted; man returns to the old condition of a hell of unending misery. (*Pl.* 1294–5 [701a–c])

Here, the story of the decline of musical judgment both presages and offers a microcosm of democracy's broader descent into anarchy: aesthetic dissolution brings political and legal dissolution in its wake. But the story is also about legal procedure in a more concrete sense. For in this scene, Plato evokes not only musical, poetic, and theatrical contests, but the Athenian lawcourt. There the audience did, quite literally, rule through "the clapping of applauders" and "the catcalls and discordant outcries of [a] crowd" that "pronounce[d] judgment by its clamors." There it must have seemed (to many) that "magistrates" had lost control, that civilization had dissolved, and that "obedience to the law" had succumbed to chaos.

The vision, here, of the theatrocracy's overthrow of what we might call "nomocracy," reiterates in explicit (if mythic) terms an opposition between legal theatricality and true law that Plato had already established many decades earlier in his famous discussion of rhetoric in the *Gorgias*.[43] Callicles, who has taken over

[43] Although the word "*nomocracy*" does not appear in Plato's lexicon, a number of people have used it to describe the regime envisioned by Plato's *Laws*. See, e.g. Strauss, *Argument and the Action of Plato's Laws*, 71.

from Gorgias as Socrates' interlocutor, has been defending rhetoric because it "preserves one's life in the law courts" (*Pl.* 293 [511b–c]). Socrates responds that he aims not at what is "most pleasant" but what is "best" (*Pl.* 302 [521d–e]). Apparently, preserving his own life (while pleasant) is not one of those things. For, if he were brought into court, he proclaims, he would refuse "to engage in those 'dainty [rhetorical] devices' that you recommend" and thus "have nothing to say for myself" (*Pl.* 302 [521d–e]). In fact (he exclaims), "it would not be surprising if I were put to death" (*Pl.* 302 [521d]): a not-so-subtle reminder that the preference for rhetoric over truth in the lawcourt was, in effect, responsible for Socrates' death.[44] In the *Laws*, the Athenian Stranger will more scathingly identify professional legal orators as "polluting and defiling parasites," peddling "a vice which cloaks itself under the specious name of an art." He will recommend stiff penalties (including the death penalty in certain cases) for "assisting another to manage his [legal business]" (*Pl.* 1487 [937d–e]). (Plato is presumably referring to both logographers and *sunêgoroi*, precursors of the modern lawyer.) In the *Gorgias*, while acknowledging that there *might* be a kind of rhetoric aimed at the good (as he does later more explicitly in the *Phaedrus*), Socrates gets Callicles to agree that he has "never seen rhetoric of this kind," nor "any such orator" (*Pl.* 286 [503a–b]). In the end, "[s]ophist and orator," says Socrates, "are the same thing, or pretty nearly so" (*Pl.* 300 [520a]).

To make his point, Socrates draws a crucial parallel between legal and theatrical rhetoric. "Do you not consider that the poets engage in rhetoric in the theaters?" Socrates asks Callicles (*Pl.* 285 [502d]). Drama is "a form of rhetoric"—"addressed to a huge mob of people... composed alike of children and women and men, slaves and free"—that flatters the "pleasure and the gratification of the spectators" (*Pl.* 285 [502b–d]). "Do you imagine that [the chorus trainer] Cinesias... is in the slightest concerned with saying anything likely to improve his hearers, or merely what will gratify the mob of spectators?" (*Pl.* 284 [501e–502a]). Similarly, legal oratory (addressed not only to citizen-jurors but to the surrounding crowd of women, slaves, and children) "produces gratification and pleasure" for the purposes of "flattery and shameful mob appeal" (*Pl.* 245 [462e], 286 [503a]). Plato here sets "pleasure" and "pain" (that is, judgment based on emotion and sensation) against "law," as he will in the famous passage in Book 10 of the *Republic* in which he explains the dangers of poetry to the city: "[W]e can admit no poetry into our city.... For if you grant admission to the honeyed Muse,... pleasure and pain will be lords of your city instead of law" (*Pl.* 832 [607a]). In the *Gorgias*, similarly, "pleasure and the gratification of the spectators" in both lawcourt and theatre stand against nomocracy: against "order and regularity of the soul, whence

[44] For a reiteration of this disavowal of lawcourt rhetoric in Socrates' actual defense speech, see *Pl.* 4 [*Apology*, 17a–18a].

men become orderly and law-abiding"; against "justice and temperance"; against "lawfulness and law" (*Pl.* 285 [502c], 287 [504d]).

The Law and Its Double: Rival Actors and the Laws as Noble Tragedy

In his tirade against theatrocracy, or his banning of dramatic poets from the city, or the parallel he draws between theatre and sophism, we can find substantiation for the textbook view of Plato as the paradigmatic antitheatricalist.[45] It is certainly true that, for him, poetic imitation (dramatic and otherwise) rouses dangerous emotions and drives: "do you think," asks Socrates in Book 3 of the *Republic*, that seeing "how Zeus lightly forg[ets] all [his] designs . . . because of the excitement of his passions, and [i]s so overcome by the sight of Hera that he . . . wants to lie with her there on the ground," do you think this "will conduce to a young man's temperance or self-control?" "No, by Zeus[!]" replies Adimantus (*Pl.* 635 [390a–c]). If poetry's arousal of sexual passions compromises "temperance" and "self-control," its arousal of pity and fear makes one weak and effeminate. The Republic must therefore "d[o] away with the lamentations of men," and indeed "the entire vocabulary of terror and fear" ("Cockytus named of lamentation loud, abhorred Styx [which] send[s] a shudder through all the hearers") "lest the habit of such thrills make [our guardians] sensitive and soft." All these are unsuited to "boys and men who are destined to be free." (They may be left "to women [and] inferior men") (*Pl.* 632 [387b–388a]). Or, as he explains more soberly in Book 10:

> [I]n regard to the emotions of sex and anger, and all the appetites and pains and pleasures of the soul which we say accompany all our actions, the effect of poetic imitation is the same. For it waters and fosters these feelings when what we ought to do is to dry them up, and it establishes them as our rulers when they ought to be ruled, to the end that we may be better and happier men instead of worse and more miserable. (*Pl.* 832 [606d])

Plato's intertwined critique of legal oratory, theatre, and poetic emotion more generally is key to his thought: at the heart of his ethics and politics. However, as many have noted, it would be misguided to treat his attack on theatre and poetry as unqualified, not only because he recognizes their power (which is what makes

[45] Plato has four basic critiques of theatre: it is false (an imitation of an imitation), sexualizing (it rouses appetites), histrionic (it is emotionally manipulative), demagogic (it leads to the rule of the demagogue through the rule of the audience). See the discussion in, for instance, Barish, *Antitheatrical Prejudice*, 5–37.

them so dangerous) but also because he recognizes their potential for good. "Let it be declared," exclaims Socrates in Book 10,

> that, if the mimetic and dulcet poetry can show any reason for her existence in a well-governed state, we would gladly admit her, since we ourselves are very conscious of her spell.... Do not you yourself feel her magic[?] Then may she not justly return from this exile after she has pleaded her defense[?] [W]e would allow her advocates... [to] show that she is not only delightful but beneficial.
> (*Pl.* 832 [607c–d])

If dramatic-lyric poetry is "unable to make good her defense," we must do everything we can to resist her: we must "preserve" ourselves "from slipping back into the childish loves of the multitude" (*Pl.* 833 [608a]). Or (switching to another time of life), we must do what we at least *try* to do when we have fallen in love with the wrong person: "even as men who have fallen in love, if they think that the love is not good for them, hard though it be, nevertheless refrain, so [must] we" (*Pl.* 833 [607e]). This is not easy. A "countercharm" is required to resist her spell (*Pl.* 833 [608a]). We might lapse. But—as we feel when we have fallen in love with the wrong person—there is also a hope that, under the right governance, the beloved might just turn out to be virtuous after all.

A famous passage in Book 7 of the *Laws* envisions precisely this kind of redemption of the beloved through the separation of good from bad in them. By way of addressing the question of whether theatre is to be allowed in Magnesia, the Athenian stranger imagines a foreign (Athenian?) tragedian approaching the Magnesian magistrates and asking: "May we pay your city and its territory a visit, sirs, or may we not? And may we bring our poetry along with us, or what decision have you reached on the point?" The magistrates respond:

> Respected visitors, we are ourselves authors of a tragedy, and that the finest and best we know how to make. In fact, our whole polity has been constructed as a dramatization of a noble and perfect life; that is what *we* hold to be in truth the most real of tragedies. Thus, you are poets, and we also are poets in the same style, rival artists and rival actors, and that in the finest of all dramas, one which indeed can be produced only by a code of true law.... So you must not expect that we shall lightheartedly permit you to pitch your booths in our market square with a troupe of actors whose melodious voices will drown our own, and let you deliver your public tirades before our boys and women and the populace at large—let you address them on the same issues as ourselves, not to the same effect, but commonly and for the most part to the very contrary. Why, we should be stark mad to do so[!] (*Pl.* 1387 [817a–c])

Here, Plato reiterates in vivid terms the *Republic*'s ban on poets, with the ban now directed not against poetry in general, but specifically against theatre. Its principal target is a tragic dramatist who seems also to be an actor himself, head of a troupe of actors planning to "pitch [their] booths in [the] market square." The ban will prevent theatre from corrupting the populace. At the same time, Plato transforms the *Republic*'s dream of a "beneficent" poetry into a positive program for a magistrate-run theatre of law: "our whole polity has been constructed as a dramatization of a noble and perfect life; that is what *we* hold to be in truth the most real of tragedies." It is a tragedy, he has just explained, not because it is sad but because, unlike comedy, it represents the "comely body and noble mind" (more or-less what most people seek in a beloved) (*Pl.* 1387 [816d–817b]).

Plato's identification of the laws as "a tragedy, . . . the finest and best we know how to make, . . . a dramatization of a noble and perfect life, . . . the most real of tragedies" is irritatingly cryptic. As a way of understanding it, critics have tended to deem it a metaphor, or, if more than a metaphor, merely a description of Magnesia's law code, not in any sense a literal counterpart to the plays put on by the troupe of traveling actors.[46] But Plato in fact gives us every reason to think of this tragedy as *performed*, in both a diffuse sense (it "dramatiz[es]" the laws by enacting them in the world), and in a far narrower and more concrete sense. If this performance is a figure for the broader "dramatization of a noble and perfect life" enacted by "our whole polity," it is not *merely* a figure: like that of the troupe of traveling actors, this dramatization takes place before spectators in the delimited time and space of performance. For in fact the youth of Magnesia perform the laws through dances and choral performances that not only represent "a noble and perfect life" but are "tragedies," in Plato's sense, because they display the "comely body and noble mind" that are the essence of tragic character (*Pl.* 1386 [816d–817b]).[47]

Plato's earlier discussion of theatrocracy helps explain how the theatre in the market square and this perfect theatre of law can be rivals. It is precisely because the boundaries between legal and theatrical institutions have become so porous—because the court has come to act like a theatre—that the actors performing in the market square pose a threat to law, and must be replaced by performers who represent "a noble and perfect life." While the two kinds of performances have different effects, they are nonetheless dangerously similar. If the traveling actors deliver speeches "not to the same effect, but commonly and for the most part to the very contrary," they are still artists "in the same style," addressing the

[46] See, for instance, Laks, "Plato's 'Truest Tragedy,'" arguing that, while Plato's ideal "political regime might be a 'drama' in a certain sense . . . it is no sort of performance of anything" (221).

[47] On the training of youth of both sexes in music and dance, see *Laws* throughout, but especially But see Folch, *City and the Stage*, describing the "performance culture" (113) that Plato envisions in the *Laws*. *Pl.* 1385–6 [814d–816d], 1250–1 [653d–654b], and 1269 [672d–e].

spectators "on the same issues as ourselves." They "are poets, and we also are poets in the same style"; they are "*rival* artists and *rival* actors"; their "minstrelsy" (he writes in the lines that follow) can be "compar[ed] with our own." Seducing women and boys with their melodious voices (those same boys once "discipline [d] [by] the official's rod"?), they threaten law's *monopoly* on theatre, the very thing on which law most depends for its persuasiveness and force. In short, Plato offers us the paradigmatic vision of the evils of theatrocracy. But at the same time, he offers us the paradigmatic vision of the virtues of legal rule through theatre, and (moreover) its possible victory: "Go to, then, ye scions of the softer Muses," the magistrates dare the actors, "exhibit your minstrelsy to [us] for comparison with our own" (*Pl.* 1387 [817d]). In Plato's account of the musical theatrocracy that will lead inexorably to a more general theatrocracy in Book 3 of the *Laws*, theatrocracy is the opposite of the rule of law, and threatens to destroy it. In his rejection of the tragedians in Book 7 of the *Laws*, theatre is law's double, its mirror image, the kind of representation to which law aspires, the sphere in which it can brook no rivals. Theatre is dangerous: it can undermine law. But it is also essential: necessary to law's representation of "a noble and perfect life."

Aristotle on *Hypokrisis* and *Pathos*

The Vulgar Crowd and the Power of Hypokrisis

Such ambivalence about legal theatricality found a more precise articulation, at once theoretical and pragmatic, in the most influential rhetorical manual ever written: Aristotle's *Rhetoric*. While the *Rhetoric* deals with three kinds of oratory—deliberative, epideictic, and judicial—judicial oratory is front and center. Aristotle saves it for last, devoting significantly more space to it than to the deliberative or epideictic. Moreover, his discussions of oratory generally are peppered with references to law, "the juror" (*dikastes*), and arguments "in court" (*en dikasterion, agora, Areopagus*).[48] In perhaps his most famous one-liner, Aristotle asserts: "a human is by nature a political animal." Thus, "anyone who is without a city . . . is either a wretch or else better than human" (*Pol.* 4 [1.2.1253a]). As at least one scholar has noted, the polis that makes us human is a space small enough for a "crier" to be heard by all and for the citizens to be "easily surveyed as a whole": in other words, a performance space (*Pol.* 165 [7.4.1326b]).[49] Moreover, in Aristotle's discussion of how the polis defines us as human, he envisions this polis-as-performance-space as, in fact, a lawcourt: "For just as when completed a

[48] See e.g. *Rh.* 2–3 [1354a–b]; 11 [1358b]; 47–8 [1374b–1375a]; 50 [1376a]; 52–4 [1377a–b]; 103–4 [1400a–b]; 126 [1410a]; 141 [1416a]; 143 [1417a].

[49] *Pol.* 165 [7.4.1326b]. See Marshall, *Vico and the Transformation of Rhetoric*, 9.

human is the best of the animals, so when separated from law and judicial proceeding he is worst of all" (*Pol.* 4 [1.2.1253a]). One might thus almost say that, for Aristotle, it is lawcourt performance that defines us as human.

If the *Politics* loftily identifies the human with legal performance, the *Rhetoric*—which is, among other things, a litigation manual—gets down to the gritty specifics of what to do there. As Aristotle explains, a handbook that "treat[s] speaking in court as [a] craft" is essential to the would-be litigant for several reasons (*Rh.* 3 [1354b]). You cannot win a case merely because the law is on your side, for laws are too imprecise to generate indisputable outcomes (*Rh.* 2 [1354a]). You cannot win a case by telling the truth, for "love," "hatred," or "private pleasure or pain overshadows [the jurors'] judgment" (*Rh.* 3 [1354b]). What you need is performance. Addressing *hypokrisis* in Book 3 of the *Rhetoric*, Aristotle explains that, while it may not be essential to *logos*, *hypokrisis* is essential to the other two means of oratorical persuasion: *ethos* (demonstrating ethical character through dignity, strength, and breeding); and *pathos* (channeling emotion through the voice and other effects) (*Rh.* 112–13 [1403b–1404a]).[50] "[D]elivery is most a factor [where] exactness is least present," where emotions are highest, "where voice is [the biggest] factor, and most of all where a loud one is" (*Rh.* 135 [1414a]). But it is always necessary.

For Aristotle, then (unlike for Plato), the orator *must* draw on the art of the actor. In fact, oratorical *hypokrisis* emerged from theatrical *hypokrisis*. The entire study of the verbal arts, including rhetoric, began in actors' and rhapsodists' attempts to theorize their art (*Rh.* 113 [1404a]). More to the point, legal *hypokrisis* is really no different from theatrical *hypokrisis*: "[w]henever delivery comes to be considered it will function in the same way as acting."[51] However, while true, this is not especially heartening. For *hypokrisis* in the lawcourt can be an ugly thing. However much we may admire orators or actors who have mastered it, it is (pardon us for saying it) "vulgar" (*Rh.* 113 [1403b]). It is concerned with "outward show," the kind of show contrived not for proof but only to "appea[l] to the listener" (*Rh.* 113 [1404a]). In a perfect world, true justice, which does not involve "entertain[ing]," but "contend[ing] by means [only] of the things at issue themselves," would triumph (*Rh.* 113 [1404a]). But given "the depravity of the citizens"—both the "weakness of the listener[s]" and their corruption—litigants can "win over the listener[s]" only by addressing "matters outside the thing at issue"

[50] Ethos has a substantial emotional element: "it makes a great difference with a view to persuading... that the speaker appear to be of a certain quality and that his listeners take him to be disposed in a certain way toward them, and if, in addition, they too will be disposed in a certain way [to him]." Ethos involves both a correct representation of character and a use of character to shape the emotions of the spectators and thus their judgments: "for things do not seem the same to those who are friendly and those who are hostile, nor [the same] to the angry and the calm but either altogether different or different in importance" (*Rh.* 55 [1377b78a]).

[51] *Rh.* 113 [1404a] (here and in a few other places in this paragraph, I modify Reeve's translations, drawing on Kennedy's in Aristotle, *On Rhetoric* [2007 ed.], 195–6).

(*Rh.* 112–13 [1403b–1404a], 148 [1419a], 3 [1354b]). Just as "actors have greater capacity" to sway audiences "than poets nowadays" (*Rh.* 112 [1403b]), *hypokrisis* has become more important than facts in legal disputes: nowadays, the best performer wins" (*Rh.* 112 [1403b]).

It is precisely for this reason that the legal orator must learn to throw "'in some of the fifty-drachma [show-]lecture,'" explains Aristotle (quoting Prodicus the sophist), or exclaim in the middle of a case, "'I'll tell you something strange, something so wondrous, you've never heard the like of it'" (*Rh.* 139 [1415b])! "[W]hen the listeners nod," or if you "have, or believe [yourself] to have, a bad case," *hypokrisis* (accompanied by a bit of drama) can wake up those snoring or conceal the case's weakness (*Rh.* 139 [1415b]). Such tricks are "outside the argument: [they] are addressed to a listener who is base, . . . since if he were not like that, there would be no need" (*Rh.* 139 [1415b]). If only "all trials were conducted as they now are [in] some cities," especially those that are well governed, the handbook writers "would have nothing to say" (*Rh.* 3 [1354a]). But in the world as it is—a world in which the art of the actor has such power (*Rh.* 112 [1403b])—the litigant must learn it or lose.

In Aristotle's description of the *hypokri*-tical orator, cheapening law by means of his "fifty-drachma [show-]lecture," we can see an echo of Plato's descriptions of the theatrical sophist-orators in the *Gorgias*, or the histrionic speakers in the *Laws*, with their "degrading appeals for mercy or unmanly pathos" (*Pl.* 1495 [949b]), or those who, "[p]ossessed by a frantic and unhallowed lust for pleasure," whip up "the catcalls and discordant outcries of the crowd" as the multitude "pronounce[s] judgment by its clamors." And in Aristotle's description of corrupt audiences, we can see an echo of Plato's throng, ruling through applause as the theatrocracy wreaks its havoc. In both, we can find the opposition between entertainment and justice. The real difference is that, where Plato sees in the march of theatrocracy a horrifying re-enactment of the "spectacle of the Titanic nature of which our old legends speak," leading to "a hell of unending misery," Aristotle sees . . . business as usual. "[S]ince the whole business of rhetoric [addresses] belief [*doxa*], one should pay the requisite attention to delivery, not because it [is] just, but because it is necessary" (*Rh.* 113 [1404a]; translation modified).

Aristotle's use of the word "*doxa*" (opinion or belief) here marks a typical, but in this context crucial, reversal of Plato's program. Plato's attack on rhetoric is, in fact, an attack on *doxa*: "the art of speech displayed by one who has gone chasing after beliefs [opinions, *doxas*], instead of knowing the truth, [is] a comical sort of art, in fact no art at all" (*Pl.* 508 [*Phaedrus* 262c]). The "finished performer" in the lawcourt, as Socrates scathingly describes him in the *Phaedrus*, is one who has chased belief, opinion, plausibility, and probability instead of truth (*Pl.* 515 [269d]):

> [T]here is . . . absolutely no need for the budding orator to concern himself with the truth . . . . In the law courts nobody cares a rap for the truth about these

> matters, but only about what is plausible. And that is the same as what is probable.... Even actual facts ought sometimes not be stated, if they don't tally with probability; they should be replaced by what is probable, whether in prosecution or defense; whatever you say, you simply must pursue this probability they talk of, and say good-by to the truth forever. Stick to that all through your speech, and you are equipped with the art complete.
>
> (*Pl.* 518 [272d–273a])[52]

The mock-advice in Socrates' portrait of the "finished [lawcourt] performer"—advice that is meant to warn aspiring orators that "probability" destroys truth—sounds like precisely what Aristotle in fact *recommends* in the *Rhetoric.*

In this, rhetoric is very like tragedy, as Aristotle describes it in the *Poetics.* There, the poet would do better to represent "something plausible though impossible [rather than] what is possible but implausible" (*Poet.* 135 [1461b]). In both legal performance and tragedy, appearances perhaps *should* not matter more than truth, but they do. In fact, Aristotle's ambivalence toward delivery in the *Rhetoric* recalls his remarks in the *Poetics* on scenic art. There, he famously insists that tragedy can achieve its effects "independent[ly] of performance and actors," and explains that spectacle is really the province only of the "the maker of masks and other stage-properties."[53] Interpreters often treat such comments as an extension of Plato's antitheatrical views. But Aristotle's dismissal of performance in the *Poetics* (like that of *hypokrisis* in the *Rhetoric*) is notably at odds with the rest of his discussion, appearing almost as a *pro forma* concession to Plato. Aristotle's story of the emergence of tragedy is the story of the emergence of theatre: Aeschylus added a second actor and "[t]hree actors and scene painting came with Sophocles" (*Poet.* 43 [1449a]). His identification of the "first component" of tragedy treats spectacle as tragedy's preeminent tool: "[s]ince the imitation is by people acting, the first component of a tragedy is of necessity the staging of the spectacle." It is this (along with song and speech) that "produce[s] the imitation" (*Poet.* 49 [1449b]). Indeed, spectacle appears to have transcendent powers for (he writes without a hint of critique), it "is capable of leading the soul" (*Poet.* 53 [1450b]).

52 See similarly the *Republic*, Bk 6: the Sophist "inculcates nothing else than these opinions of the multitude which they opine when they are assembled"; he is like one who "acquir[es] the... desires of a great strong beast" and applies such terms as good and evil "to the judgments of the great beast." He thinks "that it is wisdom to have learned to know the moods and the pleasures of the motley multitude,... grants the mob authority over himself," and is compelled "to give the public what it likes," not what "is really good and honorable" (*Pl.* 729 [493a–d]).

53 *Poet.* 55 [1450b] (translation modified, with thanks to C. D. C. Reeve for sharing his unpublished translation, on which I draw extensively in this paragraph).

The Poetics of Hypokrisis *and* Pathos

Caveats about performance out of the way, Aristotle can get to what really interests him: in the *Rhetoric*, an explanation of why we express ourselves performatively; a description of how *hypokrisis* works; and the creation of a how-to guide. Like dramatic mimesis, *hypokrisis* was born of the primal drive toward imitation. "[N]ames are imitations" not because they represent things or ideas but because "the voice [is] the most imitative of all our parts," imitating sound before meaning.[54] Vocal imitation "was there to start with" (*Rh.* 113 [1404a]): in a baby's attempt to talk, for instance, or the human attempt to communicate before language developed. *Hypokrisis* (whether in the theatre or lawcourt) is thus natural, part of the inherent imitative and communicative drive. At the same time, although the *drive* toward imitation and expression are natural, one can in fact cultivate the *arts* of imitation and expression. Actors and orators receive prizes "for their delivery" precisely because delivery is the "province of craft" (*Rh.* 112 [1404a]). Unfortunately, despite brief discussions such as Thrasymachus' *Emotional Appeals*, no treatise "systematically" explaining the art of *hypokrisis* had yet been composed (*Rh.* 112–13 [1403b–1404a]): hence the need for Aristotle's discussion.[55]

The *Rhetoric* hardly offers a complete poetics of *hypokrisis*. But it does offer a series of recommendations for performance: acting tips for the aspiring legal orator. For instance, just as the actor Theodoros could represent the voice of the "character speaking" (*Rh.* 114 [1404b]), Aristotle explains, so the legal orator should use character voices, imitating those he represents. He should learn not just from the actor's art of vocal imitation but also his expressive use of the body, costume, and props.

> [T]hose who contribute to the effect by their gestures, cries, dress, and, in general, by their dramatic manner are more pitiable.... [S]igns and actions are pitiable too—for example, the clothes of those who have suffered and any things of that sort, and the words [of] those who are in the midst of suffering, for example, of those on the very point of death—are pitiable.
>
> (*Rh.* 75 [1386a–b]; translation modified)

Here Aristotle seems to recommend that the litigant channel the kinds of scenes often represented in Athenian tragedy. Representing a deathbed scene, he must

[54] For the emergence of dramatic mimesis from this kind of primal drive toward imitation, see *Poet.* 37–41 [1448b].

[55] Neither the treatise on emotional appeals [*eleoi*, or laments meant to evoke pathos] nor Thrasymachus' *Techne Rhetorike* have survived. Theophrastus would later write a treatise on delivery that has also been lost. For a hypothetical reconstruction, see Fortenbaugh, "Theophrastus on Delivery."

speak the words of the dying with "gestures, cries," "signs and actions," "clothes," other tangible objects associated with those "in the midst of suffering," and (although he does not wear a mask as the actor does) a "dramatic manner": that is, a display of feelings writ large.

In some places in the *Rhetoric*, Aristotle seems to disparage the deployment of a "dramatic manner" and emotional manipulation generally (in terms similar to those he uses to disparage *hypokrisis* generally). Writers on oratory should not focus on "pity, anger, and such feelings of the soul": they are "outside the things at issue," merely appeals "to the juror" (*Rh.* 2 [1354a]). Citing approvingly the fact that the "court of the Areopagus... correctly legislates" against "speaking of matters outside the thing at issue" (a rule often viewed as forbidding arguments that excite the emotions), he insists that "one should not warp [the judgment of] the juror by arousing anger, fear, or pity" (*Rh.* 2 [1354a]).[56] But pathos, one of the three central components of persuasion, produces judgment: "Persuasion is through the listeners whenever they are led to feel things by the speech. For we do not give the same judgments pained and pleased, or loving and hating" (*Rh.* 6 [1356a]).[57] The fact that Aristotle provides a lengthy discussion of the emotions in Book Two and offers many recommendations for playing on the spectator's feelings reveals just how important he thinks they are to persuasion. For instance, litigants should make the audience feel anger while showing that their "opponents [are] liable for those things" that make the audience "angry" (*Rh.* 60 [1380a]). They should manipulate pity (as in the scene in which the orator acts the part of a dying man). In fact, they should "draw [the audience] toward whichever [feeling they] choose" (*Rh.* 65 [1382a]). In short, however wrong it may be "warp [the judgment of] the juror by arousing anger, fear, or pity," much of the *Rhetoric* appears, in fact, heartily to recommend it.

The *Rhetoric* not only serves as a primer in warping the jury: it attempts to anatomize what exactly happens when a litigant uses emotions to do so (one that seems to apply equally to theatre and legal oratory):

> [S]ince sufferings are pitiable when they appear close at hand, and since people do not feel pity either at all, or not to the same degree, at things ten thousand years in the past or future, since they neither expect nor remember them, necessarily those who contribute to the effect by [their] dramatic manner are more pitiable (for they make the evil appear close at hand by setting it before our eyes either as something about to happen or as something that has happened).

[56] Several late sources (Pollux, Lucian) interpret this rule as a bar to emotional appeals, and through the early modern period and beyond, commentators reiterate this view. But speeches in the homicide courts do regularly include such appeals. See the discussion in Lanni, *Law*, 97–8.

[57] See Dow, *Passions and Persuasion*, rejecting the traditional view that Aristotle's treatment of passion-arousal in the *Rhetoric* is inconsistent, and arguing that, for Aristotle, the passions are integral to reasoned judgment: emotional persuasion is a form of logical persuasion.

> And things that have just happened or are going to happen soon are more pitiable. (*Rh.* 75 [1386a])[58]

Here, scenic presence intensifies feeling: physical proximity; temporal immediacy; the visibility of the threat "before [one's] eyes," which the litigant's theatrics magnify ("gestures, cries, [and] dramatic manner," "signs and actions," "the clothes of those who have suffered," the "words [of the] suffering"). But even without visuals, the (legal) orator's vocal emotion produces the same emotion (tone, rhythm) in the audience, regardless of content: "the listeners always feel the same things as a speaker who speaks with . . . feeling, even if he says nothing" (*Rh.* 122 [1408b]) (or, in alternative translations, the jurors "surrender to the pleaders" or "suffe[r] along with the pathetic speaker, even if what he says amounts to nothing").[59] One can see in this kind of emotional *mimesis* or affective transfer-surrender something similar to what Aristotle describes in another passage: listening for their own pleasure, jurors often "surrender themselves" to the speakers (*Rh.* 3 [1354b]).

Aristotle's discussion of the use of verbal descriptions of body language as a means of persuasion further clarifies the relationship between the speaker's representation of emotion and the audience's emotional experience. Such verbal descriptions persuade not only because they vividly signify the emotions of the scene but also because they produce similar emotions in the audience: "speak on the basis of feelings," advises Aristotle, "narrating . . . the things that follow along with them." One might, for instance, say "'off he went, scowling at me,'" or, "as Aeschines says about Cratylus, . . . he was 'furiously hissing and furiously shaking his fists.'" Homer offers many examples: "'Thus she spoke, and the old nurse covered her face with her hands.' For those who start to cry put their hands over their eyes."[60] The discussion of *hypokrisis* that precedes this advice suggests that Aristotle envisions speakers enacting such gestures as they narrate them. Such descriptions, he explains, "are means of persuasion, because th[e] things [the spectators] do know"—that is, the gestures and body language the speaker evokes or enacts—"become symptoms of those they do not know" (*Rh.* 144 [1417a–b]). In such evocations, the speaker's body acts as both *symptom* of emotion (and the meaning it conveys) and its *vehicle*, transferring emotion to the audience.

[58] See, similarly, Aristotle's explanation of why "the uneducated [are] more persuasive than the well-educated in front of crowds of people": "the uneducated say things on the basis of what they know and things close at hand" (*Rh.* 95 [1395b]).

[59] Aristotle, *Art of Rhetoric* [Loeb], 9; and Aristotle, *On Rhetoric* (trans. Kennedy, 2nd ed.), 210. Reeve notes: "it is matter of how to produce a sort of feeling in the audience without regard to the things at issue, simply by the rhythm and tonality of speech, as in the case of music and rhythm in [the *Politics*]" (*Rh.* 334 [note 931]).

[60] *Rh.* 144 [1417a–b]. The line Aristotle attributes to Aeschines appears nowhere in Aeschines' extant works. It seems likely to refer to Aeschines the actor-cum-orator, but might instead refer to the Aeschines who was Socrates' disciple and a writer of Socratic dialogues. The Homer quote is from *The Odyssey* [19.361].

Catharsis as Judgment and the Mobilizing of Emotion

Emotional *mimesis* or affective transfer ("feel[ing] the same things," "suffer[ing] along with," or "surrender" to the speakers) may ride roughshod over truth. Presumably Aristotle is against this. But he does nevertheless view such emotional technique not merely as a cynical device for finessing a verdict but as a performance effect that might, under the right conditions, produce virtuous judgment. Our feelings (*pathê*) are, in fact, key to judgment, as Aristotle's definition of emotion suggests. "The feelings" he explains, "are those things due to which people, by undergoing a change, differ in their judgments, and that entail pain and pleasure—for example, anger, pity, fear, and other such things, and their contraries" (*Rh.* 56 [1378b]). Emotions (at least those that rhetoric produces) change both us and our judgments: sometimes for the worse, but sometimes for the better. Since the whole purpose of judicial rhetoric is judgment ("rhetoric is for the sake of judgment[,] for . . . a trial is a judgment") (*Rh.* 55 [1377b]), feelings matter.

How feelings might produce virtuous judgment becomes clearer if one looks at Aristotle's discussion of music in Book 8 of the *Politics*. Music represents emotion (he explains): "rhythms and melodies [have] the greatest likenesses to the true natures of anger and gentleness, . . . of courage and temperance, and of all the contraries of these" (*Pol.* 196 [1340a]). These emotional likenesses produce corresponding emotions in us: "everyone who listens to imitations comes to have the corresponding feelings" (*Pol.* 196 [1340a]). Learning to "enjoy noble melodies and rhythms" teaches pleasure in nobility itself (*Pol.* 198 [1341a]): repetition and habituation can shape virtue.[61] Since emotions are central to character ("virtue" entails "enjoying, loving, and hating in the correct way"), musical emotion "has the capacity to produce . . . character" and thus "political virtue" (*Pol.* 195–7 [1340a–b]). In fact, listening to such music, "we are altered in our souls" (*Pol.* 196 [1340a]). Unfortunately, enjoying the wrong kind of music—"only the common element in music"—can alter our souls the wrong way. However, for those of us who have a misguided fondness for "common" music (like the lower "animals [and] the majority of slaves and children"), there is still hope (*Pol.* 198 [1341a]). For when people prone to being possessed listen to music that "induce[s] a frenzy in their souls,"

> they calm down, as if they had received medical treatment and a purification. The same thing, then, must be undergone by those who are prone to pity or fear or to feelings generally. [They] get a certain purification (*tina katharsin*) and feel their burdens lightened by pleasure. (*Pol.* 200 [1342a])

[61] See Reeve's note in *Pol.* 399, note 1063.

This purification clearly does not entail the *purgation* of emotion (as some traditional explanations of catharsis would have it). Instead, it is like a medical treatment (indeed, a pleasure treatment) that calms the kinds of worries that eventually produce hysteria so that one may be sufficiently free of feverishness to put feelings to their right use. By "effect[ing] a purification" (*katharsin*) (*Pol.* 198 [1341a]), even flute-induced "frenzy" or "ecstasy" may contribute to virtue and right judgment.[62]

Scholars have rightly viewed Aristotle's discussion of catharsis in music as a key to his reference to catharsis in tragedy. He in fact cross-references these, stressing the relationship.[63] Certainly, musical emotion and the emotion that theatrical spectacle produces seem to have something in common: listening to music, "we are altered in our souls"; spectacle is similarly "capable of leading the soul" (presumably, like different kinds of music, sometimes toward virtue, sometimes toward its opposite). But the discussion of musical expression, emotion, and catharsis in the *Politics* may also be a key to understanding legal expression, emotion, and catharsis. Modern legal scholars (and public discourse) often use a textbook version of the concept of catharsis to explain what trials—particularly war crimes tribunals dealing with mass atrocity—achieve. "When justice is done, and seen to be done, it provides a catharsis for those physically or psychologically scarred: . . . [d]eep-seated resentments—key obstacles to reconciliation—are removed and people on different sides of the divide can [start with] a clean slate."[64] Here, catharsis is a vehicle of justice, standing for collective emotional purgation, psychological closure, forgiveness (perhaps even absolution), and social reconciliation. There is something of a tension between claims about the

[62] "[T]he flute has to do not with character but rather with frenzy, and so the correct occasions for its use are those where contemplation has the capacity to effect a purification rather than learning" (*Pol.* 198 [1341a]). On flute-induced frenzy or ecstasy, see e.g. *Pol.* 195, 198, 200, 201 [1340a, 1341a, 1342a–b].

[63] In the *Politics*, Aristotle explicitly identifies musical catharsis with the catharsis he references in the *Poetics*: "as to what we mean by purification, we will speak of it in simple terms now, but again and more perspicuously in our discussions concerning poetics" (*Pol.* 200 [1341b]). As Reeve notes, "[t]his extended discussion does not appear in the *Poetics* as we have it" (*Pol.* 398, note 1061]). In fact, Aristotle barely mentions catharsis in the *Poetics*, referring to it only twice and extremely briefly: "[t]ragedy through pity and fear accomplish[es] the catharsis [*katharsis*] of such emotion" (*Poet.* 47 [1449b]); Orestes was delivered from madness through catharsis (*Poet.* 91 [1455b]). However, while Aristotle's "account of music's purifying power . . . does not directly carry over to tragedy" (notes Reeve), presumably the "effect attributed to sacred melodies in [the *Politics*] is of the same sort as the one attributed [in the *Poetics*] to tragedy" (*Pol.* 399, note 1063). Moreover, Aristotle integrates a discussion of theatre audiences into his discussion of musical catharsis. (One kind of audience member is "free and well educated, the other vulgar, composed of vulgar people," but "all get a certain purification and feel their burdens lightened by pleasure") (*Pol.* 200 [1342a]). Comedy similarly achieves catharsis by refining pleasure and laughter (clearly not emotions one wishes to purge altogether). See Janko, *Aristotle on Comedy* (reconstructing *Poetics II* from the *Tractatus coislinianus*); and Watson, *Lost Second Book*, 179. The literature on catharsis is voluminous, but for two useful accounts of the vicissitudes of the history of the word (signifying, for instance, wonder, compassion, or cure), see Gobert, *Mind-Body Stage*, 50–80; and "Historicizing Emotion."

[64] Former United Nations official and Professor of International Law Kingsley Moghalu, quoted in Anders, "Therapeutic Turn," 29. For critical accounts of the common claim, see Anders, "Therapeutic Turn," especially 26–9; and Stahn, *Justice as Message*, 286, 386, 410.

virtues of catharsis as a beneficent agent of legal healing and theatrical theory's classic critique of the *Poetics*, in which catharsis instead appears as a nefarious tool of the status quo: central to a conservative program for disabling unruly popular emotion so it will cause no trouble.[65] In this vision, spectators exhaust their dangerous emotions in the theatre, which trains them to feel their feelings and then purge them, rather than to act on them. In this "Aristotelian" theatre, catharsis is an agent of stasis whose aim is to produce obedient subjects.

These visions may differ in their assessment of the political consequences of catharsis. But they both treat catharsis as a vehicle for purging emotion, rather than deploying it in the service of judgment and justice. Aristotle's discussion of music, however, suggests that he has something quite different in mind. True, catharsis "calms" the listener, acting as a kind of "medical treatment" for frenzy of the soul. But virtuous music also rouses emotion so that catharsis may mobilize it in the service of virtue. It activates not just "loving" but also "hating in the correct way," inciting the listener to action. In the lawcourt, as in music, the rousing of strong emotion—even frenzied emotion—may produce "character," "political virtue," and correct judgment. The primary aim of such emotion is not purgation, forgiveness, and closure but satisfaction through a just verdict.

Against Alcibiades: Theatrical Tears versus Righteous Outrage in the Legal Theatrocracy

Admittedly, Aristotle does not quite say this last bit (or not explicitly). But others do, or nearly so. In a speech called *Against Alcibiades* set in c.415 BCE (about thirty-five years before the publication of *The Republic*), an unknown orator who has come to be known as "Pseudo-Andocides" made a plea to the Athenian Assembly for the ostracism of the Athenian statesman and general Alcibiades.[66] Among Alcibiades' crimes (the speaker alleges), one took place in the Theatre of Dionysus: when Taureas, competing as *Choregus* against Alcibiades, had attempted to eject a non-Athenian member of Alcibiades' chorus, Alcibiades (says the speaker) drove Taureas offstage with his fists. The spectators were furious, and "showed their sympathy with Taureas and their hatred of

[65] The *locus classicus* here is, of course, Brecht's analysis of Aristotelian "dramatic" versus "epic" theatre. See e.g. Brecht, *Brecht on Theatre*, 60, 70, 78–9, 87, 135, 181, 270.

[66] *In Alc.* 559 [4.20–1]. For the debate about whether *Against Alcibiades* was delivered in an actual ostracism proceeding or offers only a fictional rendering of such a proceeding, see Maidment's introduction to the speech (*In Alc.* 534–7). While the Assembly functioned as an executive and legislative body, it also served as a judicial body: a kind of supreme court, making judgments about high-level political cases and handing down sentences. See Boegehold, *Lawcourts at Athens*, 18–19, 167–8 (on the *Heliaia*, the Assembly acting in its judicial capacity); and Lanni, *Law and Justice*, 31, 40, 121. On the judicial nature of the speech, see Andocides, *Andocides* (trans. Edwards), 200–5. Alcibiades was, of course, the famous follower of Socrates in Plato's *Symposium* and other dialogues.

Alcibiades by applauding the one chorus and refusing to listen to the other at all." But Alcibiades, who "showed such contempt for the law, was all-powerful," and so, "[p]artly from fear, partly from subservience, the judges pronounced [him] the victor, treating him as more important than their oath."[67]

Here we can find Plato's theatrocracy at work, not in a lawcourt or a musical competition but (perhaps unsurprisingly) in a theatrical competition. As in Plato's account of the musical and legal theatrocracy, there are false judges who "sho[w] contempt for the law." Unlike Plato, however, the speaker in *Against Alcibiades* is firmly on the side of the cheering spectators, whose applause stands for law against the tyranny of power. Addressing the judges in the Assembly, the speaker draws a parallel between them and the fearful and subservient judges in the theatrical competition: the "blame" for Alcibiades' judicial overthrow of the cheering demos, the speaker accuses them, "lies with you." For "[y]ou refuse to punish insolence.... That is why the young spend their days in the [law]courts instead of in the gymnasia.... they take Alcibiades as their model" (*In Alc.* 559 [4.22]). On one side are Alcibiades, the bootlicking judges, and the youth of Athens, modeling themselves on the dashing Alcibiades and making insolent speeches in the lawcourts. On the other side is the theatrical audience: attempting to enforce law through the democratic power of applause.

This accusation may appear to segue incongruously into the speaker's next accusation, but the two accusations share a central theme: rage against passive acquiescence to the status quo, and a view that theatrical arenas are places in which the representation of injustice can generate collective outrage sufficient to take action against it. (Perhaps it is no coincidence that the speech attacks Alcibiades, a devoted follower of Socrates, representative of the ability to "remain unmoved.") The second accusation charges Alcibiades with having fathered a son with a woman from Melos (which Athens had just conquered): a "woman whom he had turned from a free citizen into a slave, whose father and kinsfolk he had put to death and whose city he had made a waste," thus making "his son the deadly enemy of himself and of this city" (*In Alc.* 561 [4.22–3]).[68] The speaker sees in the birth of the son, who must commit patricide to avenge his mother, the seeds of a future tragedy akin to those shown on stage. Accusing the audience of reckless indifference, the speaker begs them to view Alcibiades' crime with the same emotions they feel in the theatre:

> When you are shown things of this kind on the tragic stage, you regard them with horror; but when you see them taking place in Athens, you remain unmoved— and yet you are uncertain whether the tales of tragedy are founded on the truth or

[67] See Andocides, *Andocides* (trans. Edwards), 203, on the fact that the dramatic festival here was the city Dionysia, and thus held in the Theatre of Dionysus.

[68] On Alcibiades' role in the attack on Melos, see Vickers, *Sophocles and Alcibiades*, 115–32.

> spring merely from the imagination of the poets; whereas you well know that these other lawless outrages, which you accept with indifference, have occurred in fact. (*In Alc.* 561 [4.23])

Isocrates—the great teacher of oratory (legal and otherwise)—had earlier made a similar point, in a much broader political critique that still seems all too resonant. "[S]ome are being put to death contrary to law in their own countries, others are wandering . . . in strange lands," the city's gates unjustly closed to them, "many [are] compelled through lack of the necessities of life to enlist, [and] are being slain":

> Against these ills no one has ever protested; and people are not ashamed to weep over the calamities which have been fabricated by the poets, while they view complacently the real sufferings, the many terrible sufferings . . . ; and they are so far from feeling pity that they even rejoice more in [others'] sorrows than in their own blessings. (*Isoc.* 1:227 [4.168–9])

The point, in both *Against Alcibiades*' and Isocrates' indictments, is not that we should weep less in the theatre; it is that we should weep more for real suffering and then act on our emotions. And the problem that both passages diagnose is not that theatre rouses emotions dangerous to the status quo (as in the textbook versions of Plato and Aristotle); it is that it rouses emotions that are *insufficiently* dangerous. Theatre produces the complacent self-satisfaction of weeping over fictional suffering, or the smug pleasure of viewing others' misfortunes as a marker of one's own deserved good fortune. Both passages imply that weeping in the theatre may drain one, leaving one exhausted and indifferent to real suffering. Both passages imply that citizens should not treat aesthetic experience as an opportunity to spend or diffuse pity and fear but as an opportunity for training themselves in real-world pity and outrage. Both passages indict complacent citizens' ability to "accept with indifference" such "lawless outrages." What both passages demand is not less emotion, but more: emotion capable of generating enough pity, fear, and (above all) anger about suffering—the "terrible sufferings" that happen every day around us—to do something about them.

Aeschines predicted that his audience would "shed more tears" over the real-world outrage of Demosthenes' crowning than "over the tragedies and the sufferings . . . presented on the stage," but apparently he was wrong. In the end, more than four-fifths of the jurors voted in favor of Demosthenes' crowning and (effectively) laughed Aeschines off stage. Punished for malicious prosecution with a fine of a thousand drachmas and prohibited from engaging in further lawsuits against his enemies, Aeschines fled Athens in humiliation and spent the rest of his life in exile as a teacher of rhetoric. Demosthenes went on to a checkered but mostly glorious career as a statesman. In the aftermath, it is not hard to imagine Aeschines reframing his prediction as an indictment similar to that of *Against Alcibiades* and Isocrates: "you . . . shed more tears over the tragedies and the sufferings of the heroes . . . presented on the stage [than] over the blindness of . . . the Athenian people."

Conclusion

Not every Athenian legal orator reproached the audience for weeping at tragedy while turning a blind eye to real world injustice. But virtually every orator did, at one time or another, attack the potential *passéism* and indifference of the spectators. Virtually all argued that, where defendants should work primarily to arouse pity, the job of the prosecution was to arouse anger and outrage.[69] Pity, anger, and outrage might sometimes be misguided. But, rightly directed, they were, it was felt, essential to producing just outcomes. I have already suggested that Aristotle offers a vision of catharsis in the *Politics* quite different from the textbook version of catharsis associated with him: a vision in which, instead of purging emotion or even simply purifying it, catharsis mobilizes it. Drawing a parallel between emotion in the theatre and that in the lawcourt, *Against Alcibiades*, Isocrates, and Aeschines similarly offer an alternative, not just to the textbook account of ancient theatrical theory but also to law-and-humanities truisms about the healing catharsis and closure that trials may offer. Instead of using the textbook reading of the *Poetics* to explain how emotion works in trials, we might use the *Politics* and *Rhetoric*—along with the impassioned pleas of *Against Alcibiades*, Isocrates, and Aeschines—to explain how emotion can work in both trials and theatre. Performance—in the theatre or lawcourt—may rouse a multitude of raging emotions.[70] These are powerful things, as Aristotle stresses: they do not necessarily disappear easily or leave you quiescent. Both trials and theatre may thus rouse feelings not to disable them but to *enable* them, to train us not to succumb to them but instead to use them to take action against wrongs. In another passage in the *Rhetoric*, Aristotle writes that "painful things are all perceptible" by the senses, "whereas the greatest evils are the least perceptible ones, for example, injustice or lack [of] wisdom. For the presence of evil does not cause any pain" (*Rh.* 65 [1382a]; translation modified). Perhaps *hypokrisis* is necessary, in both the

[69] On the importance of anger in ancient prosecution (often viewed as a vehicle of justice), see Allen, *World of Prometheus*, especially 50–1; Konstan, "Rhetoric and Emotion," 420; and, on anger generally, Konstan, *Emotions of the Ancient Greeks*, 41–76.

[70] We tend to think of pity and fear as the only emotions Aristotle associates with tragedy. But in fact he has a far more capacious conception of tragic emotion, and theatrical emotion generally: a conception closely allied with his conception of rhetorical emotion. While pity and fear may be the emotions most proper to tragedy (*Poet.* 63–9 [1452a–b]), tragedy can produce other emotions, including "anger, and others of this sort": Aristotle refers readers of the *Poetics* to the *Rhetoric* for a fuller discussion (*Poet.* 93–9 [1456a–b]).

lawcourt and theatre, to make the greatest evils perceptible to the senses. And perhaps pathos is necessary to making them painful enough for us to act against them. Legal theatricality (and the theatrocracy to which it plays) may be potentially toxic: exciting dangerous passions; encouraging mob rule; trampling reason. But it may also be the most potent tool available for stirring up emotions in the name of changing judgments, and thus the world.

2

The Roman Advocate as Actor

Actio, *Pronuntiatio*, *Prosopopoeia*, and Persuasive Empathy in Cicero and Quintilian

Introduction: Posing Fonteius

In the grand finale of his *Pro Fonteio* (*c.*69 BCE)—a defense of the praetor Marcus Fonteius—Cicero stages a family tableau to arouse pity, using embedded stage directions to direct the action and emotion of the scene. "[S]hall [the prosecution] drag and tear my client even from the embrace of that peerless though unhappy lady his mother, while you [turning to the audience] raise no finger to stay him?" cries Cicero. (Fonteius' mother embraces him.) "Shall he do so, though upon the other side a Vestal Maid casts her arms about the brother of her blood, imploring your protection, judges?" (Fonteius' sister in her sacred bridal robes embraces him on his other side.)[1] "To you a Vestal Maid extends in supplication

[1] Cicero, *Font.* 355 [46]. Throughout this chapter (as in Chapter 1), I cite first to a page number (with volume number if necessary), followed by the standard passage identification in brackets. I use the following abbreviations for frequently cited texts not otherwise identified (conforming to the abbreviation style in Hornblower, Spawforth, and Eidinow, ed., *Oxford Classical Dictionary* (2012 ed.), xxvi–liii. For Loeb editions, I use the most recently updated versions at www-loebclassics-com.

Brut. = Cicero, *Brutus*, in Cicero, *Brutus, Orator* [Loeb].

De or. = Cicero, *On the Orator* [*De oratore*] [Loeb].

Dial. = Tacitus, *Dialogus de oratoribus* in Tacitus, *Agricola, Germania, Dialogus* [Loeb].

Clu. = Cicero, *Pro Cluentio*, in Cicero, *Pro Lege Manilia, Pro Caecina, Pro Cluentio, Pro Rabirio Perduellionis.*

Font. = Cicero, *Pro Fonteio*, in Cicero, *Pro Milone* [Loeb].

Inst. = Quintilian, *The Orator's Education* [*Institutio oratoria*] [Loeb] (sometimes referenced only as "Quintilian").

Mil. = Cicero, *Pro Milone* in Cicero, *Pro Milone* [Loeb].

Off. = Cicero, *De officiis* [Loeb].

Orat. = Cicero, *Orator*, in Cicero, *Brutus, Orator* [Loeb].

Part. or. = Cicero, *De partitione oratoria* in Cicero, *On the Orator* [Loeb].

QRosc. = Cicero, *Pro Quinto Roscio comoedo* in Cicero, *Pro Publio Quinctio* [etc.] [Loeb].

Rhet. Her. = [Cicero], *Rhetorica ad Herennium* [Loeb].

Sull. = Cicero, *Pro Sulla* in Cicero, *In Catilinam I–IV, Pro Murena, Pro Sull, Pro Flacco* [Loeb].

Fonteius was accused of mistreating the inhabitants of southern Gaul, where he was praetor. On the case, see Watts' introduction, in *Mil.*, 306–7. Here and in other Cicero speeches, the Loeb translates "*iudices*" as "gentlemen," which throughout this chapter I silently change to "judges": a term that includes not only lay judges (often translated as "jurors") but also, implicitly, the audience, which included women. See Introduction, 19–21 on my use of gendered pronouns. For a persuasive argument that published speeches represent speeches as delivered (at least in Cicero's day), see Powell, "Court Procedure and Rhetorical Strategy in Cicero." On judges under the Empire (and the variable size of

Law as Performance: Theatricality, Spectatorship, and the Making of Law in Ancient, Medieval, and Early Modern Europe. Julie Stone Peters, Oxford University Press. © Julie Stone Peters 2022. DOI: 10.1093/oso/9780192898494.003.0003

the same hands which she has been accustomed to extend to the immortal gods on your behalf." (Fonteius' sister lifts her hands to the judges in a posture of religious supplication.) "Do you mark, judges, how Marcus Fonteius, brave man though he be, has at my allusion to his parent and his sister broken into sudden tears?" (Fonteius breaks into sudden tears.) "Never has he flinched upon the field, often has he dashed into the thickest of the fray fighting sword in hand against fearful odds." (While weeping, Fonteius also somehow strives to look like a man dashing into the fray.) "Yet he to-day flinches.... Marcus Fonteius,... what anguish is yours!" (*Font.* 357 [47–9]). (Fonteius flinches, displays anguish, and returns quickly to unflinching military posture, perhaps not altogether successfully: it is a difficult acting assignment.) In the emblematic tableau that closes this brief sequence, Cicero displays for the crowd a Roman citizen and military hero flanked by two sacred images of peace—the Roman mother and the Vestal Virgin—... assuming they play their parts correctly.

Cicero presumably coached the Fonteius family before the trial. But, unfortunately, in a trial as in theatre, things do not always go as planned. "Sometimes" (writes Quintilian), the client's "ignorance, lack of sophistication, stiffness, and uncouthness make the whole thing a disaster." If the "client who is being put on display" fails to "adap[t] himself to his advocate," or "resist[s]" the advocate's acting prompts, the scene turns from tragedy to farce. The advocate points to the defendant and declares: "'He stretches out his hands in supplication to clasp your knees' or 'The wretched man clings to the embrace of his children' or 'Look, he is calling me back'.... [But] the client is doing none of these things!" The more the advocate attempts to stage a *coup de théâtre* "for dramatic effect," the more chance it will backfire. He tells the girl claiming to be the defendant's sister to fall into her alleged brother's arms at a climactic moment of the speech, but... she cannot find him, she is furiously looking everywhere, dammit, where is he? (Answer: opposing counsel, none other than Quintilian himself, has helped him to make himself scarce.) Another employs a little stage trick to ensure that a child will cry in court, giving the child his lines, but when he gives the direction, "tell the judge why you are crying," the child goes rogue and answers "[because I am] being pinched by [my] *paedagogus*"! Another, deciding to rely not on his client but on his own dramatic skills, "fle[es] instantly from the benches" when "the prosecutor exhibit[s] a bloody sword" proving "the victim had been killed,... pretending to be terrified, and then... peep[s] out of the crowd with his head partly muffled up, and ask[s] whether the man with the sword ha[s] gone," raising a laugh but losing all credibility.[2] On the one hand, "real life" is a flop: too little theatre, for the client

judicial panels), see Bablitz, *Actors and Audience*, 12, 89–119 (and throughout). As should be obvious from my notes, I owe a vast debt of gratitude to Bablitz' comprehensive and erudite discussions of Roman courtrooms under the Empire.

[2] For the quotes and examples in this paragraph, see *Inst.* 3:37–41 [6.1.37–49]; and for "real life," *De or.* 2:171 [3.214].

cannot act. On the other hand, histrionics explode in your face: too much theatre (and you cannot really act either). But you *must* dramatize your client's story or your case will fail. What is the advocate to do?

No one had more to say about such scenes—and the staging of trials in general—than Cicero and Quintilian: theorists of oratory who were, at the same time, lawyers and educators interested in the pragmatics of arguing a case. Situating their thought and practices in Roman legal oratory more generally, this chapter focuses almost solely on these two figures. It does so for several reasons. Taken together, their work offers an extraordinarily extensive, detailed, and profound analysis of the nature and demands of legal oratory, the role of trial lawyers (*patroni* and *advocati*), and the ethical issues that inhere in courtroom performance.[3] Cicero wrote at least four treatises specifically devoted to oratory, all with a heavy focus on legal oratory: the three-book dialogue *On the Orator* (*c.*55 BCE); a handbook for his son Marcus called *On the Parts of Oratory* (54 or 46 BCE); and *Brutus* and *Orator* (both in 46 BCE) (as well as a fragment titled *The Best Kind of Orator* [also 46 BCE]). Quintilian's twelve-volume *The Orator's Education* (*Institutio oratoria*, *c.*95 CE) offers an exhaustive analysis of the education and art of the orator, deeply informed by his experience not only as a teacher of oratory but as a practicing legal advocate in both Rome and the provincial courts of Spain.[4] At the same time, their work exerted an unparalleled influence on later discussions of legal oratory. For theorists from antiquity through the early modern period and beyond, Cicero was revered as the greatest orator of all time, his influence arguably dwarfing that of Plato and Aristotle. Medieval commentators referenced Quintilian less frequently, but with the discovery of an entire manuscript of the *Orator's Education* in the early fifteenth century and its printing later in the century, his name came to join Cicero's, and in the early modern period he became the preeminent authority not only on rhetoric but on the specifics of courtroom persuasion.[5]

The *Orator's Education* appeared roughly a century and a half after Cicero's death, and speaks to a radically changed political and legal culture. Where Cicero wrote primarily for the courts, assembly, and senate in the Republic's tumultuous last century, Quintilian wrote primarily for the classroom under the Empire,

[3] I use the word "advocate" throughout to describe both the *patroni* of Cicero's era (generally wellborn men of leisure) and the *advocati* of Quintilian's era (often, though not always, litigation professionals). On the distinction, see Metzger, "Litigation," 275. On different kinds of lawyers under the Empire (and the differences in their status), see Bablitz, *Actors and Audience*, 141–98.

[4] During the twenty years in which Quintilian taught rhetoric in Rome, he was also active in the courts, and we know of four cases he definitely argued. See Russell's introduction in *Inst.*, 1:1–2; Bablitz, *Actors and Audience*, 3–4; and Kennedy, *Quintilian*, 16–20 (after 59 CE, Quintilian returned to Spain, probably to practice law in the provincial courts [18]). On Quintilian and law generally, see the essays in Tellegen-Couperus, ed. *Quintilian and the Law*. On Cicero as a lawyer, see the essays in Powell and Paterson, ed., *Cicero the Advocate*.

[5] On the eventual ascendency of Quintilian's *Orator's Education* "as the ultimate classical authority on eloquence," see Copeland and Sluiter, ed., *Medieval Grammar and Rhetoric*, 753.

looking back at the Republic as a distant memory. By Quintilian's era, the "decay of oratory" and the rise of the two-bit lawyer had become common *topoi*. In the *Satyricon* (*c*.54–68 CE), Petronius lays the blame at the door of ambitious parents, who push "immature schoolboys into the forum" in the view "that nothing is mightier than eloquence."[6] When "the young speakers enter court, they think they have been conveyed into another world," but they have in fact been "converted into total fools," and are "laughed at in court" as they imitate the "breezy and formless verbosity" that has "migrated from Asia to Athens, [its] breath as from some malignant star" (71–3 [2–4]). Let the young man not enter the forum, cries Petronius, until "he is replete with the learning of Socrates's school" and can "wield the heavy armor of great Demosthenes" (77 [5]). In his *Dialogue on Oratory* (*c*.102 CE), Tacitus deplores the displacement of true "orators" (distinguished for their "eloquence") by "'pleaders,' 'advocates,' 'counsel.'" His spokesman Maternus declares his determination to pursue his "long-cherished dream [of] forsaking the narrow sphere of pleading at the bar [and] cultivate eloquence in its higher and holier form" (*Dial.* 231 [1]; 237–9 [4]).

But such nostalgia for the holy oratory of Demosthenes' and Cicero's day is deceptive, for it in fact echoes precisely the kind of lament one can find in Cicero himself, who deplored "the decadence, not to say the utter extinction, of eloquence," particularly in the courtroom: today, anyone may "solici[t] ... the aid of jurisconsults or of advocates," he asserts, but "not all—no, not even many—can be ... eloquent as pleaders" (*Off.* 241 [2.19.67]). However different the political and legal cultures in which Cicero and Quintilian wrote, one can hear in their work a set of refrains. In fact, Quintilian draws so extensively on Cicero that it is sometimes hard to distinguish the two. His project was (among other things) an attempt to restore the glorious tradition of Ciceronian oratory: "[i]t was not without reason that [Cicero's] contemporaries said he was 'king' of the courts," for he was an "immortal genius" whose name has become, "for posterity, ... not so much the name of a man as a synonym for eloquence itself. Let us fix our eyes on him," urges Quintilian, "let him be the model we set before ourselves" (4:313 [10.1.109, 112]).

Although I do sometimes point to differences between Cicero and Quintilian (as above), rather than focusing on their differences I generally treat them as part of an ongoing conversation. Thus, in much of this chapter, they speak with one voice (as do Cicero's various dialogue characters, whom he tended to use as mouthpieces for his own views). While I draw on the now-extensive body of literature on performance cultures in ancient Rome and attempt to situate Cicero and Quintilian in their respective milieus, I also attempt to situate them within

[6] Petronius, *Satyricon* [Loeb], 75 [4] (translation modified; hereafter cited in the text). On the little we know of Petronius and for discussions of the date, see Schmeling's introduction, *Satyricon*, 3–5.

longer debates about the value of legal theatricality.[7] Much of the chapter is dedicated to explaining their practical instructions for legal orators and their views on legal performance. Understanding these is necessary to understanding those of the medieval and Renaissance theorists I discuss in later chapters, who take up their claims while radically altering them to suit their own courts and forms of legal pleading. My reading of Cicero and Quintilian in this chapter thus reflects centrally on some of the ongoing concerns of this book: the value and dangers of legal "theatrocracy"; the role of spectacle and emotion in persuasion; the significance of legal role-playing or impersonation; the ethics of legal performance; the distinction between the aesthetic sphere and the "real" world of law; and more.

Among other things, I argue here that Cicero and Quintilian offer an alternative to Plato's and Aristotle's more ambivalent views about theatrocratic governance and the manipulation of the judges' or jurors' emotions. For them, legal performance is at once a technology of representation and a crucial ethical practice. Vigorously representing their clients by taking on a series of masks or *personae*, advocates do not engage in hypocritical impersonation but in fact experience real emotion, which they must learn to manage through technique to prevent it from becoming disabling. Concealing such technique is not a form of illusionism but instead highlights the real stakes for their clients, rather than highlighting their own artistry. Ultimately, the ability simultaneously to access another's emotional truth while mastering it is, for Cicero and Quintilian, a model for the kind of highly skilled empathetic identification that is essential to doing justice: for one's client and in general. These issues touch not only on longstanding issues in acting theory but on longstanding debates about the political and ethical significance of rhetoric generally, debates in which Cicero is a key figure: the paradigmatic theorist of a rhetorical politics that sets itself against (most notably) Plato's idealist politics. I hope to illuminate the role that legal theatricality plays, for both Cicero

[7] On performance specifically in Cicero and Quintilian, see Hall, *Cicero's Use of Judicial Theater*; Petrone and Casamento, ed., *Lo spettacolo della giustizia*; Steel, *Reading Cicero*; Tellegen-Couperus, ed., *Quintilian and the Law* (Mastrorosa, "Quintilian and the Judges"; Bons and Lane, "*Institutio Oratoria* VI.2; and Rodríguez Martín, "Moving the Judge); Korstenko, *Cicero, Catullus, and the Language of Social Performance* (especially Ch 5–6); and Vasaly, "Masks of Rhetoric." On theatrical oratory and performance cultures in ancient Rome more generally, I am especially indebted to the chapters on "Republican Theater" and "Imperial Reenactments" in Connolly, *State of Speech*, but also to the following: the section on "Physical Technique: *Actio*" in Dinter, Guérin, and Martinho, ed., *Reading Roman Declamation*, 115–47 (Corbeill, "Physical Excess as a Marker of Genre"; and Balbo, "Between Real and Fictional Eloquence"); the section on "Oratorical Performance" in Gray, et al., ed., *Reading Republican Oratory* (especially Hilder, "Politics of *Pronuntiatio*"; and Balbo, "Traces of *Actio*"); Hall, "Roman Judges and Their Participation in the 'Theatre of Justice'"; Steel, "Tribunician Sacrosanctity and Oratorical Performance"; and Fantham, *Roman Readings* ("Orator and / et Actor" [285–301]). On masculinity as performance in ancient Rome, see Gunderson, *Staging Masculinity*; Davies, "Togate Statues and Petrified Orators"; and Gleason, *Making Men*. For helpful overviews of Roman oratory generally, see Steel, *Roman Oratory*; Kennedy, *Art of Rhetoric in the Roman World*, and his updated abridgement, *New History of Classical Rhetoric*, 102–256; and Pernot, *Rhetoric in Antiquity*, 83–201.

and Quintilian, in the development of an approach to professional and public life that is not merely prudential—not merely a pragmatic approach to the vicissitudes of the political (let alone a cynical instrument of expediency, as some have charged)—but the foundation for a committed legal and political ethics.

The Roman Legal Theatre

Courtroom as Theatre

If Roman legal practice changed considerably in the century and a half that separates Cicero from Quintilian, it was also different in the different parts of the Empire in which Cicero and Quintilian sometimes made their homes (and even in different courts in Rome itself). Nevertheless, one can identify some relative constants. Among these are features that, as in ancient Athens, helped turn important trials into great public spectacles, at once political contests and forms of mass entertainment: vast and diverse audiences (including aristocrats, plebeians, slaves, men, women, children); courts that were in open public arenas (most notably the variety of courts in the Forum); a culture of rowdy audiences (cheering, catcalling, taunting the speaker); the combination of general litigiousness and high stakes for the litigants; the political nature of trials; and the decisive role of persuasive legal oratory.[8]

That said, Roman legal practice differed from Athenian in some significant ways. Most notable among these was the fact that those deciding the outcome of a case were not hundreds of citizen-spectators but usually a single presiding judge—ranging in status from a private citizen (in the majority of cases) or a magistrate in criminal matters to the Emperor himself. A panel of additional judges or assessors (sometimes described as "jurors") often served beside the presiding judge: sometimes voting; sometimes merely serving as advisors.[9] The presiding judge usually sat alone on a raised platform or tribunal facing the spectators, with lay judges immediately below him.[10] The trial took dramatic form in the open playing space between the spectators and the judges. Benches representing each side of the case framed the space. Judges were often part of the action: during one trial in which Augustus served as judge, Archelaus (ruler of Samaria, Judea, and Idumea)

[8] On the location of courts (including the transfer from the *Forum Romanum* to the Forum of Augustus), and the variety of spaces and audience sizes (sometimes quite small), see Bablitz, *Actors and Audience*, 13–70. On litigation procedures generally, see Metzger, "Litigation." On the many kinds of "spaces of justice" in ancient Rome, see De Angelis, ed., *Spaces of Justice in the Roman World*. I follow Bablitz and others in using the word "courtroom" to designate the various kinds of spaces in which trials might be held.

[9] See Bablitz, *Actors and Audience*, 51, and on judges generally, 89–119.

[10] See Bablitz, *Actors and Audience*, 29–31, on the likelihood that only the presiding judge sat on a raised tribunal on a platform (at least during the imperial period).

embraced the Emperor's knees; during another in which Claudius served as judge, an angry defendant threw a tablet and stylus at him and ended up wounding him.[11] An equally important difference was the emergence of a class of quasi-professional legal advocates generally recognized as experts (among them Cicero himself): not officially paid in the early period, but receiving honoraria, political perks, and sometimes fame. By Quintilian's day, the profession of lawyer was firmly entrenched. Many saw professional advocacy as a possible road to social advancement, or at least a living. Lawyers struggling to establish themselves would hang around the Forum in the hope of scoring a case.[12] Some became professional accusers, serving the wealthy by attacking their enemies in the lawcourts.[13] While "the houses of distinguished jurisconsults" might be "thronged with pupils" hoping to join their number (in Cicero's description) (*Orat.* 417 [142]), and the schools of rhetoric taught oratory, there were no formal legal-educational institutions. Practicing advocates tended to learn their trade in the courts themselves, usually informally apprenticing themselves to a more experienced advocate. What they learned was not primarily legal rules (which were mostly relevant at the pretrial stage) but performance practices, for judicial oratory was still, above all, a performance art.[14]

Even more insistently than their Greek predecessors, Romans drew the parallel between law and theatre, the art of the actor and the art of the advocate. For Cicero, the Forum was a "*theatrum ingeni*" (a theatre for the talented orator): a *scaena* (scenic stage) where the advocate delivered his speech.[15] A great orator should "handl[e] . . . the business of the courts with a charm suggestive of the stage," treating "forensic" matters "scenic[ally]" ("*forenses scenica*") (*De or.* 2:25 [3.30]). For Quintilian, it was the trial audience itself that constituted the *theatrum* (3:43 [6.1.52]). The kinds of antitheatrical barbs that Athenians sometimes used against their adversaries in the lawcourt are largely absent in Roman texts.[16] When the Athenian general Iphicrates exclaimed, "my opponent's actor is better" but "my play [is] superior," he was asserting the superiority of legal substance ("my play") over mere theatrics (his opponent Aristophon's "actor"). But when Plutarch quotes him in the first century CE, he reverses the hierarchy: "the eloquence of Aristophon's orators" have quite properly defeated Iphicrates, who should have known that even the "private person of ordinary costume and mien who wishes to . . . rule the multitude [must] posses[s] persuasion and attractive

[11] Bablitz, *Actors and Audience*, 37.

[12] Bablitz, *Actors and Audience*, 151 (and generally 141–69).

[13] See the introduction to Tacitus' *Dialogus* (*Dial.*, 222–3).

[14] See Metzger, "Litigation," on the distinction between the pretrial stage, where magistrates presided, and the trial, where judges presided. In the latter, it was not laws but "the rhetorical conventions cultivated by the orators who spoke on behalf of the litigants" that governed (275).

[15] *Brut.* 22–3 [6] (describing the lawyer-orator Hortensius); *De or.* 1:455 [2.338] (describing "the orator's chief stage").

[16] See Ch 1, 28, 35–6.

speech." Iphicrates is merely a poor orator offering a weak excuse for his failure.[17] Forensic oratory may have grown debased, but not because it drew too much on theatre: rather because it drew too little on theatre, for (as Maternus' friends argue in Tacitus' *Dialogue on Oratory*) the bar needed orators with theatrical gifts. After Maternus gives a reading in which he throws "himself heart and soul into the role of Cato," determining to devote his attention to that "higher and holier form" of eloquence, theatre, Marcus Aper, one of "the leading lights of the bar at Rome," calls on him to tell him that he is now "being summoned to the forum by the long list of [his] friends' cases." Do not, begs Aper, "turn your back on your profession of... pleader[!]" (*Dial.* 233–9 [2–4]).

Although judges officially decided cases in the Roman lawcourts, the cheers or hisses of the crowd still mattered and could (as in Athens) be decisive. What Plato denounced as the theatrocracy still largely ruled the Roman legal theatre. However, where for Plato the victory of theatrocracy promised a "hell of unending misery," and for Aristotle pleasing the crowd was a sad necessity, for Cicero, the voice of the multitude could represent the voice of the Republic itself. It was not merely *acceptable* to raise "shouts of applause" (*Orat.* 508 [236]): it ought to be the speaker's central aim. Naturally, there was a certain degree of pragmatic self-interest in seeking to do so: a speaker who was "prudent and cautious" allowed himself to be "controlled by the reception given by his audience" (*Part. or.* 323 [5.15]). Speakers who wished to "win approval" must "have regard to the goodwill of their auditors, and shape and adapt themselves completely according to this" goodwill, seeking the audience's "opinion and approval" (*Orat.* 323 [24]). But applause also rewarded excellence. So seeking it was not merely prudential but principled. For the "sort of an orator a man is can only be recognized from what his oratory effects": its success "can only be judged by the assent of the multitude and the approbation of the people" (*Brut.* 157–9 [185]). This meant that (*pace* Plato), when it came to determining oratorical excellence, the audience was the highest authority: the speaker "who is approved by the multitude must inevitably be approved by the expert" (*Brut.* 157 [184]). For what was the point of eloquence (legal or otherwise) without an audience? A "speaker can no more be eloquent without a large audience than a flute-player can perform without a flute" (*De or.* 1:455 [2.338]).

Such views were more than a little idealistic, since it was standard practice for each side to have a retinue of supporters whose applause reflected team loyalty (as at a sporting event). Where a team did not seem sufficiently large, a rich litigant might hire supporters: the paid claque. The claque was regular fodder for satire.[18] Martial vividly calls up for us the image of one claque member, who "spreads his net for a dinner [when] you are... pleading a case": "'A hit!' 'A quick one!' 'Cunning!' 'Jolly good!'" cries the claque member; "'All right, you've got your

[17] Plutarch, *Moralia, Volume X* [Loeb], 177 ("Precepts of Statecraft," 801f) (translation modified).

[18] See the discussion in Bablitz, *Actors and Audience*, 136–40.

dinner,' says the rich litigant, 'Now hush.'"[19] Quintilian—writing in an era in which hiring a claque was standard practice—had contempt for the "preconcerted applause" that dignified "perverse displays of oratory" (5:273 [12.9.4]), since such applause obviously did not correlate with merit. Unlike Cicero, he could not condone those orators who were "addicted to applause" (2:281 [4.2.127]), who "prepared themselves for the applause of a large audience," and who could not "bear the silence that indicates attention, or believe in their own competence unless they have made the whole place rock with noise and clamour" (2:239 [4.2.37]). The demand for applause—and the granting of indiscriminate applause—"reeks of the theatre" (1:273 [2.2.10]).[20] The advocate's performance should "be designed [for] the judge," not the general spectators. For, after "the thunders of... perverse displays of oratory have died away to the sound of the... applause" (5:273 [12.9.4]), judges were the ones who counted.[21]

Nevertheless, as even Quintilian acknowledged, in the real world there was no bucking the theatrocracy. Given that "the feelings of audiences are fickle and the truth is exposed to so many evils," he explains, "we must fight with the weapons of art, and employ whatever means serve our purpose" (1:389–91 [2.17.29]). So, even while designing speeches for the judge, the advocate who had any hope of winning had to play to the audience. This was particularly so in the epilogue (the peroration). There, "now... in possession of the hearts of the judges... we can spread our sails" and "are allowed to release the whole flood of our eloquence," at last arriving at the key "moment to move the audience,... when we come to the phrase with which the old tragedies and comedies end: 'Now give us your applause'" (*Inst.* 3:43 [6.1.52]). The speaker thus did not merely play *to* the audience but *played* the audience: flute-players might need flutes, but they ideally played the flute, rather than the flute playing them. As Cicero had suggested in *Brutus*, one could measure the harpist's skill in playing on the strings by the sounds that emerged from the instrument; so could one measure the speaker's skill "in playing on the minds of his audience" by the emotions the audience expressed (171 [199–200]). Such skill helped one win cases, but as Tacitus' Marcus Aper suggests, the audience's adulation was a thrill in itself: "What... deference is paid to you in the law-courts! What a supreme delight it is to gather yourself to your feet, and to take your stand before a hushed audience [that] has eyes only for you! Think of the growing crowd streaming round about [you], and taking on any mood [you] wrap [yourself in!]" (*Dial.* 243 [6.4–5]).

19 Martial, *Epigrams* [Loeb], 1:147 [27]; see Bablitz, *Actors and Audience*, 127–8.

20 Quintilian is actually referring to classroom applause, but the broader context makes it clear he also has the courtroom in mind.

21 See similarly Quintilian, 1:337 [2.12.7], 2:465 [5.12.20–21], 4:273–5 [10.1.43–4]; and Seneca the Elder: "I am used to keeping my eye on the judge, not the audience" (*Controversiae* in Seneca, *Declamations* [Loeb], 1:385 [3.pr.12]).

The Art of Actio *and* Pronuntiatio

For the Roman advocate (as for the Athenian), the principal means of gaining applause and winning a case lay in *hypokrisis* (delivery), rendered as *actio* and *pronuntiatio* in Latin, and consisting (as Cicero puts it) in the control of "bodily carriage, gesture, play of features and changing intonation of voice" as well as "movement" (*De or.* 1:15 [1.18]; *Orator*, 347 [55]).[22] Romans never tired of citing the famous Demosthenes anecdote: "asked what was first in oratory, [Demosthenes] replied to his questioner, 'action' [*actio*], what second, 'action,' and again third, 'action'" (*Brut.* 125 [142]).[23] Delivery was "the most potent factor of all in oratory" (*Inst.* 4:261 [10.1.17]), the "dominant factor," explained Cicero (in a passage that was to be quoted as frequently as the Demosthenes anecdote): without it, "the best speaker cannot be of any account at all"; with it, "a moderate speaker... can often outdo the best of them" (*De or.* 2:169 [3.213]).[24] Cicero offers the example of Gnaeus Lentulus, who "won such favour by the warmth of his delivery" (his "effective use of pauses, ejaculations, a voice sonorous and agreeable") that "the qualities which he lacked were scarcely missed" (*Brut.* 201–3 [234]). Delivery spoke to both the eye and the ear. It played to both those spectators who could hear but not see (for instance, those sitting behind several rows of benches) and those who could see but not hear (for instance, those on a balcony looking down at the courtroom below).[25] It animated memorized speeches that might otherwise sound rote, particularly in the live action of the courtroom. Explaining his misgivings about giving a reading of one of his speeches, Pliny noted that not only did speeches depend on "the gestures of the speaker as he strides to and fro, the movements of his body corresponding to his changing passions." They also depended on the thrill of the courtroom.

> [S]peeches when read lose all their warmth and spirit,... since their fire is always fed from the atmosphere of [the] court: the bench of magistrates and throng of advocates, the suspense of the awaited verdict,... and the divided enthusiasm of the public.[26]

[22] See also the definitions in *Part. or.* 313 [1.3] and the *Rhetorica ad Herennium*: "Delivery [*Pronuntiatio*] is the graceful regulation of voice, countenance, and gesture" (*Rhet. Her.* 7 [1.3]). On Cicero's stress on *actio* rather than *pronuntiatio*, see Rebmann, "Pronuntiatio," col. 220–21. In Book 11, Quintilian treats the terms *actio* and *pronuntiatio* as interchangeable: "*Pronuntiatio* is called *actio* by many people. [Cicero] divides *actio* into two elements, voice and movement, and these are also the elements of *pronuntiatio*. So we are free to use both names indifferently" (5:85–7 [11.3.1]). Beyond oratory, the word "*actio*" described many kinds of action, including dramatic actions, legal actions, and pleas or speeches. See the entry for "actio" in Glare, ed., *Oxford Latin Dictionary* (1983 ed.), 30.

[23] See similarly Quintilian: "[W]hen Demosthenes was asked what was the most important thing in the whole business of oratory, he gave the prize to Delivery, and he gave it the second and the third place too, until they stopped asking; we must therefore suppose that he thought of it not just as the first faculty needed, but as the only one" (5:87–9 [11.3.6–7]).

[24] See similarly Quintilian, 5:87 [11.3.2, 5–6, 8].

[25] See Bablitz, *Actors and Audience*, 63.

[26] Pliny the Younger, *Letters* [Loeb], 1:147 [2.19].

One needed not just "innate emotion" however (*Brut.*, 85–7 [93]), for delivery was "regulated by the control of art" (*De or.* 2:173 [3.216–17]). That art was extremely difficult to master: "the actor's... art and the stage proclaim" its importance, declares Cicero, but "everyone knows how few actors... we could [ever] bear to watch!" (*De or.* 1:15 [1.18]). *Writing* a successful speech requires "but ordinary skill," he explained, but only in delivery were the orator's true "godlike power and excellence... discerned" (*De or.* 1:285 [2.120]). What made delivery still more difficult was that judges and legal audiences demanded virtuoso performance. As Tacitus complained: they would "no more put up with sober, unadorned old-fashionedness in a court of law than if you were to try to reproduce on the stage the gesture of Roscius or Ambivius Turpio" (*Dial.* 283 [20]). But one *could* nevertheless learn delivery: the voice, gestures, facial expressions, and demeanor could "be disciplined by training and method," said Quintilian (5:117 [11.3.62]). Even "natural tools" such as "voice, lungs, good looks" could be "improved by care" (5:249 [12.5.5]). Through long and dedicated study, one might ultimately acquire that "assured facility" that the Greeks called "*hexis*" (here, a kind of permanent mastery) (4:253 [10.1.1]), as well as "[t]he greatest fruit of our studies, the richest harvest of our long labours:... the power of improvisation" (4:373 [10.7.1]).

Cicero and Quintilian were both dedicated teachers of oratory. It is "glorious to teach that which it is most excellent to know," declared Cicero, defending himself from attacks on such teaching as disreputable (*Orat.* 417 [142]).[27] As Quintilian stresses at the beginning of the *Orator's Education*, he himself spent twenty years teaching before composing his *magnum opus* (*Inst.* 1:53 [1.Pr.1]). Both Cicero's and Quintilian's oratorical texts reflect their commitment to pedagogy, offering a multitude of specific instructions for the aspiring orator. Unlike Aristotle's *Rhetoric*, which became an oratorical manual almost inadvertently, Cicero's and Quintilian's writings on oratory are designedly so. Cicero produced *On the Parts of Oratory* as a handbook for his son Marcus, and explains that it is "a set of instructions" (*Part. or.* 3.9). *On the Orator* takes the form of a dialogue in which, for instance, Antonius is "a kindly and accomplished teacher" who gives Sulpicius instruction (*De or.* 1:341 [2.196]). He describes his defense of Manius Aquilius to Sulpicius "in order to help you to be wrathful, indignant and tearful in your speech-making" (although, Cicero admits, Suplicius' prosecution of Gaius Norbanus shows that he hardly needed such instruction) (*De or.* 1:339–41 [2.195–7]). Cicero's lesson in "figures" in *Orator*—an extraordinary portrait of a virtuoso orator in action—shows the extent to which he understood even instruction in verbal style as *performance* instruction. To perform "figures," the advocate

[27] *Orat.* 419 [144]. Cicero is defending the teaching of oratory by comparing it with the teaching of jurisprudence, stressing that oratory it is equally important to upholding law.

> will seem to consult the audience, and sometimes even . . . the opponent; . . . he will divert the attention of the audience from the point at issue; he will frequently provoke merriment and laughter; . . . he will warn the audience to be on their guard; he will even fly into a passion and protest violently; he will plead and entreat and soothe the audience [and] put himself on terms of intimacy with [them]; by his statement of the case he will make the scene live before our eyes. (*Orat.* 409–15 [137–9])

Aristotle had noted that no one had as yet written up the rules of delivery "systematically" (*Rhetoric*, 195 [1403b]).[28] While Cicero does not offer a systematic art of delivery, he discusses it extensively in the context of the general "theory of oratory": an art that "once seemed . . . unknown" but has fortunately now been given "order" and "correlat[ed]" to the other arts (*De or.* 1:131 [1.187–8]). Quintilian takes the program of systematizing delivery one step further, turning his accumulated experience into a comprehensive set of lessons.[29] Cicero had noted that the "body talks" and thus must "agree with the thought" (*De or.* 2:179 [3.223]). Quintilian elaborates, paying special attention to the hand: the hand's movements "almost match the entire stock of words [and], I might almost say, speak for themselves" (5:129 [11.3.85–6]). The orator was to accompany every few words with a gesture that stressed their meaning.[30] Quintilian illustrates with, among other things, a speculative reconstruction of the gestural "beats" in Cicero's *Pro Ligario*:

> *novum crimen* ("new charge")—one movement; *Gai Caesar*, a second; *et ante hanc diem* ("previous to this day"), a third; *non auditum* ("unheard of"), a fourth; then *propinquus meus* ("my relation"), then *ad te* ("before you"), then *Quintus Tubero*, then *detulit* ("brought"). (3:141 [11.3.108–9])

The Actor's Apprentice: Be Theatrical . . . But Not Too Theatrical

If Cicero and Quintilian offer extensive practical instruction in delivery, there was (according to them) one kind of practitioner who was theoretically an even more masterful teacher of delivery: the actor. Quintilian notes that Demosthenes studied with the actor Andronicus and recommends that aspiring orators do the same

[28] Aristotle, *Rhetoric* (trans. Reeve), 195 [1403b].

[29] For Quintilian's detailed gestural and vocal specifications, see his discussion of delivery in Book 11.3 (85–183). On the language of gesture in Quintilian and ancient Rome generally, see Wülfing, "Classical and Modern Gesticulation," 265–76; Aldrete, *Gestures and Acclamations*; Graf, "Gestures and Conventions"; Maier-Eichhorn, *Die Gestikulation in Quintilians Rhetorik*; and Sittl's still-classic *Die Gebärden der Griechen und Römer*.

[30] See *De or.* 5:141 [11.3.106–7]; and *Inst.* 5:141 [11.3.107–8].

(5:89 [11.3.7]). Not only the tragic actor, but the "comic actor too should be given some part . . . in so far as the future orator needs a knowledge of Delivery" (1:37 [1.11.1]). The actor, Quintilian explains, can "teach how to deliver a narrative, how to lend authority to advice, what stimulus to use in order to produce a surge of anger, what change of tone is appropriate to an appeal to pity" (1:241 [1.11.12]). One should also "study actors" in the theatre to learn how to avoid an "inelegant or ugly habit," to observe how to "control and trai[n] [the] voice, breathing, gestures and the tongue itself" (*De or.* 1:107 [1.156–7]), learning from the "tragedian's voice, and the bearing . . . of the consummate actor" (*De or.* 1:91 [1.128]). Most Romans viewed acting as a disgraceful profession.[31] And yet both Cicero and Quintilian repeatedly cite actors as models. Quintilian advises the advocate to use a "quick Delivery" like that of Roscius in comedy to "pass rapidly over things, to pile up details, and to hurry on," but "a restrained one" like that of Aesopus the tragic actor "to insist, to emphasize, and to drive points home" (5:143 [11.3.111–12]). Cicero gives specific examples. For instance,

> When Roscius speaks the lines 'since for the wise / Honour is valour's prize and not its prey,' he never uses the action at his command, but just throws them off, so that he can put his whole weight into the next lines—'But what see I? A sword-girt warrior / Seated within the sanctuary shrine!'—which he delivers with a stare of stupefied surprise. (*De or.* 2:81 [3.102])[32]

In Cicero's vision, by watching the actors' rhythms and movements, the ideal orator might himself become a consummate actor, drawing crowds of fans into court:

> [W]hen it is reported that he is going to speak let every place on the benches be taken, the judges' tribunal full, the clerks busy and obliging in assigning or giving up places, a listening crowd thronging about, the presiding judge erect and attentive; when the speaker rises the whole throng will give a sign for silence, then expressions of assent, frequent applause; laughter when he wills it, or if he wills, tears; so that a mere passer-by observing from a distance, though quite ignorant of the case in question, will recognize that he is succeeding and that a Roscius is on the stage. (*Brut.* 253 [290]).

As a Roscius performing on the stage of the courtroom, the orator was nevertheless to avoid anything that smacked too much of theatre, including obvious mimicry: do not use "stagy gestures reproducing the words"; "conve[y] . . . situation[s] and

[31] For a helpful discussion, see Edwards, *Politics of Immorality*, 98–136 ("Playing Romans").
[32] Rackham notes that we do not know the source of these lines (*De or.* 2:83).

idea[s] not by mimicry but by hints" (*De or.* 2:177 [3.220]).[33] Quintilian prohibits specific moves that had come to be associated with theatre: the "trembling hand, an import from foreign schools," is too "theatrical" [*scaenica*]" (5:139 [11.3.103]), and so is to "clap your hands" [*scaenicum*]" (5:149 [11.3.124]); it "may be sometimes acceptable to put the weight on the right foot, but only if you hold your chest level [and] this is [really] a Gesture of comedy rather than of oratory" (5:149 [11.3.125]).[34] The aspiring orator, said Quintilian, must be careful to "keep well clear of staginess" (237–9 [1.11.3]): "[e]xaggerated features and gestures" (3:77–9 [6.3.29]); "anything excessive in facial expression" (237 [1.11.3]); "pull[ing] faces, irritat[ing] by [his] gesticulations, or jump[ing] from one tone of voice to another" (5:183 [11.3.182–3]). "I do not want my pupil to be a comic actor, but an orator" (5:181 [11.3.182]). More generally, actors often had to portray women, but orators must, "[a]bove all, . . . avoid effeminate movements" (5:151 [11.3.128]). The orator "controls himself . . . by the pose of his whole body and the manly flexing of the side" (5:149 [11.3.123]). According to Cicero, the orator could occasionally indulge in a "vigorous manly throwing out of the chest, borrowed not from the stage and the theatrical profession but from the [military] parade ground or even from wrestling" (*De or.* 2:177 [3.220]). But, since the advocate's "delivery is not that of tragedy [or] of the stage," he must generally "employ only slight movements of the body" (*Orat.* 369 [86]). The orator's gestures should not be "conspicuous for . . . grossness, lest we give the impression that we are . . . day labourers" (the *Rhetorica ad Herennium* famously insisted) but nor should they be "conspicuous for . . . elegance, . . . lest we give the impression that we are . . . actors" (201–3 [3.26]). Or, as Quintilian puts it, in "our eagerness to pursue the elegance of the performer, we [must not] lose the authority of the good and grave man" (5:183 [11.3.184]).

The *Rhetorica ad Herennium*'s evident scorn for the actor's "conspicuous . . . elegance" (merely the inverse of the "day labourer['s]" "conspicuous . . . grossness") registers the kind of antitheatrical views we have come to associate with early texts. But Quintilian in fact recasts the comment, suggesting that, while the over-eager orator may *overdo* elegance, it is possible to project both "the elegance of the performer" and "the authority of the good and grave man." In fact, the kind of admiration we have seen Cicero and Quintilian express for actors comes through in all of their work. That said, there were good actors and bad actors. Bad actors and bad orators alike were "stag[y]." Worst of all were vulgar popular performers, whom the orator should never imitate. As Cicero explained, the orator "must scrupulously shun all buffoonish raillery": "all likeness to buffoons in pantomime is to be avoided" (*De or.* 1:379 [2.244]). The "rough humour of the

[33] See similarly, *Brut.* 124 [141–2]; and Quintilian: "You should refrain altogether from [mimicry] in pleading. An orator has to be very different from a dancer" (5:131 [11.3.88]). See the discussion of negative attitudes toward pantomime in late antiquity generally in Lada-Richards, "Was Pantomime 'Good to Think With'?"; and Lada-Richards, *Silent Eloquence*.

[34] See also the extended discussion with which Quintilian ends Book 11 (5:183 [11.3.182–4]).

buffoon or the stage" is "[t]otally foreign" to the courtroom (*Inst.* 3:79 [6.3.29]). "What is less becoming to an orator than a theatrical recitative which sometimes sounds like the excesses of a drunken orgy or a riotous party?" asks Quintilian. "What can be more counterproductive... than if, when what is called for is sorrow, anger, outrage, or pity," the advocate "destroys the very dignity of the court by a sort of naughty song and dance act?" (5:113–15 [11.3.57–8]).

Staging Emotion

Universal Languages: Emotion, Gesture, Voice

A "naughty song and dance act" might entertain, but it would destroy the primary aim of courtroom performance: to convey such emotions as "sorrow, anger, outrage, or pity" in order to sway both judges and audience. For Aristotle, *pathos* was merely one mechanism by which the (legal) orator changed judgments: *logos* and *ethos* played at least an equal part. Cicero and Quintilian sometimes seem to echo Aristotle in this, but they insist so frequently that the ability to produce emotion is the supreme mechanism of persuasion that emotion (*animus, adfectus*) begins to appear almost as oratory's goal, with everything else a mere servant to it.[35] "[T]he orator's chief source of power" consists "in moving the listener and in arousing his emotions" (*Brut.* 239 [276]), writes Cicero. "[I]t is in calming or kindling the feelings of the audience that the full power and science of oratory are to be brought into play" (*De or.* 1:15 [1.17]).[36] When "[p]owerful emotion... has subsided, all th[e] force and fire of oratory goes out" (*Brut.* 87 [93]). Both Cicero and Quintilian explicitly contrast all-powerful emotion to much weaker modes of persuasion (legal or otherwise). As Cicero explains,

> nothing in oratory... is more important than to... swa[y] [the hearer] by something resembling a mental impulse or emotion, rather than by judgement or deliberation. For men decide far more problems by hate, or love, or lust, or rage, or sorrow, or joy, or hope, or fear, or illusion [*errore*, mistake], or some other inward emotion, than by reality [*veritate*, truth], or authority, or any legal standard, or judicial precedent, or statute. (*De or.* 1:325 [2.178–9])

One cannot count on judgment, deliberation, reality, authority, legal standards, judicial precedents, or statutes to persuade the judge or audience. But one can count on emotion. The "orator who inflames the court accomplishes far more

[35] Cicero almost invariably uses the word *animus* for emotion, whereas Quintilian almost invariably uses *adfectus*.

[36] See similarly Quintilian: "[t]he life and soul of oratory... is in the emotions (3:49 [6.2.7]).

than the one who merely instructs it" (*Brut.* 83 [89]). "Proofs may lead the judges to think our Cause the better one," declares Quintilian, "but it is our emotional appeals that make them also want it to be so; and what they want, they also believe (3:47 [6.2.6]). It is not merely the facts that "driv[e] the judge to the conclusion": it is the advocate's ability to "arous[e] emotion which is not there or [make] an existing emotion more intense" (3:57 [6.2.24]).[37] As the orator draws toward the speech's conclusion, he should "be in possession of the hearts of the judges" (3:43 [6.1.52]). "[L]et the orator concentrate on this: 'this is the task, this the toil,'" writes Quintilian (quoting Virgil); "without this everything else is bare, thin, weak, and charmless" (3:49 [6.2.7]). When "the tears, which are the aim" of the finale "start from his eyes, is not the decision given for all to see?" (3:49 [6.2.7]).

Delivery was the principal means of stirring emotion. The entire art of delivery, explains Cicero—the "management of the voice, countenance and gestures"—is to be directed toward "arous[ing] the emotions" (*Part. or.* 351 [15.54]).[38] Delivery did its emotional work by acting on the eye and the ear, "the two senses by which" (writes Quintilian) "all emotion penetrates to the mind" (5:91 [11.3.14]). Thus, pathos needed *actio* and *pronuntiatio* as its instruments of persuasion. "[A]ll emotions inevitably languish, unless they are kindled into flame by voice, face, and the bearing of virtually the whole body," explains Quintilian: "there is no Proof... which is so secure that it does not lose its force unless it is assisted by [delivery]" (5:87 [11.3.2–3]).[39] Like the actor, the advocate had to master delivery of a wide variety of emotions and learn to move from one to another over the course of a speech, matching each emotion to its proper moment. He had to "sway [the judge's] feelings in whatever direction the situation demand[s]," sometimes "inspir[ing] in the judge a feeling of angry indignation," sometimes "mov[ing] him to tears" (*Brut.* 281 [322]).[40] "[A]s the hearers' minds are played upon" by the orator's words and actions, the judges and spectators "feel now joy now sorrow, are moved now to laughter now to tears; they show approbation detestation, scorn aversion; they are drawn to pity to shame to regret; are stirred to anger wonder, hope fear" (*Brut.* 159–61 [187–8]).[41] The trial was a contest between warring emotions: "incit[ing] the hearer to indignation" or "win[ning] the hearer over to

[37] Quintilian identifies such intensification as *deinōsis* (i.e. amplification): "language that adds force to facts which are disgraceful, cruel, or odious" (3:57 [6.2.24]); "a kind of elevation displayed in enhancing indignation and other feelings" (3:389 [8.3.88]); "Prejudice and Invocation as a means of exaggerating a charge" (4:95 [9.2.104]).

[38] See similarly *De or.*, 2:177 [3.221]: "delivery is wholly the concern of the feelings."

[39] Quintilian draws here on *Brutus*: when "[p]owerful emotion... has subsided, all th[e] force and fire of oratory goes out" (87 [93]).

[40] See similarly *De. or.*: the true orator could "by his eloquence either arouse or calm, within the souls of men, whatever passion the circumstances and occasion may demand" (1:143 [1.202]).

[41] See similarly *Orat.*: "the juror must be made to be angry or appeased to feel ill will or to be well disposed, he must be made to feel scorn or admiration, hatred or love, desire or loathing, hope or fear, joy or sorrow" (405 [131]).

pity," as the *Rhetorica ad Herennium* put it (197–199 [3.24]).[42] Advocates had to learn to use one kind of voice "to arouse the judge's indignation and a different one for arousing pity" (*Inst.* 1:225–7 [1.10.25]). In a sense (as Cicero explains), the orator had to master both tragedy and comedy (*Orat.* 387 [109]).

While the advocate might have to work hard to learn delivery, delivery in fact "started from nature" and had "a natural power of affecting us and giving us pleasure" (*De or.* 2:157 [3.197]). It had an even greater effect on "the ignorant," "the mob," and "barbarians" than on the learned precisely because it "contain[ed] a certain force bestowed by nature" (*De or.* 2:179 [3.223]). It conveyed "mental attitudes" nonverbally, attitudes that could be "inferred from the face or the walk," much like dance, which could be "understood and emotionally effective without the voice," or like the language of "dumb animals," who "reveal their anger, joy, or wish to please by their eyes or some other bodily signal" (*Inst.* 5:119 [11.3.66–7]). Communicating without words, the body spoke its own language. "[B]y action [*actio*] the body talks," explains Cicero, "and nature has given us eyes, as she has given the horse and the lion their mane and tail and ears, to indicate the feelings of the mind" (*De or.* 2:179 [3.223]). For Quintilian, the movements of the hands "almost match the entire stock of words." In fact, "[a]mid all the linguistic diversity of the peoples and nations of the world," the language of the body was "the common language of the human race" (5:129 [11.3.86–7]). Rhythm and tone also spoke. Only those who "shar[e] the same [verbal] language" can appreciate the contents of a speech and only the "clever" can appreciate "clever ideas" (*De or.* 2:179 [3.223]). But even the "unlearned crowd" can appreciate "the rhythms and pronunciations of words" because these "are rooted deep in the general sensibility, and nature has decreed that nobody shall be entirely devoid of these faculties": these "rouse us up to excitement, and smooth and calm us down, and often lead us to mirth and to sorrow" (*De or.* 2:155–7 [3.195–7]). The central reason that the "language of the body"—sound, rhythm, gesture, and facial expressions—was universally legible was that it tapped into the natural and universal language of emotion (*Orat.* 347 [55]). "[T]he same emotions are felt by all people and they both recognize them in others and manifest them in themselves by the same marks" (*De or.* 2:179 [3.223]).

Speaking Scenes: Caesar's Robe, the Blood-Bespattered Plaintiff, the Litigant's Face

If delivery spoke the universal language of emotion, so could staged objects when properly deployed. Such "real evidence" was at once evidentiary and affective: a

[42] See similarly Quintilian: the prosecution had to "stir up the judges to anger"; the defense had to "make them sympathetic," though sometimes the situation demanded the reverse (3:21 [6.1.9]).

"weapon, a footprint, blood" were (said Cicero) "silent" but emotionally charged "evidence of guilt" (*Part. or.* 399 [114]). Quintilian recommends displaying "the bloody sword, the bits of bone taken from the wound, the blood-bespattered clothing, the unbandaging of the wounds, the stripped bodies with the marks of the scourge" (3:33 [6.1.30]). Such things, he comments, "commonly make an enormous impression, because" real objects that stand for the real crime "confront people's minds directly." The visible object had the power to call up a vision of the crime itself, acting even more powerfully on the audience's imagination than *enargeia* (vivid language that produced mental images). Quintilian offers the example of Mark Antony, who displayed Caesar's bloody robe before the eyes of the crowd at his funeral:

> [i]t was known that [Caesar] had been killed; his body lay on the bier; but it was the clothing, wet with blood, that made the image of the crime so vivid that Caesar seemed not to have been murdered, but to be being murdered there and then. (3:33 [6.1.31])

The advocate could display "a picture painted on a board or a canvas, depicting the horrible event of which the judge is to be reminded," or a picture of the deceased (3:35 [6.1.32]).[43] For appeals to pity, however, it was better to stage the kind of living tableau that Cicero set up in *Pro Fonteio*: a classic device for the finale. Such appeals—"actions... used to produce tears" (as Quintilian puts it) (2:187 [4.1.14])—had their own performance rhetoric (as in Athenian courts).[44] The advocate would "brin[g] the accused into court dirty and unkempt," in *sordes* (torn and dirty clothing), "and their children and parents with them" (*Inst.* 3:33 [6.1.30]), making sure to display the most pathetic of the defendant's family members: "women, old men, wards,... children, parents, or wives" (*Inst.* 2:187 [4.1.14]).[45]

A trial scene in a first-century CE mural from Pompeii (which survives only in a drawing made in the nineteenth century) offers a dramatic image of a "blood-bespattered" victim—his body "stripped," his wounds "unbandag[ed]"—supplicating the judges on the tribunal for justice (fig. 2.1).[46]

[43] Quintilian disapproves of the practice of using pictures (3:35 [6.1.32]) and describes how a wax death mask of the defendant's husband "repeatedly raised a laugh": the stage hands kept trying to give it to the advocate at the wrong time; finally displayed, it was not affecting but hideous (3:37 [6.1.40]). On pictures to depict character in a legal narrative, see also 3:101 [6.3.72]. And see the Bablitz, "Roman Society in the Courtroom," 327; and *Actors and Audience*, 193.

[44] Quintilian notes that some might think that "calling forward the defendant, lifting up his children, leading forward his relatives, tearing one's clothes" belong to delivery, but he has addressed these elsewhere (5:177 [11.3.174]). On *sordes* and *squalor* (unkempt toilette), see Hall, *Cicero's Use of Judicial Theater*, 40–63; and Bablitz, *Actors and Audience*, 84–5, and 226, notes 84–5.

[45] See similarly Quintilian 3:35 [6.1.34].

[46] Mural from Veranius Hypsaeus' fullery (cloth dyeing and cleaning establishment) in Pompeii in Geremia Discanno's sketch (made around the time of the mural's discovery in the early nineteenth century and unfortunately the only remaining record of the original). The man is probably the victim of

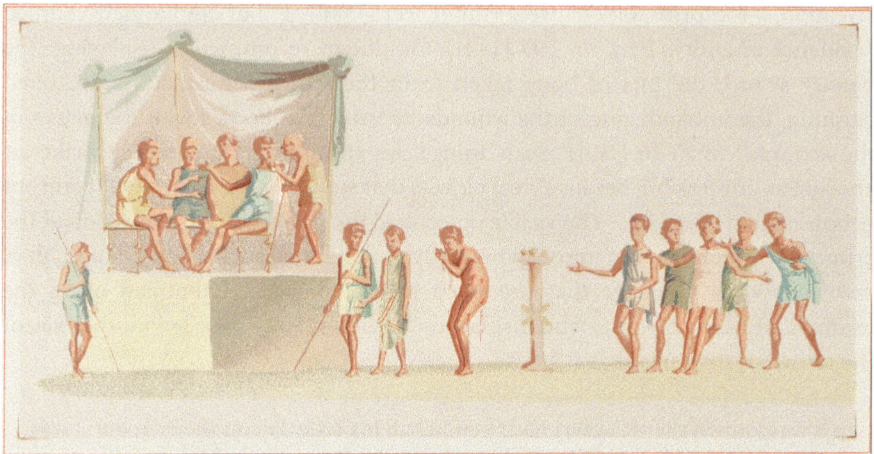

Fig. 2.1 A "blood-bespattered" victim supplicates judges for justice in a mural from Veranius Hypsaeus's fullery in Pompeii (first-century CE; sketched in the early nineteenth century).

Emil Presuhn, ed. *Pompeii: Die neuesten Ausgrabungen*, 2nd ed. (1882), 4. The Bodleian Libraries, University of Oxford, 487.8 POM.670, 4.

It may show a real event, but it also seems to offer a demonstration of how to represent a crime in court. The advocate (in the red-striped toga) addresses the court, subtly gesturing with his right hand and "employ[ing] only slight movements of the body." His subtlety contrasts with the bleeding body of the victim, who makes "the image of the crime so vivid" that it seems to be happening "then and there." The short decorative pillar with fruit on top and crossed branches on its shaft appears to stand for the union of nature and art that the victim (with his all-too-natural body) and the advocate (with his artistry) represent. The visual chiasmus of the branches may cite the importance of chiasmus in rhetoric of the kind the advocate is presumably employing. But it also perhaps stands for the thesis–antithesis structure of trials generally: the inverted parallelism through which a trial reverses an action (a wrong) in order to correct it.[47] The conjunction of the advocate's artistry and the victim's very real bleeding body seems to be doing the necessary work of "kindling the

the feast-day brawl that appears in a different portion of the mural. (He might instead be the instigator who now appears as a defendant begging for pity, in an extreme display of *squalor*, though this seems a less likely subject for sympathetic visual dramatization.) See Schefold, *Die Wände Pompejis*, 133; Sogliano, *Le pitture murali*, 134–5; Presuhn, ed. *Pompeii* (1882 ed.), 4; and David, *Patronat judiciaire*, 413–14 (fig. 4, interleaved). I am especially indebted to Jean-Michel David for his illuminating discussion there and helpful clarifications (private correspondence).

[47] See Thomas, "Chiasmus in Art and Text," 50–88, on the importance of chiasmus in both ancient rhetoric and art and, specifically, on chiasmus as "inverted parallelism" (57, 70, 80, 83).

feelings of the audience" in order to reverse and correct the wrong. The five spectators (perhaps friends or participants in the brawl) respond dramatically to the scene with emotionally demonstrative body language. But it appears hard to get the attention of the judges, who are seated comfortably under the shade of the tents on their carefully guarded platform, absorbed in a conversation with one of the guards. Astonishingly, they appear to be ignoring the victim who stands before them, naked and bleeding. The image perhaps offers an indictment of the judges: how can they shut their eyes to the bleeding man who is begging for their help? But it also seems to ask the question that Cicero and Quintilian attempt to answer: how do you make indifferent judges feel the suffering before them?

Cicero was, of course, a master of appeals for judgment or pity. As in the *Pro Fonteio* tableau, he routinely staged his clients so that their faces and postures would reveal their virtue and suffering. In attempting to "arous[e] the emotions of the jury," writes Cicero, "we are wont to use [such appeals] so piteously that we have even held a babe in our arms during the peroration." In another, "we told [the defendant] to stand up, and raising his small son we filled the forum with wailing and lamentation" (*Orat.* 403–5 [131]). In yet another case, "[t]he presence of [an] orphan and his childish weeping excited great compassion," and "by stirring the pity of the populace for little children [the defendant] snatched himself from the flames" (*Brut.* 83 [90]).[48] In fact, Cicero regularly used litigants' bodies demonstratively—both those of his clients and those on the opposing side—not just to represent pathos but also to represent ethos (both positively and negatively): his clients' virtues; the opponents' vices. Such moments spoke to both the eye and the ear, even without a wailing baby, because Cicero accompanied them with diegetic direction and explanation. Where he had himself arranged the scene, such diegesis functioned as the kind of embedded stage directions I identify in *Pro Fonteio*, serving as acting prompts for his clients. He could not use diegesis to direct adversaries in the same way, of course, but he could use it to pointedly call the audience's attention to the scene, sometimes with an indexical gesture ("[l]ook at the man, examine his expression...") (*Sull.* 387 [74]). Diegetic explanation clarified the narrative and emotional meaning of what the audience was seeing ("Do you mark, judges, how...?")

Cicero's defense of Roscius-the-actor, *Pro Quinto Roscio Comoedo* (76–66 BCE), offers a paradigmatic example.[49] Roscius, who had jointly owned a slave named Panurgus with one Fannius Chaerea, had carefully trained Panurgus for the stage. One Quintus Flavius murdered Panurgus (we do not know why or how), and later gave Roscius a farm as compensation. Fannius sued for

[48] Hendrickson notes that, defending himself from a bill of attainder charging him with massacring Lusitanians, Galba "threw himself on the mercy of the court, which in this case was the popular assembly" (notes in *Brut.* 83).

[49] For the facts of the case, see Freese's introduction and notes (*QRosc.* 266–73, 326–7, and 305 on the law that governed compensation for the murder of a slave).

his share of the farm. Cicero's defense lay largely in his comparison of Roscius' character to Fannius', illustrated (he said) in their faces, to which he pointed as evidence:

> I beg and beseech you [to] look at their faces. Do not [Fannius'] head itself, and those clean-shaven eyebrows seem to reek of malice and proclaim craftiness aloud? If one can make a guess from the silent form of a man's body, does not Fannius seem to be composed entirely of fraud, trickery, and lies from the tips of his fingers to the top of his head? (*QRosc.* 293 [20])

There was, however, one problem with this demonstration. Roscius might be "a man whom the Roman people respects [even] more highly as a man than as an actor," a man who (one can see) "has in him more good faith than art" (*QRosc.* 291 [17]). But one of the principal prongs of Cicero's argument was that it was Roscius' actor training—his great mastery of the "art" of acting—that made Panurgus valuable in the first place (*QRosc.* 295 [29–31]). As everyone knew, the actor's art was the art of "craftiness," "fraud, trickery, and lies." Moreover, most people had seen Roscius perform one of his most noted roles: Plautus' Ballio, "that most rascally and perjured pimp," the most "filthy, impure, and detested character" on the Roman stage (*QRosc.* 293 [20]). Quintilian, as we saw, worried about such indexical-demonstrative evidence of character because the client's "ignorance, lack of sophistication, stiffness, and uncouthness" often resulted in botched courtroom performances, creating a credibility problem. Cicero's problem here was the opposite one. It was precisely Roscius' acting skills—his shape-shifting embodiment of "detested character[s]" and his known skill in "perjur[y]," "fraud, trickery, and lies"—that created the credibility problem. The problem was not that Roscius-as-client was too bad an actor: it was that he was too good an actor.

Cicero, however, had a solution. In performing the role of Ballio, he says, Roscius has in fact been representing not his *own* character but that of *Fannius*. "[T]hat filthy, impure, and detested character" is nothing like Roscius but he *is* "the image of [Fannius] in manners, disposition, and life." In portraying Ballio, "Roscius has constantly portrayed [Fannius himself] brilliantly on the stage, . . . imitat[ing] him admirably in the character of the pimp." In charging Roscius with fraud, says Cicero, Fannius has confused theatre with reality: when Roscius played Ballio, the "fraud and wickedness" he portrayed was not his own but Fannius' (*QRosc.* 293 [20]). Thus, when the judges and audience look at the two faces, they should see Fannius and his mirror image: Roscius imitating Fannius as the "rascally and perjured pimp."

This solution was awkward. It undermined the contrast between Roscius and Fannius, which was its whole point. Moreover, it required the audience to engage in several leaps of the imagination: they were to look at Roscius and see Ballio, and in Ballio an image of Fannius. Requiring such imaginative leaps seemed to defeat the very purpose of indexical demonstration, which was to make ethos and pathos immediately visible. Moreover, it did not really solve the problem. When Cicero called on the audience to "look at their faces" and asked (presumably pointing at Roscius), "[c]an such an offence be fastened on this man?" (*QRosc.* 291 [17]), the audience might well have been justified in seeing not the man of "good faith" but the brilliant actor who could play any role he chose, in court as in the theatre, and answering: "yes!"

Prosopopoeia as Impersonation and Ventriloquism: Weeping for Milo in Cicero's Pro Milone

Clients might be bad at playing the correct role in court, but they were still worse at arguing *pro se.* Pondering "whether we should use the person of the litigant or an advocate" to speak, Quintilian acknowledges that "there is a free choice about this in the schools." However, "in the forum it is only rarely that a man is a suitable defender of his own Cause." Therefore, "when both possibilities are available," choose the advocate every time. Moreover, to solve the problem of the client's poor acting—or, of course, the adversary who looks altogether too credible—the advocate should not only argue the case but "take on the appropriate character": that is, he should act the parts himself (2:203 [4.1.46–7]). In this, the advocate was not merely to speak directly in others' voices but also, as Cicero had specified, employ "impersonation": "imitation of manners and behaviour, . . . given in character" (*De or.* 2:163 [3.205]). Such impersonation was a live version of the rhetorical figure *prosopopoeia*, which Quintilian defines as "fictitious speeches of other persons" (3:31 [6.1.26]). Derived from the Greek, *prosopopoeia* was (etymologically) a means of figuratively creating a face, person, or mask (*prosopon* + *poiein*, "to make" and a "face," "person," or "mask").[50] In oratory, this meant not merely personifying, or calling up an absent figure rhetorically, or speaking in another's voice, but, effectively, making one's face into another's.

[50] Rhetoricians sometimes distinguish between *prosopopoeia* (personification or giving a voice to the dead) and *ethopoeia* (speaking in the voice of actual people, impersonation). Quintilian mentions the distinction (using the word "*sermocinatio*" rather than "*ethopoeia*") but rejects it: "Some confine the term *Prosopo*poeia to cases where we invent both the person and the words; they prefer imaginary conversations between historical characters to be called Dialogues, which some Latin writers have translated *sermocinatio*. I follow the now established usage in calling them both by the same name, for we cannot of course imagine a speech except as the speech of a person" (4:51 [9.2.29–32]). In another passage, he seems to recognize the distinction: "the representation of the characters of others, which is called Ethopoeia or, as some prefer, Mimesis" (4:69 [9.2.58]). But his only other mention of *ethopoeia* is in a list of rhetorical terms (4:161 [9.3.99]) and he uses the term *prosopopoeia* throughout to denote the advocate's impersonation of real people. On the etymology of "prosopopoeia," see Greene and Cushman, ed., *Princeton Handbook of Poetic Terms*, 283. On the "prosopon" as not only person or face, but mask, dramatic part, or persona, see Napier, *Masks, Transformation, and Paradox*, 8. On the trope in Roman rhetoric, see Paxson, *Poetics of Personification*, 12–20 (18 on "to make a face," and on the lawyer as "mouthpiece," "locutionary prosthesis," or "mask").

Given that the declamation exercises of a standard Roman rhetorical education required boys to engage in oratorical *prosopopoeia* from an early age, it is not surprising that it came to occupy such a central place in legal oratory.[51] Cicero describes using such dramatic impersonation as a technique for preparing for trial: once he understands the facts of the case, alone in his room, "in my own person and with perfect impartiality I play three characters, myself, my opponent and the arbitrator" (*De or.* 1:275 [2.102]). One can see many instances of such oratorical *prosopopoeia* in both Cicero's work and the declamations ascribed to Quintilian. These declamations were, of course, school exercises, but (Quintilian explains), in real "[c]auses in which we... appear as advocates,... we use imaginary persons and speak as it were with other men's lips" (5:29 [11.1.38–42]).[52] The word *persona* could denote not only a person's role (in theatre or life) but also a theatrical mask or an individual involved in a legal case.[53] In taking on the *personae* of the characters they represented, said Quintilian, advocates were very like both "[t]ragic and comic poets" and actors. They had to "pay grea[t] attention to characters," "carefully observ[e]" the differences among them, and "provide the appropriate personalities for those to whom [they] lend [their] voice[s]" (5:29 [11.1.38–42]). Quintilian notes that he regards *prosopopoeia* as by "far the most difficult exercise," for it required great skill to play different roles convincingly (1:139–41 [3.8.49–51]). But it was a crucial skill. For "[i]mpersonations, or *prosōpopoiiai*" allowed the advocate to "display the inner thoughts of our opponents,... introduce conversations between ourselves and others, or of others among themselves,... provide appropriate characters for words of advice, reproach, complaint, praise, or pity" (4:51 [9.2.29–31]).

To illustrate courtroom *prosopopoeia*, Quintilian cites Cicero's climactic finale in *Pro Milone* (52 BCE): Cicero's speech in defense of Milo, who was accused of murdering his political rival Clodius in a violent brawl outside of Clodius' villa.[54] There, Cicero addresses the judges and audience in the voice of Milo himself, with (as he says) "those words of Milo which ring ever in my ears":

> 'Farewell!' he cries, 'farewell, my fellow-citizens!... Long may this city, my beloved fatherland, remain glorious, however ill she may have treated me! May my countrymen rest in full and peaceful enjoyment of their constitution, an enjoyment... I [will] not share.... I shall pass and go hence. (*Mil.* 111 [93])

[51] See Bonner, *Education in Ancient Rome*, 267–8, 285. For examples of *prosopopoeia* and *ethopoeia* in *progymnasmata* (textbooks written under the Roman Empire that served as the basis for teaching rhetoric and composition into the early modern period), see Kennedy, trans., *Progymnasmata*, 47–9, 84–5, 115–17, 164–6, 213–17.

[52] [Quintilian], *Lesser Declamations* (see Bailey, 1–2, on the doubtful ascription to Quintilian).

[53] Glare, ed., *Oxford Latin Dictionary* (1983 ed.), 1356.

[54] *Inst.* 3:29–31 [6.1.23–7] (and see 5:29–31 [11.1.38–42]). The trial was a huge *cause célèbre*, with a specially chosen panel of judges and armed guards holding off the mobs. Cicero delivered his speech on the last day (though not in the version we have now). Milo was condemned.

This bit of melodramatic oratory seems aimed at arousing tears, something advocates, of course, routinely attempted to do in the peroration. However, according to Quintilian, it was not easy to succeed:

> I must issue a particular warning against venturing to arouse tears, unless one has a really powerful talent. This emotion, when successfully aroused, is far the most effective of all; but if the attempt fails it is a lukewarm business, and a weak performer would do better to leave it all to the silent thoughts of the judges.

The problem was not merely (as Quintilian pointed out) that the "face, the voice, and the whole look of a defendant whom one has displayed to the court often seem ridiculous to judges whom they have failed to move." It was that advocates tended to overestimate their own skill. The "pleader should measure and estimate his strength with care, and understand the size of the task he is to undertake. There is no halfway house in this; the reward is either tears or laughter" (*Inst.* 3:39–41 [6.1.44–5]).

What made the attempt to arouse tears more difficult in Milo's case was the fact that, as Quintilian wrote, tears and "pleas for mercy [we]re not in keeping with the character of the accused": "[w]ho would have tolerated a Milo begging for his own life, when he had admitted that he had killed a man of noble birth because it had been right to do so?" (*Inst.* 3:31 [6.1.25]). Cicero had to work hard to paint Milo not as a political thug (as many viewed him) but as a hero who had saved Rome from Clodius: Clodius who was a "lunatic" who unchecked, would "[not] have restrained his unbridled lusts from your children and your wives" (*Mil.* 91 [76]). Cicero calls up an image of Milo,

> rais[ing] aloft his bloody sword, and cry[ing], 'Stand by me, fellow-citizens, and hearken! ... With this blade and this right hand have I warded from your necks the frenzy of one whom we could no longer restrain by any laws or courts, so that ... justice, equity, law, liberty, honour, and decency might yet dwell amongst us!' (*Mil.* 91–3 [76–8])

He repeatedly contrasts Milo's heroic masculinity with Clodius' effeminacy.[55] Milo does not weep. If Cicero wants tears, he is going to have to do the weeping himself. As Quintilian explains, since tears were not in keeping with Milo's character, Cicero "came forward to shed the tears in his place" (*Inst.* 3:31 [6.1.25]).

During much of the peroration, Cicero does in fact weep, then protests against his own weeping—"But no more, [i]ndeed I can no longer speak for tears, and my client forbids that tears should plead his cause" (*Mil.* 123 [105])—and weeps

[55] See e.g. *Mil.* 30 [29], 107 [89], 123 [105].

again. At the same time, he stresses that, while he is weeping for Milo, Milo's eyes are dry. In the midst of his "Farewell!" speech (playing the role of Milo), Cicero breaks character to point out Milo's stoic appearance: I weep, "[b]ut" look at him: "it is not with tears in his eyes, as I speak now, that he says this, judges, but with the same countenance that you see him wear at this moment" (*Mil.* 111 [93]). This diegetic interjection seems on its face merely to stress Milo's stoic heroism by contrasting it with Cicero's tears. But the *prosopopoeia* also offers a momentary challenge to the difference to which Cicero points. As Quintilian says, Cicero is a physical stand-in for Milo: he "came forward to shed the tears in his place." Instead of impersonating Milo's visible appearance, he seems to be portraying his internal life performatively: weeping the tears that Milo cannot show. The weeping Cicero may not be Milo. But Milo is also not Milo. For beneath his stoic mask (Cicero suggests through his *prosopopoeia*), Milo's eyes too are filled with tears.

In a famous passage in *De Oratore*, Cicero describes himself as a spectator in the theatre, "when the actor-man's eyes seemed to me to be blazing behind his mask." As the actor "lowered his voice to a plaintive tone, in the passage, 'Aged and childless, / Didst tear and bereave and didst quench me, . . . / Forgetting [thy brother's] tiny son . . . ?' I thought I heard sobs of mourning in his voice" (*De or.* 1:337 [193]).[56] Quintilian echoes this passage to explain how *prosopopoeia* (in *Pro Milone* and elsewhere) can intensify courtroom emotion. When an advocate speaks *about* the case, he explains, "the bare facts produce the effect."

> [B]ut when we pretend that the victims themselves are speaking, the emotional effect is drawn also from the persons. The judge no longer thinks that he is listening to a lament for somebody else's troubles, but that he is hearing the feelings and the voice of the afflicted, whose silent appearance alone moves him to tears; and, as their pleas would be more pitiful if only they could make them themselves, so to a certain extent the pleas become more effective by being as it were put into their mouths, just as the same voice and delivery of the stage actor produces a greater emotional impact because he speaks behind a mask [*persona*].
> (3:31 [6.1.26])

Here, Quintilian seems to be trying to reconcile his paean to *prosopopoeia* with the problem of the uncouth client. The victims' pleas would be "more pitiful if only they could make them themselves." But they cannot because, if they are bad at looking pitiful, they are even worse at speaking. So it is actually better to merely "*pretend* that the victims themselves are speaking," and delude the judge into thinking "that he is hearing the feelings and the voice of the afflicted." While the judge is listening to what he thinks are the victims' voices (which the advocate is

[56] Sutton and Rackham note that the lines are from the *Teucer*, a tragedy of Pacuvius (*De or.* 1:337).

ventriloquizing), he gazes at the victims. Another passage helps clarify Quintilian's puzzling comparison to the actor's mask. There he explains that in theatre, "artists in delivery borrow extra emotion from the masks" (5:123 [11.3.73]). Advocates, who are also "artists in delivery," can similarly "borrow extra emotion" from the victims' faces in court, adopting them as *personae*, animating them as masks for their arts of persuasion. If all goes well (and Quintilian seems skeptical), the "silent appearance" of the litigants and the advocate's voice will "mov[e] [the judge] to tears."

Emotion as Practice

Masks and Faces: Personae *and the Ethics of* Decorum

Here, appearances are all. In fact, the focus on the production of visible or "seeming" emotion pervades Roman discussions of legal performance. "[W]hen [we] seem [*videatur*] to speak under emotion, . . . we also stir the hearer," explains the *Rhetorica ad Herennium* (369 [4.55]). "[G]ood delivery ensures that what the orator is saying seems [*videatur*] to come from his heart" (*Rhet. Her.* 205 [3.27]). "[T]he perfect orator . . . will use certain tones . . . to seem [*videri*] himself to be moved" (*Orat.* 347 [55]). The advocate must "succeed in appearing [*videatur*], to those before whom he is to plead, to be such a man as he would desire to seem [*videri*]" (*De or.* 1:323 [2.176]). It would be easy to read in such advice the view that it is not truth but the *appearance* of truth that matters to law, politics, and life. In this reading, Quintilian (drawing on Cicero) promotes "pretend . . . sincerity" rather than sincerity itself. Indeed, this is how theorists often interpret Cicero and his heirs: the ultimate rhetorician, Cicero is a manipulator of appearances in the name of professional efficacy, defending a regime of politics-as-lying and promoting showmanship as the best means of managing the state.[57]

There are good reasons for these views, especially in light of Cicero's and Quintilian's assertions about the advocate's professional training and obligations. Both believe that (legal) orators must train themselves in ethical elasticity by learning to argue on both sides of the question (*in utramque partem*).[58] These exercises ready advocates for taking on roles in court: for in both *in utramque partem* exercises and in court itself, advocates must temporarily shed their own identities and beliefs (like the actor) in order to take on the *personae* (or masks) assigned to them. "[I]t is the greatest possible mistake to suppose that the speeches we lawyers have made in court contain our considered and certified opinions [or]

[57] See e.g. Zerba, *Doubt and Skepticism*, 145–207. For discussions of this position (and compelling alternative views), see Connolly, *State of Speech*; and Remer, *Ethics and the Orator*.

[58] See e.g. *Inst.* 4:263 [10.1.22–3]; and *De or.* 2:65 [3.80].

the individual personality of the advocate," declares Cicero (*Clu.* 371 [139]; translation modified). Shedding personal opinions allows advocates sometimes to defend those they know to be guilty (*Off.* 221 [2.14.51]). Defending the guilty or even vigorously defending the innocent may require advocates to suppress strict truth in the name of plausibility: for "it is sometimes the business of the advocate to maintain what is plausible, even if it be not strictly true" (*Off.* 221 [2.14.51]).

However, without losing sight of their views on the importance of strategy, one must read such claims in conjunction with Cicero's and Quintilian's general ethical commitments. As Quintilian famously put it (riffing on Cato), the orator was "a good man skilled in speaking," but, above all, "a good man" (197 [12.1.1]). In practice, Roman advocates were expected to represent not only litigants whose causes they thought just but those to whom they were socially bound: family members; friends; patrons; members of their retinue or those otherwise dependent on them.[59] But, in the ideal world, the advocate was to take on only just causes and worthy clients: he must never prosecute the innocent or defend a guilty person who is "infamously depraved and wicked" (*Off.* 221 [2.14.51]); he must defend the guilty only in the name of humanity (*Off.* 221 [2.14.51]); he must always "lend his aid to one who seems to be oppressed and persecuted by the influence of someone in power" (*Off.* 221 [2.14.51]). If truth and justice are at odds, justice should take precedence. "Judges," declares Quintilian, "can be inexperienced people who frequently need to be deceived, to save them from being wrong" (1:389 [2.17.27–8]).

Perhaps Cicero's most famous treatment of ethics is his discussion of the potential conflicts between moral rectitude and expediency (the *honestum* and the *utile*) in Book 3 of *On Duties*. The *honestum* and *utile*, he insists, are not ultimately in conflict: true honor requires expediency, and true expediency is honorable. Just as one "[cannot] divorce expediency from moral rectitude" (*Off.* 379 [3.28.101]), so one cannot divorce the appearance of right from what is truly right.[60] Addressing his son Marcus, Cicero quotes Plato, explaining that his own ethics harmonizes with Plato's ideas about the Form of the Good:

> You see here, Marcus, my son, the very form and as it were the face of Moral Goodness; 'and if,' as Plato says, 'it could be seen with the physical eye, it would awaken a marvellous love of wisdom.'

However, where Plato's point is that love of wisdom lies in seeking what *cannot* generally be seen with the physical eye (for beauty mostly leads us astray), Cicero's

[59] David, *Le patronat judiciaire*; and Bablitz, "Roman Society," 329.

[60] It is only where "knavery . . . wears the mask of wisdom" that the "expedient seems to conflict with the right" (*Off.* 343 [3.2]).

point is that it lies in seeking what can.[61] The "form [and] face of Moral Goodness" are, quite literally, the figure, face, and bearing that Marcus must show the world: the worldly "beauty [and] order" that consist in "do[ing] nothing in an improper or unmanly fashion"; the "*decorum*" that is the first principle of Cicero's situational ethics (*Off.* 15–17 [1.14–15]).

While the word "decorum" is often translated as "propriety" or simply "decorum," some scholars more accurately translate it as "fittingness," "becomingness," or "appropriateness."[62] Practicing *decorum* does not require emotional suppression: it requires the expression of emotions proper to the occasion. *Decorum* is, for Cicero, the fourth pillar of the *honestum*. In its "essential nature,... it is inseparable from moral goodness; for what is appropriate is morally right, and what is morally right is appropriate" (*Off.* 97 [1.93–4]). The fitting is always "visible fittingness." It has "three elements—beauty, tact, and taste." It

> shows itself... in every deed, in every word, even in every movement and attitude of the body. [In] standing or walking, in sitting or reclining, in our expression, our eyes, or the movements of our hands, let us preserve what we have called 'fittingness.'

Living appropriately requires role-playing: we must all strive to "work to the best advantage in that rôle to which we are best adapted" (*Off.* 117 [1.114]). Thus, "actors and orators" are models of the fitting.[63] An "actor would never step out upon the stage without a breech-cloth on, for fear he might make an improper exhibition, if by some accident certain parts of his person should happen to become exposed" (*Off.* 129–31 [1.126–9]).

Training Empathy

As an ethical practice and a model for living, fittingness—the wearing of a moral breech-cloth—sometimes required advocates, like actors, to suspend their "considered and certified opinions [or] individual personality" in order to act in a way befitting the social and emotional situation. This meant that one had to sometimes appear to be what one was not. But seeming and being were not necessarily antithetical. As many scholars have noted, by the time Cicero and Quintilian

[61] See Plato, *Collected Dialogues* (ed. Hamilton and Cairns, 1982 ed.), 497: "how passionate had been our desire for [wisdom], if she had granted us so clear an image of herself to gaze upon," but most look on it "with no reverence, and surrendering to pleasure... go after the fashion of a four-footed beast" (*Phaedrus*, [250d–e]).

[62] Throughout, I have silently changed the Loeb's translations of *decorum* (generally "propriety" or "decorum") to "the fitting" or "the appropriate."

[63] For Cicero's discussion of the theoretical virtues of the legal profession, which he associates with the gift of oratory, see *Off.* 239–41 [2.65–7].

were writing it had become a commonplace that, to stir others' emotions, actors and orators had to feel those emotions themselves.[64] Quintilian stresses that the advocate must "pretend that he is himself deeply moved, until he . . . acquires the authority that comes from sincerity": not merely apparent sincerity but actual sincerity (2:203 [4.1.46]).[65] For the true advocate (as both Cicero and Quintilian repeatedly insist), "pretense" must *become* "sincerity." Cicero explains that his sympathy for his clients is "a genuine sympathy" (*Orat.* 403 [130]), and swears (in the person of Antonius) that the emotions he shows in court are always genuine: "I give you my word that I never tried . . . to arouse either indignation or compassion, either ill-will or hatred, in the minds of a tribunal, without being really stirred myself" (*De or.* 1:335 [2.189–190]). When, defending Manius Aquilius, Antonius "called forward [his] unhappy old client, in his garb of woe, . . . tearing open his tunic and exposing his scars," it was not "by way of technique, . . . but under stress of deep emotion" (*De or.* 1:339 [2.195–196]). Cicero recognizes that cynics might be skeptical: it may "seem a mighty miracle, for a man so often to be roused to wrath, indignation and every inward emotion—and that too about other people's business." But the "power" of performing the speech "is great enough to dispense with all make-believe and trickery: for the very quality of the diction, employed to stir the feelings of others, stirs the speaker himself even more deeply than any of his hearers" (*De or.* 1:335–6 [2.191–2]).[66]

Doubtless the display of such emotions, however genuine they may be, is also instrumental. The advocate is, after all, "employed to stir the feelings of others." As Cicero acknowledges, while being "really stirred" himself, he also "worked upon [the judges'] minds, by the very feelings to which I was seeking to prompt them" (*De or.* 1:335 [2.189–90]). The purpose of "being moved by [emotions] oneself is to "arous[e] emotions" in the judges (*Inst.* 3:59 [6.2.26]): the reason that such "feelings [must] be strong in us" is that "we want [them] to be strong in the judge"; the point of being "ourselves . . . moved" is to "try to move others" (*Inst.* 3:59 [6.2.28]). Doubtless too it is not always spontaneous empathy for "other people's business" but often "by way of technique" that the advocate "give[s] an impression of reality" in order "to produce [an attitude] in the judge." But this does not make the feelings any less genuine. In fact, it is precisely "by way of technique" that we learn to "assimilate ourselves to the emotions of those who really suffer" (*Inst.* 3:59 [6.2.28]).

[64] See e.g. Balme, *Cambridge Introduction to Theatre Studies*, 18–19; and Roach, *Player's Passion* (1993 ed.), 24 (the commonplace was a "threadbare" "hand-me-down" by Quintilian's day).

[65] Quintilian has "often been moved, to the point of being overtaken not only by tears but by pallor and . . . grief" (3:63–5 [6.2.36]).

[66] In one of Cicero's more famous lines: "just as there is no substance so ready to take fire, as to be capable of generating flame without the application of a spark, so also there is no mind so ready to absorb an orator's influence, as to be inflammable when the assailing speaker is not himself aglow with passion" (*De or.* 1:335 [2.190]).

The advocate can develop such genuinely empathetic emotional impersonation through emotional training. Such emotional training was in fact part of the point of schoolroom *prosopopoeia* exercises. "Even in school," explains Quintilian,

> it is proper that the student should be moved by his subject and imagine it to be real.... We play the part of an orphan, a shipwrecked man, or someone in jeopardy: what is the point of taking on these roles if we do not also assume the emotions? (3:63 [6.2.36])

For Quintilian, students must undergo two distinctive kinds of emotional training to develop such affective *prosopopoeia*. First, they must learn to control their "[r]eal emotions,... sorrow, anger, [or] outrage, for example," which "burst out naturally [but] lack art, and have therefore to be disciplined by training and method" (5:117 [11.3.62]). Second, and far more important, they must learn to transform "[e]motions contrived by imitation"—which "involve art, [but] have no basis in nature"—into real ones (5:117 [11.3.62]). "The mere imitation of grief or anger or indignation" is not good enough and, indeed, will "be ridiculous, if we fail to adapt our feelings to the emotion as well as our words and our face" (3:59 [6.2.26]). Instead, "[l]et us identify with the persons of whose grievous, undeserved, and lamentable misfortunes we complain," urges Quintilian; "let us not plead the case as though it were someone else's, but take the pain of it on ourselves" (3:63 [6.2.34–5]).

Fortunately, Quintilian offers a detailed account of precisely how we are to do this. The "first thing for us to do... to be genuinely affected [is to] form a picture of the situation, and let ourselves be moved by it as though it was real" (5:117 [11.3.62]). Creating a mental image ("form[ing] a picture") involves something like empathetic spectatorship: just as the judge, jury, and spectators come to pity the afflicted by watching the scene of the trial, so the advocate comes to pity his client by viewing this mental picture. Unlike the scene of the trial, the picture is a mere fictional mental projection, but, like theatrical fictions, it can move one "as though it was real." The advocate's next move is to place himself within this mental picture by imagining that it is he, not his client, who is suffering: "when pity is needed, let us believe that the ills of which we are to complain have happened to us, and persuade our hearts of this" (3:63 [6.2.35]). An image triggers belief, and that belief—which requires the willing suspension of disbelief—persuades the heart. Through this process (say both Cicero and Quintilian), we "assimilate ourselves to the emotions of those who really suffer." What the heart feels is not mere artful emotional fakery but "a genuine sympathy." In those moments, we "identify with the persons of whose grievous, undeserved, and lamentable misfortunes we complain" and "take the pain of it on ourselves." One learns to do this through practice: in declamation and in the lawcourt itself. Empathetic emotion is thus, in effect, performative: the advocate develops the capacity for it by performing it until it becomes real emotion. Emotions "very like the real thing" (3:63–5 [6.2.36]) become "the real thing"; the fictitious becomes the actual; acting becomes believing; the fake becomes the true; the made-real becomes the real.

The Art of the Real

Insisting that the advocate "dispense[s] with all make-believe and trickery" when he begins to identify with his client's emotions, Cicero asks, "what can be so unreal as . . . the theatre or stage-plays?" and then proceeds to describe the "actor-man's eyes . . . blazing behind his mask," arguing that both the actor and the tragic poet who wrote the lines that so move him must have also felt the emotion deeply (*De or.* 1:337 [193–4]). We have already seen Quintilian's echo of this passage in his discussion of the power the mask lends the advocate's voice. Later, he again echoes this passage, altering its central point:

> I have frequently seen tragic and comic actors, having taken off their masks at the end of some emotional scene, leave the stage still in tears. And if the mere delivery of the written words of another can so kindle them with imagined emotions, what shall we be capable of doing, we who have to imagine the facts in such a way that we can feel vicariously the [real] emotions of our endangered clients? (3:63 [6.2.35])

Where Cicero focuses on the parity of the actor's and the tragic poet's emotions, Quintilian focuses on the disparity between the actor's and advocate's emotions. If the actor feels "imagined" emotion so intensely, how much more must the advocate feel, for he represents real danger (a contrast that recalls *Against Alcibiades*' and Isocrates' contrast between theatrical and legal emotions).[67] In Book 11, Quintilian makes a similar claim in an argument about the power of delivery:

> if [the] Delivery [of stage actors] has th[e] power to produce anger, tears, or anxiety over matters which we know to be fictitious and unreal [*fictas, inanis*], how much more powerful must it be when we really believe! (5:87 [11.3.5])

As both Cicero and Quintilian repeatedly stress, the difference between law and theatre is that law is real and theatre is fake. Oratory (including legal oratory) is "different [from acting]" because "it is a real activity, not an imitation," writes

[67] See Chapter 1, 52–4.

Quintilian (5:183 [11.3.182–3]). Or, as Cicero explains, "orators . . . are the players that act real life [whereas] actors . . . only mimic reality" (*De or.* 2:171 [3.214]). For Quintilian (as for *Against Alcibiades* and Isocrates) the reality of what is at stake in a trial—and the client's danger—should make it possible for lawcourt speakers not only to feel more than actors but also to rouse stronger emotions in their audiences. *Against Alcibiades* and Isocrates are enraged that this does not in fact happen: that audiences in fact routinely succumb to tears over theatrical fictions, but lawcourt realities leave them cold. Quintilian, on the other hand, is confident in both the power of the real and the power of the advocate to convey the reality of the real: "how much more powerful must [emotions] be when we really believe!" It may be that "men decide far more problems by . . . illusion . . . than by reality." Nevertheless, as Cicero puts it (in another context), "there can be no doubt that reality [*veritas*]"—or at least the impression of reality—"beats imitation in everything" (*De or.* 2:171 [3.216]).

Given that the impression of "reality beats imitation," it was incumbent on advocates not only to *exploit* the power of the real, but to *represent* that fact that their cases were real, not works of theatrical art. The advocate, of course, needed artistry: as Cicero points out, "if reality unaided were sufficiently effective in presentation, we should have no need at all for art" (*De or.* 2:171 [3.216]). One could not *be* artless, but one had to *look* artless. However, while the trope of legal inexperience might work for the Athenian litigant pleading *pro se*, unfortunately it would not work for the Roman advocate who regularly appeared in the courts. The artlessness effect had to lie instead in the concealment of artistry: the "first rule" of the speaker's art was "not to seem to be art," explained Quintilian (237–9 [1.11.3]). Artistry "in forensic oratory must . . . be concealed," in part because law was "concerned with real events" (2:329 [2.10.10–11]).[68] There must be no obvious show: no appearance of "excessive ingenuity" or "excessive care," which would read as "insincerity." Orators sometimes find the demand that they conceal their art "intolerable": "we think our art is wasted unless it can be seen, when the truth is that it ceases to be art once it is detected!" (2:281 [4.2.126–7]). To conceal one's artistry was not a form of deceptive illusionism: it was a way of highlighting the real emotions and the real things at stake. It may be that the orator was working his magic: but (said Quintilian), "[e]verything must seem to come from the Cause, not from the orator" (2:281 [4.2.126]). Do not pay attention to my art, said the true advocate: pay attention to what it represents because it is not my art but "the Cause" that is really important. The advocate's artful reality effect, heightened through *actio*, did not offer a mere illusion of reality (as the actor's did): it made reality appear as real as it really was.

[68] See Quintilian's minor qualification (2:329 [2.10.10–11]).

Conclusion

Giving reality the appearance of reality was, for both Cicero and Quintilian, an artistic practice but, as we have seen, also a deeply ethical one. They repeatedly refer to the suffering of their clients and the dangers they face. They believed in advocating especially for those "who see[m] to be oppressed and persecuted by the influence of someone in power," even if they did not always act on their beliefs. They knew the courtroom was a dangerous place, and recognized that inept advocacy could destroy someone's life. For better or worse, they felt that most people could not represent the urgency of their own situations persuasively: representing those who could not represent themselves was, for them, an ethical responsibility, and indeed the foundation of justice. This responsibility for justice meant worrying less about whether to act, or what to act on, than how: how to represent others or help them represent themselves; how to make their suffering or danger visible; how to feel something of what they felt in order to convey both the truth of their experience and the urgency of the cause.

Scholars in the humanities today tend to be skeptical that we can truly feel or represent another's emotional reality. Were Cicero and Quintilian deluded in their belief that they could genuinely represent their suffering clients' emotions? Did they fail to honor the alterity of a suffering they could not really know? Maybe. But when Quintilian begs, "let us not plead the case as though it were someone else's, but take the pain of it on ourselves," he recognizes the transfer of feeling from "someone else" to "ourselves" as necessary to impassioned advocacy. He asserts the value of empathetic identification against estrangement, however imperfect. In the passage in which Cicero answers skeptics who might view it as a "mighty miracle, for a man so often to be roused to wrath, indignation and every inward emotion" as he is, he notes that no one should be astonished that we feel the emotions of friends who are under attack. But nor should anyone be astonished that we feel these emotions for strangers. For, "even when defending complete strangers, we still cannot regard them as strangers, if we would be accounted good men ourselves" (*De or.* 1:337 [2.192–3]). Just as "assimilat[ing] ourselves to the emotions of those who really suffer" requires disciplined practices of empathy, so "defending complete strangers" requires learning not to "regard them as strangers." In fact, these are really the same: alien emotions become less alien; strangers become less strange.

3

Courtroom Oratory, Forensic Delivery, and the Wayward Body in Medieval Rhetorical Theory

Introduction: Alain de Lille's Rhetorica (*c.*1182–84) in the Courtroom, or How to Win a Lawsuit in the Middle Ages

In his *Anticlaudianus* (*c.*1182–84), the theologian Alain de Lille offers a portrait of "Rhetorica," among the most alluring of those seven "beautiful . . . maidens," the seven liberal arts.[1]

> [B]eauty and graceful form show Rhetorica special favor . . . Her hair, which gives the appearance of gold, and is arranged with wondrous skill, covers her neck, and in her face a fiery color plays, a purple flame on her rosy mouth that splendidly enhances her beauty. (305)

She is awash in girlish emotion: "her face is at one moment flooded with a sudden burst of tears; at the next the sunrise of a sudden smile makes it fair, wiping away the flowing tears" (305). This blushing, weeping beauty, however, suddenly metamorphoses into a brilliant jurist and master of legal argument, teaching her law students how to "plead like Cicero" (283): when to "construct objections to the charge"; when to "change [one's] plea or venue" when to "deny that a law has been broken"; how to show that one "law . . . contradicts [another], or a dissenting opinion conflicts, . . . or an ambiguity . . . gives rise to doubt" (and much, much more) (309). She explains the mysteries of the great legal speech: how it "stirs the mind of a judge, makes his ear alert, excites his interest and engages his feelings" and how it renders "the audience . . . more attentive, more easily persuaded, more favorably disposed" (307); how to "strike at the opposing position, destroy it, undermine it, tear it apart, sweep it away . . ." (309). At the same time, she

[1] Alan of Lille, *Literary Works* (trans. Wetherbee), 283 (hereafter cited in the text). I have altered Wetherbee's translation slightly, occasionally drawing on the translation in Miller, Prosser, and Benson, ed., *Readings in Medieval Rhetoric*, 223–7. On Alain's rhetoric and the potential multiple authorship of works attributed to him, see Ward, "Alan (of Lille?) as Rhetor" (particularly 156–64, 167–8, 208–16 on law). See my Introduction, 21, on my use of "courtroom"; and 19–21, on my use of gendered pronouns.

Law as Performance: Theatricality, Spectatorship, and the Making of Law in Ancient, Medieval, and Early Modern Europe. Julie Stone Peters, Oxford University Press. DOI: 10.1093/oso/9780192898494.003.0004

emblematizes oratory in action: "in her right hand she wields a trumpet, and a horn graces her left, and on this horn she sounds a call to arms" (305). "Majestically stern," she lifts her eyes, "now toward the heights; now...lower; now turning aside" (305). Displaying her "power"—"now urgent, now thundering with threats, now [with] words flashing lightning, now raining entreaties, now filling the ear with praise"—she "delivers justice" (307). Striding across the stage in her many colored robe, gazing toward the heavens, scanning the earth, thundering like Herod, inundating the ear, Rhetorica is master of the theatre of the courtroom.

Alain's portrait of Rhetorica offers a glimpse of the place of both law and oratorical performance in medieval rhetorical theory. At the same time, it hints at some of the ways that rhetorical theory might contribute to our understanding of medieval courtroom action. Historians of rhetoric have long noted the importance of law to medieval rhetoric, which developed two branches of study in the twelfth and thirteenth centuries—the *ars dictaminis* (art of letter writing) and *ars notariae* (notarial arts)—to serve the needs of expanding legal administrations.[2] Theatre historians have had much to say about the potential impact of rhetorical theory's repertoire of gestures and effects on historical acting styles.[3] Jody Enders long ago called attention to the convergence of law, rhetoric, and theatre in medieval drama and thought.[4] But rhetorical texts remain an under-exploited source of information about medieval courtrooms and courtroom experience: about what space, movement, sound, and gesture signified; how theorists thought one should act in

[2] See Martin Camargo's concise study, *Ars dictaminis, ars dictandi*, especially 18, 36–7 on the relationship of the *ars dictaminis* to legal practice; and Witt, *Two Latin Cultures*, 236–7, 253 (and generally chapters 3 and 5) on the *ars notariae*. I am indebted throughout this chapter to the extraordinarily detailed scholarship on medieval rhetoric, in particular Rita Copeland and Ineke Sluiter's indispensable annotated collection of primary sources in translation: *Medieval Grammar and Rhetoric*. In addition to the specific studies I cite below, I have also drawn extensively on Ward, *Classical Rhetoric in the Middle Ages* and "Development of Medieval Rhetoric"; Cox and Ward, ed., *Rhetoric of Cicero* (especially Ward, "Medieval and Early Renaissance Study of Cicero's *De inventione*"; Cox, "Ciceronian Rhetoric in Late Medieval Italy"; Hohmann, "Ciceronian Rhetoric and the Law"; and Milner, "Communication, Consensus and Conflict"); the essays in Carruthers, ed., *Rhetoric Beyond Words*; Kennedy, *Classical Rhetoric* (1999 ed.), 196–225; and Mack, *History of Renaissance Rhetoric*, 1–75.

[3] For the *locus classicus*, see Joseph, *Elizabethan Acting* (1951 ed.) ("stage-playing and rhetorical delivery were so alike, that whoever knows to-day exactly what was taught to the renaissance orator cannot be far from knowing at the same time what was done by the actor on the Elizabethan stage" [1]). And see Wiles, *Players' Advice to Hamlet*, 38–69 (on rhetorical performance in antiquity, and throughout on Cicero's and Quintilian's influence); and the extraordinary discussion in Roach, *Player's Passion* (1993 ed.), 23–6.

[4] Enders' groundbreaking study, *Rhetoric and the Origins of Medieval Drama*, argues that medieval drama emerged not only from church liturgy (the traditional view) but also from legal practice. While she focuses on the dramatic activities of the society of French law clerks known as the Basoche, her first two chapters examine historical ideas about judicial performance in rhetorical theory in ways that dovetail with my own discussions. See similarly the brief but evocative comments about medieval legal performance in Holsinger, "Analytical Survey 6: Medieval Literature and Cultures of Performance," 287–9; and his *Music, Body, and Desire*, on the "rich array of somatic practices and representations" that bear on "histories of the body" and that await further exploration (3).

court (and how one shouldn't); what it felt like to be there. The rhetorical theorists I examine give us a glimpse of the viscera of courtroom experience: filtered through their perceptions, agendas, and personal experiences (to be sure), often prescribing an ideal or bowing to their sources, but scrutinizing the body, voice, movements, emotions (along with fashions, hairstyles, and more), and reporting what they saw, heard, and felt.

Some of the texts I look at here have received very little critical attention: most have not been translated; one remains mostly in manuscript. They contest several views that, despite abundant contradictory evidence, persist in textbook accounts of medieval rhetoric and legal history: first, that medieval rhetorical theorists paid little-to-no attention to forensic oratory, preoccupied as they were with theology and poetry; second, that lawyers and litigants had no use for rhetorical theory, which was irrelevant in autocratic medieval courts; third, that medieval rhetorical theorists were uninterested in delivery (*actio* and *pronuntiatio*). I will address these claims below. Suffice it to say here that, as Alain's portrait of Rhetorica suggests (and as this chapter will show), not only were many medieval rhetorical theorists deeply interested in both courtroom practice and delivery. Their experiences with the courtrooms of their day (where some had in fact been parties or advocates) were central to their struggles to adapt ancient theories of delivery to medieval legal arenas. Alain's description of Rhetorica, "stir[ring] the mind of [the] judge, mak[ing] his ear alert, excit[ing] his interest and engag[ing] his feelings" may draw on ancient rhetorical theory. But it also describes his vision of how to win a case in a twelfth-century courtroom.

In the popular imagination, the medieval trial may conjure up a number of possible scenarios: a trial-by-ordeal; or a royal audience in a castle before a capricious prince (with only a court jester to defy him); or an interrogation on the Inquisitor's rack, in which the victim confesses and is dragged to the pyre. In such images, God or the Prince or the Inquisitor is all-powerful: litigants and lawyers in a courtroom—using oratory and embodied action to persuade the judges and audience—are simply not part of the picture. All of these images bear some relationship to historical institutions and practices. But if only ordeals, royal whims, or Inquisitors' zeal had decided the outcome of medieval trials, it would be hard to understand why rhetorical theorists thought that defendants, accusers, and those who interceded on their behalf had to learn the all-important art of delivery to persuade, charm, and (sometimes) entertain in the courtroom.[5]

[5] On ordeals, see Bartlett, *Trial by Fire and Water* (especially 25–33, 64, 68–9, 127–34, 144–52), describing their relative rarity, and their use primarily to decide hard cases or to absolve those who could not otherwise be proven innocent. In England, felonies were tried by ordeals of cold water and hot iron for less than a half century (from 1166 to 1215) (Kerr, Forsyth, and Plyley, "Cold Water and Hot Iron," 573). The ordeals were not instant or absolute, since signs of guilt or innocence (such as whether a wound festered) often took several days and assessors had to then interpret the outcome. Defendants were sometimes forced to undergo ordeals, but they also often elected to do so (see Tuten, "Women and Ordeals" on women's deployment of ordeals in legal negotiations.) However rare, the

In fact, even in the initial stages, plaintiffs had to use all available skills to convince the court that they had a justiciable case. Parties had to sway judges to employ their preferred form of proof. In the course of a trial, decision-makers were often unsure how to decide a case and thus open to persuasion, listening carefully to testimony and oral argument. As Archbishop Agobard of Lyon wrote in the ninth century, "judgment . . . consists in wise investigations not brutal power."[6]

Audiences also mattered. Many courts—including the public judicial assemblies, or *placita*, that spread from the Frankish kingdoms throughout much of Europe—met in public places, even in the later Middle Ages: in churches, marketplaces, open palace halls, fields, and on hills. Regulations often specified that summonses, trials, and sentences were to be public.[7] Charlemagne had an army of *missi dominici*: judges who traveled through his territories setting up temporary courts to try cases.[8] As I will suggest below, such courts were crowded: peopled by multiple accusers, defendants, witnesses, local nobility, judges, jurors or lay "judgment-finders," notaries, scribes, and (notably) general spectators. Juries or jury-like bodies were by no means exclusive to English common law courts. Often (as one document says) "all the noble men of the county, and many other men of the said county" served as juror-judges: sometimes all adult men in the region did so.[9] Even where judges and juries were expected to make decisions

ordeals did long outlast their effective abolition at the Lateran Council of 1215. Courts were still using them in the fourteenth century in Germany, southeastern Europe, and rural areas, and for proof of witchcraft throughout Europe as late as the eighteenth century.

This chapter and the next suggest how important lawyers, parties, and observers could be to outcomes. The studies to which I am most indebted for my general understanding of medieval court procedures include: Brand, *Kings, Barons, and Justices* and *Origins of the English Legal Profession*; Brundage, *Medieval Canon Law* and *Medieval Origins of the Legal Profession*; Davies and Fouracre, ed., *Settlement of Disputes*; Helmholz, *Oxford History of the Laws of England, Vol. 1*, 1–236; Hudson, *Oxford History of the Laws of England Vol. 2*; Mostert and Barnwell, ed. *Medieval Legal Process*; Pohl-Zucker, *Making Manslaughter*; Vallerani, *Medieval Public Justice*; and Vitiello, *Public Justice and the Criminal Trial*.

6 Quoted in Bartlett, *Trial by Fire and Water*, 118.

7 On the *placita* (a word that designated both the assemblies and the case records), see the studies of Frankish courts I cite immediately below. See Sexton, "Justice Seen," 309–10, on the increase in judicial activity taking place in public in the eighth-century "legal theater," the Carolingian *laubiae* (loggias) where the *placita* were often held as "stage[s]" for the performance of justice, and the Carolingian capitularies specifying that *placita* be held in public venues and that shelters be built for them ("*ad placitos observandos usus esse possit*"). On public courts generally (including outdoor courts) in the later Middle Ages, see Chapter 4, 157–60. On the public proclamation of the summons in England, see Clanchy, *From Memory to Written Record* (2013 ed.), 274–5. On the requirement that sentences be public in fourteenth-century France, see Carbonnières, *Procédure devant la chambre criminelle*, 578.

8 For details on Frankish courts under Charlemagne, see Nelson, *King and Emperor*, 198–207; Ganshof, *Frankish Institutions Under Charlemagne*, especially 76–84; and Riché, *Daily Life in the World of Charlemagne*, 259–62. See McKitterick, "King on the Move," 166, on the limits of our understanding of the nature of Charlemagne's courts.

9 Davis and Fouracre, ed., *Settlement of Disputes*, 217 (quoting a description of the ninth-century Perrecy case). And see 216–17 generally, in which they stress not only the large numbers in attendance but the collective nature of judgment: one seventh-century case was held before fifty-six people; the number of people joining decisions in Francia "seems to have been infinite"; Anglo-Saxon witness lists show "similarly large assemblies" in England. See Jolliffe, *Constitutional History of Medieval England*, 63, on the twice-yearly courts "to which the suit of all freemen is obligatory" (citing *Leges Henrici Primi*,

based in part on prior knowledge (as with the so-called "self-informing" jury of medieval England), the parties' and witnesses' demeanor and testimony could significantly affect decisions.[10] Performance (including appearance and courtroom behavior), audience responses, and the mood of the gathering could make a difference to winning or losing, often with grave consequences for life or livelihood.

Pleading as an organized profession had all but disappeared after the fall of the Roman Empire, but even in the early Middle Ages, courtroom speakers included not only litigants and judges but people skilled in persuasion (*advocati*, *adiutores*, intercessors of various kinds). Around the time that Alain's Rhetorica appeared, lawyers reemerged as a professional class. Most lawyers did not, of course, argue in court but instead served in administrative positions, as consultants, or in private transactions (as they do today); and most legal disputes, like today's, were settled before they got to court. But a class of professional advocates specializing in courtroom argument also appeared, called by various names: *causidicus* (cause speaker), *forespeca* (speaker for), *togatus* (robed one), *placitator* (pleader who pleases), *testis iuris* (witness of law), *perorator* (producer of perorations), *conteur* (reciter of counts, but also recounter of tales), *narrator*.[11]

The reemergence of the legal profession was, at least in part, the product of several interconnected twelfth-century phenomena: the rise of university law faculties; newly complex court administrations; and the proliferation of records, codes, commentaries, and procedural treatises (*ordines*) prescribing the proper

8). On collective judgment in later medieval English manorial courts, see Bailey, *English Manor*, 172–3. On juries in late medieval English ecclesiastical courts, see Helmholz, *Oxford History*, 337; and on the jury in the lawcourts of early modern Switzerland (a longstanding institution), see Potter, *Zwingli*, 97. (For many, attendance was not in fact a right but an onerous duty: see e.g. Ganshof, *Frankish Institutions Under Charlemagne*, 76–7; Hudson, *Oxford History of the Laws of England, Vol. 2*, 278; and Bailey, *English Manor*, 170–2 on punishment for failure to attend).

[10] In the past decades, scholars have challenged the classic account of the "self-informing" medieval English jury and the idea that "presentation of evidence played little or no part in the proceedings." See Musson, *Public Order and Law Enforcement*, 189. Musson describes thirteenth- and fourteenth-century English trials, in which "witnesses in court . . . could influence the course of the trial," defendants often "replied at length to the charges and the judge's questions unaided by counsel," and "onlookers" added their views. Generally, testimony and evidence, the "general demeanor of the accused," and "the way [they] handled themselves in court could be a vital factor" (*Public Order*, 188–9, 201–5).

[11] For *causidicus*, *togatus*, *placitator*, and *testis iuris*, see Brundage, "Medieval Advocate's Profession," 444; for *forespeca*, *narrator*, *conteur*, and *perorator*, see Clanchy, *From Memory to Written Record*, 275–6. Scholars generally situate the emergence of the legal profession in the twelfth or thirteenth century. On earlier advocates (including early medieval professional Irish advocates), see e.g. Davis and Fouracre, ed., *Settlement of Disputes*, 49, 89, 106, 187, and 217; Rabin, "Old English *Forespeca*"; and my discussion of Alcuin below. Studies of the profession's emergence I have found most useful include: Brundage, *Medieval Origins*; Helmholz, *Profession of Ecclesiastical Lawyers* (chapter 1, and the biographies of early ecclesiastical lawyers in chapters 5–7); Brand, *Origins of the English Legal Profession*; Padoa-Schioppa, *History of Law in Europe* (Ch 11 on the legal professions); and Altea, *Scienza e professione legale* (especially 31–63 on *causidici*, *advocati*, and other kinds of lawyers).

form of a trial (*ordo iudiciorum*).[12] Whether the lawyers who stepped up to negotiate the legal maze were more helpful than harmful was an open question. Medieval citizens were litigious, and some thought it was the lawyers' fault. By the later fifteenth century, Thomas Basin (jurist and Bishop of Lisieux) would complain that, in Normandy at least, "lawyers have spread everywhere in such great numbers in all the cities, the towns, the villages and the countryside" that they "seem truly to have in hand the whole . . . government of the province, . . . despite their common and peasant origins." This "body of lawyers gnaws at, exploits, and exhausts the whole . . . population," which is unfortunately already "by nature too inclined to litigation," and is now "dragged into ever more numerous and [in fact] nearly infinite judicial actions and disputes . . . under [the] contagious influence" of these vipers.[13] However, if lawyers were to blame for litigiousness, unfortunately you might need one. Depending on your social status, you had a good chance of ending up in a lawsuit or on the wrong end of a criminal charge. Even Basin, who so hated lawyers, found that he was "obliged to have . . . lawyers in all the tribunals of the region" to handle the "infinite number" of charges with which opposing lawyers "harrassed" him.[14] You could not win your case without a lawyer to manage the technicalities or defend you from your adversary's lawyer, who was sure to know all the tricks.

For lawyers, technical mastery was thus essential, and arguably more important than oratorical skill. But comments like Alain's that one must "make [the judge's] ear alert" and thus "excit[e] his interest and engag[e] his feelings" remind us that credible and compelling oral pleading was essential. This was the case whether the

[12] The literature on these changes is vast, but for a useful summary of their impact on courtroom argument, see Hyams, "Legal Revolution and the Discourse of Dispute" (noting that, starting in the mid-twelfth century, "experienced . . . lawyers now did much of the actual speaking in courts governed by carefully defined rules" [51]). On the proliferation of written records in England (between 1066 and 1307) and their impact on law, see Clanchy, *From Memory to Written Record*, especially 274–80. For a helpful discussion of "the resistance of oral custom to literate authoritarianism [and to] the institution of literate, centralized law" as one factor in the fourteenth-century English Peasants' Revolt, see Green, *Crisis of Truth* (especially 198). On the *ordines*, see Fowler-Magerl, *Ordines Iudiciarii*; and, for translations and discussions of a number of twelfth-century *ordines*, see Brasington, *Order in the Court*.

[13] "Sunt enim numero tam multi per civitates singulas, opida, villas et rura ubique disseminati atque dispersi . . . ut tocius profecto provincie administracionem et regimen in suis manibus habere videantur . . . licet plebeii et rusticani sint. . . . Corrodit quippe status ille advocatorum et exedit atque exsuggit totam populi substanciam; qui, cum natura satis et nimium proch dolor! proclivis sit ad lites, ex consorcio tamen et consiliis advocatorum . . . et ex hujusmodi eorum contagio . . . erroreque eis pergrato pluribus adhuc per eos et infinitis pene litibus et questionibus implicatur atque involvitur." Basin, *Apologie ou plaidoyer*, 260–2; and see Enders, "Rhetoric and Comedy," 372. On the increase in litigation in late twelfth- and early thirteenth-century England, see Hudson, *Oxford History of the Laws of England, Vol. 2* (quoting Henry II's justiciar, Richard de Lucy: "in times of old, malice did not, as now, render men pleaders or sceptics" [11]). And see the very similar complaints in fifteenth-century England quoted in Rose, "Legal Profession," 103, 114–15; and Zurcher, *Shakespeare*, 24–7 (quoting Caxton's complaint).

[14] "Hiis et nos, dum in provincia eramus, nostreque ecclesie procuracioni ac administracioni incumberemus, infinitis pene vexambamur, necesse habentes in omnibus tribunalibus patrie." Basin, *Apologie ou plaidoyer*, 262.

audience was made up of only a single judge and clerk or of the vast trial crowds I discuss in Chapters 4 and 5.[15] As R. H. Helmholz writes of late medieval and early modern ecclesiastical courts, "it was the import of the spoken word, not the probative force of documents," that counted.[16] Stylistically, the nature of "the spoken word" could differ significantly in different jurisdictions and courts, appearing sometimes as colloquial charge and counter-charge, sometimes as technical legal disputation, sometimes as a grandiloquent speech in the Ciceronian tradition. But whatever verbal style a courtroom speaker employed, body language and emotion communicated. For the theorists I discuss, the spoken word was the embodied word, as it was for their ancient predecessors, though they had very different things to say about the nature of that embodiment and what it meant in the Christian courtroom. Often radically revising or directly challenging their sources, these theorists offered, effectively, a set of distinctive theories of the legal body in performance, examining its nature, function, ethical status, expressive properties, vulnerabilities, and more. For them, the body may express the divinity of the human form; it may signify; it may entertain. Or it may be (as I suggest below) indecorous, accidental, leaky, or sublimely obscene.

Medieval Courtroom Actors

The Lawyer: Robed Vulture with Venal Tongue or Priest of the Laws?

Christian neo-Platonist critiques of surface appearances and sensory persuasions targeted, among other things, the art of rhetoric, which many identified with the decadence of pagan Rome.[17] Unsurprisingly, Augustine associates his rhetorical training and his work as a teacher of rhetoric with his legal aspirations, looking back on both with disgust. He had sought to distinguish himself as an orator "for a damnable and conceited purpose": "the objective of leading me to distinction as an advocate in the lawcourts, where one's reputation is high in proportion to one's success in deceiving people." As a teacher of "the art of rhetoric," driven "by greed," he "used to sell the eloquence that would overcome an opponent," teaching the "tricks of rhetoric" to students "'who 'loved vanity and sought after

[15] For a very concise overview of Roman and canon law trial procedure in Europe, see Padoa-Schioppa, *History of Law in Europe*, 139–50. Standard procedure in civil cases included a "dispute of the case" or "*litis contestation*," in which both parties defended their arguments before judges (140), and in criminal cases, an oral proceeding in which accusers or their relations presented their case to judges and attempted to prove it with witnesses (141). For my discussion of challenges to the classic account of the ascension of Roman-canon law on the Continent in the twelfth century, and its displacement of accusatorial by inquisitorial procedures, see Chapter 4, note 147, note 12.

[16] Helmholz, *Oxford History of the Laws of England, Vol. 1*, 334. And on the ongoing importance of oral procedures in the later Middle Ages, see Clanchy, *From Memory to Written Record*, 255–94.

[17] See the discussion in Miller, Prosser, and Benson, ed., *Readings in Medieval Rhetoric*, xiii.

a lie.'"[18] Later medieval commentators elaborated on Augustine's conjoined critique of rhetoric and law, even if they also extolled the virtues of a virtuous rhetoric. Gorgeous oratory might "stir the mind of [the] judge, make his ear alert," indeed "excite" him (as Alain said). But that was precisely what was wrong with it, as his bordering-on-lascivious portrait of Rhetorica hints (her hair falling about her neck, the "fiery color" in her face, the "purple flame on her rosy mouth"...).

The proliferation of professional lawyers in the twelfth and thirteenth centuries inevitably gave new ballast to attacks like Augustine's. In Henri d'Andeli's *Battle of the Seven Arts* (*c.*1230), for instance, "Civil Law," "Canon Law," and "Rhetoric" ride together, using their "feathered tongues" as "darts" to "pierce the hearts" of the foolish, and "snatch[ing] up many a heritage / [w]ith the lances of their eloquence."[19] That the lawyer's oratorical performance was "beguil[ing]" made it dangerous, for it employed the "shifts and colours" of rhetoric to "craftily... hide the truth."[20] To "lie like a lawyer" was proverbial.[21] "These men have taught their tongues to speak lies.... They are schooled in falsehood," Bernard of Clairvaux told the Pope in 1148. "[C]ut off their lying tongues," he urged, "and shut their deceitful mouths."[22] Appearing as "robed ones" (*togati*), lawyers were "robed vulture[s]," their costume giving credence to their "falshode" and "gyle."[23] In a dialogue between "Reason" and "Joy" in Petrarch's *Remedies for Fortune* (1360–66), Reason describes lawyers garbed at once in specious "eloquen[ce]" and the "gowns" in which they strut the legal stage. In the "legal professio[n]," declares Reason, it is "'[t]he purple or the violet robe [that] brings practice to a lawyer.... Why, no one would give Cicero himself two hundred pence nowadays unless a huge ring were blazing on his finger.'"[24] Using rich apparel as a lure, lawyers sold themselves to the highest bidders, "prostitut[ing] themselves venally for men's praise or for money," as Maurice of Saint-Victor put it.[25] The lawyer is like a "filthy whore," wrote the thirteenth-century French poet Matheolus, but "really,

[18] Augustine, *Confessions* (trans. Chadwick), 38 [3.3.6–7], 53 [4:2.2] (quoting Psalms 4:3). On the relationship between Augustine's critique of theatre and his critique of rhetoric, see Smith, "Staging the Incarnation," 125.

[19] Henri, *Battle of the Seven Arts* (trans. Paetow), 43 [65–74]. Copeland and Sluiter note that the "Lombard knight[s] / Marshalled by Rhetoric" are "lying, deceiving lawyers whose chicanery robs innocent people of their inheritances," partaking of "the long tradition that sees rhetoric in general, and especially the rhetoric of the law courts, as an art of deception" (*Medieval Grammar and Rhetoric*, 708).

[20] The lawyer at the bar will "beguile you" by taking "40 pence to take down his hood, / And speak for you a word or two": "Poem on the Evil Times of Edward II" (fourteenth-century); quoted in Rose, "Legal Profession," 1, 40. On "shifts and colors" (etc.), see Thomas Becon, *Catechism* (1844 ed.), 108; quoted in Ives, "Reputation of the Common Lawyers," 140.

[21] See e.g. the examples in Brundage, "Ethics of the Legal Profession," 240, note 11.

[22] Bernard of Clairvaux, *Five Books on Consideration*, 44 [1.10.(13)] (*De consideratione*).

[23] For "robed vulture," see Brundage, "Medieval Advocate's Profession," 444. For "falshode" and "gyle," see Brant, *Stultifera navis* [*Ship of Fools*] (trans. Barclay, 1509 ed.), fol. 149r ("onely the lawyers catchyth the avauntage" of litigiousness).

[24] Petrarch, *Remedies for Fortune*, 1:150 (dialogue 46, quoting Juvenal and John of Salisbury).

[25] Quoted in Bellomo, *Common Legal Past*, 114–15.

he's more vile." Why? "[A] whore just rents out her ass, [but] he sells . . . a member more precious than the ass": "the tongue."[26]

This vision of the lawyer as liar and whore is, of course, the portrayal one finds in medieval satires such as *Pierre Pathelin* (1457): in such texts, the lawyer is a scoundrel whose casuistic courtroom performance makes a farce of the law (though he usually gets his comeuppance). But, as so often, there was a counter-tradition, lauding the virtuous lawyer as mouthpiece of the law. As Guillaume Durand writes in his *Mirror of Law* (*c.*1276–89) (arguably the most widely consulted legal manual of the Middle Ages), through "the power [of] defence, [lawyers] often lift the fortunes of those who have been ruined." In this sense, they are "soldiers," he explains (quoting Justinian's *Code*): "[f]or these patrons of legal cases do fight. Trusting in the glorious power of eloquence, they defend the hope, life, and children of the wretched."[27] They are soldiers, explains Boncompagno da Signa in his *Newest Rhetoric* (1235), "because their tongues [a]re like sharp swords [that] cut down the bad deeds of transgressors." Patrons of legal cases, they fight alongside "princes of the city and the world" for justice. At the same time, they are "priests [*sacerdotes*] because they engage in a sacred [*sacra*] act."[28]

Statutes or the rules of legal guilds sometimes mandated behavior intended to maintain the lawyer's dignity, penalizing lawyers who insulted their adversaries, shouted in court, or used nasty language.[29] The many instructional books for lawyers—"mirrors" of law like Durand's or books instructing lawyers on their "office" or in the art of lawyers' "quibbles"—elaborated, supplementing the procedural treatises, offering performance advice aimed at upholding the dignity of the profession. Lawyers must behave courteously, control their voices and bodies, speak clearly (with voices neither too soft nor too loud), avoid grinning, chuckling, laughing, wild gestures, shuffling around the courtroom, and wearing exotic garments or dressing flamboyantly. Their attire must not be too lavish but nor should it be too ratty: they were priests and must dress accordingly.[30]

[26] The "causidic[us] . . . / Debet enim similis vel par vili meretrici, / Immo vilior est, quia, si meretrix locat anum, Hic vendit linguam, quod plus reor esse prophanum, Cum sit enim lingua membrum preciosius ano." Matheolus, *Lamentations de Matheolus* (1892 ed.), 1:283 (ll. 4579–84).

[27] Durand, *Speculum iuris* (1578 ed.), 1:178v; trans. Patrick J. Lally in Cavallar and Kirshner, ed., *Jurists and Jurisprudence*, 183–4; quoting the *Code* 2.7.14. According to Brundage, the oft-repeated claim is attributable to Emperor Leo I (457–74 CE) (*Medieval Origins*, 351).

[28] "[P]rincipes Urbis et orbis, iuxta quam militabant patroni causarum qui milites appellabantur, quoniam lingue illorum erant sicut acuti gladii quibus malefacta excedentium rescindebant. Apellabantur etiam sacerdotes qui sacra dare videbantur." Boncompagno, *Opera omnia* [*Rhetorica novissima*, 9.3.10], www.scrineum.it/scrineum/wight/index.htm (accessed July 9, 2021). The identification of lawyers as priests comes from Ulpian in Justinian's *Digest* [5.1.15.1]; see Brundage, "'My Learned Friend,'" 188 (and throughout for Brundage's richly detailed account of medieval instructions on proper behavior and attire for lawyers). On lawyers as "priests of the laws" generally, see Kelley, "'Jurisconsultus perfectus,'" 85.

[29] Brundage, "'My Learned Friend,'" 186 (and see 186–7 for similar regulations mandating brevity and clarity).

[30] Brundage, "'My Learned Friend,'" 188–90, quoting thirteenth-century jurist Bonaguida de Arezzo's *Summa introductoria super officio advocatorum* and Johannes de Deo's *Cavillationes*

Medieval writers often associated these rival visions of the lawyer with the rival visions of eloquence they found in the two most widely read rhetorical texts of the period: Cicero's *De inventione* and the *Rhetorica ad Herennium* (which medieval scholars attributed to Cicero). The *locus classicus* of this double vision of eloquence was the beginning of *De inventione*, in which Cicero acknowledges the dangers of eloquence but insists that its potential virtues outweigh those dangers. To illustrate this point, he tells a story in which a primal oratorical scene transforms the rule of violence into the rule of law. Medieval theorists often repeated this story. In the version Thierry of Chartres offers in his commentary on *De inventione* (*c.*1130–40),

> There was a time at the beginning of the world when men were savage and lived in the manner of beasts, [using] only their bodily strength, without any reason. At this time there was a certain man who was wise and eloquent, [and] recognized that . . . man was open to persuasion; and so . . . the wise man began to use eloquence and he drove out the savagery and brought men together to live by law, and he instructed the assembled people in the laws of living according to what is right.[31]

It turns out that for Thierry, the "wise and eloquent" man who persuades these "rude" and "raving" savages (424) "to live by law" is a lawyer *avant la lettre*, and that courtroom persuasion is the primary function of eloquence. The subject of rhetoric, explains Thierry, is called a "'case' [*causa*] because 'to bring a case' [*causari*] is the term used to mean 'to accuse someone of something and bring a lawsuit against him: . . . a case in the sense of a legal action about something" (413). Such cases are "[c]ivil controversies," which "customarily concern a matter of law before judges, [and] are called judicial cases" (413). Cicero's discussion of the ethical ambiguity of eloquence thus becomes, in Thierry's commentary, a discussion of the ethical ambiguity of the lawyer. In Cicero's day, explains Thierry, wise men were too "occupied [with] public affairs [to] be involved in private lawsuits." And so, unfortunately, "cunning men, busying themselves in private affairs, acquired such garrulous facility that they could thwart the truth . . . . [E]mboldened by constant practice in speaking, they brought many injuries upon citizens" (425). In both "individual law suits and public cases" today, as in Cicero's day, some misuse [eloquence]" and "put it to perverse use" (427). But, writes Thierry (quoting Cicero), the "more shamefully a most honest and worthy

advocatorum. See the discussion of Cicero's use of the word *cavillationes* (which might instead be translated as "sophistry," "cavils," or "prevarications") in Seneca the Younger, *Epistles* [Loeb], 3:277, 3:279 [111: "On the Vanity of Mental Gymnastics"].

[31] Trans. Copeland and Sluiter, ed., *Medieval Grammar and Rhetoric*, 422. Parenthetical citations refer to Copeland and Sluiter's translation. The relevant Latin passages appear in Thierry, *Latin Rhetorical Commentaries*, 52, 60–8. For the original, see Cicero, *On Invention* [Loeb], 5–7 [1.2–3].

profession [i]s abused by the folly and audacity of dull-witted and unprincipled men with the direst consequences to the state, the more earnestly should the better citizens . . . put up a resistance to them" (426).

Forensic Oratory in Medieval Theory and Practice

Thierry's and Alain's portrayals of rhetoric as courtroom oratory cut against the three persistent scholarly claims I identified earlier in this chapter: first, the claim that, with few venues for civic oratory, medieval rhetorical theorists turned away from the forensic and deliberative oratory that had preoccupied ancient theorists.[32] In fact, in most medieval theory, rhetoric appears as an applied civil science ("the art of speaking well in civic matters"): not only political but also legal matters.[33] Theorists such as Arnoul de Provence (*c.*1250) and Johannes de Dacia (*c.*1280) define rhetoric as "the science of orderly and elegant speaking for persuading the judge."[34] Jacques de Dinant regularly translates "orator" as "*advocatus*" in his commentary on the *Ad Herennium* (*c.*1291).[35] The thirteenth-century priest and poet Gautier de Metz writes: "Who knows Rhetoric well / He will know wrong [*tort*] and law."[36] Texts frequently identify the lawyer of ancient rhetorical theory with the modern lawyer, treating rhetoric as a science with practical application in the lawcourt. In his vernacular *Rettorica* (*c.*1260–62), the notary Brunetto Latini in fact worries that "a superficial reader" might conclude

[32] For a classic statement about the turn from oratory generally, see e.g. Vickers, *In Defence of Rhetoric* (in the Middle Ages, "[o]ratory was a lost art" [227]). For the more specific claim about the turn from forensic oratory, see e.g. Haskins, *Renaissance of the Twelfth Century* (1955 ed.): "Ancient rhetoric was concerned with oratory, mediaeval rhetoric chiefly with letter-writing. . . . The whole basis of such forensic oratory disappeared with the Roman political and judicial system" (138). Identifying but contesting this view, see e.g. Johnston, "Parliamentary Oratory" ("It is a truism in modern histories of rhetoric that the practice of civic oratory virtually disappeared during the European Middle Ages, [and] that the only disciplines of verbal persuasion practiced between the fall of Rome and rise of Italian humanism were the arts of versifying, letter-writing, and preaching" [99]); Ward, *Classical Rhetoric* ("rhetoricians assert that . . . the absolute nature of government banished the judicial context in which *inventio* had previously flourished, [so] medieval rhetorical treatises concern themselves principally with the devices of ornamentation" [71]); and Cox, "Rhetoric and Politics" (scholars often assert that medieval culture was "little concerned with politics as a practical application for rhetoric" [abstract]).

[33] See Copeland and Sluiter, ed., *Medieval Grammar and Rhetoric*, 56–7, 793 (describing the standard medieval Ciceronian definition of rhetoric as the "art of speaking well in civic affairs"), with examples reaching from Cassiodorus (*c.*562) to John Lydgate (*c.*1431–39). On the centrality of forensic oratory in Cassiodorus, see Kennedy, "Forms and Functions of Latin Speech," 52 (and 60–1 on Isidore of Seville's treatment of the pragmatic utility of status theory in lawcourts).

[34] "Diffinitiue sic: *Rethorica est scientia loquendi disposite et ornate ad persuadendum iudici.*" Arnoul, *Divisio scientiarum* (*c.*1250) in Lafleur, ed., *Quatre introductions*, 345 (and see Lafleur, 345, note 697–8 quoting Johannes de Dacia's *Divisio scientie* [*c.*1280], which gives the same definition).

[35] "Iacobi de Dinanto comentum Tulli," reproduced in Alessio, "Il commento di Jacques di Dinant," 860–94 (and for the probable date of composition, see Alessio's introduction, 855); and see Cox, "Ciceronian Rhetoric in Italy, 1260–1350," 251. See similarly Alan of Lille, *Art of Preaching* (trans. Evans), 152–3 ("To Orators, or Advocates").

[36] Quoted in Caplan, "Classical Rhetoric and the Mediaeval Theory of Preaching," 74, note 5.

from his book that Cicero deals *only* "with trials that take place in law courts" between "an accuser and an accused," and "with nothing else." It is, of course, true (he explains) that "no one can be a good advocate, let alone a perfect one, unless he speaks according to the art of rhetoric." But the art "is not *limited* to contending in law courts": it does really "sho[w] [you] how to speak appropriately" in cases that are "not *necessarily* to be tried in court" (all appearances to the contrary).[37]

As for the second claim—that lawyers and litigants did not bother with rhetorical theory since it was irrelevant in autocratic medieval courts—certainly thirteenth-century Italian theorist-practitioners like Latini would have disagreed. So would those who had continued to teach rhetorical theory as a practical skill throughout the Middle Ages: in the rhetorical schools that survived in Gaul, Spain, and Africa into the fifth century and in Italy into the sixth; or in the very practical *ars dictaminis* and *ars notariae*, which were not merely textual but prescribed oratorical form as well.[38] In the university liberal arts faculties (from the eleventh century on), students studying rhetoric also learned the rudiments of law.[39] Cicero's elaboration of Hermagoras' status theory, explaining how to handle different kinds of issues in (primarily) legal cases, constituted one core of rhetorical study.[40]

[37] Latini, *La rettorica* (trans. D'Ottavi), 91, 93 [sec. 76] (emphasis added). See similarly Latini's focus on forensic oratory in his discussion of rhetoric in Book 3 of *Li livres dou tresor* (the *Book of the Treasure*), [trans. Barrette and Baldwin], especially 281–5, 299–302, 320–3, 345–9, 369).

[38] Scholars have sometimes argued that it was only during the period of the communes (the eleventh through fourteenth centuries) and primarily in Italy that theorists were interested in applying rhetoric to courtroom oratory. And yet, as Kennedy writes in "Forms and Functions of Latin Speech," ancient "rhetoric was directed toward meeting the needs of speakers in a court of law" and "this judicial focus persisted as a characteristic of classical rhetorical theory even in the Middle Ages"; thus "it seems perverse to believe that medieval scholars did not expect to teach or learn something immediately applicable when they turned to the study of rhetoric" (46–8; and see 48–9 on the survival of rhetorical schools into the sixth century). On forensic oratory during the period of the communes, see Cox, "Ciceronian Rhetoric in Italy, 1260–1350" (citing, among many examples, Bartolinus de Benincasa's "enthusiastic parallel between ancient and modern forensic oratory" in his early fourteenth-century commentary on the *Rhetorica ad Herennium*). On the importance of forensic skills in the courtrooms of late medieval and Renaissance Italy generally, see Armstrong and Kirshner, ed., *Politics of Law in Late Medieval and Renaissance Italy*, 7–8, 11, 15.

[39] See Martines, *Power and Imagination* (in thirteenth- and fourteenth-century universities, "lawyers and notaries . . . heard lectures in Latin on rhetoric, dialectics, and the elements of law," with "courses in rhetoric" also "touch[ing] the art of speechmaking" [204]); and Rashdall, *Universities of Europe* (1987 ed.) (the study of "rhetoric [included] at least a preliminary initiation into the science of positive law" [1:93]; there was a "practice of learning law at school" and a "complete amalgamation of law-studies with the ordinary educational curriculum; [a]t least some rudiments of law were everywhere taught in the 'schools of the Liberal Arts' and by the masters of these arts" [1:101–2]). On the university law faculties and their relationship to the arts faculties, see Brundage, *Medieval Origins*, 219–82; Rashdall, *Universities of Europe* (1987 ed.) (especially 1:87–176, 1:254–61, 1:437–9, 2:28–31, 2:128–33, 2:140–3, 2:217–20, 3:156–7); Janin, *University in Medieval Life*, 63–71 (on the Bologna law faculty); Padoa-Schioppa, *History of Law in Europe*, 124–30; García y García, "Faculties of Law" in Ridder-Symoens, ed., *History of the University in Europe, Vol. 1*; Leader, *History of the University of Cambridge. Vol. 1*, 192–201 (on the law faculties); Barton, "Legal Faculties of Late Medieval Oxford" (in Catto and Evans, ed., *History of the University of Oxford, Vol. 2*); and Cobban, *Medieval English Universities* (especially 209–56 on academic concentrations).

[40] For helpful discussions, see Copeland, *Rhetoric, Hermeneutics, and Translation*, 67–9; and Witt, "'In the Footsteps of the Ancients'" (ancient rhetorical manuals and Cicero's *De Topica*, "served as the main texts for teaching law students to construct legal arguments" [353]).

A central pedagogic practice involved reading Seneca the Elder's model *controversiae* (fictitious legal speeches) and practicing one's own.[41] The most important rhetorical treatise of the Middle Ages—the *Ecclesiastica rhetorica* (1159–79)—was, of course, theological in nature, but it was also (as one scholar has described it) a practical "forensic rhetoric for canon law."[42] Fourteenth- and fifteenth-century humanists famously championed rhetorical training for its ability to inculcate virtue, but they also argued that it had practical value. "If students are going to be introduced to civil law," explained Battista Guarino in his "Program of Teaching and Learning" (1459), "rhetoric will prove highly useful in the analysis of judicial cases and in the explanation of many passages."[43]

Those who have studied medieval rhetoric in depth do generally recognize the importance of law to medieval rhetorical thought, but some have remained skeptical about whether theory made its way into practice.[44] And yet, not only do formal medieval courtroom speeches tend to reflect the principles of rhetorical training: speakers repeatedly testify to the use of these principles in their speeches.[45] In the oral brief he delivered at the trial of the rebel Arnulf in 995, for instance, Gerbert (later Pope Sylvester II) writes: "these are the facts that I have embellished with rhetorical material."[46] Durand—who was a professor of law in Bologna and Modena and regularly argued in the papal curia and elsewhere—

[41] See Rashdall, *Universities of Europe* (1987 ed.), 1:102 on "ordinary grammatico-legal education," which involved learning the "rhetorical rules of pleading, and practic[ing] their application [in] imaginary cases" even before the twelfth century.

[42] Caplan, "Classical Rhetoric and the Mediaeval Theory of Preaching," 74. Caplan notes generally "the alliance of rhetoric and law in the schools," and the application of the *ars dictaminis* to legal rhetoric, preparing students for positions in the ecclesiastical and state chanceries (74–5).

[43] Guarino, "Program of Teaching and Learning" (in Kallendorf, ed., *Humanist Educational Treatises*), 293.

[44] See e.g. Hohmann, "Ciceronian Rhetoric and the Law" and "Rhetoric in Medieval Legal Education"; and to a lesser extent, Ward, "Medieval and Early Renaissance Study" (especially 45–50). Despite their skepticism, Hohmann and Ward offer abundant evidence of the importance of forensic oratory to both theorists and practitioners.

[45] There has been little systematic study of the relationship between rhetorical precepts and the form or style of medieval judicial speeches. But see Kennedy's analysis of Gregory of Tours' report on the speeches in the trial of Praetextatus bishop of Rouen for plotting against the king in 577, which (Kennedy argues) adopt the techniques of "the inventional rhetoric described by Cassiodorus" ("Forms and Functions of Latin Speech," 54, and generally, 54–60). Even a glance at formal courtroom speech in the later Middle Ages shows classical rhetorical principles and strategies at work. For just a few examples, see the twelfth-century judicial speeches collected in Haye, ed., *Oratio*: mittelalterliche Redekunst in lateinischer Sprache (Guido von Bazoches [68–77]; the speeches in the *Gerichtsreden aus Lüttich* [88–109]; Laurentius of Durham [124–35]; and Stephen of Rouen [174–83]). In this light, Brundage, *Medieval Origins*, 440, cites Thomas of Marlborough's account of one thirteenth-century case and Adam Usk's defense of the earl of Salisbury. For a later period, see the speeches in Blanchard, ed., *Procès politiques au temps de Louis XI*. And see Milner, "Communication, Consensus and Conflict," on the *Avvenga Dio*, a fourteenth-century translation and paraphrase of the *Ad Herennium*, which "furnish[es] several model forensic orations which demonstrate how to accuse and defend within a court context" (387); on the emphasis in the *podestà* literature and *ars aringandi* tracts on the importance of the "ability to perform" in the courtroom (377); and, generally, on "Bolognese Ciceronianism and the Law" (388–92).

[46] See Lattin, ed., *Letters of Gerbert*, 259, 236–62 for the case generally, and 262 on the oral nature of the brief.

describes his colleagues' use of "eloquence" in court, warning students not to let style replace substance:

> Not a few navigating safely enough through the storms of eloquence come dangerously to harbour. For they begin robustly enough with their eloquent introductions, but before they arrive at the goal of their conclusion, they, very unwisely, are found wanting.[47]

Durand recommends the following strategy where one's opponent is particularly verbose (in an exemplary use of the rhetoric of anti-rhetoric). First pretend to doze off while your opponent holds forth, then rub your eyes, seem to awaken slowly, and lambaste his empty verbiage, in an address to the judge:

> You are well acquainted, my lord, with those who bring forth winds from their storehouses, and, as the Psalmist says, 'Make the clouds rise at the ends of the earth'.... [T]hey promise impossibilities and like the clouds of the prophet they stir up a haze of lies; they speak grandly and their speech is filled with falsehoods.[48]

Scholars sometimes cite a passage in the Venetian lawyer Pier Paolo Vergerio's essay on education (*c.*1401–3) as evidence that rhetoric was irrelevant to actual courtroom practice. Young Romans "once achieved great glory,... denouncing the guilty or defending the innocent," writes Vergerio. Sadly, such oratory has

> now fallen almost totally into disuse,... completely exiled from legal proceedings, where contending parties no longer use long speeches, but rather adduce laws against each other dialectically in support of their cases.

But Vergerio here merely echoes standard ancient laments about the decay of oratory. And he does so primarily in order to urge the student "nevertheless [to] work at rhetoric, so that... he can use his art to speak with polish and elaboration," principally in the courts.[49] In fact, the nearby Venetian courts were famous

[47] Durand, *Speculum iuris* (1578 ed.), 1:123r; trans. Ward, "Medieval and Early Renaissance Study," 48. Surprisingly, Ward treats this passage as evidence that oratory had little relevance in the "written context of medieval court procedure" (49).

[48] Durand, *Speculum iuris* (1578 ed.), 1:124r; trans. Brundage, "'My Learned Friend,'" 193.

[49] Vergerio, "Character and Studies" (in Kallendorf, ed., *Humanist Educational Treatises*), 51–3. For examples of use of this passage as evidence that forensic oratory was incompatible with modern legal practices, see e.g. Cox, "Ciceronian Rhetoric in Late Medieval Italy," 130; and Hohmann, "Ciceronian Rhetoric and the Law," 203 (both, however, noting that Vergerio argues for the importance of rhetoric to legal practice). While Vergerio had studied law in Bologna and Florence, he had settled in Padua, which was under Venetian control. On Vergerio's treatise and its date, see McManamon, *Pierpaolo Vergerio the Elder*, 89–103 (and 73–4 on Vergerio's argument that judicial speakers should focus less on legal technicalities and more on classical principles).

for oratory that seemed to carry on the great traditions of the ancients. The Venice Commune's attorney general Leonardo Giustinian found the demand for such oratory taxing, explaining in a 1420 letter:

> There is no kind of case, no type, no topic, finally no precept of the entire art [of oratory] in which I must not be proficient, unless I wish to fail myself.... [A]ccording to the merits and dignity of the cases, I must go now before the Doge himself, now before the Forty Judges [in the Court of the Quarantia],... now with the body of patricians. And in these places, various and wholly different forms of oratory are required.[50]

Certainly, not all courts required such elaborate oratorical skills. Lawyers in England, for instance, did tend to "adduce laws against each other dialectically in support of their cases." But dialectic and classical oratory were not necessarily viewed as antithetical. Many instead viewed them as complementary. For the rhetorical theorist Giles of Rome, for instance, rhetoric was, precisely, dialectic that could be applied to civic affairs (including legal cases).[51] For English lawyers, there was no conflict between classical "eloquence" and the legal-dialectical disputation for which they trained in moots in the Inns of Court. The early fourteenth-century *Mirrour of Justices* explains that in England, serjeants (elite lawyers allowed to argue cases in the central courts) were to be paid in proportion to both their "learning" and their "eloquence."[52]

On Forensic Delivery

Given the attention to "eloquence" generally in both medieval theory and practice, it is not surprising that medieval theorists and practitioners had much to say about what Cicero had called "the eloquence of the body."[53] As John Ward writes, from

[50] Letter to Pietro de' Tommasi (1420) quoted in Labalme, *Bernardo Giustiniani*, 23 (and in part in Cox, "Ciceronian Rhetoric in Late Medieval Italy," 130–1).

[51] Copeland and Sluiter, ed., *Medieval Grammar and Rhetoric*, 805 (discussing Giles of Rome).

[52] Horne, *Mirrour of Justices* (1903 ed.), 80 [Ch 2, sec 5: Of Countors or Pleaders]. The attribution to Horne, a learned lawyer-fishmonger, is conventional. While scholars have questioned whether the *Mirrour* accurately represents common law rules, it certainly represents attitudes. The serjeants-at-law were a highly exclusive guild with a monopoly on pleading in the central courts until that monopoly began to break down in the sixteenth century. Early modern commentators were even more explicit about the necessity of rhetorical training to legal argument, including training in the art of delivery: see Chapter 5, 204–11 and 6, 256–7, 260–2.

[53] For examples of the persistent view that medieval rhetorical theorists largely ignored delivery, see e.g. Welch, "Delivery" in Sloane, ed., *Encyclopedia of Rhetoric* ("During the medieval and Renaissance periods, delivery declined greatly because rhetoricians ignored it in favor of other rhetorical issues. The political and religious systems at work in this long period did not make delivery a compelling function of rhetoric" [218]); and Ong, "Tudor Writings on Rhetoric" (in both the Middle Ages and Renaissance, delivery became a "minor matte[r]" [52]).

late antiquity through at least the twelfth century, "all commentators recommend very close attention to the comments of the *Ad Herennium* on *pronuntiatio*" (the term medieval texts use for both vocal and bodily delivery), and "many . . . indicate that they know how to perform according to its precepts."[54] While some treat delivery only briefly, virtually all insist on its importance, regularly citing the discussions in Cicero, Quintilian, the *Ad Herennium*, Horace's *Art of Poetry*, and Seneca the Elder's *Controversiae*, as well as texts from later antiquity: Aulus Gellius' *Attic Nights*; and Fortunatianus', Gaius Julius Victor's, and Martianus Capella's treatises on rhetoric. If they paraphrase Cicero's account of the role of eloquence in the origin of law, they also rework his claims on bodily eloquence. "[L]et three tongues speak: . . . that of the mouth, [of] the speaker's countenance, [and] of gesture," instructs Geoffrey of Vinsauf in his *Poetria nova* (*c.*1200).[55] They regularly repeat Demosthenes' and Cicero's assertion that delivery is far more important than invention, arrangement, style, or memory: delivery so far surpasses the other skills, writes Alcuin, that "a speech devoid of skill may nevertheless receive applause by virtue of a speaker's excellence in Delivery, while on the other hand a speech excellent beyond description may meet contempt and mockery if it is delivered unbecomingly."[56]

Like Alain, many such theorists envision the scene of delivery as, specifically, the courtroom.[57] This includes the earliest medieval commentators on Aristotle's *Rhetoric*: the tenth-century Islamic jurist and judge Al-Farabi (Alpharabius); the twelfth-century Islamic jurist-judge and physician Ibn Rushd (Averroës); and their thirteenth-century Latin translator and commentator Hermannus

[54] Ward, *Classical Rhetoric*, 42 (and see his thorough bibliographic discussion [42]; Appendix C on "*Pronuntiatio* or Delivery in the Commentaries on the Pseudo-Ciceronian *Rhetorica ad Herennium* in the Medieval and Early Renaissance Periods" [479–87]; and his comment that the "'delivery' section of the *Ad Herennium* was continually glossed in the Middle Ages" [61]). See also Steinbrink, "Actio," col. 52–5; Rebmann, "Pronuntiatio," col. 227–30; Ziolkowski, "Do Actions Speak Louder than Words?" (generally; and see 129–30 on delivery's centrality to grammar, the *artes versificandi*, and the *scientia interpretandi*); Ward, "Master William of Champeaux"; and Camargo, "Special Delivery" (quoting, among others, Siguinus' *Ars lectoria* [1087–88]: good delivery involves "not braying with a donkey's voice, no[r] gulping like a greedy sow . . . " [175]). On medieval images that reflect ideas about delivery, see Schmitt, *Raison des gestes*; and Dodwell, *Anglo-Saxon Gestures*. In addition to the medieval discussions of delivery I analyze elsewhere in this chapter, important discussions include those in Thierry's commentary on *De inventione* (*c.*1130–40) (*Latin Rhetorical Commentaries*, 293–301); Geoffrey of Vinsauf's *Poetria nova* (orig. *c.*1200) (trans. Nims) (78–9); and his *Documentum de modo et arte dictandi et versificandi* (1213 or later) (94–5).

[55] Geoffrey of Vinsauf, *Poetria nova* (trans. Nims), 78 [VI. Delivery].

[56] Alcuin, *Rhetoric of Alcuin*, 139 (translation modified). For an example from the later Middle Ages, see Bruni, "Study of Literature" (*c.*1405) (in Kallendorf, ed., *Humanist Educational Treatises*), 105 ("Demosthenes said [delivery] was the first, the second, and the third most important acquirement of the orator").

[57] See e.g. Arnoul de Provence, who after defining rhetoric as "the science of orderly and elegant speaking for persuading the judge," defines delivery as "the measured use of voice, facial expressions, and gestures with comeliness" ("Pronuntiatio est uocis, uultus, gestus moderatio cum uenustate."). *Divisio scientiarum*, in Lafleur, ed., *Quatre introductions*, 346.

Alemannus.[58] All stress the crucial importance of delivery to conveying ethos and emotion to different kinds of audiences during legal proceedings. For Al-Farabi, these are of three different kinds: the judge; the one you must contradict (your adversary); and those you want to persuade (presumably the general audience). For both him and Ibn Rushd, the speaker's ability to use delivery to rouse the passions is crucial to judicial persuasion. Such emotions as "confusion, anguish,... desire or fear, or enthusiasm, or love, or something else" can both "incline [the judge] towards one of the two adversaries" and, at the same time, "reduce one's adversary to silence."[59] Equally crucial (explains Al-Farabi) is delivery's role in conveying ethos: the "expression of a man's face or his physiognomy, or the attitude of his limbs and their appearance, or what he does while he speaks," along with "the voice and intonation." These are "things that affirm the virtue of the speaker," he explains.[60] At the same time, as Ibn Rushd notes, delivery can help conjure the scene of a crime dramatically: a speaker "whose face has... become pale and whose voice has... risen recounting a fearful matter" can cause the listener to "imagin[e]" the scenario that the speaker wishes to convey. For both Al-Farabi and Ibn Rushd, emotional devices, voice, body, gesture, and the ethos they convey count as "Persuasive Things Which Do Not Occur by Arguments" (as Ibn Rushd puts it), but are at least as important as arguments to legal persuasion.[61]

Delivery appears in lawyers' manuals, pedagogic treatises, and rhetorical theory not merely as an art that might theoretically be useful but as one that does in fact have specific practical judicial application. Its precepts could sometimes converge with precepts from the Bible and Justinian on courtroom etiquette, as in Durand, who quotes Cicero, Juvenal, and others alongside earlier jurists. Lawyers must avoid not only a "disheveled appearance" but also "any bodily

[58] Hermannus' translation-commentaries appeared in 1256. I am indebted to the following for my discussion of Al-Farabi and Ibn Rushd: Copeland and Sluiter, ed., *Medieval Grammar and Rhetoric*, 58–9, 735–40 (and notes to their translation 740–52); Borrowman, "Islamization of Rhetoric"; Woerther, "Al-Fārābī commentateur d'Aristote"; and Bouhafa, "Rhetoric in the Court" (specifically on Ibn Rushd's use of Aristotle as a manual for practicing law in Islamic courts).

[59] Al-Farabi, *Deux ouvrages* [*Kitāb al-ḫaṭāba*], 64–8, 80; see similarly Averroës [Ibn Rushd], *Averroës' Three Short Commentaries*, 73; and Copeland and Sluiter, ed., *Medieval Grammar and Rhetoric*, 746, note 37. As several scholars point out, for Al-Farabi, one of the central functions of rhetoric was to persuade the unreasoning multitude. See e.g. Woerther, "Al-Fārābī commentateur d'Aristote," 55; and on Ibn Rushd's similar view, see Bouhafa, "Rhetoric in the Court," 75–6.

[60] Al-Farabi, *Deux ouvrages*, 78, 80, 190. The first phrases are from the French translation of his *Kitāb al-ḫaṭāba*: "l'expression du visage de l'homme ou sa physionomie, ou l'attitude de ses membres et leur aspect, ou ce qu'il fait tandis qu'il parle,... la voix et l'intonation" (78–80). The last is from his *Didascalia*: "quas firmatur virtus dictoris" (190; trans. Copeland and Sluiter, ed., *Medieval Grammar and Rhetoric*, 747).

[61] Averroës, *Averroës' Three Short Commentaries*, 73–4. Both Al-Farabi and Ibn-Rushd viewed Aristotle's *Rhetoric* and *Poetics* as part of his broader logical corpus, the "long Organon," which taught, primarily, methods of persuasion. Thus, physiognomy, posture, manner of speaking, and emotion all belong to the art of logic. See, in addition to those cited above, Watt, "Commentary on the Rhetoric," 119.

and verbal indecency, and any indecency in [their] actions." They must comport themselves "[w]ith due gravity." The lawyer's

> movements [and] bearing should be measured and grave, not headlong and rapid.... In his facial expression he should show himself affable, cheerful, and benign to the judge,...but without indiscreet laughter.... [H]e should not move with his head or his feet unduly, but let all the parts of his body play the roles they are supposed to.... 'The tongue, the feet, and the hands all have a role to perform, and the eyes also.'... In voice, he should lower it or raise it no more than is proper for the occasion.... He should move around gracefully.[62]

Even where delivery appeared in a less genteel guise, it was nevertheless clear that it was essential to courtroom success, as in Leonardo Bruni's letter to Baptista di Montefeltro (*c.*1405) (which I quote in my Introduction [20] for its reflections on gender). Among the reasons that women do not belong in the courtroom, Bruni argues, is that it would be unseemly for them to employ delivery: "why should the subtleties of [rhetoric] consume the powers of a woman, who will never see the forum?" he asks.

> That art of delivery, which the Greeks call *hypocrisis* and we *pronunciatio*, and which Demosthenes said was the first, the second, and the third most important acquirement of the orator, so far is that from being the concern of a woman that if she should gesture energetically with her arms as she spoke and shout with violent emphasis, she would probably be thought mad and put under restraint. The contests of the forum, like those of warfare and battle, are the sphere of men.... She will, in a word, leave the rough-and-tumble of the forum entirely to men.

While insisting that women must not study delivery, Bruni betrays two additional assumptions: first, the central reason that men must study rhetoric is that it is useful in courtroom argument; second, the rhetorical teachings most centrally concerned with courtroom oratory are those on delivery.

The utility of learning delivery by watching courtroom pleading in action was to become a central tenet of humanist pedagogy. In his 1492 treatise on education, Jacopo di Porcia stresses that parents should frequently take their sons to the forum to watch the highly skilled lawyers in action, not only in order to learn the secrets of legal argument but also in order to learn "lovely bodily action."[63] As in

[62] Durand, *Speculum iuris* (1578 ed.), 1:121v; trans. Lally, in Cavallar and Kirshner, *Jurists and Jurisprudence*, 215.

[63] "[C]urae parentibus etiam sit: eos ad forum frequenter secum ducere: in quo lites & controuersiae plurimae uersantur, ut peritissimos uiros tam dicentes q[uam] resepondentes audiant: nam inde et naturales rationes: quae in medium utrinq[ue]; deducunt[ur], & pulchros etia[m] corporis motus, ac cuiusq[ue]." Jacopo, *De generosa educatione liberorum* (1492 ed.), fol. VIr ("De ludis adolescentie"). Porcia also quotes the passage from Saint Jerome on the power of the live voice that Basin quotes: see Chapter 4, 156 and note 39.

the ancient rhetorical schools, teachers of rhetoric gave instruction in delivery specifically for use in the courts. In his *Five Books on Rhetoric* (*c.*1472), George of Trebizond notes that he has collected the precepts on delivery to be found in Cicero. He "will expound them" specifically for the use of "those who declaim [legal] cases" in the courts: in fact, he has "already set up quite a few people [who] practice this [profession] on a daily basis" (perhaps an advertisement for his services).[64]

A miniature in a manuscript edition of Cicero's orations (*c.*1483) depicts Cicero himself modeling techniques of courtroom delivery as he pleads a case in a fifteenth-century French courtroom (fig. 3.1): a legal orator in action, displaying "eloquence of the body" before the judges and onlookers.[65] He has extended his

Fig. 3.1 Cicero models "eloquence of the body" while arguing a case before judges and onlookers in a fifteenth-century French courtroom (1483).
By permission of the British Library. MS Harley 2681, f. 2.

[64] "Quare quae a Cicerone de pronunciatione accepimus, ea exponemus eis, qui causas declamitant (nam nonnullos iam quotidie id factitare instituimus)." Trapezuntius, *Trapezuntii Rhetoricorum libri quinque* (1538 ed.), 439 (and for his discussion of delivery generally, 429–48).

[65] Cicero before court spectators: MS Harley 2681, f. 2, British Library. The image is labeled "Pro Lege Manilia," a political speech that Cicero in fact argued before the popular assembly, but the

right hand, thumb up, forefinger gently engaged. He holds his hat in hand to show respect for the court. He raises his brow to indicate the expressive use of the face. His feet are gracefully in motion (but not vulgarly so, like a dancer or mime). The judges respond with their own expressive gestures, echoing Cicero's and signifying their mutual comprehension through the language of hands. (As in many medieval courtroom images, the disproportionately large hands of the participants represent the importance of gesture.)[66] Set in the kind of grand hall or church where trials often took place (and recalling images of such trials), the scene has a contemporary resonance, conveying the message: Cicero's bodily eloquence may serve as a model for today's legal pleader.[67]

Four Rhetorical Theorists on Courtroom Delivery

Alcuin of York (c.735–804): Allegorical Insignia, Eschatological Space, and Bodily Decorum in the Carolingian Court

In the last decades of the eighth century, Charlemagne—King of the Franks and Lombards and soon to be crowned Emperor—gathered a group of scholars-in-residence together, among them the English scholar, Alcuin of York. At Charlemagne's court in Aachen (and elsewhere), Alcuin taught a variety of subjects and wrote prolifically, producing (among other texts) his *Dialogue on Rhetoric and on Virtues* (c.784–90).[68] Charlemagne was in his mid-forties by then and had conquered much of Europe. But in the dialogue he appears as a young student eager to learn from the wise man he calls "Master." While Alcuin's lessons in rhetoric draw heavily on Cicero's *De inventione* and Gaius Julius Victor's fourth-century *Ars rhetorica*, he stresses that his dialogue introduces Charlemagne to the "civic customs" of the day and takes place "in the midst of

illustrator renders it as a courtroom scene. See the British Library catalog entry (it is "a miniature of a judge and a court in session"), and Hargreaves-Mawdsley, *History of Legal Dress*, 19–45 (on French legal dress generally) and 23–4 (on this image's specific representation of it): the Chief Justice (Premier Président) wears a silver-gray *manteau* and hood; the others wear scarlet *manteaux* lined in ermine, open only on the right side, and rigid flared *mortiers* (headdresses); the clerk at the center wears a simple *pilier*.

[66] See Caviness, "Putting the Judge in his P(a)lace," 312.

[67] See e.g. the very similar image of a trial at the Council of Constance in an edition of Ulrich Richenthal's *Chronik des Konstanzer Konzils* (1414–18), https://www.csun.edu/~hcfll004/SV1417.html, accessed March 13, 2021.

[68] *Disputatio de rhetorica et de virtutibus*. Scholars disagree on the date of the text. Here, I follow Rädler-Bohn, who dates it to *c*.784/6–90 ("Re-dating Alcuin's *De dialectica*," 77–104), persuasively contesting the argument for 801–4 in Wallach, *Alcuin and Charlemagne* (35–47) and for 794 in Howell's introduction to Alcuin, *Rhetoric of Alcuin* (5–8). My in-text citations refer to Howell's facing-page translation in *Rhetoric of Alcuin*, which I frequently modify. In some of my departures, I draw on the excellent translation of excerpts in Copeland and Sluiter, ed., *Medieval Grammar and Rhetoric*, 287–98. The dialogue uses Alcuin's adopted surname "Albinus," which I have changed to "Alcuin" to avoid confusion.

the cares of [Charlemagne's] court" (66–7).[69] Its aim is thus not merely to recover and explain ancient texts on rhetoric and virtue, but to outline a set of ideal practices for Charlemagne's court: his royal court but, still more, his lawcourts. In "Charlemagne's" summary of the topic of the *Dialogue*: "rhetoric is concerned with legal cases and public questions" (70–1). As its modern translator writes, the *Dialogue* offers "a rudimentary science of law."[70] As Alcuin leads Charlemagne through a "complete legal case" (72–3) (a pedagogic device that takes up most of the dialogue), it becomes clear that, for him, rhetoric means, principally, forensic oratory.

As Charlemagne's advisor, Alcuin regularly accompanied the itinerant court and attended its proceedings.[71] He thus had a great deal of firsthand experience of Frankish courts (and perhaps Anglo-Saxon ones as well). In his correspondence, he notes that he has helped numerous people in the cases they have brought before Charlemagne's lawcourts. That is, he regularly acted as an intercessor (*adiutor*) or advocate. He served, for instance, as intercessor on behalf of some Italian monks whose petition he also persuaded Charlemagne's Queen, Liutgarda, to support. He argued on behalf of the monks of the Abbey of Cormery (his own abbey), petitioning the King to allow them to sail ships duty-free on the Loire, the Sarthe, and some tributaries.[72] The most important case in which he was involved was in 801–2. A cleric, convicted in a public proceeding in Orléans, had escaped, fled to Tours (where Alcuin was serving as Abbot), and taken sanctuary in the Basilica of Saint Martin.[73] Acting on an extradition order issued by Charlemagne, Bishop Theodulph of Orléans sent a *posse* of armed men to drag the fugitive out of the Basilica and bring him back to suffer his punishment. Alcuin and his monks refused them entrance, standing up for the fugitive's right of sanctuary. The townspeople and peasants soon went on the attack with cudgels against the armed outsiders, who (rumor said) were desecrating the church of their patron saint. The monks got entangled in the brawl: fighting to keep the Orléans contingent out, but also to protect them from the mob. Theodulph's men

[69] Alcuin follows his sources (Cicero, Victor, Fortunatianus, and Cassiodorus) closely but very selectively. Throughout, he ignores (among other things) all of their references to conditions specific to ancient Roman legal practice. See Howell's discussion in Alcuin, *Rhetoric of Alcuin*, 22–33; and Wallach, *Alcuin and Charlemagne*, 35–47.

[70] Howell in Alcuin, *Rhetoric of Alcuin*, 62; and see Wallach, *Alcuin and Charlemagne*, 73–82 ("Legal Elements of the *Rhetoric*").

[71] For a vivid portrait of Alcuin's extensive travels (both as a member of Charlemagne's itinerant court and on his own), see Bullough, *Alcuin*.

[72] See e.g. [Alcuin], *Epistolae Karolini aevi* [*Monumenta Germaniae historica*, vol. 4, ed. Dümmler], 41 [letter 15], 154 [letter 107] (cited hereafter as [Alcuin], *Epistolae*); and Wallach, *Alcuin and Charlemagne*, 79–80. For Alcuin's acquaintance with Frankish courts generally, see Wallach, *Alcuin and Charlemagne*, 97–140.

[73] We do not know the nature of the crime but it was clearly serious. For accounts of the case, see Shoemaker, *Sanctuary and Crime*, 47–8, 75–7; Meens, "Sanctuary, Penance, and Dispute Settlement," 277–300; Collins, *Carolingian Debate Over Sacred Space*, 1–3, 91–120; and Wallach, *Alcuin and Charlemagne*, 99–124.

eventually succeeded in capturing the fugitive. Theodulf wrote to Charlemagne accusing the monks of actively participating in the brawl and naming Alcuin as instigator. Alcuin managed to clear himself, but Charlemagne, who was furious, appointed a special judge—one of the *missi dominici*—to try the monks on the charge of inciting a riot. In the course of this trial, which lasted several weeks, Alcuin acted as advocate for the accused, defending himself by extension (not entirely successfully: some of the monks were found guilty and had to undergo a punishment of lashes and chains).

Charlemagne certainly aspired to ensure procedural fairness in his courts. A capitulary from *c.*801–13 orders the *missi*:

> Do justice openly, correctly, and equitably to churches, to widows, to orphans and all others, without fraud, without corruption, without . . . abusive delays, and be watchful that all your subordinates do likewise, if you wish to be rewarded by God and by [the king] . . . . Above all be careful that no one [says] to the parties, with the idea of thwarting or delaying the exercise of justice, 'Be quiet until the *missi* are gone; we'll arrange everything later among ourselves!'[74]

As the final line suggests, such mandates were necessary, since Charlemagne's courts were not exactly citidels of justice. One of Bishop Theodulf's poems, "Verses Against Judges," describes the bribes that litigants regularly offered him in his work as one of Charlemagne's itinerant judges. "One promises crystal and Eastern jewels if I help him gain someone else's fields," declares the judge.

> [Another] in a secret whisper addresses my assistant . . . . 'I own a certain vessel ornamented with ancient figures . . . . This shall I deliver to the [judge] . . . if only he will accede to my wish' . . . . They rush to corrupt me, nor can they think that men like me are so easy unless such a one has been there before.[75]

Theodulf also gives a vivid portrayal of the judge who prefers drink to justice, and who comes to the court "all hiccups, tipsy and breathless, . . . gapes, drops, is nauseous" (93 [ll. 407–8]).

[74] "Deinde ut iustitias ecclesiarum, viduarum, orfanorum et reliquorum omnium sine ullo malo ingenio et sine ullo iniusto pretio vel sine ulla dilatione aut non necessaria mora plenitur et inreprehensibiliter et iuste ac recte per omnia faciatis, sive ad vos ipsos sive ad iuniores vestros seu ad quemcumque hominem pertinet, ut exinde et apud Deum mercedem et apud dominum nostrum bonam recipiatis retributionem . . . . Deinde obervate etiam valde, ne aut vos ipsi aut aliquis, quantum vos praevidere potestis, in vestro ministerio in hoc malo ingenio deprehensus fiat, ut dicatis: 'tacete, donec illi missi transeant, et postea faciamus nobis invicem iustitias!'" Boretius, ed., *Monumenta Germaniae historica*, 1:184; and see Halphen, *Charlemagne et l'empire carolingian*, 139.

[75] "Versus Tedulfi episcopi contra iudices" in Theodulf, *Theodulf of Orléans*, 88–90 [ll. 170–260] (all citations to Theodulf are to this poem, hereafter cited in the text; I have eliminated line breaks and removed initial line capitalization).

No one mentioned bribes or a drunken judge in the trial of the monks. But in letters to Charlemagne and others, Alcuin did vehemently protest the trial's procedures: "Surely it was not by your authority," he writes Charlemagne,

> [that] Teotbertus was sent, and remained among us for nineteen days; [and] our accusers with him? He flogged whomever he wished; sent into chains whomever he wished; . . . he called into your presence those whom it pleased him [to call].[76]

In fact, the judge, acting as *missus ad hoc*, may well have "called . . . those whom it pleased him [to call]" and not those whom it did not. In the "Verses Against Judges," Theodulf urges judges not to "allow whole hours to pass with vacuous speeches." They should "[i]mpose silence on the pleaders, both defense and prosecution, . . . each yelping his case" (100 [ll. 657, 669–70]). Alcuin based his insistence that the judge should have allowed both sides to plead their cases in part on the precedent of the Apostle Paul, who was permitted to defend himself before the Roman governor Felix (Acts 24).[77] This argument draws on precisely the passage he had used in his definition of judicial oratory in the *Dialogue*:

> Judicial [oratory] is the kind in which there is accusation and defense, as in the Acts of the Apostles, [where] we read how the Jews through a certain orator, Tertullus, accused Paul before Felix, the governor, and how Paul defended himself before the same governor. (70–3)[78]

The biblical reference, like Alcuin's classical sources, both reflects and serves as a model for trials in contemporary courts: both accuser and defendant must have an opportunity to vigorously argue their sides, with all the oratorical tools at their disposal.

Such real-world experience similarly informed Alcuin's vivid portraits of legal pleading-in-action in the *Dialogue*. Describing how a plaintiff should represent a crime of impulse, for instance, Alcuin explains that the plaintiff must

> amplify the violence and, as it were, the agitation and passion of spirit that caused the deed. And he ought to show [*ostendere*] how great is the strength of love, how

[76] "Numquid non missus auctoritatis vestrae, vir venerabilis Teotbertus, decem et novem dies pro hac inquisitione inter nos fuit; etiam et per vices accusatores nostri cum eo? Quos volebat flagellavit; quos volebat in catenam misit; quos volebat iurare fecit; quos placuit, ad vestram vocavit praesentiam." [Alcuin], *Epistolae*, 402 [letter 249]. For the five letters on the case, see 393–404 [letters 245–49].

[77] This letter is lost but Charlemagne's refutation reveals the nature of Alcuin's argument. See [Alcuin], *Epistolae*, 400 [letters 247]; and Wallach, *Alcuin and Charlemagne*, 79–80, 115.

[78] Dating the text to 801–4, Wallach argues that the *Dialogue* was a protest against the procedures used in the case, and that the text thus echoes (rather than helping formulate) Alcuin's argument in the case. He argues that Alcuin here shows Charlemagne "that legal procedure is based on an established system whose theory finds expression in the art of rhetoric and that this system includes accusation and defense, plaintiff and defendant, and the witnesses of both parties" (117, and generally 48–59, 105–26).

> profound the disturbance in an angered mind, or [one] troubled by [the] passions [that produced] the impulse; and he ought to do this in such a way that it will not seem strange [to the court that] a man disturbed by these tumults ... leaped onward to envisage, and then to direct the crime. (94–5)

Inviting the reader to envision the legal scene, Alcuin insists that the student must learn not just to "amplify" the violence narratively but learn how to *perform* "the agitation and passion of spirit that caused the deed," not merely telling but "show[ing]."

It turns out, however, that performance can go very wrong, if one is not careful. All the things that the pleader must perform—the "agitation and passion of spirit," the "profound ... disturbance," the "angered mind," the emotional "tumults"—have a tendency to produce a host of bodily and vocal deformations. One must take extra care, Alcuin warns Charlemagne. Words "should be pronounced with undistorted mouth, ... and without unseemly jeers or undue loudness of tone" (144–5). They

> should *not* be pronounced with an inhalation of breath; *nor* with an excessive quantity of breath; *nor* should they be ground out of the throat; *nor* allowed to resound in the mouth; *nor* should they be made harsh by the gnashing of the teeth; *nor* uttered by lips lax and open; ... *nor* should you shout with unbridled yelling; *nor* destroy your case with showy delivery .... [T]he speaker must necessarily take heed that ... his lips are *not* distorted, that his jaws are *not* excessively distended, that his countenance is *not* inexpressive, that his eyes are *not* fastened upon the floor, that his neck is *not* inclined to one side, and that his eyebrows are *neither* raised nor lowered .... There are truly infinite movements and expressions like these. (140–1, emphasis added)[79]

Infinite potential bodily errors? This last point is particularly disheartening.

Delivery to the rescue. We have already seen Alcuin's insistence that delivery surpasses all the other skills in importance. To emphasize the point, he asks Charlemagne: "But perhaps you think otherwise, my King"? "No," on the contrary replies Charlemagne (ever the good student). In fact, can Alcuin please say more about delivery? And, indeed, Alcuin has a lot more to say, for he proceeds to devote pages to it. Delivery, it turns out, is hard work: "[i]t is exacting," explains Alcuin, and not "so much art as it is hard labor." Learning delivery consists in a rigorous program of vocal and physical training from youth: those who would be "judged worthy of [performing] in public" must pursue "exercises in voice and diction ... with great care from [their] very early years." Such a program is

[79] Howell includes the last line in the Latin text (140) but does not translate it.

inherent in the very definition of delivery: "Delivery may be defined [as] the disciplining of the body." It involves "the regulating of the voice and body according to the dignity of thought and word." Learning delivery means learning to "control your voice, breath, body movement, and tongue" and thereby make yourself "decent" [*decet*] (138–41).

The disciplined decorum, dignity, and decency that delivery teaches, worldly as it sounds, is not merely worldly. When Alcuin's ancient sources stress that delivery produces "faith" and brings "glory," they are speaking of its contribution to the orator's credibility and the fame it can bring. Alcuin echoes them: mastery of delivery brings faith [*fidem*] and glory [*laudem*] (140–1). But he is referring to the relationship between delivery and the Christian virtues Charlemagne describes soon after: Christ (Charlemagne says) has promised "that our faithful... devotion... will bring a reward of eternal glory" (150–1). Scholars often comment on the apparent disconnect between rhetoric and the virtues in the *Dialogue on Rhetoric and on Virtues*. And yet the two are intimately linked. That Alcuin's discussion of delivery flows immediately into his famous discussion of the Christian (as opposed to pagan) virtues (146–7, 150–1) is no coincidence. For it turns out that his central precept for Christians is precisely the kind of bodily control that delivery mandates. The well-ordered Christian soul, he explains, must "rule what is lower, that is, the body," while "lov[ing] what is higher, that is, God" (152–3).

This discipline has its analogue in the decorum, dignity, and decency of the physical space of the court itself. In fact, Alcuin interrupts his discussion of impassioned live pleading to describe the courtroom, as if the stability of its fixtures might steady that dizzying scene of "agitation," "passion of spirit," "tumults," "violence." He insists that this description is a digression, not really part of the art of rhetoric, and in fact, it is almost wholly original to Alcuin.[80] To justify it, he puts a series of questions in Charlemagne's mouth, making it appear that he is merely indulging the young king's curiosity. But he clearly wants readers to visualize the setting for his lessons: aspiring legal orators are not to picture themselves in the vast and chaotic Roman lawcourts of his sources but instead in a Christian court of law, whose orderly arrangements represent justice and truth. "How many parties are customarily present in the courts of law?" asks Charlemagne. "Four," declares Alcuin, and each has a distinctive "official duty" (or "office") to discharge: the plaintiff must "amplify"; the defendant "diminish"; the witnesses bring forth "truth"; the judge bring forth "justice" (92–3). Since Alcuin has described "the persons" of the court, requests Charlemagne, can he also

[80] See Wallach, *Alcuin and Charlemagne*, 75–6. A number of later texts repeat what Wallach calls Alcuin's "*ordo*" (his courtroom description), including Petrus Helias' *Summa* (*c.*1150), the *Rhetorica ecclesiastica* (1159–79), and Geoffrey of Vinsauf's *Documentum* (1213 or later). See Fredborg, "Petrus Helias's *Summa*," 169; Geoffrey, *Documentum*, 71; and Wallach, *Alcuin and Charlemagne*, 76.

"describe the place of each in the court"? "I shall touch upon that," responds Alcuin, "although it has less to do with the precepts of rhetoric than with the decorum of official duty [*officii decorem*]" (94–5).

In using the phrase *officii decorem*—sometimes translated as "the dignity of the office" or "dignitary duties" but, literally, the decorum of duty (its grace, beauty, or harmony)—Alcuin perhaps has in mind Cicero's treatise *De officiis* (*On Duties*), which medieval scholars tended to treat as the ultimate authority on worldly ethics. For Alcuin as for Cicero, decorum (fittingness or appropriateness) defines duty. Here, the decorum of duty—realized in the pleader's body—is also visually realized in the spaces of the court.

> *Alcuin*: The judge sits on the tribunal, and before him in the middle of the court, the case for reward or for punishment is placed.... The plaintiff is on [his] left, the defendant on [his] right, and the witnesses in the rear.
>
> *Charlemagne*: Does each have his own distinctive insignia?
>
> *Alcuin*: They have. The judge is armed with the scepter of justice [equity: *aequitatis*], the plaintiff with the dagger of malice, the defendant with the shield of piety, and the witnesses with the trumpet of truth. (94–7)

Not only is delivery the ultimate godly discipline. Alcuin's visibly imagined courtroom—in which he locates that godly discipline—also offers a spatial and iconographic rendering of the virtues that must inhabit it. The list of judicial "insignia" that he gives in his courtroom description appears also in a letter to Aethelhard, Archbishop of Canterbury, *c.*802–4, in which Alcuin prays: "May your right hand be armed with the scepter of equity and your left hand distinguished with the shield of piety."[81] This imagery draws on the references to the throne, scepter, trumpets, shield, and sword that appear in a number of biblical passages, all associated with judgment and justice. These describe God on His "throne" with His "sceptre," meting out "justice" against "iniquity" (Psalms 44:7–8), donning "true judgment" and "justice" as armor, and taking "equity [*aequitatem*] for an invincible shield" (Wisdom 5:19–20).[82] The Letter to the Ephesians 6:16–17 counsels: "In all things tak[e] the shield of faith, [and] take unto you the helmet of salvation, and the sword of the Spirit (which is the word of God)."

It may at first seem surprising that in Alcuin's courtroom description, the plaintiff is necessarily armed with "malice" and the defendant with "piety": surely some plaintiffs are pious and some defendants malicious. But Alcuin's preference

[81] "Sit tua dextra sceptro equitatis armata et sinistra clipeo pietatis honesta." [Alcuin], *Epistolae*, 480 [letter 311].

[82] For all biblical passages, I quote from the Douay Reims Bible (which translates from the Latin Vulgate), though I occasionally modify the translation to more closely align with the Vulgate passages my sources would have known.

for clemency over retribution is typical of medieval theorists generally.[83] Medieval images often pitted the pious shield against the malicious sword or dagger. For instance, in one Carolingian psalter, the righteous hold up their "invincible shield[s]" to protect themselves (Psalms 63:3–5), while one of the iniquitous smiles maliciously as he sharpens his dagger on a whetstone.[84] The most important non-biblical source for such images was the fourth-century poet Prudentius' *Psychomachia*, which recounted the battle of the soul against evil.[85] Images of this battle appear in countless medieval manuscripts, showing Virtue (in various guises) using a shield to protect herself from Vice, who often has a sword or dagger. One such image, for instance, portrays a trial pitting "Greed's" malicious dagger against "Reason's" shield of piety, which protects the staff (a sort of "scepter of justice") that is a sign of her governance, while also protecting the monks who carry the law behind her (fig. 3.2).[86] If the psychomachia involved a trial of the soul, it was often figured judicially, linking the personal and the public judicial agon. Prudentius' story of this "trial" ends in the "courts" of the Temple of Wisdom, where Sapientia sits as judge on her tribunal, "reign[ing] for ever on her beauteous throne."[87]

Both the psychomachia and the proverbial "invincible shield" and "spiritual sword" were associated not merely with justice and judgment but with that ultimate moment of judgment: the Last Judgment.[88] The Book of Wisdom

[83] On the devil as prosecutor, see Shoemaker, "Devil at Law," 579–86. And see e.g. Alain de Lille, *Art of Preaching*, 153 (arguing that advocates should plead for the guilty); and Maxwell, *Art of Medieval Urbanism*, on the general medieval emphasis on mercy as equitable justice (244–5 and note 109). I am indebted here to Maxwell's discussion of Romanesque iconographic and architectural "judicial theater" generally (242), especially his analysis of the following (239–47): the figure of sword and shield in medieval renderings of Tertullian and of Prudentius' *Psychomachia*; the centrality of judgment to the psychomachia; the relationship between the personal psychomachia and the eschatological Last Judgment; the relationship between Solomon and Christ as judges in such portrayals; and depictions of the Temple of Wisdom in which the architecture of the "seat of justice, or *tribunal*" where Sapientia sits as judge is "the handwork of the Virtues" (243).

[84] Psalm 63 in Eadwine Psalter (*c.*1155–60), a copy of the image in the Utrecht Psalter (c.816–835). For the medieval theological use of "pugio," see also Spanish Dominican monk Ramon Martí's *Pugio fidei* (*Dagger of Faith*) (*c.*1278).

[85] On the particular popularity of Prudentius' *Psychomachia* in Anglo-Saxon England, see Karkov, "Broken Bodies and Singing Tongues," 115–16.

[86] St. Gallen Stiftsbibliothek Cod. Sang. 135 (*c.*1000), p. 420, https://www.e-codices.unifr.ch/en/csg/0135/438/0/ (accessed March 7, 2021). See similarly "Long-Suffering Patience" against "Anger" in a *c.*900 Prudentius manuscript, Bern Burgerbibliothek Cod. 264, pp. 78–9, https://www.e-codices.unifr.ch/en/bbb/0264/78 (accessed March 7, 2021).

[87] Prudentius, *Prudentius* [Loeb], 1:343 [*Psychomachia*, 912–15]). For an example of such images, see e.g. St. Gallen, Stiftsbibliothek, Cod. Sang. 135, p. 438, https://www.e-codices.unifr.ch/en/csg/0135/438/0/ (accessed March 7, 2021).

[88] On the appearance of Christ's "invincible shield" and "spiritual sword" in the *New Minster Charter* (966), King Edgar's coronation in 973, and their association with the Last Judgment, see Deshman, *Eye and Mind*, 122. For a pointed depiction of a woman under the Last Judgment sword holding the Trinitarian shield to defend herself, see the image from the *Lambeth Apocalypse* (*c.*1265–74) in Wogan-Browne, "'Cest livre liseez…chescun jour,'" 241–2 (fig. 18.1). On "the Last Judgment [as] an eschatological psychomachia in symbolic form" in later Doomsday plays, and specifically the "forensics" of the Last Judgment in trial scenes in which devils act as prosecutors, see Leigh, "Doomsday Mystery Play," 218 and note 21.

Fig. 3.2 "Reason" with her staff of justice and shield of piety withstands the malicious dagger of "Greed" in an illustration of Prudentius' *Psychomachia* (*c.*1000).
St. Gallen, Stiftsbibliothek, Cod. Sang. 135, p. 420—Carmina.

5:14–24 describes the Lord taking up "true judgment" and "equity for an invincible shield" as part of an apocalyptic day of reckoning on which He sends "sinners [to] hell" and the "just... receive a kingdom of glory... at the [right] hand of the Lord." In the 790s, both Alcuin and Charlemagne were preoccupied with the Last Judgment. Many believed that the year 800 (or thereabouts) would be year 6000 of the world, and that the Day of Judgment was at hand. "[W]hat a dangerous day," wrote Alcuin in a letter to Higbald, Bishop of Lindisfarne in 797, "what a fearful judgment threatens us at an uncertain time."[89] In the same letter to Aethelhard in which Alcuin described him "armed with the scepter of equity" and "the shield of piety," he wrote of his certainty that "[t]he bitter day which no one can escape will make haste and not delay." He feared that, "oppressed by the weight of my sins, I will not dare to raise my head in the sight of my Judge."[90] It was during this period that Last Judgment scenes began to appear regularly in

[89] [Alcuin], *Epistolae*, 182 [letter 124]; quoted in Garrison, "'Quid Hinieldus cum Christo?'" 240. On Alcuin's and Charlemagne's apocalyptic concerns (and those of the end of the eighth century generally), see Gabriele, *Empire of Memory*, 125–6; and Fried, "Awaiting the Last Days," 285 (on the prevalence of Last Judgment imagery in Old High German and Anglo-Saxon poetry); and see Palmer, *Apocalypse in the Early Middle Ages*, 130–58 on the complexity of reckoning the date of the apocalypse in the eighth and early ninth centuries.

[90] "Festinabit et non tardabit dies amara, quam nullus effugere valet.... Sed quantum me peccatorem scio, tantum me fateor metuere illam, ne forte, pondere peccatorum suppressus, caput in conspectu iudicis mei elevare non audeam." [Alcuin], *Epistolae*, 480 [letter 311].

churches.[91] While the courtroom, in Alcuin's description, stages the psychomachia's battle of the soul, it is also, more specifically, a Last Judgment scene resembling both verbal and visual depictions of the period. In a *c.*800 ivory panel, for instance (fig. 3.3), Christ serves as judge seated on his tribunal, as "the case for reward or punishment plays out" before him. Angels serve as witnesses blowing the "trumpets of truth" in "the rear" of the scene.[92] The saved enter heaven to Christ's right (the side of righteousness) and the condemned fall into hellmouth on His left (the *sinister* side), in the longstanding left–right symbolism on which Alcuin draws when he places his defendant to the right of the judge and his plaintiff to the left.[93] These positions call more specifically on images of the "Deesis": a scene in which Mary stands to Christ's right, defending the souls on trial (as lawyer for humankind), and John the Baptist stands to His right, sometimes prosecuting the souls on trial and urging damnation.[94] This configuration would become a standard part of Last Judgment iconography, underlining the parallel between earthly and heavenly pleading.

Given the weight of theological-allegorical imagery in the courtroom that Alcuin describes in the *Dialogue*, it is hard to reconcile this depiction with his claim that he is portraying ordinary worldly courts, and that Charlemagne can understand through "daily practice" all that he describes (90–1). And, indeed, the

[91] See Klein, "Introduction: The Apocalypse in Medieval Art," 165 (the fresco at Müstair [c.800] is one of the earliest surviving examples).

[92] Victoria & Albert Museum, Sculpture Collection, Accession number 253–1867. For the source of this image, see Apocalypse (Revelation) 8:2, which describes the "seven angels standing in the presence of God [with] seven trumpets" announcing the apocalypse. The panel, which probably originally served as the cover for an apocalypse manuscript, was created in southern Germany or northern Italy, where Charlemagne was proclaimed emperor in 800; it ended up in Rheims, approximately midway between Charlemagne's court in Aachen and Tours, where Alcuin became abbot in 796. See https://collections.vam.ac.uk/item/O90891/the-last-judgement-panel-unknown/ (accessed March 1, 2021).

[93] Alcuin has just specified that "the case [is] placed" "before [the judge] in the middle of the court," and then writes that the plaintiff and defendant are to the left and right "of the case." So the left–right perspective seems clearly that of the judge, not a viewer of the scene. For biblical left–right orientation, see the parables of the wise and foolish virgins and the separation of the sheep and goats in Matthew 25:33–4, 41, 46, in which those to the left "go into everlasting punishment" and those to the right "into life everlasting." Through at least the eighth century, these parables, with their left–right orientation, dominated images of the Last Judgment. When God's hand descends from the heavens in such images, it is always His right hand (the *Dextera Dei*). The inscription in Christ's right hand on the ivory Last Judgment panel is from Matthew 25:34, where Christ addresses those "on his right hand" with the words: "Come, ye blessed of my Father, possess you the kingdom prepared for you."

[94] The Deesis began to appear in the seventh century and was, by the tenth or eleventh century, a fixture in Last Judgment images. See the discussions in Labatt, *Emerging Iconographies*, 113–17; and Whittemore, *Mosaics of Haghia Sophia*, 22–4 (in the Deesis, the "Mother of God and St. John intercede for mankind, *pro ecclesis*, before the Supreme Judge" [24]). In a seventh-century Deesis (the earliest surviving, in Santa Maria Antiqua Church in Rome), Mary opens her hands pleadingly, while John points, in what appears a denunciation. While John does often act for the defense of humankind in such images, in the Bible his role is to denounce sin, and images tend to place him on the side of hell, portraying him with a prosecutorial dagger or sword (while Mary is on the side of heaven with a lily). For a discussion of the relationship between Charlemagne's court and mosaics like the ninth-century Deesis in the Hagia Sophia Museum (Istanbul), see James, *Mosaics in the Medieval World*, 293–333. On legal analysis in Last Judgment theology and the figure of Mary as pleader in the later Middle Ages, see Shoemaker, "Devil at Law" (especially 582–6).

Fig. 3.3 Last Judgment panel (*c.*800): Christ the Judge presides over the case for reward (on His right) and punishment (on His left) while angels blow "trumpets of truth."

real Anglo-Saxon and Frankish courts Alcuin would have known seem to bear little if any resemblance to the courtroom he describes. As I have suggested, Frankish courts—usually held in palace great halls, churches, or outdoors at traveling assizes—were far more crowded (and probably noisy) than the courtroom he describes. All free men had to attend the county courts. And present at most trials were a dizzying variety of "judgment-finders" and others, in attendance at both the county courts and the royal courts: bishops, abbots, dukes, counts, royal vassals, *gastalds*, *scabini* or *rachymburgi*, *pagenses*, *francae personae*, *procures*, *fideles*, notaries "and the rest of our faithful subjects" (as one charter describes those present in the courtroom).[95] Major trials usually included a still larger assembly. In one 782 trial, the bench alone included the king, three archbishops, a dozen or so counts, and forty-four *bonihomines*: men from the region of Trier now designated *scabini* (lay judges or jurors).[96] Bishop Theodulf describes these noisy courtrooms, full of "agitation and quarrels, . . . contention of voices" (like "raucous geese and black ravens . . . screech[ing] in chorus all at once"). To silence the noise, he urges the judge to "make threats," and have the doorkeeper try to "hold the breathless crowd in abeyance so that the raging throng does not rush in pell-mell, and so that the hall will not be overfilled with plaintive tumult" (99 [ll. 635–9], 94 [ll. 425–7]).

However, if we take Alcuin's claim to be representing real courts seriously, we can in fact see in his depiction what might be a trimmed-down, schematic version of such a court. Spatial arrangements, furnishings, attire, and physical objects often served allegorical-theological functions in depictions of courts, but so did they in actual courts. We have no contemporaneous images of Charlemagne presiding over his court, but we do have a space where he in fact presided: the chapel in the Church of the Holy Mother of God beside Charlemagne's palace at Aachen, which is still largely intact.[97] Alcuin was in residence in Aachen as it was

[95] Quoted in McKitterick, Rosamond. "King on the Move," 165. For these terms, see the sources on Frankish courts listed above.

[96] Nelson, *King and Emperor*, 200. It is not, perhaps, surprising to see large crowds at trials in Charlemagne's court, given that when Charlemagne bathed in the hot springs at Aachen, as many as one hundred members of his court bathed with him. See Einhard, *Two Lives of Charlemagne* (trans. Ganz), 34.

[97] My discussion of the chapel is indebted to the detailed analysis in Doig, "Charlemagne's Palace Chapel at Aachen." While we have no portraits of Charlemagne, we have many portraits of his grandson Charles the Bald, some of which draw on Last Judgment imagery while representing what appears to be his actual court. These images routinely show Charles "on [a] tribunal . . . armed with the scepter" (of justice), flanked by a figure bearing a shield on the left and one bearing a dagger (or sword) on the right: figures that pointedly recall the Deesis of the Last Judgment. See the discussion in McKitterick, "Charles the Bald and the Image of Kingship," noting the absence of contemporaneous images of Charlemagne (30) and reproducing two portraits of Charles that clearly draw on Last Judgment iconography (29 and 36, upper left). McKitterick notes the juxtaposition of the latter with the Adoration of the Lamb (iconographically associated with the Last Judgment). On the Carolingian "association of a terrestrial ruler with the intercessors of the Deesis to liken him to the celestial ruler Christ," and the use of this figure in the portrait of Charles in his Munich prayerbook, see Deshman, *Eye and Mind*, 121, and note 90. For the later association of a penitent Charlemagne himself with the Last Judgment, see Feltman, "Charlemagne's Sin."

being constructed (*c*.786–96), and saw the space as key to the ecclesiastical and liturgical reforms he proposed for implementation there.[98] In his *Life of Charlemagne* (*c*.817–36), Einhard describes the chapel as one of Charlemagne's major achievements.[99] Given Charlemagne's preoccupation with the Last Judgment in the 790s, it is perhaps not surprising that the domed chapel represented the Day of Judgment, both visually and spatially. As Allan Doig has pointed out, the chapel's architecture, furnishings, materials, and spatial measurements correspond in numerous respects to those describing the Last Judgment and Heavenly Jerusalem in Apocalypse (Revelation) 4 and 21. We know from medieval sources that the original painting in the dome depicted either the twenty-four Elders of the Apocalypse adoring the Lamb of God (historically associated with the Last Judgment) or Christ in Majesty in His heavenly court, surrounded by the Elders and seated on His "throne set in heaven" (Apocalypse 4:2–4), preparing to judge those below (fig. 3.4).[100] Directly below the dome is Charlemagne's matching throne, which has (astonishingly) survived for well over a millennium (fig. 3.5).[101] This throne, with its six steps, replicates that of King Solomon, whom God "set . . . upon the throne of Israel [and] appointed [king], to do judgment and justice" (1 Kings 10:9, 19). Christians viewed Solomon's throne as a forerunner of Christ-the-Judge's.[102]

The palace's main axis served as a royal processional route between Charlemagne's two thrones: that in the *Aula Regia*, where he presided over legal proceedings; and that in the chapel, where he presided over religious proceedings beneath the dome representing the Last Judgment.[103] The route, in conjunction with the image in the dome, drew the parallel between temporal judgment and the spiritual judgment that served as its model.[104] Bishop Theodulf advises judges to make this parallel explicit:

[98] See Doig, "Charlemagne's Palace Chapel," 192–3 and *History of the Church*, 109; and Kleinbauer, "Charlemagne's Palace Chapel," 2 (for the construction start date of *c*.786). Construction was completed *c*.798, two years after Alcuin had left for Tours.

[99] Einhard, *Two Lives of Charlemagne* (trans. Ganz), 30.

[100] On the debate about whether the original image in the cupola depicted the Adoration of the Lamb or Christ in Majesty, see Noble, *Images, Iconoclasm, and Carolingians*, 418, note 189. The Christ in Majesty currently in the dome is a nineteenth-century speculative reconstruction. See the discussion in Shaffer, "Recreating the Past," especially 35–6.

[101] See Doig, "Charlemagne's Palace Chapel," 183 (fig. 9.3), 187, on the dating of much of the throne to *c*.800 (by "dendrochronology"), and 182 on the relationship to the throne of Solomon. Doig notes that the moment "when Christ came again to judge the living and the dead . . . was constantly before the eyes of the Emperor in the decoration of the dome. . . . When Christ came again in power, he would occupy the throne in Judgement"; Charlemagne's own throne was "an intermediary place between earth and heaven" ("Charlemagne's Palace Chapel," 188).

[102] On the association of Frankish kings with Solomon and David, see McKitterick, "Charles the Bald," 31, 34; and Deshman, *Eye and Mind*, 201–15. On the importance of Solomon's throne in judicial iconography and architecture generally, see Maxwell, *Art of Medieval Urbanism*, 242–3.

[103] Doig, "Charlemagne's Palace Chapel," 182–3.

[104] Charlemagne's decrees banning the holding of trials in churches and their atria suggests how common the practice was (Deimling, "Courtroom," 33). And see Brundage, "'My Learned Friend,'" 185–6, on the practice of holding ecclesiastical court sessions on the porches of churches: a practice banned in some places in the later Middle Ages but that nevertheless persisted.

Fig. 3.4 Christ in His heavenly court, surrounded by the Elders and seated on His "throne set in heaven." Charlemagne's Palace Chapel, Aachen (speculative restoration of *c.*796 chapel dome).
Peter Horree/Alamy Stock Photo.

Fig. 3.5 Charlemagne's throne in his Palace Chapel in Aachen (*c.*800), replicating that of King Solomon, whom God "set . . . upon the throne of Israel [and] appointed [king], to do judgment and justice."
Image Professionals GmbH/Alamy Stock Photo.

> When you have occupied the presiding chair, looking about at the people, address them in the following language: . . . 'Be apprised of justice and the celestial commandments, which the Father on high decreed from the vault of the sky.'
>
> (94–5 [ll. 446–50])

Many medieval trials were in fact held in churches that had images of "the Father on high" in their vaulted ceilings or Last Judgment scenes (often depicted on a tympanum above the portico). From at least the twelfth century (and probably earlier), such scenes were routinely painted on courtroom walls and ceilings: in churches, palaces, town halls, and elsewhere. Some show a split scene—the temporal court below mirroring the heavenly court above—as in the painting of heavenly and earthly justice created for the city of Würzburg *c.*1400 (fig. 3.6).[105] In such images, the visible earthly court serves as artist's model for God's court while, at the same time, God's court serves as the model for the earthly court.

Alcuin seems to envision a courtroom of this kind, situating it in the Aachen chapel where, from his tribunal (sources repeatedly note), Charlemagne had a direct view onto the altars.[106] There (in the words of the *Dialogue*), "before him in the middle of the court," those pleading to God during prayer made "the case for [divine] reward or for punishment," just as those pleading to Charlemagne during legal proceedings made "the case for [temporal] reward or for punishment." If Charlemagne looked up, he would be reminded of his role as the Vicar of Christ in Majesty: exercising earthly judgment until the day when the Judge of Judges would return to judge all humankind; punishing the lawbreakers described in Apocalypse 21:8 ("the abominable, and murderers, and whoremongers . . ."); chastening plaintiffs with their daggers of malice; rewarding those who used their voices and bodies with godly decorum as shields of piety, —those who inspired faith in virtuous causes in the holy space of the courtroom.

[105] On Last Judgment images in courtrooms, see Resnik and Curtis, *Representing Justice*, 33–7; Zapalac, *In His Image and Likeness*, 26–54; Edgerton, *Pictures and Punishment*, 22–45; Huygebaert, et al., ed., *Art of Law*, 15–34 (reproducing the Würzburg image [31]); and the extensive catalog of Last Judgment images in medieval and early modern German courthouses in Troescher, "Weltgerichtsbilder in Rathäusern und Gerichtsstätten." And see fig. 0.2 (p. 14), which shows a Last Judgment image above the judges' heads.

[106] See Doig, "Charlemagne's Palace Chapel," 193; and Kleinbauer, "Charlemagne's Palace Chapel," 2.

Fig. 3.6 Heavenly justice offers a model for earthly justice in a Würzburg courtroom (*c.*1400).

Abteilung Kunst der Diözese Würzburg, Thomas Obermeier, 2021.

Boncompagno da Signa (c.1165–1240): The Leaky Body as "Organic Instrument" and Courtroom Trickster

Medieval discussions of delivery could, like Alcuin's, serve as a form of "conduct literature," akin to that in lawyers' manuals like Durand's.[107] But other discussions of delivery offered a far less normative vision than Alcuin's, and were far less optimistic about the project of taming the body. Among these was Boncompagno da Signa's. We have already seen Boncompagno praising lawyers as "priests" and "soldiers" who fight for justice.[108] As professor of rhetoric at the University of Bologna, he was in fact dedicated to training future lawyers. He had been briefly employed as a notary, and was interested in the practical application of rhetoric to law throughout his career: in 1201, he wrote a treatise proposing revisions to the statutes of the Commune of Bologna, deploring the fact that their drafters lacked all understanding of the art of rhetoric.[109] His commitment to the rhetorical training of lawyers is clear in his prefaces. In the "Testament" with which he begins his *Ancient Rhetoric* (1215–26), he declares that Rhetorica is "empress of the liberal arts" but was also born of law (both civil and canon) and that law is the noblest field for exercising rhetorical skills.[110] His *Newest Rhetoric* (1235) (he explains) is for "students of both [civil and canon] law," who "receive almost no help in learning the disciplines of the liberal arts."[111]

Like Alcuin, Boncompagno does in fact dedicate much of his *Newest Rhetoric* to forensic oratory.[112] Also like Alcuin, he stresses the practical application of his lessons: they are equally useful to plaintiffs, defendants, lawyers, and judges, who must learn to assess the performances they see in court. However, unlike Alcuin, Boncompagno is not interested in recovering ancient rhetorical theory. The precepts in the *Rhetorica ad Herennium*—familiarly called "Cicero's new rhetoric"—are utterly unsuited to contemporary courts, he declares. In fact, he

[107] On rhetoric books as conduct literature, see Johnston, "Ciceronian Rhetoric and Ethics"; and "Treatment of Speech"; and see Brundage, "'My Learned Friend,'" 185, 188–96, on lawyers guides as conduct manuals.

[108] Boncompagno, *Opera omnia* [*Rhetorica novissima*, 9.3.10]. All citations to Boncompagno are to Steven M. Wight's online edition of the *Opera omnia* (https://www.scrineum.it/scrineum/wight/index.htm, accessed July 9, 2021), with the title of Boncompagno's text and its section numbers in brackets (hereafter cited in the Latin text in my notes). Where I do not give a text title in the brackets, citations are to the *Rhetorica novissima*. Thank you to Eugene Petracca for assistance with translations.

[109] On Boncompagno's employment as a notary, see Witt, "Boncompagno and the Defense of Rhetoric," 2. On the treatise on communal statutes (the *Cedrus*), see Grévin, "Boncompagno vengé." For helpful discussions of Boncompagno's life and work, see Witt, "Boncompagno"; Sutter, *Aus Leben und Schriften*; Raccagni, "Reintroducing the Emperor"; Garbini, "Boncompagno da Signa"; and Tunberg, "What Is Boncompagno's 'Newest Rhetoric'?"

[110] "[S]it artium liberalium imperatrix et utriusque iuris alumpna" [*Boncompagnus*, prol.2.3].

[111] "[F]uit quia studentes in utroque iure modicum vel quasi nullum subsidium... habere poterant de liberalium artium disciplinis" [*Rhetorica novissima*, prol.6].

[112] As Tunberg notes, Boncompagno's *Rhetorica novissima* "is primarily designed to serve the needs of civil and canon lawyers" and teaches the "doctrine of forensic oratory" ("What Is Boncompagno's 'Newest Rhetoric'?" 301, 331).

quips, even his students find the *Rhetorica ad Herennium* "totter[ing]" (or "extinct": *cassata* [prol.7]): hence the need for his own "newest" rhetoric.

Boncompagno dedicates Book 4 to delivery. For him, delivery (*pronuntiatio*) includes not only "bodily pace, vocal extension, the meaning of words, and the manner of offering them" but also the art of dressing well, styling one's hair, and more. We might mistake him for a latter-day Alcuin when he insists, for instance, on the importance of preserving "dignified manners and approved customs" in the courtroom: "[r]everence should be shown to judges"; strive to make the "judges and listeners... benevolent and attentive" and to "find grace with everyone" through "words [and] dignity of gestures."[113] But he was famous for practical jokes, and described as a "notorious trickster" by the chronicler Salimbene da Parma.[114] According to Salimbene, in mocking imitation of a famous miracle worker, Boncompagno once promised a crowd in Bologna that he could fly through the air:

> [O]n the appointed day the entire populace congregated... Boncompagno had constructed wings for himself, and he stood on top of the mountain looking down at them. And after they had been gazing at each other for a long period of time, he shouted down to them audaciously, 'Go, with God's blessing, and let it suffice that you have looked upon the face of Boncompagno.'[115]

In fact, much of his advice to the would-be legal orator or judge takes a gravely solemn tone and then slips in a comic ending. When judges are deciding their cases, they should pay careful attention to body and dress. "According to Solomon," he writes (in far more vivid language than the Vulgate), one "should judge a man according to habit of dress, pace of feet, and smile of teeth," note if he is sufficiently "modest in dress not [to] exceed his class or office" and whether he "laugh[s] without cackling."[116]

[113] "Notantur quidem in eo habitus, gressus corporis, vocis prolatio, significatio verborum et modus proferendi" [4.3.1; and see 4.2.2, et passim]. "Reverentia debet iudicibus exhiberi.... In huiusmodi autem reverentiis honesti mores et approbate consuetudines observentur" [4.3.4]. "Quilibet prolocutor debet per verba, gestuum honestatem, iudicum et auditorum animos sibi reddere benevolos et attentos,... si penes omnes favorabilem gratiam invenire" [4.3.2].

[114] Salimbene, *Chronicle of Salimbene* (1986 trans.), 54. See Carruthers and Ziolkowski, ed. *Medieval Craft of Memory*, 103, on Boncompagno's colorful and aggressive personality and penchant for practical jokes.

[115] Salimbene, *Chronicle of Salimbene* (1986 trans.), 55. See the similar anecdote Boncompagno tells, in which he posted a letter to the university community revealing that in St. Ambrose square at noon on a particular day one "H. of Bavaria [would] "first change an ass into a lion, [then] rever[t] to an ass [but] appear horned just like a goat, [then] assume feathers like an eagle and... fly through the air [but] remain an ass at the end" (etc.). "Everyone should take care [to] face [the] sun, since otherwise none can possibly see the marvels." Teachers and students, "young men and women," "old and young" gathered in the streets and on the roofs of houses, and waited. Finally realizing it was a hoax, they retreated "in shame" [*Boncompagnus*, 1.18.14–15] (trans. Wight, in the footnotes to this passage).

[116] "Cum habitus corporis, gressus pedum et risus dentium iuxta Salomonem de homine iudicent.... [D]ebet esse modestus in habitu, quod suum ordinem vel officium non excedat,... ridere debet sine cachinno" [4.3.1]. See Ecclesiastes 19.26–7 ("[a] man is known by his look, and a wise man, when thou meetest him, is known by his countenance. The attire of the body, and the laughter of the teeth, and the

Boncompagno disapproves of speakers who "exhibit objectionable gestures" when they "rise up for speaking": for instance, "wipe their face off, and fasten their hair back behind the ears, look at their own clothes, and flare their nostrils as if a multitude of bystanders were stinking next to them."[117]

Normative prescriptions notwithstanding, Boncompagno's discussion of delivery strives not primarily to prescribe but to describe. Courtroom behavior is, for him, ever-entertaining. At the same time, he seeks to understand its causes. Two philosophical tendencies underwrite this vision of the human legal comedy. First, he tends to view behavior in medical-physiological-materialist terms: terms often stripped of theological import. At one point, reflecting on memory, he stresses that ancient Greek philosophical materialism is heresy. But what follows suggests his attraction to it. The Athenians, he explains, did not believe in the resurrection of the body, so they piled up the bodies of the dead and let them rot until they became earth. They then planted crops there and these were fruitful. Some claim that everything comes from and returns to the elements. But we of course (he adds hastily) "believe *indubitably* in the Catholic faith."[118]

Boncompagno's discussions of delivery have an even stronger materialist bent. There, he attends primarily to the mechanics of the body as it acts under the influence of the humors, with only occasional references to the role of God in the unfolding of human life (sometimes almost as an afterthought). "[D]ifferences of nature and complexion"—that is, the humors—produce different kinds of delivery, he explains. The "melancholic" speak "timidly," the "sanguine" speak "slowly," "cholerics" speak "furiously," "phlegmatics" speak between these extremes.

> Thus hoarse people and those with speech impediments, and those who have thick lips and long teeth, polypous nostrils, a weak plectrum, or a jocundly obtuse esophagus, are no good at delivery, nor can they display loveliness when they speak.[119]

As he puts it, "that which contains changes that which is contained."[120] The importance of medical-physiological features, he explains, is one reason we cannot consider delivery an "art." And that it is not an art shows that it is "not truly a

gait of the man, shew what he is"). The passage appears commonly in medieval lawyers' manuals. See the examples from Johannes de Deo's thirteenth-century *Cavillationes advocatorum* and Durand's *Speculum* quoted in Brundage, "'My Learned Friend,'" 190, note 30.

[117] Speakers must not "surgunt ad loquendum, et postea damnabiles gestus ostendunt, et abstergunt faciem, reaptant post aures capillos, propria respiciunt indumenta et corrungant nares, ac si videretur eis astantium caterva fetere" [4.2.2].

[118] "[F]idem catholicam indubitanter credimus" [8.1.16] (emphasis added).

[119] "[N]aturarum et complexionum diversitates, mortales diversimode pronuntiare noscuntur. Quidam enim pronuntiant temporale, ut sanguinei, quidam furiose ut cholerici, quidem inter utrumque ut phlegmatici, quidam timide ut naturaliter melancholici" [4.1.1.]. "Rauci siquidem, trauli et habentes grossa labia et longos dentes, poliposas nares, debile plectrum et esophagum iocunde pronuntiare non valent, neque venustatem ostendere in loquendo" [2.3.6].

[120] "[C]ontinens mutat contentum" [8.1.11].

principal part of rhetoric." "[A]rt proceeds from [both] nature and the action of the soul," and "renown in an art is granted . . . on account of one's execution," not because of a peculiarity of "one's organic instrument." Delivery, on the other hand, consists "merely in the organic instrument" [*organicum instrumentum*].[121] However, that "merely" is a ruse: for delivery somehow manages to take up an entire book in the *Rhetorica novissima*, suggesting the crucial importance of the "organic instrument."

Second, Boncompagno tends to treat the physiology driving behavior as the product not of training or divine design but of accident. It is the "accidents" of nature and physiology that determine styles of delivery (another reason we cannot consider delivery an art). He in fact seems to view the "organic" body as itself accidental rather than providential. Even the humors are "accidental complexions": they affect outcomes, but they do not determine them. The same organic features may in fact produce very different effects in different people. "In many people, a heat of ire springs forward, which, like a spark ascending to the heights, kindles equally the memorial cells and confounds [the speaker]." Others, "inflamed by a heat of ire, speak more fluently." (Indeed, Boncompagno confesses modestly that he is one of these: "the stronger the fervor of [my] ire becomes, the more . . . my delivery [is] let loose.")[122] Accidental environmental factors also influence delivery.

> Knowledge, money, nobility, power, freedom, joy, and the favor of the auditors . . . give audacity to a speaker. . . . Ignorance, poverty, baseness, weakness, servitude, sadness, [and] the opposition of the auditors take away audacity from a speaker.

Some speakers may "fluctuate in speaking and cry out with a triumphant bellowing" due to a combination of ignorance and poor impulse control. The same speaker may react differently in different environments. For instance, a speaker may be "brave and speak flamboyantly in the presence of a few people" but "tremble all over in the presence of a numerous multitude, like a twig in a river's stream." Certain experiences may even subject the humors to transformation. Too much "laborious meditation," for instance, can cause "humors [to] run into the esophagus," requiring speakers to cough "to purge their tracheal windpipe."[123] The organic

[121] "Pronuntiatio vero non est pars principalis rhetorice; immo est organicum instrumentum in sola vocis pronuntiatione consistens. . . . Sane quelibet ars a natura et anime actione procedit; unde per organici obstaculum instrumenti non admittitur artis notitia, sed effectus" [2.3.6].

[122] "[A]ccidentales complexiones iste alterabiliter permutantur" [4.1.1]. "Resultat in pluribus iracundie calor, qui velut igniculus ad suprema conscendens memoriales cellulas adurit pariter et canturbat"; others "iracundie calore succensi expeditus proloquuntur." "[Q]uanto magis fervor iracundie invalescit, tanto amplius . . . pronuntiatio expeditur" [4.1.4–5].

[123] "Scientia, pecunia, nobilitas, potentia, libertas, gaudium et favor auditorum . . . dant audaciam proloquendi . . . Ignorantia, paupertas, ignobilitas, impotentia, servitus, tristitia, contrarietas auditorum auferunt audaciam proloquendi" [4.1.2–3]. "Quidam . . . fluctuant in loquendo et boatu triumphabili proloquuntur" [4.1.6]. "[A]liquot prolocutores in paucorum presentia sunt audaces et in sermonibus

instrument, initially made to emit sparks of fire, may instead emit spit. Boncompagno's scientific materialism demands an objectivity that issues in his highly ironic take on the majesty of the body: divinely made as we may be, phlegm rises into our throats, our nostrils betray us, our "jocundly obtuse esophagus" rebels.

Instead of trying to subject those burdened with turbulent bodies to an Alcuin-style legal delivery boot camp, Boncompagno sits back and enjoys the show. Apparently, nature has a sense of humor. She and the body natural seem to be (like Boncompagno himself) incorrigible tricksters and lovers of practical jokes. Accidents are funny (at least when they don't happen to you). His attitude, however, is not that of the satirist excoriating vice but of a sympathetic ironist. Perhaps those unlucky enough to fail at delivery because they have "a defect in [their] organic instrument" are not really to blame? Such defects "must not be considered... natural vice[s]" but are rather misfortunes arising from "natural flaw[s], timidity, or momentary fear."[124] We are all victims of our bodies, temperaments, and environments. If the body gives rise to mirth, it is also full of foul fluids that may drip into your tracheal windpipe, or other places they shouldn't. This attitude is nowhere more palpable than in Boncompagno's description of the effects of fear. When those susceptible to fear stand before the multitude, dread may "so invade the spirit" that "they blanche, pale, tremble, shake, emit drops of urine, or they let loose a shameful tribute from their lower region," and thus they sadly "deliver [their speeches] into oblivion."[125] Trying to impress the judge but trembling uncontrollably, we might just have an accident in court. The body is an abject thing with a life of its own. It is unclear whether this "let[ting] loose" involves passing wind or another kind of "tribute" from one's bowels. In either case, rather than mocking the unfortunate incontinent whose body makes courtroom speech irrelevant, Boncompagno seems to be saying to judges: do not judge too harshly the one who "let[s] loose a shameful tribute from th[e] lower region" in court: it is not vice, but nature itself.

To believe that a training program like Alcuin's could produce perfect bodily control is, for Boncompagno, delusional. But his advice to law students suggests that, despite his view of the power of nature and accident, he does think it possible to nurture performance skills. How? Stop trying to constrain yourself, set your will free, and let your soul rejoice in sensory pleasure. As he explains in his discussion of memory, the student should

copiosi, sed in conspectu multitudinis numerose tanquam virgule in decursu fluminum contremiscunt" [4.1.11]. "[E]x laboriosa meditatione humores ad esophagum discurrunt. Unde prolocutores coguntur fauces... expurgare" [4.2.1].

[124] "Non debet eredi, quod sit nature vitium, sed aut pusillanimitas vel timor accidentalis" [4.1.11].

[125] "Timor horribilis et pusillanimitas abhorrenda ita invadunt animos aliquorum, quod quando sunt in multorum,... livent, pallent, trepidant, perhorrescunt, guttatim urinam emittant, vel quandoque verecundum solvunt de regione inferiori tributum, et ita mandant oblivioni [4.1.10].

> enjoy the freedom he has longed for, because ... the constraint of one's own will does great harm. Let him enjoy fresh, free air.... Let the brain be purged of phlegmatic and viscous humors. Let a salve of pearl and an electuary sometimes be enjoyed.... Sprinkle the face sometimes with napium or rose water, because from these scents the spirit is strengthened. Let pleasure be taken in the scents of spices and herbs.... Stop now and then in delightful and pleasant spots, in which one may hear nightingales and the sweet-sounding running of brooks.[126]
>
> [8.1.11]

Unsurprisingly, Boncompagno wrote a graphically entertaining manual on how to write love letters, the *Rota Veneris*, full of useful sexual advice. Somewhat surprisingly (given his paean to pleasure), he warns the student against "lasciviousness" and the "deceptive snare" of female beauty: one should meet up with women only rarely, and try to take more pleasure from "their wisdom than ... their shape."[127] It is worth briefly comparing Boncompagno's discussion of lawyers and delivery with that of the lawyer-poet Guilhem Molinier for an alternative account of the natural body as a vehicle of delivery.

Guilhem Molinier (fl. 1330–50): *Delivery According to the* Laws of Love

Molinier's discussion appears in the *Laws of Love* (*Leys d'amors*), a treatise compiled in Occitan for the Toulouse "Consistory of Joyous Knowledge" between *c.*1323 and 1356.[128] Although it primarily deals with language arts and philosophy, it is nevertheless strongly judicial in nature. Four of the Consistory's founders had

[126] "Memoratus desiderata libertate fruatur, quia ... multum obest obligatio proprie voluntatis. Utatur puro et libero aere.... Purgetur cerebrum ab humoribus phlegmaticis et viscosis. Utatur interdum diamargariton et plyris.... Aspergat aliquando faciem cum namphio vel aqua rosea, quoniam ex odoribus illis spiritus confortantur. Speciorum autem et herbarum odoribus cum intermissione fruatur, ut natura suavius delectetur.... Permaneat aliquando in locis delectabilibus et amenis, in quibus audiat philomenas et suaves rivulorum decursus" [8.1.11]. In this passage and the next, I use Sean Gallagher's translation in Carruthers and Ziolkowski, ed., *Medieval Craft of Memory*, 109.

[127] "Sit ei rarissima confabulatio mulierum et magis placeant per sapientiam quam per formam, quoniam earum pulcritudo reticulum in se continet deceptivum" [8.1.11].

[128] Molinier, *Leys d'amors* (hereafter cited in the Occitan text in my notes). Thank you to Eugene Petracca for assistance with translations, and to Laura Kendrick for generous responses to queries. I have relied primarily on Kendrick's "*Consistori del Gay Saber*" (especially 17–23) for general background and historical details; but also on Léglu, "Languages in Conflict in Toulouse," 384. For biographical information on Molinier, see Swiggers, "Guillaume Molinier" (in Stammerjohann, ed., *Lexicon Grammaticorum*, 588–9). Swiggers refers to him as "Guillaume" (listing him under "G"), but I follow most scholarship in referring to him as "Molinier." While Molinier is generally identified as the author of the *Leys*, it was a collaborative project that drew on an earlier version, as well as on such texts as Latini's *Livres dou Tresor* and judge Albertano de Brescia's *Ars loquendi et tacendi*. On its sources, see Swiggers, "Guillaume Molinier," 588; Marshall, "Observations on the Sources of the Treatment of Rhetoric"; and Fraser, "Influence of the Venerable Bede."

studied law. By the fourteenth century, the word "consistory" had come to refer specifically to judicial assemblies, so although the "Consistory" was a literary academy, it took the form of a mock legal-academic association. The society in fact met in Toulouse's small and large "consistories": the assembly rooms in the Toulouse City Hall where trials also took place. There, the group gave live performances of their work and granted academic degrees, which mimicked those of medieval university law faculties. In both the academy and the university, for instance, the aspiring doctor of laws would give a public lecture on one of the "laws" (assigned in advance), answer objections to his interpretation, and eventually host a costly celebratory feast.[129] (Women were not admitted.)

The *Laws* emerged from a desire to codify the rules that would govern the judges' decisions. The Consistory invited Molinier to undertake this codification, and he eventually became its "chancellor" (a title that had both legal and academic associations). While little is known about Molinier's life, we do know that he served primarily not as a learned jurist-consultant but as a lawyer taking on cases in the courts. He represented the city of Toulouse in tax, toll, and inheritance litigation, defended the townspeople's forestry rights, and in one case handed over an alleged murderer to the courts.[130] The fact that he was a practicing lawyer seems to have been central to his selection for the task of compiling the *Leys*, for the academy also named Marc Bartholomieu, Doctor of Laws and law professor at the University of Toulouse, as his co-consultant.[131]

Unsurprisingly, the *Laws* reflects its institutional framework in its relentlessly judicial themes and tropes, starting with the title and the "ordinances" Molinier lists, and continuing in repeated references to "law," "counsel," "judgment," "justice," and more. Rhetoric, for instance, "is that noble science through which one is able to . . . pronounce [words] founded and established in law"; it "alone is the instructor of orators," and thus "the science that teaches . . . judges and other justices and good and loyal advocates to defend, sustain and do justice."[132] Molinier has a good deal to say about his profession. He repeats some of the old saws about "malicious lawyers," citing, for instance, Bernard of Clairvaux on the "desperation" bad lawyers bring by the "assault of their words" and their habit of "subverting . . . truth by training their tongue to speak lies." They are "instructed in

[129] See Kendrick, "*Consistori del Gay Saber*," 28–9. On this structure in university law faculties, see García y García, "Faculties of Law," 399; and Rashdall, *Universities of Europe* (1987 ed.), 1:225–7 (and 1:232 on the expense of "Inception-rejoicings"). On the Consistory's emulation of both customary and university laws, see Galvez, "From the *Costuma d'Agen* to the *Leys d'Amors*," 36–7.

[130] See Jeanroy, "*Leys d'amors*" (in *Histoire littéraire de la France*, vol. 38), 140–1.

[131] See Thomas, "Bortholmieu Marc"; and Swiggers, "Guillaume Molinier" (in Stammerjohann, ed. *Lexicon Grammaticorum*), 588 (identifying him as "Marc Bartholomieu").

[132] "Rethorica . . . es aquela nobbla sciensa per laqual hom sab trobar, dictar et ordernar e dire paraulas . . . fondadas e be assetiadas en dreg. . . . [S]o es l'esenhamens de dictadors, so es la sciensa que essenha . . . jutges et autres justiciers e bos e leyals avocatz a drechura defendre, sostenere e far" (1:82–3).

falsehood, learned [in] impugning the truth."[133] But such comments primarily serve to highlight, by contrast, those "good and loyal advocates" and "the abundant benefit[s] that both the individual and the public cause receive from good lawyers," so great that it "cannot be estimated." As "great [a]s the damage that comes from malicious lawyers" is "the good that one receives from good and loyal lawyers" (1:96). Such lawyers "declare, define and determine obscure facts." Their central instrument is "their glorious voice[s]," which they use to ensure that "justice" is done "by king, prince, count, duke, baron" or other "good legal judge[s]." Paraphrasing Justinian (perhaps via Durand), he explains that they use these glorious voices to "redress and repair cases that were badly done, went askew, are fallen, and worn out; and [to] restore and protect the hope and the life of those in travail."[134]

The importance Molinier places on lawyers' "glorious voice[s]" suggests the extent to which he imagines the lawyer not primarily as a counselor or bureaucrat but as an orator. The Consistory promoted oral performance skills generally (which were essential to winning degrees and prizes), and Molinier's discussions of delivery stress the utility of delivery to a range of kinds of public speech.[135] But the strongly judicial framing and themes of the *Laws*, along with Molinier's discussion of the importance of the lawyer's voice, make it clear that he has lawyers in mind in his discussion of delivery. Echoing his predecessors, he sometimes seems to envision delivery as a disciplinary program like Alcuin's: "Delivery [*Pronunciacios*] is the worthy and noble use of words" to produce a particular "meaning and effect" through "beautiful bodily" action. It teaches that "[you must] speak with a straight face, [not] with eyes or eyebrows too high or too low, nor should you cross your body too much, or move your arms excessively, nor yell excessively" (etc.). All must be "delivered with a temperate countenance." Indeed, it is precisely a lack of temperance

[133] "[A]yssi son gran li dampnatge que veno per avocatz maliciozes.... Sant Bernat ditz enayssi, 'si cociram la dezesperacio dels mals avocatz, ni la gran guerra ni la impugnatio de lors paraulas, mays se avanso a subvertir e desviar vertat que a mantener aquela ni atrobar; aquest son aycil que han essenhadas lors lengas a dire messonjas; aquest son avizat contra drechura, instruit per falcetat, savi et aperceubut a mal far e gran parlier ad impugnar vertat'" (1:96).

[134] "[P]er aquestes paraulas... pot hom sentir e reportar que l bes fructuos que l singular e la cauza publica prendo dels bos avocatz es tan grans que no s pot estimar" (1:96). "[A]yssi cum son gran li be qu om pren dels bos e leyals avocatz, ayssi son gran li dampnatge que veno per avocatz maliciozes" (1:96). "L'Emperadors lauza bos e leyals avocatz e ditz que, 'li bon avocat am lor glorioza votz en cauzas publicas e dels privatz, so es dels singulars, los faytz escurs e doptozes declaro, definisho et determeno, so es fan definir et determenar per jutge competen... las cauzas mal faytas, biayshadas, cazutas et fatigadas dresso e reparo; e no remens l'esperansa e la vida de cels que son en trebalh e de lors successors restauro e defendo.'... Donx, segon qu'es estat dig dessus, aquest humanal profieg fan li Rey, princep, comte, duc, baro, naut justicier e li bon jutge drechurier, fazen drechura, quar ses drechura poders no dura" (1:95).

[135] See Kendrick, "*Consistori del Gay Saber*," 26.

that makes bad lawyers: they have failed to "conquer their flesh" and have thus been "conquered by it."[136]

And yet, however theologically correct such passages may be, it would be a mistake to take Molinier's admonitions about the necessity of conquering the flesh at face value, given the rest of his discussion. Sarah Kay notes that "[t]he love that this treatise aspires to regulate will ultimately be revealed as philosophy, the love of wisdom," but it is, of course, also love of another kind.[137] As Molinier's title suggests, he is clearly writing in the great tradition of works on the "laws of love," in which crisscrossing legal and amatory themes offer an ironic commentary on regulatory discourses (both judicial and theological), while also producing their own alternative form of jurisprudence.[138] If delivery serves legal "redress and repair," orators should also use their voices and bodies as instruments of pleasure. This investment in pleasure explains his use of the word "beautiful" [*bela*] to describe the body and countenance of the orator. Words spoken with such bodily beauty, he explains, are "more pleasing than words spoken otherwise, even if [the latter] are more fruitful and more useful."[139] Here, he rewrites Cicero's famous dictum. Cicero had declared that graceful delivery was more important to *persuasion* than content.[140] Molinier retains the contrast between graceful delivery and "fruitful and useful" content but revises the speaker's central aim. Any ugly speaker can find words useful to persuasion. But who cares about persuasion? It's all about pleasure.

A focus on beauty and pleasure is not perhaps surprising in a book on the laws of love. But the elevation of beauty, now the primary *aim* of delivery (rather than merely one of its vehicles), recasts the orator's body: no longer an instrument of persuasion, it becomes in Molinier's handling an "organic instrument" (to use Boncompagno's phrase), but one that is quite different from Boncompagno's humor-ridden, defective, accident-prone bag of fluids. Molinier conveys its nature in his discussion of delivery largely through recurrent *double entendres* that neither the Consistory audience nor the more general readership of a book on love could possibly have missed. In fact, the rules of the Consistory—which on their face seem to aim at prohibiting the use of poetry for the promotion of illicit

[136] "Pronunciacios es dignitatz e nobbleza de paraulas a las cauzas et als sens d'ome applicada am temprada et am bela contenensa corporal.... Am la cara dreyta deu hom parlar, no trop elevada ni trop enclinada, ni ab huelhs ni sobrecilhs trop elevatz ni trop basses, ni l cors trop crossan, ni trop brassejan, ni trop cridan, ni bas parlan, mas am votz temprada..." (1:115). "Donx si li mal avocat layshavan cobezessa, vencerian la carn; e quar no la laysho son vencut per carn" (1:96). For specific treatment of the *Leys* as "conduct literature," see Johnston, "Ciceronian Rhetoric and Ethics," 157–60, and "Treatment of Speech," 42–4.

[137] Kay, *Parrots and Nightingales*, 177.

[138] On the tradition of laws of love as "minor jurisprudence," see Goodrich, *Law in the Courts of Love*, especially 29–71.

[139] "[P]araulas am bela maniera et am bela contenensa pronunciadas, quant que sian mens utils, son leumen mays agradablas que autras estiers dichas, quant que sian mays fructuozas e mays utils" (1:115).

[140] Cicero, *On the Orator* [Loeb], 2:169 [3.213].

love—themselves promoted *double entendre*. You could write about love of God or the Virgin without challenge; but if you wrote about any other kind of love, you were to be interrogated under oath to make sure you were not promoting illicit love.[141] If you wanted to write about illicit love, you had better cast it as love of God or the Virgin.

Molinier clearly transferred the principle to his discussions of the body of the orator. If the lawyer's lying tongue was proverbial, it is a different kind of tongue that appears repeatedly—insistently—in Molinier's discussion of delivery. "Delivery requires that one exercise one's spirit, which is to say one's breath, [and] likewise body and tongue," he explains. To get the full effect of Molinier's repetition of the word "tongue," one has to imagine him reciting a portion of his treatise aloud to an assembly:

> Elocution . . . is performed with the mouth and with the artifice of the tongue. [S]ince speech comes . . . from the mouth and from the artifice of the tongue, if our speech is to be . . . good and profitable, we should restrain [the] tongue, . . . and subdue it to our power, though there is no man who can tame [the tongue] completely.[142]

That "artifice of the tongue," which however skilled cannot quite be tamed, must be "firm" (another word that appears with unmistakable point in his discussion of delivery). One must perform

> with a good and firm audacity and with such firmness . . . of body that only rarely should one be disturbed or leave off from progressing with one's matter [*materia*]; for the man who is easily disturbed shows that he has little of constancy, that is of firmness.

In fact, firmness may express audacity, but it hardly expresses control. For, explains Molinier, it is actually quite "difficult to *avoid* moving the body in accordance with the body's feelings" in the heat of the moment.[143]

Here, having recast Cicero's claim for the importance of grace to persuasion, Molinier also recasts ancient and medieval discussions of delivery as a vehicle of

[141] See Kendrick, "*Consistori del Gay Saber*," 27.

[142] "En pronunciacio es necessaris exercessis de sperit, so es de l'ale d'ome que fa mejansan l'ayre e tempransa de votz e no remens de cors e de lengua" (1:115). "Locutios . . . se fa am la boca et am l'artifici de la lenga; donx pus que paraula ve e procezish de la boca e de l'artifici de la lenga, afi que nostre parlar[s] sia be ordenatz e bos et aprofichabbles, devem metre fre e bona garda a la lenga . . . et aquela dompdar a nostre poder, quar non es homs que del tot la puesca dompdar" (1:123).

[143] "[D]eu hom parlar . . . am bona e ferma audacia et am tal fermetat e tempransa de cor que per pauca ocayso no s torbe ni layshe sa materia a proseguir; quar hom que leu se torba mostra que pauc ha de constancia, so es fermetat; pero a greu es que l cors no s mova segon la affectio del cor" (1:115–16; emphasis added).

emotional signification that functions through expressive transfer. "[M]oving the body in accordance with the body's feelings," a man communicates those feelings, he explains (with a heavily gendered repetition of the word "*hom*"). For it is "from the movements of [a man's] members" that the spectators "can come to know the desire[s] and grand passion[s] of his body." When a man moves his members in this way, he also models a practice of devotion, though devotion of a very different kind than that of Alcuin's ideal legal orator: one that draws on the classic double associations of devotion to "celestial" beauty. A man "can and should lift his hands together toward heaven," writes Molinier, "and his body, and his head, and all his members in order to better imprint devout words and other speech beneficial to public cause[s] in the hearts of the audience."[144] As the orator's members rise toward heaven (in Molinier's distinctly masculinist trope), he communicates his feelings to those who surround him, imprinting his passion and desire in their hearts (or maybe other organs). Like the lawyer's "glorious voice," this glorious body, its members divinely uplifted, serves all who attend to it, offering "redress and repair," "restor[ing] . . . the hope and the life of those in travail."

Jean de Jandun (c.1285–1328): Signifying the Passions, Warping the Judge, Entertaining the Crowd

We can see in Molinier's *double entendres* a particularly steamy version of what is otherwise a fairly standard view, drawn from ancient theory and central to medieval semiotics: the body is a signifying instrument and one of its functions is to communicate the passions. This view lies at the heart of the discussion of delivery in the work of one of Molinier's near-contemporaries, the Parisian philosopher Jean de Jandun. Jandun taught rhetoric (among other topics) in the Arts Faculty at the University of Paris.[145] He does not seem to have had the regular interaction with law students that Boncompagno had. But his *Treatise in Praise of Paris* (1323) describes (among other things) the Law Faculty in the Clos-Bruneau, with its "numerous multitude of auditors" listening avidly to the "venerable professors of ecclesiastical law." And it offers a long encomiastic description of the Palais de Justice, where, in the "vast and beautiful" Grande Chambre, are to be found the judges of the court of appeals and the king's notaries, working to ensure "the prospering of the public good," weighing requests "in the scales of equity." In the Palace too are the masters of the Parlement, with their "infallible knowledge of law and custom," launching the "lightning bolts of their sentences," which

[144] "[P]er miels enprentar las paraulas devotas e las autras mot fructuozas a la causa publica en los corages dels auzens pot hom e deu elevar las mas junctas vas lo cel, e l cors, e l cap, e totz sos membres; quar al movemen dels membres hom pot conoysher la volontat e la gran affectio del cor" (1:116).

[145] For Jandun's biography, see Bourquelot, "Jean de Jandun," 3–20; Brenet, *Transferts du sujet*, 11–13; and Schmugge, *Johannes von Jandun*, 1–41.

"send the innocent and the just into transports of joy" and drown "the evil and impious ... in bitterness and misery."[146] Unfortunately, Jandun's own encounters with the law—ecclesiastical rather than royal—were of the less-than-joyous kind. As a radical who argued for popular legal sovereignty (the multitude was the true legislator and should vote on all laws), he had to flee his beloved Paris. He remained in exile during the last decade of his life: excommunicated, summoned to appear before the papal court and, when he failed to appear, tried and condemned *in absentia* as a "perfidious heretic," subject to immediate arrest upon apprehension.[147] Although he never did come before the papal court, both his paean to the Paris Parlement and his decidedly more ironic portrayal of contemporary criminal courts make it clear that he had firsthand knowledge of the inside of a courtroom.[148]

Only fragments of Jandun's *Questions on the Third Book of the Rhetoric* (1310–26) have been published, which is surprising since his commentaries on Aristotle remained influential for centuries, appearing in numerous manuscripts and printed editions through the sixteenth century.[149] Occasionally borrowing from Cicero and Seneca, he stays primarily focused on his central purpose: the explication of Book Three of Aristotle's *Rhetoric*. In this, he draws heavily on Al-Farabi and Ibn Rushd through Hermannus' translations and commentaries, and, more immediately, on Giles of Rome's *Commentary on Aristotle's Rhetoric* (*c.*1272). Like so many medieval theorists, Giles had stressed the importance of delivery, giving it a Greek inflection: the orator must "know how to hypokritise and represent [*hypocriçare et representare*], which have great power of persuading."[150] Jandun reiterates the point, identifying the orator specifically as a litigant: "Nothing is more essential to litigation," he writes, "than showing [*ostendere*]."[151] Jandun is not particularly interested in teaching the legal orator the kind of

[146] Jean de Jandun, "Tractatus de laudibus Parisius" (in Le Roux de Lincy and Tisserand, ed., *Paris et ses historiens*), 40–3, 48–9. (Paris had a canon law faculty but no civil law faculty.) To avoid confusion, I follow many scholars in referring to Jean de Jandun as "Jandun" throughout.

[147] Bourquelot, "Jean de Jandun," 19.

[148] See the discussion in Marmo, "Carattere," 30–1 (noting that because of Jandun's familiarity with courts as well as churches, he is more interested in pragmatic oratorical problems than his most immediate source, Giles of Rome).

[149] I draw here on the sections of Jandun's *Questiones super rethoricorum tres libros* reproduced in Marmo, "Retorica e motti di spirito," 37–40 (Book 1, *Questio* 3) and Marmo, "Carattere dell'oratore," 22, 26–9 (fragments of Book 1, *Questio* 5 and Book 3, *Questio* 1). My in-text citations in the Latin refer first to the Marmo text and page number; then (in brackets) to the Leipzig manuscript's Book, *Questio*, and folio numbers. Thank you to Francesco Cassini for assistance with translations.

On Jandun's ongoing influence, see South, "John of Jandun" (observing that Jandun was one of the most important thinkers in the transmission of the Averroist tradition through the sixteenth century, and noting the large number of manuscripts and printed editions of his work [372]). For discussions of Jandun's rhetoric, see Marmo, "Carattere" and "Retorica"; and Copeland, "Pathos and Pastoralism," 102–5. For a useful discussion of Jandun's influence on Buridan's rhetoric, see Fredborg, "John Buridan on Rhetoric."

[150] "[S]ciamus hypocriçare et rep[re]sentare..., quia hab[ent] magna[m] uirtut[em] ad persuade[n]du[m]." Giles, *Commentaria in rhetoricam Aristotelis* (1968 rpt. of 1515 ed.), fol. 91r.

[151] "[A]d litigantem ni[c]hil aliud principaliter pertinet nisi ostendere" ("Retorica," 39 [1.3 fol. 266]).

disciplinary control that Alcuin advocates, nor does he dwell on the body as an organic instrument with a tendency to run amok (as Boncompagno does). But like Molinier (in a less carnal but no less passionate version), Jandun is preoccupied with delivery's power to communicate emotion and desire. He is, he declares, "a rhetor who meditates on passions": "love, hate, hope, fear, . . . mercy, anger" and more.[152] Delivery's job is to signify such emotions.

In his philosophical work generally, Jandun gives a great deal of attention to the problem of sense perceptions.[153] Drawing on both Aristotle's *De anima* and the *Rhetoric*, his *Questions on the Rhetoric* offers a compressed account of the chain reaction that eventually emerges in bodily expression. Mental concepts trigger emotions and appetites: the "affections of [both] the cognitive soul [and] the sensible appetite." Emotions and appetites then move the body to signify not only the emotions and appetites themselves but also the mental concepts that lie behind them: "one or another way of delivering the exterior voice signifies one or another kind of feeling or interior desire"; one is "a sign of the other." For instance, "a voice speaking modestly, with restraint, and slowly, signifies the modesty, restraint, and firmness of the [speaker's] mental concept and inner feeling."[154] However, following Aristotle, Jandun invests this chain reaction with ethical meaning. "[K]nowing the good or the bad"—both cognitively and through "the sensible appetite"—produces the emotions that delivery signifies. Delivery thus expresses desire for the good or fear of the bad, but it also expresses those emotions that emerge from an ethical-cognitive knowledge of good and evil. This view explains what Jandun means when he cites here Seneca the Younger's *Epistles* for the proposition that one's "speech, like [one's] life, should be well-regulated" ("refined"): speech that represents ethos (both in its content and delivery) represents an ethical life.[155] Jandun thus follows Al-Farabi and Averroës in stressing the link between ethos and pathos. Delivery conveys the ethos essential to persuasion (one must not merely have a reputation for honor but *appear* honorable); and it does so in part by conveying appropriately ethical pathos.

152 "[A]rtifex qui considerat de passionibus" ("Retorica," 37 [1.3 fol. 266r]); "amor, odium, spes, timor . . . misericordia, iracundia" ("Retorica," 38 [1.3 fol. 266r]).

153 See South, "John of Jandun," 373–4, for a concise account of Jandun's conceptions of sense perception.

154 "Et ulterius, cum ex conceptionibus anime cognoscitiue oriantur affectiones seu affectiones appetitus sensitiui . . . appetitus enim fit in actu a uirtute cognoscente bonum aut malum, 3° *De anima* et in *De motibus animalium*—rationabile est quod alius et alius modus proferendi uocem exteriorem significat alium et alium modum affectionis seu desiderii interioris. Et cum unum proportionalium sit quodam modo signum alterius, rationale est quod uox modeste et ordinate et le[n]te prolata significat modestiam et ordinationem et constantiam conceptus et affectus interioris" ("Carattere," 26–7, note 24 [3.1 fol. 316v]; I draw here on the translation in Copeland, "Pathos and Pastoralism," 105; Copeland identifies the Aristotle passage as *De anima* 431a–b).

155 "Unde etiam Seneca dicit in 40 *Epistula ad Lucilium* quod philosophi pronuntiatio sicut et uita, debet esse compta" ("Carattere," 27 note 24 [3.1 fol. 316v]). See Seneca the Younger, *Epistles*, 1:264–5 [40.2].

Jandun offers a portrait of a ranting orator to illustrate how bad delivery represents base character and the base emotions that are its source. Some speakers, he writes, try to "make up" for the fact that they have nothing to say of "value [or] verisimilitude" by "shouting, . . . with all their veins pulsating." They try to give the impression that they are "saying something tremendous, whereas in fact they are saying nothing."[156] Such ranters have learned *hypokrisis* "by practice and exercise or by imitating others." Spectators perceive that they are "blustering"—that their emotion is merely imitative—"and do not believe them." True orators, on the other hand, "are inclined by their nature to speak correctly." Here, Jandun seems to posit a relationship between "value" and "verisimilitude." Verisimilar delivery—that is, credible delivery—reflects the value of the speaker, which appears as ethos. But it turns out that credibility may after all not really rely on value. "We see some men saying something very frivolous or superficial and totally false, yet they say it so seriously and in [such] a reasonable and correct way, [that people] believe them immediately," whereas another orator who says "the same [thing] with less care would not be believed." Such speakers—speakers attentive to the power of delivery—are careful to vary their voices, sometimes speaking "discreetly" with "a low voice," sometimes "grandly" or in a "high register," sometimes if necessary even "shouting." Through delivery, they make the "frivolous or superficial [or] totally false" appear not only serious but true. These "are the [speakers] who can . . . persuade [the audience]."[157]

Alcuin and Boncompagno place the legal orator's performance in the foreground of their discussions: the judge's and audience's reception of that performance appears, if at all, almost as an afterthought. For Molinier, the audience is a susceptible mass that receives the imprint of the speaker's embodied passions, which are instantly replicated in their bodies. For Jandun, on the other hand, the judge and audience are front and center. Jandun may be interested in how delivery theoretically signifies concepts and emotions or expresses ethos. But he is still more interested in their impact on the spectator: how their "verisimilitude" may produce belief and ultimately "persuade [the audience]." When he turns explicitly to a discussion of real courtrooms, his principal concern is how to please and persuade the judge and audience through delivery and other means. This concern emerges particularly clearly in a passage in which he suddenly takes on the voice of

[156] "[C]um ipsi habent dicere aliqua parui ualoris et parum uerisimilia, recuperant in boatu et ornatu dilatando fimbrias et arterias, et uidentur magna dicere, cum nichil dicant interdum" ("Carattere," 29, note 30 [3.1 fol. 317r]).

[157] "Alii uero accipiunt istum modum per consuetudinem et artem uel per imitationem aliorum . . . et ideo putatur quod isti sunt ficti et iactatores, nec creditur eis"; "aliqui habent quasi a natura, ita quod ex sua natura indiuiduali inclinantur ad loquendum morose, discrete et pompose, cum quodam boatu et depressione uocis seu eleuatione, ut decet; et isti melius persuadent" ("Carattere," 27–8, note 27 [3.1 fol. 316v]). "[V]idemus enim quosdam homines proferre aliqua friuola et ualde superficialia—et forte falsa—qui tamen ita seriose, discrete et morose ea proferunt, ut eis statim creditur; et si unus alius diceret iila eadem, non curaretur, nec ei crederetur" ("Carattere," 27 [3.1 fol. 316v]).

an imaginary lawyer attempting to sway the judge's affections. "'My Lord,'" says the lawyer, "'this man has always been dear to your own friends, and done justly by them, and is a very loyal and valiant man.'" The judge begins to feel the love, in part thanks to the lawyer's delivery of his emotional meaning through his body and voice; watching the lawyer, the judge finds himself "desir[ing]" the client's happiness and "decide[s] that [the man] must be acquitted or rewarded." Alternatively, the lawyer can deploy negative emotions, with the appropriate accompanying tone and gestures. "'My Lord,'" says the lawyer, "'beware [!] [my client] is powerful and rich and has friends who would be seriously displeased if anything bad were to happen to him.'" Many a judge (comments Jandun) "would ... not be brave enough to render a just decision" in such a case. The judge will rule in the client's favor, "fearing that something bad might happen to him" if he fails to do so.[158]

Such scenarios are not merely hypotheticals, explains Jandun. For lawyers in contemporary courts do often use "speeches whose aim is to induce in the judge or audience some passion or passions" with the help of delivery.[159] In fact, even without a lawyer skilled in delivery, the powerful or the beautiful can often win their cases through the sheer force of the passions they produce in the judge, as recent cases show. For instance, in one case, "a poor man ... accused a very rich man of whipping him so badly that he was wounded and lost [a great deal of] blood." The judge, fearing the rich man, "sentenced ... him [merely] to avoid drinking wine for two days, and [otherwise] absolved him." In another case, "someone accused a beautiful prostitute of murder." The woman came before the judge and was "released, and not punished even the slightest bit." Jandun adds sardonically: "I shall *not* say that," just before the verdict, "the judge joyfully received the gratification of carnal pleasure": who would dare to imply such a thing?[160]

Jandun's slippage from advocating the use of both delivery and the passions to a sardonic evocation of their actual effects in the modern courtroom reveals a schism in his thinking that bears some relationship to Aristotle's own. On the one hand, one cannot deny "the power of [passionate] speeches" delivered artfully: lawyers *must* deploy these to win their cases. On the other hand, is doing so

[158] "Domine, ipse semper dilexit amicos uestros et bene fecit eis et est ualde probus et ualens homo"; "ipse iudex appetit bonum illius et ... faciliter iudicat ipsum esse absoluendum"; "Domine caueatis uobis, iste est homo potens et diues et habet amicos quibus multum displiceret malum eius"; "iudex interdum non audet reddere rectum iudicium, timens ne malum sibi contingat" ("Retorica," 38 [1.3 fol. 266r]).

[159] "Sunt autem huiusmodi sermones in proposito illi qui inducunt in iudice uel in auditoribus aliquam passionem uel aliquas passiones" ("Retorica," 38 [1.3 fol. 266r]).

[160] "Vidi quendam pauperem accusare ditissimum iudici de eo quod ipsum pauperem nequissime uerberauerat usque ad uulnera el sanguinis effusionem. Iudex sententiauit illum percussorem abstinere a potatione uini per duos dies et absoluit eum"; "pulcherrima meretrix fuit accusata de homicidio .... [I]lla domina fuit feliciter liberata .... [N]on dico quod ille iudex ab ea receperat carnalis uoluptatis iocunditatem letanter" ("Carattere," 22 note 11 [1.5 fol. 269v–70r]; emphasis added).

ethical? Is it ethical to make the "frivolous or superficial [or] totally false" appear true? It is hard to get around the fact that, when delivery and pathos serve persuasion, rich men get away with scourging poor ones and murderous whores get off scot free. To terrify a judge until he can no longer "render a just decision" is to serve injustice and falsehood. Whether "the judge love or hates [the accused]" bears no relationship to the person's guilt. For instance, if the judge hates someone accused of stealing, "it does not follow that [the person] is a thief or [even] that something was stolen."[161] Passionate speeches "distort rational judgment." Judges should really be impartial: the proper attitude is "neutrality towards the two disputants." The judge should "not incline towards one party or the other": not be "oblique or curved and distorted" but like "a straight line." Ideally, the judge should be of a "solemn" temperament, —and "be rich and influential" with many "friends, so that [he is] not corrupted by fear."[162]

However, the reality is that lawyers do use appeals to the passions—in both their speeches and delivery—and these do "incline," "curv[e]," "distor[t]," and "corrup[t]" judges. What is an honorable lawyer to do? Jandun seems determined to solve the dilemma by finding ethical arguments that can save courtroom emotional appeals. His first argument is that the lawyer must know how to use such appeals defensively against other lawyers. Defensive lawyering requires knowing how to "cope with" the emotional appeals that opposing lawyers will use "to obtain what they want" from the judge.[163] It also sometimes requires knowing how to use appeals to the passions yourself: not as your "principal strategy or frequently," but so that you can know how to counter them when others use them in order not to "be defeated by them." Jandun advises his reader to read Book 6 of the "*Nova rethorica*" (the *Ad Herennium*), as well as Seneca the Elder's legal speeches and commentaries, for useful examples.[164] His second argument is that pathos can be entertaining, and that entertainment may serve an ethical function. One unfortunately often finds judges napping on the job and the audience with them. So, when (for instance) "the judge and the audience are... tired or worn out from sitting or standing" or simply sick of listening, or when they have had enough of "bitter things," it is actually "good to insert something passionate," "comforting," "delightful," "wondrous," or even

[161] "[S]i iudex odiat ilium, non sequitur quod ille sit fur uel quod furatus fuit" ("Retorica," 39 [1.3 fol. 266]).

[162] "[U]idetur expediens esse... quod iudex precipue sit solempnis uir diues et potens amicis"; "propria et conueniens dispositio iudicis est indifferentia ad utrumque litigantium... quod non plus declinet ad unam partem quam ad aliam: ad faciendum rectam lineam non debet esse obliqua seu curva et distorta" ("Retorica," 38–9 [1.3 fol. 266]).

[163] "[E]t per hoc uenire ad intentum" ("Retorica," 39 [1.3 fol. 266]).

[164] "Si uis propriissima exempla de sermonibus passionatiuis, uide Tullium in sexto *Noue rethorice*.... Similiter plura inuenires in libro Senece qui dicitur *Liber declarationum*, siue 10 *Rethoricorum*" ("Retorica," 38 [1.3 fol. 266]).

"funny": as Cicero recommends, "make them laugh."[165] If these are forms of entertainment, they also serve justice. "[D]elightful speeches" (explains Jandun, citing Book 10 of Aristotle's *Ethics*) "make for better investigation."[166] Imagine that "someone is accused . . . of being a thief": if "the judge is delighted while listening" (rather than "saddened or angered"), he "will listen longer and more thoroughly."[167] The lawyer who deploys pathos and comedy as entertainment may in fact help the judge to do his "judging in a better way," even as he "gladdens [the auditors'] spirit through admiration" for his speech and "restor[es] them with laughter."[168]

Conclusion

For the rhetorical theorists I have looked at in this chapter, the legal actor's embodied action in the courtroom mattered, both to outcomes and to justice. All of them envision litigants and lawyers using performance to try to control, in one way or another, the scene of law: to persuade, display, seduce, trick, warp, entertain, and more. All of them place the performing body at the center of the trial process. None envisions legal decisions as subject solely to God's judgments, an all-powerful prince's capricious desires, or an Inquisitor's will. None envisions them as pure exercises in power. Their visions of embodied legal action may sometimes represent the expressive body as glorious, at other times viewing it as shameful. Theorists like Jandun may hypothesize an ethical lawcourt in which virtue acts with mechanical precision: the good lawyer's mental concept triggers virtuous emotions, which trigger virtuous bodily expression, which act on the judge to produce righteous judgment. But in the real lawcourt (sadly), money and sex hold sway unless the lawyer uses delivery as a countermeasure. Training programs like Alcuin's may strive to discipline the body's excesses. Courts may insist that everyone abide by the "decorum of duty" and stay in their proper places. But things run amock. The lawyer's "feathered," "lying," "whor[ing]" tongue may hijack truth. Legal speakers may bluster and rant "with all their veins pulsating." Their bodies may produce hideous grimaces, noxious noises, twisted postures, be bloated with warring humors, and occasionally leak. Sometimes, as their "hands [lift] together toward heaven," so does their "body, and . . . head, and all [their] members." The pleader's wayward body may express not Cicero's eloquence of the

[165] "[C]um iudex et auditores sint iam fatigati seu fessi de sedendo uel stando, . . . tunc enim bonum est interponere aliqua passionalia, utpote aliqua solaciosa seu risibilia et delectantia uel mirabilia . . . qu[a]e risum mouere possunt" ("Retorica," 39–40 [1.3 fol. 266v]).

[166] "[S]ermones delectatiui faciunt certius exquirere" ("Retorica," 40 [1.3 fol. 266v]).

[167] "[S]i proponatur coram iudice aliquem esse furem, et iudex delectetur in audiendo . . . diutius potest attendere et insistere" ("Retorica," 40 [1.3 fol. 266v]).

[168] "[S]ic animus defessus audiendo aut admiratione integratur aut risu nouatur" ("Retorica," 40 [1.3 fol. 266v]).

body but something more like communication in the Tower of Babel: thwarting intention, exploding signification, dislodging certainty. But it may also seduce, entertain, make them laugh. The next chapter will examine how the sometimes anarchic force of performance could manifest in actual legal events: thoroughly scripted trials and punishments in which the players and the crowds could go wildly off-script; top-down spectacles of power that could go bottoms-up.

4

Irreverent Performances, Heterodox Subjects, and the Unscripted Crowd from the Medieval Courtroom to the Stocks and Scaffold

Introduction: Mooning the Law with Calefurnia and Catharina Arndes

In 1482, the Archbishop of Bremen sent a deputation to the female monastery of Harvestehude (near Hamburg) to institute a series of "reforms." Throughout Germany, such reforms involved punishing the nuns for their impious accumulation of wealth by relieving them of their tableware, liturgical objects, textiles, personal property, and more (a reform recently undertaken in nearby Wienhausen). When the Archbishop's deputies arrived at the monastery, a surprise met them: a riotous crowd of townspeople, including a group of "insulting and offending women, [who], carried away in the tumult, lost their minds [and] claimed to be the counsellors of the people" (as one chronicle reports).[1]

> [M]any of them violently push[ed] themselves into the monastery, . . . climbing upon the walls and making a great noise, . . . screaming, 'Do not obey the traitors!'

Among them was a townswoman named Catharina Arndes. When the Archbishop's chaplain "kindly begged [the crowd] to calm down and stop rioting," she "rudely repulsed" him "with mocking and shameful words" and a much more expressive action: she "lift[ed] up [her] clothes," and showed him her privates.[2] Astonishingly, the strategy succeeded: the ecclesiastics fled in horror.

[1] Krantz, *Wandalia* [Bk 13, Ch 29]; quoted in Heß, "Skirts and Politics," 79. I draw on Heß's account for details of the incident. Heinrich von Schwarzburg (Heinrich XXVII) was Archbishop of Bremen 1463–96 and Bishop of Munster 1466–96. In Harvestehude, the deputation was bent on a reform that would give the Archbishop possession of the village of Wellingsbüttel, which the Hamburg city council had refused to sell him (Heß, 63).

[2] Langebek, "Des Bürgermeisters Herman Langebek *Bericht*," 342; quoted in Heß, "Skirts and Politics," 67. Catharina Arndes (or Arends) was a member of a prosperous, upper-class Hamburg family, among whom were several nuns (Heß, 71–3). It is unclear precisely what Catharina exposed to the delegation, but that they viewed it as obscene is clear from the context. Heß notes the similar use of

Law as Performance: Theatricality, Spectatorship, and the Making of Law in Ancient, Medieval, and Early Modern Europe.
Julie Stone Peters, Oxford University Press. © Julie Stone Peters 2022. DOI: 10.1093/oso/9780192898494.003.0005

Fig. 4.1 Calefurnia scolds the judge in an illustrated manuscript of the *Sachsenspiegel* (*c.*1295–1304).
Heidelberg University Library, Cod. Pal. germ. 164.

Catharina Arndes may have gotten the idea for her performance of obscenity-as-resistance from an image that circulated widely in late medieval Europe (fig. 4.1). The image originally appeared in illustrated editions of Eike von Repgow's influential compilation of Saxon law: the *Sachsenspiegel* (*Mirror of Saxons*) (*c.*1220–25), widely distributed and commonly chained to courtroom walls so that judges could easily consult it.[3] The image shows a woman named Calefurnia scolding a royal judge. The text that accompanies the image explains the legal rule it illustrates: "[n]o woman may be a pleader, nor may she bring a suit without a guardian." The reason? Calefurnia was angry "because her demands could not proceed without a spokesman," and so, "in a fit of rage," she

obscenity as resistance against the "reform" of female monasteries elsewhere: the chronicler Johannes Busch, for instance, reports that the nuns in Nuremberg's St. Katharinen monastery defeated the reformers with "unchaste manners and songs and gestures" (quoted in Heß, 69).

[3] The *Sachsenspiegel* became one of the most influential lawbooks of the Middle Ages, appearing in many languages, surviving in hundreds of manuscripts, and serving as a source of law from the time of its composition until well into the sixteenth century (and in some places through the nineteenth century). For discussions, see Dobozy, ed., *Saxon Mirror*, 1–49; Caviness, "Giving 'The Middle Ages' a Bad Name" and "Putting the Judge in his P(a)lace"; and Caviness and Nelson, *Women and Jews* (especially 74–9 on the judiciary's use of the *Sachsenspiegel* picture books chained to courtroom walls, and 58 on the representation of "ritualistic scenes" and "gestures and body language . . . encoded with legal meaning" in the images).

"misbehaved before the emperor." She thus "forfeited [for] all [women]" the right to bring a suit or plead in court.[4] In the image, Calefurnia holds her left hand over her crotch, while a peculiar hairy brush protrudes from her backside: a devil's tail? pubic hair gone wild? The Augsburg *Schwabenspiegel* (*c.*1275) explains: Calefurnia misbehaved by displaying her "*hinde schamme*" (her shameful hind parts): that is, she mooned the judge.[5] Later references elaborate. In a description of the scene in Martin Le Franc's *Champion of Women* (*c.*1440–42), one lawyer challenges another—a champion of women—to defend the indefensible Calefurnia, who (he declares) "decked herself out in her robe so badly" that she put on display her "*de profundis*," that is, she "showed her ass to the judge."[6] An image in the 1488 Lyon edition of Le Franc's text illustrates (fig. 4.2).[7]

Scholars often treat such portrayals as characteristic bits of medieval misogyny: such women are punished for their unruliness and alarming sexuality; they are victims, silenced by law. But the image in the *Sachsenspiegel* does not show a chastened Calefurnia. Her hand over her privates seems to say "*noli me tangere*!" as she aggressively leans toward the judge pointing two fingers at him, perhaps delivering a curse along with her demand. If the judge accuses her, she accuses him right back. Jehan Le Fèvre suggests something like this in his translation of the *Lamentations of Matheolus* (*c.*1380–87), declaring ambiguously that she "showed her ass in judgment" (during judgment? or in a judgment upon the judge himself?)[8] Defying the edict, Calefurnia vigorously pleads her case (*sans* guardian),

[4] Dobozy, ed., *Saxon Mirror*, 112. The image of Calefunia appears in different versions in all four of the lavishly illustrated early editions of the *Sachsenspiegel* that have survived (*c.*1295–1371). The image here is from the Heidelberg manuscript (*c.*1295–1304). The figure of Calefurnia derives from Valerius Maximus' "Carfania," whom he loosely based on the first-century BCE plebeian Caia Afrania. According to Valerius, she "was ever ready for a lawsuit and always spoke on her own behalf, . . . not because she could not find advocates but because she had impudence to spare. So by constantly plaguing the tribunals with barkings to which the Forum was unaccustomed she became a notorious example of female litigiousness, so much so that women of shameless habit are taunted with the name Carfania by way of reproach." Valerius, *Memorable Doings and Sayings* [Loeb], 2:211 [8.3]. Justinian's sixth-century *Digest* explains that the rule prohibiting women from pleading for others "goes back to a shameless woman called Carfania who by brazenly making applications and annoying the magistrate gave rise to the edict" (*Digest of Justinian* [1998 trans.], 79 [3.1.1.5]). Later medieval texts, probably drawing on the *Digest*, transformed "Carfania" into "Calefurnia" (perhaps an unconscious amalgam of the pushy Carfania and the virtuous Calpurnia, Caesar's wife). For discussions of Calefurnia, see Caviness and Nelson, *Women and Jews*, 59–60, 194–6; and Westphal, "Calefurnia's Rage" and "Bad Girls in the Middle Ages."

[5] The *Schwabenspiegel* was an adaptation of the *Sachsenspiegel*. On the *Schwabenspiegel*'s Carfania, see Caviness and Nelson, *Women and Jews*, 59; Caviness, "Putting the Judge in his P(a)lace," 316; and Westphal, "Calefurnia's Rage," 166–7, 170–3, 177–8 (stressing the *Schwabenspiegel*'s translation of the *Sachsenspiegel*'s "*Torn*" as "*Zorn*," which renders "rage" as "battle" or heroic anger).

[6] "Calfurnie . . . si mal sa robe accoustra / Que monstra son de profundis"; "son cul au juge monstra." Le Franc, *Champion des dames* (1999 ed.), 4:169 [4.18737–44].

[7] Le Franc, *Champion des dames* (1488 ed.), sig. s8r.

[8] "Son cul monstra en jugement." Matheolus and Le Fèvre, *Lamentations de Matheolus* (1892–1905 ed.), 1:52 (Le Fèvre adds these lines to his translation of Matheolus' Latin).

Fig. 4.2 Calefurnia moons the judge in an edition of Martin Le Franc's *Champion of Women* (1488).
Champion des dames (1488), sig. s8r. Newberry Library, Chicago, Special Collections.

prohibition be damned.[9] In the Lyon image, her exposure of her "*de profundis*" is clearly obscene protest, speaking the depths of her outrage. The judge appears alarmed, recoiling, his staff clutched between his legs, a sign of his body's response: what has she done to him? But the woman in attendance smiles, her hands open toward Calefurnia, seeming to applaud: a "Champion of Women."

Both the Calefurnia images and Catharina Arndes' live performance might stand as parables of how performance can upend legal scripts: the Archbishop or

[9] As Caviness and Nelson note, in the illustrated editions the page also shows a rape victim bringing a lawsuit against her rapist, i.e. another woman violating the prohibition (*Women and Jews*, 60). They stress, however, that the page represents disgraced women, and the necessity of their "forcible repression."

the *Sachsenspiegel* say one thing; but what happens in the courtroom or the streets is quite another. Most of the *Sachsenspiegel* images represent the text's official ideology: in one, God gives swords of justice simultaneously to Charlemagne and the Pope, showing ecclesiastical and secular power ruling together harmoniously; in another, the Emperor and the Pope cuddle.[10] (Never mind that Popes and Emperors were often at each other's throats.) When Calefurnia appears in these pages, disrupting judgment with her "*hindere scham*," she reminds us: life (and the unmentionable) happens, even in a courtroom.

Modern scholars have sometimes treated official legal ideologies as if they describe the participants' and spectators' actual experiences: what they actually thought and felt rather than what officials told them they were supposed to think and feel. Especially notable in this regard are accounts of the transformations that took place in the wake of the twelfth-century "legal revolution."[11] The more romanticized versions of this account explain that the whole community used to gather in open-air trials and the old ordeals to participate in the process of judgment: a collective ritual in which all partook. But as the Church and jurists took over in the twelfth century, law became an occult science that ceased to belong to the people and became the tool of a privileged class of experts. They grabbed judgment from the hands of the many and moved trials into secret chambers. What remained visible to the people were only two "rituals," which were "comprehensively stage-managed by authorities: sentencing and execution." These might appear participatory, but they were actually technologies of control: staged spectacles of "justice" that were spectacularly brutal. The people accepted them because the terror the spectacle produced also held out a promise: do not resist; repent of your sins (like the criminal on the scaffold); and you too will reap heavenly joys.[12]

[10] Caviness and Nelson reproduce both images (*Women and Jews*, 56).

[11] See Chapter 3, 93–4, on the rise of lawyers and proliferation of records and written rules, phenomena often associated with the twelfth-century legal revolution. To summarize the standard account of the twelfth-century legal revolution: Roman-canon law displaced accusatorial by inquisitorial procedures throughout the Continent. Inquisitors could initiate proceedings *ex officio*, without an accuser, and thus became both accusers and judges, interrogating the accused behind closed doors. For examples of this historiography, see e.g. Peters, *Torture*, 41–4; and Deane, *History of Medieval Heresy and Inquisition*, 100–1. See also Berman, *Law and Revolution*, for an influential (if contested) study arguing that the "revolution" in fact consisted primarily in the Church's seizure of power in the eleventh and twelfth centuries and its creation of an international legal order that produced the "Western legal tradition" as we know it.

[12] On the two "rituals," see Merback, *Thief, the Cross, and the Wheel*, 132; and, for this narrative generally, see Evans, *Rituals of Retribution*, 37; Dülmen, *Theatre of Horror*, 13, 34–9; Cohen, *Crossroads of Justice*, 54, 75 (in the early period, "judges and community could work together, expressing shared values and norms through legal rituals" [75]); and Merback, *Thief, the Cross, and the Wheel*. Merback's description of the "historic shift from one legal paradigm to another" is worth quoting at length: "Before the late Middle Ages an *accusatorial* system of criminal process predominated, in which judges had to rely on the accusations of injured parties before they could try a case; most trials were held in open-air courts and were very public occasions.... Older methods for determining guilt or innocence...took place in full view of crowds gathered for the purpose. But with the advent of an

inquisitorial criminal process in the course of the twelfth century, which gradually empowered courts to initiate investigations, make accusations, denunciations and arrests, judicial inquiries (including the use of torture) and deliberations were now conducted behind closed doors. Community participation here was denied, and as a result refocused on the two rituals that could be comprehensively stage-managed by authorities: sentencing and execution" (132).

A vast body of scholarship significantly qualifies such accounts. Even in twelfth-century Bologna—whose university was arguably at the heart of the Roman law revival—courts established new *accusatorial* procedures and these remained dominant through at least the thirteenth century. As Massimo Vallerani writes in his "Criminal Court Procedure in Late Medieval Bologna," a "new model" of "public trial... based on procedure of an accusatory type" was "shared in the civil and ecclesiastical tribunals of the late twelfth century." The new communal statutes of Bologna of 1288, for instance, included "absolute freedom to accuse." Throughout Europe, "English, German, and French professors were all active in the spread of the new model [in] local courts" (29–30). Vallerani stresses the "public and shared aspect of the trial": "the communal courts were able to accept and execute hundreds of trials, involving thousands of Bolognese citizens as litigants, *fideiussores*, advocates, and witnesses." The "convergence of so many cultural actors... produced a model of the accusatory trial that was coherent and stable over time" (30–1). Also notable "is the increase in the number of intermediaries in the trial—by the late thirteenth century *procuratores* and *fideiussores* crowded the tribunals" (32). "[F]or the jurists of the *ancien régime*, [who] founded their treatises [on] the jurisdictional acts of the tribunals, the trial was a great 'theater of the world,' a collective representation of the reality constructed by a chorus of judges, litigants, advocates, and rulers" (28) (and see Vallerani's *Medieval Public Justice*). See also Vitiello, *Public Justice*, 67–82 on the mixture of inquisitorial and accusatorial procedures in late medieval Reggio Emilia (including penalties for unproven accusations: "the late fourteenth century record at Reggio Emilia indicates neither the triumph of inquisitorial procedure nor the centralized position of the judge, but rather the synchronizing of inquisition and accusation" [80]).

As John Langbein notes, while the "outline" of "the Roman-canon prototype... had matured in the church courts by the end of the thirteenth century," it was not until the sixteenth century that "*Inquisitionsprozess*" fully took hold in most of Europe (see Langbein, *Prosecuting Crime*, 129, for a summary of the legislation in sixteenth-century Spain, Italy, Sweden, Germany, France, and the Spanish Netherlands). Even the *Constitutio Criminalis Carolina* (1530), often taken to mark the definitive transition in Germany from Saxon to Roman law, not only preserved accusatorial procedures alongside inquisitorial but treated the accusatorial as the normal form, which remained dominant through at least the sixteenth century. See Boes, *Crime and Punishment in Early Modern Germany*, 25, 45, 68, 94 (and generally on "the late fifteenth and sixteenth centur[y]... reception and integration of a foreign legal code, Roman Law, into the pre-existing *Germanische Recht* or Germanic Common Law" [25], identifying significant changes in Frankfurt with legislation introduced only in *1578* [268]). In the sixteenth century (in the German states at least), there was still lively opposition to the introduction of Roman law (see Strauss, *Law, Resistance, and the State*). See also Pohl-Zucker, *Making Manslaughter*, noting that her study of Germany 1376–1700 and other recent scholarship confirm "that the prosecution of interpersonal violence in early modern Europe continued to be influenced by 'traditional patterns of private retaliation, compensation and negotiation'" (2).

It is perhaps also worth noting that courts in which inquisitorial procedures were dominant, and (specifically) the Inquisition, often gave defendants far greater protections than those in which accusatorial procedures were dominant. Under the Inquisition, most punishments were light (penance or fines), and even corporal punishment was rare, let alone capital punishment. The Inquisition provided defendants with many more procedural safeguards than English common law courts: the right to a lawyer; legal aid; strict *habeas corpus* rules; and the promise of habitable prison conditions (specified in detail).

On safeguards in Roman-canon law procedural treatises (heavily favoring defendants), see Fowler-Magerl, *Ordines Iudiciarii*, 21–4. On legal aid in ecclesiastical courts in the twelfth century, see Brundage, *Medieval Origins*, 190–1. In medieval and Renaissance Florence, inquisitions initiated *ex officio* (by the court) had the lowest conviction rate: far lower than those initiated by accusation (Stern, *Criminal Law System*, 207). On the Inquisition's procedural protections (for a later period, but noting that safeguards were in fact *stricter* in the earlier period), see Tedeschi, *Prosecution of Heresy*, especially 135–54, and 141 on legal aid. Tedeschi notes that "a survey of the thousands of surviving sentences suggests that in actual fact milder forms of punishment prevailed, [mostly] abjurations,... fines or services,... and a seemingly endless cycle of prayers and devotions.... Despite popular notions to the

One of the central points of this chapter may seem obvious but is sometimes forgotten: law does not always follow scripts. As I note in the Introduction, even heresy and witch trials—which were supposed to be among the most secret (on the Continent at least)—were not in fact always so secret. Later in this chapter, I discuss the heresy trial of Jan Hus, at which there were hundreds of spectators. But his trial is not the only instance. At Gilles de Rais' trial for heresy and the alleged murder and sodomy of hundreds of children in 1440, "the crowd... pressed into the deliberation room" of the great upper hall of the Château La Tour Neuve on the first day of ecclesiastical proceedings. On the second day, the trial "opened in the presence of the judges and the promoter,... and in all parts of the vast hall, [there was] an ever-increasing crowd of witnesses and curious people, attracted from the city of Nantes and the whole country."[13] If inquisitorial trials were not always secret, nor were Inquisitors always all-powerful. Whether in England or on the Continent, even Inquisitors with papal bulls granting them absolute authority could encounter opposing lawyers, a host of procedural traps, and tough local opponents like Helena Scheuberin, whom I also discuss below.

One would expect fifteenth-century heresy and witch trials to be the paradigmatic instances of secret trials with all-powerful Inquisitors.[14] And yet the heresy trial and witch trial I discuss at length here both defy the dominant model, each in its own way. So do other scenes I describe: for instance, those in which raucous trial crowds pressed at the barriers and took on the guards, or impious spectators acted out at the execution site. In describing gaps between the normative ideal and actual events, this chapter extends some of the arguments of Chapter 3. There, I look primarily at theoretical texts. Here, I look primarily at historical events and their representation. There, I focus on the individual legal actor's bodily expression and experience. Here, I focus on collective events with multiple actors: crowd behavior; crowd emotion. That said, both chapters contest the persistent view that on the Continent in the later Middle Ages, so-called justice was a pure exercise in united ecclesiastical and secular power, which delivered summary judgments that it was futile to resist.

We might think Calefurnia an anomaly, but mooning the judge was actually a common medieval narrative motif, appearing in countless stories and images, representing the power of those at the bottom to use their bare backsides to stand

contrary, only a small percentage of cases concluded with capital punishment" (151). On the predominance of acquittals or settlements in late medieval Bologna, see Vallerani, "Criminal Court Procedure in Late Medieval Bologna," 34. On the light punishments in Italian courts generally and the extreme rarity of even corporal, let alone capital punishment, see Dean, "Criminal Justice in Mid-Fifteenth-Century Bologna," 26–7. In English common law courts, while defense lawyers were not allowed to argue during trials, they did work to get charges dismissed, change venue, protest jury composition, and more. For examples of English criminal defense lawyers' successes, see Bellamy, *Criminal Trial in Later Medieval England*, 100, 140.

[13] Bossard, *Gilles de Rais*, 271, 277.

[14] A thank you to Eleanor Johnson for discussions that helped me clarify my claims in this chapter, particularly about the special status of heresy and witch trials.

up to law.[15] Perhaps more important—as Catharina Arndes' act of defiance suggests, and as this chapter will show—it was not only in the world of fantasy that the accused used their bodies to defy its representatives, talked back to judges through symbolic action, chose anarchy over order, refused to follow the script. And it was not always futile to do so.

Ideals of Order, Scripted Trials, and the Disorderly Crowd

The Doge, the Judge, and the Sword: Allegorizing Justice as Terror and Pleasure in Venetian Civic Spectacle (c.1311)

In his *Splendor of the Customs of Venice* (*c*.1311), Ducal Chancellor Jacopo Bertaldo explains the meaning of the processions representing Venetian justice: the "*andate*" ("goings out") that the Doge and other magistrates performed whenever they left the Doge's palace. The "majesty of ducal glory is displayed in the regalia and rich, splendid ornament of [the Doge's] person," explains Bertaldo, "so that the good [people of Venice] may be instructed by the splendor of his grace [such that they are] amply rewarded for their goodness and obtain their lawful desires."[16] Arrayed in "regalia and rich, splendid ornament," the person of the Doge—the Republic's Chief Magistrate—represents the "splendor" of Venice and serves as a promise: be "instructed by [this] splendor" to obey the law and you will share in the prosperity it represents. The spectacle conveys its lesson as an idea, but it also instructs through affective experience. The pleasure of viewing the gorgeous display is a reward in itself for the good people's righteousness, and offers a taste of what it might be like to "obtain [your] desires." The lawful ones at least. As to the unlawful ones, the spectacle has a different message: the "judge is displayed to [the Doge's] right," explains Bertaldo, "so that evil-doers, upon seeing the judge," may be "frightened by the terror of judgment," and "taught to avoid wickedness and guard themselves against wrongdoing" (104–5). The emblematic sword of justice represents the consequences of such judgment: "the sword of the

[15] See e.g. Ziolkowski, ed., *Solomon and Marcolf*, 98–9, 237–41 on the motif of mooning in medieval and folk literature generally; and Randall, *Images in the Margins of Gothic Manuscripts*, images #533, 539, 540.

[16] The passage I discuss in this section is as follows: "Primo enim ostenditur mayestas glorie ducalis in apparatu et ornamento precioso et splendido sue persone, ut doceantur boni de splendor gracie, per suam bonitatem largiter remunerari et iusta desideria obtinere. Secundo, ostenditur iudex in dextra iudicandi malefactores, ut, iudice viso, ipsi doceantur declinare a malo et sibi cavere de faciendo malum, terrore iudicii spaventati. Tercio ostenditur ensis sive spata domini ducis, que post eum aportatur, ut doceantur de vindicta potencia et fortitudinis ducalis ad penas iudicantis incisione membrorum graviter infligendas. Et debet post dominem ducem ensis sive spata portari, quia vindicta malefactorum post iudicum fieri debet. Et nota, quod ubicumque spata portatur in publicio, iudex in dextra debet interesse." *Splendor Venetorum Civitatis Consuetudinum* (in Gaudenzi, ed., *Scripta anecdota glossatorum*), 3:104–5; and see the discussion in Barzman, *Limits of Identity*, 88.

Lord Doge is displayed... so that [people] may be taught about the justice of ducal power and strength," which inflicts "penalties with a heavy hand by the cutting of members [*incisione membrorum*]" (105).

The civic parade seeks at once to form the spectators as virtuous legal subjects and to train them in the emotions they are to feel when watching the actual spectacle of punishment. They are to experience deterrent "terror" as they watch the "heavy hand" of the law first cut off the limbs of the malefactors and ultimately cut these rotten members out of the body politic. At the same time, they are to rejoice that the "heavy hand" of the law does what is necessary to keep Venice—"that most serene Republic"—safe. The civic parade represents these emotions in its central triad: Doge, judge, and sword. It is essential (insists Bertaldo) that all three figures appear together and parade in the proper formation. "The sword must be carried behind the Doge" (he explains), "since the punishment of evildoers must happen [only] after judgment." And "wherever the sword is carried in public, the judge must be present to [the Doge's] right" (105). This order shows that judgment is founded in right and law (*dextra*). The three figures form a triangle that represents law as force but also, sequentially, justifies legal force. The Doge and the judge side-by-side embody law and judgment; the sword embodies the punishment that enacts the justice of law and judgment. In its spatial logic, the spectacle thus stands not merely for "ducal glory,... power and strength" but for that power and strength *as* justice.

Rex as Lex before the Throng in Jean Fouquet's "Lit de Justice de Vendôme" (1458)

The Venetian civic parade offers an exemplary instance of the spectacle of power as a display of sovereign legal order. Bertaldo treats the spectacle not merely as an ideal but as a description of how law actually works in Venice. In actual courts and scenes of punishment, of course, the reality could be rather different. We have what is probably a fairly realistic representation of one such court in Jean Fouquet's miniature of the "Lit de Justice de Vendôme" (1458) (fig. 4.3).[17] Portraying the treason trial of Jean, Duc d'Alençon, the miniature was completed within a month of the trial.[18] Fouquet includes portraits of the dignitaries who actually presided: under the canopy in the corner, King Charles VII (in what contemporaries called his "judiciary tribunal" or "lit de justice"); standing before

[17] Boccaccio, *Des cas des nobles hommes et femmes* [*De casibus virorum illustrium*], trans. Laurent de Premierfait (1458): Munich, Bayerische Staatsbibliothek, Codex Gall. 369, fol. 2v.

[18] On the image, see Morrison and Hedeman, *Imagining the Past in France*, 239; Hanley, *Lit de Justice*, 39–40; and Vale, *Charles VII*, 204–9 (on both image and trial, including many of the details that follow). Vale writes that the portrayal is so "faithful to the event" that it is "an almost photographic image" (206). The figure on the far right in the red hat gazing at the viewer is a self-portrait: the gaze

Fig. 4.3 The orderly court and the restless throng at the treason trial of the Duc d' d'Alençon in Jean Fouquet's "Lit de Justice de Vendôme" (1458).
Bayerische Staatsbibliothek München Cod.gall. 6 fol. 2v.

him, the king's chancellor and constable; to his left (in blue), twelve-year-old Prince Charles (etc.). Moreover, he portrays what we know to have been the

seems to communicate to the viewer that Fouquet was there and thus to authenticate his rendering. See "Fouquet: peintre et enlumineur du XVe siècle," Bibliothèque nationale de France, http://expositions.bnf.fr/fouquet/arret/26/index26g.htm (accessed April 11, 2021).

official seating plan and the decor of the great hall of the Château de Vendôme where the trial took place.[19]

Contemporary accounts of the trial stress its magnificence and the order that reigned: the majesty of the king; the sumptuousness of the fleur-de-lis fabric spread across the walls and floor; the reverential silence. "The King [was] seated triumphantly, [a] beautiful thing to see" writes the chronicler Georges Chastellain, and everyone watched "in silence." All sat "according to order and degree"; "dukes and counts [sat] just as they should ... in the correct order according to their peerage."[20] We can see such magnificence and order inside the diamond-shaped trial arena—the "parquet"—in Fouquet's miniature. The three figures under the canopy are its focal point: king, chancellor, and constable representing the union of "*Lex et Rex* ... together on that bed of Justice" (as one commentator put it).[21] The "lords temporal" and "spiritual" (peers, archbishops, bishops) take the highest seats. The next tier seats other high-ranking officials (judges and courtiers). Below them are councilors of the Parlement and civil servants. At the bottom (on the floor) are the lawyers: advocates, proctors, notaries.[22] All are similarly dressed in legal attire appropriate to their positions: all wear long colored robes, with either hoods with white miniver fur-trimmed capes or black close-fitting caps (*pilei*).[23] It is a relatively static image: most of the figures sit upright, arms folded; their faces are largely expressionless.

Laurens Girard, notary and secretary to Charles VII, commissioned the manuscript in which Fouquet's miniature appears: a manuscript of Boccaccio's treatise on the fall of the once-illustrious.[24] Fouquet's rendering of the parquet illustrates both the official royal judicial ideology for which Girard stood and the ostensible moral of Boccaccio's treatise: the King's justice punishes treason, no matter how illustrious the traitor. It is an image that Bertaldo would have approved. But Fouquet chooses not only to include but quite literally to foreground what most of the accounts of the trial ignore: the teeming crowd inside the Château that presses against the barriers surrounding the parquet. We know from Chastellain

[19] For the participants and other details, see Vale, *Charles VII*, 206–8; and Hanley, *Lit de Justice*, 39 (noting references to the king's seat as both a "judiciary tribunal" and "lit de justice"). The word "lit" in the "lit de justice" from which kings presided over cases referenced its bed-like canopy (see Hanley, *Lit de justice*, 17–22). But it clearly also referenced the Latin *lis* (plural *lites*), meaning lawsuit.

[20] "Le roy donques assis triumphamment, [qui] estoit belle chose à voir, et là ... tout le monde se disposa à silence" (3:478). Everyone "estoient assis par ordre et par degré," "ducs et contes, ainsi que aller devoient par ordre en leur pairie" (3:477). Chastellain, *Oeuvres* [*Chronique*] (1863–66, ed.), 3:477–8.

[21] Vale, *Charles VII*, 204 (citing a seventeenth-century commentator). On this arena as the "Parquet," see La Roche-Flavin, *Treze livres des parlemens de France* (1617 ed.), 300 [Bk 4, sec. 77] (describing its arrangement in ways that match both Fouquet's image and Chastellain's description [299–300]).

[22] Vale, *Charles VII*, 207–8.

[23] On the figures' attire, see Hargreaves-Mawdsley, *History of Legal Dress*, 21–3.

[24] Vale, *Charles VII*, 205.

that "the hall was also opened [publicly] and given up to everyone to come in and hear the king's sentence," and he specifies that "people of all estates" came to Vendôme for the event (not just "high and great barons, bishops, and prelates"), many traveling great distances because they knew "it must be something great and special, as it in fact was."[25] In Fouquet's miniature, the chaotic vitality of the packed crowd contrasts strongly with the scene inside the barriers. Outside, we see a patchwork of classes, genders, and attire: a motley array of local and foreign fashions, short tunics and long robes, multi-colored stockings, hats and shoes in all styles. Here, the peasants jostle with the nobility, men with women, young with old. Unlike the dignitaries inside the parquet, the spectators express a multitude of emotions: excitement, curiosity, alarm, anger, bemusement, disdain, mirth, and more. The spectators at the front pull themselves upward to peer into the trial scene, pressing their hands against the barrier. The soldiers and guards carry maces and no fewer than nine ugly bayonets, prepared to subdue anyone who gets out of line. The vignette that dominates the foreground is in fact just such a confrontation: the spectator in blue is in open defiance, ready for battle as the guard tries to push him back into the crowd: is he resisting arrest? will an all-out struggle ensue? In representing the force of law to punish defiance, Fouquet (like the Calefurnia image) places defiance front and center.

Noisy Crowds, Lawyers' Harangues, and Scripted Trials: Thomas Basin's Proposal (1455)

In his "Proposal for the Best Procedure for Hearing and Delivering Public Trials" (1455), jurist and Bishop of Lisieux Thomas Basin offers a vivid portrait of the vast crowds that routinely gathered to watch trials in high courts (parlements) throughout France.[26] In Normandy (explains Basin), one can see the worst excesses. There, at the start of a trial, a huge "multitude assembles." There is such "a grea[t] tumult of cases" that it is almost impossible even to "obtain an audience." "[H]ow great [are] the long-winded delay[s] in Normandy!" There "perhaps as many as ten thousand cases are pending," yet "a whole day is taken up

[25] Chastellain, *Oeuvres*: "Estoit aussi la salle ouverte et abandonnée à tout le monde pour y entrer et pour oïr la sentence du roy" (3:477). "Y estoient aussi tous les haulx et grans barons, évesques et prélats du royaume, . . . ensamble toutes conditions de gens autres, . . . pensant que ce devoit estre quelque chose de grant et d'espécial, comme de fait estoit" (3:467). And see Basin on the people "gathered in great numbers" ("in magno numero collectos") for d'Alençon's trial: *Histoire de Charles VII* (1933–44 ed.), 2:301.

[26] "Libellus de optimo ordine forenses lites audiendi et deferendi," in Basin, *Histoire des règnes de Charles VII et de Louis XI* (1859 ed.), vol. 4 (hereafter cited in the Latin text in my notes). See the discussion of portions of this text in Enders, *Rhetoric and the Origins of Medieval Drama*, 40–2, 96; and thank you to Eugene Petracca for assistance with translations.

with hearing one or two cases."[27] But trials in "many other provinces of this kingdom" are almost as bad, including those in "our venerable Parlement—I mean in the Grande Chambre" in the Paris Palais de Justice. "What shall we say about [our] supreme court?" Is not its trial process just as "tedious and almost as intolerably drawn-out? . . . [I]nnumerable cases fall to it daily," and because of our procedures, "some fifteen-hundred people" end up having to "occupy themselves for a whole day in hearing just one miserable case." The delays are so extreme that "almost everyone" thinks it is "better to give up from the very beginning," even when there is "certain victory."[28] Certainly, "that old proverb of the comedian [is] true: 'The highest law is the highest injury' [*Summum jus, summa injuria*]."[29]

Even worse, in Normandy and elsewhere, a "vocal audience is [actually] allowed [by] customary law," following "the custom of that most abundant marketplace": the forum. The cries of the audience turn the trial into a circus. An atmosphere of "festivity" reigns.[30] Scripture specifically prohibits being swept up in the passions of the multitude in court: "the Lord says in Exodus: 'in judgment, do not acquiesce to the opinion of the majority,'" writes Basin. And yet, in Normandy at least, "judges [do] decide cases according to the opinion of the majority of [those] present," siding with the loudest party, most of whom "are utterly ignorant of both written and customary law."[31] Ruling through applause (in an updated version of Plato's theatrocracy), the spectators control the judges.

Even worse than the crowd, however, are the lawyers. Given that they control the spectators, it is really they who control the judges. Daily their "almost

[27] "[M]ultitudo confluit negotiorum" (51). "[U]bi est major causarum concursus, ibi difficilius audientia obtinetur" (34). "[Q]uanta est prolixitas in Normannia, in plerisque causis in quibus loci sive praedii ostensio postulator" (34). "[C]uria in qua forsan causae sunt pendentes ad decem mille vel amplius, una dies in audienda vel duabus causis occupetur" (40).

[28] "Si vero consequenter ad alias curias atque tribunalia, tam illius regiae urbis Parisiensis, quam ducatus Normanniae et aliarum multarum provinciarum hujus regni respexerimus, non dissimilem fore, sed parem et consimilem dispendii prolixitatem reperiemus" (34). "Quid de curia nostri scacarii suprema dicemus? Estne in ea taediosa multis et paene intolerabilis prolixitas, tum propter innumeram causarum dietim devolutionem ad ipsam, tum propter expediendi modum, cum aliquando mille et quingentae personae ad audientiam unius miserae causae per totum diem integrum occupentur?" (35). "[O]mnium fere communi et vulgata opinione, ut melius et consultius quamplurimis foret causis justissimis ab ipso initio cedere, quam post tam molestas ac graves sumptuum et laborum jacturas victoriae indubitate eventum exspectare" (33).

[29] "Ex quibus optime verificari ostenditur vetustum illud comici proverbium: 'Summum jus, summa injuria'" (35).

[30] "Atqui consuetudo patria videtur satis hujuscemodi prolixitatibus occurrere, dummodo probe et legaliter servaretur" (39). "[J]uxta illius amplissimi fori consuetudinem" (33). "[C]um illa placitandi festivitate declamari" (51).

[31] "Dicit enim Dominus in Exodo: 'Non acquiesces in judicio plurium sententiae, ut devies a vero'" (61, citing Exodus 23:2). "[I]n plerisque curiis Normanniae observatur, quod videlicet judices ex opinione majoris numeri assistentium causas diffiniunt, quorum saepius major pars est a juris scripti et consuetudinarii penitus ignara" (61).

innumerable arguments come before the court." Every day there is both "insolence [and] begging to engross [the attention of the] audience." They thrill the audience with the "splendor," "magnificence," and "pomp" of their "verbal pleading [and] forensic oratory," inflame the audience with their "declamation," producing "feeling[s]" that become "fixed deeply in the souls of those listening." They drone on through already long-winded cases, their "superfluous and deceitful delays" drawing out each case as they "reap [their] great reward[s]." And the parties, "patiently or impatiently,... wait through [the] years" for their verdicts. When cases are finally decided, it is "wretched silver" that has decided them.[32]

There may be no remedy for "wretched silver," which can turn even the most expert of judges into "demons": "corrupt and twisted" by "perversity"; trampling justice in pursuit of "their depraved desires."[33] But Basin does have a "salubrious and effective remedy" for the theatrocracy and its insolent lawyers. He proposes that "pleading [be] done only by means of written texts" rather than being declaimed oratorically: the "verbose and trifling garrulity of [the] lawyers' haranguing" would thereby be "cut off."[34] "But perhaps" (he muses) "someone will object that I am trying to introduce a novel theory... little tested by use and experience.... Assuredly not"! For "thousands and thousands" of people have seen how in certain places "a court of twelve or thirteen [judges]" can, "during [a single] hour," dispatch as many cases as can "be done in an entire year in the court of our venerable Parlement." Where have they seen this? In his ideal of a court in the "apostolic seat" in "the city of all Christians": the Roman Rota, the Church's highest court of appeals.[35]

[32] "[P]raestat argumentum importunitas innumerabilium paene quotidie... supplicantium pro obtinenda audientia" (35). "Sed difficile atque durum erit... a placitationis verbalis seu forensis orationis pompa divellere, quae splendorem quemdam ac magnificentiam" (50). "[A]ltius audientium animis infingitur sententia a diserto oratore prolata" (51). "[S]upervacuae et frustratoriae dilationes" (37). "[D]icendi exercitationem, in qua magnus est fructus, atque orationis copiam advocatis praebere" (50). "[V]el patienter, vel impatienter ad alios annos" (35). "[M]isero... argento" (58).

[33] "[S]ed deterius forsan aestimaverim malum, juris peritiam copulatam cum perversitate et corruptione voluntatis. Nam uti daemones, quibus est perversa et in malum obstinata voluntas.... [Q]uibus est cum juris scientia perversa voluntas, tanto sunt potentiores ad exsequendum quod perverse volunt, quanto, juris scientia instructi, majorem astutiam habent ad media perquirenda quibus concupiscentias suas pravas deducant ad effectum!" (58–9).

[34] "Quid igitur? possibilene est circa hoc salubre et efficax invenire remedium?" (37). "[E]x scripto tantummodo et non verbaliter placitetur" (51). "[V]erbosa atque nugatoria plurimorum advocatorum perorantium causas garrulitas sive in placitando, sive in scribendo amputator" (37).

[35] "Sed forsan aliquis objiciet me introducere velle theoriam novam, quae minime usu et experimento probata sit. Non ego profecto id facio... sed mille et mille superstites sunt, qui pariter et melius me viderunt, cognoverunt et experimento probaverunt qualiter aliquibus in locis per curiam XII aut XIII personarum, una hora qua curia sedet, tanta et in tot causis expeditio datur, quanta fortassis in uno integro anno posset in venerabili curia parlamenti, dico in magna camera, ubi causae verbaliter placitantur" (41). "Ad romanam quippe curiam et apostolicam sedem de toto christianorum orbe causae paene innumerae dietenus per appellationes et alias deferuntur" (41).

The Rota took its name from the fact that the judges sat in the form of a wheel ("Rota").[36] The wheel signified, among other things, the kind of closed completeness, wholeness, or divine perfection that admitted of no addition or subtraction. "Oh, how greatly do we esteem it!" writes Basin. "[F]rom every Christian nation and people" come the "'judges [*auditores*] of the Rota." And yet, collectively, they form a harmonious whole, following a precisely choreographed ritual: "on the judicial days, . . . at a certain hour [of] the morning, [at] the solemn stroke of the bell, [the] lord auditors come out of their conclave and enter the great palace nearby." They all proceed "in turn and by order." There, "each sits in tribunal, separate from the others" but exactly equidistant. "At once . . . with exact diligence, the litigators [and] proctors come [before] the lord [judges]."[37] There, the lawyers and judges rapidly pass a great number of written documents back and forth: petitions, articles, depositions, explanations, scribes' reports. No one "is supplicated before an audience" and "no one complains." In such proceedings, "the truth of the matter speaks for itself." There are no "deceitful delays," litigators' tricks, shouting audiences with their ignorant judgments. Let the French follow this model![38] No more rule of the insolent lawyer or ignorant majority in court!

And yet, admittedly (writes, Basin, quoting Saint Jerome), "the performance of the live voice [*vivae vocis actus*] has [that] 'certain something of latent energy'; [the] meaning expressed by an eloquent orator is implanted more deeply in the souls of the listeners than if it were not heard [but only] read."[39] If the French were

[36] For a famous 1468 image of the auditors of the Rota seated at a round table, see Brundage, *Medieval Origins*, 422. The *c.*1483 image of Cicero pleading before judges who sit in a circular formation (fig. 3.1, 108) suggests that courts, or at least illustrators, treated the Rota's circular formation as a model. Brundage, "'My Learned Friend,'" 187, notes that advocates and proctors did actually engage in oral pleading in the Rota. For details on the medieval Roman Rota, see Salonen, *Papal Justice* (especially 42–55 on its normal procedures). I am grateful to Kirsi Salonen for clarifications about its practices.

[37] "O, quantum aestimare possumus" (43). "Ibi enim sunt . . . judices electi de omne christianorum gente et natione, qui 'auditores Rotae' appellantur" (42). "Diebus itaque juridicis . . . certa hora quam pulsus solemnis campanae omnibus palam facit, exeunt praefati domini auditores de suo conclavi et intrant palatium magnum propinquum" (44). "[V]icissim et per ordinem" (43). "[S]edet pro tribunali quilibet seorsum ab aliis per loci distantiam competentem . . . . Statim autem cum exacta diligentia veniunt litigatores et causarum procuratores ad singula dominorum" (44). By "litigatores" Basin presumably means the lawyers historians normally refer to as "advocates." Proctors were generally highly experienced in ordinary courtroom practice, but less well educated (and less expensive) than advocates, who had usually studied law in the university, and were thus equipped to handle difficult legal problems. See Brundage, "'My Learned Friend,'" 183–4 and *Medieval Origins*, 203–14; and Helmholz, *Profession of Ecclesiastical Lawyers*, 7–38.

[38] "[N]emini pro audientia supplicatur, nullus de denegata conqueritur" (41). "[R]es ipsa per se ipsam satis liquido se ostendat" (54; and see 50).

[39] "Amplius etiam habet, ut Hieronymus ait, nescio quid latentis energiae vivae vocis actus, et altius audientium animis infigitur sententia a diserto oratore prolata, quam si ab aliquo minime audita, sed scripta tantummodo legeretur" (51).

See Jerome, *Letters* [letter 53], http://www.patrologia-lib.ru/patrolog/hieronym/epist/epist03.htm (accessed April 6, 2021). Basin quotes from the following passage: "Spoken words possess an indefinable hidden power, and teaching that passes directly from the mouth of the speaker into the ears of the disciples is more impressive than any other. When the speech of Demosthenes against Aeschines was

to adopt the Rota's practices, they would, regretfully (he sighs), have to "give up their oral pleading," and thus the "pomp" and ceremony of their "forensic oratory," which "display[s] the magnificence and splendor of the courts" so brilliantly. In fact, on second thought, he would not wish to *altogether* forbid oral speech in trials, a fact underlined by his repeated references to "hearing" in his proposed proceedings: after all, the judges are *auditores* who *hear* cases (indeed, they are the "lords" of "auditors").[40] Such ambivalence may account for the fact that, in Basin's portrait of this paragon of courts, where the silent document supposedly reigns, somehow there is a lot of exciting activity. Inside the wheel of the Rota, there are twelve or thirteen judges, each with four "public notaries" at his feet. There are many lawyers in the circle ("litigators [and] proctors"). "[R]unners or attendants" run back and forth among the judges, into the back rooms and out, in a positively dizzying "vicissitude" (the whole court appears to spin like a "'Wheel'").[41] All of these people are not merely passing documents among themselves: it turns out that some of their activity is dedicated to performing for an audience. In the Rota, "[i]f something must be said against the articles or petition," Basin explains, the judge "exhibits judicially" his attack on them. These exhibitions take place before spectators whom Basin explicitly identifies as a "public audience" distinct from the judicial audience. The "lord judges si[t] before the tribunal and public audience [*publica audientia*]." They "consult, deliberate, and conclude" their cases "in public [*publice*]," and announce their decision to that public. Indeed, his entire proposal is aimed at "the Best Procedure for Hearing and Delivering Public Trials." That is, however scripted the trial, however chastened the lawyers, Basin's ideal courtroom remains—in his vision—a public theatre.[42]

Open Courtrooms, Festive "Law-Days," and the German Rechtstag as Mock Trial

That Basin envisions the chastened, controlled trial as nevertheless a kind of public theatre is not perhaps surprising. As I indicated in the Introduction,

recited before the latter during his exile at Rhodes, amid all the admiration and applause he sighed, 'if you could but have heard the brute deliver his own periods!'" New Advent, Letters of St. Jerome, https://www.newadvent.org/fathers/3001053.htm (accessed April 6, 2021; translation modified).

[40] "Sed difficile atque durum erit valde nostrates, ut arbitror, a placitationis verbalis seu forensis orationis pompa divellere, quae splendorem quemdam ac magnificentiam curiarum ostentare videtur" (50). And see 53.

[41] "Quilibet autem praefatorum dominorum quatuor publicos tabelliones secum habet" (42). "Comissiones praefatae, ut signatae sunt in pede supplicationis, auditoribus, quibus justitia partibus ministranda mandatur, per cursores seu apparitores qui eas de cancellaria recipiunt, praesentantur" (42). "[O]b quam ordinis vicissitudinem . . . curia illa Rota sive audientia Rotae appellatur" (43).

[42] "[S]i ad dicendum contra articulos vel contra libellum, similiter rationes, quibus eos impugnare credit, judicialiter exhibit" (44–5). "[P]raefati domini auditores pro tribunali et publica audientia sedent" (45). "[M]ature et graviter publice . . . consultant, deliberant, et concludunt" (43).

while some courts held trials behind closed doors, many held them in public spaces, often outdoors, even in the later Middle Ages: at natural landmarks such as hills; at columns, crosses, statues, or bridges; in places where the crime had occurred (often in public streets); in tents; or in the open market square.[43] Variants on the great public courts of the early Middle Ages—the *placita*—appeared and reappeared, in (for instance) the *Grands Jours*: courts that met in public throughout France from the thirteenth century on.[44] Among the most common locations for court sessions in the twelfth and thirteenth centuries were church porticos, vestibules, or gardens.[45] Louis IX of France heard litigants and gave judgment under an oak tree in the Forest of Vincennes or in public parks in Paris in the mid-thirteenth century.[46] The tiered stone benches where the magistrates of the city of Arles heard cases and issued judgments in the thirteenth century are still standing outside the doors of the Palais des Podestats.[47] Fourteenth- and fifteenth-century German regulations specified that trials were to be held in "public" [*offentlich*] "under the heavens": "in the open market"; in a street wide and long enough for a wagon to pass; "before the town hall . . . under the naked sky."[48] Many German images in fact show late medieval courts outdoors surrounded only by tents, or in open porticos or streets in towns.[49] In fourteenth- and fifteenth-century Cologne, courts continued to meet in open civic spaces such as marketplaces, even after the city built a set of magnificent new structures to house the expanding municipal administration.[50] Many criminal assizes took

[43] For a concise discussion of the location of ecclesiastical courts (identifying such outdoor locations), see Deimling, "Courtroom." At the end of the fifteenth century, some judicial hearings were still being held under the arcades of the Ducal Palace in Venice. In England, most ecclesiastical trials were held in churches, though (as Martin Ingram notes for the early modern period), ecclesiastical courts "sometimes left [church courtrooms] to go on circuit, and sessions were held in improvised surroundings in parish churches or in inn parlours" (*Church Courts, Sex, and Marriage in England*, 2). Courts throughout the Middle Ages and early modern period often met in informal, *ad hoc* spaces: a bishop's kitchen with the cook as witness (Hardman, *Conflicts, Confessions, and Contracts*, 43); the dining room of Doctors Commons (Senior, *Doctors' Commons*, 93–5).

[44] On the *Grands Jours*, see Trotry, *Grands jours des parlements*.

[45] On these locales for twelfth- and thirteenth-century bishops' courts, see Brundage, *Medieval Origins*, 422–4.

[46] Brundage, *Medieval Origins*, 373–4.

[47] With thanks to Francesco Cassini for discovering the site, and for photos of the benches and plaque.

[48] Maurer, *Geschichte des altgermanischen . . . öffentlich-mündlichen Gerichtsverfahrens*, 357: trials were to be held "vor dem Rathhuse . . . unter bloßem Himmel"; "an der fryn Rychs Straß so weit, brait und lang das ein Wagen durch Gericht faren mögt offenlich"; "underm Himmel"; "auf offentlichem Markte"; "bey *Sonnenschein* unnter *dem Himmel und unter keinen obendach*."

[49] For images of late fifteenth-century outdoor urban courts, see e.g. Reincke and Bolland, ed., *Die Bilderhandschrift des Hamburgischen Stadtrechts von 1497* (unpaginated, images H and L). For images of outdoor tented courts, see Tengler, *Der neü Layenspiegel* (1511), fol. 34r, 99r, 162r, 199r.

[50] Arlinghaus, *Inklusion-Exklusion*, 75–118, 376–7 (on legal space, ritual, and the public in late medieval German-speaking Cologne). Arlinghaus writes that even when courts met indoors, "the spatial concept was the same as for those municipal courts [that] work[ed] in the open [air]," noting the general scholarly consensus that the absence of dedicated courtrooms in the Middle Ages was due to the view that courts ought to be public: "the basic idea was to embed the courts into the urban space instead of taking them out" (*Inklusion-Exklusion*, 376–7).

place in marketplaces, as (quite naturally) did the English pie-powder courts for criminal and civil disputes emerging from markets and fairs.[51] In late medieval Marseille, courts met at market stalls in front of the house of a local chandler, or in front of the lower doors of Notre Dame des Accoules "above the stone drain of the apothecary."[52]

Even where courts were held indoors, these were often in public spaces: churches or open palaces halls. A late thirteenth-century royal ordinance specified that every day that the Paris Parlement met, three counsellors of the Court of Requests must sit in the corner of the great hall of the Palais de Justice, "surrounded by the ever-present noise and bustle of that tumultuous place" (as one historian writes), making themselves available to all potential plaintiffs.[53] Such courts were porous spaces: in the *c.*1483 Cicero miniature I reproduce in Chapter 3, spectators wander in through the open door in the church and peer over the backs of the judges' benches; in the 1497 image of the Hamburg municipal courtroom I reproduce in the Introduction, the crowd at the vast open window seems to be virtually inside the courtroom.[54] Town halls that held courtrooms often faced the market square to ensure that the populace could see the proceedings and have access to justice.

Large events might take place outdoors outside the city walls. In the fourteenth century, the Inquisitor Bernard Gui held huge condemnation ceremonies both in Toulouse Cathedral and outside the walls, always with an "immense crowd of clergy and people."[55] Officials like the Mayor of Hereford routinely staged court sessions on city walls or at city gates.[56] Scholars of early modern London theatre have stressed that theatres were often situated in the "liberties": outside the legal controls of the city. But so was law itself: Southampton, for instance, preserved the custom of keeping courts on hillsides by designating a mound called Cutthorn as

[51] English town courts included urban fair courts, market courts, staple courts, coroner's courts, and more. See Kowaleski, "Town Courts in Medieval England," 18. On assizes held in marketplaces (as well as town halls), see Langbein, *Prosecuting Crime*, 198.

[52] Smail, *Emotions, Publicity, and Legal Culture*, 33–4. Smail describes a 1351 Marseille town council resolution announcing that from henceforth only lawyers, procurators, and kin would be able to speak on behalf of defendants. In his view, the resolution points to "the large crowds that could forgather at the court space in the hopes of swaying the proceedings" (34); and see 224–5 and throughout on the fact that all the courts of late medieval Marseille met outdoors, and on the medieval view that "[o]utdoor and open legal ceremonies contributed to the public and honest character of the law" (225).

[53] Shennan, *Parlement of Paris* [1998 ed.], 18; and see Shennan generally on "the noise and bustle which succeeded the partial conversion of a private residence into a court of law" in the late thirteenth and early fourteenth centuries (100).

[54] See Chapter 3, fig. 3.1, 107 and Introduction, fig. 0.2, 14.

[55] See e.g. March 3, 1308: "la foule immense du clergé et du peuple"; Gui, *Livre des sentences* (2002, ed.), 1:177. (Gui repeatedly uses this and similar phrases to describe the crowd.)

[56] Johnson, *Law in Common*, 63–4, and 58–9, describing the mayor's tourn for the city wards at each of Hereford's five gates and noting that the walls of the city itself were legal spaces that served to "provid[e] a stage for court sessions" (58–9).

the site of the town leet (criminal court). In Hereford, the mayor held the city's annual "Law Day" in Tollfield outside the city walls.[57]

The phrase "law-day" appears in various forms throughout Europe—*jour de droit, dies iuris, Rechttag* or *Rechtstag*—denoting everything from general assemblies to legal festivals, general court meeting days (as in Basin's "judicial days"), specific days in a trial, or sentencing proceedings.[58] In Germany (as in much of Europe), the *Rechstage* were three days specially set aside for trials: during the first two, the parties appeared in court and argued their cases; on the last day, the court announced its decision. Though the *Rechtstage* seem often to have taken place in town halls in the late Middle Ages, regulations still specified that they should ideally be held outdoors under the open sky.[59] Often such events were seasonal (like seasonal theatrical events): on certain days of the year, people from neighboring communities and farther afield would converge for manorial courts, sheriffs' courts, assizes (or "sittings") of different bodies, or for fairs with special courts like the pie-powders.[60] The phrase "law-day" signals the fact that these were set apart from ordinary time, like holidays, contributing to their festive feel. On days on which extraordinary trials like the Duc d'Alençon's took place, one was free—as on holy days—to leave ordinary routines and go to the scene of the action. The law-day, in other words, was also a day of license.

Marketplaces were already full of activity on market days, but still noisier and more bustling on those rare and exciting occasions when a public trial or punishment was to take place there. Huge crowds gathered not only for the punishments I discuss later in this chapter but for trials and sentencing proceedings, producing the kind of carnival atmosphere Basin describes in the Norman and Paris Parlements. Trial attendees were far from sedate, and could be outright riotous.

[57] Johnson, *Law in Common*, 60–2.

[58] "Diebus . . . juridicis" (Basin, "Libellus," 44). On variants such as *jors de dret* or *jor de dreit*, see the glossary entries for "dreit (dret)" and "droytura" in Vitali, *Mit dem Latein am Ende?* 449–51; and on the Swiss version of the law day, see Gallone, *Organisation judiciaire et procédure*, 185–7, 256–9. In England, meetings of the "hundreds" courts were often called "law-days" (Jolliffe, *Constitutional History*, 63; Jones, *Gender and Petty Crime*, 14). Although the words "law-day" and "folk-moot" were not generally interchangeable, the London "law-day" was sometimes called a "Folkmoot," identifying it with early medieval lawcourts (moots or motes), often viewed as popular assemblies (Jolliffe, *Constitutional History*, 63).

[59] The word *Rechtstag* (or *Rechttag*) goes back at least to the thirteenth century and probably much earlier: defendants are granted a *Rechtstag*; plaintiffs are ordered to appear at the *Rechtstag*. See e.g. the references to the "Rechttag" in Freyberg, ed., *Sammlung historischer Schriften*, 1:325, 1:371, 3:107. On the medieval *Rechtstag*, see Knapp, *Alte Nürnberger Kriminal-Verfahren*, 131–43; and Maurer, *Geschichte des altgermanischen . . . öffentlich-mündlichen Gerichtsverfahrens*, 342. See note 48 (above) on the various codes specifying that medieval courts be held in public. Maurer notes that codes for Lübeck (1537), Württemberg (1537 and 1545), and Wurtzberg (1577–82) all specified that the *Rechtstag* was still to be held "under the heavens." And see Pohl-Zucker, *Making Manslaughter*, 202 (on the "Blood-courts" that the *Reichsvogt* held in public squares; and 227–33, 243, 246, 249, 255, 258 for additional examples of public or semi-public court locations in Württemberg and Zurich between *c.*1376 and 1700).

[60] Johnson, *Law in Common*, 63–4.

The "quarrels, brawls, bloodshed, murder, and other evils" that sometimes took place in the midst of a trial led the Council of Saumer to ban courts from meeting in churches in the mid-thirteenth century, and several later councils followed suit.[61] The Statute of Northampton of 1328 targeted precisely those rebels who went with armed followers to judicial sessions, sometimes attacking jurors en route to the proceedings.[62] It read, in part: "no Man [may] come before the King's Justices... with force and arms, nor bring [any] force in affray of the peace, [nor] ride armed by night nor by day, in Fairs, Markets, nor in the presence of the Justices or other Ministers" (notably associating sessions of the peace with fairs and markets).[63] The Statute was clearly needed (as were similar regulations in medieval Cologne).[64] In the records of Sir William Shareshull, Chief Justice of the King's Bench 1350–61, we find numerous cases in which people had caused "affray" during sessions of the peace: in-court brawls; armed assaults on justices during a trial. Groups of armed men sometimes threatened assizes (for instance in Wiltshire in 1336) or resisted the king's justices (for instance in Tredington in 1347). In one case, a crowd acting "like madmen and men possessed" imprisoned a justice of the peace in Eynsham Abbey. In another case, a knight and an esquire attacked a justice with a sword in an attempt to rescue a man who had himself been arrested for making an affray during the session.[65] During the Peasants' Revolt of 1381, law was a central target. It was rumored that the peasants were going to "kill all the lawyers" (as Shakespeare's Dick the Butcher says), and they did in fact execute many lawyers, jurors, and others with legal training.[66]

While the Statute of Northampton may have been a response to the particular vulnerability of the king's justice in the fourteenth century, and Basin's pamphlet may have been a one-off initiative, there were many people in the next two centuries who sought to restrain the unruliness of the crowd at such events. In fifteenth- and early sixteenth-century Germany, reformers launched a sustained attack on what they viewed as the disorderliness and chaos of public trials, attempting to transform these into scripted public performances before silent and reverential audiences.[67] Perhaps the most influential of these reformers was Johann Freiherr von Schwarzenberg, judge of the Episcopal Court of Bamberg,

[61] Brundage, *Medieval Origins*, 423. [62] Bellamy, *Criminal Law and Society*, 55.

[63] *Statutes of the Realm*, vol. 1 [1235–1377] (1810 ed.), 258 (2 Edward III item 3).

[64] See Arlinghaus, *Inklusion-Exklusion*, 382–3, on frequent prosecution of litigants' and lawyers' for "undisciplined behaviour" in late medieval Cologne, in violation of regulations forbidding violence or offensive speech in court.

[65] Putnam, *Place in Legal History*, 130, 147–8; and Green, *Crisis of Truth*, 411, note 12.

[66] See Green, *Crisis of Truth*, 198 (and generally 198–205); and for Dick the Butcher, Shakespeare, *Henry VI, Part 2* [4.2].

[67] On the attack on German public and oral traditions of adjudication, see Leue, *Der mündliche öffentliche Anklage-Prozeß*, 65; and Maurer, *Geschichte des altgermanischen... öffentlich-mündlichen Gerichtsverfahrens*, 306–62.

whose 1507 criminal code for Bamberg (the "*Bambergensis*") became a model for the codes that followed.[68]

Among the *Bambergensis*' prescriptions was a radical reformation of the *Rechstage*: the law days during which accused and accusers routinely confronted one another in open court in highly emotional, often dramatic encounters.[69] Some of these events were probably large, festive, unruly affairs like many other medieval "law days." Schwarzenberg was determined to "bring order" to the *Rechtstag*'s current disorder and eradicate "unseemly abuses": not only to squelch courtroom drama but also to eliminate the "superfluous questions" that he said took up most of the proceedings: questions that (he charged) serve "neither truth nor justice and in fact delay and prevent the law" from taking its proper course.[70]

A description of one public *Rechtstag* in Ulm in 1457 gives a vivid sense of what he was protesting.[71] Accusing seven men of theft, one Andrees Widenmann came into court with the stolen property as evidence. He also brought with him a team of oath-takers and the former mayor, who was to act as his lawyer. Not to be outdone, the alleged robbers brought in a judge as their lawyer. The judge acting for the defense insisted that each of the seven defendants had a right to his own lawyer in court, demanded *habeas corpus* for his clients, and asserted that they would not answer the charges until they were freed from their chains (a request that the court granted, against the plaintiff's protests). The defense had a substantive argument: there had been no theft because his clients had justifiably taken the property in a feud. But he also had many procedural objections: there were only eleven judge-assessors rather than the twelve required for a quorum; one of the oath-takers had been convicted of manslaughter so his oath was legally void; the plaintiff had bribed the oath-takers so none of their oaths were valid; the presiding judge did not have authority to issue capital sentences; moreover, he had, against strict rules, failed to remain seated throughout the proceedings. The judge acting for the defense demanded more time for his clients to acquire further proofs of their innocence and bring in more people to testify to their reputation. Ultimately, the trial judges ruled in favor of Widenmann, but the decision was a close one, clearly due to the defense's maneuvers.

In an attempt to eliminate such scenes, Schwarzenberg proposed a radical reform. Instead of a three-day proceeding, the *Rechstag* was to become a one-

[68] Schwarzenberg, *Bambergensis* (short for *Bamberger Halsgerichtsordnung* or *Constitutio Criminalis Bambergensis*).

[69] Provisions on the *Rechtstag* in Schwarzenberg's *Bambergensis* include art. 91–4, 107, 123, 217, 224, 236–9, 256, https://de.wikisource.org/wiki/Bambergische_Peinliche_Halsgerichtsordnung (accessed June 30, 2021).

[70] "[O]rdnung zubringen" (Schwarzenberg, *Bambergensis*, fol. 3v ["Die vorrede dis Buchs"]). "Item nach dem auch an uns gelangt ist das bißher an etlichen unsern halßgerichten vil uberflussiger frage gebraucht sindt die zu keiner erfarung der warheyt oder gerechtigkeyt not sein sunder alleyn das Recht verlengern und verhindern Sölche und andere unzimliche mißbreuch" (*Bambergensis*, fol. 32v [art. 121]). The word "*ordnung*" appears seventy-five times in the text.

[71] Narrated in Dülmen, *Theatre of Horror*, 34–6.

day show: a public trial-and-sentencing proceeding plus punishment rolled into one. The revamped *Rechstag* would retain many of the features of the traditional sentencing proceeding: at the "customary time of day," with the ringing of "the customary bells," the court would "assemble itself for judgment according to the dictates of good custom," with the whole town assembled to watch.[72] However, the trial portion would, in fact, be a mock trial. The judge and *Schöffen* (lay judges) would have already determined the verdict in advance behind closed doors, but all the participants would *pretend* that the trial performed for the spectators involved a genuine weighing of the evidence.

Seeking order, the *Bambergensis* "prescribed and appointed" every element, specifying not merely the general outlines but scripting every word.[73] The presiding judge, with "his staff in his hands," was to first tell his co-judges to sit down and then himself sit, ordering everyone assembled not to move till the end.[74] Participants were to recite their parts exactly as specified: no improvisation allowed. (Blanks allowed one to fill in the names of parties and crimes: "*A*" for accuser, "*B*" for criminal, "*C*" for crime, and so on.) Even the advocates were to recite from scripts:

> [*Prosecution*]: 'My Lord (name of judge): *A*, the complainant, complains against *B*, the culprit, who presently stands before the court on account of the crime of *C* which he committed . . .' [etc.]
> [*Defense*]: 'Lord judge: *B*, the accused, . . . prays that on the basis of his revealed innocence he be declared innocent with final judgment and law, . . . and that the complainant, . . . be bound to final process before the court . . . regarding punishment and compensation . . . [etc.]'[75]

The judge and Schöffen were then to appear to confer and write down their judgment but (as John Langbein writes) "this is pantomime," since they would have already met and decided on the verdict: guilty.[76]

[72] Schwarzenberg, *Bambergensis*, fol. 28r [art. 95]. Like the sixteenth-century codes for Lübeck, Württemberg, and Wurtzberg, the *Brandenburgensis* [art. 98] and *Carolina* [art. 94] specify that the reformed *Rechtstag* is to be public.

[73] Schwarzenberg, *Bambergensis*, fol. 28r [art. 95], fol. 33r [art. 123].

[74] Schwarzenberg, [*Bambergensis*], fol. 28r [art. 95].

[75] I quote here from the clearer version in the *Constitutio Criminalis Carolina*, sec. 190–1, 90 (translated in Langbein, *Prosecuting Crime*, 289–90, 302), which mostly reproduces the *Bambergensis*' provisions. For a discussion of the relationship between the *Bambergensis* and *Carolina*, see Langbein, *Prosecuting Crime*, 163–5 (the "Carolina is effectively a version of the Bambergensis" [164, note 96]). Since the advocates could be selected only from among the *Schöffen*, they were among those who had already collectively condemned the defendant.

[76] Langbein, *Prosecuting Crime*, 190. Langbein comments: "One would be hard pressed to describe the Carolina's final phase of public condemnation and execution without resort to the language of the theater. For the Rechttag is theater" (188). See also Schild, "Der 'entliche Rechtstag' als das Theater des Rechts."

Scholars have tended to interpret the reforms in the *Bambergensis* and its imitators, most notably the influential *Constitutio Criminalis Carolina* (1532), as instances of the more general transformation of accusatorial procedure into "*Inquisitionsprozess.*" (Never mind that that transformation was supposed to have already taken place in the twelfth century).[77] Many courts do seem to have implemented such reforms in one form or another. But if early sixteenth-century codes like the *Bambergensis* and *Carolina* aspired to universal law reform in the German-speaking world, they failed. For at least through the seventeenth century, accusers and accused—along with the parties' relatives, witnesses on both sides, lawyers, and sometimes audiences—continued to gather in courts for *Rechtstage*: genuine multi-day trials in which both sides argued their claims and counter-claims; victims and their relatives voiced their anger; emotions ran high.[78]

Even for courts that did try to follow the prescriptions of the new codes, visions of by-the-book performance—with no one including the defendant ever going off-script, perfect crowd docility, and the judge and Schöffen "seated in a dignified manner until the end of the proceeding"—were clearly wildly aspirational. The *Carolina* seems to recognize that audiences could not stay dignified and docile for too long, for it includes a kind of release valve in the middle of the scripted ceremony. At some point in the proceedings, "there shall be maintained (where it is customary) the practice of putting the culprit publicly in the market or square for some time in stock, pillory, or iron collar."[79] This concession to custom is a huge one. For it invites the spectators to come to the *Rechtstag* with hands and pockets full of rotting missiles and to begin pelting the "culprit" with slop and insults, perhaps even before the judge has given the order to rise. Misfires would be inevitable ("your honor, that dung ball was not meant for you!") And calming a crowd so inflamed would not have been easy. There are hints that, if there was not already trouble, there would be trouble ahead. For after the judge was to break his staff ceremonially, marking the moment in which he was to "turn over the

[77] See above, notes 11–12.

[78] I am paraphrasing the summary of later sixteenth- and seventeenth-century *Rechtstage* in Pohl-Zucker, *Making Manslaughter*, 232–3 (and see 227, 230, 243, 246, 249, 255, 258, and throughout). To mention just a few such instances, in one 1608 case in Nuremberg in which an alleged thief faced the gallows, the accused's parents, siblings, many friends, a priest, and the representatives of five different parishes showed up for the *Rechtstag*. In a 1725 case, the defendant's wife and daughter, the town priest, and seventy parents of children whom the defendant had sponsored appeared at the trial and pleaded for mercy on their knees. (Dülmen, *Theatre of Horror*, 29–30, describes both cases.) In a case from 1669/70, the University of Tübingen's criminal court insisted (against the wishes of the father of the accused) that the trial be held in public, though the university agreed to hold it earlier in the day to make it less public. (Pohl-Zucker, *Making Manslaughter*, 107–8.) In a 1661 case, there was "nothing to hear [in court] but great lamenting, bewailing, moaning and crying" and "great sighs and lamentations" (quoted in Pohl-Zucker, 243, describing "the first *Rechtstag*" in a 1661 manslaughter case, which the slayer used for the "public staging of the reconciliation process"). Statutes continued to specify that trials were to last three days. When courts combined the last two days (as many did), what they gave up (at least in seventeenth-century Zurich) was the elaborate sentencing ceremony, *not* the public trial. See Pohl-Zucker, *Making Manslaughter*, 249.

[79] *Carolina* [art. 82, 85], in Langbein, *Prosecuting Crime*, 288–9.

miserable fellow to the executioner," he was to "command the executioner by his oath faithfully to carry out the judgment delivered," then "rise from the court and *see to it* that the executioner carrie[d] out the sentence pronounced under adequate security conditions." The next provision, for the public at large, suggests why "adequate security conditions" were necessary: "the executioner is under no circumstances to be hindered"; in other words, a member of the crowd was all too likely to try to hinder him.[80]

Heretics and Witches: Staging Heterodoxy in the Fifteenth-Century Courtroom

Performing Radical Theology as Legal Counter-Narrative: The Trial and Defrocking of Jan Hus (1415)

Chapter 5 will suggest the extent to which reformers like Basin and Schwarzenberg failed in their attempts to script trials, control crowds, and get rid of grandstanding lawyers. What follows is a closer look at a trial that ended in what was supposed to be a solemn, stately, scripted sentencing proceeding (a *Rechtstag* of sorts): the trial of the Czech priest Jan Hus for heresy at the Council of Constance in 1415.[81] If we were seeking a paradigmatic example of the medieval inquisitorial trial as these are often portrayed—a secret proceeding in which an omnipotent Inquisitor subjects a prostrate victim to pitiless torture, and protest is futile—the Hus trial might at first seem like an ideal candidate. It was an ecclesiastical trial dedicated to carrying forward the Inquisition's central project—rooting out heresy—and Hus looked to many like a very dangerous heretic. Alternatively, as a trial in a papal court, one might perhaps imagine it as something like the Rota trials that Basin initially portrays: orderly, ceremonial, scripted performances before a group of judges "organiz[ed] by rank," who quietly pass their tablets and then announce their judgments to the assembly. But the Hus trial was nothing like either of these. What actually happened there reminds us how great the gap was between ideal models like Basin's or Schwarzenberg's and real trials. It offers just one example of how utopian it was to portray the Pope and Emperor ruling together in cozy harmony. And it also suggests the power of an accused heretic to rewrite the meaning of his trial performatively, even after condemnation had become certain.

[80] *Carolina* [art. 96–7], in Langbein, *Prosecuting Crime*, 292.

[81] Several descriptions of the trial survive, including three eyewitness accounts that, together, provide a level of detail unusual for medieval trials: one by Constance citizen Ulrich Richenthal; and two by the Hus devotees Petr of Mladoňovice and Jan Bradaty. I have relied primarily on these, on Provvidente, "Hus's Trial," and on Thomas Fudge's extraordinarily comprehensive and learned account (*Trial of Jan Hus*). I am grateful for his helpful comments on my discussion.

Already known for his fiery sermons, Hus began defending the teachings of John Wycliffe early in his career, attacking the sale of indulgences, defending the right of ordinary people to partake in certain rites, and condemning priests for their immorality: "but many of you are like dogs who should be put out of the house of God."[82] Such declarations did not endear him to his enemies but helped win him a huge following, which of course made him more dangerous. The Church began lodging a series of formal accusations, excommunicated him (four times), and finally, in 1414, demanded that he appear at the Council of Constance, one of whose principal aims was to crush the various heretical movements springing up across Europe.[83] Promised safe conduct, Hus made his way to Constance. There, he lived comfortably in a boarding house until Pope John XXIII suddenly had him arrested and imprisoned. Eventually, the Council put him on trial, in a series of highly public proceedings.[84]

The refitting of the Cathedral of Our Lady—where the final day of the trial was to take place—reflects the Council's aspirations.[85] Carpenters built a magnificent new high altar with "handsome throne[s]" for the Pope, one positioned so that "he might see every man clearly, down into the cathedral and everywhere," according to Constance burgher Ulrich Richenthal. They created matching thrones near the Pope's for Sigismund—"King of the Romans and Hungary" and soon-to-be Holy Roman Emperor (representing the secular power)—and the Grand Master of Rhodes (representing the sacred). They created facing tiers of seats in the nave, with seating arrangements very similar to those for trial of the Duc d'Alençon, descending by rank from princes and cardinals to the lawyers and clerical workers in the ecclesiastical beehive: "clergy, clerks, proctors, and men of that kind" (as Richenthal describes them).[86] The arrangement stood for unity, authority, and order, as well as Church hierarchy, which heretics like Hus had challenged. The Cathedral itself evoked the divine presence: it was to be a house of judgment where the Lord's most holy representative, the Pope, could, like God, see all and judge all.

Unfortunately, the Pope was not very godlike in 1415. For there were by 1415 not two but three rival popes: Pope John; Pope Benedict XIII in Avignon; Pope Gregory XII in Rome. Sigismund had called the Council to end the papal schism. Forced to attend, perhaps Pope John hoped that Sigismund would end up getting rid of his papal rivals. But the Council decided that, of all the "wicked

[82] Quoted Fudge, *Trial*, 117. For biographical details, see Spinka, *John Hus*.
[83] For an account of the cycles of accusation and excommunication between 1409 and 1414, see Fudge, "'O Cursed Judas,'" 59–70.
[84] See Fudge, *Trial*, 182–7, 240, 245, 270–85.
[85] On the refitting, see Petr of Mladoňovice (hereafter, Mladoňovic), *Relatio*, 225; Richenthal, *Chronik*, 92–3; and Fudge, Trial, 277–8.
[86] Richenthal, *Chronik*, 92–3.

popes," John was among the wickedest, and—only a week before the start of Hus's trial—deposed him.[87] He had in fact already fled Constance disguised as a laborer.[88] At one point, King Sigismund accused Duke Frederick of Austria of having carried off the Pope himself, despite the fact that the King had warned him: "[d]o not do it!"[89] Skirmishes followed. Eventually, now-Antipope John was dragged back in chains and put on trial. (As Edward Gibbon put it wryly, "the most scandalous charges were suppressed; the Vicar of Christ was only accused of piracy, murder, rape, sodomy and incest.")[90] Pope Gregory had taken his place, but just two days before Hus's final sentencing in the Cathedral, Gregory abdicated. Those who had ordered the refitting of the Cathedral perhaps thought only a miraculous *coup de théâtre* could restore the credit of the papacy: the new-and-improved Cathedral was to be its backdrop. The Pope's magnificent raised throne—from which he was to gaze down like God—was still there. But it was now *sans* Pope. (The papacy remained unfilled for another two years.) So much for unity, authority, and order.

The Hus question stirred up further dissension. Some authorities insisted on his guilt, others on his innocence, including the principal Inquisitor. Many defended Hus vigorously.[91] The issues were technical, and passionately debated. Some who thought him guilty nevertheless did not want to see him condemned, and repeatedly visited him in prison, begging him to recant. The conflict was palpable in the streets. There were pro- and anti-Hus placards posted all over town, springing up again as soon as they were torn down.[92] Given this atmosphere of conflict and chaos, it is perhaps no surprise that the trial itself was far from a solemn, orderly, perfectly choreographed event, as those who staged it might have wished. Guards armed with swords, crossbows, and long axes policed the entrance and exit to the Franciscan monastery refectory where the trial initially took place, trying to keep out rabblerousers. But many had asked that the trial be "public," and hundreds of people managed to crowd through the doors: high Church officials, nobility, proctors, secular lawyers, notaries, theologians, priests (the groundlings crowded

[87] For "wicked popes," see Mladoňovic, *Relatio*, 205–6 (quoting an unnamed monk at the trial). On the Council's struggle to maintain its authority as the court of highest jurisdiction during this period (its claim of temporary *plenitudo potestatis in foro exteriori*), and its use of heresy sentences to secure this authority, see Provvidente, "Hus's Trial," 254–6, 286. My discussion of these events draws primarily on Spinka, *John Hus*, 219–57; and Richenthal, *Chronik*, 115–27. On Pope John, the schism, and the intrigues in the Council generally, see Greenblatt, *Swerve*, 19–21, 155–81.

[88] Richenthal, *Chronik*, 115–19; Mladoňovic, *Relatio*, 120–1; Spinka, *John Hus*, 245 (for various accounts of his disguise).

[89] Richenthal, *Chronik*, 116.

[90] Gibbon, *Decline and Fall of the Roman Empire* (1993–94 ed.), 6:603.

[91] Mladoňovic, *Relatio*, 142–4 (on the Inquisitor). Mladoňovic also notes that the bishop of Nezero and barons of the kingdom of Bohemia wrote letters defending Hus, demanding a fair public hearing, and insisting that he be freed (*Relatio*, 151–4). And see Provvidente, "Hus's Trial," 264, 276.

[92] Cerretano, *Journal*, 478; and see Fudge, *Trial*, 249.

onto temporary seats).[93] All was noise and chaos: "voice[s] clamored," reports eyewitness Petr of Mladoňovice. Everyone "continued to shout simultaneously"; "tumult" prevailed.[94]

The Council had denied Hus's request for a lawyer. (He would later assert that Jesus was his lawyer.)[95] In the letters leading up to the trial, he repeatedly expressed his fervent wish to defend himself publicly: "to be heard [and] examined," not "in secret, but at a public hearing" (119; and see 145–6, 159–60). "I desire that my body be consumed by fire," he writes, "rather than that I should be so iniquitously kept out of sight by them" (164). If only he could appear at the trial, he wrote, "I imagine that many who shout would turn dumb!" (160). The Council was clearly not planning to allow him to appear in court.[96] But in a dramatic intervention on the first day of the trial, two princes charged in on horseback to report that King Sigismund had demanded that the Council allow Hus to defend himself. Hus was summarily rushed from his prison cell to the courtroom. The Council, it seems, was not fully in control.[97]

Anti-Hus Council members had tried to ensure that the guards would admit only Hus's opponents during the three days of hearings in the refectory.[98] And, indeed, of the "many [who] shouted," the anti-Hus contingent was loudest. "I [was] often overwhelmed by [the] clamour," writes Hus. "[W]hat mocking, jeering, and reviling arose against me in that assembly[!]" (210). In Mladoňovic's view, "the so-called hearings" were "in truth not hearings but jeerings and vilifications."[99] Hus "turned here and there, now to the right then to the left, then to the back, responding to those shouting and attacking him": "'See! He speaks captiously and obstinately'"; "'[l]eave off your sophistry and say 'Yes' or 'No'" (166, 214, 166)! At one point, a monk dressed in a black cape covered in shiny black satin suddenly rose up behind him and cried out, "'Lords, see to it that this Hus does not deceive himself as well as you'" (205–6)! At another point, a "fat priest, sitting in the window, [clad] in an expensive tunic... shouted: 'Do not

[93] Mladoňovic, *Relatio*, 222, 164, 167–8; Fudge, *Trial*, 278. An additional thank you to Thomas Fudge for producing a detailed calculation of likely audience size at both the hearings (100–200 people) and the sentencing proceeding (500–700 people) (email communication). Richenthal writes that twenty-nine cardinals, over three hundred abbots, bishops, and archbishops, and scores of secular dignitaries, lower-order members of the clergy, lawyers, secretaries, notaries, and others attended the Council (*Chronik*, 92–3). Given the interest of the trial, many of these must have attended the hearings as well.

[94] Mladoňovic, *Relatio*, 166, 194. All in-text page references for quotes or views I attribute to Mladoňovic here and below refer to the *Relatio*.

[95] Fudge, *Trial*, 251–2; Hus, *Letters* (1972 trans. Spinka), 145–6. All in-text page references for quotes or views I attribute to Hus here and below refer to Spinka's translation of the *Letters* unless otherwise noted.

[96] See Hus, *Letters*, 132.

[97] See Mladoňovic, *Relatio*, 165; Fudge, *Trial*, 266.

[98] Fudge, *Trial*, 11; Mladoňovic, *Relatio*, 167–8, 221–2 (noting that when the guards left, "our [friends] approached the window": presumably the guards had kept them out).

[99] Mladoňovic, *Relatio*, 163. In this paragraph, in which I evoke the mood rather than following precise chronology, parenthetical citations are to Mladoňovic unless otherwise noted.

permit him to revoke, because even if he should revoke, he will not keep it'" (217). When Hus grew silent, writes Mladoňovic, the crowd cried: "Look! Since you are silent, it is a sign that you consent to these errors!" (217). The "whole Council shouted at me," writes Hus: they all "shouted at me like the Jews [against] Jesus."[100]

And yet, not "all," either on the Council or in the room, were hostile. Some dedicated Hus supporters were there: Baron John of Chlum, Baron Wenzel of Duba, Jan Bradaty, and Mladoňovic himself.[101] Seeking to portray Hus as a martyr attacked on all sides, Mladoňovic reports only the "jeerings and vilifications." But the jeerers got their fair share of jeering too: when one attacker "began a noisy speech," reports Hus, "the crowd shouted him down." Both the Council and Sigismund (who appeared at some point in the proceedings) also sometimes intervened, for the court ordered another attacker "to keep still" and he cried out: "'Beware, lest the Council be deceived.'"[102] Far from silencing Hus, the Council repeatedly allowed him to grab the floor, which he did with gusto, using the courtroom as a cross between a pulpit and a university disputation podium. In his account, at least, he invariably emerged victorious. A Cardinal, reportedly "the highest in the Council," rose to the attack, writes Hus, but he quickly revealed his utter "lack of knowledge of the argument," and was soon reduced to silence. Immediately, "an English doctor began to argue, but he similarly floundered." Another English theologian then rose to his feet only to "[fail] in the argument" (210). After another man began to "argue noisily" only to be shouted down by the crowd, Hus stood up and cried, "'Argue boldly; I shall gladly answer you,'" but (he writes) "he likewise gave it up and ill-temperedly added: 'It is a heresy!'" (210). "They did not dare to oppose me with Scripture," he declared victoriously (196). Far from trembling before the Council, Hus scolded its members: "'I had supposed that there would be greater reverence, goodness, and better order in this Council than there is!'" he chided. "'You spoke more humbly at the castle," the presiding Cardinal observed." "[A]t the castle," Hus retorted, "nobody shouted at me, and here all are shouting!" (196). After the first day of the trial, he reported with triumph: "Two articles are already deleted [!]" (159).

Hus did not ultimately win his case. The Council found him guilty, and spent roughly a month preparing for the culminating event. This was to be, effectively, an ecclesiastical version of a *Rechtstag*: a spectacular, public, ceremonial, scripted replay of the trial leading to the climactic drama of sentence, denunciation, and punishment. A central element of the punishment was a formal defrocking: Hus

[100] Hus, *Letters*, 166, 159.

[101] Mladoňovic, *Relatio*, 221–2; Provvidente, "Hus's Trial," 283. On Jan Bradaty's presence as an eyewitness, see Fudge, "Jan Hus," 48–52. Hus describes "those gracious lords . . . who, despite all shame, stood bravely by the truth—the Czechs, Moravians, and the Poles; but especially Lord Wenceslas of Dubá and Lord John of Chlum," noting that "King Sigismund himself permitted them to be in the Council" (*Letters*, 287, and see 294).

[102] Hus, *Letters*, 210.

would, in traditional fashion, be ceremonially stripped of his priestly garments before being taken to the execution site.[103] The event, in the magisterially refitted Cathedral, would display the "reverence, piety, and discipline" so notably absent in the previous proceedings. To ensure such discipline, the Council passed a resolution of silence. There were to be no "noise[s] made with mouth, hands or feet," no "signs, words or gestures" either affirming or protesting, with severe penalties for infractions: excommunication, fines, two months in prison, and more.[104] But—unsurprisingly, given that there were now well over five hundred spectators—chaos again broke out: shouting, jeering, precisely the kinds of rude "noise[s] made with mouth, hands [and] feet" that the resolution had sought to suppress. One scholar has (perhaps extravagantly) described the crowd as "a howling mob."[105]

In the midst of this chaos was a sort of still life. High on a pedestal that stood on an elevated table in the center of the Cathedral, the Council had carefully arranged the objects for Hus's defrocking: "the vestments and the chasuble for the mass and the sacerdotal garments," as Mladoňovic describes them, along with a chalice (225). Positioned for maximum visibility, this looming centerpiece remained an ominous presence throughout what must (for some) have been an excruciatingly long morning. It began with Mass at 6 a.m., followed by a long sermon on Romans 6:6, the reading of a series of legal formulae, and a detailed review of every event in the trial from 1410 to the present.[106] For most of the Mass, the main attraction—Hus himself—was absent. In his absence, the display on the pedestal stood in as a surrogate. Sarah Beckwith has described the Mass as a "visual theophany": a palpable manifestation of God.[107] Here, an iconic still life echoing that visual theophany but uninhabited stood in wait. As an archbishop led the assembly in the Mass, the parallel would have been dramatically visible: in the central apse, the priests performing holy Mass garbed in vestments, chasuble, and sacerdotal garments, holding the sacred chalice; on the pedestal (directly in line with the altar and partially blocking it from view), a still life of their ghostly doubles, prepared for an anti-Mass of sorts.

Whether or not the trial's organizers deliberately staged this parallel, they certainly staged Hus's entrance: *after* the Eucharist (so he would not receive the blessing of the Sacrament); during "Concluding Rites." Brought through the Cathedral, he was made to mount the elevated table so that he would be visible to all. This arrangement—Hus displayed on high with the garments prepared for

[103] On the defrocking, see Fudge, *Medieval Religion*, 201–19. Fudge notes that Hus's defrocking followed traditional defrocking practices and, generally, practices of stripping and shaming malefactors: see 201–26 (the "Stripping and the Shaming of Heretics").

[104] Fudge, *Trial*, 279.

[105] Lea, *History of the Inquisition*, 2:485. (Fudge justifiably characterizes Lea's description as "overwrought" [*Trial*, 282], but it does capture something of the mood.)

[106] Fudge, *Trial*, 279–80.

[107] Beckwith, "Ritual, Church, and Theatre," 76.

his defrocking—served as a tableau illustrating the sermon that followed. The Bishop who delivered it focused on one line in Romans 6:6: "the body of sin [must] be destroyed, to the end that we may serve sin no longer." No one could miss the application to the figure before them: the man on the table, who stood throughout the sermon as "the body of sin" that the Council had to destroy.

Seven bishops performed the defrocking itself: the climax of the proceedings.[108] As they removed each of the vestments, "they pronounced in each instance an appropriate curse," writes Mladoňovic: "'O cursed Judas, because you have abandoned the counsel of peace and have counseled with the Jews, we take away from you this cup of redemption'" (120).[109] The withdrawal of "this cup of redemption" signified performatively that Hus could not hope for salvation: like Judas, he could not be redeemed. Hus's heresy had re-enacted Judas's betrayal, and that of the Jews generally: in betraying God, Hus had, effectively, joined the Jews in re-crucifying Jesus. The withdrawal of the cup thus also stood for his expulsion from Christendom, an expulsion that the bishops enacted through a performative utterance as they took the cup, in a moment that Jan Bradaty reports: "[b]y taking the chalice from you," they declared, "[we] separate you from the community" (67b). The "paper crown" that the bishops placed on his head after the defrocking reiterated this message. Its inscription read "Heresiarch" ("Arch-Heretic") and (in Bradaty's description) it had "three revolting demons drawn on it" (68a). As they placed the paper miter on Hus's head, they declared: "We commit your soul to the devil!"[110] The miter's burning devils stood for the fact that Hus was destined to burn not only at the stake but forever in hell, like Judas and the Jews. The nonverbal narrative was unequivocally clear.

There was only one problem (a perennial theatrical problem): costume changes. The vestments and chalice waiting in the still life needed to go on before they could come off, and before they could go on, the Bishops had to get Hus out of his clothes. Hus, at least, managed to find some sardonic humor in the situation, for, writes Richenthal, when they first "dressed him in a priest's habit and [then] took it off again, ... he made only a mock of that."[111] Bradaty's note on the undressing and dressing of Hus in preparation for the defrocking is terse: "in the middle of the church they stripped him of his own clothing, dressed him in his priestly

[108] Mladoňovic, *Relatio*, 229. Richenthal identifies these instead as "two cardinals, two bishops, and two bishops-elect" (*Chronik*, 132).

[109] In Jan Bradaty's account: "because you have exercised the priesthood unworthily in the manner of Judas the traitor," by "taking the chalice from you we do this day degrade, disqualify and separate you from the community of the faithful of Christ." "Passio" in Fudge, "Jan Hus at Calvary," 67a–68a. Hereafter, citations to quotes I explicitly attribute to Bradaty refer to this text (referencing the double columns with the "a" and "b" versions of the text that Fudge provides). As Fudge notes, some of the defrocked garments had specific significance: "the stole is removed, meaning such a one can no longer be regarded as a servant of the Lord; ... the chasuble is taken away, reinforcing his removal from the sacerdotal functions of the church; [the] rest of the priestly vestments are stripped from the prisoner, indicating that he has forfeited every claim to the priesthood" (Fudge, *Medieval Religion*, 204).

[110] Mladoňovic, *Relatio*, 230. [111] Richenthal, *Chronik*, 132.

vestments, and placed a chalice in his hand" (67a).[112] But the process cannot have been as streamlined as this description suggests. In order to defrock Hus, the seven bishops had to first undress Hus, then dress him, then undress him again. All while standing on a table (at least at first). Since the donning of priestly vestments did not normally take place in front of the congregation, the public dressing would have appeared as extraordinary as the undressing.[113] Mladoňovic's reference to the "vestments," "sacerdotal garments," "alb," "stole, . . . chasuble, and others" (225, 229–30) suggests that the dressing was quite laborious. If these "sacerdotal garments" included the traditional ones (as seems likely), dressing Hus required the bishops first to place an alb (a big white gown) over his head and get his arms through both sleeves, then wrap an amice around his head and neck, then drape a stole across his chest and around his back, then tie a cincture around these garments and knot it, then rest a maniple on his forearm in such a way that it would not accidentally drop off, then place a large chasuble over his head without knocking off anything else, then pull the amice back over the chasuble and fold it into a high collar. The chasuble is a stiff, bulky cape, shaped like a giant triangle that makes one feel as if one is wearing a "small house" (hence its name: *casula*).[114] It must have been challenging for seven bishops standing on a table to dress a priest in a small house. They decided to bring him down from the table to finish the job. However, once he was fully dressed in the priestly garments, he rose (explains Mladoňovic), "and ascending the table before which he was being dressed, [he] turn[ed] toward the multitude" (229).

The bishops did not prevent Hus from ascending the table. If the frocking was awkward, what really mattered was the *de*frocking: the table would serve as a stage, displaying it as visibly as possible. But Hus was determined not to waste the opportunity to use the table as his own stage—a stage that would help him, with all eyes on him before this vast "public audience," to recast the meaning of the ceremony. Throughout, he had portrayed himself as not Judas but Jesus. As the bishops had dressed him in the alb, he had declared: "'My Lord Jesus Christ, when He was led from Herod to Pilate, was mocked in a white garment.'"[115] Now, fully dressed as a priest, holding the sacramental chalice, he behaved (as Mladoňovic puts it) "as if he were about to celebrate the mass" (229): playing the role of priest-as-Christ, a double role already inherent in the Mass. As the priest donned the sacerdotal garments, he ceased to act as a mere man and instead acted in the person of Christ himself. Wearing the chasuble usually adorned with a large

[112] At one point, Mladoňovic suggests that Hus did the dressing himself, but just below describes Hus as "being dressed" by the bishops before the table (*Relatio*, 229), as do the other sources (see Bradaty, "Passio," 67a; and Richenthal, *Chronik*, 132).

[113] See Miller, *Clothing the Clergy*, 79, 174, and generally on priestly garments (with thanks to Maureen Miller for confirming that in the Western Church priests normally donned their vestments in the sacristy before Mass).

[114] See Miller, *Clothing the Clergy*, 57, on Isidore's etymology of "chasuble": "little house."

[115] Mladoňovic, *Relatio*, 229. For Christ in His white garment, see Romans 6:11.

crucifix, the body of the priest took on the cross that Jesus bore. The purple chasuble recalled the purple vestment in which Pilate's soldiers dressed Jesus as they put the crown of thorns on his head (as well as recalling the Blood).[116] In the Mass, Amalarius of Metz had explained, "the priests resemble Christ, as the bread and liquid resemble the body of Christ."[117] Resemblance here was not *mere* resemblance but the sign of the miraculous metamorphosis: the Mass did not merely represent the Passion but *was* the Passion. In the figure of the priest, the crucifixion took place anew each time. One representation of the defrocking (fig. 4.4) tellingly portrays not just a cross but a crucifixion scene on Hus's chasuble: Hus and the crucified Jesus are one.[118] Elevating the chalice—the very vessel Jesus had held at the Last Supper—Hus may have appeared to be actually performing the Mass. In the Mass, the chalice contained the Blood and thus its

Fig. 4.4 The crucified Christ superimposed on the figure of Jan Hus during his defrocking ceremony at the Council of Constance in 1415.

Ulrich Richenthal, *Das Concilium so zu Constanz gehalten ist worden* (1536), fol. 25v. Courtesy of Princeton University Library.

[116] Mark 15:16–18; John 19:1–3. [117] Quoted Beckwith, "Ritual, Church, and Theatre," 76.

[118] Richenthal, *Das Concilium so zu Constanz* (1536 ed.), fol. 25v.

elevation was a re-enactment of the resurrection. Having been, himself, elevated on the table and now elevating the chalice, at least for his followers Hus-as-Christ must have seemed to enact symbolically both Christ's resurrection and his own to come on the true Day of Judgment.

At the same time, raising the chalice was a protest. While the "cup" was never as important as the Host, access to it was a far more fraught political-theological issue.[119] Once blessed, chalices were sacred: no one but a priest, deacon, or bishop was to touch them. While the priesthood struggled to retain control of the Eucharist, a growing cult of blood kindled protests demanding access to the chalice. As Jesus had declared, the "chalice" was "the new testament in my blood, which shall be shed for you" (Luke 22:20). Where the Body (in the Host) was at rest, the Blood was in motion: it "streamed copiously as if it had been pressed out of a ripe cluster of grapes."[120] Christ bled directly into the chalice. One could drink the blood, wash in it, drown in it. It was tears for His suffering, ink for inscribing His wounds in one's heart, anointing oil, sweet milk. Why should that ecstatically living blood be reserved to priests? The Council had charged Hus with a number of wild beliefs he did not hold (for instance, that he was the fourth person of the Trinity).[121] But ultimately he did believe that anyone—priest or lay person—could participate in "the sacrament of the cup."[122] The bishops' withdrawal of the chalice thus symbolically enacted a repudiation of the heresy Hus most unabashedly embraced. And, conversely, the cup in Hus's hands, as he held it up, signified defiance: not only would he partake, defrocked or not. He would offer it to the people.

"[T]urning toward the multitude" in this moment, declaring that to recant would be to "offend the multitude to whom I have preached" (in Mladoňovic's description [229–30]), Hus clearly envisioned himself preaching to that very multitude, there in the Cathedral. During the Bishop of Lodi's sermon, the tableau had represented Hus as the silent "body of sin." The image of him now—preaching to the multitude in the sacred garments of a priest and holding the chalice (one of the attributes of John the Apostle)—offered a revision of that tableau, perhaps serving as a kind of visual counter-sermon restoring the meaning

[119] Duffy, *Stripping of the Altars*, 95–6; Rubin, *Corpus Christi*, 48–8, 291–2; Bynum, *Wonderful Blood*, 5, 93–6, 250, 258; Beckwith, *Christ's Body*, 30. With the intensification of struggles for priestly control of the Eucharist, the Church grew more adamant about this rule.

[120] From prayers on the Passion called "Fifteen Oes" (widely distributed in the fifteenth century); quoted in Bynum, *Wonderful Blood*, 12 (and, for what follows, see Bynum 11, 15).

[121] He was also wrongly charged with sharing Wycliffe's remanence theory of the Eucharist: the view that the wine and bread remained in the substance of the Eucharist. On both, see Fudge, *Trial*, 282.

[122] See *Letters*, 248 (and 140, 181–2) for Hus's discussion of lay participation in "the sacrament of the Lord's cup," and his insistence that his views on this point were not heretical. Excommunicated, he himself (according to John Foxe) "hath said mass all the ways between this and the city of Prague," asserting that "a man, being once ordained a priest or deacon, cannot be forbidden or kept back from the office of preaching" (Foxe, *Acts and Monuments* [1877 ed.], 3:437); and see Patapios, "Sub Utraque Specie."

of Romans 6.[123] There, far from urging that anyone's body be destroyed (sinful or otherwise), Paul actually mounts an attack on the "infirmity of [the] flesh": an infirmity that Hus (who was himself famously chaste) regularly denounced. The spectators cannot have forgotten Hus's attacks on the Council: an "iniquitous congregation"; a "great harlot"; an "abomination." It would take thirty years, he declared, for Constance to "rid itself of the sins which that Council has committed" there.[124] In fact, the Council had allegedly set up temporary brothels in the city (already notorious for its red-light district), and it was said that its members spent their days pursuing heretics and their nights pursuing whores.[125] In his list of those who attended the Council, Laurence of Březová includes not only "23 cardinals, 27 archbishops, 106 bishops" (and so on) but also "718 whores and public girls."[126] Cease to "obey the lusts" of "your mortal body" commands Paul, but "as you have yielded your members to serve uncleanness and iniquity, . . . so now yield your members to serve justice" (Romans 6:12, 19).

On the table stood Hus, preaching to the multitude while displaying his sanctified and holy body. At his feet were the bishops, who (everyone knew) spent their nights yielding their members up to uncleanness and iniquity in the Constance stews. The bishops must have felt that the table was a mistake after all, for they ordered Hus to descend.[127] Another mistake for, where everyone had been able to see him on the table in his priestly garments, now the defrocking was to be performed much less visibly. Moreover, getting off the table did not stop his mouth, and Hus had a very loud one.[128] "And where now is Pilate, who has removed the clothing of Christ from me?" he cried.[129] But he would "gladly embrac[e] the[ir] vilifications," for, he proclaimed (still in his loud voice), "I trust in the Lord God Almighty . . . that He will not take away from me the cup of His redemption; [I] hope to drink from it today in His kingdom."[130] And, as they placed the paper "Arch-Heretic" crown on his head, he "raised his hands and eyes to the sky" and cried out:

> My Lord Jesus Christ on account of me, a miserable wretch, bore a much heavier and harsher crown of thorns . . . . Therefore I, a miserable wretch and sinner, will humbly bear this much lighter, even though vilifying crown for His name and truth.[131]

[123] Later images of Hus holding the chalice came to associate him iconographically with John (Bartlová, "Iconography," 329).

[124] Hus, *Letters*, 196, 203–4.

[125] Fudge, *Trial*, 275–6.

[126] Březová, *Origins of the Hussite Uprising*, 53.

[127] Mladoňovic, *Relatio*, 230. Mladoňovic does not explicitly say that the bishops ordered Hus to descend, but it seems highly unlikely that he would have chosen to descend at the moment he began addressing "the multitude" unless so ordered.

[128] Mladoňovic repeatedly refers to Hus's loud voice (*Relatio*, 226, 229, 230, 232).

[129] "Relatio de concilio Constanciensi," in Novotný, ed. *Fontes rerum bohemicarum*, 13.

[130] Mladoňovic, *Relatio*, 230.

[131] "Relatio de concilio Constanciensi," in Novotný, ed. *Fontes rerum bohemicarum*, 13; Mladoňovic, *Relatio*, 230–1.

While Hus's final performance could not save him, the multitude of images that circulated in the century that followed his death often represented him during the defrocking in his full priestly garments, sometimes holding a chalice. Such images helped to inspire the vast proto-Protestant movement that spread throughout Eastern Europe in the period after his death: the Hussites, known in Czech as the *Kališníci*, or "Chalice People," who often wore the image of a chalice on their clothes, weapons, or banners.[132] In many of these images, Hus stands in the likeness of Jesus, bringing another verse from Romans 6 to mind: "in the likeness of His death, we shall be also in the likeness of His resurrection," and "death shall no more have dominion" (6:5, 6:9).

Spitting at the Inquisitor: Helena Scheuberin, Heinrich Institoris, and the Innsbruck Witch Trial (1485)

If Hus's performance did not change the verdict, making a scene in court or outside of it often could, as in the case I turn to now. Some time in late summer 1485, passersby saw an encounter in the streets of Innsbruck: the newly arrived Heinrich Institoris—"Inquisitor of Heretical Depravity" (as he described himself)—in a showdown with a local Innsbruck citizen, Helena Scheuberin.[133] Institoris had just come from Ravensburg, where he had successfully prosecuted a number of local women for witchcraft, condemning two to be burned at the stake.[134] (He would soon after publish the *Malleus maleficarum* or *Hammer of Witches* [1486]: arguably the most influential witchcraft treatise of all time).[135] Rolling into Innsbruck in late July, he immediately began posting papal bulls that declared his absolute authority to prosecute heresy, preaching against "the Heresy of Witches," and poking into local gossip.[136] As he walked by Scheuberin that day, according to him she began to "harass [him] with . . . rebukes" (197). Indeed, he complains, "I had scarcely been in town for three days" when she began her "constant rebukes" (197). When he responded by refusing to "acknowledge her" (197), shockingly, "she spat on the ground, publicly uttering these words: . . . 'Fie on you, you criminal monk! To you the falling sickness [epilepsy] should [come!]'" (197).

[132] See Fudge, *Medieval Religion*, 218.

[133] Mackay, ed., *'Unusual Inquisition'* (hereafter, "Mackay"), 149, 197. My discussion is indebted to Mackay's invaluable organization and translation of the documents from the Ravensburg and Innsbruck trials and his detailed notes (Mackay, ed., *'Unusual Inquisition'*), as well as to his collection of the original Latin and German documents (Mackay, ed., *Est insolitum inquirere taliter*). All page references to the Innsbruck trials in both the text and the notes refer to Mackay's *'Unusual Inquisition'* unless otherwise noted. The "Apostolic See" had granted Institoris the title "Inquisitor of Heretical Depravity" (Mackay, 210): for examples of Institoris' references to himself by this title, see Mackay, 144, 149, 165. On the papal bull authorizing Institoris to seek out and prosecute witches, see Wilson, "Institoris at Innsbruck," 87–90.

[134] Anna of Mindelhym and Agnes Baderin ("the Bathkeeper"). See Mackay, 22–5.

[135] On the likely composition date of the *Malleus* and its relationship to the Ravensbruck and Innsbruck trials, see 68–71; and Mackay's introduction to Institorius, *Hammer of Witches*, 4–5, 7–8.

[136] For the timeframe, see Mackay, 27–8, 33.

While we know only a few facts about Scheuberin, her vivid and powerful personality emerges from the trial record.[137] She was married to an Innsbruck burgher (204), but both before and after her marriage, she seems to have gotten around. In Institoris' malicious assessment, "she was a lax and promiscuous woman" who, "in her single years and outside of the marriage bed... had familiarity with witches and suspects in adultery, [and] maintained neither her period of time as a virgin nor her marital status without infamy" (196).[138] Her sexual freedom seems not to have harmed her marriage prospects, or her marriage, since we find her husband later pledging "all his property" to ensure that she will not "tak[e] flight" (213–14). It also allowed her (among other things) to hobnob with the nobility. At the time of the trial, she had practiced "public adultery... for many years" (as Institoris puts it) with a knight named Jörg Spiess, whom (he writes) she "so seduced in his mind that no persuasion on the part of his friends could induce him to cut off relations with her" (198).[139]

After a few months of preaching and gossip-gathering, Institoris narrowed down his long list of suspects to Scheuberin and six other women and threw them into the local jail. The deponents' allegations were colorful: primarily charges of non-diabolical *maleficium* or blasphemy (rather than the diabolical witchcraft that Institoris suspected).[140] Some had allegedly put hexes on enemies by means of garments, dead mice, voodoo dolls, bones, the thigh of an unbaptized infant, Jews' turds (42–3, 64). Others went about with black cats and dogs (115), stole milk from neighbors' cows (118), or caused impotence through gingerbread (65). One witness reported dramatically on a scene in which the "baptized Jewess" Ennel Notterin whipped an image of the crucifixion with switches and blasphemed both God and the Virgin Mary, uttering the curse: "May you have pain in your thought like Mary had when she bore Jesus in her slot" (115).[141]

Most of the reports were hearsay, and many witnesses later refused to repeat them under oath.[142] But the allegations against Scheuberin were particularly vague (as even Institoris was forced to acknowledge).[143] In addition to being "lax and promiscuous," she was (he said) "deceitful, spirited and pushy" (197). She had a bad

[137] Little has been written on the case generally, and less on Scheuberin, but see Brauner, *Fearless Wives and Frightened Shrews*, 46; and Broedel, *Malleus Maleficarum*, 1–3, 16–17, 99.

[138] For "lax and promiscuous woman," see Institoris' discussion of Scheuberin in Institoris, *Hammer of Witches*, 279. For his further comments on her alleged promiscuity, see Mackay, 198–9, 200.

[139] On the social status of the accused women, see Mackay, 56–7 (and 54 on Spiess).

[140] For a list of charges and a discussion of how they reflected Institoris' diabolical conception of witchcraft, see Mackay, 42–6, 64–6.

[141] In the original, "*sin*" (head or mind) rhymes with "*krin*" (vulgar word for vagina). I have adapted Mackay's translation ("mind" and "slot") and changed the order of the clauses to preserve the rhyme. For the original, see Mackay, ed., *Est insolitum inquirere taliter*, 27.

[142] Ammann, "Innsbrucker Hexenprocess," 25.

[143] See, for instance, his "Articles and list of questions in connection with the trial of Scheuberin": "it is difficult for her to be punished unless the preceding ones have been punished, on account of a vague adherence to very many [crimes]" (Mackay, 196) (and see 32–3 on the weakness of the evidence against her generally).

reputation. There were grave doubts about her orthodoxy. She "spat on the ground, publicly" and "utter[ed] unsalutary words": two signs Institoris would identify in the *Malleus* as evidence of diabolical influence.[144] She had dealings with persons suspected of witchcraft (37). The story of the spell Scheuberin put on a rival was, he claimed, well known: a man who "knew her carnally, just as many others had" (200), ended up taking another bride; at the wedding, Scheuberin told the bride, "[y]ou shall not have many good and healthy days here"; and indeed she had been ill ever since (171). Finally, Scheuberin may have killed the lovesick and late lamented Spiess: someone told someone that an Italian doctor had warned Spiess not to visit Scheuberin any more; gossip said that one of Spiess's female relatives had reported that Spiess had said on his deathbed, the " 'reason why I'm dying is that that woman killed me' " (166, 167, 170, 196, 199). But (the accusers admitted), it might have been poison, not witchcraft. Or maybe just food poisoning.

The weakness of the evidence against Scheuberin makes it clear that she was arrested not because she practiced magic (as several of the others probably did), but because of her willingness to tell Institoris what she thought of him to his face, fearlessly, in public, and in no uncertain terms. She had accused *him* of heresy (he reported), cursed his "grey skull" (172) upon leaving the church where he was preaching, and "was spurning and had spurned his sermons" (172), telling everyone that they should do so too (language in which he inadvertently seems to cast himself as a spurned lover: perhaps the comment on his "grey skull" stung). What seemed to gall him particularly was the *public* nature of her denunciation. As he explains, what first led him "to investigate her" was the encounter in the street in which she "publicly" spat at him, called him a criminal monk [*schnöder Mönch*], and cursed him (197). He had been posting papal bulls and delivering his pulpit jeremiads against the "Heresy of Witches." But "that woman"—"spirited," "pushy," and clearly alluring—had her own public sphere.

Scheuberin was certainly "spirited," as her encounters with Institoris suggest. Her arrest seems in no way to have crushed that spirit, for we next find her holding forth dramatically in the prison itself to the other women, the guards, and anyone else in earshot. One of those in earshot was Institoris. He heard her declaiming,

> assert[ing] to certain women standing with her that the Catholic doctrine disseminated by me in public was heretical, saying the following words:... 'When the devil leads a monk astray, he brings nothing but heresy. May the falling sickness affect him in the head!' (197–8)[145]

[144] Institoris, *Hammer of Witches*, 276.

[145] The record offers two separate accounts of this scene (Mackay, 172, 197–8), each with slightly different details, so I draw on both. The fact that Institoris describes the women as "standing with her" and gives a verbatim quote suggests that he witnessed this exchange. What follows ("When I asked the reason...") seems a direct response to her charges. On the guards, see Mackay, 212.

It seems likely that this display was a deliberate attempt to bait him. (She spoke loudly enough for him to make out her words, and when he appeared, she did not seem surprised.) Despite the fact that he had already had a similar encounter with her, and that people had told him of her public attacks on him, he was shocked and astonished. He had been told that when he was preaching "she always left the church, giving a curse with the following words: . . . 'May the falling sickness fall into your grey skull [*grauen Schädel*]! When will the Devil take you away?'" (172). But he "would never have believed that she had spoken in this way if he had not heard these words from her own mouth when she was in custody" (172).

Institoris proceeded to interrogate her, but, far from disavowing, she used the moment as an opportunity to elaborate with a new accusation:

> When I asked the reason why she asserted that the doctrine of the Church was heretical, she answered, because I had preached nothing except against *Unholden* [witches], and added that I had given the method of striking a milk jug for getting knowledge of a witch who has taken milk from the cows. (198)[146]

In describing such practices as striking the milk jug, she charges, Institoris has effectively been offering instruction in them: it is he who is spreading witchcraft, not she. Institoris protested: "I asserted that I had cited such things *against* those who would carry out such practices, *rebuking* them and not instructing them" (198; emphasis added). Her response was to declare that "in future"—after her "release"—she would continue to boycott his sermons (198). Why should she listen to a devil-led monk who preaches against witches but at the same time teaches witchcraft? Institoris was so shaken by this confrontation, and so certain that it proved her guilt, that he rushed off to get a statement from the most credible witness available: himself. Taking his own statement violated all normal procedures and, moreover, he was in such a hurry that he did not bother to gather any of the usual religious witnesses. (He seems to have grabbed one of the accused women—the widow Agnes Schneiderin—as a stand-in.)[147] He proceeded to interrogate himself, writing up a deposition that included both "the inquisitor['s]" questions of the witness and "the inquisitor['s]" answers as witness (using the third person to identify both of his roles): "[t]he inquisitor asserts that . . . "; "the inquisitor further inquired" (172).

On October 29th, Institoris, seven commissioners, three Dominicans, notaries and others gathered in the largest chamber of the Innsbruck town hall for the beginning of formal proceedings (203). Institoris expected to deliver a guilty

[146] It is unclear whether this exchange took place immediately (before the assembled women), or only later in a separate interrogation. In any case, it took place soon after, since Institoris wrote it up in his October 4th report.

[147] On the absence of the customary religious witnesses and the presence only of Schneiderin, see Mackay, 172, note 131.

verdict and "abando[n] [Scheuberin] to the secular court" that would carry out the death sentence (34, 182). In her confrontation with him in the prison, she had referred to her imminent "release" and her plans to continue her public boycott of his sermons. It is tempting to speculate that the reason she was so confident is that she was party to the plans for the scene that would unfold in court on the 29th, perhaps even helping to engineer them. Certainly, most of the officials gathered in the town hall chamber were by then less than friendly to Institoris' project. Archduke Sigismund of Tyrol and Georg Golser, Bishop of Brixen—the secular and ecclesiastical authorities in the region—had urged leniency from the start.[148] Their deputies—the Commissary General Christian Turner (standing in for the Bishop), the parish priest Sigismund Samer, and a doctor of theology named Paul Wann—attended the proceedings, and seem to have come to the courthouse with a plan for derailing Institoris' prosecution.[149] But Scheuberin's presence and leading role at most of the key moments suggests that she was not merely a helpless defendant but involved in the plan as well.

Institoris decided to call Scheuberin to the stand first, perhaps to make an example of the most defiant of the accused. But the trial offered her a new semi-public platform and the opportunity to defy him again before an audience prepared to support her. Bartholomew Hagen, the notary who would produce the trial report, hints that there was an extended showdown between the two before they even got down to business: "after *many* words were put to her by the inquisitor, she *finally* swore" on the Bible (204).[150] The showdown resulted at least in part from Institoris' determination, in the absence of better evidence, to display Scheuberin before the court as the "lax and promiscuous woman" she was, and thus make her guilt visible. He was to argue in the *Malleus maleficarum* that palpable promiscuity was evidence that a woman had become the devil's instrument: women devoted to "debauchery" and "inflamed with the purpose of satisfying their base lustings" (such as "adulteresses, female fornicators [and] concubines") are known to "engage in acts of sorcery more than do the rest."[151] Given that Scheuberin's sexual history was one of the principal pieces of evidence against her, Institoris was determined to bring it into the courtroom. "He wished to question her about her virginity and other secret matters" (204), reports Hagen.

[148] On Bishop Golser's and other officials' attitudes to Institoris' prosecutions, see Mackay, 29, 39–40; Wilson, "Institoris at Innsbruck," especially 92–100; and on Golser's role in the trial generally, Exenberger, ed., *Ein Fels in der Brandung?*

[149] Since Institoris' papal bull made it clear that he was to have sole authority as judge, the exact status of the other officials present at the trial is unclear. Several were initially appointed to "assist" Institoris (perhaps as coadjutors) (Mackay, 75), and they also clearly served to represent the Archduke's and Bishop's interests.

[150] Emphasis added. Mackay comments: "right from the start he got into some sort of wrangling with her," engaging in "pointless contentiousness," which Hagen "disdains to report" (Mackay, 34, 204).

[151] Institoris, *Hammer of Witches*, 171.

Turner however objected: he "was unwilling to take part in these matters because [they were] irrelevant" (204) (and "hardly concern th[e] case" adds Hagen) (204).

Unable to show the court just how "lax and promiscuous" Scheuberin was, Institoris was at something of a loss, and things went further downhill for him from there. After being told that he could not in fact examine Scheuberin at all because he had neglected to draw up the proper articles, he scurried off to draft them. When he returned, he found that she was already back, now with a lawyer by her side: "the venerable and outstanding gentleman, Lord Johannes Merwait of Wending, licentiate in decretals [canon law] and doctor in medicine" (205). Institoris did not like lawyers. He repeatedly cited the *Clementines* (a fourteenth-century addition to the *Corpus Iuris Canonici*), which explained that in matters of Faith, "the proceeding is summary, straightforward and informal, without the screeching and posturing of advocates in courtrooms."[152] In the articles he drew up against Scheuberin, he pointedly reiterated this claim (in terms that sound a bit like Basin's or Schwarzenberg's complaints about lawyers): "the judge has to reject obstructive exceptions, appeals and delays [and] conduct the proceedings in a straightforward, simple manner without the screeching of lawyers" (202).

Hagen's report is spare, but reading between the lines, it is possible to envision Merwait and Scheuberin working in tandem to stage-manage what followed (with the collaboration of Turner, Samer, Wann, and perhaps Hagen himself).[153] The report's phrasing—Merwait is acting "in the capacity of legal representative for said Helena Scheuberin and the other women in detention" (205)—suggests that Merwait began as Scheuberin's lawyer, and then someone (perhaps Scheuberin) decided that he should represent all of the women.[154] It also suggests that, if Merwait was their formal legal representative, Scheuberin was the women's representative: the lead defendant who, given her "spirited and pushy" personality, seems likely to have vigorously communicated to Merwait her views on how to defeat Institoris. Whatever they may have discussed, Merwait's initial defense was not based on great jurisprudential or theological principles but on minute objections to technical violations: Institoris had failed to notarize his depositions properly; he had failed to draw up articles before examining the women; he "ought to have..."; he "should have..."; "this was by no means done"; "he just

[152] Institoris, *Hammer of Witches*, 513, quoted in Mackay, 35. Institoris does acknowledge that if the accused ask for a lawyer, they must not be denied, so long as the lawyer "is a respectable and circumspect zealot for the Faith, and carefully upholds the terms for a true and circumspect representative in cases involving the Faith" (Mackay, 202).

[153] On Turner and Merwait's collusion, see, for instance, Mackay, 207, note 20.

[154] Wilson assumes that it was Golser who "recruited Merwai[t] to defend accused" ("Institoris at Innsbruck," 95), but Merwait stepped in first as Scheuberin's lawyer. Given this, it seems unlikely that Golser appointed him (he would presumably not have appointed a lawyer for only one of the accused), and far more likely that Scheuberin hired him for herself, and then agreed that he should represent all of the women.

seized the women" (206).[155] "[A]nd so he again" (and again, Merwait implies) "violated the text of the bull" (206). He has behaved as if he is above the law. Merwait's tone—cool objectivity and technical expertise—reinforced his general approach. He was a doctor of law as well as medicine (it suggested), not a "screeching and posturing" lawyer. Indeed, it was Institoris who had been "screeching and posturing" from the pulpit. Having "just seized the women," he was similarly attempting to "just seiz[e]" the law. Where Institoris thus stood for the excesses of arbitrary power, Merwait (his strategy implied) stood for the restraints of law.

One event early in the proceedings serves to dramatize this contrast. Upon arrival, Merwait explained that he had of course been properly appointed as lawyer in the case (205). But he unfortunately did not have the "mandate" with him to prove it (presumably a notarized document). To remove any possible doubts about the legality of his appearance for the defense, "he wished to show his good faith [appointment]" (205) by sending for a notary who would testify to it. Meanwhile, while waiting for the notary, he "insisted that the appointment take place anew" before Hagen (as notary) and the official witnesses (205). And so (writes Hagen), "[o]n the same day, at 12 o'clock," an hour or so after Merwait's arrival, all of the women—"Helena Scheuberin, Rosina Hochwartin, her mother Barbara, Barbara Pflüglin, Barbara Hüfeysen, Barbara Selachin, and Agnes Schneiderin"—gathered in a group in the town hall courtroom and enacted "anew" for the witnesses their formal appointment of Merwait as their lawyer. At first glance, this scene may seem insignificant: a minor bit of business to be taken care of before the main event. But Hagen emphasizes its formality: "[t]hese proceedings were conducted in the [larger chamber of the town hall], in the presence of the lord inquisitor together with [others] asked and requested as witnesses" (206). And he suggests its ritual nature. All of the women were "present in person" and, one after another, "all together and each apart, jointly and separately," repeated the proper formula. The formula was long, and, with seven women repeating it "each apart," the scene must have been quite protracted.

Perhaps the story of the notary who would testify to Merwait's previous appointment was at least a partial fiction whose purpose was to conceal his own procedural irregularities. (We never hear of this second notary again.)[156] In any case, the ceremony enacted rather than merely demonstrating: it was not *evidence* of the appointment but a legally efficacious ceremonial creation of the

[155] Merwait's claims were in fact mostly without legal foundation: see Mackay, 206–7.

[156] Merwait might have had no "mandate" at all, or one only for Scheuberin, not for the other women. If so, the supposed acting "anew" of the ceremony was not in fact a re-performance, but a legal act necessary to Merwait's appearance in court. If, on the other hand, he had already gone through the proper procedures, he could presumably have waited for the notary to appear with the mandate. In that case, it would be all the more striking that he nevertheless "insisted that the appointment take place anew."

appointment itself; a legal performative utterance in ceremonial form. At the same time, it was not merely legally utilitarian: it also served several expressive or demonstrative functions. Its overt demonstrative purpose was to "*show*" the witnesses Merwait's "good faith appointment." But it also set up the contrast between legality and arbitrary authority that Merwait's arguments would take up. Turner would ultimately declare that the whole prosecution had been "instituted in violation of the legal system" (210). The ceremony's first function was to show Merwait's own commitment to that system.

It seems possible that Scheuberin had some hand in devising the ceremony, but even if not, we can assume that she was an enthusiastic participant.[157] Performing legalism alongside Merwait and the other women gave her an opportunity to revise her previous strategies for attacking Institoris: instead of spit and curses, her weapon could now be law. Moreover, in the ceremony, law was not merely acting on her: she was acting on it. In fact, all of the women were doing so, and they were doing it together. Hagen's description registers the women's palpable collective presence and active participation: they were "present in person" as they "appointed [Merwait] as their legal representative"; they spoke first in a kind of chorus ("all together") declaring their collective will and then each in turn ("each apart"). Here, they were also (at least for the moment) freed from Institoris' illegal "seiz[ure]" of their persons, no longer prisoners but public legal actors. These were the very people (and others like them) whom Scheuberin had been working to rouse to collective action against Institoris in the church, streets, and prison. Here, they were engaging in precisely such action, action that was simultaneously demonstrative and legally efficacious.

In this, the ceremony also stood as an antidote to the scenes Institoris had been conjuring in his sermons and interrogations. It showed a covey of women pledging themselves to a male representative, purportedly revealing a previous behind-the-scenes compact with him. But instead of a diabolical scene, it was a legal one. Instead of showing witches gathered in secret covens, it showed legal citizens gathered in the town hall. For Institoris, on the other hand, the scene—in which a group of proven witches chanted in unison, ritually pledging their allegiance to their male leader—probably appeared to confirm that there were diabolical forces at work.[158] In his view, it was ultimately the power of witches like Scheuberin that defeated him.

[157] At first blush, it may seem improbable that she could have helped devise the ceremony: without legal training, she was unlikely to know about such formalities. But the fact that, at the moment that she returned to the courtroom, Merwait "likewise appeared" (Mackay, 205) suggests that they were conferring. I do not wish to overstate Scheuberin's possible role: there were others working behind the scenes. But if Merwait was initially her lawyer alone, she would, at a minimum, have had to grant him permission to represent the other women. If he said he had no mandate to do so, one can imagine her saying: "create one!"

[158] Certainly, Institoris believed that witches and sorcerers were capable of creating fantastical illusions: what was really a sabbat dance might appear to others as a harmless legal ritual in a town hall. And, unlike many theorists of witchcraft, he was certain that witches had the power to bewitch officials who failed to take proper precautions. See e.g. Institoris, *Hammer of Witches*, 548–56, on "how

The trial record reveals Merwait and Turner delivering the final blows. Merwait "rejected and rejects the lord inquisitor as . . . a suspect judge in this cause" (207), and "openly and publicly enjoined Scheuberin . . . and the other women . . . not to give the lord inquisitor any responses to his questions because he was no longer their judge" (208). He "insist[ed] on the nullity of the [Inquisitor's] proceedings" (210), and demanded that Turner "han[d] [Institoris] over to custody" (208).[159] Turner did not ultimately arrest Institoris, but he did declare the trial officially "invalidated." The women were to be released, having sworn that they would not "take flight" (212) or "inflict . . . any insult or harm on the lord inquisitor" (213), at least not "outside of lawful procedure" (213). This limit on the prohibition clearly served as a threat to Institoris: he would be liable to prosecution if he attempted to renew his witch-hunt (as he clearly hoped to do).[160] But it also served as a promise to the women and an acknowledgement of their role. If Institoris again sought their condemnation, they were free to use the kind of "lawful procedure" for which the appointment ceremony had stood—collective action, civic participation, law—to defend themselves, even if doing so meant offering him the kind of "insult" that had gotten Scheuberin into so much trouble; even if it meant answering harm with harm.

We remember Institoris, of course, because of the phenomenal success of the *Malleus maleficarum*, which would serve as the principal theoretical foundation for the execution of tens of thousands of alleged witches—mostly women—over the next two centuries. But we should also remember those like Scheuberin—largely invisible in histories of the trials—who stood up to witch-hunters like him. Scheuberin was not alone in doing so, though not all were as successful. In Ireland in 1324, the accused witch Alice Kyteler countercharged the Inquisitor Bishop Richard Ledrede with defamation and unjust excommunication and succeeded in having him arrested and dragged off to the Kilkenny Castle prison, which eventually led to his forced exile.[161] In Draguignan (in Provence) in 1439, a woman named Catherine David—given ten days to prepare her defense with the help of

[the judge] ought to forearm himself against [witches'] acts of sorcery." It is possible that he thought the Archduke's and Bishop's deputies had failed to forearm themselves and were all laboring under a diabolical delusion.

[159] As a mendicant monk who was supposed to have vowed himself to poverty (Merwait implied), Institoris could not provide surety against his flight (Mackay, 208, note 25).

[160] Instead of leaving, Institoris was still lurking in Innsbruck three months later, hoping something might change. Commenting to a "Brother Nicholas" that Institoris was perhaps senile and certainly seemed crazy, the Bishop enclosed a letter, to be conveyed to Institoris himself: "I am very astonished that you remain in my diocese, in a place so close to the court . . . . You should not be annoying to other people. [You] should depart. In fact, I actually thought that you had long since left. Good bye" (Mackay, 220–1).

[161] See the accounts in Davidson and Ward, *Sorcery Trial of Alice Kyterler*; and Callan, *Templars, the Witch, and the Wild Irish*, 117–48.

lawyers—demanded the court documents and insisted on serving as her own lawyer. By the time she had finished, the main witness against her fell to his knees before the court, admitted to having lied, and begged her forgiveness, and the Inquisitor (Father Guilhem de Malavielle) declared her innocent.[162] And in 1431, Joan of Arc—more visibly if less successfully—stood before the court in the Rouen Castle's great hall and in the market square wearing the men's clothes she refused to change, cleverly evading her judges' traps, "repl[ying] boldly to all the articles enumerated before her" without "falter[ing]" or shame.[163]

The Spectacle of Punishment Beyond the Script

Execution as "Sacred Event" and "Theater of Devotion"?

Joan's execution looked much like the kinds of classic scenes we call up when we picture the European witch trials: the innocent condemned is tied to the stake amidst the flames, while members of the frenzied mob scream "burn the witch!" It offered a spectacle of punishment that in many ways aligns with that in the dominant scholarly account I identify at the beginning of this chapter: an account that casts such spectacles as at once ruthless technologies of power (in Foucault's vision) and transcendent enactments of sacred martyrdom.[164] Such accounts describe the spectacle of punishment as "a clearly defined, ancient ritual which could not be altered" (in the words of Richard van Dülmen), with "a script" that always "remained the same," allowing the community to purge itself of evil.[165] But they also somehow argue that this ritual underwent a profound change some time in the fourteenth or fifteenth century. What had begun primarily as a ritual of retribution, they argue, was transformed in the later Middle Ages into a ritual of

[162] Aubenas, *La sorcière et l'inquisiteur*, 45–6, 49–51, 66–7.

[163] *Parisian Journal 1405–1449* (trans. 1968), 263.

[164] Foucault argues, famously, that the execution spectacle was a technology of power that replicated the crime on the tortured body. At the same time, drawing on Bakhtin's conception of the "carnivalesque," he writes that the public execution could be a "saturnalia": in "these executions, which ought to show only the terrorizing power of the prince, there was a whole aspect of the carnival, in which rules were inverted, authority mocked and criminals transformed into heroes" (Foucault, *Discipline and Punish* [1995 trans.], 60–1). On the as sacred rite and purgative sacrifice, see e.g. Cohen, *Crossroads of Justice* ("[s]ecular capital rituals were essentially rites of severance," "expulsion[s] [that] translated the exclusion from the physical to the metaphysical plane" [195]); Merback, *Thief, the Cross, and the Wheel* ("a proper execution" "held the potential to lift the miasma" of the "taint of corruption and infamy" that crime brought "upon the social body" [146]); Evans, *Rituals of Retribution* (the punishment "was a sacred ritual" that "purged the community of its blood-guilt" [85]). Merback and Evans are critical of the "ersatz anthropology," "incestuous scholarship," and racist foundations of the early twentieth-century characterization of executions as pagan earth rituals and sacrifices, in the work of, for instance, Karl von Amira, Hans von Hentig, and the German *Volkskunde* (Merback, *Thief, the Cross, and the Wheel*, 141; Evans, *Rituals of Retribution*, 3–7). Nevertheless, some of their own claims seem to echo such accounts.

[165] Dülmen, *Theatre of Horror*, 2; Prosperi, *Crime and Forgiveness*, 145.

atonement and redemption. The title of Adriano Prosperi's influential *Crime and Forgiveness: Christianizing Execution in Medieval Europe* captures the alleged change. "The noisy, ferocious spectacle," writes Prosperi, "had given way to an orderly and solemn religious ritual," a "sacred event," "a 'theater of devotion.'"[166] As Mitchell Merback writes, "compassion for the suffering martyr-criminal [took on] the status of a cultic obligation" and "the reeking scaffold [became] a surrogate altar and a place of veneration."[167] In what follows, I pursue the claims of this chapter as a whole into the arena of punishment, pointing to some of the problems with this account and sketching the outlines of an alternative: one that acknowledges the gap between penal theory and practice, the script and its performance, official proclamations and actual spectator experience.

Medieval punishments were in some ways "rituals" and they were certainly forms of spectacle. Like most medieval theatrical events, they were perambulatory and participatory, with heavily ceremonial and symbolic features. Execution rituals unfolded according to certain widespread norms: the procession often passed through sites that represented the community the criminal had violated; sometimes the executioner severed body parts that signified the crime along the way; the condemned was subjected to symbolic degradation (tethered to the tail of an animal, dragged through mud), sometimes elevated for purposes of display; afterwards dismembered body parts were exhibited at key symbolic locations. If punishments followed procedural norms, they also brought with them certain kinds of behavioral expectations. At noncapital punishments such as the pillory (blocks clamping the neck and arms), stocks (heavy leg restraints), thews (neck rings attached to posts), or tumbrels (dung carts), crowds were not merely permitted to vilify the condemned and pelt them with rotten food, mud, and dung: they were urged to do so. A fifteenth-century Dover ordinance ordered: "all the peple that will come" to the pillory are to "do [the malefactor] vylonye."[168]

Although decidedly unspectacular punishments such as fines, exile, imprisonment, or private penance vastly outnumbered spectacular ones, from at least the thirteenth century on, most jurisdictions did regularly stage spectacular public punishments for certain crimes, often for enormous crowds.[169] According to Jean

[166] Prosperi, *Crime and Forgiveness*, 144–5.

[167] Merback, *Thief, the Cross, and the Wheel*, 129. While I challenge the master narrative in these accounts, I am indebted to them for the rich evidence they provide, on which I draw freely.

[168] Carrell, "Ideology of Punishment," 305–6, quotes the Dover ordinance. For this list of punishment devices, see Masschaele, "Public Space of the Marketplace," 400, and 400–7 on marketplace punishments generally.

[169] On the predominance of unspectacular punishments, see Dean, *Crime in Medieval Europe*, 180, and "Criminal Justice in Mid-Fifteenth-Century Bologna," 26–7; Jordan, *From England to France*, 24–7; and Caviness, "Giving 'The Middle Ages' a Bad Name," 194 (and generally). For an excellent short history of the medieval revival of Roman practices of visible capital and corporal punishment, see Friedland, *Seeing Justice Done*, 23–45 (arguing that this process began around the turn of the ninth century and appeared more decidedly in the twelfth and thirteenth, but noting that many jurisdictions continued to impose punishments inconsistently: the same crime might sometimes be punished with a capital sentence, sometimes merely with a fine).

de Roye, over two hundred thousand people attended the execution of the Count of Saint-Pol for treason in 1475 (perhaps an exaggerated number but nevertheless telling).[170] Spectacular public punishments were viewed as essential to deterrence: the populace was to "witness [the] punishment as a fright and a warning."[171] Thus punishments were "by law [to] be carried out in the sight and presence of the people," producing "terror" to "serve as a warning to others."[172] Commenting on the execution of Saint-Pol, Basin notes that the king created a "spectacle" with such "*éclat*" both "to give satisfaction to [the] sentiment" of "hatred" that "the entire population had [for] the condemned" and "so that the punishment would serve everyone as an example and strike terror" into the hearts of the people.[173] Practice followed theory, in the form of new permanent gallows (usually at crossroads) and a regular practice of allowing the bodies of the executed or their severed body parts to hang in public view—on city gates, towers, bridges, and elsewhere—until they decomposed and fell by themselves.[174] Various forms of penal display could serve as frightening *aides-mémoire*, as Boncompagno da Signa explained: the "swords of justice that are carried before princes for the sake of instilling fear... have been devised for the purpose of supporting the weakness of natural memory," along with "pillories, forks, gibbets, iron chains,... eye extractions, mutilations, and various tortures of bandits and forgers."[175]

The classic account describing the shift from noisy ferocious spectacle to "solemn religious ritual" sometimes points to the various practices that came to institutionalize scaffold repentance-as-atonement. In 1312, Pope Clement V declared that the condemned must no longer be barred from confessing their sins at the final hour.[176] "Comforting societies" such as the Italian "Company of Death" formed, providing clergy to accompany the condemned to the execution site.[177] These carried *tavolette*—images of the Passion or of saints—which they held before the eyes of the condemned as they walked in procession to the scaffold. Towns constructed small chapels with images of the Passion near their gallows (in Germany, the *Armsunderkreuz*, or poor sinner's cross), so that

[170] Roye, *Journal de Jean de Roye* (1894–96 ed.), 2:361 ("IIc mil personnes et mieulx").

[171] Sentencing formula from Aargau, Switzerland; quoted in Dülmen, *Theatre of Horror*, 97.

[172] Northamptonshire *quo warranto* plea and fourteenth-century Norwich custumal, both quoted in Masschaele, "Public Space of the Marketplace," 405.

[173] "[S]pectaculum"; "Quorum ut desideriis atque odio *utcumque* satisfieret, et ut cunctis aliis exemplum et terrorem immitteret, rex ita supplicium ejus voluit esse conspicuum." Basin, *Histoire de Louis XI* (1963–72 ed.), 2:268, 2:270.

[174] See e.g. the examples in Dean, *Crime in Medieval Europe*, 126.

[175] "[C]ampanilia, berline, furce, patibula, catene ferree et gladii iustitie, quid portantur ante principes ad terrorem; exoculationes, mutilationes et diverse pene latronum [ac] falsariorum... inventa fuerunt ad substendandum imbecillitatem memorie naturalis." Boncompagno, *Opera omnia*, [*Rhetorica novissima*, 8.1.13]; trans. Sean Gallagher in Carruthers and Ziolkowski, ed., *Medieval Craft of Memory*, 111.

[176] Cohen, *Crossroads of Justice*, 198–9.

[177] See Prosperi, *Crime and Forgiveness* (especially 50–7, 107–33, 410–37); and Edgerton, *Pictures and Punishment*, 182.

the condemned could confess while gazing on these scenes.[178] Theological texts and images showed what the "good death" was supposed to look like: in these, a representative of the Church holds out a crucifix toward the condemned, who kneels, repentant.

These practices go some way to explaining the puzzling fact that medieval artists insistently represented ordinary executions as types of the crucifixion: the scaffold appears as the cross on Calvary; instruments of torture appear as instruments of the Passion; and the condemned appears as a type of the suffering Jesus.[179] Accounts of the execution spectacle as "solemn religious ritual," "sacred event," and "'theater of devotion'" are, in part, attempts to explain this puzzling fact. Performing "good death," the condemned did in fact strive to enact the likeness. Catherine of Siena's account of the execution of the nobleman Nicolas Tuldo in 1375 offers one such vision. "His will was in accord with and submissive to God's will," she writes. "[H]e arrived like a meek lamb" at the scaffold and "called the place of execution a holy place." As she placed his head on the block, "[h]is mouth said nothing but 'Gesù!' and 'Caterina!' and as he said this, I received his head into my hands,... my eyes fixed on divine Goodness."[180] In such scenes, the condemned could offer a model for the spectator: submit; act the meek lamb; in fixing your eyes on the spectacle of suffering—so like Jesus' suffering on the cross—you are fixing your "eyes... on divine Goodness," with its promise of mercy. Accounts of the 1440 execution of Gilles de Rais, rumored to have raped and murdered hundreds of children and drunk their blood, testify to the extraordinary power of this narrative to recast even the most diabolical criminals as penitent sinners.[181] At his execution, "there was a great multitude of people [there] to pray to God for the condemned."[182] Despite his "false and inhuman will," he "was very beautiful and pious" in his death.[183]

Deterrent Terror, Crowd Vengeance, and Going Off-Script

And yet, however committed the clergy and many of the condemned may have been to performing good death in the likeness of Christ, the officials who staged executions and the documents that offered justifications for the bloody spectacle virtually never mention sacrifice, atonement, or redemption. Instead, they stress

[178] Timmermann, "'Locus calvariae,'" 137–8.

[179] See Prosperi, *Justice Blindfolded*, 164–6 (specifically on the instruments of the Passion).

[180] Catherine of Siena, *Letters* (trans. Noffke), 1:87–8.

[181] For a concise account of the actual facts and skepticism about Gilles de Rais' guilt, see Fudge, *Medieval Religion*, 51–87 (on "The Strange Case of Gilles de Rais").

[182] "[F]ut grant multitude de peuple pour prier Dieu pour lesdiz condempnez." Marchegay, ed. "Récit authentique de l'exécution de Gilles de Rays," 177.

[183] "Et jà-soit-ce qu'il eût eu cette fausse et inhumaine volonté, néanmoins si eut-il à la fin très belle et dévote connoissance et repentance." Monstrelet, *Chroniques*, 7:96.

visible deterrence, collective retribution and public annihilation of criminal and crime. Public punishments regularly executed corpses, effigies, and animals, none of which could atone.[184] And the bodies that remained on the gallows till they rotted seem hardly calculated to inspire visions of divine mercy. In fact, visions of divine mercy seem to have inspired crowds far less than the models of worldly vengeance that executions offered. For crowds could remain vengeful even in the face of a stellar scaffold performance. As the cart made its way toward the gallows where Prévôt of Paris Henry de Taperel was to be shamefully hung on the common gallows, he cried out repeatedly to the "great multitude of people assembled, ... 'Good people, pray for my soul.'" But, as an eyewitness reports, all "were hoping he would ... die" and many cried "'Let him be hung!'"[185] When several alleged traitors were executed in Forlì in 1488, the crowd cut off the genitals of one and stuffed them in his mouth, "slit [another] in half" and removed the fat, "the viscera[,] and all the innards" from both men.[186] In 1381, a gang of boys cut off the hands of a man who had been executed and began playing football with them.[187] Such scenes hardly seem a renunciation of the "noisy, ferocious spectacle" in favor of "an orderly and solemn religious ritual."

It is generally recognized that botched executions, broken ropes, or wrongly withholding benefit of clergy enraged crowds. Florentine diarist Luca Landucci describes the botched execution of a young ensign in 1503, in which "the people felt such compassion" for the condemned that, instead of kneeling in prayer for divine mercy, they killed the executioner by stoning him to death "on the [very] place of justice."[188] Scholars usually take such reactions as evidence of the spectators' commitment to the execution script: "so deeply meaningful and extraordinarily important were penal rituals to members of the community, that on those rare occasions when the ritual was interrupted, the crowd immediately responded with frustration and anger, almost as if a spell had been broken."[189] But those who stage managed executions were not committed to creating spellbinding rituals. When Michelet de Terreblay, condemned for theft in 1357, confessed on the gallows to the additional crime of murder, his judges interrupted the hanging,

[184] See the discussion in Friedland, *Seeing Justice Done*, 89–116.

[185] In the "grant multitude de peuple de Paris assemblez," he cried, "'Bonnes gens, priés pour l'ame de moy.'" But "aucuns esperans que il ne mourroit mie, et lez aultres si disoient: 'Penduz soit-il!'" Hellot, ed., *Chronique parisienne anonyme*, 53 [#53].

[186] Prosperi, *Crime and Forgiveness*, 314–15. Prosperi's chapter on "Factional Conflict and Mob Justice in the Late Middle Ages" (96–106) in fact describes numerous scenes of late medieval "noisy, ferocious spectacle" that were in no sense "orderly and solemn religious ritual[s]."

[187] Prosperi, *Crime and Forgiveness*, 98. For examples of similar English execution crowds, see Royer, *English Execution Narrative*, 15–60. Writing of thirteenth- and fourteenth-century Germany, Arlinghaus similarly stresses the difference between executions and sacred rituals in his evocative contrast between the treatment of the bodies of saints after death (preciously clothed, their bodies considered intact and "fragrant" forever) and that of criminals (stripped, dragged into the street, left hanging on the gallows without burial) (*Inklusion-Exklusion*, 389–90).

[188] Landucci, *Florentine Diary*, 204.

[189] Friedland, *Seeing Justice Done*, 106.

brought him down from the scaffold, increased his sentence, and *then* proceeded to hang him, without any concern that the interruption might break the spell or that doing so might discourage confession and atonement.[190] Nor do crowds themselves seem to have treated executions as spellbinding rituals, for they often themselves went off-script: sometimes in retributive fury (as in the case of the Forlì traitors whom the crowd eviscerated); sometimes in outright rebellion against the system. In Hull in 1402, an angry crowd released inmates from the jail and stocks and attacked the mayor, shouting "doune with the maire, doune with hym."[191] When a Bologna court announced the death sentence of an alleged Cathar heretic named Bompietro in 1299, the crowd stood in the city square crying, "Death to the inquisitor!"[192] When a thief was condemned to torture in the town of Saint-Quentin in 1406, "there were at least a thousand people screaming not to kill the prisoner."[193] Such spectators were hardly acting the part of the "meek lamb" gazing upon the scaffold as a "holy . . . place of justice."

The *Carolina*'s threat of serious punishment for interference with an execution (which I note above) suggests that attempting to intervene may have been common, or at least seemed an ongoing possibility: it is "publicly proclaimed and announced—and ordered by the authorities on pain of body and property—that the executioner is under no circumstances to be hindered."[194] We can in fact see an image of a spectator attempting to stop an execution in the *Book of Misdeeds* (*Nequambuch*) from Soest (1315) (fig. 4.5).[195] A group of people holds a strap around the distraught man's waist to restrain him, their faces expressing mixed emotions: one watches the jubilant executioner with a furrowed brow expressing sorrow; another appears angry; several gaze up curiously at the two figures in the tree who look serenely down on the scene.

Politics and the Heterogeneous Crowd

Such images remind us that spectators could be as diverse as the trial spectators Fouquet represents. Accounts that portray executions as spellbinding collective rituals obscure critical differences among (for instance) nobles and peasants, scholars and illiterates, women and men, the orthodox and the heretical, upright citizens and career criminals, friends and enemies. In fact, they obscure what was probably the most important factor of all: politics. Bitter divisions produced

190 Prosperi, *Crime and Forgiveness*, 53–4.

191 Carrell, "Ideology of Punishment," 308 (also describing a similar incident in 1444 in Norwich).

192 Prosperi, *Crime and Forgiveness*, 105.

193 "[I]l se trouverent bien mil personnes qui crierent qu'on n'anerast point le prisonnier" (quoted in Gauvard, "Pendre et dépendre," 203).

194 *Carolina*, sec. 97, reproduced in Langbein, *Prosecuting Crime*, 292.

195 Soest *Nequambuch*; Stadtarchiv Soest, A 2771, illus. V; reproduced in Caviness, "Giving 'The Middle Ages' a Bad Name," 201.

Fig. 4.5 A distraught spectator restrained from attempting to stop an execution in the *Book of Misdeeds* (*Nequambuch*) from Soest, Westphalia (1315).
Stadtarchiv Soest, A 2771.

bitterly divided emotional responses. One was supposed to laugh at the villain in the stocks, but surely some spectators also wept. Many in fact wept while watching Joan of Arc burn, grieving yet honoring her exemplary death and pious martyrdom.[196] Others threw stones, viewing her as a cross-dressing virago who "would wallop [her men] hard with this stick, like a very brutal woman" (in the words of

[196] See e.g. Pernoud, ed., *Retrial of Joan of Arc*, 216–19, 223, 237, 242–3.

an anonymous Parisian chronicler), a witch who could "produce thunder and other marvels if she liked," "one wholly given over to Satan."[197] According to Guillaume de la Chambre, "the English laughed" as they watched: it was a pleasure to see her burn.[198]

For those Guillaume de la Chambre describes, jeering at Joan was at once serious political theology and sport. Far from celebrating atonement and promising redemption, the spectacle invited mockery. The executioner later lamented "the cruel way in which she was . . . made a show of" on the "tall scaffold" the English had built. But making a show of her was essential to her theological-political shaming. According to the notes of the Rouen Parlement clerk, before she was taken to the pyre, the court placed a "mitre" on her head very like Hus's, with the words "heretic, relapsed, apostate, idolater" on it, and a placard before the scaffold: "Joan, self-styled the Maid, liar, pernicious, abuser of the people, soothsayer, superstitious, blasphemer of God; presumptuous, misbeliever in the faith of Jesus-Christ, boaster, idolater, cruel, dissolute, invoker of devils, apostate, schismatic and heretic."[199] This shaming was, like Hus's, both integral to her punishment and essential to its effect.

Jeering "Like the Jews [Against] Jesus"

If penal shaming was integral to most punishments, it was at the same time associated with the crucifixion narrative. The mocking of Christ on the way to Calvary and the Ecce Homo—the scene in which Pilate displays the condemned Jesus to a crowd of Jews, declaring "Ecce Homo" ("behold the man"), and they cry "crucify him!" (John 19:6,15)—were, along with the crucifixion itself, the most widely available penal images in medieval Europe. Sometimes portrayed with realistic details such as chains and handcuffs, they could look very like contemporary sentencing proceedings or punishment scenes, as in the Swiss printmaker Urs Graf's Ecce Homo (*c.*1503), in which the crowd jeers, capers, and clamors for crucifixion (fig. 4.6).[200]

It was not only images and stories that represented these scenes, of course, but performances of the crucifixion narrative itself. By the later Middle Ages, scenes of the mocking of Christ were a regular part of the Passion plays performed annually

[197] *Parisian Journal 1405–1449* (trans. 1968), 262–3; and on members of the crowd who threw stones, Pernoud, ed., *Retrial of Joan of Arc*, 206.

[198] Pernoud, ed., *Retrial of Joan of Arc*, 216.

[199] Pernoud, ed., *Retrial of Joan of Arc*, 240, 239.

[200] Geiler von Kaysersberg, *Passio domini nostri Jesu Christi* (1508), sig. D3v. (Catalogs give a date of *c.*1503 for the image.) Merback reproduces an arguably even more realistic Ecce Homo by the Braunschweig Master (*c.*1505–6), describing it as a boisterous version of a sentencing proceeding, rescripted as a popular ritual of degradation: "the painter's apparent desire to convey the murderous hysteria of the Jews overrides his sense of judicial realism, but not by very much" (*Thief, the Cross, and the Wheel*, 132–3).

Fig. 4.6 The crowd of Jews jeers, capers, and cries "crucify him!" in Urs Graf's "Ecce Homo" (1503).

Johannes Geiler von Kaysersberg, *Passio domini nostri Jesu Christi* (1508), sig. D3v. Courtesy of Princeton University Library.

in any town large enough to have a guild. In the N-Town Plays (*c.*1450–1500), for instance, Pilate asks the crowd of Jews whether he should set Jesus free, and they all cry "Nay, nay, nay!" What should he do with Jesus then? "Crucify him! . . . crucify him!" they all cry together. And in the procession to Calvary, after four Jews nail Jesus to the cross, the stage directions instruct: "Here shall they leave off and dance about the cross."[201] Like the images, such performances stressed the parallel between the crucifixion narrative and real executions in a variety of ways. At least some cast the local executioner in the role of Christ's tormentor, as Avignon did for a 1430 Easter performance of the *Play of the Passion*.[202] Guild members were famously assigned roles appropriate to their métiers. So (for instance) the Pinners, who made nails and spikes, performed the York crucifixion and contributed to the construction of real stocks, pillories, and execution scaffolds as well.[203] Moving past actual trial-and-execution sites in a Passion play reinforced the parallel.[204] The York plays, for instance, passed several trial locations on their way to "the Pavement": a marketplace where pillories, floggings, and executions took place. It would have been hard not to identify the flogging and execution that the plays represented with the real ones in these sites.[205]

In real executions, it was natural for those who sought to cast themselves as martyrs to draw a parallel between the Passion and their own torture and execution. We have seen Hus accusing his attackers of "shout[ing] at me like the Jews [against] Jesus" and likening his miter-of-shame to Jesus' "vilifying crown" of thorns. It is not surprising that officials and religious participants like Catherine of Siena encouraged the condemned to enact a pious *imitatio Christi* on the scaffold. What is more surprising is the official use of crucifixion symbols to *shame* the condemned by casting them as Jesus in burlesque crucifixion scenes that invited mockery rather than reverence. In 1326, when Hugh Despenser the Younger—alleged sodomite, pirate, traitor, and Edward II's "husband"—was captured, a "crown of thorns" (or nettles) was placed on his head, and psalms written on his tabard. Despenser was then (wrote Jehan Le Bel) "dragged

[201] *N-Town Plays* (2007 ed.), 260–1 [play 31], 267 [play 32] (spelling modernized). See, similarly, the Benediktbeuern Passion Play, in Bevington, ed., *Medieval Drama* (2012 ed.), 217 ("Let him be crucified!"). Pamela King notes that the manuscript we possess was written for contemplative reading rather than for performance (email communication), but it surely reflects actual performances. For a close reading of the N-Town Passion analyzing its unfolding in performance, see King, *Reading Texts for Performance*, 53–60.

[202] Chiffoleau, *Justices du pape*, 239 (describing the 1430 Avignon *Jeu de la Passion de Jésus Christ* and suggesting that it was common for towns to have the executioner play the role in Passion plays).

[203] With thanks to Christopher Baswell for this vivid example, and to Pamela King for noting that, while the Pinners and Painters botch the job in the York play, they were probably also promoting their wares.

[204] See Davis, "Spectacular Death," 137, for a similar observation about Corpus Christi processions.

[205] See Teo, "Mapping Guild Conflict in the York Passion Plays," 144, noting the audience's potential identification of the actor playing Christ with criminals they had seen at these locations.

along in shame" on "the smallest, scrawniest, most wretched horse [they] could find,... through every town... accompanied by fanfares to humiliate him all the more" (a "*horridus sonus*").[206] This scene did not invite the crowd to feel "compassion for the suffering martyr-criminal." The principal aim of the spectacle was "to humiliate him," and it seems to have succeeded, for the "great popular multitude" that attended played its part in adding to the "*horridus sonus.*" Le Bel reflects popular sentiment in celebrating the execution that followed, and relishing its gory details, with no mention of atonement or redemption. Despenser was (he writes)

> tied to a tall ladder so that everyone could see him. [They] first cut off his penis and testicles because he was alleged to be a pervert and a sodomite, [then] they slit open his belly and tore out his heart and threw it in the flames to burn, because it was a false and treacherous heart.[207]

Such scenes as Despenser on his scrawny horse wearing his crown of thorns invited the crowd to behave like the mocking Jews. The images and performances of the Ecce Homo or road to Calvary that spectators had seen generally represented not a reverential body of worshippers but a mocking, jeering crowd like the crowd Graf represents. These offered the principal models for crowd behavior at sentencing proceedings and executions. When popular sentiment was against the condemned, the crowd tended to enthusiastically replicate the behavior such images depicted, as they did at Despenser's execution. Many citizens already theoretically had the experience of playing the part of jeering Jews in Passion plays, since the guilds had to recruit a substantial number of people to represent the crowd crying "crucify him" and following Jesus to Calvary. Even those people not specifically drafted to play Jews often followed the procession and joined in the cries. Jeering in a Passion play thus served as a kind of bodily and psychological training for jeering in a real execution procession.

Such performances effectively haunted real execution processions. To dance around the cross or cry "crucify him" was, of course, a means of vividly calling up the villainy of the Jews through scenic representation. Perhaps it gave performers a

[206] Le Bel, *True Chronicles* (trans. Bryant), 31; and Knighton, *Chronicon Henrici Knighton* (1889–95 ed.), 1:436 for "*horridus sonus*" and on the multitude gathered to watch. Le Bel describes Despenser's summary trial and brutal execution soon after. See also the discussions in Tarlow and Lowman, *Harnessing the Power of the Criminal Corpse*, 49–50; and Musson, *Medieval Law in Context*, 232 (including several similar examples of shameful crowns in the parade of the condemned). On the reference to Despenser as Edward's "husband," see Phillips, *Edward II*, 98 ("*rex et maritus eius*"). For a similar argument about the sometimes verging-on-blasphemous representations of Christ in Palm Sunday processions, see Harris, *Christ on a Donkey* (with a thank you to Max Harris for provocative thoughts on Palm Sunday and the liturgy).

[207] Le Bel, *True Chronicles*, 31.

deeper experience of their own complicity—as sinners—in the crucifixion.[208] But while performing the part of a jeering Jew in a Passion play may have officially been an act of solemn reverence, it did not look like one and probably did not always feel like one. Such performances must have produced, for at least some, an equivocal experience of identification with the jeering Jews, perhaps even a thrilling frisson of impiety: dallying with the demons; reveling in sacrilege. Certainly, some people found impiety irresistible, as the various cases of sacrilegious desecration suggest: Bartomeo de Cases, who confessed to desecrating images of the Virgin Mary in 1493; Antonio Rinaldeschi, found guilty in 1501 of throwing horse dung at a painting of the Annunciation on the exterior of a church (he was hanged out the window of the Florence city hall).[209] To mock Jesus with the Jews in a Passion play was to enjoy licensed impiety, and to earn special approbation if one did it with special zeal. Insofar as crowd behavior at real executions echoed the mocking of Christ, it re-enacted the crucifixion: not as a pious act of veneration, but as an opportunity for irreverent sport in which one could (unofficially) jeer like the Jew with impunity.

Penal Pleasures

Certainly, for many, watching the spectacle of punishment involved not painful penitence for one's sins but enjoyable pastime. When a fourteenth-century Florentine advice manual admonished its readers to "go to see men executed" but "*not* out of pleasure," rather only so that "it can be an example to you," it acknowledged that many did go "out of pleasure."[210] Those who arranged for "torturers dressed like devils" to ride around the alleged traitor Thomas de Turberville on the way to his execution in 1295, or who dressed executioners in garish feathered hats or skintight breeches with prominent codpieces that associated them with the devil, understood not merely the power but also the pleasure of such spectacle.[211] Certainly, there was spice in what Madeline Caviness has called "sado-erotic spectacles" of punishment, visible (for instance) in the various illustrated editions of the *Sachsenspiegel* that show half-naked women being flogged.[212] An image in the fourteenth-century *Custumal of Toulouse* shows the punishment

[208] Thank you to Eleanor Johnson for this point (and generally for inspiring conversations on the Passion plays). And see Johnson's *Staging Contemplation*, especially Ch 6 ("Laughing Our Way toward God"), 169–90, which explores, among other things, how performance may allow spectators to indulge in sinful pleasures, while ultimately seeking to inspire recognition, reform, and repair.

[209] Connell and Constable, ed., *Sacrilege and Redemption* (volume dedicated to the Rinaldeschi case); Edgerton, *Pictures and Punishment*, 47–58 (reproducing images from an anonymous early sixteenth-century panel depicting the case, including one joyfully showing Rinaldeschi *in flagrante delicto* [48]); and Crouzet-Pavan, "Emotions in the Heart of the City," 29–30 (for several similar cases).

[210] Quoted in Dean, *Crime in Medieval Europe*, 126 (emphasis added).

[211] See Davis, "Spectacular Death," 141–2; Edgerton, *Pictures and Punishment*, 134–5.

[212] Caviness, *Visualizing Women* ("Sado-Erotic Spectacles," 83–124).

of an adulterous couple: a naked woman leads a naked man by a rope attached to his penis, accompanied by a trumpeter and an armed guard.[213] In towns in southern France, if a man and woman were found naked behind closed doors or a man was found with his trousers down with a married woman, they were to run naked through the town from one gate to another: presumably through a crowd and accompanied by a whipping.[214] Ecclesiastical punishments like that for Margery Baxter in 1428 often featured flogging parades in short garments, visiting "all of the places of the market, . . . where a multitude of people is present" (as a 1447 trial report put it).[215] John Kynget's 1429 punishment mandated that he "wea[r] only a linen shirt to the length of his things" and parade around the cemetery chapel and through the marketplace while genuflecting and being solemnly flogged with a rod by the Vicar of Nedham.[216] That spectators watched with avid interest is clear. When Joan of Arc was dead (according to the Parisian chronicler), "the fire was raked back and her naked body . . . and all the secrets that could or should belong to a woman" were "shown to all the people," who "stared a long [while] at her dead body bound to the stake."[217]

The general exclusion of discussions of shaming punishments from discussions of execution-as-atonement-ritual presumes that we should divide punishments by genre: shamings in the stocks or pillory were comedy; executions were tragedy. But they had a shared repertoire: executions commonly included shaming elements similar to those in noncapital punishments; malefactors not actually condemned to death were sometimes required to parade with ropes around their necks signifying their civil death.[218] In both capital and noncapital punishments, comedy often mixed with tragedy, jeering with tears. At the end of Hus's sentencing, after the bishops managed to balance the eighteen-inch-tall "Arch-Heretic" hat with dancing devils on his head, they realized they had to take it off again because they had forgotten to "obliterate his tonsure."[219] One bishop pulled out a razor. Another pulled out a scissors. They started arguing. We must "shave [his] head all over," said one. No, "shave his head in separate squares!" said another. "[A]ll over!" "[S]eparate squares!" Hus—on his way to the stake and weeping—suddenly began to laugh at them: "Look how you cannot come together in this act of blasphemy, how will you be able to agree on others?"[220] The bishops did eventually cut his tonsure into a checkerboard and put the paper crown back on. But it is not easy to keep an eighteen-inch-tall cone on one's head, however

213 See Jones, *Secret Middle Ages*, 94.

214 See Dean, *Crime in Medieval Europe*, 130.

215 On Baxter's punishment, see Hornbeck, Lahey, and Somerset, ed., *Wycliffite Spirituality*, 329. For the quote from the trial report, see Masschaele, "Public Space of the Marketplace," 409. For many examples of malefactors paraded in their underwear or in loincloths, see Fudge, *Medieval Religion*, 209–17.

216 Hornbeck, Lahey, and Somerset, ed., *Wycliffite Spirituality*, 337.

217 *Parisian Journal 1405–1449* (trans. 1968), 263–4.

218 Cohen, *Crossroads of Justice*, 165.

219 Mladoňovic, *Relatio*, 230.

220 Bradaty, "Passio" in Fudge, "Jan Hus at Calvary," 68b.

well tied under the chin, so it must have slipped and tottered as the procession made its way to the execution site.

Conclusion

Mocked by the court, Joan herself (complained an English "doctor" at her trial) "ma[de] a mock of them" throughout.[221] Hus may have been "mocked in [his] white garment," but he mocked the mockers right back, even on the brink of execution.[222] Transforming shame into honor, he seems to have worn his Arch-Heretic hat, with its dancing devils, proudly. Certainly, for his hundreds of thousands of followers, the hat became the central icon of his martyrdom and a paradoxical signifier of his holiness: every image of the martyr-Hus burning in the pyre shows him sporting his three dancing devils (a sign of victory over the devil? or a reworking of the shaming epithet as a badge of pride?) We have a description in the *Journal of a Bourgeois of Paris* of at least one condemned man who laughed all the way to the scaffold: Pierre des Essarts, Prévôt of Paris, condemned for treason and corruption in 1413. "[D]ressed in a black checkered robe lined in sable, [with] white stockings and black slippers on his feet," dragged on a hurdle all the way from the palace to the marketplace, "he did nothing the whole time but laugh, . . . in his great majesty." Perhaps his laughter was the product of terror (many "took him for truly mad"). But it was also majestically defiant laughter that inspired not outrage but pity: "he alone laughed," whereas "everyone who saw him wept so piteously that [never were there] greater tears for the death of a man."[223] In "sado-erotic spectacles" like Margery Baxter's or John Kynget's floggings or those represented in the *Sachsenspiegel*, it is possible that people who felt unashamed of what they had done or what they believed sometimes flaunted their punishment, their half-clothed bodies in postures of defiance. Had Helena Scheuberin been required to wear the short garment that Margery Baxter wore, undergoing flogging as she paraded around the market square, it is impossible to

[221] Pernoud, ed., *Retrial of Joan of Arc*, 207.

[222] Mladoňovic, *Relatio*, 229 ("many . . . jeered at him"); Richenthal, *Chronik*, 132 ("he made only a mock of [them]").

[223] "[V]estu d'une houppelande noire dechicquetée fourrée de martres, unes chausses blanches, ungs escafinons noirs en ses piez." "[D]epuis qu'il fut mis sur la claie jusques à sa mort, il ne faisoit touzjours que rire, . . . en sa grant majesté, dont le plus des gens le tenoient pour vray foul; car tous ceulx qui le veoient plouroient si piteusement que vous ne ouyssiez oncques parler de plus grans pleurs pour mort de homme, et lui tout seul rioit." *Journal d'un bourgeois de Paris*, 32–3. According to the *Journal*, the Prévôt had granted himself lucrative posts that would have satisfied "six or eight sons of counts or knights," had engaged in "very great and cruel massacres, . . . pillaged and robbed the good inhabitants" of Paris ("who loved him so loyally"), and had planned "to betray the city and deliver it into the hands of its enemies" ("il avoit assez offices pour six ou pour huit filx de contes ou de bannerez"; "il avoit en sa voulenté . . . de faire . . . tres grans et cruelles occisions, et piller et rober les bons habitans de la bonne ville de Paris, qui tant l'aymoient loyaulment," "de trahir la ville et de la livrer es mains de ses ennemis" [33]).

imagine her—a woman who spat at the Inquisitor and charged *him* with heresy, who seduced a knight and (effectively) the monk himself—now hiding her head in shame. Instead, she would (it seems certain) have used the spectacle as a platform for protest, as Catharina Arndes and the mythic Calefurnia did: mooning the judge, earning laughter and applause, capturing the scene.

5

Performing Law in the Age of Theatre (*c.*1500–1650)

Introduction: The Priest's Bastard and the Prince's Grace: Entertaining the Polish Ambassadors in the "Greatest Theatre Ever" (1573)

In the year 1573, a delegation arrived in Paris and announced to the King's brother that he had just been elected King of Poland. Both the King and his brother were naturally very pleased. To celebrate the auspicious occasion, the King arranged a special entertainment: two celebrity lawyers—Etienne Pasquier and Barnabé Brisson—would stage a trial. Their instructions: make it diverting! Pasquier later described the scene that day: it was "the greatest theatre ever found in the Court of the Parlement," and he himself had been chosen to "plea[d] [the] case in this great theatre."[1] The spectators included the King, seated in his canopied *lit de justice*, the Princes of the Blood, Officers of the Crown, and a contingent of Polish lords and princes seated on high chairs, surrounded by the judges of the court, resplendent in their scarlet robes.[2] After paying their compliments to the illustrious attendees, the lawyers went at it (in Latin, so the Polish visitors could understand).

The facts of the case were as follows.[3] A man and his serving maid had a son out of wedlock. Fortunately, the Prince sent the father a letter declaring the child legitimate. The child grew up. His father arranged a marriage for him and, as a wedding gift, made him heir to all his worldly goods. But, plot twist: unbeknownst to all, the father was actually a priest in disguise. Fortunately, he repented, living

[1] "[F]ust plaidée une cause, en ce grand théatre" (Pasquier, *Interprétation des Institutes* [1847 ed.], 90); "au plus grand theatre qui se trouva jamais en la Cour de Parlement" (Pasquier, *Oeuvres* [1723 ed.], 2:643). All parenthetical citations to Pasquier are to the 1723 edition of his *Oeuvres*—the only complete edition—unless otherwise noted, and refer to the volume and column number (columns are separately numbered); hereafter cited in the French and Latin text in my notes.

[2] Pasquier, *Oeuvres*, 2:643; *Interprétation des Institutes*, 90.

[3] These appear in Pasquier's *Interprétation des Institutes*, 90–1 (91 for "enfant incestueux" below); and in the *Mélanges tirés d'une grande bibliothèque*, 11:191–3. The *Mélanges* (compiled in the eighteenth century) offers details not in Pasquier's accounts. I have been cautious in drawing from it since its author may simply be embroidering. But it is also possible that it draws on a sixteenth-century text that is no longer extant.

Law as Performance: Theatricality, Spectatorship, and the Making of Law in Ancient, Medieval, and Early Modern Europe. Julie Stone Peters, Oxford University Press. © Julie Stone Peters 2022. DOI: 10.1093/oso/9780192898494.003.0006

out the rest of his life in penitential poverty. Unfortunately, before doing so, he *also* made his brother (and some other relatives) heir to all his worldly goods. That created trouble. For when he died, out popped the relatives demanding the inheritance. After all, they said, the so-called heir was a bastard. Arguing for the prosecution, Brisson insisted: a priest's bastard, an "incestuous child," was no one's heir. To decide in favor of the bastard would be to sanction adultery, incest, and God only knows what else. Pasquier then took up the defense. True, the royal letter legitimating the bastard would be null and void if the young Prince's advisors had somehow forgotten to inform him that adultery was a sin. But they *had* explained this all-important fact, so the royal letter must stand as law. Certainly Pasquier condemned the vice. But the bastard child was innocent and so was his wife (who indeed did not know that her husband had ever been a bastard). And besides, the sin had been washed clean by the grace of the Prince. After much debate, the Lord Chancellor pronounced the verdict: the "incestuous child," the legitimate bastard (a bastard no more), the grace of the Prince, and the great Pasquier had won the day.

I will return to this event as another instance of the entanglement of entertainment with law and of the fictive with the real (like the thwarted trial by battle in Tothill Fields with which I begin this book). For now the event merely stands as one symptomatic example of the broader phenomenon that is at the center of this chapter: the early modern figuration of the courtroom as theatre. As we have seen, medieval commentators had a great deal to say about legal spectacle and courtroom performance. But they rarely explicitly identified such events with the performance of plays. It was only at the end of the fifteenth century that the trope identifying trials and punishments specifically with fictional stage representations began to reappear. Two phenomena classically associated with the "Renaissance" helped contribute to the trope's reappearance: renewed attention to certain ancient texts that stressed the relationship between acting and oratorical delivery; and the establishment of permanent stages in cities and courts throughout Europe, transforming theatre into a regular fixture of court and urban life. The centrality of such performance venues made theatre arguably the central prototype for spectatorship in other domains, as the pervasive "theatre of the world" trope suggests.[4] Among these domains was the modern courtroom.

Scholars of early modern law and literature have often looked at theatrical tropes as keys to understanding the relationship between theatrical representation and legal practices or ideas. The early modern commonplace that treated public

[4] For useful recent discussions of the early modern theatrical metaphor, see *Theater as Metaphor*, 1–155 (especially Marx, "Between Metaphor and Cultural Practices," 11–29, usefully distinguishing "*theatrum*" from "*scena*" and stressing the particularity of Germanic nomenclature); and see my *Theatre of the Book*, 99–100, 106–8.

executions as "tragedies" displayed on the "theatre" of the scaffold is by now familiar.[5] Studies have explored the relationship between law and the theatrical staging of jurisdiction, testimony, evidence, *mens rea*, and judicial pardon (to offer just a few examples).[6] The fact that much of this work has focused on English law and theatre is perhaps unsurprising, given the general recognition that trials in England tended to be open to the public and could sometimes seem very like theatre to contemporaries: the trial of Charles I in Westminster Hall in 1649 was one of the greatest pieces of "Theatre" ever seen (said those who staged it).[7] The largest public space in England, Westminster Hall had a capacity of several thousand, like some of the public theatres. Major parliamentary trials tended to take over the entire Hall, but even on ordinary days there were flocks of people attending trials in the Courts of King's Bench, Common Pleas, and Chancery, which shared the space (with little or no division between courts).[8] The Star Chamber has a reputation for secrecy due to its closed-door interrogations, but its trials were in fact open to the public. Writing in 1622, William Hudson noted that "young noblemen and men of quality... flock thither in great abundance, when causes of weight are there heard and determined." For exciting cases, lines outside could start forming as early as three in the morning.[9] Less prominent provincial courts could also draw crowds, especially for the most sensational trials. One pamphlet declares that "five hundred men" came to see an accused witch at the Huntington Assizes in 1593.[10] Mary Spencer, one of the accused at the 1633

[5] The *locus classicus* for conceptualizing the early modern theatre of the scaffold is, of course, Foucault's *Discipline and Punish*, which inspired a number of studies of the theatre of execution in England: see e.g. Mitchell, *Shakespeare and Public Execution*; Redmond, "Staging Executions"; Greenberg, "Tortured Mimesis." For the identification of the scaffold specifically with tragedy, see my "Short History of Scaffold Tragedy," 127–31.

[6] See Cormack, *Power to Do Justice*; Syme, *Theatre and Testimony*; Hutson, *Invention of Suspicion*; Mukherji, *Law and Representation*; Wilson, *Theaters of Intention*; and Meyler, *Theaters of Pardoning*. For some additional notable examples (by no means a comprehensive list), see Cunningham, *Imaginary Betrayals*; Dyson, *Staging Authority in Caroline England*; and Winston, *Lawyers at Play*. Studies of Shakespeare and law are especially numerous, but a few that specifically take up the question of early legal practices in addition to doctrines include: Corrigan, *Playhouse Law in Shakespeare's World*; Curran, *Shakespeare's Legal Ecologies*; Dunne, *Shakespeare, Revenge Tragedy and Early Modern Law*; Geng, *Communal Justice in Shakespeare's England*; Raffield, *Shakespeare's Imaginary Constitution*; Skinner, *Forensic Shakespeare*; Watt, *Shakespeare's Acts of Will*; and Zurcher, *Shakespeare and Law*. For a suggestive account of customary (common) law as performance, see Elsky, *Custom, Common Law, and the Constitution of English Renaissance Literature*, 103–32. For reflections on the intersections of early modern images, theatre, and law, see Goodrich's *Imago Decidendi*, *Legal Emblems and the Art of Law*, and his essay on "Law" in the *Encyclopedia of Rhetoric*.

[7] See e.g. Cook, *King Charls, His Case*, 5; and my extended discussion in "Staging the Last Judgment in the Trial of Charles I."

[8] See fig. 5.6 below.

[9] Hudson, *Treatise of the Court of Star Chamber*, 48. See Cheyney, "Court of the Star Chamber," 731, 727 (the Star Chamber "has gained a name for secrecy whereas its sessions were open practically to all comers" [727]).

[10] *Most Strange and Admirable Discoverie*, sig. N3v.

Lancaster Assize trials, claimed that "the throng [was] so great that she could not hear the evidence against her."[11]

Less attention has been paid to the relationship between law and theatre on the Continent.[12] But—as the Pasquier anecdote should suggest—courtrooms there could also seem to contemporaries very like theatres. The Paris Parlement, which Pasquier describes as a "great theatre," was already a place of vast, festive crowds in the mid-fifteenth century (if we are to believe Thomas Basin's description), and became an even more spectacular venue in the sixteenth, as will become apparent in this chapter.[13] Several different courts met inside the open Great Hall in the Palais de Justice (as courts did in Westminster Hall), sharing the space with lawyers and petitioners, legal bureaucrats, visitors, prostitutes, vendors' stalls, and itinerant hawkers. The doors that separated the Great Hall from the "Grande Chambre" where the Parlement heard cases were generally wide open. Visitors flowed through them, crowding around the bar that separated the trial arena to observe the court in action.[14] Where Basin claims that there were usually fifteen-hundred spectators at trials in some of the French parlements, Pasquier claims there were "nine or ten thousand" at the 1571 trial I analyze at the end of this chapter, with crowds blocks long trying to get into the hall in the Palais de Justice. The Paris Parlement was in some ways exceptional, but the other French parlements were also open and could sometimes draw crowds (as the 1515 image of the Toulouse Parlement reproduced in my Introduction suggests [fig. 0.4]). Like the French parlements, Venice's busy and crowded Ducal Palace was a hub of legal and other activities. There, the Quarantia courts showcased spectacular trials

[11] *Calendar of State Papers Domestic: Charles I, 1634–5* (1864 ed.), 79; quoted in Sharpe, "Women, Witchcraft, and the Legal Process," 113.

[12] But see e.g. the chapter on "Parlement comme théâtre au XVIe siècle" in Houllemare, *Politiques de la parole*, 439–86 (to which I am heavily indebted, as my notes will suggest); Biet, *Oedipe en monarchie*; Bilis, *Passing Judgment*; Carrión, *Subject Stages*; Robert, *Dramatic Justice* ("trial by theater in the age of the French Revolution"); and the essays in Dionne and Meere, eds., "Staging Justice in Early Modern France."

[13] J. H. Shennan describes the "host of judges and functionaries, plaintiffs and petitioners, barristers, solicitors and sightseers [who] thronged the narrow confines of the Palais, soon to be followed by hawkers and street-traders," who established their stalls in the "Great Hall" and "swarmed like ants into every corner of the building." While several courts met in the Great Hall, the principal court met in the Grande Chambre (built in the early fourteenth century). Only after 1539 were "extraordinary" criminal trials (i.e. those that warranted torture) held *in camera*: all other trials were open to the public. In the Great Hall, the space outside the inner parquet "was invariably filled by members of the public, for few suits involving oral pleading were heard *in camera*, and the doors separating the Great Hall from the chamber of Pleas were usually open" (Shennan, *Parlement of Paris* [1998 ed.], 68, 100–1, 105–6). The ancient Court of the *Exchequer* of Normandy (established in the early tenth century)—transformed into the Parlement of Normandy (also known as the Parlement of Rouen) in the early sixteenth century—had a long tradition of similarly public trials: for a description, see my discussion of Basin in Chapter 4, 153–5. On the establishment of the provincial parlements beginning in the fifteenth century (with procedures generally following those of the Paris Parlement), see Shennan, 83–5.

[14] For a depiction, see Jean Fouquet's painting of the trial of the Duc d'Alençon in 1458, reproduced in Chapter 4 (fig. 4.3, 151).

similar to those in Paris (as my discussion of Francesco Sansovino's *The Lawyer* below will suggest).[15]

Commentators invested the likeness between such courts and theatres with a broad array of contradictory ethical and political meanings. The trope stood for both royal magnificence and democratic populism, visibility and vainglory, transparency and trickery. At the same time, treatises dedicated specifically to oratorical delivery and studies of the art of "mute eloquence" appeared, drawing attention to the relationship between such eloquence in theatres and in courtrooms. Many gave special attention to law. Treating mute eloquence at once encyclopedically and anatomically, as evidentiary clue and as aesthetic expression, they offered tools for the detailed analysis of courtroom performance. In the cultures of critical court-watching that arose, lawyers like Pasquier could become celebrities, famous as artists not only of law but of the theatre of the courtroom. In my analysis of the murder trial of Jean Blosset, Seigneur d'Arconville at the end of this chapter, I show how these phenomena converged in a *cause célèbre* in which Pasquier harnessed the forces of that "great theatre," the Paris Parlement, through a virtuoso performance that (in his telling) reversed the crowd's determination to convict, won a complete victory for his client, and secured his reputation as the greatest of courtroom performers.

The Rhetorical Tradition and the Figure of Theatre

Delivery Handbooks for Lawyers and the Study of "Mute Eloquence"

The rhetoric books emerging from the new presses in the sixteenth century reinforced visions like that in the *c.*1483 Cicero miniature I discuss in Chapter 3 (fig. 3.1). In them, as in rediscovered texts like Cicero's *Brutus* or the complete manuscript of Quintilian's *Oratorical Education*, ancient orators were, specifically, legal advocates arguing cases in the forum.[16] Sixteenth-century

[15] In Venice, although criminal trials before the Council of Ten were held behind closed doors, both criminal and civil trials before the three Quarantia courts in the Ducal Palace (the central Venetian courts) were open to the public. See Viggiano, "Giustizia, disciplina e ordine pubblico" (especially 833–4, noting that the general audiences that attended trials in the Quarantie included a heterogeneous group of patricians and commoners, and stressing the wide and detailed debates in which lawyers on both sides engaged, and the lively and entertaining atmosphere of trials); Arato, *Parola di avvocato* (throughout, and 49, 52, 54, 56 for vivid eyewitness accounts of later public trials in Venice); Rossi, "Rhetorical Role Models," 89–91; Setti, "Avocats, procureurs, juges" (on their highly emotional nature); and my discussion of Sansovino's *L'avocato* and De Luca's *Lo stile legale* below.

[16] For the classic account of the fifteenth-century discovery of previously lost or fragmentary texts such as Cicero's *Brutus*, *De Oratore*, *Orator*, and several speeches, Quintilian's *Institution Oratoria*, new manuscripts of Tacitus' *Dialogue on Oratory*, and more, see Pfeiffer, *History of Classical Scholarship*, 3–66. Helpful sources on rhetoric generally during the period include: Mack, *History of Renaissance*

rhetorical manuals often updated such scenes, envisioning their readers as modern lawyers.[17] Leonard Cox's *Arte or Crafte of Rhethoryke* (*c*.1530), for instance, explains that "the right pleasaunt and persuadible art of Rhetorique" is "very necessary to all suche as wyll . . . be Advocates and Proctours in the law."[18] "[I]n olde tyme," writes Cox, the art of oratory "[be]longed . . . to Judges & men of law" (sig. D6v). Although the art is sadly neglected these days, it is essential to "movynge the Judges to our purpose" (sig. E6v). There is "nothynge more necessarye [than rhetoric] to quicken [lawyers] in crafty and wyse handelynge of theyr maters (sig. D6v), explains Cox, whereas without this art, "oftentymes the rude utteraunce of the Advocate greatly hindereth and [im]peyreth his clie[n]tes cause" (sig. A2v–A3r). Civil lawyer Thomas Wilson's *Arte of Rhetorique* (1553) is similarly addressed to (among others) the "Lawyer," who must learn to "myngle swete, emong the sower": presumably the sour business of law. Like Cox, Wilson warns that the lawyer ignores the art of rhetoric at his peril. It commonly happens, for instance, that "a lawyer . . . take[s] in hande a matter, concernyng life and death." After the trial, "another . . . aske[s] how he hath sped." And he is forced to confess that "in speakyng thynges inconsideratly" he "hath not onely cast awaie his clie[n]t, but undoen hymself."[19]

Wilson gives a good deal of attention to judicial speeches, which he describes as, by definition, "open": "the ORation Judiciall is, an earnest debatyng . . . of some weightie matter before a judge" in "open assemblie" and "in open audience."[20] Such descriptions spoke to the persistence of an ideal vision of judicial oratory in the ancient tradition. As in the later Middle Ages, there were skeptics who argued that legal eloquence was dead. Writing in 1528 in Basel, Erasmus describes modern courtroom speech in much the same terms that Pier Paolo Vergerio

Rhetoric; Fumaroli, *L'age de l'éloquence*, 47–70; and Kennedy, *Classical Rhetoric*, 226–58, and Kennedy, "Cicero's Oratorical and Rhetorical Legacy" (noting that Cicero's *De oratore* was the first book to be printed in Italy [492]).

17 Studies of the relationship between rhetorical theory and law during the period that have been particularly helpful to me include: Hutson, "Rhetoric and Law"; Goodrich, "Ars *Bablativa*"; Eden, "Forensic Rhetoric and Humanist Education"; Zurcher, *Shakespeare and Law*, 27–57; Perry, "Legal Handbooks as Rhetoric Books" and "Legal Rhetoric Books in England"; Schoeck, "Borromeo Rings," "Lawyers and Rhetoric," and "Rhetoric and Law"; Rossi, "Rhetorical Role Models"; and the essays in Kahn and Hutson, ed. *Rhetoric and Law in Early Modern Europe* (especially Shapiro, "Classical Rhetoric and the English Law of Evidence," 54–72).

18 Cox, *Art or Crafte of Rhetoryke*, sig. A2v (1532 ed., hereafter cited in the text). Cox's was the first rhetorical manual published in English. Its date is often wrongly given as 1524. For the conjectural date of 1530, see Carpenter's introduction to his edition: Cox, *Arte or Crafte of Rhethoryke* (1899), 5, 19. Cox's text is in part a translation of Philip Melanchthon's *Institutiones rhetorices* (1519–21).

19 Wilson, *Arte of Rhetorique*, fol. 2v, 6r.

20 Wilson, *Arte of Rhetorique*, fol. 47v–48r. Wilson seems to envision both civil and common law practitioners as potential readers, and his rhetorical texts are closely bound up with his own legal career. In exile under Mary I, he studied civil law at the University of Ferrara and received his doctorate there in 1559. The Inquisition interrogated and imprisoned him, so he had firsthand knowledge of Italian ecclesiastical court procedures. On his return to England, he issued a new edition of the *Arte*, as well as a translation of Demosthenes' orations, and began to practice law, holding a variety of judicial posts. For his biography, see Anderson, *Honorable Burden of Public Office*, 39–54.

had used a century earlier in Padua: Ciceronian oratory (he argues) has no place in modern lawcourts, where "business [is] all conducted by means of... legal terminology, by procurators and advocates who are anything but Ciceronian, before adjudicators who would think Cicero a barbarian."[21] Middle Temple member George Puttenham notes that "grave and wise counsellours... in their judiciall hearings do much mislike all [learned] rhetoricks" and "doe not use much superfluous eloquence."[22] However, like Vergerio, Erasmus and Puttenham were not dismissing judicial oratory but seeking to recast it. For Erasmus, it was sheer "effrontery" to "demand that we speak in a totally Ciceronian manner!" If you want to speak like Cicero, you "must first give us back the Rome of long ago, [the] curia, [the] laws." The great lawyer of today does not speak like Cicero but *does* "speak extempore with an unlaboured fluency," with "youthful alacrity and vitality," in speech that "flow[s] from some never-failing spring."[23] Similarly, while Puttenham rejects "*superfluous* eloquence," lawyers (in his view) must nevertheless learn to speak "cunningly and eloquently." His model is lawyer and Lord Keeper Sir Nicholas Bacon, whose speeches he has heard in the Star Chamber and "[f]rom [whose] lippes I have seene to proceede more grave and naturall eloquence, then from all the Oratours of Oxford or Cambridge."[24]

For early modern theorists of judicial oratory (as for their medieval predecessors), forensic eloquence included delivery: Cicero's "eloquence of the body." Scholars often assert that interest in delivery, already on the wane in the Middle Ages, declined still further in the Renaissance due to the advent of printing, which allegedly replaced oratory as the principal mode of communication.[25] They note, for instance, that the Lutheran theologian Philip Melanchthon—Cox's source and among the most influential rhetorical theorists of the sixteenth century—did not include delivery in his discussions. But Melanchthon

[21] Erasmus, *Literary and Educational Writings* [*Ciceronianus*], 6:405. Since "Bulephorus" and "Hypologus" represent Erasmus' own views, I do not distinguish their views from his. See similarly Cavalcanti, *Retorica*, 25–6 [Bk 1]. On Vergerio, see Chapter 3, 102.

[22] Puttenham, *Arte of English Poesie*, 116 (the attribution to Puttenham is uncertain but generally accepted). On similar advice to advocates in Castile not to engage in unnecessary, affected eloquence in their oral pleadings, see Kagan, "Lawyers and Litigation in Castile," 197.

[23] Erasmus, *Literary and Educational Writings* [*Ciceronianus*], 6:383, 6:427–8 (describing the eloquence of the jurist Ulrich Zasius).

[24] Puttenham, *Arte of English Poesie*, 116–17.

[25] The principal reference for this view is Walter J. Ong, who argues that delivery was "half-heartedly retained" in medieval and Renaissance rhetoric because it was a "reli[c] of [an] age... when expression had been more typically an oral performance and less concerned with writing than in post-Gutenberg Tudor England" ("Tudor Writings on Rhetoric," 46): a puzzling view, since Ong also notes the decline in delivery in the Middle Ages, and since Ong was an expert on Pierre Ramus, for whom rhetoric consisted *only* of delivery and style. For similar comments on the decline of delivery in the Renaissance, see Welch, "Delivery," 218; McCorkle, *Rhetorical Delivery as Technological Discourse* (the "ebbing interest in delivery that occurred in and around the fifteenth century was both a reflection of and a means by which writing and print became naturalized forms of communication" [71]); and Kendon, *Gesture* (in the Renaissance and seventeenth century, "Delivery [how to perform a speech], received but little attention" [20]). Kendon does, however, discuss several early modern manuals on delivery and gesture (22–8).

does not actually ignore delivery. Instead, he repeats the point made by such fifteenth-century humanists as Leonardo Bruni, George of Trebizond, and Jacopo di Porcia: delivery is too important to be left to mere theorizing; the aspiring orator—and especially the aspiring lawyer—must observe it in action. "*Actio*" (Melanchthon writes) is "very different now than it was amongst the ancients." Therefore, "[t]he most suitable way of learning [it]" is not from a book about ancient theory but "by imitation in the courtroom."[26]

If Melanchthon and his successors did not dedicate much space to delivery (on the theory that one could learn it only from live observation), many of the period's rhetorical theorists in fact tried to identify its precepts, often giving it extended and detailed attention.[27] Like their medieval predecessors, they continued to identify it as supreme among the canons of oratory, supporting this view with the established repertoire of ancient anecdotes and *bon mots*. (Demosthenes, when asked, what were the three most important elements in oratory? replied "Delivery, delivery, delivery!" etc.).[28] Moreover, the first books dedicated *solely* to delivery began to appear: the German doctor, musicologist, and general polymath Jodocus Willich's *Handbook on Rhetorical Delivery*, written in 1539 and published with his *Questions on Rhetorical Delivery* in 1550; the Spanish scholar Benito Arias Montano's *Book of Jeremiah, or On Delivery* (1571); the French Jesuit Louis de Cressolles' *On the Perfect Actio and Pronuntiatio of the Orator* (1620); the archaeologist Francesco Bernardino Ferrari's *The Art of Manual Speech* and *On*

[26] "Actio vero longe alia nunc est, quam qualis apud veteres fuit. Et quid maxime in agendo deceat, in foro discendum est imitatio." Melanchthon, *Schriften zur Dialektik und Rhetorik*, 276 [*Elementa rhetorices*, Bk 1, "De officiis oratoris"]. On Bruni, di Porcia, and Trebizond, see Ch 3, 106–7.

[27] In addition to those I discuss below, see the lists in Knox, "Ideas on Gesture," 109–10, notes 31 and 32. Here and below, I am indebted to Knox's comprehensive and learned account. Additional useful studies of early modern delivery and related phenomena include Wesley, "Rhetorical Delivery for Renaissance English"; Fumaroli, ed., "Rhétorique du geste et de la voix a l'age classique" (especially Fumaroli, "Corps éloquent" on de Cressoles; LeCoq, "Nature et Rhétorique" on Bulwer; and Rougement, "L'acteur et l'orateur" on the actor-orator generally); Fumaroli, *L'école du silence* (on silence and gesture in painting); Waquet, "Au 'pays de belles paroles'" (on the voice in early modern Italy); and Greenblatt, "Toward a Universal Language of Motion" (on Bulwer's *Pathomyotomia*, which outlines the universal language of the head, as well as the potential perversion of that language).

[28] Others include: the stories of Demosthenes practicing in front of a mirror and with stones in his mouth; Cicero's declaration that a great speech poorly delivered would invariably fail whereas a mediocre one delivered brilliantly could surpass all others; the story of Aeschines, who in exile in Rhodes, delivered Demosthenes' speech—the very speech that had condemned him to exile—the Rhodians applauded wildly, and Aeschines exclaimed, "'[if only] you had heard the beast himself[!]'"; and others I discuss in the body of this chapter. For the Aeschines quote, see Pliny the Younger, *Letters* [Loeb], 89 [Bk 2, letter 3] (elaborated from Cicero, *On the Orator* [Loeb], 2:171 [3.214]). For examples of these oft-repeated anecdotes and references to the importance of delivery generally in Renaissance rhetorical texts, see e.g. Talon, *Rhetorica ad Carolum Lotharingum* (1549 ed.), 66, 73, 75–6; Wilson, *Arte of Rhetorique*, fol. 119r; Cavalcanti, *Retorica* (1559 ed.), 360 [Bk 5]; Talon [and Ramus], *Audomari Talaei rhetoricae libri duo* (1569 ed.), 68; Amyot, *Projet de l'éloquence royale* (1805 ed.), 49; Wright, *Passions of the Minde* (1604 ed.), 175–6. For the classic anecdotes in their ancient and medieval versions, see Chapter 1, 32-3, Chapter 2, 65, 80, 86, Chapter 3, 104-6, and Chapter 4, 156-7, note 39.

Ancient Acclamations and Applause (1627); the English doctor John Bulwer's *Chirologia: or The Naturall Language of the Hand* and *Chironomia: or, The Art of Manuall Rhetoricke* (both 1644); Michel Le Faucheur's *Treatise on the Delivery of the Orator, or on Pronunciation and Gesture* (1657); and more.[29]

In fact, the study of delivery expanded into a much broader set of inquiries into nonverbal communication, not merely as a performance art but as an object of interpretation. In *The Advancement of Learning* (1605), Sir Francis Bacon declared that no one had yet produced a complete study of "the gestures of the bodie," and "the Motions of the countenance and parts, . . . faces and fashions of men." These "are no lesse comprehensible by art" than anatomy, "and of greater use, and advantage." For they disclose both a person's general character and "the present humour and state of the mind & will." Those who have learned to scrutinize faces, gestures, and clothing recognize that learning to interpret non-verbal signs "is a great discoverie of dissimulations, and a great direction in Businesse." For, he writes (quoting James I, in a line that would be regularly repeated in discussions of delivery), "*As the Tongue speaketh to the Eare, so the gesture speaketh to the Eye*."[30] One book in particular seemed to answer calls like Bacon's for a complete study of nonverbal communication: the lawyer and judge Giovanni Bonifacio's *The Art of Gestures, . . . Visible Speech, [and] Mute Eloquence* (1616), a more than six-hundred-page compilation of quotes and commentary on gestures, postures, deportment, clothing, and more.[31]

If Cox and Wilson stress the importance to the lawyer of studying oratory generally, both the manuals on delivery and books like Bonifacio's stress the importance to the lawyer of studying, specifically, delivery. Willich, for instance, addresses his *Questions* to Andrea Zocho, "a youth . . . dedicated to studying jurisprudence." Given the importance of public oratory to the practice of law, he explains, aspiring lawyers like Andrea need Willich's manuals, which can serve to supplement the student's "natural . . . effort[s]" with specific instruction in the

[29] Willich, *Libellus de pronunciatione rhetorica* and *Quaestiones de pronunciatione rhetorica*; Arias Montano, *Liber Ieremiae, sive de actione* (vol. 8 of the Plantin polyglot Bible); Cressolles, *Vacationes autumnales sive de perfecta oratoris actione et pronunciatione libri III*; Ferrari, *Syntagmata de artificiosa manuum loquela* (apparently lost) and *De veterum acclamationibus et plausu libri septem*; Le Faucheur, *Traitte de l'action de l'orateur, ou de la prononciation et du geste*. Books on sign language also began to emerge, such as Juan Pablo Bonet's *Reduction de las letras y arte para enseñar a ablar los mudos* (1620) (*Simplification of the Letters [of the Alphabet] and Method of Teaching Deaf Mutes to Speak*). On these texts, see Knox, "Ideas on Gesture," 110–15.

Where medieval texts primarily use the word *pronuntiatio* for delivery (denoting not only voice but gesture, deportment, and more), early modern texts use various words interchangeably. For instance, the English manuals use not only "pronunciation" but "utteraunce," as well as "delivery," "action," and sometimes "elocution" (which in some manuals includes both verbal style and bodily expression). For the English usage, see the examples below and in Chapter 6.

[30] Bacon, *Advancement of Learning* (ed. Kiernan, 2000), 94 [Bk 2].

[31] Bonifacio, *L'arte de' cenni: con la quale formandosi favella visibile, si tratta della muta eloquenza*.

"eloquence of the body."[32] Bulwer notes that "Gestures accomodated to perswade" are essential in (among other places) "courts of Common pleas."[33] The English translation of Le Faucheur's treatise is titled: *An Essay upon the Action of an Orator: as to His Pronunciation & Gesture, Useful both for Divines and Lawyers* (1680).

Bonifacio may begin his book on *The Art of Gestures* by describing his escape from the noise of the courts. He has, he writes, "worked a great part of my life in the hubbub of the forum, now as a Lawyer, . . . now as a Judge." But "sated with . . . speaking and hearing," "detesting [the courts'] odious chatter and garrulity," whenever he has been able to steal time from "the forum's confusion," he has devoted himself to "contemplat[ing] the sweetness of a virtuous silence." The fruit of this contemplation is his "work on mute eloquence."[34]

But the forum appears repeatedly as the very scene of mute eloquence. In fact, as he explains, "the knowledge of gestures has a [central] place within jurisprudence." There is a jurisprudence of contractual, ceremonial, and even criminal gestures, such as "sticking out one's tongue, or making horns at someone": in fact, there is a complete manual on such crimes called *On Gestural Offenses*.[35] Jurisprudence also includes, of course, the study of forensic oratory. Here, Bonifacio recites the old axioms: through gestures, the prosecution can make the guilt of the defendant visible to the judge; the defense can embrace the judge's knees and represent the moans and sighs and tears of his guilty client.[36] At the same time, he explains that understanding mute eloquence is crucial to judges. They can infer "from the motions, gestures, and gesticulations of the Defendant the hidden and conjectural circumstances, and discove[r] either that person's innocence or guilt." Bonifacio quotes Justinian's *Digest* on this point: "investigating the truth, the very voice yields up a great deal." Both "from speech itself and from the constancy or trepidation with which it is pronounced," "things come to light that are relevant to the illumination of truth": indeed, "every motion, gesture,

[32] Willich, *Libellus* (consecutively paginated with *Quaestiones*; hereafter cited in the Latin text in my notes): "Iodocus Willichius Andreae Zocho iurisprudentiae studiosissimo iuveni" (fol. 26r). "[U]t . . . ingenitum candorem artificio quodam iuvarem" (fol. 27r). "[Q]uandam corporis eloquentiam" (fol. 5v).

[33] Bulwer, *Chironomia*, sig. A6r (in Bulwer, *Chirologia*: the two texts were published together but are separately paginated.)

[34] "Havendo io gran parte della mia vita ne gli strepiti forensi travagliato, hora Avocato, . . . hora Giudice, . . . del parlare, e dell'udire tanto più satio, . . . quando alcun poco di tempo alle confusioni del foro io poteva sottrarre, andava la dolcezza d'un virtuoso silentio contemplando, & ogni odioso cianciume, e garralità abhorrendo, . . . mi diedi à scriver quest'opera della muta eloquenza." Bonifacio, *L'arte de' cenni*, sig. a2r (hereafter cited in the Italian and Latin text in my notes).

[35] "[H]ora è da vedere come nella giurisprudenza habbia luogo la cognitione de' cenni" (585). "E col solo gesto, e cenno si può fare ingiuria altrui; come . . . cavandogli la lingua, ò facendogli le corna, . . . di che particolarmente ha scritto Jodocho Dambudero nella sua prattica criminale nel titolo: *De iniuriis per gestus*" (586).

[36] See *L'arte*, 551; and on defense tactics, see Bonifacio, *L'arti liberali, et mecaniche*, 50–1.

and gesticulation" may be telling. This is the reason that defendants must "appear personally in the court of justice." Learning the science of mute eloquence can make "the most secret thoughts and the most concealed feelings of the souls of mortals manifest."[37]

Indeed, such penetration is the secret weapon of the lawyer as well. It is a diagnostic tool, allowing the lawyer to "foretell, from motions and gestures, the victory of his Client, or the loss of the case," just as "the good doctor can foretell the life or the death of the sick man from his motions and gestures." Such interpretation also allows the lawyer to "learn the impression he has made . . . on the souls of the Judges," determining the best techniques for "mak[ing] their feelings overflow and . . . storm[ing] their souls." The lawyer who learns to "subtly investigat[e] the will of the Judge and penetrat[e] into the inner part of his spirit" will "always be held most perfect."[38]

Learning from Roscius

Among the classic stories that Bonifacio cites as evidence of the importance of his subject are the stories of how ancient orators "learned the art of gesture from actors."[39] Such stories had almost completely disappeared from view in the Middle Ages, but they began to resurface in humanist texts in the late fifteenth century.[40] Angelo Poliziano observes in his prologue to Plautus' *Menaechmi* (*c.*1488) that "the ancients used to give young children to an actor so they could be formed in the art of *actio*"; in "doing this, we follow an ancient discipline."[41] Such stories became regular fixtures in sixteenth-century rhetorical treatises: Demosthenes learned everything he knew about delivery from the actors Andronicus and

[37] "[I]l Giudice da i moti, da i gesti, e da i cenni del Reo, ne i casi occulti, e congietturali argomenta, e scuopre ò l'innocenze, ò la colpa di quello; e perciò dice la legge: Plurimu[m] quoque in excutienda vertitate etiam vox ipsa, et cognitoris subtilis diligentia affert: nam & ex sermone, & ex eo qua quis constantia, qua trepidatione quid diceret, vel cuius [exi]stimationis quisque in civitate sua est, quedam ad illuminandam veritatem in lucem emergunt" (585; see Justinian's *Digest*, Bk 48, Tit. 18, sec. 5). "[D]a ogni loro moto, gesto, e cenno la verità del fatto" (586). "Quindi e stato introdotto, che i Rei debbano ne i casi gravi personalmente alla giustitia comparire" (585). "[C]on l'intelligenza di questi cenni i più secreti pensieri, & i più celati affetti de gli animi de' mortali si manifestano" (11).

[38] "[C]ome il buon medico da' moti, e da' cenni dell'infermo può presagire la vita, ò la morte di quello; . . . cosi l'eccellente Oratore da' moti, e da' cenni del Giudice può predire al Cliente la vittoria, ò la perdita della causa" (551–2). "Con questa cognitione de' moti, de' gesti, e de' cenni, l'Oratore conosce anco qual'impressione egli habbia fatto parlando ne gli animi de' Giudici, & in qual parte possa far i loro affeti traboccare, e più facilmente gli animi loro espugnare" (551). "E perfettissimo sarà sempre tenuto quell'Oratore, che con quest'arte sottilmente investigando la volontà del Giudice, e penetrando nell'interna parte del suo animo, potrà antivedere la riuscita del giudicio" (552).

[39] See e.g. *L'arte*, 550–1.

[40] A discussion in Petrarch offers a rare early instance (Petrarch, *Petrarch's Remedies for Fortune*, 1:84–5 [dialogue 28 on "Entertainers"]).

[41] "Dum nos sciant disciplinam antiquam sequi: / Etenim formandos comoedo veteres dabant / Pueros ingenuos, actionem ut discerent." Poliziano, *Prose volgari inedite e poesie latine e greche* (1867 ed.), 283 [Epistle 7.15].

Satyrus (they explain); Cicero learned all he knew from the tragic actor Aesopus and the comic actor Roscius.[42] Among the best-loved of these anecdotes (appearing in countless variations) is the famous story of the contest between Cicero and Roscius: a contest, but also the paradigmatic instance of actor–orator collaboration. In Sir Thomas Elyot's recounting (in his *Bibliotheca Eliotae* [1542]), Cicero challenged Roscius to see "wh[e]ther Roscius could set forthe one sentence in mo[re] fas[hi]ons of gesture and countenaunce, or he expresse the same sentence in a more diversite of eloquent wordes." Bodily eloquence appears victorious here, for "Cicero callyd [Roscius] his jewell" because of "his excellencye in pronunciation and gesture" and "[t]he excellency of this man in his arte . . . was estemed and favoured of all the Romayns."[43]

Roscius appears prominently in an image in the Dutch poet Matthijs de Castelein's *The Art of Rhetoric* (1555) (fig. 5.1). He is engaged in discussion with Quintilian, Demosthenes, Cicero, and the Roman orator Gaius Gracchus, as Rhetorica presides over the scene.[44] The composition of the image closely follows that in representations of Justice on her tribunal: for instance, the image of Justice in the Geneva Town Hall Council Chamber (*c.*1502), in which Justice appears seated, holding a sword and scales, and flanked by four representatives of ancient wisdom: Lactantius, Cicero, Aristotle, and Virgil (fig. 5.2).[45] In the Castelein image, Rhetorica's tribunal, her posture, the sword she holds, the banners, and the four ancient orators in the scene all echo those in images of Justice.

At the same time, the Castelein image also draws for its subject matter and iconography on a widely distributed representation of Rhetorica in Gregor Reisch's *Margarita philosophica* (originally 1503) (fig. 5.3).[46] There, Rhetorica presides over a courtroom scene: Cicero is in the midst of his defense of Milo, while Justinian appears in the background, holding up a book labeled "*Leges*" ("Laws"). The Castelein image replicates Reisch's composition: two men and a table to the left; three men and a bench to the right. Like Reisch's Rhetorica, Castelein's appears with a lily and a sword. Rhetorica in both of these images thus echoes the figure of Christ in Last Judgment images: like Christ, she is the ultimate judge.

While the Castelein image thus situates itself firmly in a tradition of judicial representations—reminding viewers that the orators it represents are specifically

[42] See e.g. Talon, *Rhetorica ad Carolum Lotharingum* (1549 ed.), 75; Cavalcanti, *Retorica* (1559 ed.), 361; Talon [and Ramus], *Audomari Talaei rhetoricae libri duo* (1569 ed.), 68; Wilson, *Three Orations of Demosthenes*, 111.

[43] Elyot, *Bibliotheca Eliotae*, sig. Gg4v ("Roscius"). The source of the anecdote is Macrobius' *Saturnalia* [3.14.12].

[44] Castelein, *De const van rhetoriken*, sig. *4v (immediately precedes p. 1) (written 1548 but first published 1555).

[45] Peintre murale avec la Justice (Salle du Conseil d'État, Geneva); reproduced in Resnik and Curtis, *Representing Justice*, 47 (with a thank you to Frédéric Elsig for helping me locate the original of this image).

[46] Reisch, *Margarita philosophica* ("philosophical pearl"), fol. 74r (Book 2, Tractatus 8). Reisch's text was extremely popular, published in multiple editions, and commonly used as a university textbook.

Fig. 5.1 Rhetorica presides from her tribunal while Roscius teaches acting skills to four ancient orators in Matthijs de Castelein's *The Art of Rhetoric* (1555).
Castelein, *De const van rhetoriken* (1555), sig. *4v. Ghent University Library.

Fig. 5.2 Justice presides from her tribunal flanked by four representatives of ancient wisdom: Lactantius, Cicero, Aristotle, and Virgil (c.1502).
Council Chamber in the Geneva Hôtel de Ville (Town Hall). © Office du patrimoine et des sites, Geneva—Sandra Pointet photographer, 2009.

Fig. 5.3 Rhetorica represents Justinian's Laws as she presides over Cicero's eloquent defense of Milo.

Gregor Reisch, *Margarita philosophica* (1505 ms.). Ghent University Library, BHSL.HS.0007, fol. 74r.

legal orators—it revises such representations. It is no longer Justice who serves as judge of the legal scene but Rhetorica. Where the figures flanking Justice in the Geneva Town Hall represent the supremacy of wisdom as the foundation for law, Rhetorica's legal orators in the Castelein image represent the supremacy of eloquence. The Castelein image also revises the Reisch image. For in Castelein, it is not Cicero who is at the center of the scene but Roscius. One scholar has suggested that the Castelein image represents the Rederijker stage, for which Castelein often wrote.[47] Certainly the image's identification of the ancient orators ("*rederijkers*" or rhetoricians) with the theatre would call up the association. In replacing Cicero with Roscius, Castelein places theatre at the center of the legal scene.

If eloquence is supreme, Roscius is the master who teaches the orators to deploy it through delivery. Both the image and Castelein's text make it clear that Roscius is the one in charge in the scene. In the image, he appears to be in the process of instructing the orators in how to do their job. He models a gesture, the forefinger of his right hand pointed upward indexically. Demosthenes and Quintilian mirror his hand position (though they violate one of the cardinal rules of delivery by using the left hand alone: they are clearly still learning). Castelein's text describes the art that Roscius is teaching—delivery—which trains speakers not to use vulgar, mimic "demonstrations," but instead to express themselves "through more genuine signification." They must learn to subtly "poin[t]" with "the eyes" throughout, but to express indignation they may indulge in "raising the arms up high" and "stamping [the] feet." Their "bod[ies] must be capable of great agility," for they must create "[d]ifferent personages in different actions" through "tears, sighs, voice, and eyes." In such performances (Castelein tells us), Roscius "remained the master of his time."[48]

We might take the appearance of Roscius in Castelein's Rhetoric as an expression of the renewed association of legal performance with theatre. When Willich repeats the story of the Roscius-Cicero contest, he notes that the name "Roscius" has become proverbial (fol. 4v). Roscius was not only the emblematic actor but, through his friendship with Cicero, an emblem of the successful marriage of acting and legal oratory. By the time Bulwer published his guides to the "Art of Manuall Rhetorique," he could count on readers to recognize the anecdotes that his *Chironomia* frontispiece referenced (fig. 5.4). There, Andronicus and Roscius

[47] Plett, *Rhetoric and Renaissance Culture*, 502–3 (identifying the banner as a "theatrical curtain" like that on a Rederijker stage, and asserting that the sword and lily reference "rhetoric's power to cause both war and peace" [502]). For a helpful discussion of the iconography of Rhetorica, see Kennerly and Woods, "Moving Rhetorica."

[48] "Niet met demonstratien oft zulcke mesprizijnghe, / Maer met hoesscher significatien, / Met vertoogh des vooys vul declaratien: / Dan comtere des arems ophef en risijnghe, / Pricipalick op eenighs persoons verpisijnghe: / Stampijnghe van voeten, zoo Tullius blye screef / En van als moet de ooghe doen de wisijnghe / Daer Roscius meester af tsijnen tye bleef." "Veel behendicheits, moet den lichame dooghen / Met tranen, met suchten, met vooyse, met ooghen, / Diveersche personagen maken diveersche actie." Castelein, *De const van rhetoriken*, 59 (with thanks to Rozemarijn Landsman and David Freedberg for translation of these passages).

Fig. 5.4 "Everything depends on how [a thing] is acted": Andronicus and Roscius teach *actio* to Demosthenes and Cicero; Demosthenes practices delivery in front of the mirror; Cicero calls Roscius "my delight!"; Cleon and Hortensius declaim to rapt audiences.

John Bulwer, *Chirologia* (1644), frontispiece. Call #: B5462.

teach *actio* to Demosthenes and Cicero; Demosthenes practices in front of a mirror that bears his famous words ("Delivery Delivery Delivery"); Cicero addresses Roscius with the endearment, "my delight!" (my "jewell"!). The medallions flanking "Grandiloquentia" show Cleon and Hortensius (representing politics and law) declaiming to rapt audiences. A banner declares: "everything depends on how [a thing] is acted."

Theatre and Lawyers in the Anti-Rhetorical Tradition

Humanist Legal Antitheatricality

If Roscius appears as a model orator in rhetorical manuals or in images like Castelein's or Bulwer's, elsewhere he appears in an altogether different guise. Roscius may have been "a great deale more tollerable" than the "great nu[m]ber of [today's] bungling boorders," declares the 1559 translation of German lawyer and theologian Johannes Ferrarius' treatise *On the Common Good* (1533). He may have been better than those "dissolute plaiers" who are "nothinge a shamed to exhibite the filthiest matters that thei can devise, [such] thinges, as onely minister occasion of volupteousnesse." But it was precisely his "excellencie in his arte" that made him dangerous. For his craft gave him the power to use both voice and "that gesturing, whiche Tullie . . . tearmeth, the eloquence of the bodie" to seduce both "the iye and eare" and "move any manne [to] evill."[49] Ferrarius draws an implicit parallel between Roscius' "eloquence of the bodie" and the modern "craftye" lawyer's "lawlike eloquence" (so like law in appearance, but so unlike it

[49] Ferrarius, *Woorke of Joannes Ferrarius Montanus*, title page, fol. 100v–102v (a translation of Ferrarius' *De republica bene instituenda* [1556], originally published in German as *Von dem Gemeinen nutze* [1533]). For a similar earlier example specifically targeting Roscius, see Petrarch: Roscius was a "cleve[r]" actor who arrogantly "compared acting to the art of oratory, and himself to Cicero—because he expressed the emotions of the mind and its secret conceits [through] gestures," while, "quite unabashed," he grew rich on the Romans' "depraved tastes," "vanity," and "shamelessness" (*Petrarch's Remedies for Fortune*, 1:84–5 [dialogue 28 on "Entertainers"]). See also Heinrich Cornelius Agrippa's description of the contest between Cicero and Roscius: "to exercise Stage-playing" is "a dishonest and wicked Calling"; ancient Massilia (Marseille) was quite correct in banishing actors like Roscius, for they knew that seeing the "Rapes and Adulteries" such men performed in their plays "would accustom men to the practise of [them]" (Agrippa, *Vanity of Arts and Sciences* [1676 trans.], 64). And see similarly Northbrooke's treatise against entertainments: "one Roscius a Romane and a player in Comedies (whom for hys excellencie in pronunciation and gesture, noble Cicero called his jewell) [received] a stipende of one thousande groates for every daye, [but] these are no examples for Christians to followe" (*Spiritus est Vicarius Christi in Terra*, 58–9). Ferrarius actually concludes this section by noting that the *virtuous* may safely go to the theatre and gather wisdom from "the eloquence of the bodie" (fol. 103v).

in substance). "[W]here the number of Lawyers dooe swarme and flocke together, ... every courte, every private mannes house [is] in a great sturre and tumult by [the] dissensious sutes whiche those craftye marchantes" incite. Lawyers are especially dangerous when they are "bothe practised in pleadyng, and richely clothed," for the costume and the raising of "stormye tempestes" in the courtroom seems to "promis[e] a great victorye," "stirr[ing] naughtye persones to unquietnesse." Lawyers "pric[k] forwarde" litigants who "knowe even as perfectly as they can noumber their owne fingers, that [their] sute is extreme wronge [and] contrarye to all conscience."[50]

The proliferation of theatres had, of course, intensified the kind of antitheatricality we can see in Ferrarius' discussion of Roscius. At the same time, the radical expansion of the legal profession had intensified the kind of anti-lawyer sentiment we can see in his description of lawyers. If Basin had complained about the ever-growing "body of lawyers gnaw[ing] [at] the whole... population," in the sixteenth century, throughout Europe, the profession in fact grew still more rapidly.[51] A visitor to the *chancilleria* of Valladolid in 1590 reported that there were two- to three-hundred solicitors there, all "inn- and tavern-keepers, lackeys, and other low types, [all] rob[bing] the litigants and consum[ing] their money."[52] Solicitors were the "caterpillers *del common weale*," Lord Keeper Thomas Egerton famously declared in 1596.[53] "Lawyer[s]"! a French satiric pamphlet exclaimed in 1622: the "streets of Paris are paved with them"![54]

Ferrarius' negative identification of Roscius with the eloquent but crafty lawyer reflects the broader associations between lawyers and theatre that became recurrent figures in humanist texts. In his famous letter to Emilio Barbaro of 1485, for instance, Giovanni Pico della Mirandola ventriloquizes a scholastic philosopher who has come back from the dead to defend his barbarous style.[55] Drawing on the

[50] Ferrarius, *Woorke of Joannes Ferrarius Montanus*, fol. 69v–70v. In part of this passage, Ferrarius is specifically recounting a story about Beatrice of Naples, who brough a bevy of lawyers with her to Hungary when she became queen, leading to a disastrous litigation epidemic: "where before the name of pleadyng was unknowen, now even every boie could prate thereof" (fol. 69v–70r).

[51] On the radical growth in both litigation and the profession in various places (and negative attitudes resulting from that growth), see e.g. Delachenal, *Histoire des avocats*, 117 (the number of prosecutors more than doubled in France between 1500 and 1537); Holmès, *Éloquence judiciaire*, 17 (in 1562 there were more than 400 lawyers in Paris alone); Brooks, *Pettyfoggers and Vipers*, 48–131 (admissions to the Inns of Court increased six-fold between the early sixteenth century and early seventeenth [112]); Kagan, "Lawyers and Litigation in Castile," especially 181–4, 191–5 (matriculations in Castilian law faculties soared during the sixteenth century [184]). On Basin's complaints and proposal, see Ch 3, 94, and Ch 4, 153–57.

[52] Quoted in Kagan, "Lawyers and Litigation in Castile," 191.

[53] *Att.-Gen v. Kinge* (21 May 1596) in Hawarde, *Les reportes del cases in Camera Stellata*, 45.

[54] "Advocat, les ruës de Paris en sont pavées." *Recueil general des caquets de l'acouchee*, 140.

[55] "A Ermolao Barbaro" [3 June 1485] in Pico della Mirandola, *Lettere* (ed. Borghesi), 91–9 (with passages I quote on 93–5); trans. Rebhorn, ed., *Renaissance Debates on Rhetoric*, 57–67. Citations in the text refer to Rebhorn's translation (modified).

standard opposition between scholastic logic and humanist rhetoric, the philosopher insistently figures rhetoric in theatrical terms and associates the tricks of such theatrical rhetoric with lawyers' tricks.[56] The aim of the rhetorician is nothing but to "deceive, circumvent, practice sleight-of-hand tricks," he declares,

> to transform things themselves, as if by . . . magical force, . . . so that they assume whatever face and dress you wish . . . . All this is nothing other than sheer lying, sheer imposture, sheer magic tricks, [which], like so many masks and simulacra, . . . dupes the minds of your auditors. (59)

Such sleight-of-hand magic tricks, impostures, transformations, costumes, masks, and simulacra may be "fitting for law cases," where popular judgment rules. In the courtroom and the theatre, one may be "allured by a colored complexion [and] tarry at the level of the skin, never penetrating to the marrow and the blood, which we have often seen hidden beneath a face dyed white with makeup" (60). "[F]ull of enticements and pleasure," such cosmetic enhancements may draw "the applause of the theatre" (61). Indeed, "[w]ho would not approve a delicate walk, clever hands, and playful eyes in an actor or a dancer?" asks the philosopher. But the "sodomitical," theatrical "bacchanalias" of rhetoric dishonor "the gravity and chastity" of wisdom (60). Wisdom should never have anything of the "theatrical, applause-provoking, or popular." Unlike law and theatre, it should never "accommodat[e] [itself] to the judgment of the multitude" (61).

The rhetoric-courtroom-theatre triad appears in a different configuration in the humanist scholar Juan Luis Vives' "On the Causes of the Corruption of the Arts" (1531). Where Pico's primary target is rhetoric, Vives' is law.[57] Echoing Tacitus, Seneca, Juvenal, and others, Vives offers a historical account of how rhetoric corrupted law and turned it into theatre. Rhetoric (specifically, oratory), he explains, was invented by the Sicilians, "a sharp-witted people, eloquent by nature and well-equipped to speak," who, deprived of their property, turned to the lawcourts (425–7 [4.2]). They "developed not only a more refined and polished style of speaking, but a cleverer and more argumentative one, better suited to swaying the minds of the judge and all the bystanders" (427 [4.2]). But eventually

[56] Scholars have debated whether Pico actually agrees with his scholastic philosopher. Barbaro's response suggests that he thinks Pico's ventriloquism of the scholastic is a joke, but Pico in fact seems to sympathize with his philosopher's views. For a classic account of the opposition between scholasticism and humanism that Pico channels here, see Rummel, *Humanist-Scholastic Debate.*

[57] "On the Causes of the Corruption of the Arts," part of Vives' *Twenty Books on Education* (*De disciplinis libri XX*), is translated as an appendix in Vives, *De ratione dicendi* (2018 ed. and trans.), 424–85 (hereafter cited in the text).

(and disgracefully, in Vives' narrative), judges began to prefer anything "entertaining" rather than "information about the case." Adapting their speeches "to feelings of that sort, . . . a kind of oratory was introduced into the forum that was better suited to the stage" (459 [4.21]):

> From being healthy, sober and serious, oratory became wanton and debauched, as if it had laid aside its manly garb and put on a woman's attire. The people themselves gathered in the forum and the tribunals . . . as if they were being entertained in the theatre. (459 [4.21])

We can find a similar critique in Erasmus, for whom the transformation of the courts into entertainment venues signaled the victory of emotional trickery over justice. As he declares in the *Ciceronianus* (1528), by Cicero's day "the jury expected and even demanded of the advocates an embellished style designed to please," that is,

> [one designed] to misrepresent the truth, to magnify the unimportant and make the splendid look small, which is a kind of conjuror's trick, to infiltrate the hearer's mind by deception, and finally to carry his intelligence by storm through rousing his emotions, which is putting a kind of spell on him.[58]

There ought to be a "vast difference between an actor and an orator," explains Erasmus. The former is "satisfied [only] with giving pleasure" (6:369); the latter recognizes that it is not "worth toiling such long hours merely to achieve good theatre"; toil should produce substance (6:439). Like his sources, Erasmus gives his analysis a masculinist spin. Even in Cicero's day, there were "men who still breathed that primitive austerity, [and] who wished for something sterner, less theatrical, more manly in Cicero's oratory" (6:404). "Surely you don't think" (asks Erasmus) "that something that was considered rather unmasculine in Cicero could be thought right and proper for Christians," whose aim must be living justly, not "stylish and elegant speaking," and who must distance themselves "from anything that borders on artificiality and theatrical pleasure?" (6:404–5).

In his *On the Vanity of Arts and Sciences* (1527–28), the legal scholar, physician, and occultist Heinrich Cornelius Agrippa calls upon Plato as an authority against legal theatricality. Plato excluded orators from his republic "with the same contempt [with which] he reject[ed] Players and Poets" (in the words of Agrippa's seventeenth-century translator).[59] He had good reason. "For there is

[58] Erasmus, *Literary and Educational Writings*, 6:404, 6:382 (*Ciceronianus*, hereafter cited in the text).

[59] Agrippa, *Vanity of Arts and Sciences* (1676 trans.), 36 (hereafter cited in the text).

nothing more dangerous in civil Affairs" (36), particularly in the courtroom, as the example of Demosthenes shows:

> *Demosthenes* was wont to boast among his friends, That he could sway the Opinions of the Judges, by vertue of his Eloquence, which way soever he pleased.... [Hence] [t]he *Athenians* forbad [orators] to come near the Seat of Judicature, as being perverters of Justice. (37–8)

Indeed, still today, "Eloquence being the Patroness, bad Causes are defended, the guilty are sav'd from the punishment of the Law, and the innocent are Condemned" (37). This is in large part the fault of the lawyers, most notably those who practice "the Art of Pleading,"

> an ancient, but most deceitful Calling, onely set out with the gaudy Trimming of Perswasion, which is nothing else, but to know how [to] over-rule the Judge, and to turn him and winde him at pleasure, [in] which Art there is nothing sooner prevails than Bauling and Confidence: and he is accounted the best Advocate,... who is the greatest Scolder and Brauler. (324)

For Agrippa, among the advocate's most powerful "Weapons [for] overthrow[ing] Justice" (324) is the art that Roscius set forth in "a Treatise wherein he compares Stagemotion or Action with Eloquence" (64).[60] This art—the art of "Histrionical-Rhetorical Gesticulation" (65)—does "not much diffe[r] from Stage-action" (65) in its dishonesty and wickedness. Agrippa describes certain "Mimmick Friers" who employ "Histrionical-Rhetorical Gesticulation,"

> making a thousand faces, looking with their Eyes like men distracted, throwing their Arms about, dancing with their Feet, lasciviously shaking their Loyns, with a thousand sundry sorts of wreathings, wrestings, turnings this way and that way of the whole Body, proclaiming in their Pulpits their frothy Declamations to the People. (65)

But the art also serves lawyers. In Agrippa's revision of the classic story, Demosthenes (the prototype of the modern lawyer), "being ask'd what was most efficacious in speaking, reply'd, Hypocrisie and Counterfeiting and being asked over and over again, still made the same Answer as before" (65). All "prevaricators, juggling shufflers, backbiters, sycophants, and all other leud and vile-tongu'd persons derive their malice and knavery" from such arts.

[60] On the book Roscius supposedly wrote on delivery, in which he allegedly compared acting with oratory (a book frequently mentioned in Renaissance discussions of ancient oratory), see Macrobius, *Saturnalia* [Loeb], 2:103 [3.14.12].

Oxford professor John Jewel's "Oration Against Rhetoric" (*c.*1548)—which may have begun as a burlesque of strident anti-rhetorical views but seems to enthusiastically embrace its own diatribe—provides a vivid description of lawyers engaging in the art of histrionical-rhetorical gesticulation.[61] In ancient times, (legal) orators stood lower than even those they resembled: "[a]ctors, fluteplayers, procurers, parasites, and prostitutes" (388). "But why do I go back to the ancients?" asks Jewel (389). Most lawyers today (he declares) are even worse: "much more conversant" with methods of using their "faces, their gestures, their tongues" in courtroom histrionics than they are "with the subject itself [or] with truth" (384, 388). "What do they want of such faces?" he asks.

> Why that thrashing about of the body? Why that sudden contraction? that waving of arms? that slapping of the thigh? that stamp of the foot? Why is it they speak not with the mouth, not with the tongue, not with the jaws, but with the hand, fingers, joints, arms, face, and the whole body? (383–4)

In fact, it is when their cases are weakest that lawyers employ such tricks most, says Jewel (382). Such histrionics stand against the entire edifice of law as we know it (or at least as it should be). For "if in a tangled or slippery case it is enough that a brawler and pettifogger should shout through some hours, . . . what good is the bench," asks Jewel, "what good are courts, laws, oaths, rules, . . . judges, and magistrates? Why should we appeal to the authority of witnesses, of records, of speakers, of writers, of examinations, of experts in the law?" The court is not really a lawcourt if "there is brought to the bar not an interpreter of law, . . . but a rhetor from the school! If the suit stands by the vocalizing of the orator, totters when he is hoarse, and collapses when he is silent!" (382).

In such attacks on legal theatricality, one can find critiques of the courtroom theatrocracy similar to those of Basin I discuss in Chapter 4: Pico's scholastic philosopher rejects the "theatrical, applause-provoking, or popular" lawcourt that "accommodat[es] [itself] to the judgment of the multitude"; Vives denounces the "wanton and debauched" ancient legal oratory that played to the spectators "gathered in the forum and the tribunals . . . as if they were being entertained in the theatre." The most thoroughgoing such attack appears in the philosopher Francesco Patrizi's tenth dialogue in his *On Rhetoric* (1562).[62] There, Patrizi

[61] Jewel was "Prelector in Humanities and Rhetoric" at Corpus Christi College, Oxford. As Hoyt Hudson (the oration's translator) notes, if we take the oration at face value, we must believe that Jewel "came before the assembled students, . . . announced that he would have nothing further to do with the subject of rhetoric, and urged them to study it no more." Hudson views it instead as "a *tour de force* of mingled irony, burlesque, and rhetorical display, with perhaps a modicum of serious intent" (Jewel, "Oration Against Rhetoric," in Hudson, "Jewel's Oration against Rhetoric," 374–5, hereafter cited in the text).

[62] Patrizi, *Della retorica* (1994 ed.), fol. 57r–61v; trans. Rebhorn, ed., *Renaissance Debates on Rhetoric*, 184–202. Citations in the text refer to Rebhorn's translation (modified).

explains to his interlocutor "Maresio" that oratory was born of the conjunction of tyranny and democracy: the ancient tyrant knew how to make a din; the childish people were dazed by his shouting; and the study of rhetoric was born.

> [I]n its heart, [the multitude] has a wild beast with many heads that are always barking and that . . . deafen its spirit, dazing it so that it cannot see the light or discern the truth . . . . And the master orator always has the power to awaken that beast and to make it bark from whichever . . . of its heads he pleases. (199)

Here we have the inverse of Cicero's story of the orator who tames the multitude, transforming human beasts into civilized citizens who settle their disputes through law.[63] In Patrizi's vision, the legal orator instead *rouses* the multitude to savagery, transforming it into a many-headed barking monster. Standing before this "ignorant" multitude "controlled by emotions" (200), "the orator has infinite power" (199). Patrizi stresses, however, that there is an alternative (in a discussion that echoes proposals for reform like Basin's).[64] In a few places, there are republics "ruled by the people" that "have no need of orators in the law courts" (197). In such places, "the multitude of the common people do not have power over the judges": instead, judges "make judgments according to written laws." If only in all states "everything were judged according to written laws, then judicial orators would never have appeared" (197–8). But, sadly, in most places, the lawyer rules: a liar and con man who uses performance skills solely to win a case, regardless of whether the cause is just, deceiving both judge and audience and effectively "tear[ing] the judgment out of [the judge's] hands . . . by violence" (187–8, 191).

The Forum, the Stage, and the Sewer

The Dutch engraver and publisher Crispijn de Passe's image of Rhetorica (*c.*1599) (fig. 5.5) offers an emblematic rendering of the kind of legal theatrocracy that Patrizi describes. While Rhetorica occupies the foreground, in the background is a stage on which an extremely lively dramatic performance is in progress, with a large audience in attendance.[65] The image's classical references (laurel crown, caduceus identified with Mercury) evoke the ancient world. But we are not in the ancient theatre but before a platform stage in the open streets where the popular throng gathers. There, modern Rosciuses tread the boards, seducing "the iye and

[63] Early modern theorists also often called on this narrative. See e.g. Elyot, *Boke Named the Governour*, fol. 45v. And for the medieval version, see Chapter 3, 98.

[64] See Chapter 4, 153–57.

[65] For a similar image of Rhetorica with a street theatre in the background, see Jan Sadeler's voluptuous Rhetorica (*c.*1575): https://art.famsf.org/jan-sadeler-i/rhetoric-19633010428 (accessed April 16, 2021).

Fig. 5.5 Rhetorica in the Roman Forum with a platform stage and the Cloaca Maxima in the background in Crispijn de Passe's "Rhetorica" (*c.*1599): "If I say what is to be said well, coloring the words, any cause is made good through [my] eloquence"! Engraving after M. de Vos. Wellcome Collection. Public Domain Mark.

eare" of the multitude. On stage there is a chase scene in progress. The pursuer holds his weapon in the air, theoretically to hunt down the man fleeing (stage right), but he also seems to hold the weapon over the crowd below. Rhetorica's posture (left hand raised) echoes his, cementing her identification with him. She too holds a weapon over the crowd in her left hand: her scroll, representing eloquence. If the actor here controls the crowd through his performance (his weapon, emblematically rendered in the stick he holds aloft), Rhetorica too controls the crowd through her performance (her weapon, emblematically rendered in the scroll she holds aloft). As she declares in the caption: "If I say what is to be said well, coloring the words, any cause is made good through [my] eloquence"!

This claim for the power of eloquence is also, of course, an assertion of its moral emptiness: it can make any cause—even the worst—appear good. That the kind of *causa* ("cause" or "case") that Rhetorica always wins are lawsuits—and the weapon and scroll not merely tools of social control but specifically legal tools—becomes clear when one recognizes that the setting is not just any cityscape. We are in the old Roman Forum, which many viewers would have recognized from its central identifying feature: the Cloaca Maxima, the great Forum sewer (in the lower left).[66] The Forum setting (identified with Roman legal oratory) confirms Rhetorica's association not just with theatre but with law. The two men on the right wear what appear to be lawyers' gowns and seem to be involved in legal business.[67] The image is effectively divided: the stage to the left of Rhetorica; a legal negotiation to her right. The composition calls up standard portrayals of the choice of Hercules, in which Hercules must choose between Virtue and Pleasure (the latter often rendered as a theatrical strumpet, as in Xenophon's description: "she had helped [her countenance] with an artificial white and red, and endeavoured to appear more graceful than ordinary in her mien, by a mixture of affectation in all her gestures").[68] If Rhetorica must choose between law (Virtue) and theatre (Pleasure), she seems to have made her choice. For, turning toward the stage (and turning her back on law), she looks at the viewer coquettishly, as if to say: "I'm going to the theatre! come with me!" Rhetorica's choice hints at the image's ultimate moral. While the scene is divided between theatre and law, theatre has already won. For the Forum—that iconic locale representing the great judicial oratory of the past—has a theatre at its center: a theatre where the lawyer-cum-actor can awaken that "wild beast,"

[66] Thank you to Francesco Cassini for identifying the Cloaca Maxima here.

[67] Hargreaves-Mawdsley, *History of Legal Dress*, 112 (plate 20), shows a seventeenth-century Dutch lawyer wearing an open gown similar to those in the De Passe image (and see Hargreaves-Mawdsley, 118, for a sketch of a similar barrister's gown).

[68] Xenophon, *Memorabilia* [2.1.22]. I have used Joseph Addison's vivid translation (Bond, ed., *The Tatler*, 2:100 [no. 97]; capitalization modified).

the "ignorant" multitude "controlled by emotions" and "make it bark from whichever . . . of its heads he pleases." That theatre is built on a sewer: the contents of the Cloaca Maxima gush from its mouth, figuring the gushing eloquence of actor and lawyer. As Rhetorica heads across the sewage to address the mob of spectators, rather than raising herself higher on a book of laws (as she does in many such images), she tramples the book into the mud.

The Modern Courtroom as "Theatre"

The Politics of a Trope

Complaints like those of Pico, Vives, Erasmus, and Agrippa about the theatre's domination of the forum appear in a less theoretical vein not only in images like De Passes's but in more face-to-face encounters with the modern lawcourt. From the perspective of the practitioner, Jacques Faye d'Espeisses delivered a similar protest when he complained that lawyers often came to court as if "to perform a farce," saying or doing "something indecent," and causing everyone in court "to laugh out loud: & act as [if they were] in the Hôtel de Bourgogne where the actors . . . perform in Paris: & fill the bar with laughter and mockery."[69] As Achille de Harlay was to instruct: "[w]hen pleading, you cannot allow yourself to undertake any speech that excites ridicule, which is tolerable in the comic theatre but not in the temple of sovereign Justice."[70] To describe law as theatre was to say that it was not truly law. When George Buchanan declared that the trial of the Earl of Bothwell in 1567 (for the murder of Mary Queen of Scots' husband) was "not [like] the triall of a cause in a court but the playing of a[n] enterlude upon a stage," he meant that it made a farce of proper legal protocol: "[t]here sa[t] the Judges, nat chosin to judge, but piked out to acquite"; "nathyng h[ad] be[e]n done according to the forme of law, nathing in order, nathing after the auncient usage."[71]

As Pasquier's characterization of the trial before the Polish lords and princes should suggest, however, theatre could also serve as a trope not of vilification but of glorification. Referring (twice) to the event as a "great theatre," he emphasizes the splendor of the scene. The word "theatre" could thus signal a court's "grand[eur],"

[69] "[V]enans au barreau, on diroit qu'ils [Advocats, & Procureurs] y viennent pour joüer une farce. S'il . . . dict, ou faict quelque chose indecente, . . . on se prend à rire tout haut: & faict on ce que l'on feroit en l'Hostel de Bourgoigne, où les comediens ont accoustumé de joüer à Paris: & remplit on le barreau de risées & moqueries." La Roche-Flavin, *Treze livres des parlemens de France* (1617 ed.), 310 [Bk 4, Ch 115–16], attributing the complaint to Faye d'Espeisses.

[70] "En plaidant, ne vous pouvez . . . entreietter quelque parolle qui excite risée, qui est supportable au theatre d'une comedie et non pas au temple de la Justice souveraine." Quoted in Houllemare, *Politiques de la parole*, 506.

[71] Buchanan, *Ane detectioun of the duinges of Marie Quene of Scottes*, sig. F1r, E4r (originally: *De Maria Scotorum regina* [1571]).

"magnificen[ce]," "dignity," and majesty: here quite literally due to the King's presence. But the monarch did not have to be there in person in this "great & magnificent theatre" (as Faye d'Espeisses referred to the Paris Parlement in 1585).[72] For the theatricality of the courtroom itself signified the royal presence. There, the magistrates' red robes inspired "respect & veneration for justice" (according to Faye d'Espeisses), while the space itself inspired reverence for the monarchy: its entrance decorated with reliefs representing the monarchs of France at the tops of pillars and a sun in the heavens in precious stones; the Grand Chambre where trials were held (nicknamed the "gilded chamber") draped in *fleurs de lys* tapestries.[73] As in theatre itself, the pleasure of such splendor was a political tool, satisfying the aesthetic desires of the populace, as judge Bernard de La Roche-Flavin's theatrical analogy suggests: "tragedies please less in a room, or on a rustic scaffold built of poles and hay" (he writes in his *Thirteen Books on the Parlements of France* [1617]) "than when they are recited & performed in a rich, ample & magnificent theatre."[74]

In such "grand & magnificent" theatres of law, one can arguably see the classic performance of power we often associate with Renaissance spectacle. As Jacopo Bertaldo's description of the Venetian civic procession I discuss in Chapter 4 reminds us, officials quite intentionally staged spectacles that conjoined such exquisite splendor with terror as a means of inspiring obedience to law.[75] However, like spectacles of power themselves, the trope of law as a glorious theatre was a heterogeneous tool, serving a variety of political claims, from the absolutist to the radically democratic (and sometimes both). For La Roche-Flavin, the "magnificent theatre" that is the Paris Parlement is like the court that Romulus created in ancient Rome: "a great public place in which . . . justice [is] publicly rendered."

> The ancients took it for certain [that] what was done in public, in the sight, & in the presence of all, was done with greater majesty, greater severity, & greater exemplarity.

Modern legal theatres, like ancient ones, had to be public to express the "majesty," "authority," and "severity" that would produce "terror" through example. At the

[72] "[C]e grand & magnifique theatre." Faye d'Espeisses, *Recueil des remonstrances* (1591 ed.), 25 (and for "dignité," see Houllemare, *Politiques de la parole*, 446, quoting Achille de Harlay).

[73] "[Les] robes & chaperons d'escarlate" expressed "le respect & veneration de la justice." Faye d'Espeisses, *Recueil des remonstrances* (1591 ed.), 81. See the discussion in Houllemare, *Politiques de la parole*, 110–13.

[74] "[L]es tragedies, plaisent moins en une chambre, ou sur un eschaffaut rustique basti d'eschalats, & de gazons . . . que quand elles sont recitées, & joüées en un riche, ample & magnifique theatre." La Roche-Flavin, *Treze livres des parlemens de France* (1617 ed.), 327 [Bk 5, Ch 10] (hereafter cited in the French and Latin text in my notes). La Roche-Flavin was presiding judge in the Chambre des Requêtes in the Toulouse Parlement.

[75] See Ch 4, 149–50.

same time, by rendering justice before "the sight and the ears" of all, such legal theatres served as "testimony to all the people" that justice would in fact be done.[76]

Theatre may stand for political drama and turmoil, like the dramas represented in stage tragedy: Pasquier describes himself as both "spectator" and "judge" of that "unhappy tragedy" being "played [on the stage of] this great theatre" (the imprisonment and execution of members of the ultra-Catholic League).[77] But the trope could also appear in the midst of political storms as a promise of stability, a bid for legitimacy when legal authority was in question. The "High Court of Justice" that put Charles I on trial (said the radicals at the helm) was erected for "the most Comprehensive, Impartial, and Glorious piece of Justice, that ever was Acted and Executed upon the *Theatre* of England."[78]

In such cases, a legal *coup de théâtre*—a kind of judicial *deus ex machina*—seemed to promise an end to crisis and the establishment of a new order. The theatrical state of exception was to establish the new normal. For critics, such spectacular theatre merely blinded one to the vacuum of actual judicial authority. But such critiques would have to overlook the fact that the very structure of the established legal system itself had in-built states of exception that depended on ongoing structures of legal theatre for their force. When, in his *Archeion* (*c.* 1591), William Lambarde sought to defend the extraordinary prerogatives of courts like the Star Chamber not bound by common law rules, he explained that such courts were necessary to those cases that could not be heard in ordinary courts but had "to be heard upon the *highest Stage*." This "highest stage," of course, had jurisdiction only in the "rare, extraordinary, & weighty" instances where there were no ordinary legal remedies. It was not a platform for the performance of power or the abuse of royal prerogative: it might "uphold the *Majestie* of the King," but did not represent his "infinite authoritie," only his extraordinary power to intevene in cases where the mighty had committed high crimes and misdemeanors.[79] On such a stage, the King stood *against* privilege and with the people, using equity against law. Thus, courts set upon the highest stage were paradoxically most like those other "Courts of absolute *conscience*": the "Court of *Requests*, that specially heareth the Suits of poore men," and the "*Chancerie* open to all men" (22).[80]

[76] The Forum was "une grande place publique, en laquelle pour plus grande terreur, majesté & autorité, se rendroit la justice publiquement à la veüe, aux oreilles, & au tesmoignage de tout le peuple" (296 [Bk 4, Ch 66]). "[L]es anciens ont tenu pour certain, & assuré, que ce qui se faisoit en public, en la veüe, & en la presence de tout le monde, se faisoit avec plus de majesté, plus de severité, & plus d'exemple" (298 [Bk 4, Ch 74).

[77] "S'il m'est permis, comme spectateur, de juger . . . de ceste malheureuse tragedie qui se joue sur ce grand theatre" (2:457). For the phrase generally, see e.g. Pasquier, *Oeuvres*, 2:28, 2:283, 2:539.

[78] Cook, *King Charls, His Case*, 5.

[79] Lambarde, *Archeion*, 121 (hereafter cited in the text). Although *Archeion* was written *c.*1591, it was not published until 1635: hence, presumably, the references to the King rather than the Queen.

[80] Lambarde, *Archeion*, 22.

When Lambarde describes Chancery as "open to all," he clearly means that anyone can bring suits there (even "poore men"). But Chancery is also *visibly* open, like the arenas he describes in his extended account of the history of public courts. In this account, he extols the wisdom of ancient peoples in situating courts where all could access them and making their decisions public: the ancient Israelites "pronounce[d] their *Judgements* in the Gates of every Citie" so that all could "behold the indifference of their proceedings" and no one "should need to goe out of his way to seeke *Justice*"; the Druid judges held their legal assemblies in the center of their territory "that all the people might have indifferent resort thereunto"; likewise the ancient Athenians, Romans, Saxons, Gauls, Britains, and more (6–8). It is perhaps not coincidental that the King's Bench and Chancery were both not only theoretically "open to all men" (and women) but sat—as a famous early seventeenth-century sketch shows (fig. 5.6)—literally "upon the *highest Stage*" beneath the high vaulted ceiling of Westminster Hall, open to view, so that "all men might behold" justice being done.[81] (Notably, the spectators beholding the scene in the galleries on the left are above even the court itself, though not—here at least—on stage.) Visibility "upon the *highest Stage*" and "open to all" is not the top-down display of violence that early penal theory deemed necessary to deterrence, but bottom-up open access.

In his 1617 treatise on the French parlements, La Roche-Flavin offers an extended history of open courts quite similar to Lambarde's. There he describes the "gates of cities, Temples, or public squares" that were the sites of justice for various ancient peoples, the "Tribunals, Audience halls, bars of justice, [and other] places where [the] Hebrews, Greeks, Romans, [and] the French were in ancient times accustomed to rendering justice."[82] Like Lambarde, he stresses the continuity between ancient and modern courts. Cities and towns throughout France hold trials in "Basilicas, or public squares" in "open session [*à huys ouvert*]," just as ancient peoples did. The Greeks had a "ba[r], & Audiences like those that can be seen today in our Palace [of Justice]." In fact, in Achilles' famous shield, one can see the very "form, & figure of our bars of justice": "a great people assembled around an Auditorium," filling the room with loud "murmuring." This auditorium was very like "the great halls of the Palaces" where the French parlements now hold their courts, explains La Roche-Flavin: there, "in the great halls of the Palace, which one calls 'halls [for] Audiences'"—the "Audience halls of the grand Chambre in civil trials," of "la Tournelle [in] criminal trials," and other courts—"justice [is still] rendered publicly," as it was in ancient times.[83]

[81] British Museum, Prints and Drawings, Registration number 1848,0911.748.

[82] "[P]ortes de villes, Temples, ou places publiques" (298 [Bk 4, Ch 74]). "Tribunals, sales d'Audiances, barreaux de justice, ou lieux esquels tant les Hebreux, Grecs, Romains, que François avoient anciennement accoustumé de rendre la justice" (*Treze livres*, 295 [Bk 4, Ch 63]).

[83] "[E]n ces Basiliques, ou places publiques, . . . s'il falloit ouyr les parties par Advocats, ou Orateurs, on leur donnoit Audiance à huys ouverts" (*Treze livres*, 296 [Bk 4, Ch 67]). "Les Grecs . . . avoient des

Fig. 5.6 Westminster Hall: the Courts of King's Bench and Chancery elevated "upon the highest Stage" and "open to all" (early seventeenth century sketch).

In insisting that the "rich, ample & magnificent theatre" of the courtroom serves "majesty," "authority," "severity," and "terror," La Roche-Flavin may sound distinctly antidemocratic. He believes in legal theology, ancient and modern. For the ancients, he writes, "[i]t was necessary that [courts] be public" to express the boundlessness of the divine: "justice, which is the most sacred thing in the world, cannot be done except in a public place."[84] The elevation of the tribunal expresses the loftiness of justice ("it is in the [very] nature of a Tribunal to be elevated"). And yet, for La Roche-Flavin, the function of this elevation is to ensure access to justice. "[I]f [Justice] is not elevated on her throne, if she... is not seen by all, that is not justice, it is conjuration or monopoly."[85] Here, theatrical visibility signifies both access to justice and transparency. In making itself visible, as in a theatre, law renounces both the mystifications of power and legal monopoly. As the Sieur le Castellan de Sanoc asked rhetorically in 1573, in a "great and celebrated

barreaux, & des Audiances telles que les voyo[n]s aujourd'huy en nos Palais" (295 [Bk 4, Ch 65]). Achilles' shield represented "la forme, & figure de nos barreaux de justice": "un grand peuple assemblé à l'entour d'un Auditoire... avec un fort grand murmure" (295 [Bk 4, Ch 65]). "Despuis l'establissement des Parlemens, la justice se rend publiquement es grandes sales des Palais, qu'on appelle les sales des Audiances de la grand Chambre, pour les instances civiles, & de la Tournelle, ou Criminelle pour les procez criminels" (*Treze livres*, 299 [Bk 4, sec. 75]).

[84] "Il faut que ce lieu soit public.... Aussi la justice qui est la chose du monde la plus sacrée, ne se peut traicter qu'en lieu public" (*Treze livres*, 298 [Bk 4, Ch 74]).

[85] "[C]'est le propre d'un Tribunal, d'estre eslevé" (*Treze livres*, 299 [Bk 4, Ch 77]). "[L]a justice si elle n'est eslevée en son throsne; si elle... n'est veüe de tous, ce n'est pas justice, c'est co[n]juration, ou monopole" (*Treze livres*, 298 [Bk 4, Ch 74]).

theatre, & in the presence of so many," who would "dar[e] report anything other than truth?"[86] No one (he asserts) can lie about what happens in a theatre.

Such transparency made judges accountable to the public. During a trial in the Paris Parlement, presiding judge Pierre Séguier declared: "I am in a large theatre, exposed to the view of all, in the capital city of the kingdom, accountable to the court" and (by implication) the spectators.[87] In the 1564 edition of the Dutch jurist Joost de Damhouder's treatise on the law of guardianship, we have an image in which "listeners" and "spectators" appear to be present precisely in order to hold the judge accountable (fig. 5.7).[88] Surveilling the theatre of justice from the balcony, they seem to be discussing the progress of the trial. The conjunction of "*auditores*" with "*spectatores*" (in parallel windows and sharing the balcony) makes it clear that these are general observers. But the designation "*auditores*" (which often denoted judges) also reminds us of their double role as audience members and judges of the scene. They do not watch from the *parterre* facing the judge (where one might expect spectators to be located) but instead from the position of judge. Watching from above, they take in the whole scene: the action on the floor (lawyer, wards, guardians); and the tribunal itself. The "assessores" labels clearly belong to the assessors below the windows, but the composition invites the viewer to read these as if they also explain the role of the audience in the windows: "auditor-assessors" and "spectator-assessors." Judges of the judge himself, their job is to see (and hear) and ensure that justice be done.

La Roche-Flavin's description of public justice in action suggests that holding judges accountable could be quite vocal (a description somewhat at odds with his vision of the courtroom as a place of sacred "majesty & authority"):

> The audience is the scourge of bad judges: who would whistle at them, who would make them suffer, if publicly they... committed injustice?... [W]hen the audience participates in [the lawyers' arguments] [the judge] judges quite differently.... [I]t is not only experts who can judge [a case]: everyone is capable of this: there is nothing that holds judges to their duty [more] than the fear and shame of being blamed.[89]

[86] "[Q]ui est celuy qui, d'un acte passé en un theatre si grand et si celebre, et en la presence de tant d'hommes, osast rapporter autre chose que verité." Jean Choisnin, *Mémoires ou discours au vray*, 173 (in *Collection complète des mémoires relatifs à l'histoire de France*, Vol. 38; quoting Castellan de Sanoc's speech).

[87] "Je suis en un theatre grand, exposé à la veue d'un chacun, en la ville capitale du royaume, comptable à la cour." Quoted in Houllemare, *Politiques de la parole*, 448.

[88] Damhouder, *Pupillorum patrocinium* (1564 ed.), fol. 85v. Guardianship was lucrative, so such trials were often highly contested.

[89] "L'Audiance est le fleau des mauvais Juges: qui est ce qui ne les siffleroit, qui est ce qui les souffriroit, si publiquement ils... faisoient injustice?... [Q]uand l'Auditoire participe à tout ce que les Advocats de part, & d'autre ont dict, desduict, & raisonné, il juge bien autruy.... [I]l n'y a guiere que les experts, qui en puissent juger;... tout le monde en est capable: il n'y a rien qui contienne les Juges tenants l'Audiance en leur debuoir, que la peur, & honte d'estre blasmés" (*Treze livres*, 298 [Bk 4, Ch 74]). There is a

Fig. 5.7 "Listeners" and "spectators" oversee a trial from the balcony, ensuring that justice is done in Joost de Damhouder's treatise on guardianship cases (1564).

Damhouder, *Pupillorum patrocinium* (1564), fol. 85v. The Bodleian Libraries, University of Oxford, 4° D 6(7) Jur. fol. 85v.

Judges might try to circumvent such spectatorial scrutiny, as might the lawyers and litigants seeking to bribe them. In a 1590 manuscript later published as *The Just Lawyer His Conscionable Complaint*, Lambarde describes lawyers who make deals in secret in the judge's "privy Closet" (with the help of "some score of pounds") because they "perceiv[e] their Clients businesse unable to endure the hammer of open hearing" in "open Court."[90] Here, we have a rather different vision of the "open Court" than in *Archeion*: openness in *The Just Lawyer* is a "hammer," violent in its exposure of injustice but efficacious.[91] For Lambarde (as for La Roche-Flavin), it is the rough but honest "open Court" that keeps the law righteous.

The Courtroom as Encyclopedic Anatomy Theatre: Dissecting the Legal Body

Celebrating the reopening of the Paris Parlement in 1582, Jacques Faye d'Espeisses declared: "we can rightly honor this great & magnificent theatre" with the "beautiful name: universal world!" For Faye d'Espeisses, the court was both a "great... theatre" and a "universal world" because its members had "collected [all] the celestial treasures of wisdom" and were now charged with "disclosing them [to] the whole world" in the form of decisions.[92] William West has argued that early modern theatres and encyclopedias (as both objects and concepts) shared a set of aims: the reason that so many encyclopedic compendia bore such titles as "*Theatrum*" or "*Schau-platz*."[93] Both theatres and encyclopedias promised to make the world visible in space (whether in three-dimensional spaces like the "Globe Theatre" or the two-dimensional space of the page), representing the manifold objects collected there as a totality, an entire world disclosed "to the view of all."

telling slippage in La Roche-Flavin's explanation of the "greater majesty, greater severity, & greater exemplarity" of public justice. Explaining that majesty serves the dignity of the magistrate, and exemplarity serves "discipline and terror" ("discipline & terreur"), somehow "severité" inadvertently becomes "sincerité." Publicity serves "[g]reater sincerity: because one fears failure more when there are many witnesses to debate" the case ("[p]lus de sincerité: car on y craint plus de faillier, quand il y a nombre de tesmoings, pour debattre") (*Treze livres*, 298 [Bk 4, Ch 74]).

90 Lambarde, *Just Lawyer*, 10. On the manuscript that was the basis for this pamphlet, see Prest, "William Lambarde" (especially 474–5, on the belated attribution to Lambarde).

91 The "open Court" could in fact be brutal: lawyers taunting each other; the audience shouting, whistling, or hissing; occasionally dangerous flying objects (in one famous scene, a flying brickbat). Prest, *Rise of the Barristers*, 302, 306; and for the brickbat, "Le Brickbat que Narrowly Mist" in Baker, *Collected Papers on English Legal History*, 2:1091–5. Simonds D'Ewes describes a case in the Court of Wards decided "contrarye to all mens expectations, [at] which the people gave a great shoute" and "hissed" the losing party (D'Ewes, *Diary*, 84 [1 July 1622]).

92 "Car de ce beau nom de monde universel on peut à bon droit honnorer ce grand & magnifique theatre." "[Nous] qui ayons puisé... les celestes thresors de sapie[n]ce, à nous seuls la charge est imposee de les divulguer par tout le monde." Faye d'Espeisses, *Recueil des remonstrances* (1591 ed.), 25.

93 West, *Theatres and Encyclopedias*. (Basic catalog searches show the frequency of "*Theatrum*" and "*Schau-platz*" in titles for encyclopedic compendia.)

The courtroom in Faye d'Espeisses' rendering—collecting and disclosing knowledge from all the great books—was effectively, a kind of theatre-as-encyclopedia.

Like the anatomy theatre, the courtroom as encyclopedic theatre put the body on display, simultaneously probing it for the truths it could reveal and exposing it "to the view of all."[94] An image in Jean Milles de Souvigny's *The Practice of Prosecuting Crime* (1541) (fig. 5.8) imagines the courtroom as a kind of forensic anatomy theatre.[95] In the foreground is the scene of a crime: three murder victims lie before us. The coroner and a surgeon examine the bodies, searching for evidence, while family members and other onlookers crowd around them, peering over their shoulders. The image represents this crime scene as if it is situated simultaneously in the street and in the courtroom, as if the forensic examination of the bodies is actually taking place during the trial. Courts could in fact use forensic bodily tests in the middle of a trial: for instance in "cruentation" proceedings, in which they ordered the accused to walk by or touch the body of the murder victim; if the accused was guilty, the body would begin bleeding afresh.[96] The image in Milles de Souvigny may be intended as a composite. But its representation of the crime scene as if it is in fact taking place in the courtroom implies that the trial so vividly calls the crime scene forth that those in the courtroom can see it before their very eyes. At the same time, the image draws a parallel between the surgeon's and coroner's forensic examination of bodies and the judicial examination of witnesses and parties in the courtroom. Just as the surgeon and coroner must scrutinize the bodies of the victims for evidence, so must the judges scrutinize the body language of witnesses and parties as evidence.

Such images offer a somewhat different vision of the body than those in traditional accounts of the "humanist body" (exemplified in Leonardo da Vinci's "Vitruvian Man") or the "classical" body" of the eloquent orator. If the classical body was an instrument of eloquence, Milles de Souvigny's body betrays its subjects. If "Vitruvian Man" was a complete and unified whole, Milles de Souvigny's body must be dissected as evidence. It is this latter image of the body that the anatomy books, images like Milles de Souvigny's, treatises on delivery like Willich's or Arias Montano's, or accounts of mute eloquence like Bonifacio's, all share. In Willich and Arias Montano (as in the anatomy books), the body is an amalgam of parts. These are infinite in number (because infinitely analytically

[94] On the anatomy theatres as performance sites, see e.g. Wilson, "William Harvey's Prelectiones"; and, for a slightly later period, Stafford, *Body Criticism*, 47–130. On the relationship between forensics and anatomy generally in the sixteenth century, see Shotwell, "Dissection, Techniques, Forensics and Anatomy"; and, generally, De Ceglia, ed., *Body of Evidence*. On the relationship between early modern bodily forensics and interpretation of the body in rhetorical theory, see Martin, "Francesco Casoni and the Rhetorical Forensics of the Body."

[95] Milles de Souvigny, *Praxis criminis persequendi*, fol. 8r.

[96] On the long history of cruentation in legal proceedings, see De Ceglia, "Saving the Phenomenon" (noting the variety of names for such proceedings: *cruentatio cadaverum*; *Bahrrecht*, *Bahrprobe*, *Bahrgericht*, *Blutungsrecht*; *jus* or *judicium feretri*, *sandapilae*, *cruentationis*, or *aimatoxis*; "bier right" (etc) [24]). I am indebted to John Kuhn for drawing my attention to these proceedings and their ongoing use in the later seventeenth century.

Fig. 5.8 The courtroom as forensic anatomy theatre in Jean Milles de Souvigny's *The Practice of Prosecuting Crime* (1541).

Milles de Souvigny, *Praxis criminis persequendi* (1541), fol. 8r. Beinecke Rare Book and Manuscript Library, Yale University.

divisible) and each is separable from the body as a whole, as the body-part headings in Willich's text suggests: "head"; "eyes"; "forehead"; "eyebrows"; "nostrils"; "cheeks"; "lips"; "teeth"; "chin"; "neck"; "throat"; "shoulders"; "arms"; "hands"; "fingers"; "chest"; "belly"; "sides"; "knees"; "feet."[97] Arias Montano includes all these and adds a score of his own (including liquids): "elbow," "back," "diaphragm," "viscera," "loins," "rear end," "hair," "ear," "beard," "tongue," "flesh," "heart," "bones," "femur," "horns" (figurative, he stresses), "blood," "tears."[98] While the headings isolate each part, the sheer number of parts follows the logic of the encyclopedic catalog, offering up a bodily version of the *copia* and *accumulatio* prized by so many rhetorical theorists.

The story about the contest between Roscius and Cicero, in which Cicero challenges Roscius to "set forthe one sentence in mo[re] fas[hi]ons of gesture and countenaunce" than Cicero can in words, offers a gestural analogue to this kind of anatomical copia. Erasmus in fact uses the anecdote in *On Copia* (1512) as an illustration of precisely such gestural copia.[99] But treatises like Willich's, Arias Montano's, or Bonifacio's seek not merely to set forth more (more body parts, more gestures), but to focus microscopically on their details. In his *Retorica* (1559), Bartolomeo Cavalcanti praises modern studies of gesture not only for considering "almost every part of the body" but for studying each through "extremely minute observations."[100] In a section called "Desire to See Everything," Bonifacio explains that the judge must "peer into the cracks" because "[y]ou get a big light from a small hole."[101] Here, minutiae count. The treatises are at once exhaustive and dissective: drawing on illustrations from literary texts, the Bible, medicine, the observation of customs; identifying geographical differences, physiological deviations, historical transformations. They may isolate body parts: the cheeks, for instance, "signify arrogance and pride when inflated, . . . but also irascibility" and, when released, "sadness and despair," and "laughter" is also "related to these spots."[102] But they also contextualize body parts, analyzing

[97] "De capite," "De oculis," "De fronte," "De superciliis," "De naribus," "De buccis," "De labiis," "De dentibus," "De mento," "De cervice," "De collo," "De humeris," "De brachiis," "De manibus," "De digitis," "De pectore et ventre," "De lateribus," "De genibus," "De pedibus" (Willich, *Libellus*, fol. 12v–19v, 38r–41v).

[98] "Cubitus," "Dorsum," "Praecordia," "Viscera," "Lumbi," "Tergum," "Capillus," "Auris," "Barba," "Lingua," "Caro," "Cor," "Ossa," "Foemur," "Cornu," "Sanguis," "Lachrymae" (Arias Montano, *Liber Ieremiae*, 7–15).

[99] Erasmus, *Literary and Educational Writings*, 2:298 [*De copia*, 2.2].

[100] "Il gesto é stato considerato . . . quasi in tutte le parti del corpo, & con minutißime osservationi." Cavalcanti, *Retorica* (1559 ed.), 361 [Bk 5]. Perhaps Cavalcanti has Willich's rhetorical handbooks in mind. Arias Montano's would appear a little over a decade later.

[101] "Voler veder il tutto": "Iudex cuncta rimari debet, ciò è per rimas inspicere, e come disse colui da picciolo pertugio cavare gran luce" (Bonifacio, *L'arte*, 141).

[102] "Proximum his [naribus] locum buccae retinent, quae inflatae arrogantium et fastum, apud Horatium tamen et iracundiam significant his, verbis: Quin Iuppiter ambas Iratus buccas inflet. Demissae autem tristitiam et desperationem. Huius quoque loci sunt, quae apud rhetores de risu memoriae prodita sunt" (Willich, *Libellus*, fol. 15r).

them in relationship to a host of variables: manners, habits, dress, style (annoyingly frequent changes in "the fashion [of] one's dress"); iconic objects such as the staff, crown, or sword; actions such as kissing, weeping, singing, blowing; or practices such as wearing clothes or being naked.[103]

Pasquier's Hands

An essay by Pasquier, "Apology for the Hand" (*c.*1583), is like the treatises in its understanding of body parts not only as instruments of intentional signification (as for Cicero and Quintilian) but as situational objects whose meaning derives from complex networks of practices, signs, and tropes. The "Apology" offers an encyclopedic account of the hand's many social uses and meanings, while highlighting its role as a lawyer's tool-of-the-trade. It begins with a story. Attending the special judicial sessions ("Grands Jours") held in Troyes in 1583, "Monsieur Pasquier Advocate of the Parlement of Paris" meets a Flemish painter and hires him to paint his portrait. Sitting for the portrait, Pasquier asks to be posed with a book in his hands. The painter says: too late; I've already painted you without hands. Pasquier makes up a distich on the spot: "Here Pasquier has no hands," for Roman law "decreed that lawyers have no hands."[104] (The Roman *Lex Cincia* prohibited advocates from taking payment for their services.) Pasquier treats the distich as a preemptive strike against any who might quip that his hands (like all lawyers' hands) do not appear because they are dirty and greedy and hidden in shame. Far from it, for he is (he asserts) one of the judicial nobility in the tradition of the ancient Romans, working not for dirty lucre but for the benefit of humankind.

The story draws on a tradition of painting judges without hands, signifying that they must not (cannot?) take bribes.[105] But it was also apparently more or less true. At Pasquier's request, the painter included the distich in the portrait, and it went viral, setting off a storm of poems about lawyers' hands: "Epigrams, Sonnets, Odes, Elegies," roughly one hundred and thirty in number, by all the lawyer-poets in Troyes.[106] The painting proved an irresistible invitation to lawyer jokes. But it also inspired poetic rejoinders to such jokes, defending the lawyer's hands as noble instruments, persuasively eloquent, bringing pleasure to spectators

[103] "Est enim quotannis alia atq; alia stolae ratio & permutatio" (Willich, *Libellus*, fol. 42v); and see e.g. Arias Montano, *Liber Ieremiae*, 20, 15.

[104] "Nulla hîc Paschasio manus est, lex Cincia quippe Caussidicos nullas sanxit habere manus" (2:206; as above, all parenthetical citations are to Pasquier, *Oeuvres* [1723 ed.], unless otherwise noted).

[105] See Resnik and Curtis, *Representing Justice*, 44–6 (on the iconography of handless "Theban judges" and the occasionally handless figure of Justice herself).

[106] "[E]ntre six ou sept vingts, tant Epigrammes, que Sonnets, Odes & Elegies" (2:207). Pasquier offers two accounts of this incident: 2:203–12; and 2:1001–48, containing the poems the incident produced.

through their beauty and grace. In the "Apology" and his own poetic contributions, Pasquier elaborates. As the stories of Demosthenes, Roscius, and Cicero show (he explains), the lawyer's delivery depends singularly on his hands (2:209). He needs his hands to defend his clients (as well as to defend himself from poverty) (2:1008). His hands can make appeals, stop an adversary, express defiance or blame, "all without the use... of language."[107] They represent all the passions of the soul (2:209). They entertain. They persuade. What is the lawyer's most vital member? No, not his tongue: his hands (2:210). So, you who make lawyer jokes, you of "dark and slimy minds" (2:207), beware! "He who challenges Pasquier in a hazardous case," will discover, to his woe, "that lawyers have two hands," all the better to crush you in court![108]

The Legal Entertainment Industry

Learning from Marino's Evil Cousin

In Francesco Sansovino's *The Lawyer* (1554), a dialogue on how to practice law in the courts of the Venetian Ducal Palace, two budding lawyers decide to visit a veteran in the profession, Messer Lorenzo, to gather wisdom about becoming a lawyer.[109] What do the "fair young" Marino and his sidekick Felice know already? asks Messer Lorenzo. Well, Marino has a cousin who knows the Palazzo inside out and has explained everything to him. First of all, his cousin has told him that he must not shy away from being "impulsive, insolent and shameless." For entering the Palazzo means learning to leave behind all "caution,... humility, [and] modesty." He must pay no heed to Cicero's advice to learn doctrine. "Ignore him," Marino's cousin has explained. Ideally, "be ignorant,... not like Socrates, but *really* ignorant."[110] Before the trial, make sure you have planted "your own people in the crowd": they should "pretend not to know you"—only your brilliant reputation—and "prais[e] you to the stars." You should also make sure that during the trial, while you work yourself up into a "heat," there are "people stirring up the crowd." "[S]tart [by] denigrating the other party and the opposing lawyer,... then shout, laugh, cry, and swear as much as you can." That's how to get both the

[107] "[L]e tout sans l'usage... de la langue" (2:209).

[108] "Sed qui Paschasium dubiâ de lite moratur, / Caussidicos binas discit habere manus" (2:207). This line comes from a Latin epigram that Pasquier quotes twice enthusiastically (2:207, 2:1002), attributing it to the lawyer Antoine Mornac.

[109] Sansovino, *L'avocato* (1586 ed.), fol. 1r–v (hereafter cited in the Italian text in my notes); and see the discussion in Rossi, "Rhetorical Role Models," 89–91.

[110] "[I]o voglio primariamente ch'in cambio di portare in Palazzo prudenza e verecundia che si chiama modestia... tu si imprudente e sfacciato e senza alcuna vergogna e che tu non sappia cosa veruna non al modo di Socrate, ma che tu sia veramente ignorante del tutto" (fol. 5v–6r; emphasis added).

audience and "the judges . . . on your side." Each drop of sweat dripping from your brow is actually a coin dropped in your purse, because "the audience, seeing how deeply and wholeheartedly you defend your causes, will rush to your house," you will suddenly have more cases than you can handle, and you will grow rich as Croesus. That is how to "become a supreme lawyer."[111]

Unfortunately, sighs Messer Lorenzo, Marino's cousin is right about how to become a famous lawyer. But, unlike his cousin, Marino is virtuous: it would not become him to use methods that are "less than honest." Even in these sadly fallen times he can become "great and famous" by honest means.[112] Marino must shun at all cost the kind of ignorant, vulgar, blatant histrionics of his evil cousin. Instead, he must practice learned, refined, *subtle* histrionics. Or so Messer Lorenzo's advice suggests (if one reads selectively). Lawyers like Marino's cousin, of course, use cheap tricks to get the audience on their side, causing ignorant audiences to "ceaselessly marvel." Though these "shock" and "alarm" the more knowing, Marino and Felice must nevertheless learn to do something similar: not merely "put someone else's desires into words and win cases" but "also please the audience and move them to astonishment."[113] Admittedly, Messer Lorenzo also instructs Marino and Felice in the fundamentals of legal argument, court procedures, jurisdictional matters, ethics. "Defend the innocence of the poor man against the insolence of the rich one"; never "defend what is wrong."[114] But

[111] "E così con confusione entra a dir male della parte e dell'Avocato contrario . . . esclama, ridi, piangi e finalmente impreca in tutti i modi ch'i giudici facciano per te . . . . Voglio poi che tu abbia alcuni tuoi partiali amici, clienti, sollicitatori i quali si sfingendo di non ti conoscere . . . si spargino tra le persone lodandoti fino alle stelle"; "gli ascoltanti, vedendo che tu difendi le cause, ti corrono a casa"; "senza alcun dubbio, diverrai sommo avocato" (fol. 7r–v). In his treatise *On Legal Style* (1674), Giovanni Battista de Luca describes Venetian lawyers in terms very similar to Sansovino's. Lawyers in Rome (he explains) may be too dignified to use "the clamor, the weeping and sighing, the laughter, the jokes, the gestures, and the wanton movements" that the ancients employed ("i clamori, i pianti e sospiri, il riso, le facezie, i gesti, e gli azzi, o cose simili"). But in republics like Venice or other places that still "retain the ancient customs," especially before judges who are "legally illiterate" ("vulgarly, we call them idiots, or indeed pectorals": presumably because they judge from the chest), lawyers "*must* imitate the style of ancient [advocates] as much as possible, adorning [their] speech with . . . gestures and actions" (and even "jokes") "to give grace to speech, and to keep the audience attentive and stirred up, so that talking only about the [case itself] does not bore them." ("[A]vanti giudici, e magistrati, i quali legalmente si dicono non letterati, e volgarmente diciamo idioti, ovvero pettorali secondo l'accennata usanza di quelle citta, le quali si governino a forma di repubblica, o che non essendo tali di presente, lo siano state per lo passato, sicche si ritengano tuttavia le antiche usanze: ed in tal caso si debba imitare al possibile lo stile degli oratori, e declamatori antichi, . . . ornando il discorso con . . . facezie, e con i gesti ed azzi per dar grazia al parlare, e per tener attentati e sollevati gli uditori, accio il parlare de' soli motivi della causa non gli arrechi noia"). De Luca, *Lo stile legale* [2010 ed.], 144–5 [Ch 14]; emphasis added).

[112] "Ma à voi non si convien usar termini che sian meno che honesti, percioché essendo ripieno di buone cose, dovete ricordarvi che voi s[i]ete in un tempo che vi puo far grande e riputato con quel veri mezzi" (fol. 7v).

[113] Spectators "si maravigliano senza fine." The lawyer who uses such tricks "sbigottisce e spaventa ogni bon intelletto" (fol. 2v). However, "[n]on basta adunque che l'Avocato sappia solamente esporre l'altrui desiderio . . . ma bisognia che piaccia agli ascoltanti e che li muova a maraviglia" (fol. 4r–v).

[114] "[N]on debbiate difendere il torto: difendette [*sic*] l'innocenza del povero contro l'insolenza del ricco" (fol. 17v).

much of his advice is about how to grow bold in court and use performance to vanquish your adversary. Becoming a "real lawyer" requires not just intellect and truth but embellishing your speeches with the entire repertoire of rhetorical "ornaments."[115] The "young lawyer is naturally timorous," but with practice can "become fearless and at home with the judges."[116] Practice "declaiming," he advises Marino; practice pleading "on both sides of the case."[117] Once you are in the courtroom, feel free to start by attacking your "adversary's traits," using "all those parts of [the] art [that] make you a maestro."[118] In fact, "use . . . any device to achieve victory."[119] If you "use your weapons" (those secret weapons "only you really know"), you will be able to "move the judges," the "audience [will] prefer to listen to you" than to your adversary, and you will sail to victory.[120]

Critical Court-Watchers and the Feverish Crowd

The courtroom culture that Sansovino describes—in which lawyers did all they could to stir up the crowd, and those best at doing so became legal celebrities—was (as I have suggested) particularly intense in locales like Venice or Paris: locales with large, prestigious, public courts, long traditions of courtroom oratory, and the kinds of vast audiences I describe at the beginning of this chapter. There, just being one in the teeming crowd could excite the most intense emotions. "There is no passion as great as that of [a] trial," wrote Louis Dorléans in 1607. "A trial is a fever, . . . an apoplexy" that ravishes "all one's limbs, & [all] one's soul."[121] But elsewhere, too, the general spectator might attend trials for the intense pleasures they could offer. The Scottish poet John Barclay notes in his *Mirror of Minds* (1614) that "nothing is more delightful" than the "spectacle of the courts and judges."[122] "[I]f thou lovest to be among the trouble of the court" (as he does, he confesses),

[115] "Avocati . . . che sanno che cosa s'aspetti all'ornamento"; "[i]l vero Avocato" (fol. 2v).

[116] "Bisogna . . . che il giovane che è timoroso, impari prima a parlare al cospetto de' Giudici, da poi fatto ardito e domesticato col giudice" (fol. 15v).

[117] Argue "per l'una parte, e per l'altra, e s'essercita declamando" (fol. 14v).

[118] "[T]occ[a] brevemente le qualità dell'adversario con tutte quelle parti di che l'arte vi fa maestro" (fol. 16r).

[119] "Usate . . . ogni artificio per acquistar la vittoria" (fol. 17v).

[120] "[I]n che modo si movino i giudici" (fol. 5r). "Osservando adunque i detti ordini e altri che voi stesso sapete, non potrà mai esser . . . che gli ascolta[n]ti non v'odino più volentieri voi che quell'altro" (fol. 16v).

[121] "[I]l n'y a passion si gra[n]de que celle des proces . . . . C'est une fievre que le proces, voire une apoplexie qui frappe tous les membres, & parties de l'esprit." Dorléans, *Ouvertures des parlements* (1607 ed.), 243.

[122] Barclay, *Icon animorum, or, The Mirror of Minds* (2013 ed.), 305 (hereafter cited in the text).

> the very noise of [the people] running up and down and [their] different looks, some animated with fear, some exulting with hopes, will so take up thy mind and eyes that thou wilt think thou beholdest a pleasant scene of human madness. (305)

In the courtroom itself, "it is wonderful how great a reverence" the assembled judges could "strike into you" in all their "majesty," offering a "delightful spectacle." There, one could "sit as it were in the haven, [and] securely look upon the stormy sea, and see these Neptunes governing the waves according to their own beck" (303). (Lest he seem too callous, Barclay adds a qualification—delightful, of course, only to those with "no hopes or fears depending upon their sentences [303]—and a caution: "while thou enjoyest, thou shalt not withstanding with fearless sighs grieve sometimes for the miseries of others" [305]). If reverence or grieving are not to your taste, he writes (growing snarkier), you might take wicked pleasure in the judges' "*want* of sense and eloquence" and enjoy "giv[ing] sentence upon the judges themselves" (305; emphasis added). Or you might find equal entertainment in the slippery "subtlety of the advocates, whose eloquence is there [for] sale, displaying itself in ostentation . . . and pompous language, . . . enough to give thee a delight sweet" (305).

Such critical spectators could be keen observers. Books like Bonifacio's urged court watchers to scrutinize "every motion, gesture, and gesticulation" and spectators seem often to have done so, minutely detailing their observations. In the sensational treason trial of Charles de Gontaut, Duc de Biron in 1602, his arrogant posture helped to condemn him, explains La Roche-Flavin, "because, being seated on the bench to be heard, he advanced his right foot & held his coat turned up under his arm, which he held arched, [his] only act of bravery."[123] In France in particular, where debates about theatrical style could become virulently political, courtroom observers could scrutinize lawyers as intensely as they did actors. Pasquier's friend Antoine Loisel writes of his admiration for Pierre Robert, who "did not know much [about law]" but was a "man of a beautiful presence, voice, and movements." Pierre Versoris' delivery was also "beautiful and agreeable," except for one small "vice": "he pronounced . . . an A for an E, and an E for an A."[124] In his 1590 treatise on French eloquence, Guillaume du Vair noted that Barnabé Brisson might be admired for his moving expressions of pathos, but his *actio* was hopelessly turgid, for "[h]e always had the same posture, his collar tilted

[123] "[C]ar estant assis sur le scabeau pour estre ouy, il advançoit le pied droit, & tenoit le manteau retroussé soubs le bras, qui tenoit en arcade, seul geste de braverie" (La Roche-Flavin, *Treze livres*, 314 [Bk 4, Ch 132]).

[124] Robert "n'en sçavoit past tant; mais il estoit homme d'une belle presence, voix et action" (94). "[L]a voix [et] l'action" of Versoris "estoit belle et agreable. . . . Vray est qu'il avoit un vice, qui est qu'il prononçoit ordinairement un A pour un E, et un E pour un A" (106). Loisel, *Pasquier ou Dialogue des advocats* (1844 ed.), 83–4, 94, 106.

and his eyes raised high," as if afraid "of being distracted by what he saw" and forgetting his lines.[125] In a satiric pamphlet, François Garasse (writing under a pseudonym) compared Louis Servin to a peacock, incessantly preening himself: "a gesture, an eye, a voice, a support of the whole body that preaches nothing but a pure [vain]glory."[126]

The great legal orator was an artist who knew that audience pleasure—narrative and aesthetic—was key to winning a case. As Guillaume du Vair said, the lawyer must "tickle the ears of the audience, as an affected courtesan does in a theatrical scene."[127] On the one hand, lawyers must "adapt themselves to the passions of their audience" (as one rhetorical theorist wrote).[128] On the other hand, the goal was not to be a slave to the emotion of the crowd but its master. Lawyers often bragged that they had turned a hostile crowd.[129] Writing in 1559, one "R. B. Lawyer" describes a case in the Parlement in Aix-en-Provence in which Jean Charrier, Advocate General for the King, represented "two poor nephews tricked by their uncle" who were "bereft of defense": "a pitiful case." (The uncle had promised to make them his heirs but instead cruelly left his fortune to some good-for-nothing monks.) "[I]f you had heard [the Advocate General], as I did," writes R. B., "you would have [been] like all the spectators amazed and ravished with admiration for the grace, & force of his eloquence," such eloquence as had "never [been] known or felt before."

> [W]ith his modest countenance, & the grave movements of his body, [he] spoke with such a clear, and sweet voice that when he came to the apostrophes, & other emotional places, he so powerfully moved the Court, & the whole Audience, that he drew tears from [the Judges], & as for the audience, the greatest part melted in tears.

All were certain that "the rigor of the law" would prevail. But "such was the grace of his delivery, & force of his eloquence" that he won a judgment for the "poor nephews" "beyond all expectation."[130]

125 "Il avoit tousjours une mesme posture, le col un peu tourné et les yeux levez en haut, ce que quelques uns disoient qu'il faisoit de peur d'estre diverty par la veuë." "Mais quant à l'action, il l'avoit tres-mauvaise." Du Vair, *De l'éloquence françoise* (1908 ed.), 137–8.

126 "[U]n geste, un oeil, une voix, un maintien de tout le corps qui ne presche autre chose qu'une pure & fine gloire." Garasse, *Banquet des sages*, 48.

127 "[C]hatoüiller les oreilles de l'auditeur, comme feroit une courtisane affettee en une scene de comédie." Du Vair, *De l'éloquence françoise* (1908 ed.), 166.

128 One must "s'accomoder aux passions de ses auditeurs." Du Perron and Renouard, *Fleurs de l'éloquence françoise*, 158; quoted in Holmès, *L'éloquence judiciaire*, 33.

129 See e.g. Marion, *Plaidoyez de M. Simon Marion* (1594), 142; and Pasquier on the Arconville case (below).

130 "[U]ne cause pitoyable abandonné de defense,... deux pauvres nepveux trompez par un leur oncle." "[S]i tu l'eusses ouy, comme moy, tu fusses demeuré avec les autres auditeurs esmerveillé, & ravy en admiration de la grace, & force de l'eloquence: laquelle les Advocatz... n'avoyent encores cogneue, ne sentie." "[L]'Advocat general avec sa contenance modeste, & grave remuement de son

As Charrier's defense suggests, to produce the desired emotions while entertaining the spectators, lawyers borrowed from theatre, drawing on comic and tragic stock figures and classic narrative arcs, relying on their tried-and-true emotional effects. While importing such conventions, they also inevitably imported the performance conventions that brought these to life. In one trial in Paris in 1600, for instance, a young man had been murdered, the mother accused her landlord, and he was subjected to torture and on the brink of being condemned for the murder when two thieves confessed to the crime. The landlord charged the mother with false prosecution and claimed damages for the torture and suffering he had undergone. Both lawyers worked to capitalize on the emotions this "very tragic" event would inevitably produce. As the collection of *Notable Trials and Trial Speeches* by Louis Servin reports, the famous Monsieur Anne Robert argued first for the landlord:

> If this woman represents to you the devotion and sorrow of a mother, imagine, Messieurs, the miserable groans of this innocent in the midst of the cruelty of [torture], having then no other feeling than his pain.

Arguing for the mother, the equally famous Antoine Arnauld contrasted his own speech with Robert's: Robert "represented to you his complaints with an elegant discourse full of artifice and of the force of eloquence," whereas from the defense "you will hear [instead] the sobs and groans of a poor mother transported by sorrows and reduced [to] despair." Assuming her persona to make those sobs and groans audible right there in the courtroom, Arnauld cried out: "there, my son, my poor son, I will still call [you] night and day even though you do not respond." The verdict: the mother's sobs and groans won the day.[131]

The world of humanist theory sometimes seems very remote from actual practice in the courts. But humanist critics of legal performance like Erasmus, Agrippa, Jewel, or Patrizi seem to have had precisely such scenes in mind. Practitioners could echo their critiques. In a letter to his son Theodore offering

corps prononcea avec une voix claire, & doulce de telle sorte, que qua[n]d il vint aux apostrophes, & autres lieux d'affection, il esmeut si tresfort la Cour, & tout l'Auditoire, qu'à la plus grand part de messieurs les Senateurs il arracha les larmes des yeux,... & quant aux auditeurs, la plus gra[n]d part fondoit en larmes.... [T]elle estoit la grace de la prononciation, & force de l'eloquence" that "par dessus l'expectation" and against "la rigueur du droict," he won the case. Charrier, *Memorable action judiciaire*, 4–5.

131 "Et si cette femme vous represente la pieté & les regrets d'une mere, imaginez vous Messieurs, les miserables gemissemens de cét innocent au milieu de la cruauté d'une question ordinaire & extraordinaire, n'ayant lors autre sentiment que de ses douleur" (854). "[Robert] vous a representé ses plaintes avec un discours élegant remply d'artifice & de force d'eloquence: & au contraire de nostre part vous n'entendrez que sanglots & gemissemens d'une pauvre mere transportée de douleurs, & reduite en toutes sortes de desespoirs" (855). "Là mon fils, mon pauvre fils je r'appelleray nuict & jour encores que tu ne me respondes point" (857). Servin, *Actions notables et plaidoyez* (1640 ed.), 854–7; see the discussion in Houllemare, *Politiques de la parole*, 466–8.

advice on how "to be [a] good Lawyer," Pasquier urges Theodore to place honor before all else: "[f]ight for truth & not for victory"; arm yourself to "fell vice, virtuously defend the afflicted poor," and stand up to those who "abuse their authority and greatness to the ruin of the weakest."[132] Dishonorable lawyers may try to sway the crowd, with their "Rhetorical elegance & hypocrisy," and sometimes they manage to "better please the ears." But they will not ultimately persuade. However true it may be that "this noble exercise" (pleading) means that the lawyer has "more in common with the ancient Roman Orator than the Jurisconsult," as "a good father" Pasquier will not teach his son the cheap theatrical tricks of the ancient courts.[133] However, like the advice of Sansovino's Messer Lorenzo on how to be a good lawyer, Pasquier's is somewhat equivocal. "Do not expect here that I will teach you all those masks of oratory that . . . the ancient Greeks & Romans" used, he declares, or "the art of moving the passions of those who listen." "Do not expect that I will teach you . . . the variety of ways [to] diversify [your] eloquence," the "lovely rhythmic closing of a clause, [or the] infinity of beautiful florets with which their books & teachings are packed," he writes, evidently carried away with enthusiasm for his theme. "Do not expect that I will teach you . . . the lovely management of [the Orator's] body & his voice" that Demosthenes identified as "the first, second, & third part of Orator[y]" and that is so essential to persuasion. "[A]ll the artifice that I intend to give you here" (writes Pasquier), lies in this one lesson: "use no artifice."[134] And yet, the end of the letter seems somehow to have forgotten its beginning. For, as he tells Theodore, the greatest "spur exciting us to do well"—more inspiring than the need to persuade the judges or do right by our clients— is knowing that "we must please and satisfy the ears of a great Theatre."[135]

In the trial with which I begin this chapter, the job the King gave Pasquier and Brisson was, of course, precisely to "please and satisfy the ears of a great Theatre."

[132] "[D]e quelle façon doit estre le bon Advocat" (2:229) (the editor's side note describing the letter). "Combattez pour la verité, & non point pour la victoire"; "soit armée . . . pour terrasser le vice, soustenir vertueusement le pauvre affligé, faire pavois de vostre conscience contre les efforts des plus puissans, qui veulent abuser de leur authorité & grandeur à la ruine des plus foibles" (2:231). (As above, all parenthetical citations are to Pasquier, *Oeuvres* [1723 ed.], unless otherwise noted; I have silently corrected the numbers of pages 2:229–2:230, which are mispaginated.)

[133] "[A]pportez tant d'élegances & hypocrisies de Rhethorique, . . . vous delecterez davantage les aureilles de ceux qui vous escoutent, mais les persuaderez beaucoup moins." "[D]'autant que ce noble exercice a plus de participation avec l'ancien Orateur de Rome que Jurisconsulte, je vous diray deux mots" (2:231), "comme bon pere" (2:232).

[134] "N'attendez point icy que je vous enseigne tous ces masques d'oraison qui nous furent representez en ce subjet par les anciens Grecs & Romains, en combien de façons il faut diversifier son bien dire, la maniere de remuer les passions de ceux qui escoutent, la closture aggreable d'une clausule, & une infinité de belles fleurettes dont leurs livres & enseignemens sont farcis, . . . [e]t ce que Demosthéne disoit que la premiere, seconde, & troisieme partie de l'Orateur gisoit en une belle ordonnance de son corps & de son parler." "Tout l'artifice que j'entends icy vous donner, est de n'user point d'artifice" (2:231).

[135] "Et sur tout, . . . on a de contenter & satisfaire aux oreilles d'un grand Theatre, qui n'est pas un petit aiguillon pour nous exciter à bien faire" (2:230).

The case at issue—featuring the priest, his servant, their bastard son, the son's wife, and the greedy relatives—sounds uncannily like the improbable hypotheticals that students in the Inns of Court and universities debated in moots and other disputations (which I discuss in Chapter 6).[136] But the case was not a hypothetical. The relatives, having lost in the court of first instance, had appealed to the Parlement. There, the verdict was not only binding but treated as precedent. As Pasquier observed later, the decision was "very notable [and] has since served as law."[137] The parties were perhaps surprised that their case—which must have been very real to them, with all its lies, betrayals, and shameful revelations—was to be served up as entertainment for the Polish lords and princes. But no one, least of all Pasquier, seems to have thought twice about the parties' feelings or even worried that calling on big-name lawyers to make it as entertaining as possible might compromise its fairness. When he writes about the trial, he stresses the honor of having been chosen to entertain the Polish delegation in "the greatest theatre that was ever found in the Court of the Parlement," and basks in the reflected glory of the august audience. What made him a courtroom maestro—as all accounts of his trials suggest—was ignoring his advice to Theodore on "how to be a good Lawyer" and instead using "the art of moving the passions of those who listen," the "masks of oratory," the "lovely management of [the] body [and] voice" to "please and satisfy the ears of [that] great Theatre."

Pasquier Defends "the Slaughterer": The Trial of Jean d'Arconville (1571)

In January 1571, neighbors reported that the home of the lawyer Simon Bobie—where one normally heard Bobie and his wife in heated arguments that often came to blows—had been suspiciously quiet for days. When police entered, they found the bodies of Bobie's wife, their two small children, a nurse, and a chambermaid: all brutally murdered. Rings, candelabras, and a coat had been thrown into the privy, and all left in chaos, but nothing had been stolen: not (it seemed) the work of a thief, but of someone avenging a wrong. Informed of the historic enmity between Bobie and Jean Blosset Seigneur d'Arconville, officers arrested Arconville and dragged him through the streets of Paris lashed to a cob horse "as if he had already [been] convicted of the crime."[138] A few days later they took the rest of his

[136] See e.g. "Le Virge," in which there is a bastard son, another son who suddenly becomes a monk, the mother of the bastard who subsequently marries, deaths, suits, and countersuits about property (see Baker, *Third University of England*, 15–16; and my discussion in Chapter 6, 279).

[137] It was a decision "fort notable, et qui du depuis a servi de loy" (Pasquier, *Interprétation des Institutes* [1847 ed.], 91).

[138] [C]omme s'il eust esté jà atteint & convaincu du crime" (Pasquier, *Oeuvres* [1723 ed.], 2:312).

household—his wife, their servants (male and female), their laborers—transporting them through the streets in carts. "[W]ho [is] it[?]" the people asked the guards as the procession passed. "[T]he slaughterer," they answered, and "the wife of the slaughterer." "[T]here was no one," declared Pasquier, "who did not believe they were complicit in the execrable crime."[139] So, naturally, he took the case for the defense.

Pasquier loved nothing better than a high-profile case in which the odds were against him. In 1564, as a young unknown, he had won a verdict on behalf of the University of Paris against the Jesuits, describing the arena as the "great theatre of the Court of the Parlement of Paris," where he had performed "in the presence of an infinite number of people."[140] The Arconville case was even more of a *cause célèbre*: one that could make him or break him. There were no witnesses: the case depended entirely on circumstantial evidence, which meant (he was to brag later) that it depended solely on the "wits [*esprits*] of the lawyers." Whatever the truth of the matter, it was clever lawyering that would be victorious. The lawyer for the prosecution was the eminent Brisson (who would, of course, be Pasquier's antagonist before the Polish ambassadors two years later). Pasquier declared to Brisson on the courtroom floor, "you [M]aster Barnabé Brisson," by "means of your speech," have "been the principal instrument" of Arconville's ill-fame. "I wish to make this my quarrel, and [I] take your Plaidoyer as a throwing down of the gauntlet.... I accept[!] I thus now enter the field to do combat with you head-to-head"![141]

On the day of the trial, the Salle Saint-Louis—the criminal courtroom in the Palais de Justice—was packed with spectators, the crowd overflowing and filling the streets. "Never were more people to be found at a trial," writes Pasquier. The public was in a frenzy of outrage at the acts of "the Slaughterer," so "everyone raced" to the Palais, "as if to a fire." The courtroom was in an uproar: the "extraordinary racket of the people" was deafening. Pasquier tried to speak, but "an infinite murmuring arose from the whole audience"; he waited for it to die down, began to speak again, and "here my speech was once more taken away by the people"; this too eventually died down, he began to speak again, and there was a "third charge of the people," which "made the color rise in my face." Giving vent

[139] [Q]ui c'estoit [?]" "[L]'assommeur [et] la femme de l'assomeur" (2:317). "[I]l n'y eust aucun qui ne creust, qu'ils estoient complices du crime execrable" (2:312).

[140] "[E]n ce grand theatre de la Cour de Parlement de Paris, en presence d'une infinité de gens, [j'ai] plaid[é] pour l'Université de Paris, contre les Jesuites" (1:891).

[141] "Cette cause despendoit... des esprits de ceux qui devoient plaider" (2:312). "[J]'ay grand interest que sa reputation ne demeure engagée envers le peuple, dont vous, maistre Barnabé Brisson, avez esté le principal instrument, par vostre Plaidoyé; je veux faire de sa querelle la mienne, & prendre votre Plaidoyé, comme un cartel de deffy, que j'accepte. J'entre doncques maintenant en champs clos, pour vous combattre, teste à teste" (2:319–20).

to "a bittersweet anger" that offered "some relief," he raised his voice: "in vain" (he cried) do "I come to persuade you of the justice of my cause...." As he writes, "everyone [was] against me."[142]

The "two great buttresses of [Brisson's] case," writes Pasquier, were the universal "compassion... for his client [Bobie] & the common belief that prejudiced the people against us."[143] Clearly determined to exploit that compassion, Brisson made sure that Bobie appeared in the courtroom not as an accuser vengefully pursuing the murderer of his wife, children, and servants, but instead as a victim: a man crumpled at the feet of his lawyer, weeping. Pasquier—worried that he might appear callous in further "afflict[ing] a person afflicted" (so *visibly* afflicted)—proclaimed that he "share[d] with the people in [their] compassion" for Bobie.[144] At the same time, equally aware of the power of the visible scene, he created a parallel tableau whose intention was clearly to trump Brisson's, and eventually to turn it against him. As Pasquier later described the scene: "At the feet of Monsieur Brisson was Bobie, who was not without tears in his eyes: [but] at mine was [Arconville], & with him his weeping wife, and also his two small children."[145] The parallel Pasquier then drew between the two families—equally innocent and equally suffering—effectively explained the tableau. His stress on "seeing" suggests that he gestured toward these figures as he spoke:

> Great is the compassion that one finds in seeing a mother, a nurse, two small children, and one chambermaid, all innocent persons, having been cruelly assassinated. No less great is that [which arises from] see[ing] a husband, a wife, laborers, servants male and female, all innocent persons, led through the streets of Paris in carts, ignominious prisoners,... their small children left alone in their house at the mercy of swine.[146]

[142] "Jamais plus de peuple ne se trouva en cause;... chacun y accouroit comme au feu" (2:312). "[S]'excite un bourdonnement infiny de toute l'assistance;... icy la parole m'est derechef enlevée par le peuple;... troisiesme recharge du peuple... [q]ui me fit monter la couleur au visage, & lors d'une douç'aigre cholere, m'ayant donné quelque respit, eslevant ma voix; en vain (dy-je) viendroy-je pour vous persuader de la justice de ma cause." "[P]ar le tintamarre extraordinaire du peuple,... je cogneu que chacun, en cette cause, estoit prevenu contre moy" (2:313).

[143] "[L]a compassion qu'on prenoit de sa partie, & la creance commune dont le peuple estoit prevenu contre nous, luy estoient deux grands arcboutants de sa cause" (2:313).

[144] "Ce n'est pas que... je ne contribü avecques le peuple à cette compassion,... & [j'ai] quitter je ne sçay quoy de la force que j'apporte en mes autres causes, pour ne vouloir affliger une personne affligée" (2:314).

[145] "Aux pieds de Monsieur Brisson, estoit Bobie, qui ne manquoit de larmes à ses yeux: aux miens, estoit le Gentil-homme, & avec luy sa femme larmoyante, comme aussi deux petits enfans" (2:312).

[146] "Grande est la compassion qui s'est trouvée, de voir une mere, une nourrice, deux petits enfans & une chambriere, toutes personnes innocentes, avoir esté cruellement assassinées; non moins grand est celle... de voir un mary, une femme, mestayers, serviteurs & servantes, tous innocents, menez par cette ville de Paris, ignominieusement prisonniers, par chartées,... leurs petits enfans laissez seuls en leur maison, à la mercy des pourceaux" (2:313).

This parallel inevitably called to mind the scene that was haunting the public imagination: a bloody vision of the murdered mother, nurse, small children, and chambermaid. But Pasquier used the parallel in an attempt to recast that haunting image. One finds "compassion . . . in seeing," actually seeing (he suggests here). And what the audience actually saw before them was not the murdered victims but a tragic family scene, featuring the heartrending image of a suffering man, weeping wife, and two small suffering children, whom Pasquier had surely artfully posed, and who created a piteous picture: notably, not at Brisson's feet but at his own.

If the tableau functioned affectively, co-opting the compassion that was one of the two central buttresses of Brisson's case, Pasquier also used it to challenge the other buttress: the "belief that prejudiced the people against us." He did so by using Arconville's "face [and] countenance" as a form of physiognomic evidence. Arconville's face served as a prop as Pasquier led the audience through his own conversion from skepticism to belief. At their first meeting, Pasquier reports, Arconville told him "the tale of his innocence," but Pasquier did not believe his words alone. Instead, he tested the tale's veracity by scrutinizing Arconville's face and body for signs. "I evaluated his face" carefully, "sound[ing] him to the depths [and] from all sides, as if I had been his judge." After this thorough live examination, Pasquier was persuaded. For he saw in him signs that were a "guarantee" of his innocence.[147] Reporting this meeting as he pointed to the accused, he invited the audience similarly to scrutinize Arconville's face and body for the "guarantee[s]" of innocence that he had found (again, probably after some coaching to ensure that Arconville could keep the proper expression in place for the duration). The family scene helped. Not only did the children serve as a metonymy for Arconville's innocence. The contrast between Madame d'Arconville's tears and Arconville's dry eyes provided an image of stoic innocence that Pasquier would exploit later in the trial: in the courtroom, Bobie is manipulating you with his "tears, which are the arms of women," not of honorable men like my client.[148]

Impugning the sincerity of Bobie's tears, Pasquier underlined a thematic contrast he had been carefully developing over the course of the trial: the contrast between visible truth and concealed falsehood. This idea appeared in its starkest form at a turning point in Pasquier's performance, when he shifted suddenly from begging sympathy for the Arconvilles to righteous indignation (one of his signature performance techniques). To do so, he called up a new character: "the Gascon valet." Why had no one noticed that the Bobies' "Gascon valet" vanished on the day of the crime? And, more to the point, why had no one noticed that, "instead of casting his eyes in search of the Gascon," Bobie had given the Gascon "leisure to

[147] "[J]e n'avois assuré l'asseurance de mon plaidoyé, que sur la face, & contenance de ma partie" (2:313); "m'ayant fait recit de son innocence, je le consideray au visage, & sondai au vif de toutes façons, comme si j'eusse esté son juge: & ne trouvant rien en luy, que l'assurance d'un homme innocent . . . " (2:311).

[148] "[V]ous me payez de larmes, qui sont les armes des femmes" (2:318).

disappear"?[149] (The Gascon remained nameless and never appeared in court.) At this stage in the trial, Pasquier had clearly stopped worrying about appearing to "afflict a person afflicted." For, in the dramatic *peripeteia* that followed, he went on the attack. It was not merely that Bobie was complicit in the Gascon's disappearing act (and, by implication, in the murders). Bobie had tried to deceive the court about his real motive: not justice but greed. For, while he had been displaying himself to the audience as a weeping victim, he had in fact "covert[ly]" been acting as a party to the case: an accuser seeking Arconville's confiscated property as damages. Working behind the scenes and "under cover," inspired by avarice, he had been the true "conductor of th[e] fabricat[ed]" charges against Arconville.[150]

Earlier, Pasquier had presented himself as a once-greedy and hypocritical lawyer who had been converted to altruism. What had motivated him in all of his previous cases (he said), was a "sack [of] coins." (At that point, the audience broke into cries of outrage: clearly part of Pasquier's plan as a set-up for his next sentence.) However, what had motivated him in this case was not money but Arconville's innocent face.[151] That face became a theme throughout the trial. As Pasquier began to attack Bobie, he again conjured the contrast between the hypocritical lawyer and the innocent face of the wrongfully accused Arconville. But this time, instead of merely pointing to Arconville, he dramatized it. Playing the role of Arconville, he went face-to-face with Bobie, now casting not himself but Bobie as the hypocritical lawyer: "as for the three thousand écus of reparation [you] demand of me, you are joking" (cried "Arconville"-as-played-by-Pasquier, performing outraged innocence). "[F]or having, against God, & against reason, afflicted me, I [should] pay the penalty[?] You demand recompense from me, [but] I demand reparation against you"! you who have used nothing but "dissimulation & hypocrisy."[152]

It was here that Pasquier called upon the figure of theatre to clarify the relationship between his claims against Bobie and what the audience could see with their own eyes. "[P]laying" a "role," declares Pasquier—a "character that Master Barnabé Brisson wanted [his client] to play"—Bobie "never dared to present himself in the theatre with open face before the first Judge." Now he must shed his mask:

> [Y]ou master Simon Bobie, who are a Judge and a Lawyer, must . . . declare whether you are [a] civil party in this case or not. . . . [B]anishing all

[149] "Bobie . . . avoit un valet Gascon" (2:316); "au lieu de jetter ses yeux sur la recherche du Gascon, . . . luy donnant loisir de s'evanoüir, il ramentoit la vieille querelle" (2:317).

[150] "[Bobie] se tient clos & couvert"; "[il a] esté conducteur de cest orne, à couvert" (2:317).

[151] "[E]n toutes les autres [causes], je me rendois capable par le sac & pieces qu'on m'apportoit: mais [en] cette-cy, . . . que [par] la face, & contenance de ma partie" (2:313).

[152] "[C]oncernant les trois mille escus de reparation que demandez contre moy, vous estes un mocqueur . . . Que pour m'avoir, contre Dieu, & contre raison affligé, je paye l'amende! Vous me demandez recompense, dont je demande reparation contre vous"; "dissimulation & hypocrisie" (2:324).

> hypocrisy, . . . you must . . . declar[e] [yourself], before this great tribunal, where the face of God resides, that is to say, of truth.[153]

Here, "theatre" is not (as one might expect) identified with the lies of the hypocritical lawyer; but set in *antithesis* to lies and hypocrisy. It is a place of exposure: before "the first Judge," but also before His worldly equivalent, the judges in "this great tribunal." They can scrutinize Bobie, his face open before them ("*à face ouverte*") to determine the truth, just as Pasquier had scrutinized Arconville's face, "sound[ing] him to the depths from all sides, as if I had been his judge." Given that "the face of God, . . . that is to say, of truth" resides in "this great tribunal," Pasquier insists, truth will out. Bobie may try to hide behind the mask of his silent tears. But the open theatre will expose their hypocrisy and the *hypokrisis* that lies behind them.

There is, of course, a fundamental irony in this rendering of the legal theatre as a divine tribunal that exposes the subterfuges of hypocrisy and *hypokrisis*. For at the very moment that Pasquier was demanding that Bobie cease his role-playing and expose his true face to the tribunal, Pasquier himself was of course acting the role of Arconville, in a calculated dramatization of injured victimhood and righteous indignation. However righteous Pasquier's *hypokrisis* (hypokrisis *à face ouverte*), here in the "theatre" of "this great tribunal"—this "Theatre of Justice and Truth," (as De Luca was to call it)—*hypokrisis* reigns.[154]

Describing his trial techniques years later, Pasquier bragged of the brilliant performance that led to his victory. For the court fully and conclusively exonerated Arconville; and, while no one charged Bobie with the murder, the court held him liable for wrongful prosecution, condemning him to pay a three thousand *livre* fine plus costs, damages, and interest. Comparing himself to Cicero, whose defense of Ligarius succeeded in reversing the judgment of the great Julius Caesar himself, Pasquier writes: "*I* could boast of having had . . . a happier success." For that "great Orator conquered the judgment of [one] man, [but] I that of nine or ten thousand," nine or ten thousand who upon "leaving [the courtroom] were [no longer] in any doubt."[155] At one point during his summation, Pasquier asked Bobie, "What? You have lost your tongue?" and then turned to the judges: "Ah [*Hé*]! truly, Messieurs, I recognize that [it] is not to him that I must address my

[153] "[Q]uelque personnage que Maistre Barnabé Brisson ait voulu jouer pour luy" (2:314), "quelque rolle que Bobie joüast sous la custode, . . . ne s'osa-t'il jamais presenter sur le theatre, à face ouverte, devant le premier Juge" (2:320). "[V]ous, Maistre Simon Bobie, qui estes Juge & Advocat, m'ayez presentement à declarer, si estes ma partie civile en ceste cause, ou non . . . . [B]annissant toute hypocrisie, . . . vous ayez à me faire la declaration que je vous demande, devant ce grand tribunal, où reside la face de Dieu, c'est-à-dire, de verité" (2:318).

[154] De Luca, *Theatrum veritatis, et iustitiae.*

[155] "[J]e me puis vanter avoir eu lors un plu Council Chamber, Geneva Town Hall (*c.*1502).s heureux succez, que Ciceron pour Ligarius . . . . En cela ce grand Orateur vainquit l'opinion d'un homme, & moy celle de neuf ou dix mille, qui, . . . sortants n'en faisoient point la petite bouche" (2:314).

speech, but to you." But in fact Pasquier had been addressing the "nine or ten thousand" spectators all along. Indeed, as he insisted, it was "not only you, Messieurs, [who must] be the judges, but . . . the whole people, who have come here in a tidal wave to hear us."[156] That "great tribunal, where the face of God reside[d]" was a "theatre" where the parties stood "*à face ouverte*, before the first Judge": God, perhaps, but also the Godlike audience. And more Godlike still was the lawyer who could, through his performance in that great tribunal—that great theatre—command even such gods.

[156] "Quoy? vous avez perdu la parole? Hé! vrayement, Messieurs, je recognois avoir tort; ce n'est à luy auquel je dois adresser ma parole, ains à vous" (2:318); "non seulement vous, Messieurs, soyez les juges, mais aussi tout le peuple, qui est icy venu en flote, pour nous escouter" (2:320).

6
Legal Performance Education in Early Modern England

Introduction: Rehearsing the Revels in St. Dunstan's Tavern (1628–29)

In his "Annals," Bulstrode Whitelocke describes the scene in St. Dunstan's Tavern, where he and about twenty other "young gentlemen of good birth, quality, & fortune" spent their time in the winter of 1628–29.[1] They were all members of the Middle Temple, one of the four Inns of Court where young men trained to become lawyers while enjoying the pleasures of London. They met in the tavern, "in the great new built roome there, called the Oracle of Apollo," to "consult about carrying on, of their great affayre," the revels: the entertainments—including music and dancing, witty orations, performance of plays and masques, and more—that took place over the three-month long Christmas "vacation" in the Inns. Bulstrode had been chosen as the Middle Temple's Master of the Revels, making him responsible for both planning and practice sessions in the tavern. Gathering there, the young men engaged in high-spirited revelry that sometimes bordered on riot. For (writes Bulstrode) "among so many young gallants, of warme spirits, . . . differences & contests would sometimes arise." He would sometimes find them, "in the midst of their quarrells, . . . with swords drawne one against another." But they also "exercise[d] both their wits & bodyes" through performance training of various kinds: "practis[ing] their dauncing"; rehearsing the theatrical entertainments they would perform at the revels; and "improv[ing] their judgements & knowledge [by] putting of cases." Like the moots, case-putting was one of the many mock trial "learning exercises" in which students regularly engaged in the Inns as training for courtroom argument. Bulstrode stresses the difference between such serious courtroom practice and revelry: engaged in case-putting, the students "did appear togither, much more like to grave antients in a Councell chamber"—that is, like senior lawyers—"then to young revellers in an house of drinking." But he also stresses the relationship between lawyers and revellers. Case-putting, he suggests, is in fact a form of revelry, and "appear[ing]" like a "grave antien[t]" (performing the role of lawyer) a form of theatre.

[1] BL Additional MS 53726 fol. 45 (col. 1–f) and fol. 46 (col. 2), excerpted in Nelson and Elliott, Jr., ed., *Inns of Court*: 1:223–4.

Law as Performance: Theatricality, Spectatorship, and the Making of Law in Ancient, Medieval, and Early Modern Europe. Julie Stone Peters, Oxford University Press. © Julie Stone Peters 2022. DOI: 10.1093/oso/9780192898494.003.0007

This chapter explores one facet of legal education in early modern England: the training in courtroom performance and general carriage that taught the aspiring lawyer not just the tools of persuasion but the all-important art of *acting* like a lawyer. In what follows, I explore the various kinds of performance education that law students received: from tutors and books; courtroom observation; dancing, singing, and fencing lessons; theatrical activities; and, most important of all, the moots and other performance exercises that gave future lawyers practice in courtroom argument and demeanor. While my other chapters range across Western Europe, here I focus only on England, with occasional comparisons to Continental legal education. Given the distinctiveness of the Inns of Court and Chancery (the lesser Inns where students usually began their training), early modern commentators often felt they had to explain and defend English legal education at length. Thus, while the archive of sources on early modern Continental legal education is limited, there is an abundant archive of sources on English legal education, much of it describing the hothouse atmosphere of the Inns in intimate detail and offering extended comparison to life in the universities.[2]

It was in the Inns that most English lawyers received their training: only the Inns taught common law, and common law overwhelmingly dominated English legal practice. For this reason, scholars who have studied early modern English legal education have generally focused solely on the Inns. However, to ignore the role of the universities in educating future lawyers is to lose a substantial part of the story of English legal education. Henry VIII shut down the canon law faculties in 1535, but the Oxford and Cambridge civil law faculties continued to train students for ecclesiastical and civil law positions. Even more important, the undergraduate arts faculties offered significant pre-legal education. As in the medieval universities—students doing the arts course also learned the rudiments of law: important training, since, according to Victor Morgan, the majority of university undergraduates would go on to work in courts in some capacity.[3]

[2] In this chapter, I am particularly indebted to the following sources on the Inns: Baker, *Oxford History of the Laws of England, Vol. 6*, 445–72 and *Legal Education in London*; Baker and Thorne, ed. *Readings and Moots at the Inns of Court*; and Prest, *Inns of Court under Elizabeth I and the Early Stuarts.* On civil-ecclesiastical law training in England, see Helmholz, *Profession of Ecclesiastical Lawyers*, 39–58 (on education) and *Oxford History of the Laws of England, Vol. 1*, 237–309 (on the early modern period); and on the ecclesiastical courts generally during the period, Outhwaite, *Rise and Fall of English Ecclesiastical Courts.* On legal education in the early modern English universities, see Levack, "Law" (in Tyacke, ed., *History of the University of Oxford, Vol. 4*); Wijffels, "Disputations en droit à l'Université de Cambridge"; and Baker, "750 Years of Law at Cambridge." On the early modern English universities generally, see Morgan and Brooke, *History of the University of Cambridge, Vol. 2*; Brockliss, *University of Oxford*; Thompson, *Universities in Tudor England*; and Costello, *Scholastic Curriculum at Early Seventeenth-Century Cambridge.* On early modern Continental legal education, see Ridder-Symoens, ed., *History of the University in Europe, Vol. 2* (599–609 for Brockliss's description of the law faculty curriculum); and Grendler, *Universities of the Italian Renaissance* (430–73 on the law faculties).

[3] On the study of forensic oratory in the Cambridge Arts faculty, see Jardine, "Humanism and the Sixteenth Century Cambridge Arts Course," 20; and Morgan and Brooke, *History of the University of Cambridge, vol. 2*, 133–4 (the vast majority of Cambridge undergraduates would ultimately use their university training in "the law courts, [and] the judicio-administrative-political meetings of quarter

While the Inns take center stage in this chapter, they cannot be treated in isolation. For there was a constant flow of people and ideas between the Inns and universities, traveling in both directions.[4] In the 1590s, James Whitelocke (Bulstrode's father) somehow managed to be a student at both St. John's College and the Middle Temple simultaneously, running back and forth between Oxford and London and "Keeping thus by turnes in bothe places": at first secretly; eventually, with the leave of his college president, who found it handy to have a runner for errands in the city.[5] Polemicists may have emphasized the rivalry between the common law taught in the Inns and the civil law taught in the universities. But many enthusiastically championed learning both bodies of law (stressing their similarities rather than their differences).[6] Even in practice they were far from hermetically sealed off from each other, for civil lawyers often served in common law courts and vice versa.[7] Those who compared the Inns to the universities tended to stress not their differences but what they shared. The Inns were the "third university of England," as Sir George Buc famously put it, and "as worthily stiled an university" as all the others (Oxford, Cambridge, Angiers, Perugia, Salamanca, and more), having not only "the stile" but also the "title [of] a chiefe and principall universitie."[8]

sessions and assizes" [133]). The typical trajectory was to spend a few years in the university (without taking a degree) and then move on to an Inn. From 1590 to 1640, well over half of practicing common lawyers had attended a university as well as an Inn (Prest, *Rise of the Barristers*, 111–12). Students seeking civil law degrees usually began with an undergraduate arts degree and then went on to the law faculty, but in English universities (unlike in most Continental universities), one could in fact get a Bachelor of Law without an arts degree.

[4] To offer just a few examples, Abraham Fraunce studied philosophy for eight years at St. John's College Cambridge before entering Gray's Inn, where he completed the *Lawiers Logike* he had begun at Cambridge (addressed to both "the Gentlemen of Grays Inne" and those "fine University men" who would eventually "apply their heads to the study of the Law" [1588 ed., sig. ¶2r]). Thomas Sackville studied at Cambridge and Oxford, went on to the Inner Temple, and then later became Chancellor of Oxford. Alberico Gentili, Regius Professor of Civil Law at Oxford, was admitted to Gray's Inn in 1600 and began practicing law in London, but also served in the (civil law) Admiralty Court as standing advocate for Spain from 1605 to 1608 (Gentili, *Wars of the Romans*, xxvii).

[5] Whitelocke, *Liber famelicus*, 14–15.

[6] For a few examples, see Elyot, *Boke Named the Governour*, fol. 54v–55r (praising civil law); Whitelocke, *Liber famelicus*, 14 (he "began to joyne the study of the common law withe the civill" because he "saw how great use" ecclesiastical lawyer Richard Cosin "made of his knoledge [*sic*] of the common law"); Fulbeck[e], *Parallele or Conference of the Civill Law*; Fulbecke, *Direction or Preparative to the Study of the Lawe*, fol. 72v–81v ("Table of certain words in the Interpretation whereof the Common Law of this Realme and the Civill Law doe seeme to agree"); Waterhouse, *Fortescutus Illustratus*, 223–4, 236, 249–51 (arguing for the importance of civil law). Several civil law professors championed studying common law in universities alongside civil law, most notably John Cowell.

[7] See Helmholz, "Civilians in the Common Law Courts"; and Siepp, "Reception of Canon and Civil Law in the Common Law Courts." On civil lawyers in England generally, see Levack, *Civil Lawyers in England*; and Squibb, *Doctors' Commons*.

[8] Buc, "Third Universitie of England" in Stow, *Annales* (1615 ed.), sig. Mmmm3r–v (965–6, but volume erratically paginated). See also his comparison of degrees and ranks in the Inns with university degrees (sig. Nnnn3r [969]). Such comparisons differed. Sir Henry Spelman compared barristers to bachelors, apprentices to masters, and serjeants to doctors (Baker, *Collected Papers*, 1:34). For Coke, "Mootemen," "Utterbarristers," "Readers," "Benchers, or Auncients," and "Serjeants" were equivalent

Both common and civil law students later pursued a variety of careers—political, diplomatic, academic—and sometimes no career at all, planning to live not "by the practise [of law], but onely uppon their fathers allowance" (as Sir John Fortescue put it).[9] Some remained in the lower echelons of the profession, working as solicitors ("petty foggers of the lawe" as William Harrison famously called them), or low-level clerks.[10] But many who trained as lawyers in the Inns set about to become barristers and hoped to become serjeants-at-law (the highest-ranked barristers), arguing cases in court before judges and ideally eventually becoming judges themselves.[11] This education could be grueling. In the preface to Abraham Fraunce's *Lawiers Logike* (1588), a fictional common lawyer proudly describes the study of common law as "hard, harsh, unpleasant, unsavory, rude and barbarous."[12] For those serious about becoming lawyers, studying in the Inns probably did entail much that was "hard, harsh, [and] unsavory": memorization of writ forms, pleadings, rules, maxims and more (mostly in law French), as well as digging through the "vaste volumes" in which the common law was "confusedly scattered and utterly undigested" (in Fraunce's description).[13] While civil law was supposed to be more "constant and philosophicall," "more methodically, and… eloquently put downe," more "elegant and delectable" than common law (according to Fraunce), studying it required one to grind through what Sir Thomas Elyot described as "the great fardelles and trusses of the most barbarouse autours stuffed with innumerable gloses: wherby the most necessary doctrines of lawe…be mynced into fragmentes."[14]

At the same time, students in both the universities and the Inns engaged in other more pleasurable learning activities. Most prominent among these were moots and disputations (words that Buc uses interchangeably—"disputations

to Oxford's "Sophisters, Bachellors, Masters, [and] Doctors" (*Tierce part des reportes* [1610 ed.], sig. D4r–D4v). And see Waterhouse, *Fortescutus Illustratus* (the degree of serjeant is equivalent to a "Doctorship of the Law" [547]).

9 Fortescue, *De laudibus legum Angliae* (1616 ed.), fol. 115r. This may in fact have described the majority of students. Certainly, absentee rates during the required "learning vacations" were high (Prest, *Inns of Court*, 15–16).

10 Harrison's "Historicall description of Brytaine" (Bk 3, Ch 3) in Holinshed, *Firste [Laste] Volume of the Chronicles* (1577 ed.), fol. 100r.

11 For a discussion of the shifting status of different members of the legal profession, see Brooks, *Pettyfoggers and Vipers*; Prest, *Rise of the Barristers*; and Baker, *Oxford History of the Laws of England, Vol. 6*, 437–43 and *Common Law Tradition*, 78–87. The serjeants originally had a monopoly on pleading before the central courts, but with the demand for lawyers in the sixteenth century, the rules were relaxed, and "utter-barristers" (initially, a designation applicable only to one's status in an Inn) were allowed to plead in the central courts. See Baker, *Common Law Tradition*, 82–4 (in 1547, qualification for practicing at the bar of the central courts was redefined by the judges to be five years' standing as an utter barrister [84]). Although the term "barrister" was not used in the earlier period to denote lawyers who argued in court, I use it as the general term.

12 Fraunce, *Lawiers Logike*, sig. ¶2v (a "Tenurist," that is, one who knows Thomas Littleton's *Tenures*).

13 Fraunce, *Lawiers Logike*, sig. ¶3v. For a study of the extensive reading list of Thomas Egerton when he was at Lincoln's Inn, see Knafla, "Law Studies of an Elizabethan Student."

14 Fraunce, *Lawiers Logike*, sig. ¶¶1r–v; Elyot, *Boke Named the Governour*, fol. 53r.

which they call mootes," "Mootes or disputations"—stressing the parallel between Inns and universities).[15] These exercises not only taught legal substance but offered essential practice in courtroom performance. Under various names, they took place in one form or another in both the Inns and universities nearly daily: in the Inns, as "bolts," "case-putting," "chapel," "house," "term," "hall" and "library" moots (and more); in the universities, in ordinary and extraordinary, "*quadragesimals*" (during Lent), Act and Commencement disputations (inception or "*vesperia comitorum*"), and more.[16] Such exercises could range from informal practice sessions with a tutor to highly ceremonial public "performances" (as contemporaries often referred to them) with large audiences.[17] All were central to the learning process, but the more formal ones were the ultimate tests of knowledge and skill. These served effectively as examinations and graduation exercises, necessary to advancement in both the Inns and universities. As Sir John Baker writes: "the bachelor, the doctor and the serjeant all created themselves, by performing the exercise or pleading which carried them up the step"; the "process of graduation was inseparable from the performance of moots."[18] I focus primarily on what these exercises meant for students in the most formative period of their education. But everyone performed in them: in the universities, all from beginning students to doctors; in the Inns, "inner-barristers" (the most junior members), "utter-barristers" (those who could argue at "the bar"), "readers" (who gave lectures, generally in order to qualify as benchers); and "benchers" (the senior barristers who governed the Inns).[19] The use of the word "apprentices of the law" for some of the highest-ranking barristers suggests that all were in a sense apprentices.[20]

[15] Buc, "Third Universitie of England," sig. Nnnn3r, Nnnn4r (paginated as 969, 971). Fortescue similarly draws the parallel (*De laudibus legum Angliæ* [1616 ed.], fol. 56r). On the parallel structure of university law faculty disputations and moots, and of their graduation exercises, see Baker and Thorne, ed., *Readings and Moots*, 2:xvii–xxv, lvi–lvii. For the parallel between the readings and lectures, and between the moots and disputations, see Freda, "Legal Education in England and Continental Europe," 256–60. For clarity, I reserve the word "disputations" for those exercises that took place in the universities, using "moots" as shorthand for the various kinds of case-putting exercises in the Inns (following Baker and Thorne, ed., *Readings and Moots*, 2:xvi).

[16] On the variety of forms the mock trial exercises in the Inns took, see Baker and Thorne, ed., *Readings and Moots*, 2:lxxiv–lxxxv. For their frequency, see the 1613 schedule in Dugdale, *Origines Juridiciales*, 268–70. On the various sorts of disputations in the universities, see Morgan and Brooke, *History of the University of Cambridge, vol. 2*, 186; and Costello, *Scholastic Curriculum at Early Seventeenth-Century Cambridge*, 15–16.

[17] For an early example of the word "perfor[m]" to designate a learning exercise, see e.g. the record from Furnival's Inn in 1422 ("Here began an Exercise of Learning not before mencyoned and was to be performed..." [quoted in Bland, *Early Records of Furnival's Inn*, 26]). For later examples, see e.g. D'Ewes, *Diary* (ed. Bourcier), 61, 92, 108, 129 (etc.); and the many instances I quote throughout this chapter.

[18] Baker and Thorne, ed., *Readings and Moots*, 2:lvii.

[19] As Baker stresses, "the bar" and "bench" were physical objects in the Inns that came to stand for certain achievements. Thus, one could be an "utter-barrister" without being qualified to argue at the bar in an actual court (Baker, *Oxford History of the Laws of England, Vol. 6*, 458).

[20] On the designation "apprentice," see Baker, *Readers and Readings*, 11; Baker and Thorne, ed., *Readings and Moots*, 2:lvi and note 281; and Baker, *Collected Papers*, 1:33–6 (apprentices were "fully fledged advocates below the degree of serjeant" [1:33], usually readers or benchers). The distinguished

Although we know a tremendous amount about the moots (thanks to the work of legal historians), their portrayal in the records that have survived is fairly schematic, with little detail on how they unfolded as events and lived experiences: the specifics of their staging; the participants' demeanor, gestures, and affect; the nature of the audience members and their reactions. Those who recorded moot cases or arguments preserved these primarily as teaching texts, leaving out all the details they thought inessential to learning law. The rules outlining their procedures give formulae for exercises but generally prescribe rather than describing. The descriptions we do have are either fragmentary or written by apologists for the Inns like Buc, who render the moots in idealized terms. Such sources—if taken at face value—clearly do not tell the whole story. To envision the moots fully, we have to read between the lines. As I will suggest, the much richer accounts we have of university disputations and of revels (in both the Inns and the universities) help us to do so: not because the norms for university disputations were the same as those for moots (let alone those for the revels) but because these performances help make certain obscure aspects of the moots visible. Together, all of these performances not only served as forms of courtroom rehearsal: they also helped to shape the identity of the lawyer and forge a set of sometimes contradictory visions of what it meant to be a member of the profession.

Directions for the Study of Law: Learning to Act Like a Lawyer

Rhetorical Education as (Legal) Performance Training

In his *Boke Named the Governour* (1537), Sir Thomas Elyot proposed an educational program for—among others—young men destined for the bar and bench. In a chapter on "Howe the studentes in the lawes of this realme, maye [learn from] the lessons of sō[n]dry doctrines," he argues that future lawyers should study, above all, the ancient orators.[21] Some might worry that "the swetnesse" of such study would "utterly withdrawe the myndes of yonge men from the more necessary studye of the lawes" (fol. 52v). But in fact, the ancient orators teach precisely the skills needed not only for courtroom pleading but for practicing such pleading in moots:

lawyer Edmund Plowden referred to himself when he was in his 50's as "un apprentice de le comen ley" (*Les comentaries ou les reportes de Edmunde Plowden* [1571], title page). And see Waterhouse's comment: "the travel and pains in the abstruse study of the Common-Law, is such, that when [common lawyers] have studied as long as their bodies will endure, or their eyes assist them; yet after all, do not arrive to be Doctors, Professours, Exprofessours; but in the most accumulate advances are but Apprentisii & servientes ad legem" (*Fortescutus Illustratus*, 139).

[21] Elyot, *Boke Named the Governour*, fol. 50v–56r (fol. 53r on studying ancient orators), hereafter cited in the text.

> [I]n the lernyng of the lawes of this realme, there is at this day an exercise, wherin is a maner of a shadowe or figure of the auncient rhetorike. I meane the pleading used in courte & Chancery called motes. (fol. 53r–v)[22]

The moots are merely a "shadowe or figure" of ancient oratory because, frankly, the students are no Ciceros. But they do employ the classical canons of rhetoric: *inventio* when they invent arguments; *dispositio* when they arrange the pleas; and *memoria* when they memorize their parts.[23] Replacing the "barberouse" law French in which participants argued with pure French or Latin would easily remedy the absence of *elocutio*. As for *pronuntiatio* (delivery), despite the fact that English lawyers *never* attempt to "ste[er] [the] affectiō[n]s of the minde" (perhaps Elyot is joking?), some lawyers do "pronounce right vehemē[n]tly" (at least when "wel reteyned"). In any case, "in arguynge theyr cases," the students even now lacke very lytell of the hole art" (fol. 53v–54r). If they were educated to be "depely lerned in the arte of an oratour [as well as] the lawes of this realme," then "fewe men in consultations, shuld (in myne opinion) compare with our lawyars" who would, by this means, be "brought to be perfect oratours." Such perfect orators would have all of the qualities that Cicero required: "the sharpe wyttes of logitians, the grave sentences of philosophers, the elegancie of poetes, the memory of civi[l] [lawyers]," and, not least, "the voice and gesture of them that can pronounce comedies" (fol. 54r–v).[24]

In his *Direction or Preparative to the Study of the Lawe* (1600), William Fulbecke makes a similar claim about the education of future lawyers, though in somewhat less elevated terms: a young boy's

> parents and tutors in the University should have principall regard, that he who is to addresse himselfe to the study of the lawe, may be fitt with a plausible grace to discourse and dispute. (fol. 39r)[25]

In theory, most young gentlemen were in training to discourse and dispute gracefully from an early age. John Stanbridge's 1509 Latin textbook, for instance, includes classic prescriptions: however pleasant the child's speech, "[i]t is a rude maner [to] stande styll lyke an asse" or "to be wanderynge of eyes, pykyng or

[22] As Baker and Thorne note, one of the normal fourteenth-century meanings of "to moot" was to plead a case in court (*Readings and Moots*, 2:xlix). Elyot makes it clear he is referring to a learning exercise: his reference to court and chancery is merely an analogy (this exercise is like the moots actually used in court). On the earlier history of the word "moot," see Chapter 4, note 58.

[23] See the discussion in Eden, "Forensic Rhetoric and Humanist Education," 24.

[24] See Cicero, *On the Orator* [Loeb], 1:89–91 [1.28] ("in an orator we must demand the subtlety of the logician, the thoughts of the philosopher, a diction almost poetic, a lawyer's memory, a tragedian's voice, and the bearing almost of the consummate actor").

[25] Fulbecke, *Direction or Preparative to the Study of the Lawe*, fol. 39r (all parenthetical citations to Fulbecke, sometimes listed as "Fulbeck," are to this text unless otherwise noted).

playenge ye foole with his hande and unstable of foote"; rather, "gesture [must] be comely with semely & sobre movynge: somtyme of the heed somtyme of the hande & fote: and as the cause requyreth with all the body."[26] Pedagogic manuals like John Brinsley's *Ludus Literarius, or the Grammar Schoole* (1612) stress the importance of teaching not only verbal skills but delivery, which goes by a variety of names that denote both vocal and bodily style: "pronunciation," "utteraunce," "deliveraunce," or sometimes "elocution" (incorporating classical *elocutio*, *actio*, and *pronuntiatio*).[27] Students, explains Brinsley, are to "pronounce [their] Theam without book," while the master examines their performance as they speak, evaluating "audacitie, memory, gesture, pronuntiation."[28]

These were not merely theoretical desiderata: English grammar schools in fact put such principles into practice in days packed with oral performances, frequent assessments of delivery, and basic lessons in classical oratory.[29] A school commonplace book from the 1590s records one such lesson, explaining that "action" (*actio*) is called the "eloquence of the bodye, or a shadowe of affect," and that the speaker needs "three springes which flowe from one fountayne": "*vox, vultus, vita.* Voyce, countenance, life."[30] *Prosopopoeia* and *ethopoeia* remained important, not only as composition exercises but also as performance skills, involving, for instance, the use of the voice to make "lamentable imitacion, upon the state of any one" (according to Richard Rainolde's *Booke Called the Foundacion of Rhetorike* [1563]).[31] Many masters used theatre to train their students in performance skills. For instance, Winchester headmaster Christopher Johnson explained in the 1560s that "those stage plays which we have lately exhibited to the view" helped teach "what must be pronounced with what expression, with what gestures": how "there should be in the voice a certain amount of elevation, depression, and modulation, in the body decorous movement without prancing

[26] Stanbridge, *Vulgaria of John Stanbridge*, 114 (italics and line breaks removed). See also Enterline's discussion of Mulcaster's "loud speaking" (or "vociferation") exercises (*Shakespeare's Schoolroom*, 33). Unsurprisingly, the books on elementary education quote the classic stories on delivery. See e.g. Mulcaster, *First Part of the Elementarie*, 19; and the commonplace book cited by Enterline, *Shakespeare's Schoolroom*, 39.

[27] See e.g. Doddridge (following Melanchthon and Cox): "Eloquution doth consist of three things, first, of the voyce as the instrument, 2, the words that are the subject; 3, the manner of doing, which is the forme of delivery" (*English Lawyer*, 25).

[28] Brinsley, *Ludus Literarius*, 177–8.

[29] See Wesley, "Rhetorical Delivery for Renaissance English," 1267, on daily schedules for grammar schools such as Merchant Taylors', Westminster, Norwich, and Harrow and on inter-school performance events. My discussion of grammar school performance education is greatly indebted to Wesley's essay and to the account in Enterline, *Shakespeare's Schoolroom* (especially 9–61); and see Joseph, *Elizabethan Acting* (especially 9–17).

[30] Quoted in Enterline, *Shakespeare's Schoolroom*, 40.

[31] Rainolde, *Booke* (1563 ed.), fol. 49r. See Wesley, "Rhetorical Delivery for Renaissance English," 1275; Enterline, *Shakespeare's Schoolroom*, 31, 79–88, 92–4, 127–42; and the discussion of medieval schoolboys' training in *prosopopoeia* and emotional identification in Woods, *Weeping for Dido*.

around, sometimes more quiet, at others more vehement."[32] Looking back on the origins of his career as lawyer and judge, James Whitelocke was to stress the success of such training: "yeerly [headmaster Richard Mulcaster] presented sum playes to the court, in whiche his scholers [were] actors, and I on[e] among them, and by that meanes taughte them good behaviour and audacitye."[33]

The universities offered students a more advanced form of such performance training. From at least the mid-sixteenth century, the undergraduate program involved intensive rhetorical study that entailed reading, among other things, the great texts on oratory, as well as some foundational legal texts.[34] Cambridge Master Richard Holdsworth, for instance, assigned the students he tutored "Justinians Institutions w:ch are the grounds of Civil Law," along with Cicero's and Demosthenes' orations, Cicero's *On the Orator*, Quintilian's *Orator's Education*, Seneca's *Controversies*, and various texts on "Modern Oratorie."[35] All these could teach the student "the nature of mens passions & affections, how to raise & move them, & how to allay quiet & change [them]" so "that Auditors may hear with delight & you goe through it with ease" (2:643). "[N]o piece of scholarship is more usefull, & necessarie" (2:644), he insists. Without it,

> [l]earning though never so eminent, is in a manner voide & useless, without [it] you will be bafeld in your disputes, disgraced, & vilified in Publicke examinations, laught at in speeches, & Declamations. You will never dare to appear in any [disputation] of credit in ye University. (2:637)

Putting principles into practice was crucial. "At the begining of [the third] quarter, [you] are to begine to dispute [in] your Tutors Chambers, & so continue that exercise through all your studies, & in every faculty," explains Holdsworth (2:636). Doing so involved developing not only verbal skills but also performance skills. Another Cambridge tutor, James Duport offers lessons in piety, study habits, and conduct (do not "pic[k] your Nose" in "your Tutors Chamber"), but intersperses these lessons with performance advice: "be sure you speake audibly, & tractably, aloude, & leisurely"; "[s]lubber not over your exercises in a slight and carelesse perfunctory manner, as if you performed them *per formam* only." And "[w]hen you dispute, . . . take heede of that dull, cold, idle, way of reading Syllogismes out of

32 Recorded in a student notebook; quoted in Enterline, *Shakespeare's Schoolroom*, 43 (and, for further examples, Enterline 41–3; and Wesley, "Rhetorical Delivery for Renaissance English," 1268, 1280).

33 Whitelocke, *Liber Famelicus*, 12.

34 On the new rhetorical program for first-year students instituted in 1559, see Costello, *Scholastic Curriculum*, 41, 43–4. On rhetoric and dialectic in the universities generally, see Mack, *Elizabethan Rhetoric*, 48–75.

35 Holdsworth, "Directions for a Student in the Universitie," in Fletcher, *Intellectual Development of John Milton*, 2:634–46; hereafter cited in the text. (Most scholars accept the attribution of the "Directions" to Holdsworth, who became a Fellow of St. John's College in 1613.) See also the extensive list of legal texts in the anonymous mid-seventeenth-century "younger schollers" reading list (DeJordy and Fletcher, ed. *"Library for Younger Schollers,"* 46, 52–4, 58–61).

a paper." It was "not enough barely to pronouce, & propound your Arguments," you had to express them with "life and courrage."[36] Like grammar school students, university students could learn such "life and courrage" from performing in plays. Writing *c.*1600 to his son John who was at Queens' College Cambridge, Thomas Isham draws on classical precedent to recommend learning from actors (sounding much like Elyot):

> the best orrators in tymes past as Cicero amongst the Romans, and Demostines amongst the Grecians... learned of stage players to pronounce playnelie to speake ellequentlie, to act there speeches properlie.... lett not then that be contemptable unto yow which wise menn hereto fore highlie have esteemed.[37]

University statutes could in fact mandate the performance of plays for such purposes, as a Queen's College statute did in 1558–59, requiring the Greek master and examiner to put on plays before Christmas so that the students would not "remain crude in pronunciation and gesture and unpolished."[38] For Doctor of Civil Law William Gager, who directed students in his own Latin plays at Oxford in the 1580s and 90s, university theatre allowed students "to trye their voyces, and confirme their memoryes; to frame their speeche; to conforme them[selves] to convenient action."[39] Thus, most students entering the Inns already had substantial training in delivery, through exercises that served (as Peter Mack writes) "as preparation for mock-trials at the Inns of Court."[40]

Scholars of early modern English legal education have debated the extent to which rhetorical education penetrated the Inns.[41] Doubts about its importance

[36] Duport, "Rules to Be Observed by Young Pupils & Schollers in the University," in Trevelyan, "Undergraduate Life Under the Protectorate," 329–30 (hereafter cited in the text). Duport was a tutor at Trinity College, Cambridge, between 1635 and 1664. See Van Miert, "Disputation Hall in the Seventeenth-Century Dutch Republic," 217 for similar performance advice in Dutch texts.

[37] Isham Correspondence 14 (May 9, 1600?), Northamptionshire Archives; quoted in part in Morgan and Brooke, *History of the University of Cambridge*, 137. With thanks to Andrew North of the Northamptonshire Archives and Heritage Service for locating this letter and confirming the identities of Thomas Isham and his son John, who matriculated at Queens' in 1597.

[38] Nelson, ed., *Cambridge* (1989), 2:1130. Similarly, in 1546, Queens' College had required that all scholars below the level of master of arts attend and occasionally participate in drama. See Clopper, *Drama, Play, and Game*, 61.

[39] Letter reproduced in Young, "William Gager's Defence of the Academic Stage," 614. See also Northbrooke's comment: students may perform in "Comedies, and suche lyke things... both in the Universities, and [other] Schooles... for learning and utterance [delivery's] sake," so long as the plays "be not mixt with any ribaudrie and filthie termes" or "vaine and wanton toyes of love" (*Spiritus est Vicarius Christi* [1577], 75–6).

[40] Mack, *Elizabethan Rhetoric*, 66.

[41] Such debates are quite similar to those I note in Chapters 3 and 5 about the extent to which rhetorical theory penetrated legal practice in earlier periods. The sustained skepticism seems surprising, since it is impossible to ignore the impact of rhetorical education on (among other things) law students' and lawyers' commonplace books and the classical orations delivered during the revels, which both imitated and parodied the lessons of rhetorical education. For accounts detailing this influence, see e.g. Goodrich, "Ars *Bablativa*" (especially 56–69); Schoeck, "Borromeo Rings," "Lawyers and Rhetoric,"

there perhaps arise from the fact that some early moderns themselves denied that rhetoric—and humanist education generally—were of use to common lawyers. Elyot is clearly answering those who argued that "the swetnesse" of rhetorical study *would* "utterly withdrawe the myndes of yonge men from the more necessary studye of the lawes." Fraunce is clearly answering those who thought that "elegant, conceipted, nice, and delicate" university studies *were* incompatible with study of the "hard, harsh, unpleasant, unsavory" but all-important common law (sig. 2r).

And yet, if there were detractors, Elyot and Fraunce were far from alone in viewing rhetorical study as valuable to both law students and practicing English lawyers. When Puttenham praises Nicholas Bacon's eloquence in the Star Chamber (superior to that of "all the Oratours of Oxford or Cambridge"), he notes that Bacon was often to be found "in his gallery alone with the works of *Quintilian* before him."[42] It may be (said the Richard Mulcaster) that "no English man [will] prove a *Tullie* or like to *Demosthenes*" using the same techniques that the ancients "used in their spacious and great courts." But nevertheless, an Englishman "maie prove verie comparable to them [in] the eloquence" used in his own.[43] It is clearly such views that prompted some of the recommendations in "the Bacon report" (as it is often called): a description of and set of recommendations for the Inns drawn up for Henry VIII in 1539–40 by a committee consisting of Nicholas Bacon and several other Inn members.[44] The Bacon report proposed, among other things, that the Inns implement the equivalent of university rhetorical training. Three days per week, someone with "excellent knowledge in the *Latine* and *Greek* tongue" should "read some Orator, or book of Rhetorick, . . . openly to all the Company," and some of the moots should be replaced with "dayly Declamations . . . in *Latine*."[45] The Inns never implemented these proposals, a fact that some have taken as evidence that the governors decided that rhetorical training was irrelevant to common law education. However, it is possible that the governors failed to implement the proposals because they recognized that students were already getting such training in other forms. The moots themselves appeared as one such form of training. Richard Huloet defined "[to] Declame" in his 1552 dictionary as to "exercise fayned argument in pleadynge, used among

and "Rhetoric and Law." On common lawyers' commonplacing books and notebooks, see Mack, *Elizabethan Rhetoric*, 104–8 (on John Manningham's Middle Temple diary); Williams, "Medieval Book and Early-Modern Law," 58–9; and Brooks, *Law, Politics and Society*, 66.

42 Puttenham, *Arte of English Poesie*, 116–17 (and see Chapter 5, 206). Bacon had risen to the position of Lord Keeper of the Great Seal by the time of Puttenham's account.

43 Mulcaster, *First Part of the Elementarie*, 257.

44 The "Bacon report" consists of two reports by the committee, which included Bacon (Francis' father), Thomas Denton, and Robert Cary. Waterhouse, *Fortescutus Illustratus*, 539–46, includes complete copies of the originals (now lost).

45 Waterhouse, *Fortescutus Illustratus*, 541.

lawers called mooting."[46] If for Buc and others the moots were university-style disputations, they were also (for Huloet at least) declamations in law French comparable to the "dayly Declamations" in Latin that the Bacon report recommends.

Manuals for the English Law Student

One of the other ways students got rhetorical training was, of course, by "read[ing] some Orator, or book of Rhetorick" in the privacy of their chambers. Thomas Wilson's extremely popular *Arte of Rhetorique* (1553) was just one of the many concise, English rhetorical manuals available to those who did not want to take the time to read those heavy Greek and Latin treatises that university tutors like Holdsworth assigned.[47] Gabriel Harvey's copy of Quintilian famously contained the following note: "Wilson's Rhetorique & Logique, the dailie bread of owr com*m*on pleaders, & discoursers:" clearly at least some lawyers—and, presumably, law students—were getting their rhetorical instruction from such books.[48] In Chapter 5, I note how many early rhetorical manuals seem to envision lawyers as potential readers. But one might equally say that they envision law *students* as potential readers. Leonard Cox explains that he wrote his *Art or Crafte of Rhetoryke* (*c.*1530) for "the profyte of yonge studentes" (rhetoric is necessary to those who wish to become "Advocates and Proctours in the law").[49] Wilson explains that he has framed his book as a series of "Lessons," in order to teach, among other things, "pleadyng at the Barre."[50] Fraunce addresses the preface to his *Lawiers Logike* "especially [to] the Gentlemen of Grays Inne," publishing his *Arcadian Rhetorike* as its companion volume. (Both appeared in 1588, the year he himself was called to the bar.)[51] Middle Templar John Hoskyns addresses his rhetorical handbook, *Direcciõns for Speech and Style* (*c.*1599), to a "yonge maiste[r] of the Temple."[52]

[46] Huloet, *Abecedarium anglico latinum*, sig. H2v.; quoted in Mack, "Declamation in Renaissance England," 130.

[47] Unless otherwise noted, all parenthetical citations to Wilson are to the *Arte of Rhetorique* (1553 ed.), which went through nine editions before 1585. For a discussion of the period's manuals generally, see Chapter 5, 204–8 (as well as the discussions of the relationship between rhetoric and law that I cite above). For studies specifically of the English manuals, see Mack, *Elizabethan Rhetoric*, 76–102; and Perry, "Legal Handbooks as Rhetoric Books" and "Legal Rhetoric Books in England."

[48] Harvey, *Gabriel Harvey's Marginalia*, 122.

[49] Cox, *Art or Crafte of Rhetoryke*, sig. A2v (1532 edition, hereafter cited in the text). Cox's dedication stresses his identity as both a university lecturer and schoolmaster who has "charge of the instruction & bryngynge up of... youth" who may eventually become civil law practitioners.

[50] Wilson, *Arte of Rhetorique*, fol. 58r (here, specifically on the *exordium*). On Wilson's legal interests and career, see Chapter 5, note 20.

[51] *Lawiers Logike*, sig. ¶1r. Fraunce entered his *Arcadian Rhetorike* into the Stationers Register three weeks after *Lawiers Logike*, having noted there that one must "joy[n] Rhetorike with Logike" (fol. 120r). On the Stationers Register entry, see Seaton's introduction to Fraunce, *Arcadian* (1950), vii.

[52] Osborn, *Life, Letters, and Writings*, 117 (reproducing the *Direcciõns*, 114–66).

Alongside such rhetorical manuals, a distinctive kind of manual began to emerge in the seventeenth century. These were similar in some ways to the earlier "mirrors" of law in serving as both guides to practice and lawyers' conduct literature, but they had titles that specifically targeted the English law student: *Direction or Preparative to the Study of the Lawe* (1600); *A Due Direction for the Study of the Law* (1629); *The English Lawyer... Expressing the Best Qualities Requisite in the Student Practizer* (1631); *Treatise [on] the Lawes... Very Usefull and Commodious for all Students* (1651); *Perfect Guide for a Studious Young Lawyer* (1654); *Directions for the Study of the Law* (1662).[53] These advised the law student on how to study, ethics, style, manners, and courtroom behavior. They specified (among other things) the proper physical regimen for the aspiring lawyer. "A Student must in his diet be temperat, and abstinent," explains Fulbecke.

> A fat and full belly yeeldeth nothing to a man but grosse spirits, by which the sharp edge of the minde is dulled and refracted, and too much meate cast into the stomack doth ingender nothing but cruditie and diseases.

Indeed, one must avoid "all voluptuousnes and lust," for instance "covetuosnes [*sic*], excesse of diet, wantonnes, and all other unlawfull delights."[54] Such bodily care was necessary because legal argument was a bodily practice. "Mans body," writes John Doddridge in *The English Lawyer*, is an "instrument and organ for the operation of the powers of the soule." Law students must strive to make their bodies "more apt instrument[s]" for their work.[55] As Fraunce and Wilson had stressed, bodily care was especially essential to delivery: "[w]alking a litle after supper, annoynting, moderation of diet, and such like bodilie pleasures keepe the voyce in temper" (writes Fraunce) and "helpe muche to have a good deliveraunce" (writes Wilson).[56]

Both law student manuals and rhetoric books could correct unfortunate bodily habits. As Fulbecke explains, "by nature we hold that fast which in our tender yeares we conceive, and the worse sort of things do stedfastly abide in us" (fol. 39r). Wilson offers a long catalogue of such "worse sort of things": the "thousand... faultes" of "bothe... speache, and... gesture" that his book seeks to correct.

[53] Fulbecke, *Direction or Preparative*; Doddridge, *Lawyers Light* and *English Lawyer*; Noy, *Treatise of the Principal Grounds and Maximes of the Lawes*; Fidell, *Perfect Guide for a Studious Young Lawyer*; Phillips' *Studii Legalis Ratio*.

[54] Fulbecke, *Direction or Preparative*, fol. 12v (hereafter cited in the text). For a discussion of the manuals' regulatory nature and their stress on bodily care, see Goodrich, *Law in the Courts of Love*, 72–94 (especially 80–3).

[55] Doddridge, *English Lawyer*, 18 (probably written in the 1620s but published posthumously in 1631; hereafter, in-text citations to Doddridge, occasionally spelled Doderidge or Dodderidge, refer to *The English Lawyer* unless otherwise noted).

[56] Fraunce, *Arcadian Rhetorike*, sig. I7r; Wilson, *Arte of Rhetorique*, fol. 119r.

> One pipes out his woordes so small through defaulte of his wynde pype, that ye woulde thinke he whisteled. [An]other speakes, as though he had Plummes in his mouthe. [Some] blowes at their noistrelles. [Some] gruntes lyke a Hogge. Some cackels lyke a Henne, or a Jack Dawe. [Some] whynes lyke a Pig. [Some] noddes their head at every sentence. An other winckes with one [e]ye, and some with both....

And so on: Wilson offers over forty examples, providing such suggestions for correction as "gaping wyde, or singyng plaine song, & counterfeityng those that do speake distinctly," or putting stones under one's tongue like Demosthenes (fol. 119r–v). Or one could use a music teachers' trick: gag children's mouths to train them to pronounce words distinctly (though, regrettably, "the love... is gone of bringyng up children to speake plainely" so no one gags them today) (fol. 119v).

The aims of such correctives are those we have seen again and again in discussions of delivery and of courtroom demeanor generally. Stressing the importance of "Voyce, Countenance[,] Gesture," repeating the classic stories about Demosthenes and Cicero, the manuals insist that delivery "speaks": "as the Tongue speaketh to the Ear, so the Gesture speaketh to the Eye," writes William Phillips in his *Studii Legalis Ratio, or, Directions for the Study of the Law* (quoting Bacon).[57] They insist that delivery must be not only "soun[d]" but "swee[t]," for pleasure is a vehicle of persuasion.[58] They insist that it convey emotion, though not too much emotion for the lawyer must observe "decorum," preserving a "Manly moderation of the Voyce, Countenance and Gesture, &c," and thus must neither feel nor show excess passion.[59] They list the traditional dangers of excess emotion, but with a renewed emphasis on avoiding indecency and ensuring that one does not become an object of ridicule. "[E]ven in the heat of disputation," explains Fulbecke, you "must bee free from anger" because anger can lead you "both to give and suffer undecent speeches." Be neither "drye and faynt" in your delivery, nor "importunate[ly] garrul[ous]": such garrulity is "troublesome" to one's adversary, "to the Judge loathsome, [and] to thy selfe shamefull." In "all thynges *decorum* must be observed," he explains, "least that which wee saye, doe turne to laughter, or loathing, and purchase the name of folly."[60] As

[57] Phillips quotes Bacon's *Advancement of Learning* without attribution (see *Advancement* [2000 ed.], 94 [Bk 2]). Bacon attributes the quote to James I. See Chapter 5, 208.

[58] Phillips, *Studii Legalis Ratio*, 19; Doddridge, *English Lawyer*, 25.

[59] Phillips is extreme in insisting that one "avoid *all* passion, *and shew* thereof," advice that seems to contradict the entire rhetorical tradition's stress on the use of expression of the emotions for persuasion. He argues that passion "puts all into confusion": it "discomposeth the Speaker"; it takes away "the force and weight" of the speech, putting it "out of joint"; "[i]t taketh away the grace of the delivery" (*Studii Legalis Ratio*, 21–2).

[60] Fulbecke, *Direction or Preparative*, fol. 40r, 42v. (Fol. 42v–43r is missing in the EEBO 1600 edition, but can be found online in the identically foliated 1620 edition). Perhaps Fulbecke borrows from Fraunce's warning that anger leads to indecency: beware of "fall[ing] to threatning and railing with undecent tearmes" (*Lawiers Logike*, fol. 101v).

Doddridge insists, you must *never* become "the subject of dirision" (33). Phillips echoes Doddridge when he stresses that the student must develop "a Delivery full of Dignity, without Affectation, . . . and set forth with Gravity" (20). "Gravity" (says Phillips) is in fact, the "first" of "the Moral Qualifications requisite in our Student": the quality "best becoming him" because law is a profession that inherently "laies claim" to "Gravity" (38).

The Noble Arts and Courtroom Carriage

"Gravity," however, had to be accompanied by "grace" in "delivery," "discourse," and "disput[ation]," as the manuals stress.[61] Learning such grace required training and practice: among the reasons that students in the Inns learned not just law but singing, dancing, fencing, deportment, and dress. For Fortescue and others, such lessons were essential to inculcating all the "cōmendable qualities requisite for Noblemen."[62] University students strove to acquire such skills as well.[63] Oxford professor (and Bishop of Salisbury) Seth Ward noted that, in order to become "Rationall and Gracefull speakers, students often undertook "lighter Institutions and Exercises" before "[t]heir removall [from] hence [to] the Innes of Court."[64] Both the Inns and the universities normally condoned such studies: according to university tutors, dancing was "an exercise well beseminge a gentleman and noe hindrance to his study," and a good singing voice was "a qualitie in it selfe not to be discomended."[65]

A romanticized account of the Inns in Gerard Legh's *Accedens of Armory* (1562) suggests the importance of such skills to the practice of law. In the Inner Temple, he writes, there is a

> store of Gentilmen of the whole Realme, that repaire thither to learne to rule, and obeye by lawe, [and] to use all other excercises of bodye and minde [to] adorne by speaking, coũ[n]tenaunce, gesture, & use of apparel, the person of a gentleman.[66]

Training in speech, countenance, gesture, and mode of dress is at once training in delivery and a status "adorn[ment]" that fashions the student into a representative

[61] See e.g. Phillips, *Studii legalis*, 22; Fulbecke, *Direction or Preparative*, fol. 39r.

[62] Fortescue, *De laudibus legum Angliæ* (1616 ed.), fol. 114v (mentioning "*sing[ing]*," "all kinde of harmony," "*dauncing, & other Noble mens pastimes*").

[63] Morgan and Brooke, *History of the University of Cambridge*, 134, 139.

[64] Ward, *Vindiciæ Academiarum*, 50. Ward is actually complaining that such light exercises get in the way of studying natural philosophy, which is far more important.

[65] Quoted in Morgan and Brooke, *History of the University of Cambridge, vol. 2*, 138.

[66] Legh, *Accedens of Armory* (1568 ed.), fol. 119v. See Goodrich's extended discussion of this incident in *Law in the Courts of Love*, 72–7 (stressing the symbolics of banqueting, i.e. "eating law").

of the rule of law. As a form of discipline, it inculcates the self-mastery required of one who is law's representative (one who "obey[s] by lawe"). At the same time, such training gives the student the demeanor and "person of a gentleman" equally necessary to ruling by law. For Fulbecke, the law student must learn such "curtesie" for it

> setteth in order, garnisheth and graceth the other giftes of the minde, without which they shoulde be unsavorie, and want applause.... This I commend to the student as a principall meane to gaine favour, love, and good entreatie. (fol. 16r)[67]

Observing lawyers in action in court showed students firsthand how important such physical training and lessons in personal appearance were to gaining "applause" in the actual practice of law. Attending the courts in session was an essential part of legal study in both the Inns and the universities. During term, common law students usually spent their mornings in Westminster Hall observing cases from the "crib": the specially designated area where they were close enough to get pointers from the judges.[68] Civil law students observed and trained in the extremely active university courts—which handled litigation and breaches of the peace involving anyone associated with the university—as well as in the various ecclesiastical courts in Oxford and Cambridge.[69] For civil law students, apprenticeship in the courts was the necessary transition between university and practice.[70] For common law students, carefully observing the courts might get one closer to serving as a serjeant in such courts.

One went, of course, to see how law worked and to hear the arguments, but also to see how grace, dignity, gravity (etc.) were to be expressed in the heat of courtroom argument. In the crib, one might be close enough to hear vocal intonations and

[67] See similarly Elyot's description of the importance of a man's "beautie or comelynesse in his countenance, langage and gesture," and "sobre demeanure, deliberate and grave {pro}nunciation, [and] excellent temperance," allowing his "wordes or countenances" to, in themselves, serve as "a fyrme and stable lawe" (Elyot, *Boke Named the Governour*, fol. 99r–v). For a helpful discussion of the specifically legal meaning of "courtesy," see Zurcher, *Spenser's Legal Language*, 163–4.

[68] Lawyers stressed the importance of observing both moots and courts (one reason, they argued, that the common law "universities" had to be in London). See e.g. Fortescue, *De laudibus legum Angliæ* (1616 ed.), fol. 112v–113r; Buc, "Third Universitie of England," in Stow, *Annales* (1615 ed.), sig. Nnnn3r (paginated as 969); and Phillips, *Studii Legalis*, 184. As Wilfrid Prest points out, this system of education-through-observation goes back at least to the time of the earliest yearbooks (*Inns of Court*, 131).

[69] See Shepard, "Legal Learning and the Cambridge University Courts," on the high volume of litigation in these courts and the constant presence of university law students as trainees and proctors there, as well as in the Bishop of Ely's Consistory Court and Archdeacon's Court in Cambridge and the Archidiaconal Court of Berkshire in Oxford. Many went on to become advocates in these courts, other ecclesiastical courts, or the admiralty courts.

[70] See Helmholz, *History of the Canon Law and Ecclesiastical Jurisdiction*, 223 (on the "year of silence" before ecclesiastical lawyers could practice, and their training through "repeatedly witnessing a court in session").

observe facial expressions and gestures. When Edward Waterhouse advises students "to repair on Court-dayes to the Courts, and there to take notes and observe," he explains that they must observe not merely the arguments but also the "*carriages* of persons... therein," which "is very advantageous to the profit of the Student, who there may learn much... to his after-improvement."[71] Some students apparently did so. Admitted to the Inner Temple in 1607, Thomas Wentworth spent seven years in "constant attendance" at the Star Chamber (according to one contemporary), gathering "many directions for his carriage toward the publick."[72] Simonds D'Ewes similarly regularly attended Star Chamber trials before his call to the bar, later recollecting his admiration for Francis Bacon's "eloquent expression of himself and his graceful delivery" (though he lambastes Bacon's for his "vices").[73]

Practicing Performance: Moots and Disputations

Rehearsal and Mimesis

If reading manuals, taking dancing and singing lessons, and observing trials was important to the law student's education, what was most important (everyone agreed) was practicing what one had learned. "[P]ractise and exercise is all in all," explains Fraunce.[74] "What maketh the lawyer to have suche [excellent] utteraunce?" asks Wilson. Answer: "Practise," which "in all thynges is a sovereigne meane, most highly to excell" (fol. 3r). "[E]very art by continual exercise doth receive increase," writes Fulbecke, but law is a "professio[n] which *consist[s]* in practise," so lawyers are especially in need of practice.[75] "[P]rivate and home exercise" might be helpful to the law student, he explains, but "publike exercise must ensue" (fol. 42r). For the law student must not "see[k] that in hymselfe, which is to bee done and performed in a multitude" (fol. 39v).

71 Waterhouse, *Fortescutus Illustratus*, 535 (emphasis added).

72 Quoted in Prest, *Inns of Court*, 131 (attributing the observation about Wentworth to Sir George Radcliffe).

73 D'Ewes, *Autobiography*, 1:191, 1:220. (On Bacon, D'Ewes adds: "yet his vices were so stupendous and great, as they utterly obscured and out-poised his virtues" [1:191], presumably referring to his homosexuality and prodigality.) On the Continent, law students similarly attended the courts to learn delivery. Antoine Loisel noted that he went to the Paris Parlement as a student in the mid-sixteenth century to learn from Advocat-du-Roi Jean-Baptiste Dumesnil: it was he "whom I most wanted to resemble because of the purity and fluidity of his language, the grace and softness of his eloquence, his voice, and his delivery." Loisel, *Pasquier ou dialogue des advocats* (1844 ed.), 83–4. French law students trained for several years as auditors (*escoutants*), watching trials in action and often modeling their own performances on those of the advocates. See Houllemare, *Politiques de la parole*, 170–1.

74 *Arcadian Rhetorike*, sig. I7r.

75 Fulbecke, *Direction*, fol. 41v (quoting the second-century jurist Ulpius Marcellus), fol. 39r (emphasis added).

> [T]he Student of the lawe . . . must live in great celebritie in the assembly of the people, and in the middest of the common weale. Let him therefore enure himselfe from his youth, to frequent assemblyes: let him not be afrayde of men, nor appalled or tymerous through a shadowed kinde of life. (fol. 39r–v)

Study was pointless without practice. "[I]n vaine shall a man passe away the night without slepe, or the day without recreation, in vaine shall he run over the volumes of the Law, in vaine shall hee inquire after the opinions of the learned" if he does not practice "perform[ing] in a multitude" (fol. 41v, 39v).

In offering practice "perform[ing] in a multitude," the moots were, effectively, rehearsals for courtroom performance. Moots, explains Fulbecke, are like the "smal skirmishes" that train young soldiers "for more valerous and haughtie proceedinges." Like soldiers, "Gentlemen students of the Law ought by domestical Moots to exercise and conforme themselves to greater & waightier attempts." For "such a shadowed kind of contention doth open the way, and give courage unto [students] to argue matters in publique place and Courts of Recorde" (fol. 41r). As the publisher of *Choice Cases for Moots . . . Very Useful [for] Students of the Common Lawes* notes, "the well performances of private Exercises in the *Inns of Court* Conduce to the more Elaborate and Publick Arguings in *Westminster-Hall*."[76] In fact, the moot system involved not one kind of rehearsal but a series of nested rehearsals (rehearsals for rehearsals): students began with the "smal[lest] skirmishes" (private rehearsals in their tutors' chambers), and then went on to "waightier attempts," which were rehearsals for still "waightier attempts." Participants advanced by performing in a certain number of exercises of increasing difficulty.

The moots were "private" or "shadowed" insofar as they were mere rehearsals for the real encounters to come in the "Publick" sphere of the courts. But they did attempt, insofar as possible, to imitate the "Courts of Recorde" in Westminster Hall. Contemporaries touting their virtues stressed their likeness to real trials. In "all their open disputations," explains the Bacon report, members of the Inns follow "the forme[s] used amongst the Judges and Serjeants." One "Inner-Barreste[r]" (acting as "Serjean[t]") is "as it were retained with the Plaintiff in the Action, and the other with the Defendant." They "doe in *French* openly declare unto the Benchers" (acting as "Judges") "some kinde of Action," reciting the pleadings "by heart," one "taking the part of the Plaintiff, and the other the part of the Defendant, . . . even as the Serjeants doe at the barr in the King's Courts, to the Judges."[77] The "forme[s]" the Bacon report cites referred to the forms of the pleadings. But they also implicitly referenced the material "forms": benches that

[76] Hughes, *Hughes's Quaeries*, sig. A3r–A3v ("To the Students of . . . *Grayes-Inn*, and of the rest of the Honourable Inns of Court").

[77] Waterhouse, *Fortescutus Illustratus*, 544–5.

could be rearranged in the form of a courtroom, producing a bench, a bar, and a place for the make-believe "Serjeants" to face the make-believe "Judges."

The historians who have looked specifically at university law faculty disputations stress two things: first, like moots, they served as practical training for courtroom argument; and, second, they were, in effect, "mock trials."[78] Like moots, they began with a fictional legal case that gave rise to several disputed legal questions, each of which required a specific form of legal action. The disputants acted as litigants or lawyers arguing before a jurist acting as judge, who would give the decision or ruling at the end. Historians have suggested that the disputation form more generally may have emerged from legal disputations or mock trials in the university, and that it retained marks of its juridical origins even outside the law faculties.[79] They have noted the prevalence of legal terminology, metaphors, or structures in early modern disputations generally. For instance, the German educator Johann Conrad Dannhauer writes in his *Idea of a Good Disputator* (1629): "the roles of the respondent [are] like the roles of a defendant in court."[80] The respondent was in fact sometimes called the "defendant."[81] When undergraduates performed disputed legal questions or disputations in the "*genre judiciali*" (as they often did), they were effectively practicing performing legal argument before a judge.[82] Fraunce describes disputations generally as if they were moots or mock trials. They are "exercises" (the normal word for moots) that give students "particular practise" and serve as "triall[s] of their skil" in "civill assembl[ies]."

[78] See e.g. Fransen, "Questions disputées dans les facultés de droit," 231–3, 275 (disputations were fictitious trials that prepared students for the practice of law); Freda, "Legal Education in England and Continental Europe," 255 (disputations "were aimed at preparing the prospective lawyers for the court" [255]; "the role of litigants was taken by the students on both sides of the Channel" [258]); Weijers, *In Search of the Truth*, 164 (legal disputations treated "concrete problems of daily life"); Clarke, "Western Canon Law in the Central and Later Middle Ages," 273–4 (the *causae* were designed to teach students how to solve legal problems they might face in court and may have served as the basis for moots [273]); Kantorowicz, "*Quaestiones disputatae* of the Glossators," 1, 4–5, 20–21; Baker and Thorne, ed., *Readings and Moots*, 2:xvi–xviii (medieval law faculty disputations were structured like cases and involved hypotheticals meant to engage relevant legal issues); and, for the early modern period, Prest, *Inns of Court*, 116 (like the Inns, the English universities grounded formal teaching in aural exercises that involved debating a hypothetical case or set of circumstances involving one or more controversial questions of the law). Some Continental law professors staged mock trials quite similar to moots: for instance, Paulus Merula of Leiden had students learn the details of a case and then take turns playing the judge, prosecutor, defendant, and other roles in a trial (Ahsmann, "Teaching the *Ius Hodiernum*," 429–8).

[79] Chang, "From Oral Disputation to Written Text," 132; Kantorowicz, "*Quaestiones disputatae* of the Glossators," 21; Rodda, *Public Religious Disputation in England*, 21 (on legal terminology and legal similitudes in early modern disputations generally); and Makdisi, "Scholastic Method in Medieval Education," 645, 648–60 (disputations originated in Islamic legal debates).

[80] Dannhauer, *Idea boni disputatoris*, 98–9; quoted in Felipe, "Burden of Proof in Post-Medieval Disputation," 43. See similarly Scharf, *Processus disputandi* (1635), 134; and see Felipe generally on juridical analogies in university disputations and the "jurisprudential analogies sometimes used to describe the roles and duties of the respondent and opponent, the status of the thesis, and the process of disputation itself" (40).

[81] For an English example of the respondent as "defendant," see Fraunce, *Lawiers Logike*, fol. 101r.

[82] On advice to students performing in the genre "judiciali," see Duport, "Rules to Be Observed by Young Pupils & Schollers in the University," 329.

Fraunce's principal models for such exercises are Edmund Plowden's common law case reports, which he reproduces in lengthy law French excerpts.[83]

Public Spectacle, Battle, Theatre, Farce

It was not merely practice performing that moots and disputations offered but practice "perform[ing] in a multitude." Contemporaries often referred to the more formal moots as "public exercises" or "open disputations."[84] For the "*grand Mootes*... performed at the Inns of Chancery, in the time of the *grand Readings*," as William Dugdale describes them, spectators came not only from all of the Inns but the broader legal community.[85] Sir Thomas Smith, Regius Professor of Civil Law in Cambridge, for instance, enjoyed attending the public exercises in the Inns, and seems not to have been daunted by the fact that they were largely performed in law French.[86] The public university disputations could draw still broader audiences, attracting not only spectators from across the academic community but family members, townspeople, and even London tourists.[87] Many such spectators would not have understood the words (in Latin), but there was plenty of pomp and ceremony to keep them entertained. For graduation day exercises in Cambridge, for instance, the bell would ring and the "Esquire Bedle"—the master of ceremonies (in a tall hat and gown carrying the mace)—would lead a procession arranged in order of seniority from the college to each of the schools, pausing at each door and declaring, "*Segnour Doctour, bona nova, bona nova* [good news, good news]." All would then proceed to the disputation site and (as one account describes it) "whan the Doctour is enteryde the chayer," a kind of tribunal, "the Responsall shall enter hys stall [and] make Cursy to hym, & after turne them to the Responsall, & make Cursy to hym." Speeches and prayers would follow before the disputants got to the main "Act": the disputation itself.[88]

[83] *Lawiers Logike*, fol. 101r, 120r; and see the long selections from Plowden and other reporters in law French (fol. 12r–15v, 23v, 24v–25r, 26r–27r, *et passim*). Fraunce explains in his preface: the reason he is including examples "out of our Law bookes" is that "our Law is most fit to expresse the praecepts of Logike" (though he also includes poetic examples for those "who never learne[d] Lawe") (sig. ¶1v).

[84] For "open disputations" and "public exercises," see Waterhouse, *Fortescutus Illustratus*, 545, 532 (the student attends "frequent exercises both publick and private" [532]); and see e.g. D'Ewes, *Autobiography*, 1:218, 1:219, 1:221 (the moots are "public" exercises); Dugdale, *Origines Juridiciales*, 290 ("Exercises, or other publick Occasions").

[85] On the "grand moots" attended by students from the other Inns and the broader legal community, see Dugdale, *Origines Juridiciales*, 159–60, 243, 274–5, 281–2, 288, 313 (hereafter cited in the text); Baker, *Legal Profession and the Common Law*, 17; and Baker and Thorne, ed., *Readings and Moots*, 2:xxv.

[86] See Smith's Inaugural Oration, whose Latin text is excerpted in Maitland, *English Law and the Renaissance*, 90.

[87] Haugen, "Imagined Universities," 323; and on the graduation disputation ceremonies generally, see Shugar, "St. Mary the Virgin," 315; and (for Continental universities) Weijers, *In Search of the Truth*, 164.

[88] Costello, *Scholastic Curriculum*, 16 (describing the account in Esquire Bedell Matthew Stokes's book).

Even with their more limited audience, the "public" exercises in the Inns involved similar solemn ceremonial. At the Lent readings, for instance, the Reader would avoid being seen in public for a week so "that his entrance may be with the more state," explains Dugdale. He would then appear in the Church "accompanyed by [all the] Benchers [and] attended by [at least] twelve or fourteen Servants [in] one livery." After parading to the Inns of Chancery, he would "tak[e] his place in the Hall, in a Chair, at the upper end of the Bench Table." Challengers, which included "Judges or Serjeants at the Law [in] their purple Robes, and Scarlet Hoods," were positioned at fixed locations in the hall, ready to take him on. When the reader had completed his task, "the young Students, and many others, do usually accompany him for [his return] journey, bringing him forth of the Town, with great state and solemnity."[89]

Performing for such public audiences, disputants (in both disputations and moots) sought not only to win, but to win applause (whatever form that might take). "Be over carefull to performe your Acts well," advises Holdsworth, "that you may be encouraged by the applause" (2:653). Performance skills were, as always, essential. We have already seen James Duport's admonition that one must not perform disputations "as if you performed them *per formam* only," and he adds specifics similar to those in the manuals. "In your disputations, be not too cold, & faint, nor yet too hot, & fiery, fierce, and wrangling.... [A] sober, calme, sedate deportment of speech is best even in disputing" (330). Theatrical training helped. In his *Apology for Actors* (1612), Thomas Heywood claimed that university theatre taught the "bold Sophister, to argue *pro et contra*" in "publicke exercise[s]" with "judgement," to "keepe a decorum in his countenance" and not "to buffet his deske like a mad-man."[90] According to Sir Thomas Smith, such ideals—boldness but decorum, liveliness but calm—were not merely prescriptive but in fact described the performances he saw, both in Cambridge disputations and in the moots he attended in London. The Inns may be "remote... from our university's education," but "you would not find missing from them the vigor of your dialectic or the splendor of your eloquence," he declared in his inaugural address as Regius Professor of Law in 1542. "Dear God!... with what ease and abundance, with how much grace and beauty" they perform in the moots, in a style that is "calm and impartial and flowing as a fluid stream," a style (he implies) that is just as graceful and beautiful as that of Cambridge disputations.[91]

[89] Dugdale, *Origines Juridiciales*, 206, 208.

[90] Heywood, *Apology for Actors*, sig. C3v–C4r.

[91] "At vero nostrates, et Londinenses iurisconsulti, quibuscum disputare, cum ruri sim et extra academiam, non illibenter soleo, qui barbaras tantum et semigallicas nostras leges inspexerint, homines ab omnibus suis humanioribus disciplinis et hac academiae nostrae instructione semotissimi, etiam cum quid e philosophia, theologiave depromptum in quaestione ponatur, Deus bone! quam apte, quamque explicate singula resumunt, quanta cum facilitate et copia, quantaque cum gratia et venustate, vel confirmant sua, vel refellunt aliena! Certe nec dialecticae vim multum in eis desideres, nec

Unfortunately, not all disputants had learned these lessons, or perhaps none of them had. For only in idealizing accounts like Smith's do the performances appear "calm and impartial." "[A]dmit your ignorance[!]" cried the defendant, an undergraduate named Boyes, in the heat of a *c.*1600 Cambridge disputation on the criminological question: does the threat of punishment deter crime? "[Y]ou are overwhelmed with the force of [my] argument," cried the attacker in response. "[T]hink up some way of escape" if you can, with your "cunning and twisty" "verbal juggling[!]" he taunted. "The glory of the stage is the actor, of the lecture room the philosopher," so enough with the theatrics! sneered Boyes. "Either carry on the disputation as befits the part you are playing, or be quiet"! But as soon as Boyes had done with one opponent, up rose the second, with the war cry: "I will slit your throat with your own sword" (*Tuo gladio jugulabo*!)[92] Describing the civil law disputation staged for Queen Elizabeth in 1566, Oxford college dean John Bereblock captures the atmosphere typical of even more ordinary disputations: the proctors "impelled [the] usually peace-loving men into battle." The first attacker "flew without delay" at the defendant with "exceptional intensity," drawing "admiration from all" (not least the Queen) "for his vehemence and thirst for victory." After him, "the next soldier in the battle line" "hunt[ed] [the respondent] down and [was] hard on his heels," so "no matter which way he turned" there was no escape.[93]

While ferocious (or perhaps because ferocious), disputations could also be highly entertaining. In a letter to Sir Dudley Carleton after he attended a series of disputations performed in Cambridge for James I in 1614, John Chamberlain assessed the quality of the "acts" in terms one might use to describe a variety show: "the divinity act was performed reasonably well, but not answerable to the expectation; [and] the law and physic acts stark naught." (The "philosophy act," however, "made amends" by featuring a dispute about whether dogs could make syllogisms, which James apparently interrupted by speculating on his own dog's syllogistic thinking, imagining the dog saying to himself something to the effect of: I rout a hare, I realize I need help, I bay to call the pack; how can "this [be]

eloquentiae splendorem. Eorum oratio est Anglicana quidem, sed non sordida, non inquinata, non trivialis, gravis nonnunquam et copiosa, saepe urbana et faceta, non destituta similitudinum et exemplorum copia, lenis et aequabilis, et pleno velut alveo fluens, nusquam impedita." Smith, Inaugural Oration, in Maitland, *English Law and the Renaissance*, 89–90. Smith is urging students to study civil law, arguing that if common lawyers can perform with such "grace and beauty" in barbaric law French, Cambridge students steeped in rhetoric can do still better.

[92] Rembert, *Swift and the Dialectical Tradition*, 200–1; and Costello, *Scholastic Curriculum*, 21. I have selectively excerpted for effect. This is the only Cambridge disputation for which we have a complete transcript. See the discussion in Costello, 19–24; and Rembert's excerpt and translation of the first opponent's disputation on the first question (198–201). Boyes' task was to attack the syllogism: "Where knowledge of a thing suffices, experience of the thing ought more than suffice. But even the experience of punishment is not sufficient deterrent. Therefore, much less the threat of punishment" (Costello, 21).

[93] For the account by Bereblock (or Bearblock), see Plummer, ed., *Elizabethan Oxford*, 115–50; translated in Shugar, "St. Mary the Virgin," 339.

contrived and carried on without the use and exercise of understanding"? asked the king. Ironic, said the moderator, for "whereas in the morning... the *Lawyers* could not [make *Syllogisms*], now every Dog could, especially his Majesties.")[94]

Audiences seem to have treated disputations as a cross between theatre and blood sport. A Cambridge decree of 1600 orders there to be no more "standinge upon stalles, knockinge, hissinge and other imoderate behaviour" during the disputations. One Oxford don complains of "the great riots, tumults, abuses and disorders at [the] time of disputations in schooles."[95] In a sweeping attack on disputation as a practice in 1624, Pierre Gassendi captures the combination of violence and theatricality that seems to have characterized not only those in Oxford and Cambridge but disputations on the Continent as well. The disputants' behavior

> make[s] disputations into public spectacles, so that the common people attend as spectators, and all that matters is the urge to conquer. [In these] theatrical gatherings, you can see [the disputants'] minds becoming so fevered that they... do everything but throw sticks and stones in their frenzy.... Who could restrain his laughter when he sees how one of these gladiators, when reduced to desperation, will confuse the issue with shouting and even entertain the audience with taunts so that they break into applause while he is speaking?

For Gassendi, the disputations are gladiatorial contests in which the "fevered... frenzy" of the combatants, determined to "conquer" their enemies, satisfies the spectatorial blood lust of the "common people." At the same time, these "public spectacles" are "theatrical" events in which the performers "entertain the audience" until "they break into applause."[96]

Impersonation, Make-Believe, and the Mise-en-Abîme

Accounts of the exercises in the Inns are quite different. According to all reports, these were serious affairs. As Buc describes the Lent and August readings, they were "performe[d] with much magnificence, and solemnity."[97] Most sources seem to confirm this portrayal: the moots were serious; mooters argued law and only law; no one insulted opponents or made the audience laugh. But the insistence

[94] Hardwicke, *Miscellaneous State Papers*, 1:395; Costello, *Scholastic Curriculum*, 24–6.

[95] Morgan and Brooke, *History of the University of Cambridge, vol. 2*, 129–30.

[96] Gassendi, "Exercitationes paradoxicae adversus Aristoteleos," in *Opera omnia* (1658 ed.), 3:106; trans. Haugen, "Imagined Universities," 333 (translation modified).

[97] Buc, "Third Universitie of England," sig. Nnnn2v (paginated as 974); and see sig. Nnnn3r (paginated as 969).

of people like Buc that moots *were* in fact disputations raises a question: how different were they? We know that students in the Inns were often very badly behaved. They engaged in "excesse of entertainment" during the Lent readings; "br[o]ke open the dores of the hall, butterie and kitchin [and] sett up comons and playe."[98] We know that they misbehaved in lesser ways in the moots: they routinely failed to know their parts "without book" (stumbling or reading from crib notes); they came to moots booted or wearing hats; they entered the buttery and kitchen against orders; they failed to show up (a "Moot-fayl") or sometimes outright refused to moot.[99] On at least one occasion, a mooter became so belligerent that his next scheduled opponent was too terrified to show ("his heart failed, and he sent word he was sick").[100] The moots were "quarrels" that the students fought "with weapons both offensive and defensive."[101] Perhaps the moots were not always so "calm and impartial." Perhaps they were not always so magnificently solemn either.[102]

Certainly, they had an element of ritual solemnity, but with a good deal of theatre thrown in. In Middle Temple moots—whose general procedures appear typical of moots generally—the students who were to play plaintiff and defendant would approach those who were to play judges (lined up at a bay window "according to their antiquity"), make "a low obeysance," and ask "whether it be [the judges'] pleasure to hear a Moot," in a kind of prologue that announced the start of the play.[103] The bay window was one of several places in the hall invested with ritual significance, along with the "screen" (the great oak partition that lined the entrance), buttery door (behind the screen), and "cupboard" (table where utter barristers could be "called to the bar") (fig. 6.1).[104] These served as important stations in the choreography of the exercises, which required considerable agility and lightness on one's feet. (All those dancing lessons must have helped.) In the Inner Temple "imparlance exercise," for instance, "the pannier-man blows the horn... immediately after supper," an utter- and inner-barrister leap "behind the screen," then pop out again and return to the forms, then soon jump up again and head toward the screen, followed by a train of twelve inner-barristers and at least six utter-barristers, all of whom now crowd behind the screen. There is also some going up and down: all the inner- and utter-barristers "go down and attend behind the screen, and as the bench comes down they all go up." At that point, the three "judges" rise, go to "the buttery door" (which served as "Sanctuary" for offenders who had missed dinner), and "se[t] their backs against [it]," critiquing the mootmen's performances as they bar the door (as if to say, we are the law! no

98 Prest, *Inns of Court*, 108; Baker, *Oxford History of the Laws of England, Vol. 6*, 462.

99 See e.g. Dugdale, *Origines Juridiciales*, 148, 199, 213, 244, 279–80, 282–83, 289, 314–15, *et passim*.

100 D'Ewes, *Autobiography*, 1:302.

101 Plowden, *Plowden's Quaeries*, sig. A4v.

102 See Del Mar, "Ludic Legal Pedagogy," on their "ludic quality."

103 Dugdale, *Origines Juridiciales*, 208–9.

104 Gray's Inn Hall in Fitzgerald, *Picturesque London*, 112.

Fig. 6.1 Gray's Inn Hall with tables, benches, cupboard, and screen used in "performance . . . exercises."

Fitzgerald, *Picturesque London*, 112. The Bodleian Libraries, University of Oxford, G.A. Lond. 4° 164, 112.

sanctuary!) The mootmen attempt a defense (from amidst the crowd behind the screen?) Everyone eventually goes home. And the next day they do it again (with variations): "the horn blows," all the students and utter-barristers go behind the screen, and so on.[105]

I have deliberately left out the legal content here, in part because it does not map easily onto procedure in the exercises, in part in order to highlight all the "going and coming" (as the text calls it): behind screens and against doors, up and down levels. But legal content started, of course, with the case. Cases were fictional

105 Inner Temple "imparlance exercise"; reproduced in Baker and Thorne, ed., *Readings and Moots*, 2:cxci–cxciii. These exercises offered practice in asking for a continuance, compressing several different moments in a proceeding. The buttery had special significance. As Dugdale explains, normally, only "ancients" were allowed to enter it (279), but the buttery also served as a sanctuary: "If any offendor escape from the Lieutenant into the Buttery, and bring into the Hall a Manchet [small wheat loaf] upon the point of a knife, he is pardoned: For the Buttry, in that case is a Sanctuary" (156–7).

and many were old: based on scenarios to be found in medieval moot-books.[106] The moot-books contained stories repeatedly retold in variant forms (like *commedia dell'arte* scenarios or early modern plays), featuring such pre-Reformation figures as monks, abbots, and prioresses alongside stock characters—"Kate Pan," "Cat ith' Panne," "John a Style"—which made the cases seem like a cross between fairy tale and farce.[107] They often had baroque plotlines filled with improbable events, superfluous details, surprise characters ("the stranger"), sudden twists of fate, and more bastards than could possibly ever have come before courts of law.[108] In one Inner Temple exercise from around 1590, for instance, "John Style" has died childless, so the land (says the plaintiff) reverts to him, but (plot twist) Style's "wife [was] secretly pregnant with a son who was afterwards born and is still alive at Dale," not (it turns out) a bastard, so, too bad for the plaintiff: he's out on his ear.[109]

All of this puts a slightly different spin on the Bacon report's enthusiastic assertion that the mooters behave "even as the Serjeants doe at the barr in the King's Courts."[110] (Defending "John Cat ith' Panne" against a monk who was the brother of the prioress who was the secret love child of the stranger who, it turns out, had willed the property to the woman justice of the peace, and so on, was not the kind of case that usually came before the royal courts.)[111] The simile—"even as . . . "—marked the likeness, but also the difference: "as it were retained with the Plaintiff" was not the same as "is." In "taking the part of the plaintiff [or] defendant," mooters rehearsed the roles they hoped one day to assume as lawyers. But the fact that such impersonation was, visibly, mere impersonation underlined the make-believe quality of the whole ritual.

In fact, the impersonations required a hefty suspension of disbelief. For starters, the two junior mootmen, who generally appeared as sidekicks of the more senior

106 Baker and Thorne, ed., *Readings and Moots*, 2:lii. Cases disputed in the university law faculties were similar in this respect. They came largely from classic texts of Roman-canon law, so the parties and other characters invariably had Roman names—Titius, Sempronius, Seia—sounding much like characters in Roman plays.

107 Baker and Thorne note that to turn "cat in pan" meant to flip something suddenly, as in a case or a legal argument. (They include a sketch from one of the moot-books of a cat being flipped in a pan, identifying the case.) *Readings and Moots*, 2:xlii.

108 For examples of monks, abbots, and friars in seventeenth-century moot-books, see e.g. Clayton, *Topicks in the Laws of England*, 17, 27, 40, 45, 48, 80, 82, 112–13; Gregory, *Gregories Moot-Book*, 3, 8–10, 17, 21, 519, 650, 724–5, 765; Plowden, *Plowden's Quaeries*, 17, 88. On "Kate in the Pan," "Jacob and Esau," "Hobbe et John" (or variants), see Baker and Thorne, ed., *Readings and Moots*, 2:lii, 2:xli, 2:clxxxv–clxxxix. Examples of a "stranger" who appears on the scene are too numerous to list, but see e.g. Plowden, *Plowden's Quaeries*, 5, 18, 21, 36 (etc).

109 Baker and Thorne, *Readings*, clxxxv–clxxxix.

110 For the Bacon report's comparison, see Waterhouse, *Fortescutus Illustratus*, 545.

111 For my slightly parodic composite case, see the above citations. As Baker and Thorne comment: the stories reflected a "love of the improbable," full of "expectant heirs becoming monks and then inconveniently returning to life when claimed by deserted fiancées," and raising questions such as "whether a woman justice of the peace could send her own husband to gaol" or "how a person could be a villein every other day of his life and a free man on alternate days" (*Readings and Moots*, 2:lxii).

mootmen who argued the cases, represented the clients. But because these students recited the pleadings, they also represented those clients' attorneys. This made a certain kind of sense: it realized through performance the legal fiction that the attorney was not merely representing the client but *was* the client. But it required students to perform a double impersonation. For instance, in an Inner Temple exercise from *c.*1590, during the roll call (role call?), the court called the name of the plaintiff, "Thomas Massingberd," and the student acting as both "Massingberd" and the attorney for "Massingberd" answered "[h]ere by his attorney."[112] "Massingberd" was "[h]ere" in the person of his attorney, who was, of course, really a student pretending to be the attorney. The indexical invocation ("[here]") of the presence of the client emphasized the fact that the client disappeared in the attorney: the attorney was, for those purposes, the client. But it also emphasized the fact that the attorney was not really present either, only his student stand-in.

Certain moots multiplied such visibly layered impersonations still further by having students perform roles normally performed by more senior members of the Inns. For instance, during certain vacations (as the Bacon report explains), instead of benchers performing the role of judges, utter-barristers would "sit down on the bench in the end of the Hall, whereof [the benchers] take their name," where normally only benchers sat, and perform the role of benchers performing the role of judges.[113] And instead of utter-barristers performing the role of serjeants, inner-barristers would perform the role of utter-barristers performing the role of serjeants, who, of course, represented their clients. This meant performing something like a play within a play within a play, in a dizzying representational *mise-en-abîme*. Since it took years to graduate to each level, mooters might engage in such rehearsals for rehearsals for years. Lawyers of all kinds certainly engaged in more oral argument in the Inns than they ever did in real courts. Some never succeeded in practicing in the central courts, or (in fact) any courts at all.[114] So participants might slowly advance but never actually get past rehearsals. And even when they did, there was more make-believe to come. For the ceremony that created the serjeant-at-law involved an exercise very like a moot, in which the serjeant-elect and a senior serjeant played the role of parties in a feigned tenancy case.[115] It must often have seemed like rehearsals all the way down.

112 Imparlance exercise, reproduced in Baker and Thorne, ed., *Readings and Moots*, 2:clxxxv–clxxxix.

113 Waterhouse, *Fortescutus Illustratus*, 545.

114 For the strict limits on the number of students the Inns could call to the bar, see Prest, *Inns of Court*, 53. While the Inns often ignored those limits, as Prest notes, "call to the bar was by no means an inevitable prelude to practice as counsel at the Westminster courts, or indeed anywhere else. Although 2,138 barristers were called by the four inns between 1590 and 1640, [a] list of practising counsel from the reigns of James I and Charles I includes only 489 names" (53).

115 See Baker, *Oxford History of the Laws of England, Vol.* 6, 421; and Baker, *Order of Serjeants at Law*, 91–2.

Through such performances, one fashioned oneself into a lawyer by first pretending to be one. In Baker's words, lawyers "created themselves, by performing the exercise[s]." In a sense, this is how all professionals create themselves. But the multiple layers of impersonation in the moots complicated matters. The student was not really the lawyer he pretended to be, a "professo[r] of gravitie" and "excellent and chiefe Pillar, prop and Ornament of his profession"; nor was he the client whom he was supposedly representing. The use of students' names as part of the fiction complicated things still further. The secondary characters might be "John a Style" and "Kate Pan," but the parties normally had the participating students' names. For instance, in the *c.*1590 Inner Temple exercise, the client "Massingberd" (present in the person of his "attorney") was, in fact, a student named Massingberd (the real Massingberd), pretending to be the client "Massingberd" in the person of his "attorney": in other words, Massingberd was pretending to be "Massingberd." In the moot, Thomas Massingberd became a fictional character: if he was not really the lawyer or the client, perhaps he was not even himself. Mooting strove to make the make-believe courtroom seem real, but it also made the real seem make-believe.

When a student playacted his fictional alter ego ("[h]ere by his attorney"!), even if he performed with poker-faced seriousness, the performance seems likely to have sometimes raised a laugh. The benchers appear to have frowned upon treating the moots as frolics in any sense. But there must have been a perpetual temptation to bring the mood of the revels into the moots: students were used to hamming it up in the revels, and it is not really credible to imagine them invariably rising above such temptations in the moots. Lessons in *ethopoiea* and *prosopopoeia* taught students how to project emotion through performance. Mooting offered superb opportunities for exaggerating emotion to the point of parody. If students used *each other's* names as parties (as they may have done), the performance could have been still funnier.[116] For instance, the student answering that Massingberd was "[h]ere" might not be Massingberd, but a student doing an imitation of his friend Massingberd, who was in fact watching the impersonation from the audience. It would have been tempting for the students representing the plaintiff and defendant to switch names: so William Lockey, performing the role of plaintiff "Thomas Massingberd," might attack defendant "William Lockey"; and Massingberd, performing the role of defendant "William Lockey," might attack plaintiff "Thomas Massingberd." With nearly infinite possible variations and new crops of students appearing every year, such sport was unlikely to grow stale.

The same students who indulged in exuberantly obscene legal double-entendres in the revels would surely have at least cracked a smile at all the things "Kate Pan"

[116] Baker writes that "members used each other's names as parties" (*Oxford History of the Laws of England, Vol. 6*, 458): he probably means that they used their own, but it seems quite possible that mooters indulged in the temptation to mix up the names to keep things interesting.

or "Cat ith' Panne" (with her many bastard sons) could do to the other characters in the scenarios. In one case—"Le Virge," or "The Rod"—what is at issue is a tenancy "by the rod" or "verge," a word that had multiple meanings. It was a stick or rod that tenants held while swearing fealty to the Lord of the Manor, the tract of land to which this ceremony entitled them, and also, by the by, a slang word for "the male organ" (as the OED primly puts it).[117] When the moot case was performed in 1529 (taking up all of the autumn vacation), the newly admitted inner-barrister John Tawe performed as the defendant "John Tawe," who had penetrated this "verge" in violation of "the services which belong to the aforesaid verge," and must come to Westminster to show "why the aforesaid verge" is his "verge" rather than, for instance, the "verge" of one of the plaintiffs, "Thomas Moigne" (played by utter-barrister Thomas Moigne). Since the land changes hands many times, the mooters must repeatedly insist (effectively): "the rod is mine!" Certainly in the revels, tenancy "by the verge" offered endless fodder for such jokes (often sophomoric, routinely sexist, raising a laugh even where not in themselves particularly funny). For instance, in the 1594–95 Gray's Inn revels (which I discuss below), one of the Prince's subjects holds a tenancy "in Tail-general" and another "by the Veirge," where he provides the Prince's entourage with "eight Loins of Mutton, which are sound, well fed, and not infectious," as well as "Coneys" and other "dainty Morsels" (clear references to the "nuns" aka whores who are part of the scenario).[118] Given the ubiquity of such jokes, could the students have simply ignored the repetition of the word "verge" (and the potential slippage between "verge" as rod and "verge" as virgin)? In fact, the creators of the scenario (utter-barristers) seem likely to have chosen the theme precisely because the jokes would make the lesson memorable.

Moots were, of course, not supposed to involve such madcap merriment: they were supposed to teach law. Fulbecke warns students categorically that they must not let their theatrical frolics creep into their training in lawyerly demeanor, in a passage that pilfers from Pico della Mirandola's famous letter to Emilio Barbaro:

> *Rethoricke* I graunt is a pleasant thing, and full of delite. But in professors of gravitie, neither comely nor commendable. Who would not allowe a tripping gate, nimble handes, glauncing eyes in a Stageplaier or dauncer. But [if] the

[117] I derive details here from the 1527 Latin scenario (and its translation) in Baker and Thorne, ed., *Readings and Moots*, 2:clxxxii–clxxxv (and see the picture illustrating the case [2:xxxix]). I have modified the translation to represent the word the students would have used during the moot, the law French, "*verge*," which the Latin renders as "*virgata*" and Baker and Thorne translate as "virgate." For the law French "*verge*," see Baker, *Manual of Law French*, 212 (the *Manual* does not include alternatives such as "virgate"). Baker, *Third University of England*, 15–16, offers a summary of the case that is quite different from the 1527 scenario, but even livelier (with a woman who marries a lord after giving birth to both a bastard and a legitimate son, who becomes a monk, and so on). On "verge" as a slang word, see the *Oxford English Dictionary* entry.

[118] *Gesta Grayorum* (1688 ed.), 13.

> professor of the Law should affect [this style], he should not speake like a Lawier.... *Cicero* when he treateth of matters of Law, speaketh like a Lawyer, and a Lawyer must speake as the Law doth speake.[119]

Inserting the passage into a lesson about law students' professional training, Fulbecke transforms its meaning. Where Pico identifies law with rhetoric and theatre (all involve "sheer lying, sheer imposture, sheer trickery"), Fulbecke reclaims law as the vocation that stands *against* rhetoric and theatre. The aspiring "professor of the Law" is a "professo[r] of gravitie," quite unlike "Stageplaier[s] or dauncer[s]," with their "tripping gate, nimble handes, glauncing eyes." To "celebrate the feast of *Bacchus* in the Temple of *Vesta*" (that sacred Temple that is the storehouse of the law) is to dishonor law (fol. 20v). In the guise of urging the student to "speak like a Lawier" (a language that may be "rude in sound, yet [is] preignant in sense" [fol. 21v]), Fulbecke here revisits his earlier warning against "voluptuousnes," "lust," and "unlawfull delights" generally: beware "the feast of *Bacchus*"; beware the "Stageplaier or dauncer." The pleasure that students in the Inns took in theatre was proverbial. Fulbecke seems to realize that prohibiting them from attending theatre would be futile.[120] But, a warning:

> O delicate fellow, when you go to the Theater or dauncing Schoole repose your selfe wholy in your eares, but when you come to heare matters of weight handled & discussed, rest not upon your senses, but upon your mind & understanding.
> (fol. 21v–22r)

Go to the theatre if you must. But do not be carried away by the "tripping gate, nimble handes, glauncing eyes [of] a Stageplaier or dauncer." Do not let your senses ("voluptuousness," "lust," "unlawfull delights") carry away your judgment. And do not, above all, bring theatre into the Temple of Law.

Theatre in the Temple of Law: What the Revels Taught

Defending Academic Theatre: Impersonation and Dissimulation for Lawyers

The theatre had, of course, long been in the Temple of Law, not merely figuratively but literally: in the Inns' "Christmas" revels; in university plays associated with the

[119] Fulbecke, *Direction and Preparative*, fol. 20v–21r. (Fulbecke does not credit Pico.) On Pico's letter, which itself draws on Quintilian's distinction between the advocate-orator and the dancer (Quintilian, *Orator's Education* [Loeb], 5:131 [11.3.88]), see Chapter 5, 217–18.

[120] For the avid theatrical attendance of students in the Inns, see e.g. Nash, *Pierce Penilesse*, sig. F3r; Prynne, *Histrio-Mastix*, sig. **3v ("one of the first things" the "Innes of Court men... learne as soone as they are admitted [is] to see Stage-playes").

law faculties and colleges. Both Inns and universities generally condoned such activities, but not everyone was happy about it. Lady Anne Bacon wrote to her son Anthony at Gray's Inn in 1594: "I trust they wyll not mum nor mask nor synfully revell at Grayes Inne."[121] There were those who shared Lady Bacon's view that to "mum," "masque," or "revel" in law school (or any school) was sinful. Perhaps the most vociferous of these was John Rainolds, a lecturer in Greek and Divinity at Oxford, and Dean of Lincoln College. In the 1590s, Rainolds engaged in a series of nasty battles with colleagues over university theatre. His attacks were the usual antitheatrical ones: theatre trained students in vice, idleness, lying, and cross-dressing. (He himself, he confessed, had been guilty of that sin in his youth when he shamefully played the role of Hippolyta before the whole court).[122] His two principal antagonists were both law professors: William Gager (who, as we saw, directed students in his own Latin plays); and Alberico Gentili, Regius Professor of Civil Law at Oxford and future member of Gray's Inn. When Gager decided he had had enough quarreling, Gentili took over, and he and Rainolds carried on a series of highly public attacks and counterattacks in letters, lectures, and treatises. These included Gentili's *Two Disputations: On Not Censuring Actors and Audiences of Fictional Representations*; and *On the Abuse of Lying* (delivered as lectures in 1597 and published in 1599); and Rainolds' *Th'Overthrow of Stage-Playes* (1599), which incorporated some of Gager's and Gentili's letters with all of Rainolds' responses.[123]

The dispute was about academic theatre for university students generally, but Gentili stresses his role as a lawyer and teacher of law who is invested in training future lawyers. He is engaging in the controversy, he explains, not as a theologian

[121] Bacon, *Letters of Lady Anne Bacon*, 198.

[122] Boas, *University Drama*, 232–3 (with a thank you to Daniel Blank for first calling my attention to this controversy); and see Blank's "Actors, Orators."

[123] Briefly, the controversy began when Rainolds refused to attend the performance of three of Gager's Shrovetide plays. A virulently antitheatrical character named "Momus" and an epilogue that mocked Momus' views appeared in the plays. Rainolds (probably correctly) assumed that he was the target. Gager published *Momus* as an appendix to his *Ulysses Redux* (1592). He and Gager began to exchange angry letters. Gentili entered the fray by publishing a defense of poetry and of acting grounded in arguments from civil and ecclesiastical law: *Commentatio ad Legem III Codicis de professoribus et medicis* (1593) (*Commentary on the Third Law of the [Justinian] Code "On Teachers and Doctors"*). Gentili's lectures (published as *Alberici Gentilis Disputationes Duae: I. De actoribus & spectatoribus fabularum non notandis. II. De abusu mendacii*) and Rainolds' *Th'Overthrow of Stage-Plays* followed.

Gentili is primarily known today for his foundational *De Jure Belli* (*On the Law of War*). He was an Italian convert to Protestantism who fled Italy, began teaching at Oxford, and was named Regius Professor in 1587. He had worked as a lawyer and judge in Italy, and continued to practice law in England. See note 4, above.

On *Momus* and for the translation of some of Gager's letters, see Young, "Elizabethan Defence of the Stage" and "William Gager's Defence of the Academic Drama." For a translation of the Gentili-Rainolds letters, see Gentili and Rainolds, *Latin Correspondence*. I have used J. W. Binns' translation of Gentili's "*Commentatio ad Legem III*" in Binns, "Alberico Gentili in Defense of Poetry and Acting," 229–72 (hereafter, "*Commentatio*"). I am grateful to Francesco Cassini for assistance with translations from Gentili's *Alberici Gentilis Disputationes Duae* (hereafter, "*Disputationes*").

but as one whose job is to "teach the boys [as a] lawyer."[124] In defending theatre, he "bring[s] [a] gift to those who study law, [and who] wish . . . to be rightly called, jurists": the gift is a lecture on the law of theatre and a defense of university theatre.[125] His qualifications as a jurist make him an expert on the subject, he argues. Although divines like Rainolds may lay claim to expertise on the Scriptures, what is at issue here is the Commandments in "the second table," which belong to the lawyers: those "are ours."[126] He is ashamed of Tertullian, "whom they deem one of us lawyers," for his "worthless" reasoning in his attack on "the buskined tragic actors and the fictive masks of the players" (reasoning no real lawyer would employ).[127] Gentili will show everyone what real legal reasoning looks like. By way of displaying his skills in legal reasoning, he proceeds to treat the debate as if it were a law faculty disputation on the question: is theatre legal? (A version of this question had in fact been the subject of an Oxford disputation in 1584.)[128] His style is at once combative and full of the kind of labyrinthine quibbling and verbal juggling typical of university disputations.[129] But if one looks past the truculence and the many layers of minute quibbles, two central claims emerge: university acting is legal under biblical, ecclesiastical, and civil law; the reason it is legal is that its educational utility outweighs its dangers.

Gentili's two central arguments in defense of these propositions, which he elaborates most fully in his *Two Disputations*, are on their face fairly conventional. First, theatre teaches delivery. Supporting this claim, he quotes the same passage from Cicero's *On the Orator* that Elyot does: the orator must have not only wit, wisdom, eloquence, and "the memory of [the] lawye[r]," but also "the voice of [the] tragedia[n] and the gesture[s] of . . . the finest acto[r]."[130] Second, theatre (particularly comedy) cures vice. Since teaching virtue requires representing vice, one cannot censure actors for performing depraved parts (for instance, a villain or "drunkard").[131] And, just as "the actor [must] sho[w] off at one moment bulky

124 Gentili and Rainolds, *Latin Correspondence*, 39, 45.

125 Gentili, "*Commentatio*," 251.

126 Gentili and Rainolds, *Latin Correspondence*, 39.

127 Gentili and Rainolds, *Latin Correspondence*, 41.

128 The question was, "should the theater be allowed in a well-governed state?" See Shugar, "St. Mary the Virgin," 321–2.

129 Gentili's principal argumentative strategy throughout the dispute is what Puttenham calls "to confesse and avoid," a "figure . . . much used by our English pleaders in the Starchamber and Chancery" (Puttenham, *Arte of English Poesie*, 190). Gentili hedges his arguments with disclaimers (probably as a defense against increasing antitheatricality in Oxford). His disclaimers make for confusing reading, since, in admitting the truth of many of Rainolds' charges, Gentili often sounds as antitheatrical as Rainolds himself. However, all of his contributions to the dispute ultimately defend university theatre.

130 "[I]n oratore non modo . . . memoriam iurisconsultorum, sed etiam vocem tragoediorum et gestus . . . summorum actorum requirit" (*Disputationes*, 108).

131 "[C]um de ebrio . . . incidisset oratio" (*Disputationes*, 8, and see 49–50); "*Commentatio*," 269; and Gentili and Rainolds, *Latin Correspondence*, 61–3. Elyot offers a similar defense: "by the same argumente not onely enterludes in englyshe but also sermones, wherin some vyce is declared, shulde be to the beholders and herers lyke occasion to encreace sinners" (*Boke Named the Governour*, fol. 49r). Rainolds exaggerates these positions by way of parody: "you declared [stageplayers] positively necessary for the perfection of poetry, for the skill of oratory, for the curing of diseases of the body and the

Hercules, at another effeminate... Venus," so the orator must "mimic [various] characters" and can do so without "incur[ring] disgrace."[132] In fact, it is not just actors and orators who take on different roles at different moments (his rhetoric implies): everyone does. "[E]veryone puts on the shoes of those they must represent": everyone must, in the course of things, "reproduce characters, faces, words, and deeds."[133]

The view that role-playing is built into everyday life—that we must represent ourselves by reproducing the "characters, faces, words, and deeds" appropriate to our role—is, of course, implicit in the "theatre of the world" trope and in the more general rhetorical attitude often associated with Renaissance ideas about the theatre of everyday life. This attitude is captured in a famous passage in Thomas More's *Utopia* (1516). Philosophy (More tells the impolitic Raphael) demands that we behave with Ciceronian "decorum" or "fittingness."

> [She] knows her own stage, and thus ordering and behaving herself in the play in hand, plays her part accordingly with comeliness, uttering nothing out of due order and fashion.

Performing the wrong role at the wrong time (he explains) would be like charging onto the stage during the performance of a comedy by Plautus and performing a scene from a Senecan tragedy.[134]

Gentili may in fact have this passage in mind in "On the Abuse of Lying," for there he calls upon a lesser-known passage in More to substantiate a similar point about role-playing. However, his account of the necessity of role-playing is actually far more radical than More's. His fellow lawyer the "brilliant Thomas More" (he writes) notes that in "certain ceremonies" one must perform actions that do not represent one's real thoughts, for instance, "when a bishop is created, he must refuse twice and say the third time that he accepts against his will."[135] Is

vices of the soul" (Gentili and Rainolds, *Latin Correspondence*, 57). One of the things that particularly incenses him is that some of the actors in Gager's *Rivales* portrayed drunkards (*Latin Correspondence*, 61–3).

[132] "[H]istrio nunc Herculem robustum ostendit, nunc mollis in Venerem frangitur" (Gentili, *Disputationes*, 9).

[133] "[Q]uisque in eam se induit personam quam refert"; "Dico referendas esse oratori personas, referendos vultus,... dicta referenda et facta" (*Disputationes*, 9, 49). See, similarly, Julius Caesar Scaliger (one of Gentili's heroes), more explicitly linking such representation with classical *prosopopoeia*: the poet, historian, philosopher, or orator "in judicial speaking" and elsewhere "injects personifications," sometimes speaking "in his own person," sometimes "in that of another" (Scaliger, *Select Translations from Scaliger's Poetics*, 7).

[134] More, *Complete Works*, 4:99 (translation modified, drawing on More, [*Utopia*] [1551 ed.], sig. F5r–v). For a discussion of this passage and the "rhetorical attitude" generally, see Zurcher, *Shakespeare and Law*, 48.

[135] "[Q]ui creatur episcopus, bis negare habeat, id velle se, et tertio dicere, nolentem velle" (*Disputationes*, 153). Gentili is paraphrasing a passage in More's "History of King Richard III": "menne must sommetime for the manner sake not [show] what they knowe. For at the consecracion

this lying? Certainly not. "On the Abuse of Lying" pointedly extends the first disputation's defense of "Actors and Audiences of Fictional Representations": there is clearly a relationship between Gentili's treatment of acting in fictional representations in the first disputation and his treatment of lying in the second disputation. Antitheatrical literature had, of course, long insisted that acting was a form of lying. In the *Commentary* on Justinian, Gentili had offered a classic riposte to the charge (similar to that in Sir Philip Sidney's *Defence of Poesie*): poets and painters—and, by extension, actors—are not liars, for "both poetry and painting feign under the image of truth."[136] But in "On the Abuse of Lying," Gentili reverses the traditional charge. To "mimic characters" in the course of performing our roles, "to reproduce faces, words, and deeds," "to put on the shoes of those [we] must represent" may *require* dissimulation. That is, doing our jobs right as actors on the stage of the world may require lying.

"On the Abuse of Lying" is, of course, purportedly a critique of the abuse of lying. But in the course of distinguishing use from abuse, Gentili ends up offering a ringing defense of the useful lie, elaborating on the many circumstances in which lying is not only appropriate but virtuous. Given the fact that he was Regius Professor of Law, and given his focus on law in the *Two Disputations*, Gentili could probably count on his colleagues and students to recognize the double meaning of "*Actoribus*" in the title of the first disputation: *actores* were actors, but also lawyers (advocates or prosecutors). Thus to defend *actores* from censure was to defend not only actors but lawyers. This passage might have recalled for some Raphael's description in *Utopia* of lawyers as those who "instruct with deceit" or "disguise": More's defense of playing one's part with decorum is, implicitly, a defense of the profession of law, with its necessary lies and disguises.[137] This view—only implicit in More but explicit in Gentili—is actually quite different from Sidney's view that aesthetic feigning is distinct from lying. In defending poets (and, by extension, actors) from the charge of "falshood," Sidney draws a famous analogy with lawyers. Some charge poets with pretending to "an actuall truth," which, "not beeing true, prooves a falshood." But (he asks), "doth the Lawyer lye then, when under the names of *John a stile*, and *John a noakes*, hee puts his case?" Sidney's rhetorical question is clearly meant to draw an emphatic "no!" He explains: "[T]hat is easily answered. Theyr naming of men, is but to make theyr picture the more lively."[138] But "On the Abuse of Lying" suggests that

of a bishop, every man woteth well" that the bishop "purposeth to be [a bishop]. And yet must he bee twise asked whyther he wil be bishop or no, and he muste twyse say naye, and at the third tyme take it as [if he were] compelled ther unto" (More, *Complete Works*, 2:80).

[136] Gentili, "*Commentatio*," 252. In the *Defence of Poesie* (also published as *Apologie for Poetrie*), written *c.*1579–80 but not published until 1595, Sidney famously argued that the poet "nothing affirmes, and therefore never lyeth" (*Apologie for Poetrie*, sig. G4v).

[137] More, [*Utopia*], sig. O2r ("deceit" here is sometimes translated as "disguise"); More, *Complete Works*, 4:195.

[138] Sidney, *Apologie for Poetrie*, sig. H1r.

Gentili would have answered with an enthusiastic "yes!" Lawyers are also actors of "*fabulae*" (fictions) when they "pu[t] on the shoes of those they must represent": they too are liars deploying the useful lie. Here, instead of deflecting the age-old charge that lawyers are by nature liars, Gentili heartily embraces it: yes, lawyers are liars; lying is essential to their role. Civil law "do[es] not condemn a necessary lie," he insists, indeed it welcomes such lies. "This is the opinion of the jurists, [a]nd the jurists do not lie," he adds with an implied wink, for, of course, he himself is a jurist: who can tell whether he is lying or not?[139]

Gentili's discussion of the virtues of professional dissembling may put a slightly different spin on the advice on appearances in manuals like Fulbecke's or Phillips'. We have already seen that, for Phillips, the "first" of "the Moral Qualifications requisite in our Student" is an appearance of "Gravity." How is he to "la[y] claim" to that moral qualification? He must work on his "outward behaviour, and the private and subtil motions and labour of [his] Countenance"; and he must "order [his] Gesture and Habit."[140] Ordering one's "Habit" here is, of course, a figure for all the ways in which the young lawyer must regulate his appearance. But to "order [one's] Habit" is also, quite literally, to order a well-tailored suit. For "Behavior is as it were [a] Garment" (42), writes Phillips. It "ought to have the Conditions of a Garment; for it ought to be made in fashion, it ought not to be too curious, it ought to be shaped so as to set forth any good making of the minde, and hide any deformity" (42). Phillips thus draws all of the criteria for the lawyer's behavior from the world of tailoring: it must be fashionable, but not so *ostentatiously* fashionable as to make one too remarkable ("curious"). It should highlight one's assets and conceal one's flaws. It should be artful, but the student must not try too hard to be artful. For "if... outward Carriage be intended too much, it passeth into Affectation" (39). It is essential to affect an absence of affectation.

In Phillips' discussion of how to "speak" (and look) "like a Lawier," he does not explicitly advocate lying. But he does advocate such layers of "pretend[ing]" (59) and "Dissimulations" (60) that, if they are not lies, they are very like. For instance, if the young lawyer's behavioral "Garment" does not fully conceal his central flaw, he must actively "pretend the vertue that shadoweth it" (59), making a flaw appear to be a virtue. "[I]f he be dull, he must affect Gravity" (60) (advice which—given the importance of "Gravity" to projecting lawyerliness—makes the profession of lawyer well suited to the constitutionally dull). If the dissimulation of a virtue matching his actual flaw is insufficient to hide that flaw, the young lawyer must engage in a higher-order dissimulation: a dissimulation of dissimulation (reminiscent of the moots). He must pretend that he is merely *pretending* to be dull, incompetent, or lazy, but that he is in reality scintillating, skilled, and enterprising. And he must hint at some plausible reason for hiding these vast abilities, "to give

139 "Sic iurisconsulti. Et ipsi tamen iurisconsulti non mentiuntur" (*Disputationes*, 153).
140 Phillips, *Studii Legalis Ratio*, 38–9.

colour that his true wants are but . . . Dissimulations" (59–60). Doing so repeatedly should secure a reputation for secret virtue. And if *that* is still not enough, the student must use "Confidence, . . . the last, but surest Remedy": a remedy that "doth fascinate and bind Hand and Foot, those that are either shallow or weak in judgement, which are the greatest Part" (60). In other words, you need not worry, for you have an audience of fools, so "pretending," "Dissimulations," and general bluster will turn you into a proper lawyer.

When Francesco Sansovino describes Marino's evil cousin in *The Lawyer* (1554) pretending that he has more cases than he can handle, it is satire.[141] When Phillips describes precisely the same strategy, it is advice. The person one might imagine as the most pious and uncompromising lawyer of the seventeenth century—John Cook, soon-to-be-prosecutor of Charles I and enthusiastic regicide—describes the same strategy in his *Vindication of the Professors & Profession of the Law* (1646), a text that outlines "what manner of persons Christian magistrates, judges, and lawyers ought to be" (1646). But instead of attacking such charades as patent falsehoods, he fondly describes them as what we all do:

> I cannot but smile many times, to see a company of hypocrites as wee are, stirring up and downe in our Gownes, making men believe that we are full of employment; and so we are indeed in a perpetuall motion, measuring the length of the Hall, [without] a Motion perhaps from the first day of the Tearme to the last.[142]

He cannot help smiling that he too is a member of this "company of hypocrites."

The Trial of the Sorcerer in Gray's Inn (1594): The Lawyer as Lord of Misrule

On December 29th, 1594 in the Gray's Inn Hall, several hundred people assembled to observe the proceedings of a Commission of *Oyer and Terminer*—a criminal assize court—specially convened to try an alleged sorcerer. The crown charged him with having used witchcraft to cause the riot that had broken out at the revels the night before. The festivities (in honor of the Prince) had erupted into "Disorders" and "Tumults" so great that the guests of honor had fled, and all the long and careful planning had gone for naught. The "Lawyers of the Prince's Council" had launched an investigation, resulting in indictments that "preferred Judgments thick and threefold" against the prisoner.[143]

[141] Sansovino, *L'avocato*, fol. 6v. [142] Cook, *Vindication of the Law*, 40.

[143] *Gesta Grayorum* (1688 ed.), 22–3. Unless otherwise noted, parenthetical citations refer to this edition.

On the day of the trial, the jury that the Sheriff had impaneled—twenty-four men who were "to give their Verdict upon the Evidence"—seated themselves in the courtroom. The prisoner had been in the stocks, but a Lieutenant brought him to the courtroom, and there he was "arraigned at the Bar." Standing before the jury and the assembled spectators, the Clerk of the Crown proceeded to read the indictments:

> [The prisoner] caused the Stage to be built, and Scaffolds to be reared... to increase Expectation, [and] caused divers [people] of good Condition, to be invited to our Sports.... [Then] he caused Throngs and Tumults, Crowds and Outrages, to disturb our whole Proceedings. And Lastly, [he] foisted a Company of base and common Fellows, to make up our Disorders with a Play of Errors and Confusions, [to our] Discredit.... All which were against the Crown and Dignity of our Sovereign Lord, the Prince of *Purpoole*. (23)

The prisoner, however, protested adamantly that he was innocent, and begged that his petition to the court be read by the "Master of Requests" (Judge of the Court of Requests, where people who could not afford ordinary writs could sue).[144] The Master agreed and read the petition as follows:

> [It was] the Knavery and Juggling of the Attorney and Sollicitor [that] brought all this Law-stuff on purpose to blind the Eyes of... all the honourable Court,... mak[ing] them think, that those things which they all saw... actually performed, were nothing else but vain Illusions, Fancies, Dreams and Enchantments,... wrought and compassed by the Means of a poor harmless Wretch, that never had heard of such great Matters in all his Life.

Moreover, said the petition, the Prince's Council (made up largely of "Lawyers") was guilty of "soundly mis-govern[ing]" the Commonwealth. All listened, and unfortunately many agreed: there had been "divers Instances of great Absurdities"; the petition's allegations could not be denied. And so, in a dramatic reversal, "thereupon the Prisoner was freed and pardoned" and the Attorney, Sollicitor, Judge, and their legal collaborators (presumably the Prince's lawyers) dragged off to the stocks.[145]

[144] See Bland in *Gesta Grayorum* (1968 ed.), 98 note 28.

[145] The text says that "the Attorney, Sollicitor, Master of the Requests, and those that were acquainted with the Draught of the Petition, were all of them commanded to the Tower" (24), which means the stocks, since the "Stocks were graced with th[e] Name" the "Tower" (23). I interpret "those that were acquainted with the Draught of the Petition" as those who knew the Sorcerer was innocent but collaborated with the Attorney (etc.) in framing him (but it is equally possible that the identification of the guilty parties merely follows the nonsense logic of farce).

Scholars who are familiar with this mock trial, which the students of Gray's Inn staged during their Christmas revels in 1594–95, know it primarily for one reason: the "Play of Errors and Confusions" that the Sorcerer allegedly substituted for the planned revels (and that the "Company of base and common Fellows" performed) was none other than *A Comedy of Errors*. The "night of errors" (recounted in the *Gesta Grayorum*, the report on the 1594–95 revels) has received considerable critical attention. But there has been surprisingly little discussion of the trial of the Sorcerer. Those who do mention it tend to stress the fact that the Sorcerer is charged with the creation of theatrical illusions: in this view, what is on trial is the power of theatre itself as a form of "Sorcer[y] and Inchantmen[t]."[146] But, according to the verdict, at least, the Sorcerer is in fact merely "a poor harmless Wretch," victim of a legal frame-up.[147] The people actually responsible for error, confusion, and falsehood are the lawyers: the Attorney, the Sollicitor, the Prince's Lawyers, and the Judge. Their "Knavery and Juggling" brought "all this Law-stuff on purpose to blind the Eyes" of the court. It is "Law-stuff" that is the real sorcery or illusionism.

"Law-sports" in both the Inns and universities were often, of course, full of "Law-stuff": insider jokes burlesquing legal terminology (usually with scatological or bawdy connotations). We have already seen the obscene play on such phrases as "in Tail-general" and "by the Veirge." In the *Gesta Grayorum*, several of the Prince's subjects similarly hold the town of Knightsbridge "by Villenage in base Tenure" (and are charged with cleaning all the "Sluces, Passages, strait Entrances, and dangerous Quagmires" and "laying Stones in the Pits and naughty places" of the "common High and Low-Ways") (13). The "nuns" perform "Night-Service in *Cauda*" ("in the tail"). St. Giles is held "by Cornage in *Cauda*" (12), and Tottenham "in free and common Soccage, [by] rendring to the Master of the Ward rope so much Cunny-Furr as will serve to line his Night-Cap" (12).[148] Law-sports often burlesqued the kinds of real legal proceedings for

[146] See e.g. Nelson and Winston, "Drama of the Inns of Court," 98–9 (the trial is about the revels themselves, which "frequently descended into chaos and a promiscuous mixing of the sexes; about the staging of plays . . . ; and about attitudes towards professional players, including Shakespeare's company"); and Whitworth's note in Shakespeare, *Comedy of Errors*, 4 (the " 'sorcerer or conjuror' . . . was presumably the member of the Inn responsible for organizing the evening's entertainment."; some think it may have been Francis Bacon). For additional brief discussions of the trial, see e.g. McCoy, "Law Sports and the Night of Errors," 289 (the "trial echoes many of the themes of the play and concludes with the familiar reversals of feasts of misrule"); Cormack, "Locating *The Comedy of Errors*" (the trial and the revels generally were "jurisdictional exercise[s]" in which the Inns explored their own jurisdictional autonomy).

[147] If the verdict is correct, the Sorcerer did not produce the "Representations and Shews" or "Confusion and Errors," and in fact the court charges him primarily with having *prevented* the planned entertainments, raising expectations for the theatrical evening and then dashing them (though, admittedly, also foisting the *Comedy of Errors* on them).

[148] For clarification of the meaning of these phrases, I am indebted to Bland's introduction to the *Gesta Grayorum* (1968 ed.), 95–7, which draws on John Cowell's law dictionary and offers many additional examples.

which students were training, offering (as Martin Butler writes) "both parody [and] homage."[149] Through such burlesque, wrote the author of the *Gesta Grayorum*, "we ... mock[ed] ... at our own Follies" (24).[150]

In both the Inns and the universities, such conjoined parody and homage targeted many social forms and practices, not solely legal ones. But there was a great tradition of lawyer satire in such plays as *Club Law* (*c*.1599–1600) or George Ruggle's *Ignoramus* (1615) (both of them acted in Clare Hall, Cambridge).[151] And general university traditions of revelry—particularly those associated with the public disputations—often offered legal lampoon. There, satiric speeches—sometimes in the form of mock disputations—were delivered by an officially designated student jester: in Oxford the "*terrae filius*" (son of the soil); in Cambridge the "*tripose*" or "prevaricator" (a quibbler, equivocator, or outright liar).[152] These were highly theatrical. One member of the Cambridge community complained to Archbishop William Laud in 1636:

> St Mary's Church at every great Commencement, is made a Theater, & the Prevaricatours stage, wherein he acts, & setts forth his prophane and scurrilous jests besides diverse other abuses & disorders then offered in that place.[153]

They also often took the form of legal satire, sometimes in the form of burlesque legal oratory. For the lawyer-playwright Thomas Baker, the *terrae filius* was a "University Jester" whose speech was "a sort of Law-Oratory without Truth, or Modesty."[154] These "University Jester[s]" often targeted the officials responsible for enforcing the university's legal regulations. For instance, the *terrae filius* sometimes took on the persona of the Bedell, who—in addition to being Master of Ceremonies in disputation processions—policed the university for curfew

[149] Butler, "Legal Masque," 184.

[150] For a discussion of the precise parallels between mock legal proceedings and real ones (focusing on the arraignment of the lovers in *Le Prince d'Amour* [performed 1597–98] and Marston's *Fawne*), see Finkelpearl, "Use of the Middle Temple's Christmas Revels," 201–5 (the "sequence of events at a regular trial was paralleled step by step" [202]).

[151] *Club Law* satirizes the Cambridge town (versus gown), but one of its principal targets is John Yaxley, "a pretie pettifogging Lawyer [who will] drawe bloud of theise gentle Athenians" (*Clare Hall*, xlii, 18). *Ignoramus* satirizes Cambridge Recorder and common lawyer Francis Brackyn. The lawyer satire is broad enough that Edward Coke also thought he was a target. See Chamberlain, *Letters of John Chamberlain*, 1:597–8.

[152] On the mock disputations, see Henderson, "Erudite Satire," 139–44. The "*tripose*" referred to a student reading for the undergraduate Tripos exam, but the name offered opportunities for jokes about being three-legged. The "praevaricator" served in graduate disputations, including those of the law faculty. On the long tradition of satiric disputation in European universities (reaching back at least to the thirteenth century), see Corbellari, *Voix des clercs*.

[153] Quoted in Nelson, *Early Cambridge Theatres*, 78 (and see Nelson on the persistent identification of the commencement stage as a "theatre," from at least 1498 [78]).

[154] Baker, *Act at Oxford* (1704), 49–50 (listing "Law-Oratory" as only one form of satire). Baker's *Act* directs much of its satire at an Oxford Doctor of Civil Law (41).

violations, drunkenness, and other infractions.[155] A Cambridge decree of 1628 suggests that university magistrates and laws were a common *tripose* target: "prevaricators, triposes, and other disputants should [h]ereafter abstain from mimic salutations and gesticulations, ridiculous jokes and scurrilous jeers, at the laws, statutes or ordinances of the University, or the magistrates" (including, presumably, this very ordinance).[156] Hogarth's frontispiece to Nicholas Amhurst's *Terrae-Filius* (1726) shows what appears to be an ecclesiastical court in an Oxford disputation hall punishing Amhurst for having gone too far as *terrae filius* in his "scurrilous jeers, at the laws" (fig. 6.2): those Amhurst has slandered rip off his wig, while a member of the court tears his book in two.[157]

Terrae filius or *tripose* satire in fact often went too far: the universities regularly expelled—and even occasionally imprisoned—the offenders (including Amhurst himself).[158] In fact, revels in both the universities and the Inns often got out of hand. In 1519, the Lincoln's Inn governors "ffrom hensforth uttrely banyshed" "Jack Strawe & all his adherent*es*" as too incendiary. Several years later, the Lord of Misrule accidentally killed someone.[159] In the Cambridge colleges, students sometimes punished those who refused to participate in the revels by "stanging" them: tying them to a pole and carrying them through the courts of the college.[160] In 1628, the selection of a Lord of Misrule at Pembroke College in Cambridge ended in a drunken riot.[161] One might think that such riotous behavior would lead these institutions to ban revels and the figures who stood for misrule. But in fact, university statutes *mandated* the appearance of the *terrae filius* and *tripose*. And the Inns not only tolerated the revels but penalized those who refused to participate. Any member appointed to the grand Christmas "Parliament" who failed to serve was to be fined, "at the discretion of the Bench," as well as everyone who failed to attend "the solemn Revells."[162] Dugdale outlines early regulations mandating the revels and the "Exercises of Dancing" during the Christmas season: on one occasion, every tenth barrister was "put out of Commons, for examples sake, because the whole Bar offended by not Dancing on *Candlemass* day preceding, according to the *antient Order* of this Society"; if they ignored this rule again, they were told, "they should be fined or disbarred."[163] Why?

[155] Henderson, "Erudite Satire," 164.

[156] Quoted in Costello, *Scholastic Curriculum*, 27.

[157] For the view that the image represents an ecclesiastical court, see Paulson, *Hogarth's Harlot*, 370, note 114, noting also that the location is probably the Sheldonian Theatre in Oxford.

[158] See Haugen, "Imagined Universities," 318, 335; Henderson, "Erudite Satire," 144, 148, 161; Feingold, "Humanities" (*History of the University of Oxford, Vol. 4*), 304.

[159] The Lincoln's Inn banishment of Jack Straw is quoted in Nelson and Elliott, Jr., ed., *Inns of Court*: 1:xix; and for this incident and the 1524 Lord of Misrule accident, see Baker, *Oxford History of the Laws of England, Vol. 6*, 462. For several more examples of riotous behavior in the Inns, see Butler, "Legal Masque," 181, 184–5.

[160] Morgan and Brooke, *History of the University of Cambridge*, 144.

[161] Morgan and Brooke, *History of the University of Cambridge*, 142–3.

[162] Dugdale, *Origines Juridiciales*, 153, 213.

[163] Dugdale, *Origines Juridiciales*, 246.

Fig. 6.2 An ecclesiastical court in an Oxford disputation hall punishes a *terrae filius* for scurrilous jeers at the laws in Hogarth's frontispiece to Nicholas Amhurst's *Terrae-Filius* (1726).

Amhurst, *Terrae-Filius*. The Bodleian Libraries, University of Oxford, Douce A 466.

Contemporaries offered several explanations, and scholars have elaborated on these. First, recreation was necessary "after serious Affairs," serving "as Sauces for Meats of better Nourishment" (explains one of the Prince's Councilors in the *Gesta Grayorum*).[164] At the same time, the revels *were* "serious Affairs," communicating politics and raising important legal issues in the guise of entertainment—a view that many scholars have pursued through serious analysis not only of tragedy in the Inns but of such apparently frivolous entertainments as the 1594 Gray's Inn law-sports.[165] The revels also provided behavioral and professional training: they taught students "how to use themselves" (as the Bacon report put it) both in the courtroom and when fraternizing with nobility.[166] Like the moots, the revels were "Performance . . . Exercises," serving as an extension of both rhetorical training and the professional performance training I have been exploring throughout this chapter: one observer particularly notes the "good utterance" of a performer in the Gray's Inn *Masque of Mountebanks* in 1617–18.[167] Hinting at the relationship between these two kinds of "Performance . . . Exercises," the Prince burlesques the instructions one could find in the manuals (sounding decidedly like Fulbecke or Phillips): gentlemen must not "faint or fail in Courage, or Countenance, Semblance, Gesture, Voice, Speech," but must instead represent "the Profession, Practice and Perfection of a compleat and consummate Gentleman" (implicitly, a "Gentleman of Gray's Inn," one studying for the profession and practice of law).[168] Presumably, the revels taught one not only how to perform that "Profession" (by offering performance practice) but also how *not* to perform it (how not to behave like a Lord of Misrule).

However, I would like to suggest that the "law-sports"—in their similarity to the moots—taught something else as well. We can see the constant interchange between law-sports and moots in Bulstrode Whitelocke's description of the concurrent rehearsals for the revels and "putting of cases" in St. Dunstan's Tavern (with which I began). Revels ceremonial closely paralleled mooting

[164] *Gesta Grayorum* (1688 ed.), 41. (It is, of course, a law student representing the Councilor who makes this point.)

[165] See e.g. Raffield, "Elizabethan Rhetoric of Signs" ("the masques . . . presented resonant images of the ideal polis: a Utopian vision of the English state, in the governance of which common lawyers would play a crucial role" [246]); Winston, *Lawyers at Play* (examining the politics of numerous plays performed in the Inns); Cunningham, "'So Many Books, So Many Rolls of Ancient Time'" (on *Gorboduc*); Butler, "Legal Masque of Humanity" (on *The Triumph of Peace*); and for studies of the legal significance of *Comedy of Errors*, see note 146, above; Zurcher, "Consideration, Contract, and the End of the *Comedy of Errors*" (on language of *assumpsit* and ideas about the changing law of contract); and Dente, "Renaissance Actors and Lawyers" (on the play's representation of contracts). But see Elton, *Shakespeare's Troilus and Cressida*, for a reading of the play as festive revelry.

[166] Waterhouse, *Fortescutus*, 546.

[167] For the revels as "Performance . . . Exercises," see *Gesta Grayorum*, 20. On the revels as rhetorical training, see e.g. Bland, "Rhetoric and the Law Student"; and Perry, "Legal Rhetoric Books in England," 7. For "good utterance," see Nelson and Elliott, Jr., ed., *Inns of Court*: 1:xxvi and 2:697, quoting Gerard Herbert.

[168] *Gesta Grayorum*, 16. The Prince has granted a pardon with some exceptions, including for those who fail in performance (with sexual connotations).

ceremonial (and vice versa). According to Sir John Spelman, when the Christmas Prince or "king" was chosen in Gray's Inn *c.*1500, he was to replicate parts of the mooting ritual. He must

> sit in the middle of the high bench [and] choose the officeres, who were previously ordained by the fellowship at the Cupboard. And then the wardens of the wax shall take the torches, and the cupbearer and the carver shall give bread and ale to the king.[169]

Participants performed both moots and revels in the Inns' grand halls. There, mock trials like the trial of the Sorcerer mimicked the arrangements of the moots, using the benchers' raised dais for the Prince and his councilors, and creating a bar out of the "forms" (whatever adjustments burlesque elements may have required).[170] One wonders whether students sometimes experienced a bit of recursive dysphoria when they went to the courts in the morning, performed in a moot in the afternoon in a space set up like the Court of Common Pleas, and performed in a mock trial like that at Gray's Inn not long after, in a space set up like a moot. Just as the moots echoed real trials, mock trials in the revels echoed the moots, both in some ways parodying their parent forms. Even revels that did not involve mock trials were similar to the moots in certain respects. Like these, they were "Performance... Exercises" that revolved around narratives of imaginary worlds, combining fairy tale with farce, mixing knights, mighty princes, and "nuns" (of various sorts) with prosaic modern characters (often, students rendered as fictional representations of themselves).

[169] Translated in Nelson and Elliott, Jr., ed., *Inns of Court*, 1:xix. For further examples of revels ceremonial that closely paralleled that of moots, see e.g. Dugdale, *Origines Juridiciales*, 161, 198, 204–5, describing (for instance) the following choreography for offering wafers and Ipocras (sweet wine) to the Judges during the "solemn Revells": "When the last measure is dancing, the *Reader* at the Cupboard, calls to one of the Gentlemen of the Bar, as he is walking or dancing with the rest, to give the Judges a Song,... after which, all the rest of the Company follow, and... [w]hilst they are thus walking and singing, the *Reader* with the white Rod, departs from the Cupboard, and makes his choice of a competent number of Utter-Baristers, and as many under the Bar, whom he takes into the Buttry; where, there is delivered unto every Barister, a Towell, with Wafers in it; and unto every Gentleman under the Bar, a wooden Bowl, filled with Ipocras, with which they march in order into the Hall, the *Reader* with his white Rod, going formost. And when they come... opposite to the Judges, the Company divide themselves, one half (aswell Baristers, as those under the Bar) standing on the one side of the *Reader*; the other on the other side," at which all serve the judges and make "solemn Congee[s]" (deep bows). *Origines Juridiciales*, 205.

[170] The Prince, acting as judge, "ascended his Throne at the high End of the Hall" (25), on the dais where the benchers sat (usually acting as judges); "His Counsellors and great Lords were placed about him, and before him; below the Half-pace, at a Table" (where moot-men would normally sit below benchers) "sate his learned Council and Lawyers" (9). The prisoner was "arraigned at the Bar" (23). Gray's Inn paid a carpenter in 1571–72 "for mendynge formes and tables in the hall after the great Showe" (quoted in Nelson and Elliott, Jr., ed., *Inns of Court*, 1:xxxviii). For further details on the arrangement of the hall, see Girouard, "Halls of the Elizabethan and Early Stuart Inns of Court." And see Goodrich, *Law in the Courts of Love*, 79–80, on the "commons" where both exercises and revels were held (simultaneously regulated and festive).

These similarities might warrant using moots to shed light on revels, illuminating the revels' fundamental seriousness, as so many scholars have done. But they might also warrant using revels to shed light on moots, illuminating the moots' fundamental revelry. So, for instance, while *Comedy of Errors* may be a play that explores jurisdiction, *assumpsit*, contract, citizenship and exile, it may at the same time capture the revelry of the moots, with their fast-paced repartee, twinning, multiple identities, and screwball misrecognitions. Contemporaries describe the moots as "solemn." But they also describe the revels as "solemn": the Inns "keep a solemn *Christmas*," notes the Bacon report; there are "solemn Revells" during the Christmas season.[171] The revels did have a certain ritual solemnity, but that solemnity could quickly slide into mock solemnity. The revels are "solemn foolerie," writes John Evelyn.[172] Surely the "solemn foolerie" of the revels sometimes served to reveal the foolish solemnity of the moots.

Satiric culture traveled between the Inns and universities: when Oxford expelled John Hoskyns for his *terrae filius* speech in 1592, he promptly entered the Middle Temple, where he performed the speech again at the Middle Temple revels.[173] Many of those who performed the moots had first spent several years in the university performing in (and watching) university disputations, effectively learning how to use serious oral arguments to entertain a crowd. Certainly, in university disputations, the boundary between the solemn exercises and their satiric double (the *terrae filius* and *tripose* speeches) was highly porous. Gassendi tells us that the entertaining taunts in serious disputations regularly had the audience in stitches ("[w]ho could restrain his laughter[?]"). The 1628 Cambridge decree orders not just *triposes* but "*other disputants*" to immediately stop engaging in "mimic salutations and gesticulations, ridiculous jokes and scurrilous jeers": the regular disputant, it seems, was often hard to distinguish from the *tripose*.

In both the Inns and the universities, while students trained themselves for serious argument, they also trained themselves to perform an officially sanctioned sendup of the law, learning legal burlesque not only conceptually, but with their voices, bodies, facial muscles. Those returning to serious "Law-stuff" after the Christmas season and performing at the very same faux "bar" where they had represented farcical lawyers during the revels might have found it hard to moot

[171] At these, an utter-barrister "sing[s] a Song to the Judges, Serjeants, or Masters of the Bench," and then the inner- and utter-barristers "perform a second solemn Revell before them" (Dugdale, *Origines Juridiciales*, 161).

[172] Evelyn, *Diary*, 3:307 (referring to the 1662 revels involving the "Prince de la Grange" at Lincoln's Inn). On the revels as a "subgenre of *serio ludere*" ("rites of violence," incorporating "satire and burlesque"), see O'Callaghan, "'Jests, stolne from the Temples Revels.'"

[173] Hoskyns rewrote the speech substantially for performance in the Inns. He performed it at the 1597–98 Christmas revels (and possibly earlier as well). See Osborn, *Life and Letters of John Hoskyns*, 10–11, 98–102 (reproducing the speech 100–2), and 222–3, 258. And see *Le Prince d'Amour* (1660 ed.), 37–40 (Hoskyns' role is "Clerk of the Council" and the speech is supposedly "*ex tempore*").

with a straight face. Having to argue for one's rightful tenancy "by my rod," or plead the case of "Thomas Massingberd" whose very livelihood depended on the secret love child of "John Cat ith' Panne," would not have helped. Especially if one *was* Thomas Massingberd. While the revels burlesqued the moots, the moots (drawn irresistibly into imitation of their festive double) could surely sometimes burlesque themselves. Here, there was an implicit logic of resemblance: if moots were like real courtrooms, and revels were like moots, revels were like real courtrooms; thus, conversely, real courtrooms were like revels.[174]

In a sense, the verdict in the trial of the Sorcerer captures this logic of resemblance among learning exercises, revels, and real trials. In condemning not theatre but "the Knavery and Juggling" of the lawyers as the real sorcery or illusionism, the verdict evokes the historical association of legal rhetoric with theatrical tricks and impostures.[175] It echoes classic lawyer satire: lawyers bend your mind; they make you doubt what you saw. But the verdict in fact offers an even more searing critique of law than classic lawyer satire. For the "Juggling... Law-stuff" that the verdict describes actually works not precisely like theatre but like a mirror image of theatre. Theatre makes you think that "Illusions, Fancies, Dreams and Enchantments" are being "actually performed" before your eyes. Law as performed in the revels, on the other hand, "blind[s] the Eyes" of all present by "mak[ing] them think, that those things which they all saw... *actually performed*, were nothing else but vain Illusions, Fancies, Dreams and Enchantments" (emphasis added). That is, when you watch these law-sports you may think you are seeing only theatre. But the revels—with all their theatrics, illusionism, and cruel jokes—show law as it really is. This is how law is "actually performed." This is as real as law gets.

Conclusion

At least some of those who partook of revels in the Inns or universities seem to have imbibed the view that law, cruel and tragic as it might sometimes be, was also

[174] One might draw a parallel here not only with the European tradition of satiric disputation but with the tradition more specifically of burlesque trials that were at once learning exercises, forms of revelry, and very like real trials. The clerks of the Basoche in Paris were given *causes grasses* to perform during Mardi Gras in the fifteenth and sixteenth centuries ("fat cases" for Fat Tuesday), possibly arguing them in the Grand Chambre of the Parlement itself where real cases were heard. (See Bouhaïk-Gironès, *Clercs de la Basoche*, 161–8, noting that several of the *causes grasses* found in the registers of the Paris Parlement use real lawyers' names, and arguing that they were probably performed there.) In Bernard de la Roche-Flavin's description, the proctors would choose a case and give it to the "young lawyers, who would plead it, to incite and move the audience to laughter." "Bien est vray qu'es Audiances, qu'on appelloit grasses le temps passé,... qui estoit choisie, ou reservée par les Procureurs, pour la faire plaider à un des jeunes Advocats." In these, "il n'estoit pas seulement loisible de rire, mais permis aux Advocats qui la plaidoyent, d'inciter, & esmouvoir l'Auditoire à rire." La Roche-Flavin, *Treze livres des parlemens de France* (1617 ed.), 310 [Bk 4, Ch 115–16].

[175] See e.g. Pico's letter (note 119 above, and Chapter 5, 217–18).

a practice of "solemn foolerie": that those who trained in it either came to see the foolishness in its solemnities or were solemn fools. The lawyer-playwright Richard Brathwait—who studied law at both Cambridge and Gray's Inn—found himself unable to practice law with any seriousness:

> *I went to* John a Styles, *and* John an Okes,
> *And many other Law-baptized folkes,*
> *Whereby I set the practise of the Law*
> *At as light count as turning of a straw.*[176]

However "baptized" in the schools of law, he felt his calling was not law but poetry (and, in particular, satire), in part due to a formative event at Oxford: his performance as *terrae filius c.*1607–8. It was the "performance of [that] exercise," he writes, that led him to put himself "forward [generally] in Publique Exercises": disputations both in the university and in Gray's Inn. But that performance also gave him an identity (as he wrote) "whose *Style* I have, and shall ever retaine, the *Sonne of Earth; Terrae Filius.*"[177] In such legal burlesques as *A Solemn Jovial Disputation [on] the Law of Drinking* (1617)—precisely the kind of "solemn foolerie" the revels taught—one can see Brathwait still performing the *terrae filius* a decade or so later.[178] Once a *terrae filius,* always a *terrae filius.* Once a Lord of Misrule, always a Lord of Misrule. Performing in revels changed who you were.

So did disputations. A character named "Irony" in a 1678 school entertainment argues that performing "*Disputations* in Schools" trained students in "*Ironical* dissimulation."[179] The "counterfeiting [of] *Voice* [and] *Gesture*" in such disputations, explains Irony, demands the presence of Irony himself, for "[i]f I did not spirit them, *Voice* would be a pittiful *Babble* and *Gesture* a miserable *Gesticulation*" (116–17). But one should not fear "*Ironical* dissimulation": it is "useful and laudable," as "necessary to the practice of *Vertue* as to the propagation of *Vice*" (118). Performing in the revels, of course, required "*Ironical* dissimulation" writ large. But so did disputations and moots generally. If, as Baker writes, lawyers "created themselves, by performing the exercise[s]," that self-creation involved not merely skills training or a change in status. Pretending to be a lawyer

176 Brathwait, *Shepheards Tales,* 13. For Brathwait's biography, see Bowes, *Richard Brathwait.*

177 Brathwait, *Spiritual Spicerie,* 424, 426 (a spiritual autobiography and devotional text distinctly satiric in tone). There seems to be no authoritative record of his performance as *terrae filius,* but he was at Oxford 1605 to *c.*1608, and was likely to have performed in the latter end of this period.

178 *A Solemn Jovial Disputation* is in fact Brathwait's translation of *Disputatio inauguralis theoretico-practica jus potandi* (1616) by "Blasius Multibibus" (a pseudonym formerly identified as Brathwait's).

179 Shaw, *Words Made Visible,* 118, 116 (hereafter cited in the text). I have taken the passage somewhat out of context, for Irony in fact claims a much wider dominion (in a defense of Machiavellian dissimulation and a rhetorical cynicism characteristic of the Restoration): "[t]he whole World would be a rude lump if I did not form it.... All that write not as they speak, all that speak not as they think, all that think not according to truth, all that intend not as they pretend, all that practise not as they profess, all that look one way and row another, are my Subjects" (117).

on a daily basis by practicing "*Ironical* dissimulation" offered professional formation of a far more thoroughgoing kind. In daily moots and disputations, students took on roles "whose *Style*" they were "ever [to] retaine." Nearly every day, they "created themselves, by performing... exercise[s]" in "*Ironical* dissimulation." Nearly every day, they counterfeited not only their clients but themselves, in performances in which their own names became the names of characters they impersonated. Nearly every day, they dramatized the legal profession through "Performance... Exercises" that were halfway between solemn rehearsal and farce, and yet very like the real thing.

Epilogue

The history I have traced did not, of course, end abruptly in or around the year 1678. In fact—as theatres proliferated and the modern entertainment industry began to emerge, proffering a set of new tropes for performance—one could argue that it had only just begun. When the novelist Frances Burney was asked how she had "been entertained" at the trial of Warren Hastings in 1788, she cried: "'Entertained[!]...you ask after my amusement as if I were at an opera or a comedy" but "it is quite too serious and too horrible for entertainment."[1] Law was not entertainment, opera, comedy, theatre. And yet, for legal philosopher Jeremy Bentham (writing just a few years later), that was precisely what it was. The courtroom, he writes, "[is a] theatre of justice," where "the sports of the imagination" shown in the theatre "give place to the more interesting exhibitions of real life." In the courtroom, spectators "imbibe, without intending it, and without being aware of it, a disposition to be influenced [by] the love of justice."[2] There, the

> byestanders at large [receive] instruction, not the less impressive and beneficial from its [appearance as] simple entertainment. Here [is] a theatre: the suit at law, the drama; parties, advocates,...judge, and jury, the *dramatis personae* and actors; the bye-standers, the audience.[3]

The great Sir Francis Bacon, Bentham notes, had once declared that law should take "*Nihil ex scenâ*": "nothing from the theatre." But he is wrong, insists Bentham. In law there must be "*Multum ex scenâ*": "*much from the theatre.*" For Bacon (writes Bentham), "*Scena*"—theatre—means "*lying.*" But legal theatre is not lying but in fact lying's opposite. Legal theatre offers transparency, demonstrative visibility. "To say, *Multum ex scenâ*," he writes, "is to say, lose no occasion of speaking to the eye. In a well-composed committee of penal law, I know not a more essential personage than the manager of a theatre."[4]

[1] Burney, *Diary* (1910 ed.), 1:446–7.

[2] Bentham, *Works* (1962 ed.), 5:21, col. 2, 5:577, col. 1. ("Letters on Scotch Reform," first published in 1808, but reiterating the similar arguments Bentham made in his 1791 *Panopticon*, postscript).

[3] Bentham, *Works*, 2:137, col. 2 (*Principles of Judicial Procedure*, [*c.*1820–27]), where Bentham is actually envisioning this scene as the result of one of his proposals for judicial reform.

[4] Bentham, *Works*, 4:80, col. 1 (*Panopticon*, postscript, arguing specifically for penal theatre but also reversing Bacon's claim about trial procedure). In the passage Bentham quotes, Bacon is arguing that courts must deal only with real cases, not cases by "fained parties" (essentially, fictional test cases): "*Nil habeat Forum ex scenâ*"; the court should have nothing to do with fictional matters (matters brought

Law as Performance: Theatricality, Spectatorship, and the Making of Law in Ancient, Medieval, and Early Modern Europe. Julie Stone Peters, Oxford University Press. © Julie Stone Peters 2022. DOI: 10.1093/oso/9780192898494.003.0008

One can track the idea that theatre is essential to the courtroom in its classic form well into the twentieth century (and beyond). Texts like Michel Le Faucheur's *Essay upon the Action of an Orator: as to His Pronunciation & Gesture, Useful [for] Lawyers* (1680) continued to draw on ancient precepts for *hypokrisis*, *actio*, *pronuntiatio*, appearing in ever-updated versions: in Jean-Sifrein Maury's *Principles of Eloquence for [the] Bar* (with a chapter "On Oratorical Delivery") (1782); William C. Robinson's *Forensic Oratory: A Manual for Advocates* (with sections titled "Of voice," "Of gesture") (1893); or *The Professional Voice: Practical Lessons [for] the Bar [and] Theatre* by Dr. Pierre Bonnier (consultant at the Comédie-Française and Opéra-Comique) (*c.*1908).[5] The four-page list of "do's" and "don't's" in Peter Joseph Cooke's *Forensic Eloquence; or, The Eloquence of the Bar* (1897) offers specifics: "Do not place your thumbs in the armholes of your waistcoat; do not clutch your coat or gown with your hands"; "Do not twist your moustache"; "Do not jerk your body or bend your knees spasmodically when pressing home . . . your narrative"; "Be natural, decisive, spontaneous, and sincere." Modern, but—waistcoat and moustache aside—suspiciously like Quintilian. The "most eminent actors and actresses of the day [know]" that it "all amount[s] to this —Be natural!" declares one theorist.[6] Do not "ris[k] becoming a declaimer or an actor" or speak with "theatrical pomp," declares another. And yet—insists the first—"you must be at once an actor and a comedian."[7]

Lest you think such advice belongs to a bygone era, read manuals for the aspiring courtroom lawyer, or better yet, go online: "remember that the courtroom is a theater" (as one website on cross-examination advises). "Do not disappoint your jury. [M]ake sure [your performance] has maximum dramatic effect—without being overly dramatic."[8] An article titled "Acting Effectively in Court: Using Dramatic Techniques" urges: transfer techniques "from theater to the courtroom"; train your voice; block your movements; learn to express emotion; and employ "character voices," as in the following script, in which counsel for the defense addresses the jury.

"from the stage"). Bacon, "A Proposition to His Majesty . . . Touching the Compiling and Amendment of the Laws of England" (*c.*1616) in Bacon, *Resuscitatio*, 278. I am grateful to Alan Stewart for helping me locate this passage.

5 Le Faucheur, *Traitté de l'action de l'orateur, ou de la Prononciation et du geste* (1657) (trans. *Essay upon the Action of an Orator* in 1680); Maury, *Principes d'éloquence, pour . . . le barreau*" (section "*De l'action oratoire*"); Robinson, *Forensic Oratory*; Bonnier, *La voix professionelle: Leçons pratiques de physiologie appliquée aux . . . Barreau, Théâtre.*

6 Cooke, *Forensic Eloquence*, 19–23.

7 "[O]n risque facilement de devenir un déclamateur et un comédien"; "une pompe factice et théâtrale." Mareille, *La plaidoirie sentimentale*, 21, 290 (both a history and a practical guide); Cooke, *Forensic Eloquence*, 116.

8 Gerald A. Klein, "The Art of Cross-Examination," Klein & Wilson, https://www.kleinandwilson.com/publications/the-art-of-cross-examination/ (accessed July 13, 2021).

> If you had been in Billy Bob's shoes that night at the Commodore Club you would have seen that Joe Willie had fire in his eyes and smelled the alcohol on his breath. If you had been in Billy Bob's shoes that night at the Commodore Club, you would have thought:
>
> (*Now with a slight drawl*)
>
> Joe Willie doesn't understand that I'm in love with Beth. Beth told me how violent he gets when he's drinkin.' How he's capable of just about anything.

But "BE NATURAL." Do not be overly dramatic. For "[t]he courtroom is *not* a stage.... Theater is make believe, while the world that revolves around our practice of law is harsh reality."[9] In other words, be theatrical. But not too theatrical. For (as the judge and bailiff repeatedly admonished during the Michael Jackson trial in 2005): "the courtroom is not a theatre."[10]

In each such declaration one can find not only a poetics of legal performance but also a distinctive theory of law. In "The Path of Law" (1897), Oliver Wendell Holmes writes that the lawyer's task is to "eliminat[e]... all the dramatic elements with which his client's story has clothed [the case]." For Holmes, insisting that law is not drama means that it is a cool machine that operates without moral judgment, emotion, or extraneous detail. Law is merely a neutral set of "prophesies... that if a man does or omits certain things he will be made to suffer in this or that way by judgment." The "lawyer does not mention that his client wore a white hat,... while Mrs. Quickly would be sure to dwell upon it," since the lawyer "foresees that the public force will act in the same way whatever his client had upon his head."[11] (Holmes is of course wrong—and "Mrs. Quickly" right—about whether you might "suffer... by judgment" or by the violence of "public force" because of what you wear or how you look.) In 1962, defending the rule that banned television cameras from the courtroom, one-time Dean of Harvard Law School Erwin Griswold wrote: "[a] courtroom is not a stage; and witnesses and lawyers, and judges and juries and parties, are not players, [and a] trial is not a drama." For Griswold, insisting that law is not drama means that its central function is the search for truth. "[A] courtroom is a place for ascertaining the truth in controversies among men, and has no other legitimate function" (no other?)[12] If each such declaration harbors a poetics and a theory of law, each also

[9] Fiedler, "Acting Effectively in Court: Using Dramatic Techniques," 23 (emphasis added). See similarly Ball, *Theater Tips and Strategies for Jury Trials.*

[10] "Reporter's Log: Michael Jackson Trial," BBC News, 1 June, 2005, http://news.bbc.co.uk/2/hi/entertainment/4511991.stm (accessed June 20, 2021).

[11] Holmes, *Collected Legal Papers*, 168–9 ("The Path of Law").

[12] Griswold, "Standards of the Legal Profession," 616, col. 1, col. 3. See similarly Dershowitz, "Life is Not a Dramatic Narrative": "When we import the [dramatic] narrative form of storytelling into our legal system, we confuse fiction with fact and endanger the truth-finding function of the adjudicative process" (101).

harbors a politics, a praxis, an applied ethics. In her 1963 report on the Eichmann trial, Hannah Arendt described the auditorium where the trial took place as "a theater... complete with orchestra and gallery, with proscenium and stage, and with side doors for the actors' entrance": an ideal setting for the prosecutor's "theatrics." But "Justice does not permit" theatrics, she proclaims: "it demands seclusion, it permits sorrow rather than anger."[13] For Arendt, insisting that law is not drama means that it is not to be a stage for aggrandizing the banality of evil, but instead to be a place of mourning. As Arendt knew, in legal performance, there can be a very great deal at stake.

Championing legal positivism, Bentham was writing at the moment when the great traditions of legal oratory were allegedly fading under the rules and regulations of the modern administrative state. He was writing at the moment when (according to Foucault) "the great spectacle of physical punishment disappeared," "the theatrical representation of pain" was no longer punishment's central technology of power, and punishment was becoming "the most hidden part of the penal process."[14] But positivism did not in fact herald the end of legal oratory: the courtroom remained for Bentham (as for many of his contemporaries) a "Judicial Theatre."[15] And punishment did not go underground. Performance forms merely changed. The nineteenth century was the age of the scandalous trial, with mass attendance fueled by mass journalism. It was an age in which—alongside an ongoing culture of spectacular public punishment—an industry of prison tourism blossomed, funding the incipient prison-industrial complex.[16] Newly organized and newly visible police forces appeared alongside new cultures of surveillance. Film and television cameras made their way into the courtroom, transforming legal spectacle into recorded light and sound shows, collapsing distance. The Internet multiplied these into an infinitude of fragments, fracturing time and space. As fast as old cultures of legal spectacle faded, new ones arose.

No one living in the age of late modern mass media—when moving images have taken over the public sphere and brought the courtroom into the palms of our hands—would now say that law takes "*[n]ihil ex scenâ*": "nothing from the theatre." Streaming across our ubiquitous screens, legal performances are with us whenever we care to look—the fictional sometimes inseparable from the real. Glancing at our devices, there is no escape from crime scene or trial footage, police dashcam videos, chokeholds caught on camera mingling promiscuously with prison reality shows, COPS, Law and Order reruns, Judge X (replicated in infinite

[13] Arendt, *Eichmann in Jerusalem* (1994 ed.), 4, 6.

[14] Foucault, *Discipline and Punish* (1995 ed.), 14, 9.

[15] The figure appears throughout his work, most insistently in the constitutional code Bentham published in 1827, in which he repeatedly envisions "Actors on the Judicial Theatre" as "*Performers in the Judicial Drama.*" Bentham, *Works* (1962 ed.), 9:459, col. 1–2 (and see 9:157, 466, 474, 481, 486, 491, 493, 501, 538, 540, 561–3, 569, 571, 579, 581–2, 585).

[16] For a discussion of nineteenth-century prison tourism, see Miron, *Prisons, Asylums, and the Public*; and my "Penitentiary Performances."

knockoffs). Those of us who are privileged—probably most of my readers and I myself—live law mostly not face to face but as media theatre. We may be its subjects but we also consume it: as news; as entertainment. Legal philosophers and historians still sometimes tell us that law is a set of rules, doctrines, or concepts. They still sometimes tell us that we live under the "rule of law, not men."[17] But in an era in which showmanship, Twitter, and videobytes can determine the outcome of the most momentous legal events, it seems clear that we instead live under the rule of theatre, in a twenty-first-century version of Plato's theatrocracy but on speed.

However different our own legal cultures may look from those of premodern and early modern Europe, we remain, in various ways, heirs to the tradition I have described in these pages. The questions that recur throughout this book are among the most important we ask ourselves: about the ethics of law-as-entertainment; about the relationships among aesthetics, emotion, and legal or political action; about the courtroom representation of atrocity. We echo early legal theorists when we ask, for instance, about the appropriate limits on video evidence (prejudicial or probative?); whether judges should instruct juries to ignore a defendant's appearance and demeanor; whether police training should include video games and if so, how; whether executions should be televised; whether prison reality shows exploit prisoners; whether programs like "Scared Straight" actually scare anyone straight. Like early theorists, we mistrust courtroom theatrics and the manipulation of emotion. And yet we recognize that law is a performance art, and the communication of emotion central to the work it does. Like them, we fear that repeated exposure to stories of atrocity dulls our sense of outrage and makes us feel helpless; we worry that the spectacle of suffering, instead of acting as protest, may instead inadvertently offer perverse pleasures, if only the pleasure of indulging one's own sympathy. And yet we know that atrocity must be visible if there is to be redress. Like them, we fear that teaching law students performance arts offers them training in specious persuasion and outright dissembling. But we also view such arts as the necessary weapons of justice. Like them, we protest the sway of "trial by media" and fear its affiliation with a demagoguery that stirs up popular fears and leads the people to trample the laws. And yet we view the secret trial as a tool of tyranny and the public trial as essential to democracy, which, despite all, still seems better than the alternative. Like them, we know that performance matters to how we make law and how it makes us. This book constitutes not an ending to that story, but its beginning.

[17] See e.g. Kahn, "Freedom, Autonomy, and the Cultural Study of Law": since Thomas Paine's announcement that "law is king," there has "been an unbroken, public commitment to the idea that we live under the rule of law, not men" (noting, however, the failure of this normative proposition as a descriptive claim) (165).

Works Cited

Primary Sources

Aeschines. [*The Speeches of Aeschines*]. *Against Timarchus, On the Embassy, Against Ctesiphon*. Trans. Charles Darwin Adams. [Loeb Classical Library.] Cambridge: Harvard University Press, 1919.

Agrippa, Heinrich Cornelius. *The Vanity of Arts and Sciences*. London: Samuel Speed, 1676.

Alain de Lille [Alan of Lille]. *The Art of Preaching*. Trans. Gillian R. Evans. Piscataway, NJ: Gorgias Press, 2010.

Alain de Lille [Alan of Lille]. *Literary Works*. Trans. Winthrop Wetherbee. Cambridge: Harvard University Press, 2013.

[Alcuin of York.] *Epistolae Karolini aevi*. [*Monumenta Germaniae historica*, vol. 4.] Ed. Ernst Dümmler. Berlin: Weidman, 1895.

Alcuin of York. *The Rhetoric of Alcuin & Charlemagne*. Trans. Wilbur Samuel Howell. New York: Russell & Russell, 1965.

Al-Farabi [Fārābī.]. *Deux ouvrages inédits sur la réthorique [sic]: I. Kitāb al-ḫaṭāba. II. Didascalia in Rethoricam [sic] Aristotelis ex glosa Alpharabi*. Eds. J. Langhade and M. Grignaschi. Beirut: Dar el-Machreq, 1971.

Amhurst, Nicholas. *Terrae-Filius: Or, The Secret History of the University of Oxford*. London: R. Francklin, 1726.

Amyot, Jacques. *Projet de l'éloquence royale, composé pour Henry III, roi de France*. Versailles: Lamy, 1805.

Andocides. *Andocides*. Trans. Michael Edwards. Warminster: Aris & Phillips, 1995.

Arendt, Hannah. *Eichmann in Jerusalem: A Report on the Banality of Evil*. Rev. ed. New York: Penguin, 1994.

Arias Montano, Benito. *Liber Ieremiae, sive de actione*. Antwerp: Christopher Plantin, 1571.

Aristotle. *The Art of Rhetoric*. Trans. John Henry Freese. Rev. trans. Gisela Striker. [Loeb Classical Library.] Cambridge: Harvard University Press, 2020.

Aristotle. *On Rhetoric: A Theory of Civic Discourse*. 2nd ed. Trans. George A. Kennedy. Oxford: Oxford University Press, 2007.

Aristotle. *Poetics*. In *Poetics. Longinus: On the Sublime. Demetrius: On Style*. Trans. Stephen Halliwell, et al. Rev. ed. [Loeb Classical Library.] Cambridge: Harvard University Press, 1999, 1–142.

Aristotle. *Politics: A New Translation*. Trans. C. D. C. Reeve. Cambridge: Hackett, 2017.

Aristotle. *Rhetoric*. Trans. C. D. C. Reeve. Cambridge: Hackett, 2018.

[Aristotle]. *Rhetoric to Alexander*. In Aristotle, *Problems Books 20–38 and Rhetoric to Alexander*. Trans. Robert Mayhew and David C. Mirhady. [Loeb Classical Library.] Cambridge: Harvard University Press, 2011, 450–641.

Augustine. *Confessions*. Trans. Henry Chadwick. Oxford: Oxford University Press, 1991.

Averroës [Ibn Rushd]. *Averroës' Three Short Commentaries on Aristotle's "Topics," "Rhetoric," and "Poetics."* Trans. Charles E. Butterworth. Albany: State University of New York Press, 1977.

Bacon, Anne. *The Letters of Lady Anne Bacon*. Ed. Gemma Allen. Cambridge: Cambridge University Press, 2014.

Bacon, Francis. *Resuscitatio, or, Bringing into Publick Light Severall Pieces... Hitherto Sleeping*. London: Sarah Griffin for William Lee, 1657.

Bacon, Francis. *The Advancement of Learning*. [*The Oxford Francis Bacon*, vol. 4.] Ed. Michael Kiernan. Oxford: Clarendon Press, 2000.

Baker, Thomas. *An Act at Oxford: A Comedy*. London: Bernard Lintott, 1704.

Ball, David. *Theater Tips and Strategies for Jury Trials*. Notre Dame: National Institute for Trial Advocacy, 1994.

Basin, Thomas. *Apologie ou plaidoyer pour moi-même*. Trans. Charles Samaran and Georgette de Groër. Paris: Société d'édition "Les Belles Lettres," 1974.

Basin, Thomas. *Histoire de Charles VII*. Trans. Charles Samaran. 2 vols. Paris: Société d'édition "Les Belles Lettres," 1933–44.

Basin, Thomas. *Histoire de Louis XI*. Trans. Charles Samaran and M.-C. Garand. 3 vols. Paris: Société d'édition "Les Belles Lettres," 1963–72.

Basin, Thomas. "Libellus de optimo ordine forenses lites audiendi et deferendi" ["Projet de réforme en matière de procédure."] In *Histoire des règnes de Charles VII et de Louis XI, Vol. 4*. Ed. J. Quicherat. Paris: J. Renouard et Cie, 1859, 27–65.

Barclay, John. *Icon animorum, or, The Mirror of Minds*. Trans. Thomas May. Ed. Mark T. Riley. Louvain: Louvain University Press, 2013.

Becon, Thomas. *The Catechism of Thomas Becon*. Ed. John Ayre. Cambridge: The University Press, 1844.

Bénet, Armand, ed. *Procès verbal fait pour délivrer une fille possédée par le malin esprit à Louviers*. Paris: Progrès Médical, A. Delahaye et Lecrosnier, 1883.

Bentham, Jeremy. *The Works of Jeremy Bentham*. Ed. John Bowring. 11 vols. New York: Russell & Russell, 1962.

Bernard of Clairvaux. *Five Books on Consideration: Advice to a Pope*. Trans. John D. Anderson and Elizabeth T. Kennan. Kalamazoo: Cistercian Publications, 1976.

Bertaldo, Jacopo. *Splendor Venetorum civitatis consuetudinum*. Ed. Francisco Schupfer. In *Scripta anecdota glossatorum, Vol. 3*. Ed. August Gaudenzi. Torino: Bottega d'Erasmo, 1901, 104–5.

Bertrand, Nicolas. *Opus De Tholosanorum Gestis*. Toulouse: Johannis Magni Johannisi, 1515.

Bevington, David, ed. *Medieval Drama*. Rev. ed. Indianapolis: Hackett, 2012.

Blackstone, William. *Commentaries on the Laws of England*. [*The Oxford Edition of Blackstone*.] Ed. David Lemmings. 4 vols. Oxford: Oxford University Press, 2016.

Boguet, Henry. *Les procès inédits de Boguet en matière de sorcellerie dans la grande judicature de Saint-Claude, XVIe-XVIIe siècles*. Ed. Francis Bavoux. Dijon: Imprimerie Bernigaud et Privat, 1958.

Boncompagno da Signa. "Il I libro del *Boncompagnus* di Boncompagno da Signa: edizione critica e glossario." Ed. Martina Basso. Thesis. University of Padua, 2015–16. http://tesi.cab.unipd.it/50282/1/MARTINA_BASSO_2015.pdf. Accessed March 4, 2021.

Boncompagno da Signa. *Opera omnia Boncompagni (1194–1243)*. In *Medieval Diplomatic and the 'Ars Dictandi.'* Ed. and trans. Steven M. Wight. Los Angeles: Steven M. Wight, 1998. http://www.scrineum.it/scrineum/wight/index.htm. Accessed July 13, 2021.

Boncompagno da Signa. *Rhetorica novissima*. In *Scripta anecdota glossatorum* [Bibliotheca iuridica medii aevi]. Vol. 2. Ed. Augusto Gaudenzi. Bologna: Societatis Azzoguidianae, 1892, 249–297.

Bond, Donald F., ed. *The Tatler*. 3 vols. Oxford: Clarendon Press, 1987.

Bonet, Juan Pablo. *Reduction de las letras y arte para enseñar a ablar los mudos*. Madrid: Francisco Abarca de Angulo, 1620.
Bonifacio, Giovanni. *L'arte de' cenni con la quale formandosi favella visibile, si tratta della muta eloquenza*. Vicenza: Francesco Grossi, 1616.
Bonifacio, Giovanni. *L'arti liberali, et mecaniche, come siano state dagli animali irrationali agli huomini dimostrate*. Rovigo: Daniel Bissuccio, 1628.
Bonnier, Pierre. *La voix professionelle: leçons pratiques de physiologie appliquée aus carrières vocales*. Paris: Bibliothèque Larousse, 1908.
Boretius, Alfredus, ed. *Monumenta Germaniae historica. Legum sectio II, Capitularia regum Francorum*. 4 vols. Hanover: Bibliopolii Hahniani, 1980–84.
Brant, Sebastian. *Stultifera navis* [*Ship of Fools*]. Trans. Alexander Barclay. London: Richard Pynson, 1509.
Brathwait, Richard. *The Shepheards Tales*. London: Richard Whitaker, 1621.
Braithwait, Richard. *A Spiritual Spicerie, Containing Sundrie Sweet Tractates of Devotion and Piety*. London: George Hutton, 1638.
Brand, Paul A., ed. *The Earliest English Law Reports*. 4 vols. London: Selden Society, 1996–2007.
Brecht, Bertolt. *Brecht on Theatre: The Development of an Aesthetic*. Trans. John Willett. New York: Macmillan, 1964.
Březová, Laurence of. *Origins of the Hussite Uprising: The Chronicle of Laurence Březová (1414–1421)*. Ed. Thomas A. Fudge. New York: Routledge, 2020.
Brinsley, John. *Ludus Literarius: Or, the Grammar Schoole*. London: Thomas Man, 1612.
Bruni, Leonardo. "The Study of Literature." In *Humanist Educational Treatises*. Ed. Craig W. Kallendorf. Cambridge: Harvard University Press, 2002, 92–125.
Buc, Sir George. "The Third Universitie of England. Or A Treatise of the Foundations of all the Colledges, Auncient Schooles of Priviledge, and of Houses of Learning, and Liberall Arts, Within and About the Most Famous Cittie of London." In Stow. *Annales*, 958–988 (volume not consecutively paginated).
Buchanan, George. *Ane Detectioun of the Duinges of Marie Quene of Scottes thouchand the Murder of hir Husband*. London: John Day, 1571.
Bulwer, John. *Chirologia, or, The Naturall Language of the Hand [and] Chironomia, or, The Art of Manual Rhetoricke*. London: Thomas Harper, 1644.
Burney, Frances. *The Diary and Letters of Madame D'Arblay*. Ed. Sarah Chauncey Woolsey. 2 vols. Boston: Little Brown, 1910.
Burtt, J. O., trans. *Minor Attic Orators, Volume II: Lycurgus. Dinarchus. Demades. Hyperides*. [Loeb Classical Library.] Cambridge: Harvard University Press, 1954.
Calendar of State Papers Domestic: Charles I, 1634–5. Ed. John Bruce. London: British History Online, 1864. http://www.british-history.ac.uk/cal-state-papers/domestic/chas1/1634-5, accessed April 14, 2021.
Carruthers, Mary, and Jan M. Ziolkowski, eds. *The Medieval Craft of Memory: An Anthology of Texts and Pictures*. Philadelphia: University of Pennsylvania Press, 2002.
Castelein, Matthijs de. *De const van rhetoriken*. Ghent: Jan Cauweel, 1555.
Catherine of Siena. *The Letters of Catherine of Siena*. Trans. Suzanne Noffke. 4 vols. Tempe, AZ: Arizona Center for Medieval and Renaissance Studies, 2000.
Cavalcanti, Bartolomeo. *La Retorica*. Ferrara: Gabriel Giolito, 1559.
Chamberlain, John. *The Letters of John Chamberlain*. Ed. Norman Egbert McClure. 2 vols. Philadelphia: American Philosophical Society, 1939.
Charrier, Jean. *Memorable action judiciaire de maistre Jean Charrier*. Aix: Thomas Maillou and Marie d'Herbes, 1559.

Chastellain, Georges. *Oeuvres de Georges Chastellain*. Ed. Kervyn de Lettenhove. 8 vols. Brussels: F. Heussner et al., 1863–1866.

Choisnin, Jean. *Discours au vray, de tout ce qui s'est faict & passé pour l'entiere negociation de l'election du Roy de Polongne* [1574]. In *Collection complète des mémoires relatifs à l'histoire de France*. Vol. 38. Ed. Claude Petitot. Paris: Foucault, 1823.

Cicero, Marcus Tullius. *Brutus, Orator*. Trans. G. L. Hendrickson and H. M. Hubbell. Rev. ed. [Loeb Classical Library.] Cambridge: Harvard University Press, 1962.

Cicero, Marcus Tullius. *De inventione, De optimo genere oratorum, Topica*. Trans. H. M. Hubbell. [Loeb Classical Library.] Cambridge: Harvard University Press, 1949.

Cicero, Marcus Tullius. *De officiis*. Trans. Walter Miller. [Loeb Classical Library.] Cambridge: Harvard University Press, 1913.

Cicero, Marcus Tullius. *In Catilinam I-IV, Pro Murena, Pro Sulla, Pro Flacco*. Trans. C. MacDonald. [Loeb Classical Library.] Cambridge: Harvard University Press, 1977.

Cicero, Marcus Tullius. *On the Orator*. Trans. E. W. Sutton. 2 vols. Rev. ed. [Loeb Classical Library.] Cambridge: Harvard University Press, 1948.

Cicero, Marcus Tullius. *Pro Lege Manilia, Pro Caecina, Pro Cluentio, Pro Rabirio Perduellionis*. Trans. H. Grose Hodge. [Loeb Classical Library.] Cambridge: Harvard University Press, 1927.

Cicero, Marcus Tullius. *Pro Milone, In Pisonem, Pro Scauro, Pro Fonteio, Pro Rabirio Postumo, Pro Marcello, Pro Ligario, Pro Rege Deiotaro*. Trans. N. H. Watts. Rev. ed. [Loeb Classical Library.] Cambridge: Harvard University Press, 1953.

Cicero, Marcus Tullius. *Pro Publio Quinctio, Pro Sexto Roscio Amerino, Pro Quinto Roscio Comoedo, De Lege Agraria*. Trans. John Henry Freese. [Loeb Classical Library.] Cambridge: Harvard University Press, 1930.

[Cicero, Marcus Tullius]. *Rhetorica ad Herennium*. Trans. Harry Caplan. [Loeb Classical Library.] Cambridge: Harvard University Press, 1954.

Clayton, John. *Topicks in the Laws of England: Containing Media, Apt for Argument and Resolution of Law Cases*. London: William Leake, 1647.

Club Law, a Comedy Acted in Clare Hall, Cambridge, about 1599–1600. Ed. G. C. Moore Smith. Cambridge: The University Press, 1907.

Coke, Edward. *Le tierce part des reportes del Edward Coke attorney generall le Roigne* [1602]. London: Companie of Stationers, 1610.

Cook, John. *King Charls, His Case, or, An Appeal to All Rational Men Concerning his Tryal at the High Court of Justice*. London: Giles Calvert, 1649.

Cook, John. *The Vindication of the Professors & Profession of the Law*. London: Matthew Walbancke, 1646.

Cox, Leonard. *The Art or Crafte of Rhetoryke* [c.1530]. London: Robert Redman, 1532.

Cox, Leonard. *The Arte or Crafte of Rhethoryke* [c.1530]. Ed. Frederic Ives Carpenter. Chicago: University of Chicago Press, 1899.

Cressolles, Louis de. *Vacationes autumnales sive de perfecta oratoris actione et pronunciatione libri III*. Paris: Sebastien Cramoisy, 1620.

Dannhauer, Johann Konrad. *Idea boni disputatoris et malitiosi sophistae*. Strasbourg: Wilhelm Christian Glaser, 1629.

Damhouder, Joost de. *Praxis rerum civilium*. Antwerp: Joannem Bellerum, 1567.

Damhouder, Joost de. *Praxis rerum criminalium*. Antwerp: Joannem Bellerum, 1562.

Damhouder, Joost de. *Pupillorum patrocinium*. Antwerp: Johannem Bellerum, 1564.

Davidson, L. S. and J. O. Ward, eds. *The Sorcery Trial of Alice Kyteler: A Contemporary Account (1324) Together with Related Documents in English Translation*. Binghamton: Center for Medieval and Early Renaissance Studies, 1993.

De Luca, Giovanni Battista. *Lo stile legale*. Eds. Guido Alpa, Andrea D'Angelo, and Aldo Mazzacane. Bologna: Il Mulino, 2010.

De Luca, Giovanni Battista. *Theatrum veritatis, et iustitiae*. 21 vols. Rome: Corbelletti, 1669–1681.

Demosthenes. *De Corona, De Falsa Legatione, XVIII, XIX*. Trans. C. A. Vince and J. H. Vince. [Loeb Classical Library.] Rev. ed. Cambridge: Harvard University Press, 1939.

Demosthenes. *Orations XXI-XXVI*. Trans. J. H. Vince. [Loeb Classical Library.] Cambridge: Harvard University Press, 1935.

Demosthenes. *Orations XXVII-XL*. Trans. A. T. Murray. [Loeb Classical Library.] Cambridge: Harvard University Press, 1936.

Demosthenes. *Private Orations XLI-XLIX*. Trans. A. T. Murray. [Loeb Classical Library.] Cambridge: Harvard University Press, 1939.

Demosthenes. *Private Orations L-LVIII, In Neaeram LIX*. Trans. A. T. Murray. [Loeb Classical Library.] Cambridge: Harvard University Press, 1939.

D'Ewes, Simonds. *The Autobiography and Correspondence of Sir Simonds D'Ewes*. Ed. James Orchard Halliwell. 2 vols. London: R. Bentley, 1845.

D'Ewes, Simonds. *The Diary of Sir Simonds D'Ewes (1622-1624): journal d'un étudiant londonien sous le règne de Jacques Ier*. Ed. Elisabeth Bourcier. Paris: Publications de la Sorbonne/Didier, 1974.

Doddridge, John. *The English Lawyer*. London: Assignes of I. More Esq, 1631.

Doddridge, John. *The Lawyers Light: Or, a Due Direction for the Study of the Law*. London: Beniamin Fisher, 1629.

Dorléans, Louis. *Les ouvertures des parlements auxquelles sont adjoustées cinq remonstrances*. Paris: G. Des Rues, 1607.

Dugdale, William. *Origines Juridiciales, or, Historical Memorials of the English Laws*. London: The Author, 1666.

Du Perron, Jacques, and Nicolas Renouard. *Les fleurs de l'éloquence françoise*. Paris: A. Estoc, 1615.

Duport, James. "Rules to Be Observed by Young Pupils & Schollers in the University." In G. M. Trevelyan, "Undergraduate Life Under the Protectorate." *The Cambridge Review*, 64 (1943), 328–30.

Durand, Guillaume [with additions by Johannes Andreae and Baldus de Ubaldis]. *Speculum iuris*. Leiden: Philippi Tinghi, 1578.

Du Vair, Guillaume. *De l'eloquence françoise et des raisons pourquoy elle est demeuree si basse*. Ed. René Radouant. Paris: Société française d'imprimerie et de librairie, 1908.

Dyer, Sir James. *Reports of Cases in the Reigns of Hen. VIII, Edw. VI, Q. Mary, and Q. Eliz*. Ed. John Vaillant. London: J. Butterworth, 1794.

Einhard and Notker the Stammerer. *Two Lives of Charlemagne*. Trans. David Ganz. London: Penguin, 2008.

Elyot, Sir Thomas. *Bibliotheca Eliotae / Eliotis librarie*. London: Thomae Berthelet, 1542.

Elyot, Sir Thomas. *The Boke Named the Governour*. London: Thomas Berthelet, 1537.

Erasmus, Desiderius. *Literary and Educational Writings*. [*Collected Works of Erasmus Vol. 23–29*.] Eds. A. H. T. Levi, et al. 7 vols. Toronto: University of Toronto Press, 1978–1986.

Evelyn, John. *Diary of John Evelyn*. Ed. E. S. de Beer. 6 vols. New York: Oxford University Press, 2000.

Faye d'Espeisses, Jacques. *Recueil des remonstrances faites en la cour de parlement de Paris aux ouvertures des plaidoiries*. La Rochelle: H. Haultin, 1591.

Fenner, Dudley. *The Artes of Logike and Rethorike*. Middelburg: R. Schilders, 1584.

Ferrari, Francesco Bernardino. *De veterum acclamationibus et plausu libri septem*. Milan: Collegium Ambrosianum, 1627.

Ferrarius, Johannes. *A Woorke of Joannes Ferrarius Montanus Touchynge the Good Orderynge of a Common Weale*. Trans. William Bavand. London: John White, 1559.

Fidell, Thomas. *A Perfect Guide for a Studious Young Lawyer*. London: The Author, 1654.

Fiedler, Donald B. "Acting Effectively In Court: Using Dramatic Techniques." *The Champion* 25 (July, 2001), 18–23.

Fortescue, Sir John. *De laudibus legum Angliae writen by Sir John Fortescue L. Ch. Justice, and after L. Chancellor to K. Henry VI* [c. 1470]. London: Companie of Stationers, 1616.

Foxe, John. *The Acts and Monuments of John Foxe*. Ed. Josiah Pratt. 8 vols. 4th ed. London: The Religious Tract Company, 1877.

Fraunce, Abraham. *The Arcadian Rhetorike*. London: Thomas Orwin, 1588.

Fraunce, Abraham. *The Arcadian Rhetorike* [1588]. Ed. Ethel Seaton. Oxford: B. Blackwell, 1950.

Fraunce, Abraham. *The Lawiers Logike: Exemplifying the Praecepts of Logike by the Practise of the Common Lawe*. London: Thomas Newman and T. Gubbin, 1588.

Freyberg, Maximilian Prokop von, ed. *Sammlung historischer Schriften und Urkunden, geschöpft aus Handschriften*. 4 vols. Stuttgart: n.p., 1836.

Fulbecke, William. *A Direction or Preparative to the Study of the Lawe*. London: Thomas Wight, 1600.

Fulbeck[e], William. *Parallele or Conference of the Civill Law, the Canon Law, and the Common Law of this Realme of England*. 2 vols. London: Thomas Wight, 1601–2.

Garasse, François ["Sieur Charles de L'Espinoeil"]. *Le banquet des sages dressé au logis et aux despens de M Louys Servin*. N.p.: n.p., 1617.

Gassendi, Pierre. *Opera omnia in sex tomos divisa*. 6 vols. Lyon: Laurent Anisson and Jean Devenet, 1658.

Geiler von Kaysersberg, Johannes. *Passio domini nostri Jesu Christi, ex evangelistarum textu*. Strasbourg: Johann Knoblouch, 1508.

Gentili, Alberico. *Alberici Gentilis Disputationes Duae: I. De actoribus & spectatoribus fabularum non notandis. II. De abusu mendacii*. Hanau: Antonius, 1599.

Gentili, Alberico. "*Commentatio ad Legem III Codicis de professoribus et medicis*." In J. W. Binns, "Alberico Gentili in Defense of Poetry and Acting." *Studies in the Renaissance* 19 (1972), 229–72.

Gentili, Alberico. *The Wars of the Romans: A Critical Edition and Translation of De armis Romanis*. Eds. Benedict Kingsbury and Benjamin Straumann. Trans. David Lupher. Oxford: Oxford University Press, 2011.

Gentili, Alberico, and John Rainolds. *Latin Correspondence by Alberico Gentili and John Rainolds on Academic Drama*. Trans. Leon Markowicz. Salzburg: Institut für Englische Sprache und Literatur, 1977.

Geoffrey of Vinsauf. *Documentum de modo et arte dictandi et versificandi (Instruction in the Method and Art of Speaking and Versifying)*. Trans. Roger P. Parr. Milwaukee: Marquette University Press, 1968.

Geoffrey of Vinsauf. *Poetria nova*. Trans. Margaret F. Nims. Rev. ed. Toronto: Pontifical Institute of Mediaeval Studies, 2010.

Gesta Grayorum, or, The History of the High and Mighty Prince, Henry Prince of Purpoole. London: William Canning, 1688.

Gesta Grayorum; or, The History of the High and Mighty Prince Henry, Prince of Purpoole [1688]. Ed. Desmond Bland. Liverpool: Liverpool University Press, 1968.

Gibbon, Edward. *The Decline and Fall of the Roman Empire*. 6 vols. New York: Alfred A. Knopf, 1993–94.

Giles of Rome. *Commentaria in Rhetoricam Aristotelis*. [Facsimile reprint of Venice 1515 ed.] Frankfurt: Minerva, 1968.

Gregory, Arthur, and William Hughes. *Gregories Moot-Book... Inlarged by William Hughes*. London: H. Twyford, T. Dring, and J. Place, 1663.

Griswold, Erwin N. "The Standards of the Legal Profession: Canon 35 Should not Be Surrendered." *American Bar Association Journal* 48 (July 1962), 615–18.

Guarino, Battista. "A Program of Teaching and Learning." [*De ordine docendi et studendi*]. In *Humanist Educational Treatises*. Ed. Craig W. Kallendorf. Cambridge: Harvard University Press, 2002, 260–309.

Gui, Bernard. *Le livre des sentences de l'inquisiteur Bernard Gui: 1308–1323*. Ed. and trans. Annette Pales-Gobilliard. 2 vols. Paris: CNRS, 2002.

Harvey, Gabriel. *Gabriel Harvey's Marginalia*. Ed. G.C. Moore Smith. Stratford-upon-Avon: Shakespeare Head Press, 1913.

Hawarde, John. *Les reportes del cases in Camera Stellata, 1593 to 1609: From the Original Ms. of John Hawarde*. Ed. William Paley Baildon. London: Privately printed, 1894.

Haye, Thomas, ed. *Oratio: mittelalterliche Redekunst in lateinischer Sprache*. Leiden: Brill, 1999.

Hellot, Amédée. ed. *Chronique parisienne anonyme du XIVe siècle*. Nogent-le-Rotrou: Daupeley-Gouverneur, 1884.

Henri d'Andeli. *The Battle of the Seven Arts: A French Poem*. Trans. Louis John Paetow. Berkeley: University of California Press, 1914.

Herodotus. *Books V-VII*. Trans. A. D. Godley. [Loeb Classical Library] Cambridge: Harvard University Press, 1922.

Heywood, Thomas. *An Apology for Actors*. London: Nicholas Okes, 1612.

Holdsworth, Richard. "Directions for a Student in the Universitie." In Harris Francis Fletcher, *The Intellectual Development of John Milton*, Vol. 2. Urbana: University of Illinois Press, 1961, 623–64.

Holinshed, Raphael. *The Firste [Laste] Volume of the Chronicles of England, Scotlande, and Irelande... Untill the Yeare 1571*. London: John Hunne, 1577.

Holmes, Oliver Wendell. *Collected Legal Papers*. New York: Harcourt, Brace and Company, 1921.

Hornbeck II, J. Patrick, Stephen E. Lahey, and Fiona Somerset, eds. *Wycliffite Spirituality*. New York: Paulist Press, 2013.

Horne, Andrew. *The Mirrour of Justices*. Trans. William Hughes. Ed. William C. Robinson. Washington, DC: J. Byrne, 1903.

Hughes, William. *Hughes's Quaeries, or, Choice Cases for Moots*. London: George Dawes, 1675.

Huloet, Richard. *Abcedarium anglico latinum, pro tyrunculis Richardo Huloeto exscriptore*. London: William Riddel, 1552.

Hus, Jan. *The Letters of John Hus*. Trans. Matthew Spinka. Manchester: Manchester University Press, 1972.

Institoris, Heinrich. *The Hammer of Witches: A Complete Translation of the Malleus Maleficarum*. Trans. Christopher S. Mackay. Cambridge: Cambridge University Press, 2009.

Isocrates. *Isocrates*. Trans. George Norlin and Larue Van Hook. 3 vols. [Loeb Classical Library.] Cambridge: Harvard University Press, 1928–45.

Jandun, Jean de. "Tractatus de laudibus Parisius / Traité des louanges de Paris." In *Paris et ses historiens aux XIVe et XVe siècles*. Eds. Antoine J. V. Le Roux de Lincy and L. M. Tisserand. Paris: Imprimerie impériale, 1867, 32–79.

Jewel, John. "Oration Against Rhetoric." In Hoyt Hudson, "Jewel's Oration against Rhetoric: A Translation." *Quarterly Journal of Speech* 14:3 (1928), 374–92.

Justinian. *The Digest of Justinian*. Trans. Alan Watson. 2 vols. Philadelphia: University of Pennsylvania Press, 1998.

Kennedy, George A., ed. and trans. *Progymnasmata: Greek Textbooks of Prose Composition and Rhetoric*. Leiden: Brill, 2003.

Klein, Gerald A. "The Art of Cross-Examination." Klein & Wilson [rpt. from *OCTLA Gavel*, Fall 2010], https://www.kleinandwilson.com/Publications/The-Art-Of-Cross-Examination.shtml. Accessed June 20, 2021.

Knighton, Henry. *Chronicon Henrici Knighton*. Ed. Joseph Rawson Lumby. 2 vols. London: H. M. Stationery Office, 1889–95.

Krantz, Albertus. *Wandalia*. Cologne: J. Soter, 1519.

Lafleur, Claude, ed. *Quatre introductions à la philosophie au XIIIe siècle*. Montréal: Institut d'Études Médiévales, 1988.

Lambarde, William. *Archeion, or, A Discourse upon the High Courts of Justice in England*. London: Henry Seile, 1635.

Lambarde, William. *The Just Lawyer His Conscionable Complaint against Auricular or Private Informing and Soliciting of Judges*. London: George Purslowe, 1631.

Landucci, Luca. *A Florentine Diary from 1450 to 1516*. Trans. Alice de Rosen Jervis. New York: Dutton, 1927.

Langebek, Herman[n]. "Des Bürgermeisters Herman Langebek Bericht über den Aufstand zu Hamburg im Jahre 1483." In *Hamburgische Chroniken in nierdersächsischer Sprache*. Ed. Johan Martin Lappenberg. Hamburg: Perthes & Mauke, 1861, 340–75.

Latini, Brunetto. *The Book of the Treasure*. Trans. Paul Barrette and Spurgeon Baldwin. New York: Garland, 1993.

Latini, Brunetto. *La rettorica*. Trans. Stefania D'Agata D'Ottavi. Kalamazoo: Medieval Institute Publications, 2016.

Lattin, Harriet Pratt, ed. *The Letters of Gerbert, with His Papal Privileges as Sylvester II*. New York: Columbia University Press, 1961.

La Roche-Flavin, Bernard de. *Treze livres des parlemens de France*. Bordeaux: Simon Millanges, 1617.

Le Bel, Jehan. *The True Chronicles of Jean Le Bel 1290–1360*. Trans. Nigel Bryant. Woodbridge: Boydell Press, 2011.

Le Faucheur, Michel. *Essay upon the Action of an Orator: As to His Pronunciation & Gesture, Useful [for] Lawyers*. London: Nicholas Cox, 1680.

Le Faucheur, Michel. *Traitté de l'action de l'orateur, ou de la Prononciation et du geste*. Ed. Valentin Conrart. Paris: A. Courbé, 1657.

Le Franc, Martin. *Le champion des dames*. Lyon: n.p., 1488.

Le Franc, Martin. *Le champion des dames*. Ed. Robert Deschaux. 5 vols. Paris: Honoré Champion, 1999.

Legh, Gerard. *The Accedens of Armory* [1562]. London: Richard Tottel, 1568.

Loisel, Antoine. *Pasquier ou dialogue des advocats du Parlement de Paris*. Ed. André-Marie-Jean-Jacques Dupin. Paris: Videcoq, 1844.

Lysias. *Lysias*. Trans. W. R. M. Lamb. [Loeb Classical Library.] Cambridge: Harvard University Press, 1930.

Mackay, Christopher, ed. *Est insolitum inquirere taliter: Latin and German documents from Heinricus Institoris's witch hunts in Ravensburg and Innsbruck.* Leiden: Brill, 2021.
Mackay, Christopher, ed. *'An Unusual Inquisition': Translated Documents from Heinricus Institoris's Witch Hunts in Ravensburg and Innsbruck.* Leiden: Brill, 2020.
Macrobius. *Saturnalia.* Trans. Robert A. Kaster. 3 vols. [Loeb Classical Library.] Cambridge: Harvard University Press, 2011.
Maidment, K. J., trans. *Minor Attic Orators, Volume I: Antiphon. Andocides.* [Loeb Classical Library.] Cambridge: Harvard University Press, 1941.
Marchegay, P., ed. "Récit authentique de l'exécution de Gilles de Rays et de ses deux serviteurs: le 26 Octobre 1440." *Revue des provinces de l'Ouest* 5 (1857), 177–79.
Mareille, Vital. *La plaidoirie sentimentale en France.* Paris: A. Pedone, 1907.
Marion, Simon. *Plaidoyez de M. Simon Marion, avec les arrêts donnez sur iceux.* Paris: n.p., 1594.
Martial. *Epigrams.* Trans. D. R. Shackleton Bailey. 3 vols. [Loeb Classical Library.] Cambridge: Harvard University Press, 1993.
Matheolus and Jean Le Fèvre. *Les Lamentations de Matheolus et le livre de leesce de Jehan Le Fèvre, de Resson.* Ed. A.-G. van Hamel. 2 vols. Paris: É. Bouillon, 1892–1905.
Maury, Jean-Sifrein. *Principes d'éloquence pour la chaire et le barreau.* Paris: Antoine Boudet, 1782.
Melanchthon, Philipp. *Schriften zur Dialektik und Rhetorik: Principal Writings on Rhetoric.* Eds. Stefan Strohm, William P. Weaver, and Volkhard Wels. Berlin: De Gruyter, 2017.
Mélanges tirés d'une grande bibliothèque, Vol. 11 ["L": "De la lecture des livres françois, septieme partie: Grandes affaires & plaidoyers du seizieme siecle"]. Paris: Moutard, 1780.
Milles de Souvigny, Jean. *Praxis criminis persequendi.* Paris: Simonem Colinaeum, Arnoldum et Carolum Les Angeliers, 1541.
[Molinier, Guilhem]. *Las Leys d'amors: Manuscrit de l'Académie des Jeux Floraux.* Ed. Joseph Anglade. 4 vols. Toulouse: E. Privat, 1919–20.
Monstrelet, Enguerrand de. *Chroniques d'Enguerrand de Monstrelet.* Ed. J.-A. Buchon. 15 vols. Paris: Verdiere Libraire, 1826–27.
More, Sir Thomas. *The Complete Works of St. Thomas More.* 15 vols. in 20. New Haven: Yale University Press, 1963–97.
More, Sir Thomas. [*Utopia.*] *A Fruteful, and Pleasaunt Worke of the Beste State of a Publyque Weale, and of the Newe Yle Called Utopia.* Trans. Ralph Robinson. London: Abraham Vele, 1551.
The Most Strange and Admirable Discoverie of the Three Witches of Warboys. London: Thomas Man and John Winington, 1593.
The Most Wonderfull and True Storie, of a Certaine Witch named Alse Gooderige of Stapen Hill. London: n.p., 1597.
Mulcaster, Richard. *The First Part of the Elementarie.* London: Thomas Vautroullier, 1582.
Nash, Thomas. *Pierce Penilesse his Supplication to the Divell.* London: John Busby, 1592.
Nelson, Alan H., ed. *Cambridge* [Records of Early English Drama]. 2 vols. Toronto: University of Toronto Press, 1989.
Nelson, Alan H., and John R. Elliott, Jr., eds. *Inns of Court.* [Records of Early English Drama.] 3 vols. Cambridge: D. S. Brewer, 2010.
Nietzsche, Friedrich. *The Birth of Tragedy and the Case of Wagner.* Trans. Walter Kaufmann. New York: Vintage, 1967.
Northbrooke, John. *Spiritus est Vicarius Christi in Terra. Treatise wherein Dicing, Dauncing, Vaine Plaies or Enterludes [are] Reprooved.* London: George Bishop, 1577.

Novotný, Václav, ed. *Fontes rerum bohemicarum, Vol. 8*. Prague: Nákladem nadání Františka Palackého, 1932.
Noy, William. *A Treatise of the Principal Grounds and Maximes of the Lawes of this Nation*. London: W. Lee, D. Pakeman, R. Best and G. Bedell, 1651.
The N-Town Plays. Eds. Douglas Sugano and Victor I. Scherb. Kalamazoo, MI: Medieval Institute Publications, 2007.
A Parisian Journal 1405–1449. Trans. Janet Shirley. Oxford: Clarendon Press, 1968.
Pasquier, Etienne. *L'interprétation des Institutes de Justinian*. Ed. Charles Giraud. Paris: Videcoq ainé and A. Durand, 1847.
Pasquier, Etienne. *Les oeuvres d'Estienne Pasquier*. 2 vols. Amsterdam: la Compagnie des libraires associez, 1723.
Patrizi, Francesco. *Della retorica: dieci dialoghi*. Ed. Anna Laura Puliafito Bleul. Lecce: Conte, 1994.
Pernoud, Régine, ed. *The Retrial of Joan of Arc: The Evidence at the Trial for Her Rehabilitation, 1450–1456*. Trans. J. M. Cohen. New York: Harcourt, Brace, 1955.
Petrarch, Francesco. *Petrarch's Remedies for Fortune Fair and Foul: A Modern English Translation of De remediis utriusque fortune*. Trans. Conrad H. Rawski. 5 vols. Bloomington: Indiana University Press, 1991.
Petronius. *Satyricon*. In Petronius and Seneca, *Satyricon and Apocolocyntosis*. Trans. Gareth Schmeling. [Loeb Classical Library.] Cambridge: Harvard University Press, 2020, 3–451.
Phillips, John. *The Examination and Confession of Certaine Wytches at Chensforde in the Countie of Essex*. London: William Pickering, 1566.
Phillips, William. *Studii legalis ratio, or, Directions for the Study of the Law*. London: Francis Kirkman and Henry Marsh, 1662.
Pico della Mirandola, Giovanni. *Lettere*. Ed. Francesco Borghesi. Florence: Leo S. Olschki, 2018.
Plato. *The Collected Dialogues of Plato*. Eds. Edith Hamilton and Huntington Cairns. Princeton: Princeton University Press, 1963.
Pliny the Younger. *Letters and Panegyricus*. Trans. Betty Radice. 2 vols. [Loeb Classical Library.] Cambridge: Harvard University Press, 1969.
Plowden, Edmund. *Les Comentaries, ou les Reportes de Edmunde Plowden un Apprentice de le Comen Ley*. London: Richard Tottel, 1571.
Plowden, Edmund. *Plowden's Quaeries, or, A Moot-Book of Choice Cases*. London: Ch. Adams, J. Starkey, and Tho. Basset, 1662.
Plummer, Charles, ed. *Elizabethan Oxford: Reprints of Rare Tracts*. Oxford: Oxford Historical Society at the Clarendon Press, 1887.
Plutarch. *Moralia, Volume X*. Trans. Harold North Fowler. [Loeb Classical Library.] Cambridge: Harvard University Press, 1936.
Plutarch. *Plutarch's Lives*. 11 vols. Trans. Bernadotte Perrin. [Loeb Classical Library.] Cambridge: Harvard University Press, 1914–26.
Poliziano, Angelo. *Prose volgari inedite e poesie latine e greche edite e inedite di Angelo Ambrogini Poliziano*. Ed. Isidoro Del Lungo. Florence: G. Barbèra, 1867.
Porcia, Jacopo di. *De generosa educatione liberorum*. [Treviso]: Gerardus de Lisa, 1492.
Le Prince d'Amour; or the Prince of Love. London: William Leake, 1660.
Prudentius. *Prudentius*. Trans. H. J. Thomson. 2 vols. [Loeb Classical Library.] Cambridge: Harvard University Press, 1949–53.
Prynne, William. *Histrio-mastix: The Players Scourge, or, Actors Tragaedie*. London: Michael Sparke, 1633.
Puttenham, George. *The Arte of English Poesie*. London: Richard Field, 1589.

[Quintilian]. *The Lesser Declamations*. Trans. D. R. Shackleton Bailey. [Loeb Classical Library.] Cambridge: Harvard University Press, 2006.

Quintilian. *The Orator's Education*. Trans. Donald Russell. 5 vols. [Loeb Classical Library.] Cambridge: Harvard University Press, 2001.

Rainolde, Richard. *A Booke Called the Foundacion of Rhetorike*. London: John Kingston, 1563.

Rainolds, John. *Th'Overthrow of Stage-Playes*. Middelburg: Richard Schilders, 1599.

Rebhorn, Wayne, ed. *Renaissance Debates on Rhetoric*. Ithaca: Cornell University Press, 2000.

Recueil general des caquets de l'acouchée. Ou discours facecieux, où se voit les moeurs, actions, & façons de faire des grands & petits de ce siecle. Paris: n.p., 1623.

Reincke, Heinrich, and Jürgen Bolland, eds. *Die Bilderhandschrift des Hamburgischen Stadtrechts von 1497*. Hamburg: Broschek Verlag, 1968.

Reisch, Gregor. *Margarita philosophica* (1505 ms.). Ghent University Library, BHSL. HS.0007.

Richenthal, Ulrich von. *Das Concilium so zu Constanz gehalten ist worden*. Augsburg: H. Steyner, 1536.

Robinson, William C. *Forensic Oratory: A Manual for Advocates*. Boston: Little, Brown, 1893.

Roye, Jean de. *Journal de Jean de Roye, connu sous le nom de Chronique scandaleuse, 1460–1483*. Ed. Bernard de Mandrot. 2 vols. Paris: Librairie Renouard, H. Laurens, 1894–96.

Ruggle, George. *Ignoramus*. Ed. E. F. J. Tucker. Hildesheim: G. Olms, 1987.

Salimbene da Parma. *The Chronicle of Salimbene de Adam*. Trans. Joseph L. Baird, Giuseppe Baglivi, and John Robert Kane. Binghamton, NY: Medieval & Renaissance Texts & Studies, 1986.

Sansovino, Francesco. *L'avocato: dialogo nel quale si discorre tutta l'auttorità che hanno i Magistrati di Venezia, con la pratica delle cose giudiciali del Palazzo* [1554]. Venice: Troiano Navò, 1586.

Scaliger, Julius Caesar. *Select Translations from Scaliger's Poetics*. Trans. Frederick Morgan Padelford. New York: H. Holt, 1905.

Scharf, Johann. *Processus disputandi de requisitis, moribus, et principiis disputantium*. Wittenberg: Wusthi[i] [and] Röhnerus, 1635.

Schwarzenberg, Johann Freiherr von. [*Bambergensis*]. *Bambergische Peinliche Halsgerichtsordnung* [1507]. https://de.wikisource.org/wiki/Bambergische_Peinliche_Halsgerichtsordnung. Accessed July 13, 2021.

Seneca the Elder. *Declamations*. Trans. M. Winterbottom. 2 vols. [Loeb Classical Library.] Cambridge: Harvard University Press, 1974.

Seneca the Younger. *Epistles*. 3 vols. Trans. Richard M. Gummere. [Loeb Classical Library.] Cambridge: Harvard University Press, 1917–25.

Servin, Louis. *Actions notables et plaidoyez de Messire Louis Servin* [1613]. Rev. ed. Paris: Estienne Richer, 1640.

Shakespeare, William. *The Comedy of Errors*. Ed. Charles Whitworth. Oxford: Oxford University Press, 2008.

Shaw, Samuel. *Words Made Visible, or, Grammar and Rhetorick Accommodated to the Lives and Manners of Men*. London: Daniel Major, 1678–79.

Sidney, Sir Philip. *An Apologie for Poetrie*. London: Henry Olney, 1595.

Smith, Thomas. *De republica Anglorum*. London: Gregorie Seton, 1583.

Stanbridge, John. *Vulgaria Sta[n]brige*. London: Wynken de Worde, 1509 [?].

Stanbridge, John, and Robert Whittinton. *The Vulgaria of John Stanbridge and the Vulgaria of Robert Whittinton.* Ed. Beatrice White. London: K. Paul, Trench, Trubner & Co., 1932.
Statutes of the Realm, Vol. 1 [1235-1377]. London: n.p., 1810.
Stow, John. *The Annales, or a Generall Chronicle of England.* London: Thomas Adams, 1615.
Stow, John. *The Chronicles of England from Brute unto this Present Yeare of Christ.* London: Ralphe Newberie, 1580.
Tacitus. *Agricola, Germania, Dialogus.* Trans. M. Hutton and W. Peterson. Rev. trans. R. M. Ogilvie, E. H. Warmington, and M. Winterbottom. [Loeb Classical Library.] Cambridge: Harvard University Press, 1970.
Talon, Omer [and Petrus Ramus]. *Audomari Talaei rhetoricae libri duo.* Basil: Nicolai fratris, 1569.
Talon, Omer. *Rhetorica ad Carolum Lotharingum.* Paris: Matthaei Davidis, 1549.
Tengler, Ulrich. *Der neü Layenspiegel: Von rechtmässigen ordnungen in Burgerlichen und peinlich[e]n Regimenten.* Augsburg: Rynman, 1511.
Theodulf of Orléans. *Theodulf of Orléans: The Verse.* Trans. Theodore M. Andersson, Åslaug Ommundsen, and Leslie S. B. MacCoull. Tempe: Arizona Center for Medieval and Renaissance Studies, 2014.
Theophrastus of Eresus. *Theophrastus of Eresus: Sources for His Life, Writings, Thought, and Influence.* Eds. and trans. William W. Fortenbaugh, et al. 2 vols. Leiden: Brill, 1992.
Thierry of Chartres. *The Latin Rhetorical Commentaries.* Ed. Karin Margareta Fredborg. Toronto: Pontifical Institute of Mediaeval Studies, 1988.
Trapezuntius, Georgius [George of Trebizond]. *Trapezuntii Rhetoricorum libri quinque.* Paris: Christiani Wecheli, 1538.
Tuvill, Daniel. *Essaies Politicke, and Morall.* [London]: Mathew Lownes, 1608.
Valerius Maximus. *Memorable Doings and Sayings.* Ed. D. R. Shackleton Bailey. 2 vols. [Loeb Classical Library.] Cambridge: Harvard University Press, 2000.
Vergerio, Pier Paolo. "The Character and Studies Befitting a Free-Born Youth" [*De ingenuis moribus et liberalibus adulescentiae studiis liber.*] In Craig W. Kallendorf, ed. *Humanist Educational Treatises.* Cambridge: Harvard University Press, 2002, 2–91.
Vives, Juan Luis. *De ratione dicendi: Critical Edition with Introduction, Translation, and Notes.* Ed. and trans. David Walker. Leiden: Brill, 2018.
Vives, Juan Luis. [*De tradendis disciplinis.*] *Iohannis Ludovici Vivis Valentini... De disciplinis.* London: William Stansby, 1612.
Vives, Juan Luis. *Vives On Education: A Translation of the De tradendis disciplinis of Juan Luis Vives.* Trans. Foster Watson. Cambridge: University Press, 1913.
Ward, Seth. *Vindiciae Academiarum: Containing some Briefe Animadversions upon Mr Websters Book Stiled, The Examination of Academies.* Oxford: Thomas Robinson, 1654.
Waterhouse, Edward. *Fortescutus Illustratus, or a Commentary on That Nervous Treatise de Laudibus Legum Angliae.* London: Thomas Dicas, 1663.
Whitelocke, James. *Liber famelicus of Sir James Whitelocke, a Judge of the Court of King's Bench in the Reigns of James I and Charles I.* Ed. John Bruce. London: Camden Society, 1858.
Willich, Jodocus. *Libellus de pronunciatione rhetorica... Quaestiones de pronunciatione rhetorica.* Frankfurt on the Oder: Eichorn, 1550.
Wilson, Thomas. *The Arte of Rhetorique for the Use of all Suche as are Studious of Eloquence.* London: Richard Grafton, 1553.
Wilson, Thomas. *The Rule of Reason, Conteinyng the Arte of Logique.* London: Richard Grafton, 1551.

Wilson, Thomas. *The Three Orations of Demosthenes Chiefe Orator among the Grecians*. London: Henry Denham, 1570.
Wright, Thomas. *The Passions of the Minde in Generall*. 2nd ed. London: Walter Burre [and Thomas Thorpe], 1604.
Ziolkowski, Jan M., ed. *Solomon and Marcolf*. Cambridge: Harvard University Press, 2008.

Secondary Sources

Ahsmann, Margreet. "Teaching the *Ius Hodiernum*: Legal Education of Advocates in the Northern Netherlands (1575–1800)." *Tijdschrift voor Rechtsgeschiedenis / Revue d'Histoire du Droit / The Legal History Review* 65:4 (1997), 423–57.
Aldrete, Gregory S. *Gestures and Acclamations in Ancient Rome*. Baltimore: Johns Hopkins University Press, 1999.
Alessio, Gian Carlo. "Il commento di Jacques di Dinant all 'Rhetorica ad Herennium.'" *Studi medievali*, 3rd series, 35:2 (1994), 853–94.
Allen, Danielle S. *The World of Prometheus*. Princeton: Princeton University Press, 2009.
Altea, Maria Grazia Merello. *Scienza e professione legale nel secolo XI: ricerche e appunti*. Milano: A. Giuffrè, 1979.
Anders, Diana Elizabeth. "The Therapeutic Turn in International Humanitarian Law: War Crimes Tribunals as Sites of 'Healing'?" PhD diss. University of California, Berkeley, 2012.
Anderson, J. M. *The Honorable Burden of Public Office: English Humanists and Tudor Politics in the Sixteenth Century*. New York: Peter Lang, 2010.
Ammann, Hartmann. "Der Innsbrucker Hexenprocess von 1485." *Zeitschrift des Ferdinandeums für Tirol und Vorarlberg*, ser. 3, 34 (1890), 1–87.
Archer, Jayne Elisabeth, Elizabeth Goldring, and Sarah Knight, eds. *The Intellectual and Cultural World of the Early Modern Inns of Court*. Manchester: Manchester University Press, 2013.
Aubenas, Roger J. *La sorcière et l'inquisiteur: épisode de l'Inquisition en Provence*, 1439. Aix-en-Provence: La Pensée universitaire, 1956.
Bablitz, Leanne. *Actors and Audience in the Roman Courtroom*. London: Routledge, 2007.
Bablitz, Leanne. "Roman Society in the Courtroom." In *The Oxford Handbook of Social Relations in the Roman World*. Ed. Michael Peachin. Oxford: Oxford University Press, 2011, 317–34.
Bailey, Mark. *The English Manor c.1200–1500*. Manchester: Manchester University Press, 2002.
Baker, John H. "750 Years of Law at Cambridge: A Brief History of the Faculty of Law, to Commemorate the Opening of the New Building" [pamphlet]. Cambridge: Faculty of Law, University of Cambridge, 1996.
Baker, John H. *Collected Papers on English Legal History*. 3 vols. Cambridge: Cambridge University Press, 2013.
Baker, John H. *The Common Law Tradition: Lawyers, Books and the Law*. London: Hambledon Press, 2000.
Baker, John H. *Legal Education in London, 1250–1850*. London: Selden Society, 2007.
Baker, John H. *Manual of Law French*. Aldershot: Scolar Press, 1990.
Baker, John H. *The Order of Serjeants at Law*. London: Selden Society, 1984.
Baker, John H. *Oxford History of the Laws of England, Vol. 6: 1483–1558*. Oxford: Oxford University Press, 2003.

Baker, John H. *Readers and Readings in the Inns of Court and Chancery*. London: Selden Society, 2000.

Baker, John H. *The Third University of England: The Inns of Court and the Common-Law Tradition*. London: Selden Society, 1990.

Baker, John H., and Samuel E. Thorne, eds. *Readings and Moots at the Inns of Court in the Fifteenth Century*. 2 vols. London: Selden Society, 1954–90.

Balbo, Andrea. "Between Real and Fictional Eloquence: Some Observations on the *Actio* of Porcius Latro and Albucius Silus." In Dinter, Guérin, and Martinho, eds. *Reading Roman Declamation*, 134–47.

Balbo, Andrea. "Traces of *Actio* in Fragmentary Roman Orators." In Gray, et al., eds. *Reading Republican Oratory*, 227–46.

Balme, Christopher B. *The Cambridge Introduction to Theatre Studies*. Cambridge: Cambridge University Press, 2008.

Barish, Jonas A. *The Antitheatrical Prejudice*. Berkeley: University of California Press, 1981.

Bartlett, Robert. *Trial by Fire and Water: The Medieval Judicial Ordeal*. Oxford: Oxford University Press, 1988.

Barton, J. L. "The Legal Faculties of Late Medieval Oxford." In *History of the University of Oxford, Vol. 2: Late Medieval Oxford*. Eds. J. I. Catto and Ralph Evans. Oxford: Oxford University Press, 1993, 281–313.

Barzman, Karen-edis. *The Limits of Identity: Early Modern Venice, Dalmatia, and the Representation of Difference*. Leiden: Brill, 2017.

Beckwith, Sarah. "Ritual, Church and Theatre: Medieval Dramas of the Sacramental Body." In *Culture and History, 1350–1600: Essays on English Communities, Identities and Writing*. Ed. David Aers. New York: Harvester Wheatsheaf, 1992, 65–89.

Bellamy, John G. *Criminal Law and Society in Late Medieval and Tudor England*. New York: St. Martin's Press, 1984.

Bellamy, John G. *The Criminal Trial in Later Medieval England: Felony before the Courts from Edward I to the Sixteenth Century*. Toronto: University of Toronto Press, 1998.

Bellomo, Manlio. *The Common Legal Past of Europe, 1000–1800*. Trans. Lydia G. Cochrane. Washington, DC: Catholic University of America Press, 1995.

Berman, Harold. *Law and Revolution: The Formation of the Western Legal Tradition*. Cambridge: Harvard University Press, 1983.

Berry, D. H., and Andrew Erskine, eds. *Form and Function in Roman Oratory*. Cambridge: Cambridge University Press, 2010.

Berry, Herbert. *The Noble Science: A Study and Transcription of Sloane Ms. 2530, Papers of the Masters of Defence of London, Temp. Henry VIII to 1590*. Newark: University of Delaware Press, 1991.

Bers, Victor. "Dikastic Thorubos." *History of Political Thought* 6:1/2 (1985), 1–15.

Bers, Victor. *Genos Dikanikon: Amateur and Professional Speech in the Courtrooms of Classical Athens*. Washington, DC: Center for Hellenic Studies, 2009.

Bers, Victor. "Performing the Speech in Athenian Courts and Assembly Adjusting to Fit the *Bēma*?" In Kremmydas, Powell, and Rubinstein, eds., *Profession and Performance*, 27–40.

Biet, Christian. *Oedipe en monarchie: tragédie et théorie juridique à l'âge classique*. Paris: Klincksieck, 1994.

Biet, Christian, and Laurence Schifano, eds. *Représentations du procès: droit, théâtre, littérature, cinéma*. Nanterre: Université Paris X-Nanterre, 2003.

Blanchard, Joël, ed. *Procès politiques au temps de Louis XI: Armagnac et Bourgogne*. Geneva: Droz, 2016.

Bland, D. S., ed. *Early Records of Furnival's Inn*. Newcastle upon Tyne: Department of Extra-Mural Studies King's College, 1957.

Bland, D. S. "Rhetoric and the Law Student in Sixteenth-Century England." *Studies in Philology* 54 (1957), 498–508.

Blank, Daniel. "Actors, Orators, and the Boundaries of Drama in Elizabethan Universities." *Renaissance Quarterly* 70 (2017), 513–47.

Blanshard, Alastair J. L. "The Permeable Spaces of the Athenian Law-Court." In *Space, Place, and Landscape in Ancient Greek Literature and Culture*. Eds. Kate Gilhuly and Nancy Worman. Cambridge: Cambridge University Press, 2014, 240–76.

Boegehold, Alan L. *When a Gesture Was Expected: A Selection of Examples from Archaic and Classical Greek Literature*. Princeton: Princeton University Press, 1999.

Boegehold, Alan L. *The Lawcourts at Athens: Sites, Buildings, Equipment, Procedure, and Testimonia*. Athens: American School of Classical Studies at Athens, 1995.

Bonner, Stanley F. *Education in Ancient Rome*. New York: Routledge, 2012.

Boas, Frederick S. *University Drama in the Tudor Age*. Oxford: Clarendon Press, 1914.

Boes, Maria R. *Crime and Punishment in Early Modern Germany: Courts and Adjudicatory Practices in Frankfurt am Main, 1562–1696*. Farnham, Surrey, England: Ashgate, 2013.

Bons, Jeroen, and Robert Taylor Lane. "*Institutio Oratoria* VI.2: On Emotion." In Tellegen-Couperus, ed. *Quintilian and the Law*, 129–44.

Borrowman, Shane. "The Islamization of Rhetoric: Ibn Rushd and the Reintroduction of Aristotle into Medieval Europe." *Rhetoric Review* 27:4 (2008), 341–360.

Bossard, Eugène, ed. *Gilles de Rais: maréchal de France, dit Barbe-Bleue (1404–1440)*. Paris: H. Champion, 1886.

Bouhafa, Feriel. "Rhetoric in the Court: Averroes on Testimonial Witnessing and Oaths." In Woerther, ed. *Commenting on Aristotle's Rhetoric*, 64–88.

Bouhaïk-Gironès, Marie. *Les clercs de la Basoche et le théâtre comique (Paris, 1420–1550)*. Paris: Honoré Champion, 2007.

Bourquelot, Emile. *Jean de Jandun et ses oeuvres*. Paris: Alphonse Picard et Fils, 1908.

Bove, Laurent, et al., eds. *Théâtre & justice*. Paris: Quintette, 1991.

Bowes, John. *Richard Brathwait: The First Lakeland Poet*. Ings, Cumbria: Hugill, 2007.

Brand, Paul A. *Kings, Barons, and Justices: The Making and Enforcement of Legislation in Thirteenth-Century England*. Cambridge: Cambridge University Press, 2003.

Brand, Paul A. *The Origins of the English Legal Profession*. Oxford: Blackwell, 1992.

Brasington, Bruce C. *Order in the Court: Medieval Procedural Treatises in Translation*. Leiden: Brill, 2016.

Brenet, Jean-Baptiste. *Transferts du sujet: la noétique d'Averroës selon Jean de Jandun*. Paris: Vrin, 2003.

Brockliss, L. W. B. *The University of Oxford: A History*. Oxford: Oxford University Press, 2016.

Broedel, Hans Peter. *The Malleus Maleficarum and the Construction of Witchcraft: Theology and Popular Belief*. Manchester: Manchester University Press, 2003.

Brooks, C. W. *Law, Politics and Society in Early Modern England*. Cambridge: Cambridge University Press, 2008.

Brooks, C. W. *Pettyfoggers and Vipers of the Commonwealth: The 'Lower Branch' of the Legal Profession in Early Modern England*. Cambridge: Cambridge University Press, 1986.

Brownlee, Peter. "The Administration of Justice in Ancient Athens and in Plato's Laws—Some Comparisons." *Politics* 12:1 (1977), 116–20.

Brundage, James A. "The Ethics of the Legal Profession: Medieval Canonists and Their Clients." *Jurist* 33:2 (1973), 237–48.

Brundage, James A. "The Medieval Advocate's Profession." *Law and History Review* 6:2 (Autumn, 1988), 439–464.

Brundage, James A. *Medieval Canon Law*. London: Routledge, Taylor and Francis, 2014.

Brundage, James A. *The Medieval Origins of the Legal Profession: Canonists, Civilians, and Courts*. Chicago: University of Chicago Press, 2008.

Brundage, James A. "'My Learned Friend': Professional Etiquette in Medieval Courtrooms." In *Readers, Texts, and Compilers in the Earlier Middle Ages: Studies in Medieval Canon Law in Honour of Linda Fowler-Magerl*. Eds. Martin Brett and Kathleen G. Cushing. Farnham, Surrey: Ashgate, 2009, 183–96.

Brundage, James A. *The Profession and Practice of Medieval Canon Law*. Burlington, VT: Ashgate/Variorum, 2004.

Buckler, John. "Demosthenes and Aeschines." In *Demosthenes: Statesman and Orator*. Ed. Ian Worthington. New York: Routledge, 2000, 114–58.

Bullough, Donald A. *Alcuin: Achievement and Reputation: Being Part of the Ford Lectures Delivered in Oxford in Hilary Term 1980*. Leiden: Brill, 2004.

Butler, Martin. "The Legal Masque: Humanity and Liberty at the Inns of Court." In Hutson, ed. *Oxford Handbook of English Law and Literature*, 180–97.

Buxton, Richard G. A. *Persuasion in Greek Tragedy: A Study of Peitho*. Cambridge: Cambridge University Press, 1982.

Bynum, Caroline Walker. *Wonderful Blood: Theology and Practice in Late Medieval Northern Germany and Beyond*. Philadelphia: University of Pennsylvania Press, 2007.

Callan, Maeve Brigid. *The Templars, the Witch, and the Wild Irish: Vengeance and Heresy in Medieval Ireland*. Ithaca: Cornell University Press, 2015.

Camargo, Martin. *Ars dictaminis, ars dictandi*. Turnhout: Brepols, 1991.

Camargo, Martin. "Special Delivery: Were Medieval Letter Writers Trained in Performance?" In Carruthers, ed. *Rhetoric Beyond Words*, 173–189.

Caplan, Harry. "Classical Rhetoric and the Mediaeval Theory of Preaching." *Classical Philology* 28:2 (1933), 73–96.

Carbonnières, Louis de. *La procédure devant la chambre criminelle du parlement de Paris au XIVe siècle*. Paris: Champion, 2004.

Carruthers, Mary, ed. *Rhetoric Beyond Words: Delight and Persuasion in the Arts of the Middle Ages*. Cambridge: Cambridge University Press, 2010.

Carsten, Stahn. *Justice as Message: Expressivist Foundations of International Criminal Justice*. Oxford: Oxford University Press, 2020.

Carrión, María M. *Subject Stages: Marriage, Theatre, and the Law in Early Modern Spain*. Toronto: University of Toronto Press, 2010.

Cartledge, Paul. "'Deep Plays': Theatre as Process in Greek Civic Life." In *The Cambridge Companion to Greek Tragedy*. Ed. P. E. Easterling. Cambridge: Cambridge University Press, 1997, 3–35.

Casamento, Alfredo, and Gianna Petrone, eds. *Lo spettacolo della giustizia: le orazioni di Cicerone*. Palermo: Flaccovia, 2006.

Cavallar, Osvaldo, and Julius Kirshner. *Jurists and Jurisprudence in Medieval Italy: Texts and Contexts*. Toronto: University of Toronto Press, 2020.

Caviness, Madeline H. "Giving 'The Middle Ages' a Bad Name: Blood Punishments in the Sachsenspiegel and Town Lawbooks." *Studies in Iconography* 34 (2013), 175–235.

Caviness, Madeline H. "Putting the Judge in his P(a)lace: Pictorial Authority in the Sachsenspiegel." *Österreichische Zeitschrift für Kunst und Denkmalpflege* 54 (2000), 308–320.

Caviness, Madeline H. *Visualizing Women in the Middle Ages: Sight, Spectacle, and Scopic Economy*. Philadelphia: University of Pennsylvania Press, 2001.

Caviness, Madeline H., and Charles G. Nelson. *Women and Jews in the Sachsenspiegel Picture-Books*. Turnhout: Brepols/Harvey Miller, 2018.

Chang, Ku-ming (Kevin). "From Oral Disputation to Written Text: The Transformation of the Dissertation in Early Modern Europe." *History of Universities* 19:2 (2004), 129–87.

Cheyney, Edward P. "The Court of the Star Chamber." *The American Historical Review* 18:4 (July 1913), 727–50.

Chiffoleau, Jacques. *Les justices du pape: délinquance et criminalité dans la région d'Avignon au quatorzième siècle*. Paris: Publications de la Sorbonne, 1984.

Clanchy, M. T. *From Memory to Written Record, England 1066–1307*. 3rd ed. Malden, MA: Wiley-Blackwell, 2013.

Clarke, Peter D. "Western Canon Law in the Central and Later Middle Ages." In *The Oxford Handbook of European Legal History*. Eds. Markus D. Dubber, Mark Godfrey, and Heikki Pihlajamäki. Oxford: Oxford University Press, 2018, 265–286.

Clopper, Lawrence M. *Drama, Play, and Game: English Festive Culture in the Medieval and Early Modern Period*. Chicago: University of Chicago Press, 2001.

Cobban, Alan B. *The Medieval English Universities: Oxford and Cambridge to c.1500*. London: Routledge, 2017.

Cohen, Esther. *The Crossroads of Justice: Law and Culture in Late Medieval France*. Leiden: Brill, 1993.

Cohen, Esther. "'To Die a Criminal for the Public Good': The Execution Ritual in Late Medieval Paris." In *Law, Custom, and the Social Fabric in Medieval Europe*. Eds. Bernard S. Bachrach and David Nicholas. Kalamazoo, MI: Western Michigan University Press, 1990, 285–304.

Collins, Samuel W. *The Carolingian Debate over Sacred Space*. New York: Palgrave Macmillan, 2012.

Connell, W. J., and G. Constable, eds. *Sacrilege and Redemption in Renaissance Florence: The Case of Antonio Rinaldeschi*. Toronto: Centre for Reformation and Renaissance Studies, 2008.

Connolly, Joy. *The State of Speech: Rhetoric and Political Thought in Ancient Rome*. Princeton: Princeton University Press, 2007.

Copeland, Rita. "Pathos and Pastoralism: Aristotle's *Rhetoric* in Medieval England." *Speculum* 89: 1 (Jan 2014), 96–127.

Copeland, Rita. *Rhetoric, Hermeneutics, and Translation in the Middle Ages: Academic Traditions and Vernacular Texts*. Cambridge: Cambridge University Press, 1991.

Copeland, Rita, and Ineke Sluiter, eds. *Medieval Grammar and Rhetoric*. Oxford: Oxford University Press, 2009.

Corbeill, Anthony. "Physical Excess as a Marker of Genre in the Elder Seneca." In Dinter, Guérin, and Martinho, eds. *Reading Roman Declamation*, 115–33.

Corbellari, Alain. *La voix des clercs: littérature et savoir universitaire autour des dits du XIIIe siècle*. Geneva: Droz, 2005.

Cormack, Bradin. *A Power to Do Justice: Jurisdiction, English Literature, and the Rise of Common Law, 1509–1625*. Chicago: University of Chicago Press, 2007.

Cormack, Bradin. "Locating The Comedy of Errors." In Archer, Goldring, and Knight, eds. *Intellectual and Cultural World of the Early Modern Inns of Court*, 264–85.

Corrigan, Brian Jay. *Playhouse Law in Shakespeare's World*. Madison, NJ: Fairleigh Dickinson University Press, 2004.

Costello, William T. *The Scholastic Curriculum at Early Seventeenth-Century Cambridge.* Cambridge: Harvard University Press, 1958.

Courtenay, William J., and Karl B. Shoemaker. "The Tears of Nicholas: Simony and Perjury by a Parisian Master of Theology in the Fourteenth Century." *Speculum* 83:3 (2008), 603–28.

Cox, Virginia. "Ciceronian Rhetoric in Italy, 1260–1350." *Rhetorica: A Journal of the History of Rhetoric* 17:3 (Summer 1999), 239–88.

Cox, Virginia. "Ciceronian Rhetoric in Late Medieval Italy." In Cox and Ward, eds. *Rhetoric of Cicero in Its Medieval and Early Renaissance Commentary Tradition*, 109–135.

Cox, Virginia, and John O. Ward, eds. *The Rhetoric of Cicero in its Medieval and Early Renaissance Commentary Tradition.* Leiden: Brill, 2006.

Crawley, Charles. *Trinity Hall: The History of a Cambridge College 1350–1975.* Cambridge: The College, 1976.

Crouzet-Pavan, Elisabeth. "Emotions in the Heart of the City: Crime and its Punishment in Renaissance Italy." In *Violence and Emotions in Early Modern Europe.* Eds. Susan Broomhall and Sarah Finn. London: Routledge, 2016, 21–35.

Cunningham, Karen. *Imaginary Betrayals: Subjectivity and the Discourses of Treason in Early Modern England.* Philadelphia: University of Pennsylvania Press, 2002.

Cunningham, Karen. "'So Many Books, So Many Rolls of Ancient Time': The Inns of Court and Gorboduc." In *Solon and Thespis: Law and Theatre in the English Renaissance.* Ed. Dennis Kezar. Notre Dame: University of Notre Dame Press, 2007, 197–217.

Curran, Kevin. *Shakespeare's Legal Ecologies.* Evanston, IL: Northwestern University Press, 2017.

Cushman, Stephen, and Roland Greene, eds. *The Princeton Handbook of Poetic Terms.* 3rd ed. Princeton: Princeton University Press, 2016.

David, Jean-Michel. *Le patronat judiciaire au dernier siècle de la République romaine.* Rome: École française de Rome, 1992.

Davies, Glenys. "Togate Statues and Petrified Orators." In Berry and Erskine, eds. *Form and Function in Roman Oratory*, 51–72.

Davies, Wendy, and Paul Fouracre, eds. *The Settlement of Disputes in Early Medieval Europe.* Cambridge: Cambridge University Press, 1986.

Davis, James. "Spectacular Death: Capital Punishment in Medieval English Towns." In *Death in Medieval Europe: Death Scripted and Death Choreographed.* Ed. Joëlle Rollo-Koster. New York: Routledge, 2017, 144–62.

Dean, Trevor. *Crime in Medieval Europe: 1200–1550.* New York: Routledge, 2014.

Dean, Trevor. "Criminal Justice in Mid-Fifteenth-Century Bologna." In *Crime, Society and the Law in Renaissance Italy.* Eds. Trevor Dean and K. J. P. Lowe. Cambridge: Cambridge University Press, 1994, 16–39.

Deane, Jennifer Kolpacoff. *A History of Medieval Heresy and Inquisition.* Lanham, MD: Rowman & Littlefield, 2011.

De Angelis, Francesco, ed. *Spaces of Justice in the Roman World.* Leiden: Brill, 2010.

De Ceglia, Francesco Paolo, ed. *The Body of Evidence: Corpses and Proofs in Early Modern European Medicine.* Leiden: Brill, 2020.

De Ceglia, Francesco Paolo. "Saving the Phenomenon: Why Corpses Bled in the Presence of their Murderer in Early Modern Science." In De Ceglia, ed. *Body of Evidence*, 23–52.

Deimling, Barbara. "The Courtroom: From Church Portal to Town Hall." In *The History of Courts and Procedure in Medieval Canon Law.* Eds. Wilfried Hartmann and Kenneth Pennington. Washington, DC: Catholic University of America Press, 2016, 30–50.

Delachenal, Roland. *Histoire des avocats au Parlement de Paris, 1300–1600.* Paris: E. Plon and Nourrit et cie, 1885.
Del Mar, Maksymilian. "Ludic Legal Pedagogy: Mooting in Early Modern England." In *Law and Poetics in Early Modern England and Beyond.* Ed. Subha Mukherji. Basingstoke, Hampshire: Palgrave, 2022 (forthcoming).
Dente, Carla. "Renaissance Actors and Lawyers: Instability of Texts and of Social Trafficking: *The Comedy of Errors.*" *Pólemos* 8:2 (2014), 309–20.
Dershowitz, Alan M. "Life is not a Dramatic Narrative." In *Law's Stories: Narrative and Rhetoric in the Law.* Eds. Peter Brooks and Paul Gewirtz. New Haven: Yale University Press, 1996, 99–105.
Deuel, Leo. *Testaments of Time: The Search for Lost Manuscripts and Records.* New York: Knopf, 1965.
Dillon, Janette. *The Language of Space in Court Performance, 1400–1625.* Cambridge: Cambridge University Press, 2010.
Dinter, Martin T., Charles Guérin, and Marcos Martinho, eds. *Reading Roman Declamation: Seneca the Elder.* Oxford: Oxford University Press, 2020.
Dionne, Valérie M., and Michael Meere, eds. "Staging Justice in Early Modern France." [Special issue.] *Early Modern French Studies*, 42:2 (2020), 105–217.
Dodwell, C. R. *Anglo-Saxon Gestures and the Roman Stage.* Cambridge: Cambridge University Press, 2000.
Doig, Allan. "Charlemagne's Palace Chapel at Aachen: Apocalyptic and Apotheosis." In *Bishop Robert Grosseteste and Lincoln Cathedral: Tracing Relationships between Medieval Concepts of Order and Built Form.* Eds. Nicholas Temple, John Shannon Hendrix, and Christian Frost. Farnham, Surrey: Ashgate, 2014, 179–200.
Doig, Allan. *A History of the Church Through Its Buildings.* Oxford: Oxford University Press, 2021.
Donavin, Georgina, and Denise Stodola, eds. *Public Declamations: Essays on Medieval Rhetoric, Education, and Letters in Honour of Martin Camargo.* Turnhout: Brepols, 2015.
Dow, Jamie. *Passions and Persuasion in Aristotle's Rhetoric.* Oxford: Oxford University Press, 2015.
Dülmen, Richard van. *Theatre of Horror: Crime and Punishment in Early Modern Germany.* Trans. Elisabeth Neu. Cambridge: Polity Press, 1990.
Duncan, Anne. *Performance and Identity in the Classical World.* Cambridge: Cambridge University Press, 2006.
Dunne, Derek. *Shakespeare, Revenge Tragedy and Early Modern Law.* Basingstoke, Hampshire: Palgrave Macmillan, 2016.
Dyson, Jessica. *Staging Authority in Caroline England: Prerogative, Law and Order in Drama, 1625–1642.* Farnham, Surrey: Ashgate, 2013.
Easterling, Pat. "Actors and Voices: Reading Between the Lines in Aeschines and Demosthenes." In Goldhill and Osborne, eds., *Performance Culture and Athenian Democracy*, 154–65.
Eden, Kathy. "Forensic Rhetoric and Humanist Education." In Hutson, ed. *Oxford Handbook of English Law and Literature*, 23–40.
Eden, Kathy. *Poetic and Legal Fiction in the Aristotelian Tradition.* Princeton: Princeton University Press, 1986.
Edgerton, Samuel. *Pictures and Punishment: Art and Criminal Prosecution During the Florentine Renaissance.* Ithaca: Cornell University Press, 1985.
Edwards, Catharine. *The Politics of Immorality in Ancient Rome.* Cambridge: Cambridge University Press, 1993.

Edwards, Mike. "*Hypokritēs* in Action: Delivery in Greek Rhetoric." In Kremmydas, Powell, and Rubinstein, eds., *Profession and Performance*, 15–25.

Elsky, Stephanie. *Custom, Common Law, and the Constitution of English Renaissance Literature*. Oxford: Oxford University Press, 2020.

Elton, W. R. *Shakespeare's Troilus and Cressida and the Inns of Court Revels*. New York: Routledge, 2016.

Enders, Jody. "Rhetoric and Comedy." In MacDonald, ed. *Oxford Handbook of Rhetorical Studies*, 365–74.

Enders, Jody. *Rhetoric and the Origins of Medieval Drama*. Ithaca: Cornell University Press, 1992.

Enterline, Lynn. *Shakespeare's Schoolroom: Rhetoric, Discipline, Emotion*. Philadelphia: University of Pennsylvania Press, 2012.

Evans, Richard J. *Rituals of Retribution: Capital Punishment in Germany, 1600–1987*. New York: Oxford University Press, 1996.

Exenberger, Andreas, ed. *Ein Fels in der Brandung? Bischof Golser und der Innsbrucker Hexenprozess von 1485*. Kufstein: IMT-Verlag, 2015.

Farenga, Vincent. *Citizen and Self in Ancient Greece: Individuals Performing Justice and the Law*. Cambridge: Cambridge University Press, 2006.

Fantham, Elaine. *Roman Readings: Roman Response to Greek Literature from Plautus to Statius and Quintilian*. New York: De Gruyter, 2010.

Feingold, Mordechai. "The Humanities." In *The History of the University of Oxford [Vol. 4]: Seventeenth-Century Oxford*. Ed. Nicholas Tyacke. Oxford: Clarendon Press, 1997, 211–358.

Felipe, Donald. "Burden of Proof in Post-Medieval Disputation: Early Leibniz and Disputation Handbooks." In *Early Modern Disputations and Dissertations in an Interdisciplinary and European Context*. Eds. Meelis Friedenthal, Hanspeter Marti, and Robert Seidel. Leiden: Brill, 2021, 34–64.

Filmer, Reginald Mead. *A Chronicle of Kent 1250–1760*. London: Clear Copies, 1967.

Finkelpearl, Philip J. "The Use of the Middle Temple's Christmas Revels in Marston's 'The Fawne.'" *Studies in Philology* 64:2 (April 1967), 199–209.

Fitzgerald, Percy. *Picturesque London*. London: Ward & Downey, 1890.

Folch, Marcus. *The City and the Stage: Performance, Genre, and Gender in Plato's Laws*. Oxford: Oxford University Press, 2015.

Fortenbaugh, William W. "Theophrastus on Delivery." In *Theophrastus of Eresus: On His Life and Work*. Vol. 2. Eds. William W. Fortenbaugh, Pamela M. Huby, and Anthony A. Long. New Brunswick: Transaction Publishers, 1985, 269–88.

Foss, Edward. *Memories of Westminster Hall*. 2 vols. New York: J. Cockcroft, 1874.

Foucault, Michel. *Discipline and Punish: The Birth of the Prison*. Trans. Alan Sheridan. 2nd Vintage ed. New York: Vintage, 1995.

Fowler-Magerl, Linda. *Ordines Iudiciarii and Libelli de Ordine Iudiciorum (From the Middle of the Twelfth to the End of the Fifteenth Century)*. Turnhout: Brepols, 1994.

Fransen, Gérard. "Les questions disputées dans les facultés de droit." In *Les Questions disputées et les questions quodlibétiques dans les facultés de théologie, de droit et de médecine*. Eds. Bernardo C. Bazàn, et al. Turnhout: Brepols, 1985, 225–77.

Fraser, Veronica. "The Influence of the Venerable Bede on the Fourteenth-Century Occitan Treatise *Las Leys d'Amors*." *Rhetorica* 11:1 (Winter 1993), 51–61.

Freda, Dolores. "Legal Education in England and Continental Europe between the Middle Ages and the Early Modern Period: A Comparison." In *Comparative Legal History*. Eds.

Aniceto Masferrer, Kjell A. Modéer, and Olivier Moreteau. Cheltenham, UK: Edward Elgar, 2019, 242–60.

Fredborg, Karin Margareta. "Petrus Helias's *Summa* on Cicero's *De Inventione*." *Traditio* 64 (2009), 139–82.

Fried, Johannes. "Awaiting the Last Days... Myth and Disenchantment." In *Apocalyptic Time*. Ed. Albert I. Baumgarten. Leiden: Brill, 2000, 283–303.

Fried, Johannes. *Charlemagne*. Trans. Peter Lewis. Cambridge: Harvard University Press, 2016.

Friedland, Paul. *Seeing Justice Done: The Age of Spectacular Capital Punishment in France*. Oxford: Oxford University Press, 2012.

Fudge, Thomas A. "Jan Hus at Calvary: The Text of an Early Fifteenth-Century 'Passio.'" *Journal of Moravian History* 11 (Fall 2011), 45–81.

Fudge, Thomas A. *Medieval Religion and its Anxieties: History and Mystery in the Other Middle Ages*. New York: Palgrave Macmillan, 2016.

Fumaroli, Marc. *L'âge de l'éloquence: rhétorique et "res literaria" de la Renaissance au seuil de l'époque classique*. Paris: Champion, 1980.

Fumaroli, Marc. "Le corps éloquent: une somme d'*actio et pronuntiatio rhetorica* au XVIIe siècle; les *Vacationes autumnales* du P. Louis de Cressolles (1620)." In Fumaroli, ed., "Rhétorique du geste et de la voix à l'âge classique," 237–64.

Fumaroli, Marc. *L'école du silence: le sentiment des images au XVIIe siècle*. Paris: Flammarion, 1994.

Fumaroli, Marc, ed. "Rhétorique du geste et de la voix à l'âge classique." [Special issue.] *XVIIe siècle*, 33(3):132 (July–Sept. 1981), 235–368.

Furley, Robert. *A History of the Weald of Kent*. Ashford: H. Igglesden, et al., 1871–74.

Gagarin, Michael, and David Cohen, eds. *The Cambridge Companion to Ancient Greek Law*. Cambridge: Cambridge University Press, 2005

Gallone, Paolo. *Organisation judiciaire et procédure devant les cours laïques du Pays de Vaud à l'époque savoyarde (XIIIe-XVIe siècle)*. Lausanne: Bibliothèque historique vaudoise, 1972.

Galvez, Marisa. "From the *Costuma d'Agen* to the *Leys d'Amors*: A Reflection on Customary Law, the University of Toulouse, and the *Consistori de La Sobregaia Companhia del Gay Saber*." *Tenso* 26:1–2 (Spring-Fall 2011), 30–51.

Ganshof, François-Louis. *Frankish Institutions Under Charlemagne*. Trans. Bryce Lyon and Mary Lyon. Providence: Brown University Press, 1968.

Garapon, Antoine. *L'âne portant des reliques: essai sur le rituel judiciaire*. Paris: Le Centurion, 1985.

Garbini, Paolo. "Boncompagno da Signa da retore a storiografo." *Reti medievali rivista* 19:1 (2018), 556–70.

García y García, Antonio. "The Faculties of Law." In *A History of the University in Europe, Vol. 1: Universities in the Middle Ages*. Ed. H. de Ridder-Symoens. Cambridge: Cambridge University Press, 1992, 388–408.

Garrison, Mary. "'Quid Hinieldus cum Christo?'" In *Latin Learning and English Lore: Studies in Anglo-Saxon Literature for Michael Lapidge, Vol. 1*. Eds. Katherine O'Brien O'Keeffe and Andy Orchard. Toronto: University of Toronto Press, 2005, 237–59.

Gauvard, Claude. "Pendre et dépendre à la fin du Moyen Âge: les exigences d'un rituel judiciaire." In *Riti e rituali nelle società medievali*. Eds. Jacques Chiffoleau, Lauro Martines, and Agostino Paravicini Bagliani. Spoleto: Centro italiano di studi sull'alto Medioevo, 1994, 191–211.

Geng, Penelope. *Communal Justice in Shakespeare's England: Drama, Law, and Emotion.* Toronto: University of Toronto Press, 2021.

Gernet, Louis. *Recherches sur le développement de la pensée juridique et morale en Grèce.* Paris: Ernest Leroux, 1917.

Gewirtz, Paul. "Narrative and Rhetoric in the Law." In *Law's Stories: Narrative and Rhetoric in the Law.* Eds. Peter Brooks and Paul Gewirtz. New Haven: Yale University Press, 1996, 2–13.

Girouard, Mark. "The Halls of the Elizabethan and Early Stuart Inns of Court." In Archer, Goldring, and Knight, eds. *Intellectual and Cultural World of the Early Modern Inns of Court*, 138–56.

Glare, P. G. W., ed. *Oxford Latin Dictionary.* Rev. ed. Oxford: Clarendon Press, 1983.

Gleason, Maud W. *Making Men: Sophists and Self-Presentation in Ancient Rome.* Princeton: Princeton University Press, 1995.

Gobert, R. Darren. "Historicizing Emotion: The Case of Freudian Hysteria and Aristotelian 'Purgation.'" In *Emotion, Place and Culture.* Eds. Mick Smith, et al. Burlington, VT: Ashgate, 2009, 57–76.

Gobert, R. Darren. *The Mind-Body Stage: Passion and Interaction in the Cartesian Theatre.* Stanford: Stanford University Press, 2013.

Goodrich, Peter. "Ars *Bablativa*: Ramism, Rhetoric, and the Genealogy of English Jurisprudence." In *Legal Hermeneutics: History, Theory, and Practice.* Ed. Gregory Leyh. Berkeley: University of California Press, 1992, 43–82.

Goodrich, Peter. *Imago Decidendi: On the Common Law of Images.* Leiden: Brill, 2017.

Goodrich, Peter. "Law." In *Encyclopedia of Rhetoric.* Ed. Thomas O. Sloane. Oxford: Oxford University Press, 2001, 417–26.

Goodrich, Peter. *Law in the Courts of Love: Literature and Other Minor Jurisprudences.* New York: Routledge, 1996.

Goodrich, Peter. *Legal Emblems and the Art of Law: Obiter Depicta as the Vision of Governance.* Cambridge: Cambridge University Press, 2014.

Goodrich, Peter, and Thanos Zartaloudis, eds. *The Cabinet of Imaginary Laws.* New York: Routledge, 2021.

Graf, Fritz. "Gestures and Conventions: The Gestures of Roman Actors and Orators." In *A Cultural History of Gesture: From Antiquity to the Present Day.* Eds. Jan Bremmer and Herman Roodenburg. Cambridge: Polity Press, 1991, 36–58.

Graham, Clare. *Ordering Law: The Architectural and Social History of the English Law Court to 1914.* London: Routledge, 2016.

Gray, Christa, et al., eds. *Reading Republican Oratory: Reconstructions, Contexts, Receptions.* Oxford: Oxford University Press, 2018.

Green, Richard Firth. *A Crisis of Truth: Literature and Law in Ricardian England.* Philadelphia: University of Pennsylvania Press, 1999.

Greenberg, Marissa. "Tortured Mimesis: Representing Punishment in Early Modern London." PhD diss., University of Pennsylvania, 2005.

Greenblatt, Stephen, ed. *Cultural Mobility: A Manifesto.* Cambridge: Cambridge University Press, 2010.

Greenblatt, Stephen. *The Swerve: How the World Became Modern.* New York: W. W. Norton, 2011.

Greenblatt, Stephen. "Toward a Universal Language of Motion: Reflections on a Seventeenth-Century Muscle Man." In *Choreographing History.* Ed. Susan Leigh Foster. Bloomington: Indiana University Press, 1995, 25–31.

Grendler, Paul F. *The Universities of the Italian Renaissance*. Baltimore: Johns Hopkins University Press, 2002.

Grévin, Benoît. "Boncompagno vengé ou l'infiltration des statuts communaux italiens par la rhétorique (XIIIe-début XVe siècle)." In *Les statuts communaux vus de l'extérieur dans les sociétés méditerranéennes de l'Occident (XIIe-XVe siècle)*. Ed. Didier Lett. Paris: Éditions de la Sorbonne, 2020, 225–57.

Gunderson, Erik. *Staging Masculinity: The Rhetoric of Performance in the Ancient World*. Ann Arbor: University of Michigan Press, 2000.

Hall, Edith. "Lawcourt Dramas: The Power of Performance in Greek Forensic Oratory." *Bulletin of the Institute of Classical Studies* (1995), 39–58.

Hall, Edith. *The Theatrical Cast of Athens: Interactions Between Ancient Greek Drama and Society*. Oxford: Oxford University Press, 2006.

Hall, Jon. *Cicero's Use of Judicial Theater*. Ann Arbor: University of Michigan Press, 2014.

Hall, Jon. "Roman Judges and Their Participation in the 'Theatre of Justice.'" In Papaioannou, Serafim, and da Vela, eds. *Theatre of Justice*, 243–62.

Halphen, Louis. *Charlemagne et l'Empire carolingien*. Paris: A. Michel, 1968.

Hanink, Johanna. "Courtroom Drama: Aeschines and Demosthenes." In *Lycurgan Athens and the Making of Classical Tragedy*. Cambridge: Cambridge University Press, 2014, 129–59.

Hanley, Sarah. *The Lit de Justice of the Kings of France: Constitutional Ideology in Legend, Ritual, and Discourse*. Princeton: Princeton University Press, 1983.

Hardman, Elizabeth L. *Conflicts, Confessions, and Contracts: Diocesan Justice in Late Fifteenth-Century Carpentras*. Leiden: Brill, 2016.

Hargreaves-Mawdsley, W. N. *A History of Legal Dress in Europe Until the End of the Eighteenth Century*. Oxford: Clarendon Press, 1963.

Harris, Edward M. *Aeschines and Athenian Politics*. New York: Oxford University Press, 1995.

Harris, Edward M. "Law and Oratory." In *Persuasion: Greek Rhetoric in Action*. Ed. I. Worthington. London: Routledge, 1994, 130–51.

Harris, Max. *Christ on a Donkey: Palm Sunday, Triumphal Entries, and Blasphemous Pageants*. Leeds: Arc Humanities Press, 2019.

Haskins, Charles Homer. *The Renaissance of the Twelfth Century*. Cambridge: Harvard University Press, 1955.

Haugen, Kristine. "Imagined Universities: Public Insult and the *Terrae filius* in Early Modern Oxford." *History of Universities* 16 (2001), 1–31.

Hayaert, Valérie. "The Paradoxes of Lady Justice's Blindfold." In *The Art of Law: Artistic Representations and Iconography of Law and Justice in Context, from the Middle Ages to the First World War*. Eds. Stefan Huygebaert, et al. New York: Springer, 2018, 201–21.

Helmholz, R. H. "Civilians in the Common Law Courts, 1500–1700." In *English Legal History and Its Sources: Essays in Honour of Sir John Baker*. Eds. David Ibbetson, Neil Jones, and Nigel Ramsay. Cambridge: Cambridge University Press, 2019, 342–57.

Helmholz, R. H. "Continental Law and Common Law: Historical Strangers or Companions?" *Duke Law Journal*, 6 (Dec., 1990), 1207–28.

Helmholz, R. H. "The Education of English Proctors, 1400–1640." In *Learning the Law: Teaching and the Transmission of English Law, 1150–1900*. Eds. Jonathan Bush and Alain A. Wijffels. Rio Grande, OH: Hambledon Press, 1999, 191–210.

Helmholz, R. H. *Oxford History of the Laws of England, Vol. 1: The Canon Law and Ecclesiastical Jurisdiction from 597 to the 1640s*. Oxford: Oxford University Press, 2004.

Helmholz, R. H. *Profession of Ecclesiastical Lawyers: An Historical Introduction.* Cambridge: Cambridge University Press, 2019.

Henderson, Felicity. "Erudite Satire in Seventeenth-Century England." PhD diss. Monash University, 2002.

Herman, Susan N. *Right to a Speedy and Public Trial: A Reference Guide to the United States Constitution.* Westport, CT: Greenwood, 2006.

Hesk, Jon. *Deception and Democracy in Classical Athens.* Cambridge: Cambridge University Press, 2000.

Hesk, Jon. "The Rhetoric of Anti-Rhetoric." In Goldhill and Osborne, eds., *Performance Culture and Athenian Democracy*, 201–30.

Heß, Cordelia. "Skirts and Politics: The Cistercian Monastery of Harvestehude and the Hamburg City Council." *Medieval Feminist Forum: A Journal of Gender and Sexuality* 47:2 (2012), 57–92.

Hibbitts, Bernard J. "Coming to Our Senses: Communication and Legal Expression in Performance Cultures." *Emory Law Journal* 41:4 (Fall 1992), 873–960.

Hibbitts, Bernard J. "Making Motions: The Embodiment of Law in Gesture." *The Journal of Contemporary Legal Issues* 6:1 (1995), 51–81.

Hilder, Jennifer. "The Politics of *Pronuntiatio*: The *Rhetorica ad Herennium* and Delivery in the Early First Century BC." In Gray, et al., eds. *Reading Republican Oratory*, 213–26.

Hobsbawm, Eric and Terence Ranger, ed. *The Invention of Tradition.* Cambridge: Cambridge University Press, 2012.

Hohmann, Hanns. "Ciceronian Rhetoric and the Law." In Cox and Ward, eds. *Rhetoric of Cicero in Its Medieval and Early Renaissance Commentary Tradition*, 193–207.

Hohmann, Hanns. "Rhetoric in Medieval Legal Education: Libellus Pylei Disputatorius." *Disputatio: An International Transdisciplinary Journal of the Late Middle Ages* 4 (1999), 59–73.

Holmès, Catherine E. *L'Éloquence judiciaire de 1620 à 1660: reflet des problèmes sociaux, religieux et politiques de l'époque.* Paris: A. G. Nizet, 1967.

Holsinger, Bruce W. "Analytical Survey 6: Medieval Literature and Cultures of Performance." *New Medieval Literatures* 6 (2003), 271–311.

Holsinger, Bruce W. *Music, Body, and Desire in Medieval Culture: Hildegard of Bingen to Chaucer.* Stanford: Stanford University Press, 2001.

Hornblower, Simon, Antony Spawforth, and Esther Eidinow, eds. *The Oxford Classical Dictionary*, 4th ed. Oxford: Oxford University Press, 2012.

Houllemare, Marie. *Politiques de la parole: Le Parlement de Paris au XVIe siècle.* Geneva: Droz, 2011.

Hudson, John. *Oxford History of the Laws of England, Vol. 2: 871–1216.* Oxford: Oxford University Press, 2012.

Hutson, Lorna. "Rhetoric and Law." In MacDonald, ed. *Oxford Handbook of Rhetorical Studies*, 397–408.

Hutson, Lorna. *The Invention of Suspicion: Law and Mimesis in Shakespeare and Renaissance Drama.* Oxford: Oxford University Press, 2007.

Hutson, Lorna, ed. *The Oxford Handbook of English Law and Literature, 1500–1700.* Oxford: Oxford University Press, 2017.

Huygebaert, Stefan, et al., eds. *The Art of Law: Three Centuries of Justice Depicted.* Tielt: Uitg. Lannoo N. V., 2016.

Hyams, Paul. "The Legal Revolution and the Discourse of Dispute in the Twelfth Century." In *The Cambridge Companion to Medieval English Culture.* Ed. Andrew Galloway. Cambridge: Cambridge University Press, 2011, 43–65.

Hyams, Paul. "Trial by Ordeal: The Key to Proof in the Early Common Law." In *On the Laws and Customs of England: Essays in Honor of Samuel E. Thorne*. Chapel Hill: University of North Carolina Press, 1981, 90–126.

Ingram, Martin. *Church Courts, Sex, and Marriage in England, 1570–1640*. Cambridge: Cambridge University Press, 1987.

Isham, Sir Gyles. "Historical and Literary Associations of Lamport." *Northamptonshire Past and Present* 1–2 (1948), 17–32.

James, Liz. *Mosaics in the Medieval World: From Late Antiquity to the Fifteenth Century*. Cambridge: Cambridge University Press, 2017.

Janin, Hunt. *The University in Medieval Life, 1179–1499*. Jefferson, NC: McFarland & Co, 2008.

Janko, Richard. *Aristotle on Comedy: Towards a Reconstruction of Poetics II*. London: Duckworth, 1984.

Jardine, Lisa. "Humanism and the Sixteenth Century Cambridge Arts Course." *History of Education* 4:1 (1975), 16–31.

Jeanroy, Alfred. "*Les Leys d'amors*." In *Histoire littéraire de la France, Vol. 38: Suite du quatorzième siècle*. Paris: Imprimerie nationale, 1949, 139–233.

Johnson, Eleanor. *Staging Contemplation: Participatory Theology in Middle English Prose, Verse, and Drama*. Chicago: University of Chicago Press, 2018.

Johnston, Mark D. "Ciceronian Rhetoric and Ethics: Conduct Literature and 'Speaking Well.'" In Cox and Ward, eds. *Rhetoric of Cicero in its Medieval and Early Renaissance Commentary Tradition*, 147–64.

Johnston, Mark D. "Parliamentary Oratory in Medieval Aragon." *Rhetorica* 10:2 (Spring 1992), 99–117.

Johnston, Mark D. "The Treatment of Speech in Medieval Ethical and Courtesy Literature." *Rhetorica: A Journal of the History of Rhetoric*. 4:1 (Winter 1986), 21–49.

Johnson, Tom. *Law in Common: Legal Cultures in Late-Medieval England*. Oxford: Oxford University Press, 2020.

Jolliffe, J. E. A. *The Constitutional History of Medieval England: From the English Settlement to 1485*. London: Adam and Charles Black, 1937.

Jones, Karen. *Gender and Petty Crime in Late Medieval England: The Local Courts in Kent, 1460–1560*. Woodbridge: The Boydell Press, 2006.

Jones, Malcolm. *The Secret Middle Ages*. Westport, CT: Praeger, 2002.

Joseph, B. L. *Elizabethan Acting*. London: Oxford University Press, 1951.

Jordan, William Chester. *From England to France: Felony and Exile in the High Middle Ages*. Princeton: Princeton University Press, 2015.

Kagan, Richard L. "Lawyers and Litigation in Castile, 1500–1750." In *Lawyers in Early Modern Europe and America*. Ed. Wilfrid Prest. London: Croom Helm, 1981, 181–204.

Kahn, Paul W. "Freedom, Autonomy, and the Cultural Study of Law." In *Cultural Analysis, Cultural Studies, and the Law: Moving Beyond Legal Realism*. Eds. Austin Sarat and Jonathan Simon. Durham: Duke University Press, 2003, 154–87.

Kahn, Victoria, and Lorna Hutson, eds. *Rhetoric and Law in Early Modern Europe*. New Haven: Yale University Press, 2001.

Kamali, Elizabeth Papp. *Felony and the Guilty Mind in Medieval England*. Cambridge: Cambridge University Press, 2019.

Kantorowicz, Hermann. "The *Quaestiones disputatae* of the Glossators." *Tijdschrift voor Rechtsgeschiedenis* 16 (1939), 1–67.

Kay, Sarah. *Parrots and Nightingales: Troubadour Quotations and the Development of European Poetry*. Philadelphia: University of Pennsylvania Press, 2013.

Kelley, Donald. "Jurisconsultus perfectus: The Lawyer as Renaissance Man." *Journal of the Warburg and Courtauld Institutes* 51 (1988), 84–102.

Kelly, Henry Ansgar. *Inquisitions and Other Trial Procedures in the Medieval West.* Burlington, VT: Ashgate/Variorum, 2001.

Kendon, Adam. *Gesture: Visible Action as Utterance.* Cambridge: Cambridge University Press, 2004.

Kendrick, Laura. "The *Consistori del Gay Saber* of Toulouse (1323-circa 1484)." In *The Reach of the Republic of Letters: Literary and Learned Societies in Late Medieval and Early Modern Europe.* Eds. Arjan van Dixhoorn and Susie Speakman Sutch. Leiden: Brill, 2008, 17–32.

Kennedy, George A. "Cicero's Oratorical and Rhetorical Legacy." In *Brill's Companion to Cicero: Oratory and Rhetoric.* Ed. James M. May. Leiden: Brill, 2002, 481–501.

Kennedy, George A. *Classical Rhetoric and its Christian and Secular Tradition from Ancient to Modern Times.* 2nd ed. Chapel Hill: University of North Carolina Press, 1999.

Kennedy, George A. "Forms and Functions of Latin Speech, 400–800." *Medieval and Renaissance Studies* 10 (1979), 45–73.

Kennedy, George A. *New History of Classical Rhetoric.* Princeton: Princeton University Press, 1994.

Kennedy, George A. *Quintilian.* New York: Twayne, 1969.

Kennedy, George A. *The Art of Persuasion in Ancient Greece.* Princeton: Princeton University Press, 1963.

Kennedy, George A. *The Art of Rhetoric in the Roman World, 300 B.C.–A.D. 300.* Princeton: Princeton University Press, 1972.

Kennerly, Michele, and Carly S. Woods. "Moving Rhetorica." *Rhetoric Society Quarterly* 48:1 (2018), 3–27.

Kerr, Margaret H., Richard D. Forsyth, and Michael J. Plyley. "Cold Water and Hot Iron: Trial by Ordeal in England." *The Journal of Interdisciplinary History* 22:4 (Spring, 1992), 573–95.

Kezar, Dennis, ed. *Solon and Thespis: Law and Theater in the English Renaissance.* Notre Dame: University of Notre Dame Press, 2007.

King, Pamela M. *Reading Texts for Performance and Performances as Texts: Shifting Paradigms in Early English Drama Studies.* Ed. Alexandra F. Johnson. Abington, Oxon: Routledge, 2021.

Kleinbauer, W. Eugene. "Charlemagne's Palace Chapel at Aachen and Its Copies." *Gesta* 4 (Spring 1965), 2–11.

Knafla, Louis A. "The Law Studies of an Elizabethan Student." *Huntington Library Quarterly* 32:3 (May 1969), 221–240.

Knapp, Hermann. *Das alte Nürnberger Kriminal-Verfahren bis zur Einführung der Carolina.* Berlin: L. Simion, 1891.

Knox, Dilwyn. "Ideas on Gesture and Universal Languages, c.1550–1650." In *New Perspectives on Renaissance Thought: Essays in the History of Science, Education and Philosophy in Memory of Charles B. Schmitt.* Eds. John Henry and Sarah Hutton. London: Duckworth, 1990, 101–36.

Konstan, David. "Rhetoric and Emotion." In *A Companion to Greek Rhetoric.* Ed. Ian Worthington. Oxford: Blackwell, 2007, 411–25.

Konstan, David. *The Emotions of the Ancient Greeks: Studies in Aristotle and Classical Literature.* Toronto: University of Toronto Press, 2007.

Korobkin, Donald R. "Bankruptcy Law, Ritual, and Performance." *Columbia Law Review* 103:8 (Dec. 2003), 2124–59.

Korstenko, Brian A. *Cicero, Catullus, and the Language of Social Performance*. Chicago: University of Chicago Press, 2001.

Kowaleski, Maryanne. "Town Courts in Medieval England: An Introduction." In *Town Courts and Urban Society in Late Medieval England, 1250–1500*. Eds. Richard Goddard and Teresa Phipps. Woodbridge: Boydell Press, 2019, 17–42.

Kremmydas, Christos, Jonathan Powell, and Lene Rubinstein, eds. *Profession and Performance: Aspects of Oratory in the Greco-Roman World*. London: University of London, 2013.

Labalme, Patricia H. *Bernardo Giustiniani: A Venetian of the Quattrocento*. Rome: Edizioni di Storia e Letteratura, 1969.

Labatt, Annie Montgomery. *Emerging Iconographies of Medieval Rome: A Laboratory of Images in the Eighth and Ninth Centuries*. Lanham, MD: Lexington Books, 2019.

Lada-Richards, Ismene. "Was Pantomime 'Good to Think With' in the Ancient World?" In *New Directions in Ancient Pantomime*. Eds. Edith Hall and Rosie Wyles. Oxford: Oxford University Press, 2008, 285–313.

Lada-Richards, Ismene. *Silent Eloquence: Lucian and Pantomime Dancing*. London: Duckworth, 2007.

Laks, André. "Plato's 'Truest Tragedy': Laws Book 7, 817a–d." In *Plato's 'Laws': A Critical Guide*. Ed. Christopher Bobonich. Cambridge: Cambridge University Press, 2010, 217–31.

Lang, Mabel L. *Life, Death, and Litigation in the Athenian Agora*. Princeton: American School of Classical Studies at Athens, 1994.

Langbein, John H. *Prosecuting Crime in the Renaissance: England, Germany, France*. Cambridge: Harvard University Press, 1974.

Lanni, Adriaan. *Law and Justice in the Courts of Classical Athens*. Cambridge: Cambridge University Press, 2006.

Lea, Henry Charles. *A History of the Inquisition of the Middle Ages*. 3 vols. New York: Harper, 1887.

Leader, Damian Riehl. *A History of the University of Cambridge, Vol. 1: The University to 1546*. Cambridge: Cambridge University Press, 1988.

LeCoq, Anne-Marie. "Nature et rhétorique: de l'action oratoire à l'éloquence muette (J. Bulwer)." In Fumaroli, ed., "Rhétorique du geste et de la voix à l'âge classique," 265–77.

Léglu, Catherine. "Languages in Conflict in Toulouse: 'Las Leys d'Amors.'" *Modern Language Review* 103:2 (Apr. 2008), 383–96.

Leiboff, Marett. *Towards a Theatrical Jurisprudence*. New York: Routledge, 2019.

Leiboff, Marett, and Sophie Nield, eds. *Law's Theatrical Presence*. [Special Issue: *Law, Text, Culture* 14:1] (2010).

Leigh, David J. "The Doomsday Mystery Play." *Modern Philology* 67:3 (1970), 211–23.

Leue, Friedrich Gottfried. *Der mündliche öffentliche Anklage-Prozeß und der geheime schriftliche Untersuchungs-Prozeß in Deutschland*. Aachen and Leipzig: Jacob Anton Mayer, 1840.

Levack, Brian P. *The Civil Lawyers in England, 1603–1641: A Political Study*. Oxford: Clarendon Press, 1973.

Levack, Brian P. "Law." In *History of the University of Oxford, Vol. 4: Seventeenth-Century Oxford*. Ed. Nicholas Tyacke. Oxford: Oxford University Press, 1997, 559–65.

Levenson, Laurie L. "Courtroom Demeanor: The Theater of the Courtroom." *Minnesota Law Review* 92:3 (Feb. 2008), 573–633.

Loftie, W. J. *The Inns of Court and Chancery*. London: Seeley, 1893.

MacDonald, Michael J., ed. *The Oxford Handbook of Rhetorical Studies*. Oxford: Oxford University Press, 2017.

Mack, Peter. "Declamation in Renaissance England." *Papers on Rhetoric: Proceedings of the Seminars held at the Scuola Superiore di Studi Umanistici, Bologna* 8 (2007), 129–55.

Mack, Peter. *Elizabethan Rhetoric: Theory and Practice*. Cambridge: Cambridge University Press, 2002.

Mack, Peter. *A History of Renaissance Rhetoric, 1380–1620*. Oxford: Oxford University Press, 2011.

Maier-Eichhorn, Ursula. *Die Gestikulation in Quintilians Rhetorik*. Frankfurt: P. Lang, 1989.

Maitland, Frederic William. *English Law and the Renaissance*. Cambridge: The University Press, 1901.

Makdisi, George. "The Scholastic Method in Medieval Education: An Inquiry into Its Origins in Law and Theology." *Speculum* 49:4 (1974), 640–661.

Marmo, Costantino. "Carattere dell'oratore e recitazione nel commento di Giovanni di Jandun al terzo libro della Retorica." In *Filosofia e teologia nel Trecento: studi in ricordo di Eugenio Randi*. Ed. Luca Bianchi. Louvain-la-Neuve: Fédération internationale des instituts d'études médiévales, 1994, 17–31.

Marmo, Costantino. "Retorica e motti di spirito: una 'quaestio' inedita di Giovanni di Jandun." In *Semiotica: storia, teoria, interpretazione: saggi intorno a Umberto Eco*. Eds. Patrizia Magli, et al. Milan: Bompiani, 1992, 25–41.

Marshall, Christopher W., and Stephanie Van Willigenburg. "Judging Athenian Dramatic Competitions." *Journal of Hellenic Studies* 124 (2004), 90–107.

Marshall, David L. *Vico and the Transformation of Rhetoric in Early Modern Europe*. Cambridge: Cambridge University Press, 2010.

Marshall, J. H. "Observations on the Sources of the Treatment of Rhetoric in the 'Leys d'Amors.'" *Modern Language Review* 64:1 (Jan, 1969), 39–52.

Martin, John Jeffries. "Francesco Casoni and the Rhetorical Forensics of the Body." *Journal of Medieval and Early Modern Studies* 45:1 (2015), 103–130.

Martines, Lauro. *Power and Imagination: City-States in Renaissance Italy*. Baltimore: Johns Hopkins University Press, 1988.

Marx, Peter W. "Between Metaphor and Cultural Practices: *Theatrum* and *Scena* in the German-Speaking Sphere before 1648." In Penskaya and Küpper, eds. *Theater as Metaphor*, 11–29.

Masschaele, James. "The Public Space of the Marketplace in Medieval England." *Speculum* 77:2 (2002), 383–421.

Mastroberti, Francesco. "Sul caso della tranese Giustina Rocca e sulla donna *arbiter* nella dottrina giuridica tra Medioevo ed Età Moderna." In *La donna nel diritto, nella politica e nelle istituzioni*. Eds. Francesco Mastroberti and Riccardo Pagano. Bari: Università degli Studi di Bari Aldo Moro [*Quaderni del Dipartimento Jonico*, n.1], 2015, 105–19.

Mastrorosa, Ida. "Quintilian and the Judges: Rhetorical Rules and Psychological Strategies in the 4th Book of the *Institutio Oratoria*." In Tellegen-Couperus, ed. *Quintilian and the Law*, 67–80.

Maurer, Georg Ludwig von. *Geschichte des altgermanischen und namentlich altbairischen öffentlich-mündlichen Gerichtsverfahrens*. Heidelberg: Mohn, 1824.

McBain, James. "'Attentive Mindes and Serious Wits': Legal Training and Early Drama." In Hutson, ed. *Oxford Handbook of English Law and Literature*, 80–96.

McCorkle, Ben. *Rhetorical Delivery as Technological Discourse: A Cross-Historical Study*. Carbondale and Edwardsville: Southern Illinois University Press, 2012.

McCoy, Richard C. "Law Sports and the Night of Errors: Shakespeare at the Inns of Court." In Archer, Goldring, and Knight, eds. *Intellectual and Cultural World of the Early Modern Inns of Court*, 286–301.

McKitterick, Rosamond. "Charles the Bald and the Image of Kingship." *History Today* 38:6 (June 1988), 29–36.

McKitterick, Rosamond. "A King on the Move: The Place of an Itinerant Court in Charlemagne's Government." In *Royal Courts in Dynastic States and Empires: A Global Perspective*. Eds. Jeroen Duindam, Tülay Artan, and Metin Kunt. Leiden: Brill, 2011, 145–69.

McManamon, John M. *Pierpaolo Vergerio the Elder: The Humanist as Orator*. Tempe, AZ: Medieval & Renaissance Texts & Studies, 1996.

Meens, Rob. "Sanctuary, Penance, and Dispute Settlement Under Charlemagne: The Conflict Between Alcuin and Theodulf of Orléans over a Sinful Cleric." *Speculum* 82 (2007), 277–300.

Meineck, Peter. *Theatrocracy: Greek Drama, Cognition, and the Imperative for Theatre*. London: Routledge, 2018.

Merback, Mitchell B. *The Thief, the Cross, and the Wheel: Pain and the Spectacle of Punishment in Medieval and Renaissance Europe*. Chicago: University of Chicago Press, 1999.

Metzger, Ernest. "Litigation." In *The Cambridge Companion to Roman Law*. Ed. David Johnston. New York: Cambridge University Press, 2015, 272–98.

Meyler, Bernadette. *Theaters of Pardoning*. Ithaca: Cornell University Press, 2019.

Miller, Joseph M., Michael H. Prosser, and Thomas W. Benson, eds. *Readings in Medieval Rhetoric*. Bloomington: Indiana University Press, 1973.

Miller, Maureen C. *Clothing the Clergy: Virtue and Power in Medieval Europe, c. 800–1200*. Ithaca: Cornell University Press, 2014.

Milner, Stephen J. "Communication, Consensus and Conflict: Rhetorical Precepts, the *Ars Concionandi*, and Social Ordering in Late Medieval Italy." In Ward and Cox, eds. *Rhetoric of Cicero in its Medieval and Early Renaissance Commentary Tradition*, 365–408.

Miron, Janet. *Prisons, Asylums, and the Public: Institutional Visiting in the Nineteenth Century*. Toronto: University of Toronto Press, 2011.

Mitchell, Charles. *Shakespeare and Public Execution*. Lewiston, NY: Edwin Mellen Press, 2004.

Morgan, Victor, and Christopher Brooke. *A History of the University of Cambridge, Vol. 2: 1546–1750*. Cambridge: Cambridge University Press, 2004.

Morrison, Elizabeth, and Anne D. Hedeman. *Imagining the Past in France: History in Manuscript Painting, 1250–1500*. Los Angeles: Getty Publications, 2010.

Mostert, Marco, and P. S. Barnwell, eds. *Medieval Legal Process: Physical, Spoken and Written Performance in the Middle Ages*. Turnhout: Brepols, 2011.

Mukherji, Subha. *Law and Representation in Early Modern Drama*. Cambridge: Cambridge University Press, 2006.

Musson, Anthony. *Medieval Law in Context: The Growth of Legal Consciousness from Magna Carta to the Peasants' Revolt*. Manchester: Manchester University Press, 2001.

Musson, Anthony. *Public Order and Law Enforcement: The Local Administration of Criminal Justice 1294–1350*. Woodbridge, Suffolk: Boydell Press, 1996.

Musson, Anthony. "Visualising Legal History: The Courts and Legal Profession in Image." In *English Legal History and its Sources: Essays in Honour of Sir John Baker*. Eds. David

Ibbetson, Neil Jones, and Nigel Ramsay. Cambridge: Cambridge University Press, 2019, 203–22.

Napier, A. David. *Masks, Transformation, and Paradox*. Berkeley: University of California Press, 1986.

Neilson, George. *Trial by Combat*. Glasgow: William Hodge, 1890.

Nelson, Alan H. *Early Cambridge Theatres: College, University, and Town Stages, 1464–1720*. Cambridge: Cambridge University Press, 1994.

Nelson, Alan H., and Jessica Winston. "Drama of the Inns of Court." In *A New Companion to English Renaissance Literature and Culture*. 2 vols. Ed. Michael Hattaway. Malden, MA: Wiley-Blackwell, 2010, 2:94–104.

Nelson, Janet L. *King and Emperor: A New Life of Charlemagne*. Berkeley: University of California Press, 2019.

Noble, Thomas F. X. *Images, Iconoclasm, and Carolingians*. Philadelphia: University of Pennsylvania Press, 2009.

Ober, Josiah. *Mass and Elite in Democratic Athens: Rhetoric, Ideology, and the Power of the People*. Princeton: Princeton University Press, 2009.

O'Callaghan, Michelle. "'Jests, stolne from the Temples Revels': The Inns of Court Revels and Early Modern Drama." In *Drama and Pedagogy in Medieval and Early Modern England*. Eds. Elisabeth Dutton and James McBain. Tübingen: Narr Francke Attempto, 2015, 227–52.

Ong, Walter J. "Tudor Writings on Rhetoric." *Studies in the Renaissance* 15 (1968), 39–69.

Osborn, Louise Brown. *The Life, Letters, and Writings of John Hoskyns, 1566–1638*. New Haven: Yale University Press, 1937.

Outhwaite, R. B. *The Rise and Fall of English Ecclesiastical Courts, 1500–1860*. Cambridge: Cambridge University Press, 2006.

Padoa-Schioppa, Antonio. *A History of Law in Europe: From the Early Middle Ages to the Twentieth Century*. Trans. Caterina Fitzgerald. Cambridge: Cambridge University Press, 2017.

Palmer, James T. *The Apocalypse in the Early Middle Ages*. Cambridge: Cambridge University Press, 2014.

Papaioannou, Sophia, Andreas Serafim, and Beatrice da Vela, eds. *Theatre of Justice: Aspects of Performance in Greco-Roman Oratory and Rhetoric*. Boston: Brill, 2017.

Patapios, Hieromonk. "Sub Utraque Specie: The Arguments of John Hus and Jacoubek of Stříbro in Defence of Giving Communion to the Laity Under both Kinds." *The Journal of Theological Studies*, new ser., 53:2 (2002), 503–22.

Paterson, Jeremy, and Jonathan Powell, eds. *Cicero the Advocate*. Oxford: Oxford University Press, 2004.

Paulson, Ronald. *Hogarth's Harlot: Sacred Parody in Enlightenment England*. Baltimore: Johns Hopkins University Press, 2003.

Paxson, James J. *The Poetics of Personification*. Cambridge: Cambridge University Press, 1994.

Penskaya, Elena, and Joachim Küpper, eds. *Theater as Metaphor*. Berlin: De Gruyter, 2019.

Peponi, Anastasia-Erasmia, ed. *Performance and Culture in Plato's Laws*. Cambridge: Cambridge University Press, 2013.

Pernot, Laurent. *Rhetoric in Antiquity*. Washington, DC: Catholic University of America Press, 2005, 1–56.

Perry, Lisa Anne. "Legal Handbooks as Rhetoric Books for Common Lawyers in Early Modern England." In *Learning the Law: Teaching and the Transmission of Law in*

England, 1150–1900. Eds. Jonathan A. Bush and Alain Wijffels. Rio Grande, OH: Hambledon Press, 1999, 273–85.
Perry, Lisa Anne. "Legal Rhetoric Books in England, 1600–1700." PhD. diss., University of Maryland at College Park, 1998.
Petch, Simon. "Borderline Judgments: Law or Literature?" *Australian Journal of Law & Society* 7 (1991), 3–15.
Peters, Edward. "Juristic Theology? Medieval and Early Modern European Perspectives on Crime and Punishment." In *Perspectives on Punishment: An Interdisciplinary Exploration*. Ed. Richard Mowery Andrews. New York: Peter Lang, 1996.
Peters, Edward. *Torture*. Rev. ed. Philadelphia: University of Pennsylvania Press, 1996.
Peters, Julie Stone. "Law as Performance: Historical Interpretation, Objects, Lexicons, and Other Methodological Problems." In *New Directions in Law and Literature*. Eds. Elizabeth Anker and Bernadette Meyler. New York: Routledge, 2017, 193–209.
Peters, Julie Stone. "Legal Performance Good and Bad." *Law, Culture, and the Humanities* 4:2 (Spring 2008), 179–200.
Peters, Julie Stone. "Mapping Law and Performance: Reflections on the Dilemmas of an Interdisciplinary Conjunction." In *Oxford Handbook of Law and Humanities*. Eds. Maksymilian Del Mar, Bernadette Meyler, and Simon Stern. Oxford: Oxford University Press, 2020, 199–215.
Peters, Julie Stone. "Penitentiary Performances: Spectators, Affecting Scenes, and Terrible Apparitions in the Nineteenth-Century Model Prison." In Umphrey, Douglas, and Sarat, eds., *Law and Performance*, 18–67.
Peters, Julie Stone. "Staging the Last Judgment in the Trial of Charles I." *Representations* 143 (Summer 2018), 1–35.
Peters, Julie Stone. *Theatre of the Book 1480–1880: Print, Text, and Performance in Europe*. Oxford: Oxford University Press, 2000.
Pfeiffer, Rudolf. *History of Classical Scholarship from 1300 to 1850*. Oxford: Clarendon Press, 1976.
Phillips, Seymour. *Edward II*. New Haven: Yale University Press, 2010.
Plett, Heinrich F. *Rhetoric and Renaissance Culture*. Berlin: De Gruyter, 2004.
Pohl-Zucker, Susanne. *Making Manslaughter: Process, Punishment, and Restitution in Württemberg and Zurich, 1376–1700*. Leiden: Brill, 2017.
Potter, G. R. *Zwingli*. Cambridge: Cambridge University Press, 1976.
Powell, J. G. F. "Court Procedure and Rhetorical Strategy in Cicero." In Berry and Erskine, eds. *Form and Function in Roman Oratory*, 21–36.
Prest, Wilfrid R. *The Inns of Court under Elizabeth I and the Early Stuarts 1590–1640*. Totowa, NJ: Rowman and Littlefield, 1972.
Prest, Wilfrid. *The Rise of the Barristers: A Social History of the English Bar 1590–1640*. Oxford: Clarendon Press, 1986.
Prest, Wilfrid. "William Lambarde, Elizabethan Law Reform, and Early Stuart Politics." *Journal of British Studies* 34:4 (Oct. 1995), 464–80.
Presuhn, Emil, ed. *Pompeii: Die neuesten Ausgrabungen von 1874 bis 1878*. 2nd ed. Leipzig: T. O. Weigel, 1882.
Prosperi, Adriano. *Crime and Forgiveness: Christianizing Execution in Medieval Europe*. Trans. Jeremy Carden. Cambridge: Harvard University Press, 2020.
Prosperi, Adriano. *Justice Blindfolded: The Historical Course of an Image*. Trans. John Tedeschi and Anne C. Tedeschi. Leiden: Brill, 2018.
Putnam, Bertha H. *The Place in Legal History of Sir William Shareshull, Chief Justice of the King's Bench, 1350–1361*. Cambridge: Cambridge University Press, 1950.

Rabin, Andrew. "Old English *Forespeca* and the Role of the Advocate in Anglo-Saxon Law." *Mediaeval Studies* 69 (2007), 223–53.
Raccagni, Gianluca. "Reintroducing the Emperor and Repositioning the City Republics in the 'Republican' Thought of the Rhetorician Boncompagno da Signa." *Historical Research* 86:234 (2013), 579–600.
Radin, Max. "The Right to a Public Trial." *Temple Law Quarterly* 6:3 (April 1932), 381–99.
[Rädler]-Bohn, Eva M. E. "Alcuin's Heirs: The Early Reception of Alcuin's *De rhetorica* and *De dialectica*." PhD diss. Cambridge University, 2003.
Rädler-Bohn, Eva M. E. "Re-dating Alcuin's *De dialectica*: or, Did Alcuin Teach at Lorsch?" *Anglo-Saxon England* 45 (2016), 71–104.
Raffield, Paul. "The Elizabethan Rhetoric of Signs: Representations of *Res Publica* at the Early Modern Inns of Court." *Law, Culture and the Humanities* 7:2 (2010), 244–63.
Raffield, Paul. *Shakespeare's Imaginary Constitution: Late Elizabethan Politics and the Theatre of Law*. Oxford: Hart, 2010.
Rancière, Jacques. *The Philosopher and His Poor*. Trans. John Drury, Corinne Oster, and Andrew Parker. Durham: Duke University Press, 2003.
Randall, Lilian M. C. *Images in the Margins of Gothic Manuscripts*. Berkeley: University of California Press, 1966.
Rashdall, Hastings. *Universities of Europe in the Middle Ages*. Eds. F. M. Powicke and A. B. Emden. 3 vols. Rev. ed. Oxford: Clarendon Press, 1987.
Read, Alan. *Theatre & Law*. London: Palgrave, 2016.
Redmond, Sarah N. "Staging Executions: The Theater of Punishment in Early Modern England." PhD diss., Florida State University, 2007.
Rebmann, F. "Pronuntiatio." In *Historisches Wörterbuch der Rhetorik*. Eds. Gert Ueding, et al. Tübingen: Niemeyer, 2005, vol. 7, columns 212–47.
Rembert, James A. W. *Swift and the Dialectical Tradition*. Basingstoke, Hampshire: Macmillan Press, 1988.
Remer, Gary A. *Ethics and the Orator: The Ciceronian Tradition of Political Morality*. Chicago: University of Chicago Press, 2017.
Resnik, Judith, and Dennis Curtis. *Representing Justice: Invention, Controversy, and Rights in City-States and Democratic Courtrooms*. New Haven: Yale University Press, 2011.
Riché, Pierre. *Daily Life in the World of Charlemagne*. Trans. Jo Ann McNamara. Philadelphia: University of Pennsylvania Press, 1978.
Ridder-Symoens, H. de, ed. *A History of the University in Europe, Vol. 2: Universities in Early Modern Europe (1500–1800)*. Cambridge: Cambridge University Press, 1996.
Roach, Joseph R. *Cities of the Dead: Circum-Atlantic Performance*. New York: Columbia University Press, 1996.
Roach, Joseph R. *The Player's Passion: Studies in the Science of Acting*. 2nd ed. Ann Arbor: University of Michigan Press, 1993.
Robert, Yann. *Dramatic Justice: Trial by Theater in the Age of the French Revolution*. Philadelphia: University of Pennsylvania Press, 2018.
Rodda, Joshua. *Public Religious Disputation in England, 1558–1626*. Farnham, Surrey: Ashgate, 2014.
Rodríguez Martín, José-Domingo. "Moving the Judge: A Legal Commentary on Book VI of Quintilian's *Institutio Oratoria*." In Tellegen-Couperus, ed. *Quintilian and the Law*, 157–68.
Rossi, Giovanni. "Rhetorical Role Models for 16th to 18th Century Lawyers." In Tellegen-Couperus, ed. *Quintilian and the Law*, 81–94.

Rougemont, Martine de. "L'acteur et l'orateur: étape d'un débat." In Fumaroli, ed., "Rhétorique du geste et de la voix à l'âge classique," 329–33.

Royer, Katherine. *The English Execution Narrative, 1200–1700*. London: Pickering & Chatto, 2014.

Rubinstein, Lene. *Litigation and Cooperation: Supporting Speakers in the Courts of Classical Athens*. Stuttgart: F. Steiner Verlag, 2000.

Rummel, Erika. *The Humanist-Scholastic Debate in the Renaissance & Reformation*. Cambridge: Harvard University Press, 1995.

Salonen, Kirsi. *Papal Justice in the Late Middle Ages: The Sacra Romana Rota*. London: Routledge, Taylor & Francis Group, 2016.

Salter, H. E., and W. H. Stevenson. *The Early History of St. John's College, Oxford*. Oxford: Oxford Historical Society, 1939.

Schäfer, Thomas. *Imperii insignia, sella curulis und fasces: zur Repräsentation römischer Magistrate*. Mainz: Verlag P. von Zabern, 1989.

Schechner, Richard. *Between Theater and Anthropology*. Philadelphia: University of Pennsylvania Press, 1985.

Schechner, Richard. *Performance Studies: An Introduction*. 3rd ed. New York: Routledge, 2013.

Schefold, Karl. *Die Wände Pompejis: topographisches Verzeichnis der Bildmotive*. Berlin: DeGruyter, 1957.

Schild, Wolfgang. "Der 'entliche Rechtstag' als das Theater des Rechts." In *Strafrecht, Strafprozess und Rezeption: Grundlagen, Entwicklung und Wirkung der Constitutio Criminalis Carolina*. Eds. Peter Landau and Friedrich-Christian Schroeder. Frankfurt: V. Klostermann, 1984, 119–44.

Schild, Wolfgang. *Die Geschichte der Gerichtsbarkeit*. Hamburg: Nikol Verlag, 2003.

Schoeck, Richard. "The Borromeo Rings: Rhetoric, Law, and Literature in the English Renaissance." In *Rhetoric and Pedagogy Its History, Philosophy, and Practice: Essays in Honor of James J. Murphy*. Eds. Winifred Bryan Horner and Michael Leff. Mahwah, NJ: Lawrence Erlbaum Associates, 1995, 261–76.

Schoeck, Richard. "Lawyers and Rhetoric in Sixteenth-Century England." In *Renaissance Eloquence: Studies in the Theory and Practice of Renaissance Rhetoric*. Ed. James J. Murphy. Berkeley: University of California Press, 1983, 274–91.

Schoeck, R. J. "Rhetoric and Law in Sixteenth-Century England." *Studies in Philology* 50:2 (1953), 110–27.

Senior, William. *Doctors' Commons and the Old Court of Admiralty: A Short History of the Civilians in England*. London: Longmans, Green, 1922.

Serafim, Andreas. *Attic Oratory and Performance*. New York: Routledge, 2017.

Serafim, Andreas. "'Conventions' in/as Performance: Addressing the Audience in Selected Public Speeches of Demosthenes." In Papaioannou, Serafim, and Vela, eds., *Theatre of Justice*, 26–41.

Setti, Cristina. "Avocats, procureurs, juges: rhétorique et praxis dans le procès pénal vénitien." In *Récit et justice: France, Italie, Espagne, XIV*ᵉ*-XIX*ᵉ *siècles*. Eds. Lucien Faggion and Christophe Régina. Aix-en-Provence: Presses universitaires de Provence, 2014, 105–19.

Sexton, Kim. "Justice Seen: Loggias and Ethnicity in Early Medieval Italy." *Journal of the Society of Architectural Historians* 68:3 (Sept. 2009), 309–37.

Shaffer, Jenny H. "Recreating the Past: Aachen and the Problem of the Architectural 'Copy.'" PhD diss., Columbia University, 1992.

Shapiro, Barbara J. "Classical Rhetoric and the English Law of Evidence." In Kahn and Hutson, eds., *Rhetoric and Law in Early Modern Europe*, 54–72.
Shepard, Alexandra. "Legal Learning and the Cambridge University Courts, c. 1560–1640." *Journal of Legal History* 19:1 (1998), 62–74.
Shennan, J. H. *The Parlement of Paris*. Rev. ed. Thrupp, Stroud, Gloucestershire: Sutton, 1998.
Shoemaker, Karl. "Regarding Untimeliness: Medieval Legal History and Modern Law," *Critical Analysis of Law* 2 (2015), 199–213.
Shoemaker, Karl. "The Devil at Law in the Middle Ages." *Revue de l'histoire des religions* 228:4 (2011), 567–86.
Shoemaker, Karl. *Sanctuary and Crime in the Middle Ages, 400–1500*. New York: Fordham University Press, 2011.
Shotwell, Allen. "Dissection Techniques, Forensics and Anatomy in the 16th Century." In De Ceglia, ed. *Body of Evidence*, 107–118.
Shugar, Debora. "St. Mary the Virgin and the Birth of the Public Sphere." *Huntington Library Quarterly* 73:3 (2009), 313–46
Siepp, D. J. "Reception of Canon and Civil Law in the Common Law Courts before 1600." *Oxford Journal of Legal Studies* 13:3 (Fall 1993), 388–420.
Simon, Goldhill, and Robin Osborne, eds. *Performance Culture and Athenian Democracy*. Cambridge: Cambridge University Press, 1999.
Sittl, Karl. *Die Gebärden der Griechen und Römer*. Leipzig: B. G. Teubner, 1890.
Skinner, Quentin. *Forensic Shakespeare*. Oxford: Oxford University Press, 2014.
Smail, Daniel Lord. *Emotions, Publicity, and Legal Culture in Marseille, 1264–1423*. Ithaca: Cornell University Press, 2003.
Smith, James K. A. "Staging the Incarnation: Revisioning Augustine's Critique of Theatre." *Literature and Theology* 15:2 (June 2001), 123–139.
Smith, Pliny B. "The Oration on the Crown." *Illinois Law Review* 2 (1908), 496–514.
Sogliano, Antonio. *Le pitture murali campagne scoverte negli anni 1867–79*. Naples: Detken & Rocholl, 1879.
South, James B. "John of Jandun." In *A Companion to Philosophy in the Middle Ages*. Eds. Jorge J. E. Gracia and Timothy B. Noone. Malden, MA: Blackwell, 2003, 372–76.
Spinka, Matthew. *John Hus: A Biography*. Princeton: Princeton University Press, 1968.
Squibb, G. D. *Doctors' Commons: A History of the College of Advocates and Doctors of Law*. Oxford: Clarendon Press, 1977.
Stacey, Robin Chapman. *Dark Speech: The Performance of Law in Early Ireland*. Philadelphia: University of Pennsylvania Press, 2007.
Stafford, Barbara Maria. *Body Criticism: Imaging the Unseen in Enlightenment Art and Medicine*. Cambridge: MIT Press, 1992.
Steel, Catherine. *Reading Cicero: Genre and Performance in Late Republican Rome*. London: Duckworth, 2005.
Steel, Catherine. *Roman Oratory*. Cambridge: Cambridge University Press, 2006.
Steel, Catherine. "Tribunician Sacrosanctity and Oratorical Performance in the Late Republic." In Berry and Erskine, eds., *Form and Function in Roman Oratory*, 37–50.
Steinbrink, B. "Actio." In *Historisches Wörterbuch der Rhetorik*. Eds. Gert Ueding, et al. Tübingen: Niemeyer, 1992, vol. 1, columns 43–74.
Strauss, Gerald. *Law, Resistance, and the State: The Opposition to Roman Law in Reformation Germany*. Princeton: Princeton University Press, 1986.
Strauss, Leo. *The Argument and the Action of Plato's Laws*. Chicago: University of Chicago Press, 1975.

Sutter, Carl. *Aus Leben und Schriften des Magisters Boncompagno: ein Beitrag zur Italienischen Kulturgeschichte im Dreizehnten Jahrhundert*. Freiburg: Akademische Verlagsbuchhandlung von J. C. B. Mohr, 1894.

Swiggers, Pierre. "Guillaume Molinier." In *Lexicon Grammaticorum: A Bio-Bibliographical Companion to the History of Linguistics*. Ed. Harro Stammerjohann. 2nd ed. Tübingen: Niemeyer, 2009, 588–9.

Syme, Holger Schott. *Theatre and Testimony in Shakespeare's England: A Culture of Mediation*. Cambridge: Cambridge University Press, 2012.

Tarlow, Sarah, and Emma Battell Lowman. *Harnessing the Power of the Criminal Corpse*. Cham: Springer International Publishing/Palgrave Macmillan, 2018.

Tedeschi, John. *The Prosecution of Heresy: Collected Studies on the Inquisition in Early Modern Italy*. Binghamton: Medieval & Renaissance Texts & Studies, 1991.

Tellegen-Couperus, Olga, ed. *Quintilian and the Law: The Art of Persuasion in Law and Politics*. Louvain: Leuven University Press, 2003.

Teo, Kevin. "Mapping Guild Conflict in the York Passion Plays." In *Performing Environments: Site-Specificity in Medieval and Early Modern English Drama*. Eds. Susan Bennett and Mary Polito. New York: Palgrave Macmillan, 2014, 141–58.

Thomas, Antoine. "Bortholmieu Marc collaborateur de Guilhem Molinier." *Romania* 41:163 (1912), 418–19.

Thomas, Edmund. "Chiasmus in Art and Text." *Greece & Rome* 60:1 (2013), 50–88.

Thompson, Craig R. *Universities in Tudor England*. Washington, DC: Folger Shakespeare Library, 1959.

Thomson, Alexander Douglas. *Euripides and the Attic Orators: A Comparison*. Athens: Macmillan and Company, Limited, 1898.

Timmermann, Achim. "'Locus calvariae': Walking and Hanging with Christ and the Good Thief, c.1350–c.1700." *Artibus et Historiae* 35:69 (2014), 137–161.

Todd, S. C. "Law and Oratory at Athens." In Gagarin and Cohen, eds., *Cambridge Companion to Ancient Greek Law*, 97–111.

Troescher, Georg. "Weltgerichtsbilder in Rathäusern und Gerichtsstätten." *Westdeutsches Jahrbuch für Kunstgeschichte: Wallraf-Richartz Jahrbuch* 11 (1939), 139–214.

Trotry, G. *Les grands jours des parlements*. Paris: Librairie générale de droit & de jurisprudence, 1908.

Tunberg, Terence O. "What Is Boncompagno's 'Newest Rhetoric'?" *Traditio* 42 (1986), 299–334.

Tuten, Belle Stoddard. "Women and Ordeals." In *Conflict in Medieval Europe: Changing Perspectives on Society and Culture*. Eds. Warren C. Brown and Piotr Górecki. New York: Routledge, Taylor and Francis Group, 2016, 163–74.

Umphrey, Martha Merrill, Lawrence Douglas, and Austin Sarat, eds. *Law and Performance*. Amherst, MA: University of Massachusetts Press, 2018.

Vale, M. G. A. *Charles VII*. Berkeley: University of California Press, 1974.

Vallerani, Massimo. "Criminal Court Procedure in Late Medieval Bologna: Cultural and Social Contexts." In *Violence and Justice in Bologna: 1250–1700*. Ed. Sarah Rubin Blanshei. Lanham, MD: Lexington Books, 2018, 27–53.

Vallerani, Massimo. *Medieval Public Justice*. Trans. Sarah Rubin Blanshei. Washington, DC: Catholic University of America Press, 2012.

Vasaly, Ann. "The Masks of Rhetoric: Cicero's *Pro Roscio Amerino*." *Rhetorica* 3:1 (Winter 1985), 1–20.

Vickers, Brian. *In Defense of Rhetoric*. Oxford: Clarendon Press, 1988.

Vickers, Michael. *Sophocles and Alcibiades: Athenian Politics in Ancient Greek Literature.* New York: Routledge, 2014.
Viggiano, Alfredo. "Giustizia, disciplina e ordine pubblico." In *Storia di Venezia: dalle origini alla caduta della Serenissima, Vol. 6: Dal rinascimento al barocco: politica e cultura.* Ed. Gaetano Cozzi and Paolo Prodi. Rome: Istituto della enciclopedia italiana, 1994, 825–57.
Vitiello, Joanna Carraway. *Public Justice and the Criminal Trial in Late Medieval Italy: Reggio Emilia in the Visconti Age.* Leiden: Brill, 2016.
Walker, David M. *The Oxford Companion to Law.* Oxford: Clarendon Press, 1980.
Wallach, Luitpold. *Alcuin and Charlemagne: Studies in Carolingian History and Literature.* 2nd ed. Ithaca: Cornell University Press, 1968.
Waquet, Françoise. "Au 'pays de belles paroles': Premières recherches sur la voix en Italie aux XVIe et XVIIe siècles." *Rhetorica* 11:3 (Summer 1993), 275–92.
Ward, John O. "Alan (of Lille?) as Rhetor: Unity from Diversity?" *Papers on Rhetoric* 5 (2003), 141–227.
Ward, John O. *Classical Rhetoric in the Middle Ages: The Medieval Rhetors and Their Art 400–1300, with Manuscript Survey to 1500 CE.* Leiden: Brill, 2019.
Ward, John O. "The Development of Medieval Rhetoric." In MacDonald, ed. *Oxford Handbook of Rhetorical Studies*, 315–28.
Ward, John O. "Master William of Champeaux and Some Other Early Commentators on the Pseudo-Ciceronian *Rhetorica ad Herennium.*" In Donavin and Stodola, eds. *Public Declamations*, 21–44.
Ward, John O. "The Medieval and Early Renaissance Study of Cicero's *De Inventione* and the *Rhetorica ad Herennium*: Commentaries and Contexts." In Ward and Cox, eds. *Rhetoric of Cicero in Its Medieval and Early Renaissance Commentary Tradition*, 3–75.
Watson, Walter. *The Lost Second Book of Aristotle's "Poetics."* Chicago: University of Chicago Press, 2012.
Watt, Gary. *Shakespeare's Acts of Will: Law, Testament, and Properties of Performance.* London: Bloomsbury Publishing, 2016.
Watt, John. "The Commentary on the Rhetoric by Bar Hebraeus." In Woerther, ed. *Commenting on Aristotle's Rhetoric*, 116–131.
Weber, Samuel. *Theatricality as Medium.* New York: Fordham University Press, 2004.
Weijers, Olga. *In Search of the Truth: A History of Disputation Techniques from Antiquity to Early Modern Times.* Turnhout: Brepols, 2013.
Welch, Kathleen E. "Delivery." In *Encyclopedia of Rhetoric.* Ed. T. O. Sloane. Oxford: Oxford University Press, 2006, 217–20.
Wesley, John. "Rhetorical Delivery for Renaissance English: Voice, Gesture, Emotion, and the Sixteenth-Century Vernacular Turn." *Renaissance Quarterly* 68:4 (Winter 2015), 1265–96.
West, Robin. "Adjudication Is Not Interpretation: Some Reservations about the Law-as-Literature Movement." *Tennessee Law Review* 54:2 (1987), 203–78.
West, William N. *Theatres and Encyclopedias in Early Modern Europe.* Cambridge: Cambridge University Press, 2002.
Westphal, Sarah. "Bad Girls in the Middle Ages: Gender, Law, and German Literature." *Essays in Medieval Studies* 19:1 (2002), 103–19.
Westphal, Sarah. "Calefurnia's Rage: Emotions and Gender in Late Medieval Law and Literature." In *The Representation of Women's Emotions in Medieval and Early Modern Culture.* Ed. Lisa Perfetti. Gainesville: University Press of Florida, 2005, 164–90.
Wheatley, Edward. *Stumbling Blocks Before the Blind: Medieval Constructions of a Disability.* Ann Arbor: The University of Michigan Press, 2010.

Whittemore, Thomas. *The Mosaics of Haghia Sophia at Istanbul: Fourth Preliminary Report Work Done in 1934–28: The Deesis Panel of the South Gallery*. Boston: Byzantine Institute, 1952.

Wijffels, Alain. "Disputations en droit à l'Université de Cambridge sous le règne élisabéthain." *Mémoires de la Société pour l'histoire du droit et des institutions des anciens pays bourguignons, comtois et romands* 57 (2000), 113–30.

Wiles, David. *The Players' Advice to Hamlet: The Rhetorical Acting Method from the Renaissance to the Enlightenment*. Cambridge: Cambridge University Press, 2020.

Williams, Ian. "A Medieval Book and Early-Modern Law: Bracton's Authority and Application in the Common Law c. 1550–1640." *Tijdschrift voor rechtsgeschiedenis* 79:1 (2011), 47–80.

Wilson, Eric. "Institoris at Innsbruck: Heinrich Institoris, the *Summis Desiderantes* and the Brixen Witch-Trial of 1485." In *Popular Religion in Germany and Central Europe, 1400–1800*. Eds. Bob Scibner and Trevor Johnson. New York: St. Martin's Press, 1996, 87–245.

Wilson, Luke. *Theaters of Intention: Drama and the Law in Early Modern England*. Stanford: Stanford University Press, 2000.

Wilson, Luke. "William Harvey's *Prelectiones*: The Performance of the Body in the Renaissance Theater of Anatomy." *Representations* 17:17 (Winter 1987), 62–95.

Winston, Jessica. *Lawyers at Play: Literature, Law, and Politics at the Early Modern Inns of Court, 1558–1581*. Oxford: Oxford University Press, 2016.

Witt, Roland G. "Boncompagno and the Defense of Rhetoric." *Journal of Medieval and Renaissance Studies* 16:1 (Spring 1986), 1–31.

Witt, Ronald G. *'In the Footsteps of the Ancients': The Origins of Humanism from Lovato to Bruni*. Leiden: Brill, 2000.

Witt, Ronald G. *The Two Latin Cultures and the Foundation of Renaissance Humanism in Medieval Italy*. Cambridge: Cambridge University Press, 2012.

Woerther, Frédérique. "Al-Fārābī commentateur d'Aristote dans les Didascalia in Rethoricam Aristotelis ex glosa Alpharabii." In Woerther, ed. *Commenting on Aristotle's Rhetoric*, 41–63.

Woerther, Frédérique, ed. *Commenting on Aristotle's Rhetoric, from Antiquity to the Present / Commenter la Rhétorique d'Aristote, de l'Antiquité à la période contemporaine*. Leiden: Brill, 2018.

Wogan-Browne, Jocelyn. "'Cest livre liseez . . . chescun jour': Women and Reading c.1230–c.1430." In *Language and Culture in Medieval Britain: The French of England c.1100–c.1500*. Eds. Jocelyn Wogan-Browne, et al. York: York Medieval Press, 2009.

Woods, Marjorie Curry. *Weeping for Dido: The Classics in the Medieval Classroom*. Princeton: Princeton University Press, 2019.

Woodward, William Harrison. *Vittorino da Feltre and Other Humanist Educators*. New York: Bureau of Publications, Teachers College, Columbia University, 1964.

Wülfing, Peter. "Classical and Modern Gesticulation Accompanying Speech: An Early Theory of Body Language by Quintilian." In Tellegen-Couperus, ed. *Quintilian and the Law*, 265–75.

Young, Karl. "An Elizabethan Defence of the Stage." In *Shakespeare Studies by Members of the Department of English of the University of Wisconsin*. Madison: The University, 1916, 103–24.

Young, Karl. "William Gager's Defence of the Academic Stage." *Transactions of the Wisconsin Academy of Sciences, Arts, and Letters* 18 (1916), 593–638.

Yunis, Harvey. "The Rhetoric of Law in Fourth-Century Athens." In Gagarin and Cohen, eds., *Cambridge Companion to Ancient Greek Law*, 191–208.

Zapalac, Kristin Eldyss Sorensen. *In His Image and Likeness: Political Iconography and Religious Change in Regensburg, 1500–1600*. Ithaca: Cornell University Press, 1990.

Zerba, Michelle. *Doubt and Skepticism in Antiquity and the Renaissance*. Cambridge: Cambridge University Press, 2012.

Ziolkowski, Jan M. "Do Actions Speak Louder than Words? The Scope and Role of *Pronuntiatio* in the Latin Rhetorical Tradition, with Special Reference to the Cistercians." In Carruthers, ed. *Rhetoric Beyond Words*, 124–150.

Zurcher, Andrew. "Consideration, Contract, and the End of *The Comedy of Errors*." *Law and Humanities*, 1:2 (2007), 145–166.

Zurcher, Andrew. *Shakespeare and Law*. London: Bloomsbury, 2010.

Zurcher, Andrew. *Spenser's Legal Language: Law and Poetry in Early Modern England*. Rochester, NY: D. S. Brewer, 2007.

Index

Note: Bold = pages with substantial discussion of the topic. Italics = pages with an image relevant to the topic. References are to pages and their footnotes. I include references to footnotes only where a substantive discussion of the topic does not appear in the main text on that page.